Client/Server Survival Guide

Third Edition

Robert Orfali • Dan Harkey • Jeri Edwards

WILEY COMPUTER PUBLISHING

JOHN WILEY & SONS, INC.

New York   Chichester   Weinheim   Brisbane   Singapore   Toronto

Publisher: Robert Ipsen
Editor: Theresa Hudson
Managing Editor: Angela Murphy
Text Design & Composition: Robert Orfali, Dan Harkey, and Jeri Edwards
Graphic Art: David Pacheco

Library of Congress Cataloging-in-Publication Data:

ISBN 0-471-31615-6

Printed in the United States of America
10 9 8 7 6 5 4 3

Foreword

by Zog the Martian

Captain Zog

Greetings, Earthlings! I'm Zog, the captain of the Martian team. My team and I first visited earth over five years ago to understand what client/server was all about. During that visit, we discovered the **Client/Server Survival Guide** and found it to be absolutely vital in our mission to explore this new technology. So we were very excited to hear about this third edition. We returned to Earth to pick up a copy of this new book. It was just what we were looking for. It gives us an update on all the new technologies we've been hearing about—including distributed objects, Web application servers, Enterprise JavaBeans, data warehousing, TP Monitors, Object Transaction Monitors, MOM, XML/DOM, LDAP, DBMSs, CORBA, COM+, WEBEM, and Groupware.

It's hard to believe the pace at which you Earthlings keep coming up with new technologies. You seem to be reinventing client/server every year. We thought the Java Web was the hottest thing in the universe. Now we hear that even Java is not enough; you also need an Object Web. Or, as the authors put it, you need "to morph distributed objects with the Web." Yes, things keep changing so fast that this third edition reads like a new book. Over a third of the material is completely new, and the rest was completely updated. Not a single page was left untouched since our last visit. Does it ever stop? Don't get me wrong: I know it's not the authors' fault that things keep changing so fast. They're just trying to help us understand these constant upheavals, which is why we keep buying their books.

So what did I like about this book? It felt like it was talking directly to me and to my crew in a friendly voice. That's very important when you're from a foreign planet. We like books that are painless, fun to read, and contain good Martian humor. We were apprehensive at first about client/server technology. The first edition helped us overcome this barrier. The second edition helped us understand how the Web transformed client/server. Then here comes this new edition with a ton of new technologies. As it turns out, the timing is perfect. We now believe that objects are the only way to build an intergalactic client/server Web. Yes, we will be connected to the Internet. Hopefully, our Java objects will be connected to yours.

In summary, this new Survival Guide helped us understand the "latest and greatest" client/server technology and how to use it in practical Martian situations. The personal touch was great; it felt like we had our own private tour guides. The artwork and cartoons were wonderful. I love to see pictures of myself in books (and especially on the cover). The Soapboxes really helped us understand the issues and what the latest Earthling debates are all about. We like to hear strong opinions instead of just sterilized information. I cannot recommend this book enough to my fellow Martians. Through this foreword, I highly recommend this book to you Earthlings. If I can understand this intergalactic client/server technology, so can you.

Zog

Preface

Client/Server: The Perpetual Revolution

Client/server computing has created a deep paradigmatic shift in our industry. It's replacing monolithic mainframe applications with applications split across client and server lines. The client—typically a PC—provides the graphical interface, while the server provides access to shared resources—typically a database. Distributed objects and the Internet are a paradigm shift within a paradigm shift—they're a new client/server revolution within the client/server revolution. Objects break up the client and server sides of an application into smart components that can play together and roam across networks. The Java Web is the killer application that is bringing objects to the masses. The combination of distributed objects and the Web (or the *Object Web*) is reinventing client/server computing.

Why Another Revolution?

So why is there another client/server revolution when the first one is still in full swing? The answer—as usual—is newer and better hardware and the demand for applications that match the new hardware. The first client/server revolution was driven by new hardware—PCs and Ethernet LANs forever changed the way we interact with our applications. Gone are the green-screen uglies associated with terminal-attached mainframes. Instead, we have GUIs.

The second client/server revolution is also being fueled by advances in hardware. This time, Wide Area Networks (WANs) are breaking the proximity barriers associated with Ethernet LANs. The telephone companies and WAN providers are getting ready to unleash almost unlimited bandwidth—they're wiring the entire planet for fiber-optic speeds.

Millions of us are getting a firsthand taste—thanks to the Internet—of the joys of intergalactic networking. We aren't satisfied with just navigating through information and chatting; we also want to conduct our business on these networks. Money is already changing hands on the Web. In the age of intergalactic transactions, there's no going back to single-server, departmental client/server LANs. The Java Web has changed that forever.

The Object Web

We may soon have millions of servers interconnected across the planet at ten times LAN speeds. This is the good news. The bad news is that our existing client/server infrastructure is geared for single-server departmental LANs; it cannot cope with the new intergalactic demands—millions of servers and applications that can spawn trillions of distributed transactions. 3-tier client/server solutions using distributed objects and the Web—or the *Object Web*—are our only hope for dealing with the new infrastructure requirements. Distributed Web objects—such as JavaBeans, CORBA Beans, Enterprise JavaBeans, and COM+ components—are changing the way we architect, develop, package, distribute, license, and maintain our client/server software. A new breed of *Object Transaction Monitors (OTMs)* built on top of Object Request Brokers, TP Monitors, and the Internet promises to provide the ultimate middleware for running these Web-based components.

We Live in Uncertain Times

A paradigm shift is akin to a revolution: Dominant structures crumble, vacuums are created, and the world is in turmoil. The transition period is marked by confusion, deep uncertainty, and exhilaration. Confusion is the result of seeing familiar bedrock structures disappear. Uncertainty comes from not knowing what the next day will bring. And the exhilaration comes from realizing the new possibilities that are being created by the new paradigm. **Client/Server Survival Guide** is our attempt to understand this revolution. The emerging 3-tier client/server paradigm is fielding a lineup of competing technologies, each vying to become the new emperor. We hope the new emperor will have clothes.

And We Can't Turn Back the Clock

Before we tell you all about this book, let's answer some questions that we've been wrestling with: Is intergalactic client/server just a passing fad? Is the Object Web a figment of the imagination? Can things go back to the way they were? We're the first to admit that client/server and the Web have become the industry's most overhyped and overloaded terms, but they're not a passing fad. This is because the world is populated with more than 150 million networked PCs that need to be served in the style they expect. The Web is the application; distributed services everywhere extend the client's universe. And in the age of the Internet, these services must be provided on an intergalactic scale. Servers are expected to do a lot more work for their Web-based clients. Yes, the revolutionary chaos of the client/server world may make some of us yearn for the good old days, but the time machine only marches forward.

What This Survival Guide Covers

This Survival Guide explores client/server computing from the ground up. It consists of ten parts; each one can almost be read independently. We'll give you a short description of what the parts cover. If you find the terminology too foreign, then by all means read the book to find out what it all means.

■ **Part 1** starts with an overview of what client/server is and what the fuss is all about. We develop a 3-tier client/server model that will serve as a roadmap for the rest of the book. We go over the state of the client/server infrastructure to provide a feel for how much of it is already here, and what remains to be built. We take a close look at how much bandwidth we can expect, and when.

■ **Part 2** examines the client/server capabilities of our current crop of operating systems—including Windows 98, NT 5.0 (or Windows 2000), Mac OS X, Linux, the Unixes, OS/2, and NetWare 5.0. We feel like war correspondents covering the battlefield of the operating system wars. We also look at how Internet appliances, shippable places, and Webtops are changing the client landscape.

■ **Part 3** explores the NOS and transport middleware substrate. We take a look at communication stacks, RPCs, MOMs, event channels, publish-and-subscribe, global directories, Kerberos security, and single logon. The Internet is becoming the mother of all NOSs. Consequently, we go over Internet NOS technology such as LDAP directories, X509v3 digital certificates, public/private keys, Secure Electronic Transactions (SET), IPSec, SSL, S-HTTP, VPNs, and firewalls.

■ **Part 4** explores the very popular database server model of client/server. We cover SQL-92, SQL3, ODBC, JDBC, SQLJ, OLE DB, ADO, DRDA, stored procedures, and triggers. We spend a lot of time looking at new database technologies such as data warehouses, data marts, OLAP, ROLAP, HOLAP, data mining, and data replication.

■ **Part 5** explores the TP Monitor model of client/server. We cover the different transaction types—including flat transactions, sagas, nested transactions, chained transactions, and long-lived transactions. We bring you up-to-date on what's happening with TP Monitors. Then we dive into the great debate that's pitting the TP Lite model offered by the database servers against the TP Heavy model offered by TP Monitors. We explain why TP Monitors are needed in a world dominated by database servers.

■ **Part 6** explores the groupware model of client/server. We look at the world of Lotus Notes, Exchange, Collabra, GroupWise, and interpersonal applications. We look at workflow and e-mail Internet standards such as Wfmc, SWAP, jflow, SMTP, IMAP4, POP3, and S/MIME. Groupware shows us what client/server can really do—its paradigm goes much further than just recreating mainframe-like applications on PCs.

■ *Part 7* explores the distributed object model of client/server. We explain the role of Object Request Brokers (ORBs)—such as CORBA, RMI, and DCOM. We explain how objects are packaged as components. We look at client-side component models such as ActiveX and JavaBeans. We also look at the new server-side components models—including Enterprise JavaBeans, CORBA Beans, and NT 5.0's COM+. Finally, we look at a new generation of Object Transaction Monitors (OTMs)—such as BEA's M3, Oracle's Application Server 4.0, IBM's WebSphere/Component Broker, and Microsoft's MTS—that act as server-side component coordinators. We explore how objects, components, and OTMs can be used to create a new generation of client/server information systems.

■ *Part 8* explores the Internet from a client/server perspective. We start with the Web as we know it today. Then we look at Java objects and new Web compound document standards such as XML, DOM, and XSL. Finally, we look at how distributed objects, components, and the Web are morphing into a new *Object Web*. This is real revolutionary technology that's going to completely overhaul the way we build client/server systems.

■ *Part 9* is about how to manage client/server applications. The biggest obstacle to the deployment of client/sever technology is the lack of integrated system management platforms. Fortunately, the situation is changing. We will look at new Web-based frameworks that may help us manage our distributed applications. We also cover system management standards, such as SNMPv3, MIB, RMON2, CMIP, DMI, CORBA, X/Open, WEBEM, CIM/XML, and JMAPI 2.0.

■ *Part 10* is about how to design, build, and deploy 3-tier client/server applications. We look at what tools can and cannot do for you. This part ends our journey and ties all the pieces together.

We cover products in all these areas. We also look at technology and market trends and introduce the key players.

What's New in This Edition?

We thank the 170,000 readers of our two previous editions for continuing to make this book a bestseller. As a result, our publisher asked us to do another "minor" update to bring the book up-to-date. As usual, we discovered that there's no such thing as a minor update in the client/server field. Time is measured in dog years. Almost everything in the book had changed. So the minor upgrade became another eight-month effort. The result is this new book. Over a third of it is entirely new material. Almost every page in the old book was updated. It was an amazing amount of work. We pity the practitioners of client/server because the field is a moving target; it takes a certain amount of stability to develop applications. We also pity the readers of our previous editions because you must now read an entire new book. There are no shortcuts. Of course, we kept some of the old cartoons. The Martians appear to be timeless.

How To Read This Book

As we recommend in all our books, the best way to approach this Survival Guide is to ask your boss for a one-week, paid sabbatical to go sit on a beach and read it. Tell him or her that it's the cheapest way to revitalize yourself technically and find out all there is to know about client/server technology, which now covers almost the entire computer science discipline. Once you sink into that comfortable chair overlooking the ocean, we think you'll find the book a lot of fun—maybe even downright relaxing. You won't get bored; but if you do, simply jump to the next part until you find something you like. You can jump to any part of the book and start reading it. We recommend, however, that you carefully go over the cartoons so that you have something to tell the boss back at the office.

What Are the Boxes For?

We use shaded boxes as a way to introduce concurrent threads in the presentation material. It's the book version of multitasking. The Soapboxes introduce strong opinions or biases on some of the more controversial topics of client/server computing. Because the discipline is so new and fuzzy, there's lots of room for interpretation and debate—so you'll get lots of Soapboxes that are just another opinion (ours). The Briefing boxes give you background or tutorial type information. You can safely skip over them if you're already familiar with a topic. The Detail boxes cover some esoteric area of technology that may not be of interest to the general readership. Typically, the same readers that skip over the briefings will find the details interesting (so you'll still get your money's worth). Lastly, we use Warning boxes to let you know where danger lies—this is, after all, a Survival Guide.

Who Is This Book For?

This book is for anybody who's associated with the computer industry and needs to understand where it's heading. We are all involved with client/server technology in some form or another—as users, IS managers, students, integrators, system developers, and component developers. All new software is being built using some form of client/server technology.

We hope you enjoy the reading, the cartoons, and the Soapboxes. Drop us a line if you have something you want to "flame" about. We'll take compliments too. We're relying on word-of-mouth to let people know about the book, so if you enjoy it, please spread the word. Finally, we want to thank you, as well as our Martian friends, for trusting us to be your guides.

Contents at a Glance

Contents

Part 4. SQL Database Servers

Chapter 10. SQL Database Servers

Chapter 11. SQL Middleware and Federated Databases

Chapter 12. Data Warehouses: Information Where You Want It . 261

Chapter 13. EIS/DSS: From Queries, To OLAP, To Data Mining. 289

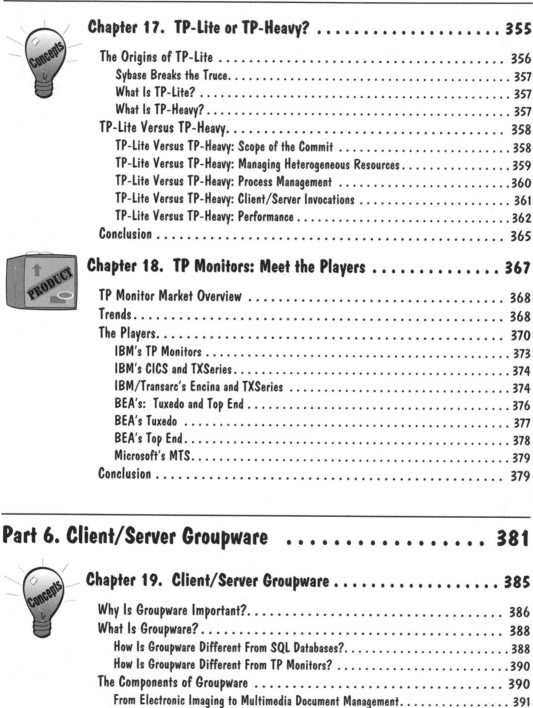

Chapter 27. Web Client/Server: The Interactive Era. 579

Chapter 28. Web Client/Server: The Distributed Object Era. . . . 593

Part 9. Distributed System Management 649

Part 1
The Big Picture

An Introduction to Part 1

Welcome to our client/server planet. We hope you will like it here, because there's no turning back now! You've long passed the point of no return. Don't panic: You're in good hands. We'll somehow find our way through the swamps, deserts, and roaring waters. We will show you how to avoid the dangerous paths infested with rattlesnakes and scorpions. Our adventure will be challenging—and exciting. In the course of the journey, we may even help you find the fabled land of client/server "milk and honey."

Part 1 of any good Survival Guide always starts with mapping the treacherous terrain. This is where you get the bird's-eye view of things—continents, oceans, forests, and Manhattan traffic jams. We create such a map for the world of client/server.

We start with an overview of what client/server is and what the fuss is all about. We explain what client/server computing can do, as well as what makes a product client/server. Then we develop a game using client/server building blocks that will help you navigate through the treacherous terrain. Finally, we go over the state of the client/server infrastructure—the equivalent of roads, bridges, and airports for client/server.

Chapter 1

Your Guide to the New World

Don't stand in the doorway
Don't block the hall
For he that gets hurt
Will be he who has stalled...
For the times they are a-changin'

— *Bob Dylan, 1963*

THE GOOD OLD DAYS

Back in the days when mainframes roamed the Earth, life was simple. The big choice of the day was how to pick the "right" computer vendor. And there were only a few you could choose. Once that choice was behind you, everything else fell into place. A staff of superbly trained analysts supervised the powering up of a great big box with a matching operating system. Data communications specialists could fine-tune, in a matter of hours, the octopus-like front-end network that brought hundreds of remote terminals into the fold. They were followed by storage specialists who would hook up "farms" of disk and tape drives. Maintenance and system management were built into every component. If anything went wrong, you knew exactly who to call—your on-site systems engineer.

If you had to write applications, your vendor would provide the "right" set of top-down methodologies, case tools, and run-time subsystems. There were, of course, five-year plans and grand architectures to help you design your future growth and budget for it. Most importantly, there was job security, a career path, and a bright future for everybody in the computer industry. And revenues were good for mainstream computer vendors and for the niche players that marketed within their orbits. These were the good old days before the client/server and "open" systems revolution.

LIFE AFTER THE REVOLUTION

Life is not as simple in the new world of client/server and open systems. Client/server computing is the ultimate "open platform." Client/server gives you the freedom to mix-and-match components at almost any level. You can put together an incredible variety of networked client and server combinations. Everything in the client/server world is sold *a la carte*.

At every turn, you will be presented with a Chinese restaurant menu of choices: Which server platform? Which client platform? Which network protocols? Which distributed computing infrastructure? Which database server? Which set of middleware? Which component model? Which system management base? If you get past the first set of choices, you will face even tougher new choices in the area of client/server application development and tools. There are at least five major technologies that can be used to create client/server applications: database servers, TP Monitors, groupware, distributed objects, and Web application servers. Which one is best?

You're the one who makes the tough decisions in this new world order. To succeed, you'll need to pick the right client/server platform, tools, vendors, and architecture base. You must identify and ride the *right* client/server technology wave. If the winning wave is distributed objects, it doesn't make sense to invest time and energy writing stored procedures for database servers. But if you pick the object wave too soon, it may shipwreck your business. So it's important that you know exactly what the technology can do for you at a given point in time. To figure this out, you must be able to sort your way through the marketing slogans and architectural promises. Most importantly, you need to know exactly what existing products can do for you *today*.

The good news in all of this is that client/server technology is liberating, flexible, and allows you to do the great things we will describe later in this book. The bad news is that you're on your own. The vendors will sell you their products at

near-commodity prices, but you'll have to figure out how to make the pieces work together. If they don't work, it's your problem. No promises were made when the goods were sold. Yes, system integrators can help, but they don't come cheap. So what happened to the good old days? They're gone. Vendors now sell piecemeal components. Everything is unbundled. Even service is priced separately. In this new *a la carte* world, you are the system integrator.

THE SURVIVAL PLAN

We, the authors, have been roaming in the wilderness for quite some time, and the result is this Client/Server Survival Guide. It will help you survive, but it won't be easy. Nobody, unfortunately, has that magic map with all the correct paths. We will share with you our insights, which—when combined with yours—may help you take the least treacherous path. A Survival Guide is more than just a map. It contains instructions for how to find food, build shelter, navigate in strange terrain, and protect yourself from snakes and scorpions. We'll provide all of this.

We will first go over the client and server sides of the equation. We will then work on the slash (/) in client/server—that's the glue that ties the client with the server. We will go over the five leading technologies for developing client/server applications: database servers, TP Monitors, groupware, distributed objects, and the Web.

Next, we explain how these technologies are morphing into what we call the *Object Web*. Finally, we conclude by covering system management platforms and tools.

Chapter 2

Welcome to Client/Server Computing

> In no way does Internet computing replace client/server computing. That's because it already is client/server computing.

> — Herb Edelstein, Principal
> Euclid Associates

At times, it seems as if everyone associated with computing has something to say about the client/server relationship. In this chapter, you get one more "definitive" viewpoint of what this all means. We will first look at the market forces—including the Internet and ERP—that are driving the client/server industry today. After coming this far, we feel we can handle even more danger in our lives, so we tackle the big issue of trying to answer the question: *Just what is client/server anyway?* We then get into a diatribe on fat clients versus fat servers (or 2-tier versus 3-tier). Finally, we peek through our crystal ball to give you a little glimpse of where things are going with the client/server industry. And we introduce the forthcoming *intergalactic* client/server era.

THE CLIENT/SERVER COMPUTING ERA

Client/server computing is an irresistible movement that is reshaping the way computers are being used. Although this computing movement is relatively young, it is already in full force and is not leaving any facet of the computer industry untouched. In addition, the Internet is like a tsunami; it is introducing a new form of client/server computing—*intergalactic* client/server. It's a revolution within the revolution.

What will the brave new world of client/server computing look like? What effect will it have on IS shops? What does it mean to compete in an open client/server computing market? What new opportunities does it create for software developers? Let's try to answer these questions now.

What's the Real Client/Server Vision?

Client/server computing has the unique distinction of having strong champions across the entire spectrum of the computer industry. For the "PC can do it all" crowd, client/server computing means scrapping every mainframe that can't fit on the desktop and the demise of host-centric computing. For mainframe diehards, client/server computing means unleashing a new breed of "born-again" networked mainframes that will bring every PC in the enterprise back to the fold. For the middle-of-the-roaders, client/server means a new era of Internet-based co-existence and openness in which all can play.

There is some truth in all these visions. Client/server computing provides an open and flexible environment where mix-and-match is the rule. The client applications will run predominantly on wired PCs and other desktop machines that are at home on networks and LANs. The successful servers will also feel at home on the network; they will know exactly how to communicate with their PC clients. Beefy PCs make natural superservers. For mainframes to succeed as servers, however, they will have to learn how to meet PCs as equals on the network. In this world of equals, mainframe servers cannot treat PCs as dumb terminals. They need to support peer-to-peer protocols, interpret PC messages, service their PC clients' files in their native formats, and provide data and services to PCs in the most direct manner. Ultimately, the server platform with the best cost/performance and the most services wins.

Client/Server and the "New IS"

The reason for IT decentralization was that many individuals were not strong enough to drive a common direction across units and functions and deliver the required services. So we decentralized IT as the only alternative. That's harder to do now in more electronically integrated enterprises.

> — *Ralph Szygenda, CIO*
> *General Motors*
> *(May, 1998)*

Client/server application development requires hybrid skills that include transaction processing, database design, communications experience, graphical user interface design, and Internet savvy. The more advanced applications require a knowledge of distributed objects and component infrastructures. Mastering these skills will require renaissance programmers who can combine the best of "big-iron," reliability-driven thinking with the PC LAN traditions. Where will these renaissance programmers come from? Will IS shops be able to provide solutions and services in this new computing environment? Or, will that service be provided by consultants and system integrators who have taken the time to learn these new skills?

Most client/server solutions today are PC LAN implementations that are personalized for the group that uses them. Everything from LAN directories to security requirements must be properly configured, often by the users themselves. IS departments have the skills to not only manage and deploy large networks but also to provide interoperability standards. They also know how to fine-tune applications, distribute fixes, and ensure data integrity. IS traditionally caters to the large data centers—not to the line departments that own the PCs and LANs. The key is for them to do what they do well in a distributed client/server environment where they share the power, responsibility, computing know-how, and financial budgets with the line business managers (the end-users). Consequently, distributing some of the IS function is essential.

Client/server computing may be best served by two-tiered IS organizations: a line IS for managing and deploying departmental systems, and an enterprise IS for managing the global network, intra- and inter-company applications and for setting the interoperability and component infrastructure standards. This type of aligned federation will not only preserve departmental autonomy but will also allow the local departmental LANs to be part of the multiserver, multivendor global network.

Competition in the Client/Server Market

Client/server, the *great equalizer* of the computer business, encourages openness and provides a level playing field on which a wide variety of client and server platforms can participate. The open client/server environment serves as the catalyst for "commoditizing" hardware and system software. The PC is a good example of a computer commodity; it can be obtained from multiple suppliers and is sold in very price-competitive market situations. LAN adapters, modems, communication protocol stacks, network routers, and bridges are also commodities. On the software side, PC operating systems, SQL Database Management Systems (DBMSs), Web servers and browsers, ERP applications, and LDAP directories are approaching commodity status. Distributed object infrastructures built on CORBA and COM are also becoming ubiquitous. These trends are good news for computer users.

But where are the *great differentiators* that will set vendors apart in this highly competitive commodity environment? What will happen to the computer vendors when commodity-priced client/server computing power satisfies the needs for computerization as we know it today?

Computer vendors will in the short run differentiate themselves by the power of the superservers they provide. This will last until commodity operating systems start to routinely support multiprocessor clustered hardware platforms. We anticipate that the most sustained differentiation will be in the area of new client/server software and not hardware platforms. PCs and client/server solutions will unleash a massive new wave of computerization. For example, VRML and multimedia enhanced client/server solutions have ravenous appetites for storage, network bandwidth, and processing power. These solutions will easily consume the new supply of low-cost client/server systems, as long as software providers can create enough applications.

We foresee a brave new era of ubiquitous client/server computing. Clients will be everywhere. They will come in all shapes and forms—including desktops, network computers, pen tablets, intelligent devices, Internet appliances, mobile personal communicators, Java cards, TV set-top boxes, smart books, robots, automobile dashboards, and myriads of yet-to-be-invented, information-hungry devices. These clients, wherever they are, will be able to obtain the services of millions of other servers. In this brave new world, every client can also be a server. To give you an idea of the size of this new market, IDC forecasts that by the year 2001, the shipping volume of Internet-connected consumer devices alone will top 41 million per year. These non-PC devices will account for almost 50% of Internet client unit shipments by 2002.[1] This bullish view of the industry puts us in the camp of those who believe that *the supply of low-cost MIPs creates its own demand*.

The Internet and Intranets

Transactions over the Web are pennies for every dollar that they cost if done in other ways.

> — **Jon Ziegler, Java Commerce Manager**
> **Sun**
> **(May, 1998)**

The World Wide Web (or the "Web") is redefining client/server computing. In many cases, it is causing departmental LANs and corporate WANs to morph into the Internet—technically, they're *intranets* because they hide behind firewalls. But these intranets are breaking down the traditional barriers between departmental and enterprise client/server computing. Instead, we have webs of servers that are interconnected at an intergalactic level. The corporate LANs and WANs become part of the Internet, and vice versa. Some corporations are extending the firewall to include their suppliers and customers. These intercorporate webs—called *extranets*—are becoming the backbone for Internet-based commerce (see Figure 2-1). An extranet creates a secure tunnel between two companies over the public Internet. It is also used to connect remote employees to the corporate network via the Web. The technology to create these secure tunnels is called *Virtual Private Networks* (VPNs). The good news is that there are now Internet-based security standards for creating these VPNs.

Doing business on the Web—or *e-commerce*—is the next big thing for the Internet. According to IDC, the number of home Internet users will increase from about 48 million worldwide in 1997 to nearly 160 million in 2001. This is a 35% year-on-year growth. The amount of Internet commerce originating from the home will increase also, from $5 billion in 1997 to $59 billion 2001.[2] This enormous rate of growth in consumer-to-business transactions will be overshadowed by the even more phenomenal growth in business-to-business transactions. This extranet-based commerce is expected to grow from $7 billion in 1997 to over $300 billion in 2002.[3] Forrester Research is even more bullish—they predict $327 billion by 2000. In either case, these numbers are huge. To deliver on this potential, businesses spent

---

[1] Source: IDC, *Death of the PC-Centric Era* (May, 1998). This projection covers Internet-connected appliances such as NetTVs, screen phones, gaming devices, NCs, and small hand-held devices.

[2] Source: IDC, *Internet Commerce: Where Is the Money? Who Are the Players?* (January, 1998).

[3] Source: U.S. Department of Commerce, *The Emerging Digital Economy* (April, 1998).

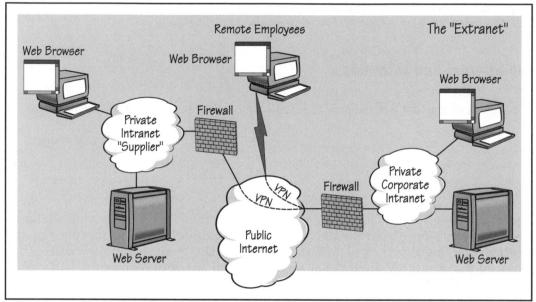

Figure 2-1. Extranets Create VPNs Over Public Internet to Connect Private Intranets.

$2.7 billion in 1997 on equipment, software, and services to develop and deploy Internet commerce capabilities. BRG forecasts that Internet commerce technology and services spending will balloon to $148 billion by 2001. This will happen as Internet commerce penetrates mainstream businesses and as those businesses and their service providers build out the infrastructure to support surging transaction volume.[4]

ERP: The Shrink-Wrapped Client/Server Craze

It seems the entire business world is under the spell of the vendors of ERP systems, which hope to solve year 2000 problems and hope to save on development costs, or some combination of the two.

— Sean Gallagher, Columnist
PC Week
(August, 1998)

So where are the shrink-wrapped client/server applications? The closest thing to a shrink-wrapped client/server market are the so-called *Enterprise Resource*

---

4 Source: Business Research Group, *U.S. Internet Commerce Market Forecasts* (May, 1998).

Planning (ERP) applications from companies like SAP, Oracle, PeopleSoft, Baan, Intentia, and J.D. Edwards. These vendors provide packaged client/server solutions for back-office enterprise functions such as accounting, payroll, human resources, financials, and manufacturing. And, they are now expanding their client/server suites to the front-office and vertical application space. For example, the ERP vendors now offer client/server solutions for consumer packaged goods, automotive, sales force automation, online catalogs, retail, oil and gas, supply-chain management, banking, and electronic commerce.

A good ERP system lets you manage from a single user interface many of the key functions in an enterprise. Of course, you must purchase all the pieces from the same ERP vendor to get this type of integration. The good news, however, is that the newer ERP products are being built on top of an open distributed object infrastructure such as CORBA/JavaBeans or COM/ActiveX. They are also being integrated with messaging systems, data warehouses, workflow engines, and the Web. As a result, the ERP market is booming (see Figure 2-2). In 1997, SAP's sales were $3.36 billion (a 62% growth). PeopleSoft grew by 81% to $815 million. Baan grew by 65% to $684 million. And, Oracle reported $1.16 billion in ERP enterprise application revenues. As you can see from these numbers, IS is buying packaged client/server applications by the truckload.

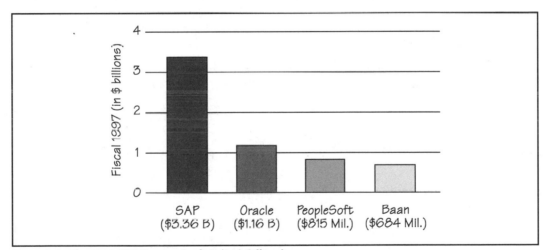

Figure 2-2. The 1997 ERP Revenue Leaders (in $ Billions).

So is ERP the client/server silver bullet we've all been waiting for? Can you now close this book and buy your client/server solutions off-the-shelf? Not yet. Here's why:

■ ***ERP systems are not really turn-key.*** A typical ERP system gives you an 80% solution. You must still implement the remaining 20% to fit your enterprise needs. In the end, you will pay more for customizing this last 20% than for the entire ERP application. It is not unusual for companies to spend millions of dollars to implement an ERP system. The big consulting houses—such as Arthur Andersen and Price Waterhouse—have made a ton of money helping large companies customize their ERP software.

■ ***ERP requires the re-engineering of a company's process and culture***. With solutions like SAP you must change your operations and processes to match the logic of the ERP package.

■ ***ERP must be integrated with the rest of the IS environment.*** Most companies don't start with green-field applications. Consequently, they must build the infrastructure that ties their new ERP package with their existing mainframes, DBMSs, data warehouses, Web servers, e-mail systems, and LAN-based applications.

■ ***ERP applications don't give you a competitive advantage.*** ERP systems are "me-too" applications. Forrester calls them "bread-and-butter apps" (see Figure 2-3); everybody has one. However, in today's world, IT systems have become a competitive weapon. For example, companies like Cisco, Dell, FedEx, Wells Fargo, and Amazon.com use the latest Web technology to effectively compete and expand their businesses. Web-based electronic businesses require a strong corporate identity that you cannot get from an off-the-shelf package. To compete effectively, you must create custom-built systems using best-of-breed tools, DBMSs, and middleware.

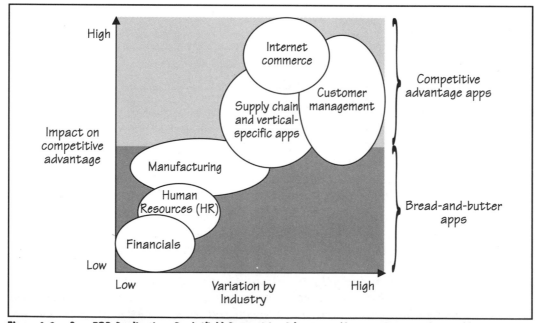

Figure 2-3. Core ERP Applications Don't Yield Competitive Advantage (Source: Forrester Research).

In summary, there are no silver bullets in the client/server business—the discipline is far too competitive and cutting-edge. However, ERP systems are great for automating well-understood functions and processes. An ERP system helps you offload the development and maintenance of the more mundane IS functions. In theory, this gives you more time to focus on the cutting-edge, bet-your-company applications. It's a win-win situation.

WHAT IS CLIENT/SERVER?

Even though client/server is the leading industry buzzword, there is no consensus on what that term actually means. So, we have a fine opportunity to create our own definition. As the name implies, clients and servers are separate logical entities that work together over a network to accomplish a task. So what makes client/server different from other forms of distributed software? We propose that all client/server systems have the following distinguishing characteristics:

- **Service:** Client/server is primarily a relationship between processes running on separate machines. The server process is a provider of services. The client is a consumer of services. In essence, client/server provides a clean separation of function based on the idea of service.

- **Shared resources:** A server can service many clients at the same time and regulate their access to shared resources.

- **Asymmetrical protocols:** There is a many-to-one relationship between clients and server. Clients always initiate the dialog by requesting a service. Servers are passively awaiting requests from the clients. Note that in some cases a client may pass a reference to a *callback* object when it invokes a service. This lets the server call back the client. So the client becomes a server.

- **Transparency of location:** The server is a process that can reside on the same machine as the client or on a different machine across a network. Client/server software usually masks the location of the server from the clients by redirecting the service calls when needed. A program can be a client, a server, or both.

- **Mix-and-match:** The ideal client/server software is independent of hardware or operating system software platforms. You should be able to mix-and-match client and server platforms.

- **Message-based exchanges:** Clients and servers are loosely coupled systems that interact through a message-passing mechanism. The message is the delivery mechanism for the service requests and replies.

- **Encapsulation of services:** The server is a "specialist." A message tells a server what service is requested; it is then up to the server to determine how to get the job done. Servers can be upgraded without affecting the clients as long as the published message interface is not changed.

- *Scalability:* Client/server systems can be scaled horizontally or vertically. Horizontal scaling means adding or removing client workstations with only a slight performance impact. Vertical scaling means either migrating to a larger and faster server machine or distributing the processing load across multiple servers.

- *Integrity:* The server code and server data is centrally managed, which results in cheaper maintenance and the guarding of shared data integrity. At the same time, the clients remain personal and independent.

The client/server characteristics described here allow intelligence to be easily distributed across a network. These features also provide a framework for the design of loosely-coupled, network-based applications.

WILL THE REAL CLIENT/SERVER PLEASE STAND UP?

Many systems with very different architectures have been called "client/server." System vendors often use client/server as if the term can only be applied to their specific packages. For example, file server vendors swear they first invented the term, and database server vendors are known in some circles solely as *the* client/server vendors. To add to the confusion, this book adds distributed objects, TP Monitors, groupware, and the Internet to the list of client/server technologies. So who is right? Which of these technologies is the real client/server? The answer to both of these questions is all of the above.

The idea of splitting an application along client/server lines has been used over the last twelve years to create various forms of networked software solutions. Typically, these solutions are built on top of off-the-shelf *middleware* software packages (we explain middleware in the next chapter). Each of these solutions, however, is distinguished by the nature of the service it provides to its clients, as shown in the following sections.

File Servers

With a file server, the client (typically a PC) passes requests for file records over a network to the file server (see Figure 2-4). This is a very primitive form of data service that necessitates many message exchanges over the network to find the requested data. File servers are useful for sharing files across a network. They are indispensable for creating shared repositories of documents, images, engineering drawings, and other large data objects.

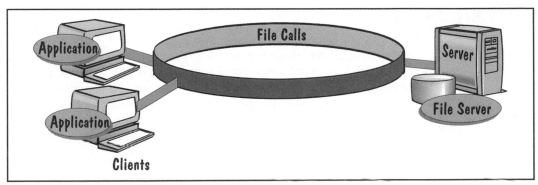

Figure 2-4. Client/Server With File Servers.

Database Servers

With a database server, the client passes SQL requests as messages to the database server (see Figure 2-5). The results of each SQL command are returned over the network. The code that processes the SQL request and the data reside on the same machine. The server uses its own processing power to find the requested data instead of passing all the records back to a client and then letting it find its own data, as was the case for the file server. The result is a much more efficient use of distributed processing power. With this approach, the DBMS server code is shrink-wrapped by the vendor. However, you must create the SQL tables and populate them with data. The application code resides on the client. So you must either write code for the client application or you can buy a shrink-wrapped query tool. Database servers provide the foundation for decision-support systems that require ad hoc queries and flexible reports. They also play a key role in data warehousing.

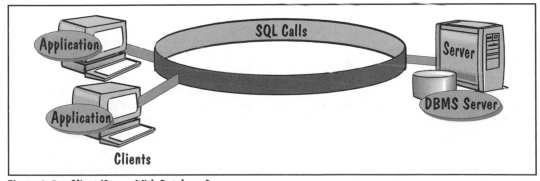

Figure 2-5. Client/Server With Database Servers.

Transaction Servers

With a transaction server, the client invokes *remote procedures* (or *services*) that reside on the server with an SQL database engine (see Figure 2-6). These remote procedures on the server execute a group of SQL statements. The network exchange consists of a single request/reply message (as opposed to the database server's approach of one request/reply message for each SQL statement in a transaction). The SQL statements either all succeed or fail as a unit. These grouped SQL statements are called *transactions*.

With a transaction server, you create the client/server application by writing the code for both the client and server components. The client component usually includes a Graphical User Interface (GUI). The server component usually consists of SQL transactions against a database. These applications are called *Online Transaction Processing*, or *OLTP*. They tend to be mission-critical applications that require a 1-3 second response time 100% of the time. OLTP applications also require tight controls over the security and integrity of the database. Two forms of OLTP will be discussed in this book: *TP-Lite*, based on the stored procedures provided by database vendors; and *TP-Heavy*, based on the TP Monitors provided by OLTP vendors.

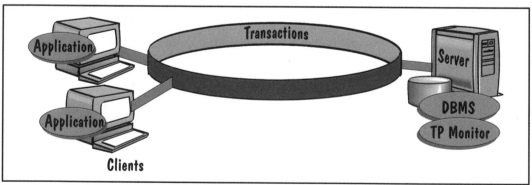

Figure 2-6. Client/Server With Transaction Servers.

Groupware Servers

Groupware addresses the management of semi-structured information such as text, image, mail, bulletin boards, and the flow of work. These client/server systems place people in direct contact with other people. Lotus Notes and Microsoft Exchange are the leading examples of such systems, although a number of other applications—including document management, imaging, multiparty applications, and workflow—are addressing some of the same needs. Specialized groupware software can be built on top of a vendor's canned set of client/server APIs. In most cases, applications are created using a scripting language and form-based interfaces provided by the vendor. Typically, the communication middleware between the client and the server is vendor-specific (see Figure 2-7).

However, many groupware products now use e-mail as their standard messaging middleware. In addition, the Internet is quickly becoming the middleware platform of choice for groupware. Both Netscape and IBM/Lotus are moving their products in this direction.

Figure 2-7. Client/Server With Groupware Servers.

Object Application Servers

With an object server, the client/server application is written as a set of communicating objects (see Figure 2-8). Client objects communicate with server objects using an *Object Request Broker (ORB)*. The client invokes a method on a remote object. The ORB locates an instance of that object server class, invokes the requested method, and returns the results to the client object. Server objects must provide support for concurrency and sharing. The ORB and a new generation of CORBA *application servers* bring it all together. After years of incubation, "real

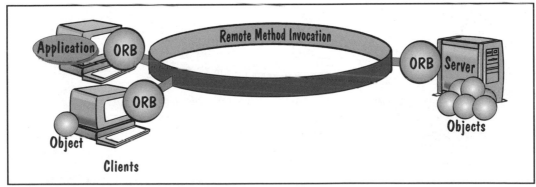

Figure 2-8. Client/Server With Distributed Objects.

life" commercial ORBs are now in production. Examples of commercial ORBs that comply with the Object Management Group's CORBA standard include Iona's *Orbix*, Inprise's *VisiBroker*, ICL's *DAIS*, JavaSoft's *Java IDL*, BEA's *ObjectBroker*, IBM's *SOM*, and Expersoft's *PowerBroker*.

CORBA is also the foundation technology for the *Enterprise JavaBeans* component model. A new generation of CORBA application servers—also called *Object Transaction Monitors (OTMs)*—provide server-side component coordination services. Examples of CORBA application servers are BEA's *M3*, IBM's *Component Broker*, Oracle's *Application Server 4.0*, GemStone's *GemStone/J*, Persistence's *PowerTier for EJB*, Sun's *NetDynamics 4.0*, Sybase's *Jaguar CTS*, and Inprise's forthcoming *Application Server*. However, CORBA is not the only game in town. Microsoft has its own ORB called the *Distributed Component Object Model (DCOM)*. DCOM is the foundation technology for Microsoft's enterprise software and also its *ActiveX* component model. The *Microsoft Transaction Server (MTS)* is the application server for ActiveX components. You should note that the latest name for this technology is *COM+* (Microsoft also calls it *DNA*).

Web Application Servers

The World Wide Web is the first truly intergalactic client/server application. This new model of client/server consists of thin, portable, "universal" clients that talk to superfat servers. In its simplest incarnation, a Web server returns documents when clients ask for them by name (see Figure 2-9). The clients and servers communicate using an RPC-like protocol called HTTP. This protocol defines a simple set of commands; parameters are passed as strings, with no provision for typed data.

The Web client/server model is evolving. More specifically, the Web and distributed objects are starting to come together to provide a very interactive form of client/server computing. We call this new convergence the *Object Web*. Java applets

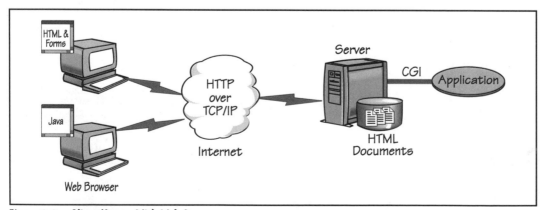

Figure 2-9. Client/Server With Web Servers.

and CORBA-enabled browsers are the first manifestations of this new Object Web. The next step is the componentization of the Web. For example, we are starting to see the deployment of *JavaBeans* on the client and *Enterprise JavaBeans* on the server. These client and server beans talk to each other via CORBA or HTTP. In Microsoft's parallel universe, the Object Web is based on ActiveX components that communicate via either a COM+ or HTTP pipe.

Web application servers are a new class of Internet software. They augment standard HTTP servers with server-side component frameworks. Functionally, they are very similar to object servers. Soon, you won't be able to tell the difference between the two. For example, in the Microsoft world, the MTS distributed object server is also the Web application server of choice. MTS is tightly integrated with Microsoft's IIS HTTP server; it uses IIS as an HTTP front-end. In the CORBA/Java world, Enterprise JavaBeans are becoming the common currency of Web application servers. In addition, most servers manage ordinary CORBA objects. Finally, some of these servers also provide COM/CORBA bridges. Examples of CORBA/Java Web application servers are Netscape/Kiva's *Application Server*, BEA's *WebLogic*, Bluestone's *Sapphire Web*, IBM's *WebSphere*, SilverStream's *SilverStream Application Server 2.0*, Novera's *jBusiness Application Server*, and HAHT's *HAHTsite Application Server 4.0*.

FAT SERVERS OR FAT CLIENTS?

So far, we've shown you that client/server models can be distinguished by the service they provide. Client/server applications can also be differentiated by how the distributed application is split between the client and the server (see Figure 2-10). The *fat server model* places more function on the server. The *fat client model* does the reverse. Groupware, transaction, and Web servers are examples of fat servers; database and file servers are examples of fat clients. Distributed objects can be either.

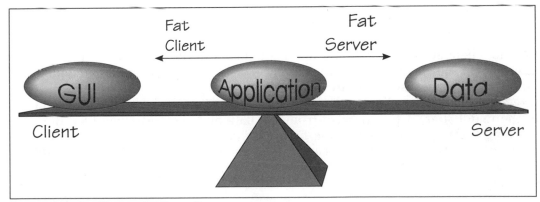

Figure 2-10.   Fat Clients or Fat Servers?

Fat clients are the more traditional form of client/server. The bulk of the application runs on the client side of the equation. In both the file server and database server models, the clients know how the data is organized and stored on the server side. Fat clients are used for decision support and personal software. They provide flexibility and opportunities for creating front-end tools that let end-users create their own applications.

Fat server applications are easier to manage and deploy on the network because most of the code runs on the servers. Fat servers try to minimize network interchanges by creating more abstract levels of service. Transaction and object servers, for example, encapsulate the database. Instead of exporting raw data, they export the procedures (or methods in object-oriented terminology) that operate on that data. The client in the fat server model provides the GUI and interacts with the server through remote procedure calls (or method invocations).

Each client/server model has its uses. In many cases, the models complement each other, and it is not unusual to have them coexist in one application. For example, a groupware imaging application could require an "all-in-one" server that combines file, database, transaction, and object services. Fat servers, used for mission-critical applications, represent the new growth area for PC-based client/server computing.

2-TIER VERSUS 3-TIER

High-brow client/server pundits prefer to use terms like 2-tier, 3-tier, and N-tier client/server architectures instead of fat clients and fat servers. But it's the same basic idea. It's all about how you split the client/server application into functional units that you can then assign either to the client or to one or more servers. The most typical functional units are the user interface, the business logic, and the shared data. There many possible variations of multi-tier architectures depending on how you split the application and the middleware you use to communicate between the tiers (see Figure 2-11).

In 2-tier client/server systems, the application logic is buried either inside the user interface on the client or within the database on the server (or both). Examples of 2-tier client/server systems are file servers and database servers with stored procedures. In 3-tier client/server systems, the application logic (or process) lives in the middle-tier; it is separated from the data and user interface (see the next Warning box). Processes become first-class citizens; they can be managed and deployed separately from the GUI and the database. Examples of 3-tier client/server systems are TP Monitors, Object Transaction Monitors, and Web application servers.

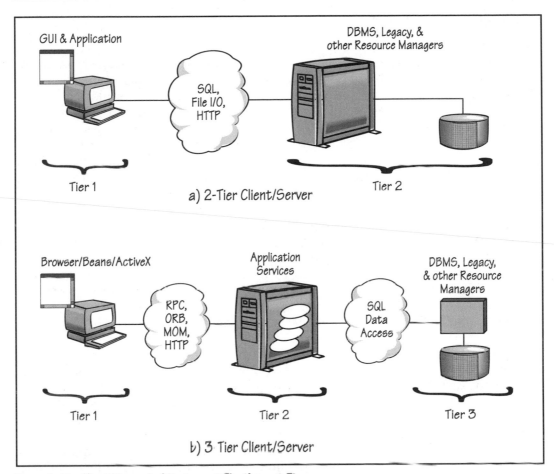

Figure 2-11. Client/Server Architectures: 2-Tier Versus 3-Tier.

3-Tier Is an Overloaded Word

Warning

3-tier is an overloaded word in the client/server literature. It was first used to describe the physical partitioning of an application across PCs (tier 1), departmental servers (tier 2), and enterprise servers (tier 3). Later it was used to describe a partitioning across client (tier 1), local database (tier 2), and enterprise database (tier 3). Now, the in-vogue definition is client (tier 1), application server (tier 2), and database server (tier 3). ❑

2-Tier Hits a Brick Wall

Simplicity is the biggest factor driving the popularity of 2-tier client/server. 2-tier is great for creating applications quickly using visual builder tools. Typically, these are departmental applications, such as decision support and small-scale groupware, or simple Web publishing applications. However, as successful departmental applications started to roll out, IS began to depend on 2-tier for mission-critical applications. They soon discovered that the architectures and tools they used so successfully for 2-tier didn't scale up. Applications that worked perfectly well in prototypes and small installations fell apart when put into large-scale production. Projects went over budget to create workarounds.

2-tier client/server can be a system management nightmare when you deploy it beyond the departmental LAN. It is especially hard to deploy and manage fat clients on the intergalactic net. Typically, IS does not own the remote desktops, so it can't control the software that runs on them. By the mid-90s, the total cost of ownership of 2-tier client/server systems had become a major issue. It seemed the client/server revolution had hit a brick wall—the systems could not scale or be managed. Naturally, some pundits started to declare that client/server had failed.

What really happened was that client/server was undergoing a transition—it had outgrown its departmental origins. We are now deploying core, enterprise-wide, 3-tier client/server applications that serve thousands of enterprise clients. As we move to e-commerce, these applications will span across enterprises. With the Internet, servers can get requests from any of the world's millions of connected browsers. Consequently, we have moved past the traditional 2-tier client/server world that we cut our teeth on. We now face a complex world where applications are split into hundreds of components and distributed across multiple servers—a world of 3-tier (and N-tier) applications.

Client/server architecture is moving to multiple tiers to deal with this new reality. The brick wall we encountered was simply a shortcoming of the 2-tier architecture. N-tier eliminates this shortcoming. As far as we can tell, there are no scalability limits in this new architectural model.

3-Tier to the Rescue

3-tier is the new growth area for client/server computing because it meets the requirements of large-scale Internet and intranet client/server applications. In theory, 3-tier client/server systems are more scalable, robust, and flexible. In addition, they can integrate data from multiple sources. 3-tier applications are easier to manage and deploy on the network—most of the code runs on the servers, especially with zero-footprint technologies like Java applets and beans. Also, 3-tier applications minimize network interchanges by creating abstract levels of service. Instead of interacting with the database directly, the client calls business logic on the server. The business logic then accesses the database on the client's behalf. 3-tier substitutes a few server calls for many SQL queries and updates, so it performs much better than 2-tier. It also provides better security by not exposing the database schema to the client and by enabling more fine-grained authorization on the server.

How Does 2-Tier Compare With 3-Tier?

Table 2-1 compares the 2-tier and 3-tier approaches. When client/server was a departmental or campus-based phenomenon, the shortcomings of 2-tier weren't very important. They certainly didn't outweigh the advantages provided by 2-tier's ease of development. But as client/server grew up to run mission-critical applications—especially those of intergalactic proportions—3-tier became essential.

Table 2-1. 2-Tier Versus 3-Tier Client/Server.

	2-Tier	3-Tier
System administration	Complex (more logic on the client to manage)	Less complex (the application can be centrally managed on the server—application programs are made visible to standard system management tools)
Security	Low (data-level security)	High (fine-tuned at the service, method, or object type level)
Encapsulation of data	Low (data tables are exposed)	High (the client invokes services or methods)
Performance	Poor (many SQL statements are sent over the network; selected data must be downloaded for analysis on the client)	Good (only service requests and responses are sent between the client and server)
Scale	Poor (limited management of client communications links)	Excellent (concentrates incoming sessions; can distribute loads across multiple servers)
Application reuse	Poor (monolithic application on client)	Excellent (can reuse services and objects)

Table 2-1. 2-Tier Versus 3-Tier Client/Server. (Continued)

	2-Tier	3-Tier
Ease of development	High	Getting better (standard tools can be used to create the clients, and tools are emerging that you can use to develop both the client and server sides of the application)
Server-to-server infrastructure	No	Yes (via server-side middleware)
Legacy application integration	No	Yes (via gateways encapsulated by services or objects)
Internet support	Poor (Internet bandwidth limitations make it harder to download fat clients and exacerbate the already noted limitations)	Excellent (thin clients are easier to download as applets or beans; remote service invocations distribute the application load to the server)
Heterogeneous database support	No	Yes (3-tier applications can use multiple databases within the same business transaction)
Rich communication choices	No (only synchronous, connection-oriented RPC-like calls)	Yes (supports RPC-like calls, but can also support connectionless messaging, queued delivery, publish-and-subscribe, and broadcast)
Hardware architecture flexibility	Limited (you have a client and a server)	Excellent (all three tiers may reside on different computers, or the second and third tiers may both reside on the same computer; with component-based environments, you can distribute the second tier across multiple servers as well)
Availability	Poor	Excellent (can restart the middle tier components on other servers)

Components: When 3-Tier Is N-Tier

The middle tier in most 3-tier applications is not implemented as a monolithic program. Instead, it is implemented as a collection of components that are used in a variety of client-initiated business transactions (see Figure 2-12).

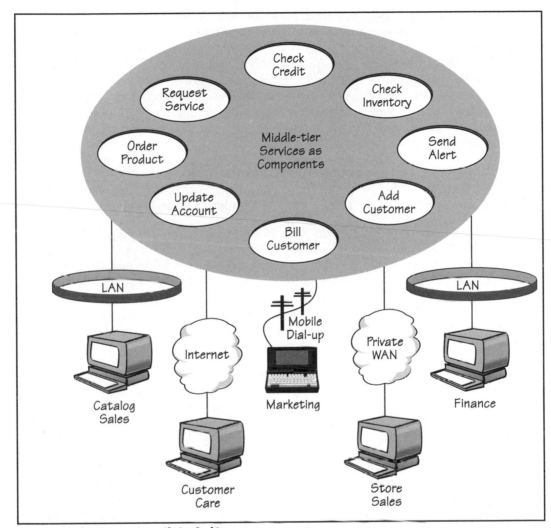

Figure 2-12. Components in an N-tier Architecture.

Each component automates a relatively small business function. Clients frequently combine several middle-tier components within a single business transaction. A component can call other components to help it implement a request. In addition, some components may act as gateways that encapsulate legacy applications running on mainframes. So, most of the time 3-tier is really N-tier.

Component-based applications offer significant advantages over monolithic applications. When you design the middle tier as a component-based application, you obtain the following benefits:

- ***You can develop big applications in small steps.*** Component-based architectures allow you to develop large mission-critical applications as small projects. When you use this step-wise development method, you can put initial versions of applications into production faster. It also reduces your risk. Standish Group reports that the larger a project grows, the more it is likely to fail. They found that 53% of IT projects fail. Small projects that are developed by just four people over four months have the best chance for success. Components lend themselves well to this small-team, incremental development approach.

- ***Applications can reuse components.*** Unlike object-oriented languages that focus on source code reuse, you reuse components as binary "black boxes." You can recombine them in different ways, depending on the application.

- ***Clients can access data and functions easily and safely.*** Clients send requests to components to execute a function on their behalf. The server components encapsulate the details of the application logic and thus raise the level of abstraction. Clients do not need to know which database is being accessed to execute the request. And they do not need to know if the request was sent to another component or application for execution. Encapsulation provides consistent, secure, auditable access to data and eliminates random, uncontrolled updates coming from many applications at once.

- ***Custom applications can incorporate off-the-shelf components.*** Enterprises gain tremendous benefits by buying ready-made components that are packaged as applications. They can also mix and match suites from different software vendors. However, this mix-and-match capability requires some semantic glue (see the next Warning box).

- ***Component environments don't get older—they only get better.*** Component-based systems grow beyond a single application to become the basis for suites of applications. You can assemble applications very quickly by building new clients, adding a few new middle-tier components, and reusing a number of existing components. You can update components without changing your clients. And you can add new capabilities as your business needs them.

Component Glue Not Necessarily Included

Warning

Mixing and matching components sounds wonderful—and is wonderful. Standard middleware allows seamless communications between clients and server components, as well as between server components. But buying component suites that use the same middleware—even loosely coupled, dynamic messaging mechanisms such as queues and publish-and-subscribe—does not guarantee plug-and-play capability. Components must know how to access each other semantically. One frequently used mechanism for combining component suites is to develop a new client application that bolts them together. Or, a component suite offered by a major software vendor can be used as a framework to which smaller vendors add function. In all cases, someone must provide the glue. ❏

When Should You Use 3-Tier?

According to GartnerGroup, 33% of all client/server applications are using the 3-tier model in 1998. This means that 3-tier is rapidly growing in popularity, but 2-tier is far from dead. There are still a number of applications that are ideal for 2-tier architectures. So, how do you know which model to use? We like GartnerGroup's answer to this question (see Figure 2-13). The figure shows that—for smaller projects—2-tier applications are easier to develop than 3-tier. However, as applications become more complex, 2-tier applications become exponentially harder to develop.

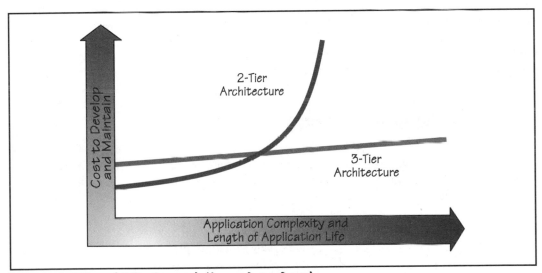

Figure 2-13. 2-Tier and 3-Tier Compared. (Source: GartnerGroup.)

So, where is the crossover point? According to GartnerGroup, you should use 3-tier if your application has any of the following characteristics:

- Many application services or classes—more than 50

- Applications programmed in different languages or written by different organizations

- Two or more heterogeneous data sources—such as two different DBMSs or a DBMS and a file system

- An application life that is longer than three years—especially if you expect many modifications or additions

- A high-volume workload—more than 50,000 transactions per day or more than 300 concurrent users on the same system accessing the same database

- Significant inter-application communication—including inter-enterprise communication such as *Electronic Data Interchange* (*EDI*)

- The expectation that the application will grow over time so that one of the previous conditions will apply

Generally speaking, it has become a safe bet to implement your applications using a 3-tier client/server architecture—especially if you pick a solid infrastructure. In today's world of intranet and Internet applications, 3-tier is the odds-on favorite. It lets you start small—both in scale and function—and then grow your application to intergalactic proportions. It also lets you create a catalog of custom and purchased components that you quickly assemble to produce new applications. You can publish the interfaces to these components and use GUI tools to access them. Consequently, departmental programmers can include them in their applications. You can even encapsulate and "reuse" legacy applications.

INTERGALACTIC CLIENT/SERVER

The Network Economy is fed by the resonance of two stellar bangs: the collapsing microcosm of chips and the exploding telecosm of connections... Curious things start to happen when you connect all to all.

> — *Kevin Kelly, Editor*
> *Wired Magazine*
> *(September, 1997)*

Client/server applications stand at a new threshold brought on by: 1) the exponential increase of low-cost bandwidth on Wide Area Networks—for example, the Internet and AOL; and 2) a new generation of Web-enabled desktops and devices. This new threshold marks the beginning of a transition from 2-tier *Ethernet* client/server to N-tier *intergalactic* client/server. Clients and servers do not have to be co-located on the same campus any longer—they can be a world away. We call this "the irrelevance of proximity."

A Revolution Within the Revolution

The bottom line is that the center of gravity is shifting from single-server, 2-tier, LAN-based departmental client/server to a post-scarcity form of N-tier client/server where every machine on the global "information highway" can be both a client and a server. This is really a revolution within the client/server revolution. You may want to fasten your seat belts. This second revolution promises to be just as traumatic as the one we just went through when client/server applied a giant chainsaw to mainframe-based monolithic applications and broke them apart into client and server components. Table 2-2 contrasts these two eras of client/server computing. As you can see, the requirements of intergalactic client/server are many orders of magnitude greater than those of departmental client/server. Our applications have outgrown their old departmental boundaries and spilled over into an interconnected world. Intergalactic applications introduce new and more stringent requirements. N-tier client/server architectures are designed to meet this new challenge.

Table 2-2. Web Client/Server Versus Traditional Client/Server.

Application Characteristic	Intergalactic Era Client/Server	Ethernet Era Client/Server
Number of clients per application	Millions	Less than 100
Number of servers per application	100,000+ "Server-mania" with many heterogeneous servers performing different roles	1 or 2
Geography	Global	Campus-based
Server-to-server interactions	Yes	No
Middleware	ORBs on top of Internet	SQL and stored procedures
Client/server architecture	3-tier (or N-tier)	2-tier
Transactional updates	Pervasive	Very infrequent
Multimedia content	High	Low
Mobile agents	Yes	No
Client front-ends	OOUIs, JavaBeans, Webtops, browsers, and shippable places	Fat GUI clients
Timeframe	1998 and beyond	1985 till present

The Intergalactic Vision

The big insight for the next ten years is this: What if digital communications were free? The answer is that the way we learn, buy, socialize, do business, and entertain ourselves will be very different.

— *Bill Gates, Chairman*
Microsoft

When it comes to intergalactic client/server applications, the imagination is at the controls. The promise of high bandwidth at very low cost has conjured visions of an information highway that turns into the world's largest shopping mall. The predominant vision is that of an electronic bazaar of planetary proportions—replete with boutiques, department stores, bookstores, brokerage services, banks, and travel agencies. Like a Club Med, the mall will issue its own electronic currency to facilitate round-the-clock shopping and business-to-business transactions. Electronic agents of all kinds will be roaming around the network looking for bargains and conducting negotiations with other agents. Billions of electronic business transactions will be generated on a daily basis. Massive amounts of multimedia data will also be generated, moved, and stored on the network.

Obviously, what we're describing is not the Internet as we know it today—there is a lot more to this vision than just surfing through hypertext webs of HTML-tagged information. We're talking about transaction rates that are thousands of times larger than anything we have today. In addition, these transactions are going to be more long-lived and complex. The data these transactions operate on will also be more complex and rich in multimedia content. So we're talking about the next generation of Internet technology, which we call the *Object Web* (see Part 8). This technology will also be used on small "i" Internets—or intranets—including LANs, interbusiness networks, and private wide-area networks.

What Do We Need?

Some key technologies are needed at the client/server application level to make all this happen, including:

■ *Rich transaction processing*. In addition to supporting the venerable flat transaction, the new environment requires nested transactions that can span across multiple servers, long-lived transactions that execute over long periods of time as they travel from server to server, and queued transactions that can be used in secure business-to-business dealings. Most nodes on the network should be able to participate in a secured transaction; superserver nodes will handle the massive transaction loads.

- **_Roaming agents_**. The new environment will be populated with electronic agents of all types. Consumers will have personal agents that look after their interests; businesses will deploy agents to sell their wares on the network; and sniffer agents will be sitting on the network, at all times, collecting information to do system management or simply looking for trends. Agent technology includes cross-platform scripting engines, workflow, and Java-like mobile code environments that allow agents to live on any machine on the network.

- **_Rich data management_**. This includes active multimedia compound documents that you can move, store, view, and edit in-place anywhere on the network. XML provides the foundation technology for this type of mobile document management. Of course, this environment must also be able to support existing record-based structured data and SQL databases.

- **_Intelligent self-managing entities_**. With the introduction of new multi-threaded, high-volume, network-ready desktop operating systems, we anticipate a world where millions of machines can be both clients and servers. However, we can't afford to ship a system administrator with every $99 operating system or $15 Internet appliance. To avoid doing this, we need distributed software that knows how to manage and configure itself and protect itself against threats.

- **_Intelligent middleware_**. The distributed environment must provide the semblance of a single-system image across potentially thousands of components running on hundreds of servers. The middleware must create this Houdini-sized illusion by making all servers on the global network appear to behave like a single computer system. Users and programs should be able to dynamically join and leave the network, and then discover each other. You should be able to use the same naming conventions to locate any resource on the network.

This is a tall order of requirements. Can our client/server infrastructure—conceived to meet the needs of the single-server Ethernet era—meet the new challenges? Is our client/server infrastructure ready for intergalactic prime time? Can our existing middleware deal with millions of objects that can be both clients and servers? We answer these questions in the rest of this book.

CONCLUSION

Client/server has outgrown its departmental origins. We are now deploying client/server applications that serve thousands of enterprise clients.[5] These applica-

---

[5] Our coauthor, Jeri Edwards, documents some of these large applications in her case-study book called **3-Tier Client/Server At Work, Revised Edition** (Wiley, 1999).

tions often run on many servers and consist of hundreds of software components. They run the core functions within an enterprise. And these client/server applications are going intergalactic. With the Internet, servers can get requests from any of the world's millions of connected PCs.

In this new world, transactions can come from consumers (via Internet applications), from suppliers or distributors (via inter-company extranets), or from your own far-flung employees. Intergalactic client/server will allow enterprises to thrive in a quickly changing business climate—where they are driven by new demands that must be fulfilled in "Internet years." Here are some examples:

■ Businesses will increasingly compete by being the first to market with new electronic goods and services. Their success will be determined by their applications.

■ Companies will create *virtual corporations* through alliances with a shifting set of partners. This will allow them to react quickly to new opportunities—and maintain a tight focus on their "core competencies."

■ Roles and relationships between enterprises will shift frequently as industries realign. Successful companies will use these dislocations to increase market-share and to acquire a dominant industry position. The current corporate trend toward mergers and acquisitions will escalate.

Intergalactic client/server will both enable and drive these massive changes. It will change the way many industries operate.

Chapter 3

Client/Server Building Blocks

---

*W*hat are you able to build with your blocks? Castles and palaces, temples and docks.

— *Robert Louis Stevenson*
A Child's Garden of Verses

We are all familiar with the concept of *architecture* as applied in the construction of buildings. Architectures help us identify structural elements that may be used as building blocks in the construction of ever-more complex systems. Just like we buy homes instead of plans, users in the computer industry buy solutions to business problems, instead of grand client/server architectures. But architecture determines the structure of the houses, high rises, office buildings, and cities where we live and work. In the computer analogy, architecture helps us determine the structure and shape of the client/server systems we can build to meet various needs.

The "million-dollar" architectural questions we will cover here are: How is the application split between the client and the server? What function goes in the client and what function goes in the server? Can the client/server model accommodate businesses of all sizes? How are the new tribes of nomadic laptop users brought into the client/server fold? Can client/server play in the home? Where do peer networks fit in this picture? Will client/server disappear in a post-scarcity computing world?

CLIENT/SERVER: A ONE-SIZE-FITS-ALL MODEL

Can a single client/server model accommodate all these types of users? We think we have such a model. It is deceptively simple, and it works well with today's technologies. It is ideally suited for dealing with the needs of a *post-scarcity computing* world, where client/server becomes the ultimate medium for sharing and collaborating.

The model we present in this section is really a game of putting together things with building blocks. We will show you how we can meet a wide spectrum of client/server needs—from the tiny to the intergalactic—with just three basic building blocks: a client, a server, and the slash (/) that ties the client to the server (see Figure 3-1). Kids of all ages will love this game. It should help you identify some durable structures in the design of client/server systems.

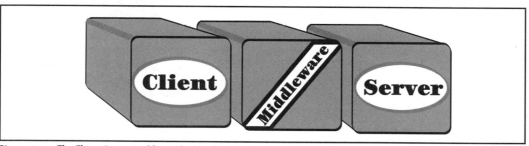

Figure 3-1. The Three Basic Building Blocks of Client/Server.

In the next few sections, we explain (and illustrate) how the building-block arrangements are used in four situations:

- *Client/server for tiny shops and nomadic tribes* is a building-block implementation that runs the client, the middleware software, and most of the business services on the same machine. It is the suggested implementation for the one-person shops, home offices, and mobile users with well-endowed laptops. This is a new opportunity area for client/server technology.

- *Client/server for small shops and departments* is the classic Ethernet client/single-server building-block implementation. It is used in small shops, departments, and branch offices. This is the predominant form of client/server today.

- *Client/server for intergalactic enterprises* is the multiserver building-block implementation of client/server. The servers present a single-system image to the client. They can be spread throughout the enterprise, but they can be made to look like they're part of the local desktop. This implementation meets the initial needs of intergalactic client/server computing.

■ *Client/server for a post-scarcity world* transforms every machine in the world into both a client and a server. Personal agents on every machine will handle all the negotiations with their peer agents anywhere in the universe. This dream is almost within reach.

You will discover many similarities in the four arrangements. This is because they all use the same type of software, middleware, and communications infrastructure.

Client/Server for Tiny Shops and Nomadic Tribes

The nice thing about client/server is that it's infinitely malleable. It is easy to run the client and server portion of an application on the same machine. Vendors can easily package single-user versions of a client/server application (see Figure 3-2). For example, a client/server application for a dentist's office can be sold in a single-user package for offices consisting of a single dentist and in a multiuser package for offices with many dentists. The same client/server application covers both cases. The only caveat is that you need to use an operating system that is robust enough to run both the client and server sides of the application.

The example of the tiny dentist's office also works for the tiny in-home business office and the mobile user on the road. In all cases, the business-critical client/server

Figure 3-2. Client/Server for Tiny Shops and Nomadic Users.

application runs on one machine and does some occasional communications with outside servers to exchange data, refresh a database, and send or receive mail and faxes. For example, the one-person dentist's office may need to communicate with outside servers such as insurance company billing computers. And, of course, everyone needs to be on the Internet, even dentists.

Client/Server for Small Shops and Departments

The client/server architecture is particularly well-suited for the LAN-based single server establishments. So, it's no wonder that they account for around 70% of today's client/server installations. This is the "archetypical" Ethernet model of client/server. It consists of multiple clients talking to a local server (see Figure 3-3). This is the model used in small businesses—for example, a multiuser dentist office—and by the departments of large corporations—for example, the branch offices of a bank.

The single-server nature of the model tends to keep the middleware simple. The client only needs to look into a configuration file to find its server's name. Security is implemented at the machine level and kept quite simple. The network is usually relatively easy to administer; it's a part-time job for a member of the group. There are no complex interactions between servers, so it is easy to identify failures—they're either on the client or on the local server.

Braver souls may be using their server to interact in a very loosely-coupled way with some enterprise server. For example, data (such as a price list) may be downloaded once a day to refresh the local server. Or inventory data may be uploaded to an

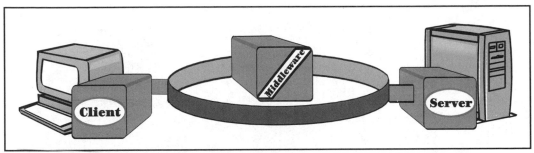

Figure 3-3. Client/Server for Small Shops and Departments.

enterprise server using a WAN or the public Internet. Fax and mail can be sent or received any time through the mail server gateway. Typically, the software that interacts with remote servers will reside on the departmental server.

Departmental servers will continue to be popular, even in large enterprises, because they provide a tremendous amount of user autonomy and controls. Users feel that it is *their* server, and they can do anything they please with it. A departmental server's applications typically address the specific needs of the local clients first, which makes users very happy. With fiber optics and high-speed ATM connections, it will be hard to detect a performance difference between a local departmental server and an enterprise server a continent away. However, the psychology (and politics) of ownership will always provide a powerful motivator for holding on to that local server.

In summary, this implementation of client/server uses our three building blocks to create the classical single-server model of client/server that is so predominant in the Ethernet era. This model works very well in small businesses and departments that depend on single servers or on very loosely-coupled multiserver arrangements.

Client/Server for Intergalactic Enterprises

The client/server enterprise model addresses the needs of establishments with a mix of heterogeneous servers. This is an area that's getting a lot of industry attention as solutions move from a few large computers to multiple servers that live on the Internet, intranets, and corporate backbone networks (see Figure 3-4). One of the great things about the client/server model is that it is upwardly scalable. When more processing power is needed for various intergalactic functions, more servers can be added (thus creating a pool of servers), or the existing server machine can be traded up for the latest generation of superserver machine.

We can partition servers based on the function they provide, the resource they control, or the database they own. In addition, we may choose to replicate servers for fault tolerance or to boost an application's performance. There can be as many

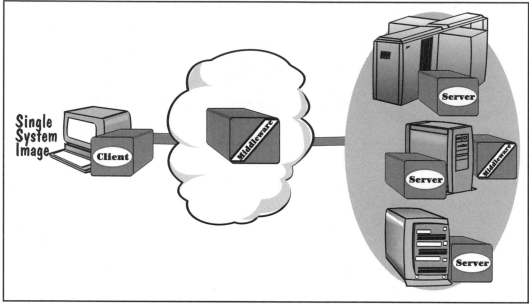

Figure 3-4. Client/Server for Intergalactic Enterprises.

server combinations as your budget will tolerate. Multiserver capability, when properly used, can provide an awesome amount of compute power and flexibility, in many cases rivaling that of mainframes.

To exploit the full power of multiservers, we need low-cost, high-speed bandwidth and an awesome amount of middleware features—including network directory services, network security, remote procedure calls, and network time services. Middleware creates a common view of all the services on the network, called a "single-system image" (see the next Briefing Box).

Good software architecture for intergalactic enterprise client/server implementations is all about creating system "ensembles" out of modular building blocks. With some practice, you may develop creative skills akin to those of a symphony composer in the articulation of software components that run on multiple servers. You will need to find creative ways to partition work among the servers. For example, you may partition the work using distributed objects. You will also need to design your servers so that they can delegate work to their fellow servers. A complex request may involve a task force of servers working together on the request. Preferably, the client should not be made aware of this behind-the-scenes collaboration. The server that the client first contacts should be in charge of orchestrating the task force and returning its findings to the client.

Intergalactic client/server is the driving force behind middleware standards such as distributed objects and the Internet. We're all looking for that magic bullet that will make the distributed multivendor world as integrated as single-vendor mainframes. Tools for creating, deploying, and managing scalable client/server applications are getting a lot of attention. There are fortunes to be made in intergalactic client/server because nobody has yet put all of the pieces back together.

Client/Server for a Post-Scarcity World

In this section, we up the ante. We will investigate what new systems can be created on a client/server platform when memory and hardware become *incredibly afford-able*. Every machine is both a client and a full-function server (see Figure 3-5). We call this plentiful environment *the post-scarcity world*. We imagine the typical post-scarcity machine as a $2000 cellular notebook powered by a top-of-the-line processor and loaded with 100 MBytes of RAM and 100 GBytes or more of disk space. And, of course, this machine runs all the middleware that vendors will be able to dream of over the next few years.

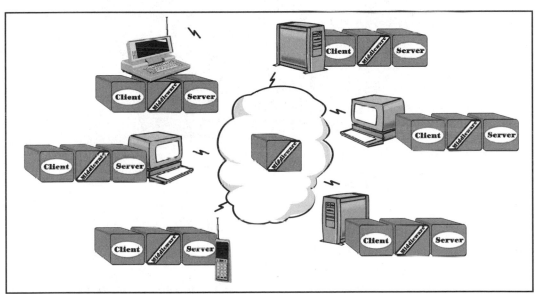

Figure 3-5. Client/Server for a Post-Scarcity World.

What do we do with all this power other than run middleware? What happens when every machine in the world becomes a universal server and client? Because every machine is a full-function server, we should assume it will run, at a minimum, a file server, database server, workflow agent, Object Transaction Monitor, and Web server—all connected via an ORB. This is in addition to all the client software and middleware.

What we're saying is that in the next few years, a hundred million machines or more may be running *almost all* the forms of client/server software described in this book. This should be good news to TP Monitor, ORB, groupware, Internet, and database vendors—it's a huge opportunity. Are they thinking about it? Do they have the proper packaging and marketing channels to go after it? After you read this book, you'll have a better appreciation for how complex, powerful, and essential this software is. So who will manage and run all that software on behalf of the user? *Personal agents*, of course (see the next cartoon).

INSIDE THE BUILDING BLOCKS

In the last sections, we introduced the three *building blocks* of client/server: the client, the server, and the middleware slash (/) that ties them together. Figure 3-6 peels the next layer off the onion and provides more detail about what goes into each of the building blocks. What you see in this figure is, in a nutshell, the entire client/server software infrastructure. Let's go over the pieces:

■ *The client building block* runs the client side of the application. It runs on an Operating System (OS) that provides a Graphical User Interface (GUI) or an Object Oriented User Interface (OOUI) and that can access distributed services, wherever they may be. Thin clients require a Web browser to download

JavaBeans and applets on demand. In all cases, the operating system most often passes the buck to the middleware building block and lets it handle the non-local services. The client also runs a component of the *Distributed System Management (DSM)* element. This could be anything from a simple agent on a managed PC to the entire front-end of the DSM application on a managing station.

■ ***The server building block*** runs the server side of the application. The server application typically runs on top of some shrink-wrapped server software package. The five contending server platforms for creating the next generation of client/server applications are SQL database servers, TP Monitors, groupware servers, object servers, and the Web. The server side depends on the operating system to interface with the middleware building block that brings in the requests for service. The server also runs a DSM component. This could be anything from a simple agent on a managed PC to the entire back-end of the DSM application (for example, it could provide a shared object database for storing system management information).

■ ***The middleware building block*** runs on both the client and server sides of an application. We broke this building block into three categories: transport stacks, network operating systems (NOSs), and service-specific middleware. Middleware is the nervous system of the client/server infrastructure. Like the other two building blocks, the middleware also has a DSM software component.

The Distributed System Management application runs on every node in a client/server network. A *managing* workstation collects information from all its *agents* on the network and displays it graphically. The managing workstation can

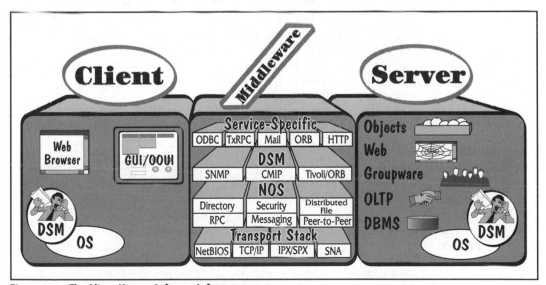

Figure 3-6. The Client/Server Software Infrastructure.

also instruct its agents to perform actions on its behalf. Think of management as running an autonomous "network within a network." It's the "Big Brother" of the client/server world, but life is impossible without it.

So What Is "Middleware"?

Briefing

Mid.dle.ware: 1) a hodgepodge of software technologies; 2) a buzzword; 3) a key to developing client/server applications.

— Information Week

Middleware is now everywhere and everything, so pervasive that it has passed into the realm of the non-entity.

— Clara H. Parkes, Editor
DBMS Magazine
(May, 1998)

So what exactly is middleware? First, it's a large software market that generated $1.7 billion in 1997. According to IDC, this market will grow to $7 billion in 2002—a 408% increase (Source: IDC, *Middleware: 1998 Worldwide Markets and Trends*, May, 1998). Now, the hard part. Middleware is a vague term that covers all the distributed software needed to support interactions between clients and servers. Think of it as the software that's in the middle of the client/server system. In this Survival Guide, we refer to middleware as the slash (/) component of client/server. In this first approximation, middleware is the glue that lets a client obtain a service from a server.

Where does middleware start, and where does it end? It starts with the API set on the client side that is used to invoke a service, and it covers the transmission of the request over the network and the resulting response. Middleware does not include the software that provides the actual service—that's in the server's application's domain; nor does it include the database. On the client side, middleware does not include the user interface—that's in the client's application domain.

Pipes and Platforms

The middleware boundaries have become murkier as we move to 3-tier and N-Tier client/server. You may recall from the last chapter that in this new architecture model, the bulk of the application logic runs on one or more servers in the middle tier. In addition, the application may consist of hundreds of independently written components, objects, or services. In other words, the middle-tier application may consist of hundreds or thousands of moving parts. So what makes the middle-tier act as a single system (or application)? You guessed it—the *middleware*.

In N-tier environments, the middleware must also provide a platform for running server-side components, balancing their loads, managing the integrity of transactions, maintaining high-availability, and securing the environment. It must also provide pipes that allow server components to communicate using a variety of metaphors. Of course, the middleware is still responsible for providing client/server communication pipes. So we propose a new metaphor for describing middleware in N-tier client/server environments, which we call *pipes and platforms* (see Figure 3-7). Here's a brief explanation:

- **Pipes** provide the intercomponent (and interapplication) communication services. Examples of pipes are RPCs, MOMs, and ORBs. Pipes also include wire-level security such as SSL, as well as directory services such as LDAP.

- **Platforms** are the application servers that run the server-side components. You can typically use them across multiple operating systems to provide a unified view of the distributed environment. Examples of platforms are TP Monitors, Object Transaction Monitors, and Web Application Servers. Note that the platform for the client side is not part of the middleware equation; it is typically either a Web browser or the operating system.

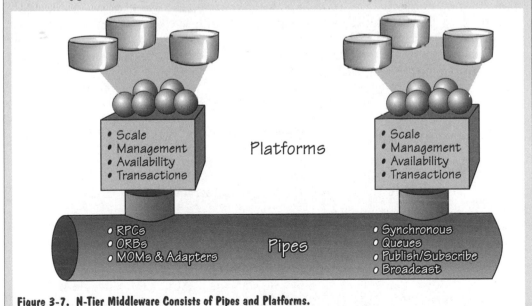

Figure 3-7. N-Tier Middleware Consists of Pipes and Platforms.

Pipes Come in All Shapes

We further divide pipes into two broad classes:

■ *General pipes* provide the substrate for most client/server interactions. They include the communication stacks, distributed directories, authentication services, network time, remote procedure calls, and queuing services. This category also includes the network operating system extensions such as distributed file and print services. Products that fall into the general middleware category include LDAP, X.500, firewalls, certificate servers, SSL, DCE, MS-RPC, Named Pipes, TCP/IP, APPC, IPX/SPX, and NetBIOS. We also include the Message-Oriented Middleware (also known as MOM) products from IBM, BEA, TIBCO, Microsoft, Peerlogic, and Neon Systems.

■ *Service-specific pipes* accomplish a particular client/server type of service. They include:

♦ Database-specific middleware such as ODBC, JDBC, SQLJ, DRDA, EDA/SQL, SAG/CLI, OLE DB, OQL, and Oracle SQL*Net.

♦ OLTP-specific middleware such as Tuxedo's ATMI and /WS, Encina's Transactional RPC, X/Open's TxRPC and XATMI, CORBA's OTS, and Microsoft's DTC and TIP.

♦ Groupware-specific middleware such as MAPI, VIM, JavaMail, SMTP, Web/NNTP, S/MIME, POP3, IMAP, Workflow, and Lotus Notes calls.

- ◆ Object-specific middleware such as OMG's CORBA/IIOP, Microsoft's COM+, and JavaSoft's RMI-over-IIOP.

- ◆ Internet-specific middleware such as HTTP, CGI, XML, and SET.

- ◆ System management-specific middleware such as SNMP, CMIP, RMON, DMTF, WFM, JMAPI, WEBEM, and ORBs.

You can probably tell by now that middleware was created by people who love acronyms. To the best of our knowledge, few technologies have as many buzzwords and acronyms as client/server middleware. We will cover, in gruesome detail, the middleware standards that apply to the different client/server application types. By the time you finish reading this Survival Guide, you'll know exactly what all these middleware acronyms mean. In the meantime, please bear with us as we gradually pull together the pieces of this story. ❏

Server-to-Server Middleware

Middleware does not include the software that provides the actual service. It *does*, however, include the software that is used to coordinate inter-server interactions (see Figure 3-8). Server-to-server interactions are usually client/server in nature—servers are clients to other servers, and vice versa. So a server can play both client and server roles. Most modern software (even within operating system kernels) follows the client/server paradigm.

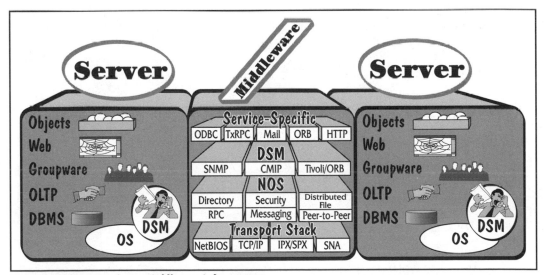

Figure 3-8. Server-to-Server Middleware Infrastructure.

However, some server-to-server interactions require specialized server middleware. For example, a two-phase commit protocol may be used to coordinate a transaction that executes on multiple servers. Servers on a mail backbone typically use special server-to-server middleware for doing store-and-forward type messaging. Databases and groupware servers use daemons to automatically replicate data.

The Client/Server Roadmap

The building blocks we just described will serve as our roadmap throughout this Survival Guide. It will keep you from getting lost in the client/server maze. In the next chapter, we look at the state of the networking infrastructure: When can we expect bandwidth heaven? *Part 2* covers what clients and servers need from an OS. *Part 3* is about the intergalactic NOS. We then start our ascent into the application space by covering the five competing technologies for intergalactic client/server: *Part 4* covers SQL databases and data warehousing; *Part 5* covers TP Monitors; *Part 6* covers groupware; *Part 7* covers distributed objects, components, and Object Transaction Monitors (OTMs); and *Part 8* covers the Internet, Web Application Servers, E-Commerce, and the Object Web that brings all these technologies together. We're almost there. *Part 9* is about how to manage these systems; it deals with the issues of distributed systems management. Finally, *Part 10* introduces a model for looking at client/server application tools and speculates on where all this is going.

Chapter 4

The Road to Bandwidth Heaven

If something inert is set in motion, it will gradually come to life.

— Lao Tzu

We hope to have convinced you that our planet will soon be covered with ubiquitous client/server webs. Using these webs, we will be able to communicate more effectively with other humans—customers, suppliers, the boss, coworkers, family, and friends. We will also be able to communicate with the everyday machines that serve us—cars, gas pumps, TV sets, smart cards, Java-based *Jini* devices, and even intelligent homes.

This chapter provides an overview of the extensive networking infrastructure that supports these client/server webs. Even though this book is really about client/server software, we need to take a short detour to look at the physical networking infrastructure on which the software builds. Today, it is a very extensive infrastructure that can interconnect every network on the planet. But for intergalactic client/server computing to really take off, these webs must become even more ubiquitous. They must extend deep into our homes. Just as importantly, they must

provide low-cost, abundant bandwidth. So what is the state of this infrastructure? When can we expect this bandwidth heaven? What obstacles remain? These are the questions we need to answer in this chapter.

SO WHAT DOES A MODERN NETWORK LOOK LIKE?

A physical network is a collection of communication links, cables, routers, switching equipment, and the transport stacks that glue it all together. Networks can be divided into two broad categories: *Local Area Networks (LANs)* that cover short distances—typically a building or campus—and *Wide Area Networks (WANs)* that cover extended geographical areas. A WAN may use physical links from multiple carriers. This section explains how LANs and WANs are interconnected into global backbones. And we briefly explain where transport stacks fit in this equation.

Bridges, Routers, IP Switches, and Gateways

*U*ntil recently, you had the router camp and the switch camp, but those walls are coming down.

> — Matthew Bross, CTO
> Williams Communications Group
> (June, 1998)

Transport stacks—for example, TCP/IP, NetBIOS, IPX/SPX, DECnet, AppleTalk, and SNA/APPN—provide reliable end-to-end communications across WANs and LANs. So how do these protocols provide end-to-end networking on a global scale? They use the magic of LAN/WAN/LAN interconnect technology—such as routers, bridges, and gateways—to transport multiprotocol traffic across a campus or wide area network in an integrated fashion. Groups can decide for themselves what protocols to run on their local networks. And they can leave it up to the backbone providers to collect these protocols and route them across networks.

Figure 4-1 shows how bridges, routers, and gateways are used in a modern backbone network. As you can see, today's enterprise networks consist of a combination of LANs, including Token Rings and Ethernets; WANs, including public and private packet-switched networks that run X.25, Frame Relay, and ATM; and the bridges, routers, and gateways that provide the internetworking, multiprotocol "glue" that ties the LANs and WANs together.

Bridges are computers or devices that interconnect LANs using link-layer routing information and physical addresses; protocols that do not support internetworking, like NetBIOS, are bridged. *Routers* interconnect LANs using protocol-dependent

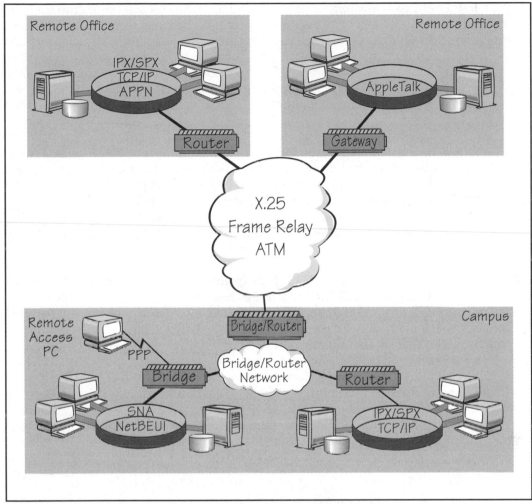

Figure 4-1. Creating a Modern Backbone With Bridges, Routers, and Gateways.

routing information. Routers create and maintain dynamic routing tables of the destinations they know. They are typically used with protocols that support a network layer—such as TCP/IP, IPX/SPX, APPN, XNS, AppleTalk, and OSI. *Multiprotocol Routers* support different combinations of network layer protocols. *Bridge/Routers* are single devices that combine the functions of bridges and routers. *Gateways* are devices that perform brute force translations between protocols. They are used in situations where the backbone can only support one protocol, and all other protocols get translated to it.

Bridge/Routers started as a bottom-up phenomenon—they solved practical problems and were not part of a grand architecture. The router products from Cisco, Bay Networks, 3Com, Motorola, and IBM can now encapsulate NetBIOS, AppleTalk,

SNA, and IPX/SPX to allow only a single protocol to run on the backbone (usually IPX/SPX, APPN, or TCP/IP). The industry is still learning how to make these products work in environments that require the load balancing of traffic between links and the handling of high-priority traffic. Bridges use fixed-path, one-route-only schemes; only a few know how to re-route traffic to alternate paths when a link fails. While they can handle any LAN-based protocols, they do not perform very well when large amounts of broadcast packets are propagated throughout the network.

But the fast-growing Bridge/Router industry—$5.2 billion in 1997—is extremely competitive, and it will undoubtedly solve these problems. For example, the newest routers use specialized protocols to determine the best paths for network traffic and can even perform load balancing across multiple parallel paths. In addition, they filter traffic and control broadcast storms, such as those generated by TCP/IP. Routers are also used as low-level firewalls between intranets and the public Internet.

In the old days, you could always tell a bridge from a router by the OSI layer in which they operated. Bridges simply forwarded link-layer frames (layer 2), while routers looked at routing information (layer 3) to perform routing calculations and forward IP frames. However, a new generation of IP-switching devices is starting to encroach on the turf of traditional routers by making routing decisions based on layer 3 information. These so-called *Layer-3 Switches*—pioneered by Bay Networks and Ipsilon Networks in 1997—use semiconductor switches to directly stuff the forwarding addresses in a link-layer packet based on IP routing information. As a result, these switches are able to forward IP traffic at wire speeds—several million packets per second. Non-IP packets take the slower path through traditional routers. We will have more to say about IP-switching when we cover ATM later in this chapter.

The Transport Stacks Middleware

The Bridge/Router phenomenon is not the only area that experienced great progress. Modern operating systems—like Unix, Windows 98, Windows NT, Mac OS, OS/2, and NetWare—are much more network friendly. They've introduced features that allow multivendor communication stacks and network adapters to easily plug into them. And they also make life easier for programmers by providing APIs that are stack independent.

Here's a summary of some of the new operating system features that make that possible:

■ *The stack sandwich* provides the hooks for snapping multivendor protocol stacks into an operating system. To accommodate multivendor networks, modern operating systems must support multiple protocols, redirectors, and APIs. To do that effectively, the operating system must provide well-defined interfaces between components. A modern operating system usually "sand-wiches" the transport stacks between a transport-independent interface at the top of the stacks and a logical interface to the network device drivers at the bottom of the stacks (see Figure 4-2).

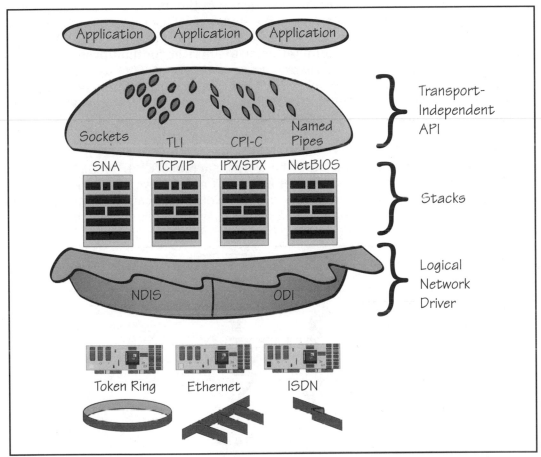

Figure 4-2. The Stack Sandwich.

■ **The logical network driver** provides a single interface to all the network adapters. This interface between the network adapter and the transport stacks is particularly important. The last thing vendors who provide transport stacks want is to write a driver for every possible network adapter. And, of course, network adapter vendors want to avoid having to interface to every possible stack. Microsoft/3Com's *NDIS* and Novell's *ODI* are the two most widely supported de facto standards for interfacing protocol stacks to network adapter device drivers. They do so by providing a logical network board that makes it easy to interface different network adapters with multiple protocol stacks (see Figure 4-2). Transport stack providers can use NDIS or ODI as the common interface to all network adapters. And network adapter vendors can use NDIS or ODI as the top layer for their network drivers. NDIS and ODI take care of sending and receiving data and managing the adapter card.

■ ***The transport-independent APIs*** sit on top of the transport stacks and allow developers to plug their programs into a single interface that supports multiple protocols. The *Sockets* interface is becoming the premier choice on most operating system platforms for interfacing to multivendor multiprotocol stacks. Other choices include the *Transport Layer Interface (TLI)* used in NetWare and many Unix implementations; *CPI-C*, the modern SNA peer-to-peer API that can now run over both SNA and TCP/IP stacks; and *Named Pipes*, which runs on top of NetBIOS, IPX/SPX, and TCP/IP stacks.

■ ***The protocol matchmakers*** allow applications written for a specific transport, such as SNA, to run across other networks, such as TCP/IP or IPX/SPX (see Figure 4-3). This strategy eliminates the need for gateways and works well with existing applications. For example, a Lotus Notes application written for Net-BIOS could be made to run over SNA networks without changing a line of code.

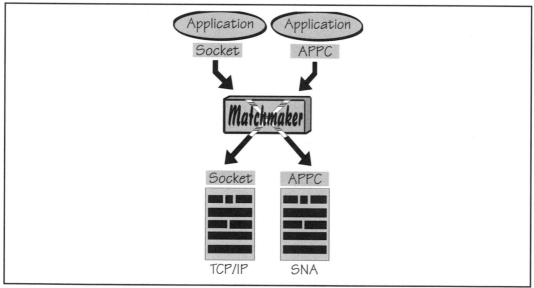

Figure 4-3. The Protocol Matchmaker.

In summary, today's network environment is a truly heterogeneous hodgepodge of protocols and media options. Network routers, gateways, switches, and bridges insulate the application developer from having to worry about cabling, network adapters, or protocol transport choices. Multiprotocol API sets make it easier for service providers to develop client/server applications that run over multiple protocol stacks. And we're getting closer to the day when client/server programs can be plugged into any protocol stack (on any machine) almost as easily as appliances plug into electrical outlets.

IS BANDWIDTH HEAVEN AROUND THE CORNER?

Is bandwidth heaven around the corner? To answer this question, we must first take a stab at defining bandwidth heaven, and then we can determine if the networking infrastructure can meet our expectations. As you will discover, some of us are already in bandwidth heaven. For the rest of us, a few more roadblocks need to be overcome before we get there.

Boundless Bandwidth: How Much Is Enough?

So how much bandwidth do you need? It really depends on your tastes (see Table 4-1). If you have expensive tastes, then you will need at least 9 Mbit/s to get high-quality video, audio, and data on your network connections. Many of us will be in heaven with just under 1 Mbit/s—at least until we compare ourselves with the Joneses. According to Morgan Stanley's U.S. Investment Research Group, the typical user's demand for bandwidth grows between 16 and 55 times over a three-year period. So it's all very subjective. In this book, we define heaven as 2 Mbit/s or more of dedicated, isochronous bandwidth.

Table 4-1. How Much Bandwidth Do You Need?

Content	Bandwidth Requirements	Remarks
Audio		
■ CD quality	706 Kbit/s	44,100 samples/sec, 16-bit per sample
■ Digital phone quality	64 Kbit/s	8,000 samples/sec, 8-bit samples
Minimum-quality, full-motion video	566 Kbit/s	1024 X 768 pixels, 30 frames/sec 3 colors; 8 bits each
TV-quality, full-motion video		
■ Uncompressed	96 Mbit/s	
■ MPEG-2 compression	6 Mbit/s	
Data requirements	2 Mbit/s	For LAN-speed responsiveness

Must It Be Isochronous?

First, what is an *isochronous* network? It's a network that provides very low and predictable node-to-node delays (or latencies). Isochronous networks are capable of dealing with the steady, immediate delivery, and high-bandwidth requirements of multimedia technology. For example, networks that support desktop training videos or videoconferencing need to supply, on demand, 1.5 Mbit/s (or more) to each PC. We can accommodate some of that demand by exploiting the prioritized traffic services of existing Token Ring and Ethernet networks. Higher-priority frames are assigned to the delay-sensitive traffic. But what we really need are high-speed networks with separate voice/video and data traffic channels (also called virtual circuits) that can guarantee a fixed delivery time for multimedia traffic (see the next Briefing box).

What's a Virtual Circuit?

Briefing

Virtual circuits are like the phone system. They get established when two nodes need to communicate, and then get relinquished after they're not needed. Because video and voice are carried over the network in streams within virtual circuits, delays are low and constant. For example, the WAN-based Frame Relay packet-switching technology uses virtual circuits to allocate bandwidth on demand and optimize the use of the existing bandwidth.

In contrast, today's LAN technology allocates bandwidth by *contention*. Everybody is bidding with everybody else to obtain the use of the broadcast medium. To get on the LAN, you must either wait for a token (Token Ring) or start broadcasting; you must be prepared to back off if you detect a collision (Ethernet). Contention methods cannot guarantee deterministic response times (or delays). It's a matter of luck, and things get worse around rush hour. The situation can be improved by assigning priorities, but there's still contention within the same priority levels.

Some of the new isochronous LAN technologies propose a *hybrid* environment that allocates a certain amount of bandwidth to contention traffic and gives the rest to virtual circuits. For example, isochronous FDDI allocates a certain percentage of the network bandwidth to multiple 64 Kbit/s virtual circuits and gives the remainder to normal contention-based data.

Another approach is to use LAN switches to eliminate contention. For example, *Switched Ethernet* provides a dedicated 10 Mbit/s pipe to each station by giving it its own LAN segment; each cable segment is directly wired to a centralized Ethernet switch, which acts as a hub. The hub provides a high-speed internal bus to switch packets between multiple cable segments; it still offers 10 Mbit/s to each station. Many LAN switches are designed to be interconnected via high-speed uplinks such as FDDI (100 Mbit/s), Fast Ethernet (100 Mbit/s), and, in limited situations, ATM (up to 2.4 Gbit/s), and Gigabit Ethernet. LAN switching is big business; according to the Dell'Oro Group, LAN switches and shared hubs generated sales of $9 billion in 1997.

Asynchronous Transfer Mode (ATM) is the ultimate isochronous technology. It allocates LAN/WAN bandwidth on demand via virtual circuits. ATM uses high-speed, hardware-based, circuit-switching technology that is potentially capable of unleashing an awesome amount of isochronous bandwidth at very low cost (every node is given its own dedicated LAN segment into the switch). ❑

How Much Bandwidth Can We Really Expect?

You're only as fast as your weakest link.

— *Gopi Bala, Senior Analyst*
Yankee Group

The amount of bandwidth you get generally depends on which side of the firewall you're on. Many corporate users are already in bandwidth heaven, at least on their LANs. However, if you're outside the corporate firewall, you're probably in "bandwidth hell"—this includes home users, mobile users, and corporate users when they're outside their inner sanctum. In addition, even traffic on corporate LANs must occasionally traverse a slow WAN—the big cloud in the sky—to connect with other LANs in far-away places (see Figure 4-4).

Assuming no contention, the bandwidth you get at work is primarily a function of the capacity of your LANs, WANs, and the links that connect them. The bandwidth you get at home is primarily determined by the link that connects you to an access point—or *Point of Presence (POP)*—on the WAN; it is also a function of the capacity of the WAN. Finally, if you're a mobile user, the bandwidth you get will be determined by your wireless link to the WAN or LAN. So to understand bandwidth, we need to look at the performance of the five potential chokepoints: LANs, WANs, LAN-to-WAN, home-to-WAN, and wireless-to-WAN. The next five sections give you a quick update of the state of these five networking technologies and their infrastructures.

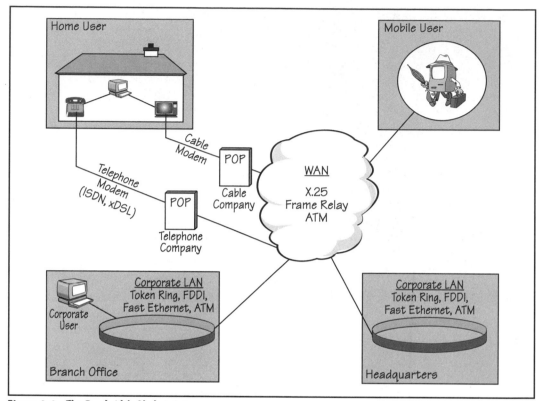

Figure 4-4. The Bandwidth Chokepoints.

The State of the LAN

As you can see from Table 4-2, LANs are not the bottleneck in our quest for bandwidth heaven. It also appears that Ethernet now owns the LAN at any speed. Although ATM can be used in LANs, it remains more expensive than Ethernet at any given speed. ATM's niche is on the WAN, where it has many advantages. In mid-98, the IEEE 802.5 committee finally ratified the 100 Mbit/s *High-Speed Token Ring (HSTR)* standard. However, it may be too little, too late.

So on the eve of its 25th anniversary, Ethernet is a $10 billion industry with more than 100 million users (Source: Dell'Oro Group estimates). The "classic" 10 Mbit/s contention-based Ethernet is now the entry-level. But, as we explained in the previous briefing, you can use switched Ethernet to give each user a dedicated 10 Mbit/s of bandwidth for an additional $10 per port. If this is not enough, you can move to Fast Ethernet using existing wiring. Even though this technology is less than four years old, it is now in the mainstream. According to Dataquest, Fast Ethernet sales surpassed the $1 billion mark in the second quarter of 1998.

Table 4-2. LAN Transmission Technologies.

LAN Type	Speed	Marketshare	Adapter Cost	Deployment
Ethernet	10 Mbit/s	>50%	Under $70	Widespread (Over 70 million nodes)
Token Ring	4/16 Mbit/s	<18%	Under $180	Flat market (20 million nodes)
Fast Ethernet	100 Mbit/s	<30%	Under $140	Growing very rapidly
FDDI	100 Mbit/s	<1%	Under $1,000	Declining marketshare
Gigabit Ethernet	1 Gbit/s	<1%	$1000 and up	Growing rapidly
ATM	25 Mbit/s-2.4 Gbit/s	<1%	$500 and up	Declining marketshare as a LAN replacement

Gigabit Ethernet is the new kid on the block. However, it is already a stable technology based on the new *IEEE 802.3z* standard. There are quite a few products that implement this new standard, and they are selling well. The bad news is that Gigabit Ethernet does not support existing twisted-pair cabling; it only runs on fiber. The other bad news is that the technology is still too costly for your ordinary client PCs. However, it may be affordable for server backbones. According to Dell'Oro Group, the Gigabit Ethernet market will reach $1.3 billion by the year 2000. And, vendors are already working on Fast Gigabit, which operates at 10 Gbit/s; it will be used initially to interconnect Gigabit switches.

The State of the WAN

Putting large file-oriented applications over WANs is like herding hippos through a garden hose.

— David Willis
Network Computing

WAN performance is primarily determined by two factors: 1) the switches that route data across networks, and 2) the type (and quality) of the wide-area cabling infrastructure. For example, the faster switches require a fiber-optic cabling infrastructure to achieve their maximum speeds. Yes, the physical world still matters when it comes to networks.

Table 4-3 shows the progression of physical links that are used in WAN backbones. Until recently, the Internet backbone was a collection of T3 lines. The Web almost brought the Internet to its knees just carrying text and occasional pictures. So T3 is not enough. As a result, Internet backbone providers are now stepping up to ANSI's

Table 4-3. WAN Backbone: Physical Interconnect Technology.

Line Type	Speed		Comments
T1 (or DS1)	1.54	Mbit/s	North American standard
E1	2.04	Mbit/s	European CCITT standard
E2	8.44	Mbit/s	European CCITT standard
E3	34.36	Mbit/s	European CCITT standard
T3 (or DS3)	44.73	Mbit/s	North American standard
OC-1	51.84	Mbit/s	Sonet fiber standard
OC-2	103.68	Mbit/s	Sonet fiber standard
OC-3	155.52	Mbit/s	Sonet fiber standard
OC-12	622.08	Mbit/s	Sonet fiber standard
OC-24	1.244	Gbit/s	Sonet fiber standard
OC-48	2.488	Gbit/s	Sonet fiber standard
OC-96	4.976	Gbit/s	Sonet fiber standard
OC-192	10	Gbit/s	Sonet fiber standard
OC-768	40	Gbit/s	Sonet fiber standard

Synchronous Optical Network (Sonet) transmission standards for high-speed fiber-optic links. The Sonet standard is specified in multiples of 51.84 Mbit/s. The top-of-the-line is OC-192, which specifies a line speed of 10 Gbit/s; ANSI is now working on 40 Gbit/s Sonet (and higher). Today, Sonet tops out at OC-96 speeds. We can extrapolate that by the year 2000, OC-192 speeds will be typical. The Sonet physical layer also specifies a ring-like wiring topology for instantly rerouting traffic around outages.

The good news is that all the major carriers worldwide are deploying Sonet on their backbones. And many are starting to offer Sonet services to corporate users and Internet service providers but it's not cheap. By the year 2000, most public WANs will be close to 100% Sonet. In the U.S., most long distance carriers have installed Sonet fiber coast-to-coast, and many local carriers are installing Sonet fiber rings within major cities. Sprint is the furthest along, with 100 interconnected Sonet rings, which cover 85% of its customers. By mid-99, Sprint expects to add 70 more rings to cover all its customers. Sprint is now carving out Sonet OC-12 trunks into lower-capacity T1 and T3 circuits and selling them to individual users; the idea is to provide a low-cost fiber service at the low-end.

Sonet is basically a physical layer fat-pipe technology. Data must be framed to travel over it. So now that Sonet is being deployed around the world, the question is: What will be used to push data on these fat pipes? Of course, one of the answers must be ATM; it was designed from day one to support switching speeds of up to 2.488 Gbit/s. In addition, some of the newer IP switches can go directly to Sonet thus bypassing ATM and its "cell tax" altogether (see the next Briefing box). A compromise is to provide IP packet switching over ATM hardware (bypassing the ATM software). So what is this packetizing all about?

Modern WANs make use of packet-switching technology to provide the link layer on top of T1, T3, or Sonet physical backbones. Packet switches break data streams into packets that they then launch into the network. The address headers are used to direct each packet to its destination. You should note that protocols like TCP/IP or IPX/SPX run on top of these packet-switched networks.

Table 4-4 compares the three leading packet-switching technologies—*Frame Relay, Switched Multimegabit Data Services (SMDS)*, and *Asynchronous Transfer Mode (ATM)*. Clearly, ATM gives us the best bandwidth. However, Frame Relay is a seasoned technology that works on the existing T1 WAN infrastructure. SMDS is mostly used in Europe as a precursor to ATM. Both Frame Relay and SMDS can run on top of ATM packet switches (see the next Briefing box). The bottom line is that the intergalactic WAN backbone seems to be in good shape. The carriers can supply all the bandwidth we are willing to pay for.

Table 4-4. WAN Backbone: The Packet-Switching Alternatives.

WAN Technology	Maximum Speed	Applications	Packet Size	Deployment
Frame Relay	45 Mbit/s (T3/E3)	Data/voice	Variable length 4,096 bytes max	Wide
SMDS	45 Mbit/s (T3)	Data	Variable length 9,188 bytes max (can be broken into 53-byte cells)	Limited and declining
ATM	2.4 Gbit/s (OC-48)	Data, voice, and video	53-byte cells	Limited but growing

The State of the LAN-to-WAN Interconnect

Today's LANs connect to WANs via routers. The router connects to either a private or public WAN via dedicated leased lines (usually T1 or T3). The switching technology is typically Frame Relay, X.25, or just point-to-point (PPP). Some of the larger corporations are now using ATM-over-Sonet (or ATM-over-xDSL) for their LAN-to-WAN connections. Others are looking at intranet service providers as a way to replace private networks with public WANs.

In contrast to individuals, corporations can require a guaranteed "fat pipe" (or *quality of service*) from their WAN providers via bandwidth reservation schemes such as the Internet's *Resource Reservation Protocol (RSVP)*. And corporations can afford to maintain sophisticated high-speed routers on their premises. This means that the LAN becomes just another segment on the WAN. Consequently, the technology that we described in the previous section applies to the LAN-to-WAN connection. So today's LAN-to-WAN connection is Frame Relay; tomorrow's connection will be ATM. And if ATM runs on the LAN, separate routers won't even be required. The LAN simply morphs into the WAN. There is no longer an impedance mismatch.

B-ISDN: Frame Relay, SMDS, and ATM

Briefing

The public network, which is essentially 20 years old, has been overwhelmed by the sudden and dramatic increase in traffic. And conditions are getting worse.

> — Joe McGarvey
> Inter@ctive Week

Fiber optics is taking us from a modest to an almost infinite bandwidth, with nothing in between.

> — Nicholas Negroponte, Author
> Being Digital

What Is Frame Relay?

Frame Relay is currently the most popular packet-switching technology for WANs. According to a 1998-survey by the *Frame Relay Forum*, some 38,000 companies now use a half-million Frame Relay ports. Most customers still run their Frame Relay over low-speed (56-Kbit/s to 64 Kbit/s) lines, according to the survey, and voice accounts for only 1% of the traffic.

The technology first appeared in 1992 as a streamlined implementation of the older X.25 packet-switching technology. Frame Relay can route variable-length packets at megabit speeds over existing routers, switches, and other HDLC-based equipment; it only requires a software upgrade. In contrast, X.25 can only deliver a maximum of 64 Kbit/s over the same physical infrastructure. Frame Relay achieves its magic by bypassing error checks at each network segment (the midpoints). Instead, it relies on the endpoints to provide end-to-end error checking.

In addition to connecting LANs, Frame Relay's virtual circuits can connect to both the Internet and SNA. The demand for Frame Relay is still very strong. According to the Vertical Systems Group, the total market for Frame Relay equipment and services will grow from $6.1 billion in 1997 to $14.6 billion in the year 2000. Note that Frame Relay is being continuously improved. For example, scalability was always an issue because the technology was designed to operate at T1 speeds or less. However, equipment suppliers were able to boost its top transmission speed to 45 Mbit/s (or T3/E3-speeds). In 1997, MCI became the first carrier to offer 45 Mbit/s Frame Relay service.

What Is SMDS?

SMDS was originally designed to fill the gap for high-speed WAN services until ATM became widely available. It supports variable-length packets that can be broken into ATM-size fixed cells to facilitate the migration. SMDS today can run at T3 speeds (45 Mbit/s); it obtains its high throughput by not providing support for virtual circuits—each packet is on its own. In contrast, both ATM and Frame Relay support virtual circuits. SMDS is not a runaway market success. It became available at about the same time as Frame Relay. It seems users felt more comfortable with Frame Relay because its virtual circuits were an obvious substitute for private lines. In the U.S., only MCI offers SMDS services. The other major carriers seem to have passed over SMDS in favor of Frame Relay and ATM. In June 1998, MCI announced it will cease marketing the service to new accounts; it will continue to support existing SMDS customers and help them migrate to ATM.

What Is ATM?

ATM may not be gaining much acceptance in LANs, but it is the darling of the WAN industry—and its greatest hope for the future. More than 70% of today's Internet traffic is carried across backbones in ATM cells. ATM is a packet-switching protocol that achieves very high speeds by using fixed-length data cells—or packets on top of *virtual circuits*. *Permanent Virtual Circuits (PVCs)* are statically assigned; *Switched Virtual Circuits (SVCs)* are dynamic. In either case, a virtual circuit can guarantee quality of service—including bandwidth and priority.

ATM was designed from the start to mix different types of traffic—including data, voice, and video. ATM's system of transmitting small 53-byte cells of information—or packets—is flexible enough to work at capacities ranging from megabits to gigabits (see Figure 4-5). The small, fixed size cell makes it possible to implement very high-speed switches in hardware. ATM's bandwidth is demand-based and scalable, meaning that each node can access the network at the speeds required by an application. Initially, ATM promised to provide seamless networking and remove the current distinctions between LANs and WANs. However, at this stage, ATM is only being used on WANs, where it is gaining acceptance for being both reliable and scalable; it is the only technology that offers guaranteed *Quality of Service (QoS)* transmissions. To keep pace with rising demand for Internet access, ISPs are buying OC-3 and OC-12 ATM ports for their backbone infrastructures in droves.

More than 35 vendors make ATM equipment and switches—including Fore Systems, 3Com, Bay Networks, IBM, Cisco, Madge, Motorola, and Nortel. A few of these switches have throughput capacities approaching 50 Gbit/s. What's surprising is that some of this equipment even interoperates. Currently, all the major local and long-distance telephone carriers in the U.S. and Canada offer ATM. Nearly every carrier says its ATM network will handle all types of traffic—including Frame Relay and SMDS. And most carriers offer Frame Relay to ATM conversions.

The price of an ATM connection is declining by about 40% each year. In addition, the maximum speed of an ATM connection appears to be doubling every year; it could reach 10 Gbit/s by 2000. So it shouldn't come as a surprise that the ATM market is growing. According to the Vertical Systems Group, the total demand for ATM services and equipment will grow from $2.2 billion in 1997 to $7.3 billion in the year 2000.

Of course, ATM still faces some very stiff competition. As we explained in the last section, Gigabit Ethernets are giving ATM a run for the money on LAN backbones. ATM may counter by always being faster and more scalable. On the WAN, ATM faces competition from both Frame Relay and IP Layer-3 switches. ATM will counter with its unique features such as virtual circuits and fixed-sized small cells to provide guaranteed QoS. ATM is already the carrier of choice for Frame Relay packets on high-speed data backbones.

However, ATM must still deal with its IP problem. If you think about it, the inventors of ATM designed a new packet-switched network from scratch without paying attention to the ubiquity of TCP/IP. Of course, with the explosion of the Internet, no one can afford to ignore the needs of IP (or treat it just like any other protocol). To succeed, ATM must go out of its way to become more IP-savvy. ATM's *Multiprotocol Over ATM (MPOA)* may not be enough. The predominance of IP demands more special treatment. Today, IP packets are being transferred over ATM networks at very high speeds. For example, MCI runs IP reliably on its 622-Mbit/s ATM backbone right now. However, there is routing intelligence in the IP packet that needs to be transferred to the Layer-2 ATM virtual circuit mechanism. This is where the newer IP-switching technologies come into the picture. The ATM answer is to incorporate this technology directly into the ATM switch.

Of course, there are some who don't want to pay for the 5-byte header (or cell tax) ATM imposes on IP. They don't want to segment IP packets into multiple ATM cells, each with its 5-byte overhead. They feel that *IP-over-Sonet* is all you need to move IP traffic over the Internet—the IP frame is mapped straight into the STS-3c frames of a Sonet link. However, this is not a solution for moving voice, video, and multi-protocol data over the same highway. In today's world, voice is still the biggest source of revenue for the backbone carriers. It doesn't make sense for them to impose an "IP cell tax" on every voice packet. So ATM may still be the best compromise for moving data, voice, and video over a common intergalactic highway.

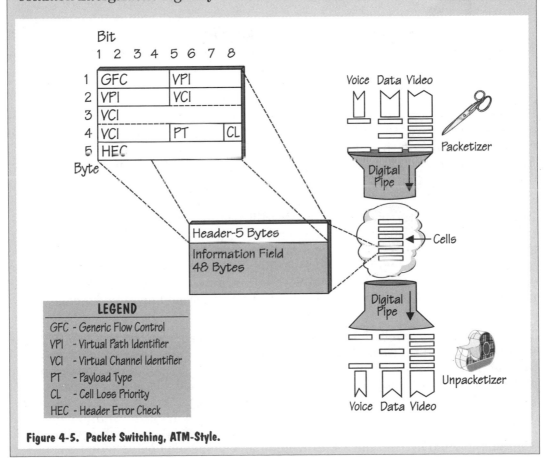

Figure 4-5. Packet Switching, ATM-Style.

What Is B-ISDN?

So what is the *Broadband-Integrated Services Digital Network (B-ISDN)*? The CCITT defines B-ISDN as a cell-switched WAN that supports speeds of over 1.54 Mbit/s. B-ISDN is really ATM over Sonet. The B-ISDN standard defines an *ATM adaptation layer (AAL)* that is responsible for mapping data, voice, and video information to and from ATM-defined cell formats. So B-ISDN is really the Information Highway built on fiber links and ATM switches. SMDS and Frame Relay are the precursors to this technology. ❑

The State of the Home-to-WAN Connection

So which is it going to be: the thick white coaxial cable coiled up behind your television set? Or the thin plastic phone cord behind your desk?

— Mike Mills
Washington Post
(July, 1998)

So how do we bring the digital highway into the home? As most Internet Web users are painfully aware, the home is on the wrong side of the bandwidth track. To extend the WAN into the home requires a solution to the impedance mismatch (or bottleneck) created by the "last mile" of telephone cable that connects homes and offices to the long-distance service providers.

In the U.S. alone, telephone companies still own more than 167 million pairs of copper wire local loops (there are over 650 million telephone lines in the world). But, over the past decade, the long-distance carriers replaced their copper wire backbones with a network of superfast, high-bandwidth, low-tariff, and fiber-optic cables (i.e., Sonet). However, bringing these advantages into the home requires the upgrading of that last mile of local cable to fiber—a mind-boggling expense.

Today's 56-Kbit/s (well, 53-Kbit/s) modems are pushing the analog telephone system to the limit. These "blazingly fast" modems won't deliver their advertised throughput, except under prime conditions. But there's good news on the horizon in the form of two competing technologies from the local telephone companies that promise to speed up the local loops without replacing the existing wiring: *Integrated Services Digital Network (ISDN)* and the new *Digital Subscriber Line (xDSL)* set of services. And if these don't work out, there's always the *cable modem* alternative from the cable TV companies (see the next Briefing box).

Eventually, fiber-optic cable will be strung into homes. Fiber is several hundred times faster than even coaxial cable, and more versatile. U.S. local phone companies are already expanding fiber beyond their switching offices to the curbs of their residential customers. They will eventually extend it all the way into the home. Pacific Bell—which covers all of California—is leading the pack. In addition, some cable operators (such as Time Warner) are installing fiber as a replacement for coax. Table 4-5 compares these various alternatives (also see the next Briefing box).

Table 4-5. The Home-to-WAN Connection: Comparing the Alternatives.

Connection Technology	Speed	When Available	Comments
V.34	28.8 Kbit/s	Now	■ Dial-up analog modem ■ Modem under $50
V.90	56 Kbit/s	Now	■ Dial-up analog modem ■ Modem under $150
ISDN BRI	128 Kbit/s	Now	■ Dial-up digital modem ■ $200 for ISDN modem ■ $100 service installation ■ $40 per month + usage
ISDN PRI	1.544 Mbit/s	Now	■ Requires T1 ■ $500 - $750 per month
T1	1.544 Mbit/s	Now	■ Leased line ■ More than $700 per month
HDSL	up to 1.5 Mbit/s	Now	■ Uses existing telephone wire ■ 2 twisted-pairs ■ $300 installation ■ More than $300 per month
ADSL	up to 6 Mbit/s up to 640 Kbit/s (return)	Now	■ Asymmetrical bandwidth ■ Single twisted-pair ■ $300 installation ■ $100-$300 per month (includes Internet service)
Cable modem	up to 10 Mbit/s	Now	■ May require separate phone return ■ $100 installation ■ $100 Ethernet adapter ■ $40 per month (includes Internet service and cable modem rental)
B-ISDN (ATM/Sonet)	100 Mbit/s (and up)	2000	■ Bandwidth Nirvana ■ Voice, multimedia, and data ■ Requires fiber to the curb

FYI

Briefing

Medium Bandwidth:
ISDN, xDSL, and Cable Modems

What Is ISDN?

In the annals of telecommunications, few technologies have been as widely touted and as widely scorned as ISDN.

> — Paul Korzeniowski
> InternetWeek
> (April, 1998)

ISDN—not to be confused with B-ISDN—is a digital telephony technology that supports the high-speed transfer of voice and data over 24 gauge telephone lines. The most prevalent ISDN service is the *Basic Rate Interface (BRI)*, also known as *2B + D*. This service works over regular telephone lines by creating two independent 64 Kbit/s "B channels" for information (data or voice), and one 16 Kbit/s "D channel" for signaling and placing calls. The Basic Rate telephone line is clocked at 192 Kbit/s and uses time division multiplexing to allocate the two B and D channels; the extra 48 Kbit/s is reserved. Basic Rate uses the standard 4-wire telephone jack that is used in homes and offices. A higher-capacity version of ISDN is also available; it is called the *Primary Rate Interface (PRI)*, or *23B + D*. PRI can deliver 1.544 Mbit/s, but it is rarely used.

ISDN BRI is the digitization of the telephone line. It is five times faster than anything you can do with a modem today. In addition, ISDN provides a lower-cost form of communication because it charges by connect time (like normal voice calls) rather than by the packet (like some packet-switched WANs). Its higher speeds can reduce the connect time and save you some money. Today, more than 80% of U.S. homes can access ISDN. In contrast, more than 90% of European phones are ISDN-friendly. As of March 1997, there were over 5.3 million BRI installations worldwide. ISDN has traditionally been popular in Europe—Germany and France—where it's growing at 40% per year. ISDN is also doing well in the U.S. According to Dataquest, the number of ISDN lines in the U.S. hit 1.1 million in 1997; this number is expected to reach 1.6 million in 1998, and then double to 3.1 million in 2001. The current popularity of ISDN can be attributed to better pricing, packaging, and deployment of the technology by the U.S telephone companies. In addition, many Internet ISPs are now aggressively marketing ISDN. For $100, UUNet—a national ISP—will coordinate with local carriers the installation of ISDN. As a result, half the company's new customers are going with ISDN.

According to the Dataquest study, ISDN represents fewer than 5% of new customer access lines in 1997. So why isn't everyone using ISDN? The problem with ISDN is that it may be too little, too late. Detractors argue that 128 Kbit/s does not provide enough bandwidth for multimedia; it's not worth the pain to upgrade. At the low-end, it's much easier to go with a 56 Kbit modem. If you really need the bandwidth, you are better off going with either xDSL or cable modems—especially if they are offered in your area (see the following).

What Is xDSL?

The real battle for consumer Internet access will be cable modems vs. ADSL.

> — *Peter E. Dyson, Seybold Analyst*
> *(June, 1998)*

DSL was developed at Bellcore Labs as a way to use existing telephone twisted-pair wires to deliver low-cost video on demand in competition with cable modems. Like ISDN, DSL can combine both data and voice over the same wire. So if you subscribe to a DSL service, you will be able to cancel your second phone line. The "x" in *xDSL* stands for a variety of DSL technologies that are currently finding their way into the market. For example, *High-Bit-Rate Digital Subscriber Line (HDSL)* delivers 1.5 Mbit/s of bandwidth over the two telephone twisted-pairs that are found in most U.S. homes. The beauty of HDSL is that it offers repeaterless spans of 15,000 feet over existing copper loops. In contrast, a T1 circuit requires the carrier to install repeaters every 6,000 feet, and the last one can't be more than 3,000 feet from your home. The newer *Single-Line Digital Subscriber (SDSL)* operates at the same rates as HDSL, but it uses a single twisted-pair. It's range is also more limited.

Another variation of HDSL—called the *Asymmetric Digital Subscriber Line (ADSL)*—offers up to 8 Mbit/s downstream (to the home) and up to 640 Kbit/s upstream (to the telephone company). Asymmetrical, in this case, means that the line has more bandwidth going into the home than out. ADSL runs on a single telephone twisted-pair; its repeaters can span 18,000 feet. *R-ADSL* operates within the same transmission rates as ADSL, but it adjusts dynamically to various lengths and quality of the twisted-pair. *ADSL Lite* (also known as *g.lite*) is a lower-speed version of ADSL that eliminates the need for the telephone company to install a splitter to separate data from voice; it also covers a longer distance than full-rate ADSL. This lite version of ADSL is being spearheaded by Compaq, Intel, Microsoft, and almost every telco in existence (more on this later).

Finally, there is the super-fast *Very High Bit-Rate Digital Subscriber Line (VDSL)*; it will be able to support up to 52 Mbit/s downstream and 2.3 Mbit/s upstream over a single twisted-pair. However, the maximum range for this technology is 4,500 feet. Don't hold your breath waiting for VDSL. It's currently only a set of requirements for providing video-on-demand in an HDTV environment.

As you can tell from this brief introduction, the various xDSL technologies are differentiated by the following trade-offs: 1) distance versus speed, 2) upstream/downstream symmetry, and 3) ease-of-installation. Of course, these technologies are at different levels of market acceptance and deployment: HDSL is the oldest, VDSL is vaporware, ADSL is the most popular, and ADSL Lite has the most backers. Table 4-6 demonstrates some of these trade-offs. You should note that almost 75% of U.S. homes are within 18,000 feet of a telephone company's central office. This means that most homes can be serviced by one xDSL technology or another.

Table 4-6. Comparing the xDSL Flavors.

xDSL Technology	Maximum Speed		Max Distance (in feet)	Usage
	Downstream	Upstream		
ADSL Lite	1 Mbit/s	384 Kbit/s	22k-25k	Internet home access (easy installation)
ADSL/R-ADSL	8 Mbit/s	1.54 Mbit/s	12k	High-speed Internet access
	1.54 Mbit/s	1.54 Mbit/s	18k	
HDSL	1.54 Mbit/s	1.54 Mbit/s	15k	T1 replacement (requires two twisted-pairs)
	2.05 Mbit/s	2.05 Mbit/s	15k	E1 replacement (requires three twisted-pairs)
SDSL	1.54 Mbit/s	1.54 Mbit/s	10k	T1 replacement (requires single twisted-pair)
	2.05 Mbit/s	2.05 Mbit/s	10k	E1 replacement (requires single twisted-pair)
VDSL	52 Mbit/s	2.3 Mbit/s	1k	Video-on-demand Internet access for HDTV.
	13 Mbit/s	1.5 Mbit/s	4.5k	

By the middle of 1998, local telephone companies were introducing ADSL on an unprecedented scale throughout the U.S, Canada, Singapore, Switzerland, and Finland. In April, GTE announced rollouts in 16 states (via 300 POPs) throughout the U.S. In June, U.S. West completed a 40-city rollout based on Cisco/Netspeed DSL modems. In July, UUNet started offering 768 Kbit/s DSL access from all its 54 domestic POPs. In August, Pacific Bell deployed DSL to more than 200 California communities, reaching over 3 million businesses and homes. PacBell charges a flat $200 per month for bidirectional 384 Kbit/s DSL-based Internet access. For $339, you can get speeds of 1.5 Mbit/s downstream and 384 Kbit/s upstream. Currently, ADSL modems sell for about $250. However, Compaq is incorporating DSL modems into all its PCs and laptops for free. So we expect other PC manufacturers to follow suit. In addition, Microsoft is including DSL drivers in Windows 98.

The next step is for ADSL Lite to hit the market. The supporters of this new standard hope to have plug-and-play DSL products on the market by early 1999. The goal of the *Universal ADSL Working Group (UAWG)*, which is developing the new standard, is to make DSL as ubiquitous (and user-friendly) as telephone modems or Ethernet cards. It will be something that you buy off-the-shelf at your local CompUSA. In addition to the telephone companies, UAWG includes members from the PC industry like Intel, Microsoft, and Dell. The idea is to make DSL Lite a seamless end-to-end solution—just plug the PC into the phone. The coalition does not want to repeat the mistakes that made ISDN a relative failure. So it set out to create a mass market for DSL.

One of the first items the new group addressed was how to eliminate the $300 (or more) ADSL installation charge. It also wanted to make life easier for the telephone companies who are unwilling to send their technicians to open people's PCs, install cards, and deal with software issues. The problem is that ADSL requires a splitter to separate voice from data on the telephone line. Installing this splitter requires a "truck roll" from the telephone company. So ADSL Lite is splitterless (see Figure 4-6). But, there's no free lunch. So in this case, you lose some speed.

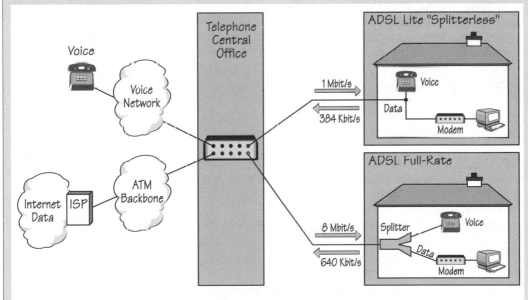

Figure 4-6 Splitterless ADSL Lite Versus Full-Rate ADSL.

In summary, xDSL is screamingly fast when compared with ISDN. It's also a lot less costly. ADSL Lite will help accelerate the DSL mass market, which should further bring down prices. However, ADSL Lite's most formidable competitor is cable. So be sure to read the next section before you decide to jump on the DSL bandwagon.

What Are Cable Modems?

We see cable providers as formidable competition. We want to target the existing copper facility as an alternative to cable modems for Internet access.

> — **John Cahill, Co-chair**
> **Universal ADSL Working Group**
> **(April, 1998)**

Of course, the telephone companies are not the only ones trying to solve the last-mile problem. They face stiff competition from the cable TV companies. There are now 1.3 million miles of cable that snake past 95% of all U.S. households. Cable has over 65 million subscribers in the U.S. and 157 million worldwide.

The secret weapon of the cable companies is a cheap cable modem that can provide more than 10 Mbit/s of bidirectional data to the home by transmitting data over a portion of the cable bandwidth. Low-cost—under $200—cable modems are now available from 3Com (U.S. Robotics), Bay Networks, Samsung, Panasonic, Terayon, Toshiba, Analog Devices, Rockwell Semiconductor, Intel, Cisco, and Hayes. In late 1997, the cable industry completed a slew of new standards. Consequently, modems from these different vendors should interoperate. The industry even has a *Cable Lab Group* that tests for compliance with the new standards. As a result, cable modems are becoming commodities. Today's typical cable modem supports downstream rates of up to 40 Mbit/s and upstream rates of up to 10 Mbit/s. It also provides a 10/100 Mbit/s Ethernet interface. You connect your computer to the cable modem via a standard Ethernet adapter (see Figure 4-7).

Even though the modems are bidirectional, most home cable systems are unidirectional—the bandwidth only comes into the home. So, in general, you will be using the cable modem to download information from the WAN at Ethernet speeds and a plain old telephone modem to upload (or return) information. Of course, this solution is not very satisfactory—it still requires a telephone line. So most cable companies are upgrading their cable to provide true bidirectional data. By the end of 1997, 20% of U.S. homes had two-way cable. The cable companies predict they will complete the rollout by the year 2000. Goldman Sachs estimates that 40 million homes in the U.S. will be two-way enabled by 1999. Today, Time Warner leads the way with 90% of the homes they "pass." In June 1998, the TCI upgrade was 60% completed when

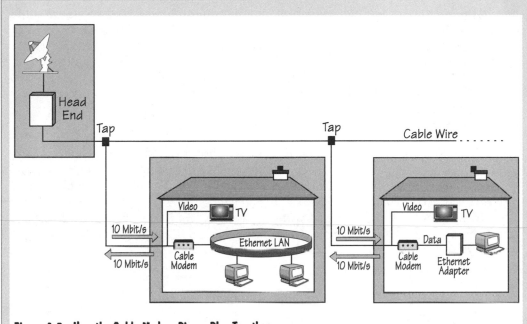

Figure 4-7. How the Cable Modem Pieces Play Together.

AT&T announced it would acquire the company for $48 billion. As part of this acquisition, AT&T plans to infuse another $1.3 billion to complete the upgrade of the TCI two-way service.

The cable backbone is extremely Internet-savvy. A well-funded start-up called *@Home* has partnered with nine of the 12 largest cable companies in the U.S. to provide a high-speed Internet *Point of Presence (POP)* at the cable head-end. It uses an ATM backbone to offer a very high-speed "shadow Internet" consisting of four high-speed POPs and 19 regional data centers that provide massive local Internet caching for high-speed data delivery to cable head-ends. The company also offers a VPN called @Work. Note that @Home does not own any of the cable infrastructure. It simply provides the Internet service. For $40 per-month, you can obtain cable-based Internet service even if you don't subscribe to the cable company's TV service (@Home receives one-third of the take). Two other pioneering cable ISPs are Time Warner's *RoadRunner* business unit and Media-One *Express*. All these ISPs are starting to service businesses as well as homes.

With the TCI deal, AT&T, the world's largest telephone company, did the unthinkable—it cast its vote for cable. So does this mean cable has already won the battle for the single home wire? The answer is that it's still up for grabs. Cable modems have a one-year solid head start over DSL. However, being a shared medium, cable modem introduces two problems that DSL does not have: 1) congestion on the wire as more users are added, and 2) inherently insecure communications.

So if 100 subscribers are concurrently active on a 10 Mbit/s shared segment, the bandwidth available to each is only 100 Kbit/s. In contrast, DSL is point-to-point. Of course, there is nothing to prevent the cable operators from segmenting their systems to accommodate a growing number of users. For example, they could put the 100 users on ten segments. To deal with the security issue, you must use SSL (or some other form of Internet security) to protect your important communications end-to-end. If you really want to play it safe, you should go with a firewall-based VPN service like @Work.

Another concern you often hear is that cable is not reliable. Can you depend on a cable TV operator for your data access? What kind of support service can you expect? How much down-time is there? Of course, this is where the value-added infrastructure of systems like @Home come into play. We also expect cable operators to manage their networks more proactively. In the past, they relied on users to call them when the picture turned blurry. But, data is a new world. ❏

The State of the Wireless-to-WAN Connection

Be-all end-all wireless-communications technology always seems a couple of years away.

> — *Angela Hickman*
> *PC Magazine*
> *(May, 1996)*

The Internet is both a blessing and a curse for wireless.

> — *Yankee Group*
> *(January, 1998)*

Wireless networks promise to provide the ultimate connection to the digital highway by letting you communicate "anywhere, anytime." With the mobile workforce growing at nearly 15% per year, wireless is becoming a necessity. But while cellular phones are everywhere (over 200 million in 1998), ubiquitous wireless data connections are still far off in the future.

Table 4-7 compares the leading wireless data technologies. Not one is ideal for high-volume traffic. So you may have to live with your wired connections for another two years, until the new *Low Earth Orbit (LEO)* satellites give us all the bandwidth we need in the friendly skies.

Table 4-7. The Wireless Alternatives.

Wireless Service	Bandwidth	Call Setup Time	Pricing
Cellular-Switched	14.4 Kbit/s (or less)	30 secs	By-the-minute (10 cents per minute)
Cellular-Packet (CDPD)	19.2 Kbit/s (or less)	5 secs	By-the-packet (5 to 20 cents per KByte)
Private Packet Radio	19.2 Kbit/s	5 secs (or more)	By-the-packet (15 cents per KByte)

But first, what is the state of today's wireless WAN connection? Here's a quick update on what's available:

- **Circuit-switched cellular** simply provides a modem that lets you connect your laptop with a cellular phone. And you can still use your cellular phone for voice (but not at the same time). So all you need to go wireless is a cellular phone and a cellular modem. Of course, you must still pay cellular rates by the minute (10 cents or more), which is where the fun stops.

- **Cellular Digital Packet Data (CDPD)** lets you transmit data packets over unused portions of the existing cellular network. CDPD can dynamically pick the open voice channels and use them for data traffic. You will need a CDPD modem to get on the network, and you then pay by-the-packet. You will be charged between 5 to 20 cents per KByte on the average; most carriers vary prices according to volume. CDPD modems do not require an existing cellular phone—they include their own radio transceivers. There are a variety of CDPD modems—from PC cards to cell phones with digital modems. Note that CDPD was designed to operate at speeds of 19.2 Kbit/s. However, actual throughputs are closer to 10 Kbit/s.

- **Private packet radio providers** offer a nationwide wireless alternative to the cellular network. The two leading private packet radio providers in the U.S. are *RAM Mobile Data* and *Ardis*. RAM (now BellSouth) claims that it can provide two-way wireless services to over 95% of the U.S. urban population (it covers 260 metropolitan areas). Ardis—from American Mobile Satellite Corporation, Motorola, and IBM—is available in most U.S. cities. In addition, AT&T spent $12.6 billion to acquire McCaw Cellular Communications to round-out its end-to-end wireless suite of offerings. AT&T/McCaw provides a single wireless network based on CDPD and PCS that covers 80% of the U.S.

In addition to these nationwide services, you should shop around for local wireless alternatives. For example, in the San Francisco Bay Area and Seattle, Ricochet (*http://www.ricochet.net*) offers unlimited wireless Internet access for a flat fee of \$29.95 per month. In addition, you must purchase a wireless modem for about \$200. Ricochet built its own private packet radio network by mounting digital repeaters on city street lights (on the average, one repeater each 1/2 mile). Your authors are all Ricochet users. Once you taste the freedom of unlimited wireless communications, it's hard to go back.

Data Standards for the Friendly Skies

Briefing

The ideal wireless panacea would be to tell people they can take their laptop computer on the road and have it work as if it were wired into their company's LAN.

— Dan Croft, Senior VP
Ardis

But who will maintain order in the friendly skies? Currently, each wireless network provider is building its own "skyway." To bring order out of that chaos, the IEEE 802.11 committee was given the thankless task of creating standards for wireless networks. The standards are intended to cover the following areas: wireless modems, APIs, PCMCIA devices, data security in the sky, bridges from wired-to-wireless LANs, guidelines to prevent broadcast interference, and a media-access protocol for radio and infrared transmissions. The good news is that after three long years in gestation, the IEEE 802.11 standard was finally approved in July 1997. In addition to the IEEE standard, an NDIS standard for wireless was completed in early 1996. This means that existing communication stacks will be able to transparently access any wireless modem—including cellular, Ardis, CDPD, RAM, and future PCS networks. These standards will make wireless more affordable and easier to deploy. In May 1998, the first 802.11-compliant products were shipped by Lucent, BreezeCom, and Aironet. ❑

Personal Communication Service

The up-and-coming attraction in the wireless world is PCS—the all-digital alternative to today's cellular network. So where did the additional PCS bandwidth come from? It came from the U.S. federal regulators—the FCC. The FCC allocated 140 MHz of government-held radio frequency to be auctioned to private developers. This is four times the spectrum originally allocated to the cellular phone industry. The allocated frequencies—between 1.85 GHz and 1.99 GHz—can be supported by low-cost, low-power, small-cell, one-chip transceivers. The first auction was held in March 1995; the government sold an 80 MHz chunk of the PCS spectrum for $7.7 billion. Since then, the government has collected a total of $23 billion from 15 FCC auctions (you can find the gory details at *http://www.fcc.gov/wtb/auctions.html*). This is one way to get rid of the U.S. federal deficit.

PCS is digital. So in theory it should be very data friendly. Three all-digital access technologies are vying to replace the venerable CDPD: *Time Division Multiple Access (TDMA)*, *Code Division Multiple Access (CDMA)*, and *Global System for Mobile Communications (GSM)*. In Europe, the PCS counterpart is called the *Personal Communications Network (PCN)*. PCN operates in the 1.8 GHz frequency range; it uses GSM. According to Yankee Group, GSM will grow worldwide from 64 million subscribers in 1997 to 248 million subscribers by 2002. During this same period, CDMA will grow from 6 million to 92 million, and TDMA will grow from 9 million to 59 million.[1] In the U.S., more than 50% of PCS carriers have chosen CDMA; the rest are almost equally divided among GSM and CDMA.

The bad news is that none of these technologies provide the kind of bandwidth we have come to expect from xDSL or cable modems. TDMA supports 14.4 Kbit/s, CDMA 13 Kbit/s, and GSM 9.6 Kbit/s. These numbers are nothing to write home about. The PCS equipment suppliers are trying to solve this bandwidth problem with a proposed standard called *Wideband CDMA*. It should provide 64 Kbit/s uplink speeds and downlink speeds of up to 384 Kbit/s.

LEOs to the Rescue

The next big jump in wireless data speeds will come from *Low Earth Orbit (LEO)* satellites. By the year 2001, these low-orbit satellites will be able to provide to anyone on this planet bidirectional data speeds in excess of 2 Mbit/s—some LEOs even promise speeds of up to 155 Mbit/s. According to BYTE's John Montgomery, the price of these services will be competitive with what you're paying for your land-based services. To get there, more than 400 LEO satellites will be launched in the next few years by well-financed ventures such as *Teledisc*, Motorola's *Celestri*, Loral's *Cyberstar*, and Alcatel's *Skybridge*. According to the FCC, you will be able to use this bandwidth for Internet access, e-mail, telemedicine, direct-to-home video, transaction processing, and news gathering. LEOs will open up entire new industries that can take advantage of low-cost and ubiquitous wireless data.

---

[1] Source: Yankee Group, *The Impact of the Internet on Mobile Computing and Wireless Data* (January, 1998).

CONCLUSION

Bandwidth is intrinsically abundant.

> — *George Gilder*
> *(November, 1995)*

There are a whole lot of people out there needing a whole lot of bandwidth. And we'll need every hose we have to put out that fire: fiber, ATM, Sonet, xDSL, Gigabit Ethernet, cable modems, satellites, and probably a few that haven't been thought of yet.

> — *John Montgomery*
> *BYTE Magazine,*
> *(November, 1997)*

In conclusion, the global networking infrastructure is coming together at a fast pace. Everything can physically exchange bits with everything else via the magic of WANs and routers. The next step is to do something meaningful with these bits, which is what client/server computing is all about. Of course, without low-cost and abundant bandwidth, client/server will remain a departmental technology. We hope to have made the case that abundant bandwidth is already here for most corporate users. For the home user, it appears to be just around the corner.

Will the cost of bandwidth come down? Yes, especially in the U.S. The *Telecommunications Act of 1996* has unleashed intense competition between long-distance carriers, local carriers, and cable companies. They can now all play in each other's turf. It's goodbye to the age of the telephone monopoly. As George Gilder points out, bandwidth is intrinsically plentiful. It's also intrinsically cheap. For example, one Mbit/s of xDSL bandwidth is an order of magnitude cheaper than its T1 equivalent. Of course, supply also creates its own demand.

Part 2
Clients, Servers, and Operating Systems

An Introduction to Part 2

Now that you've got the "bird's-eye" view, are you ready for some action? We've got a dangerous journey ahead. Did you bring your bullet-proof vests? We're only going to cross an active war zone. No, it's not Star Wars. It's the client/server operating system wars, and they're just as dangerous. You'll feel the bullets coming right out of the book. But don't worry. You're in good hands.

Part 2 is an overview of what clients and servers do in life and what they require from their operating systems. We'll briefly look at various OSs and see what they have to offer on both the client and server sides. There's no right or wrong when it comes to OSs—it's one big balancing act with hundreds of shades of gray. Everything is fuzzy and constantly in flux. If you make the wrong decision or ride the wrong client/server wave, you simply go broke (or take the next spaceship back to Mars). Some of the big players in client/server can afford to take a more secular view of OSs by simply porting to all the platforms. If you can afford to be secular, do it. Otherwise, you'll have to pick your OSs very carefully.

Chapter 5

Clients, Servers, and Operating Systems

Look at every path closely and deliberately. Try it as many times as you think necessary. Then ask yourself, and yourself alone, one question...Does this path have a heart? If it does, the path is good; if it doesn't, it is of no use.

— Carlos Castaneda
The Teachings of Don Juan

This chapter starts with a brief description of what typical clients and servers do in life. We then examine what each side of the client/server equation needs from an operating system. By the time you reach the end of this chapter, you should be better prepared to know what to look for in a client/server platform.

THE ANATOMY OF A SERVER PROGRAM

The role of a server program is to *serve* multiple clients who have an interest in a shared resource owned by the server. This section describes a day in the life of a typical server. Here's what a typical server program does:

■ *Waits for client-initiated requests*. The server program spends most of its time passively waiting on client requests, in the form of messages, to arrive over a communication session. Some servers assign a dedicated session to every client. Others create a dynamic pool of reusable sessions. Some provide a mix of the two environments. Of course, to be successful, the server must always be responsive to its clients and be prepared for *rush hour traffic* when many clients will request services at the same time.

■ *Executes many requests at the same time*. The server program must do the work requested by the client promptly. Clearly a client should not have to depend on a single-threaded server process. A server program that does not provide multitasking will run the risk of having a client hog all the system's resources and starve out its fellow clients. The server must be able to concurrently service multiple clients while protecting the integrity of shared resources.

■ *Takes care of VIP clients first*. The server program must be able to provide different levels of service priority to its clients. For example, a server can service a request for a report or batch job in low priority while maintaining OLTP-type responsiveness for high-priority clients.

■ *Initiates and runs background-task activity*. The server program must be able to run background tasks triggered to perform chores unrelated to the main program's thrust. For example, it can trigger a task to download records from a host database during non-peak hours.

■ *Keeps running*. The server program is typically a mission-critical application. If the server goes down, it impacts all the clients that depend on its services. The server program and the environment on which it runs must be very robust.

■ *Grows bigger and fatter*. Server programs seem to have an insatiable appetite for memory and processing power. The server environment must be upwardly scalable and modular.

WHAT DOES A SERVER NEED FROM AN OS?

In distributed computing environments, operating system functions are either *base* or *extended* services. The base services are part of the standard operating system, while the extended services are add-on modular software components that are layered on top of the base services. Functionally equivalent extended services are usually provided by more than one vendor. There is no hard rule that determines what gets bundled in the base operating system and what goes into the extensions. Today's extensions are usually good candidates for tomorrow's base system services.

Base Services

It should be apparent from the previous description that server programs exhibit a high level of concurrency. Ideally, a separate task will be assigned to each of the clients the server is designed to concurrently support. Task management is best done by a multitasking operating system. Multitasking is the natural way to simplify the coding of complex applications that can be divided into a collection of discrete and logically distinct, concurrent tasks. It improves the performance, throughput, modularity, and responsiveness of server programs. Multitasking also implies the existence of mechanisms for intertask coordination and information exchanges.

Servers also require a high level of concurrency within a single program. Server code will run more efficiently if tasks are allocated to parts of the same program rather than to separate programs (these tasks are called *coroutines* or *threads*). Tasks within the same program are faster to create, faster to context switch, and have easier access to shared information. Figure 5-1 shows the type of support that servers require from their operating system. Let's go over the server operating system requirements.

- ■ *Task Preemption*. An operating system with preemptive multitasking must allot fixed time slots of execution to each task. Without preemptive multitasking, a task must voluntarily agree to give up the processor before another task can run. It is much safer and easier to write multitasking server programs in environments where the operating system automatically handles all the task switching.

- ■ *Task Priority*. An operating system must dispatch tasks based on their priority. This feature allows servers to differentiate the level of service based on their clients' priority.

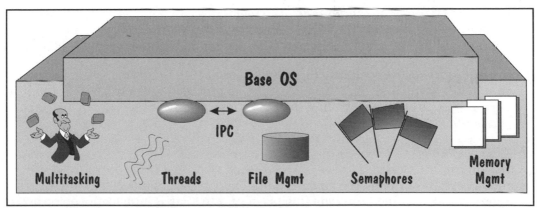

Figure 5-1. What Server Programs Expect From Their Operating System.

- *Semaphores*. An operating system must provide simple synchronization mechanisms for keeping concurrent tasks from bumping into one another when accessing shared resources. These mechanisms, known as *semaphores*, are used to synchronize the actions of independent server tasks and alert them when some significant event occurs.

- *Interprocess Communications (IPC)*. An operating system must provide the mechanisms that allow independent processes to exchange and share data.

- *Local/Remote Interprocess Communications*. An operating system must allow the transparent redirection of interprocess calls to a remote process over a network without the application being aware of it. The extension of the interprocess communications across machine boundaries is key to the development of applications where resources and processes can be easily moved across machines (i.e., they allow servers to grow bigger and fatter).

- *Threads*. These are units of concurrency provided within the program itself. Threads are used to create very concurrent, event-driven server programs. Each waiting event can be assigned to a thread that blocks until the event occurs. In the meantime, other threads can use the CPU's cycles productively to perform useful work.

- *Intertask Protection*. The operating system must protect tasks from interfering with each other's resources. A single task must not be able to bring down the entire system. Protection also extends to the file system and calls to the operating system.

- *Multiuser High-Performance File System*. The file system must support multiple tasks and provide the locks that protect the integrity of the data. Server programs typically work on many files at the same time. The file system must support a large number of open files without too much deterioration in performance.

- *Efficient Memory Management*. The memory system must efficiently support very large programs and very large data objects. These programs and data objects must be easily swapped to and from disk, preferably in small granular blocks.

- *Dynamically Linked Run-Time Extensions*. The operating system services should be extendable. A mechanism must be provided to allow services to grow at run time without recompiling the operating system.

Extended Services

Extended services provide the advanced system software that exploits the distributed potential of networks, provide flexible access to shared information, and make the system easier to manage and maintain. They also make it easier for independent software vendors (ISVs) and system integrators to create new server applications. Figure 5-2 shows some of the extended services server programs can expect either from their OS or from a best-of-breed middleware package. You should note that in intergalactic networking situations, the middleware becomes the OS. So many corporations are standardizing on middleware (or even on a DBMS package—like Oracle) to provide a meta-layer of heterogeneous glue. We'll return to this important topic in later chapters.

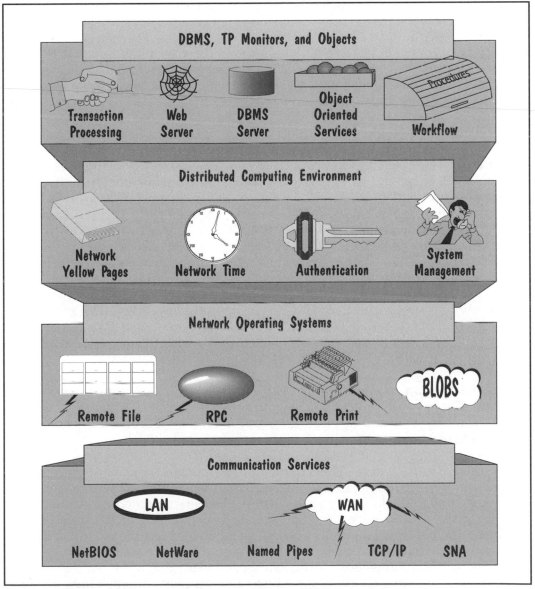

Figure 5-2. What Server Programs Hope To Get From Their Extended Operating Systems.

Let's go over these extended services, starting from the bottom layer and working our way up. Some of these expectations read more like wish lists. Others are so commonly used that they may eventually find their way into most operating systems.

■ ***Ubiquitous Communications***. The operating system extensions must provide a rich set of communications protocol stacks that allow the server to communicate with the greatest number of client platforms. In addition, the server should be able to communicate with other server platforms in case it needs assistance in providing services.

■ ***Network Operating System Extensions***. The operating system extensions must provide facilities for extending the file and print services over the network. Ideally, the applications should be able to transparently access any remote device (such as printers and files) as if they were local.

■ ***Binary Large Objects (BLOBs)***. Images, video, graphics, intelligent documents, and database snapshots are about to test the capabilities of our operating systems, databases, and networks. These large objects (affectionately called BLOBs) require operating system extensions such as intelligent message streams and object representation formats. Networks must be prepared to move and transport these large BLOBs at astronomic speeds. Databases and file systems must be prepared to store those BLOBs and provide access to them. Protocols are needed for the exchange of BLOBs across systems and for associating BLOBs with programs that know what to do when they see one.

■ ***Global Directories and Network Yellow Pages***. The operating system extensions must provide a way for clients to locate servers and their services on the network using a global directory service. Network resources must be found by name. Servers must be able to dynamically register their services with the directory provider.

■ ***Authentication and Authorization Services***. The operating system extensions must provide a way for clients to prove to the server that they are who they claim to be. The authorization system determines if the authenticated client has the permission to obtain a remote service.

■ ***System Management***. The operating system extensions must provide an integrated network and system management platform. The system should be managed as a single server or as multiple servers assigned to domains. An enterprise view that covers multiple domains must be provided for servers that play in the big leagues. System management includes services for configuring a system and facilities for monitoring the performance of all elements, generating alerts when things break, distributing and managing software packages on client workstations, checking for viruses and intruders, and metering capabilities for pay-as-you-use server resources.

- ***Network Time***. The operating system extensions must provide a mechanism for clients and servers to synchronize their clocks. This time should be coordinated with some universal time authority.

- ***Database and Transaction Services***. The operating system extensions must provide a robust multiuser Database Management System (DBMS). This DBMS should ideally support SQL for decision support and server-stored procedures for transaction services. The server-stored procedures are created outside the operating system by programmers. More advanced functions include a *Transaction Processing Monitor (TP Monitor)* for managing stored procedures (or transactions) as atomic units of work that execute on one or more servers.

- ***Internet Services***. The Internet is a huge growth opportunity for servers. We expect that over time the more common Internet services will become standard server features—including HTTP daemons, Secure Sockets Layer (SSL), firewalls, Domain Name Service, HTML-based file systems, and electronic commerce frameworks.

- ***Object-Oriented Services***. This is an area where extended services will flourish for a long time to come. Services are becoming more object-oriented. The operating system will provide object broker services that allow any object to interact with any other object across the network. The extended operating system must also provide object interchange services and object repositories. Client/server applications of the future will be between communicating objects (in addition to communicating processes).

As you can see, extended does mean "extended." It covers the universe of current and future services needed to create distributed client/server environments. No current operating system bundles *all* these extended functions, but they're all aspiring to do so. Of course, the downside is that the functions that are bundled with the OS are usually not best-of-breed. In addition, they tend to be platform-specific, which locks you into a particular operating system. The distributed system world is by definition heterogeneous and multiplatform. So in general, it's better to standardize on a multiplatform set of extended services, which is where middleware comes into play.

SERVER SCALABILITY

What are the upper limits of servers? The limits really depend on the type of service required by their clients. One safe rule is that clients will always want more services, so scalable servers are frequently an issue. Figure 5-3 shows the different levels of escalation in server power. It starts with a single PC server that reaches its limits with the top-of-the-line processor and I/O power. The next level of server power is provided by superservers populated with multiprocessors. If that is not enough power, the client/server model allows you to divide the work among different servers. These multiservers know no upper limits to power. But they must know how to work together.

Multiservers (or *clusters*) are used in environments that require more processing power than that provided by a single server system—either SMP or uniprocessor (see the next Briefing box). The client/server model is upwardly scalable. When you need more processing power, you can add more servers (thus creating a pool of servers). Or, the existing server machine can be traded up to the latest generation of PC superserver machine. Multiservers remove any upward limits to the growth of server power. Ordinary servers can also provide this power by working in all kinds of ensembles using middleware.

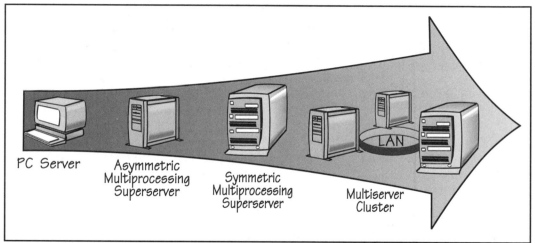

Figure 5-3. The Server Scalability Story.

MULTIPROCESSING SUPERSERVERS

Briefing

If you need more server power, you'll be looking at a new generation of *superservers*. These are fully-loaded machines; they include multiprocessors, high-speed disk arrays for intensive I/O, and fault-tolerant features. Operating systems can enhance the server hardware by providing direct support for multiprocessors. With the proper division of labor, multiprocessors should improve job throughput and server application speeds. A multiprocessor server is upwardly scalable. Users can get more performance out of their servers by simply adding more processors instead of additional servers. Multiprocessing comes in two flavors: asymmetric and fully symmetric (see Figure 5-4).

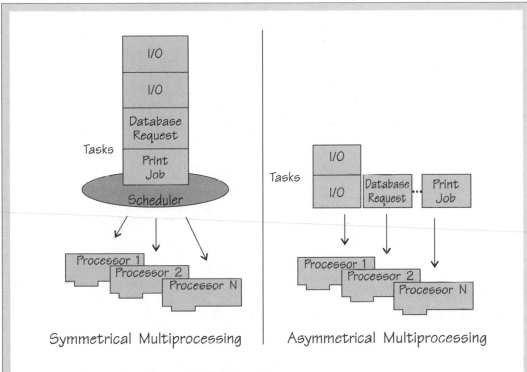

Figure 5-4. Symmetric and Asymmetric Multiprocessing.

Asymmetric multiprocessing imposes hierarchy and a division of labor among processors. Only one designated processor, the master, can run the operating system at any one time. The master controls (in a tightly-coupled arrangement) slave processors dedicated to specific functions such as disk I/O or network I/O. A coprocessor is an extreme form of codependency; one processor completely controls a slave processor through interlocked special-purpose instructions. The coprocessor has unique special-purpose hardware that is not identical to the main processor. An example is a graphic coprocessor.

Symmetric Multiprocessing (SMP) treats all processors as equals. Any processor can do the work of any other processor. Applications are divided into threads that can run concurrently on any available processor. Any processor in the pool can run the operating system kernel and execute user-written threads. Symmetric multiprocessing improves the performance of the application itself, as well as the total throughput of the server system. Ideally, the operating system should support symmetric multiprocessing by supplying three basic functions: a reentrant OS kernel, a global scheduler that assigns threads to available processors, and shared I/O structures. Symmetric multiprocessing requires multiprocessor hardware with some form of shared memory and local instruction caches. Most importantly, symmetric multiprocessing requires new applications that can exploit multithreaded parallelism. The few applications on the market that really exploit SMP are SQL DBMSs and TP Monitors. Note that the SMP architecture requires cache synchronization between processors. Consequently, it is not fault-tolerant.

The mass-market server operating systems—including Unix, NetWare, OS/2, and NT—all support SMP. These operating systems run on commodity super-server platforms; the hardware vendors have been gearing up for these OSs for quite some time. Commodity Intel-based servers supplemented with SMP are powerful enough to handle more than 80% of client/server application needs. These servers can run ordinary PC software and have a strong affinity with clients. In some cases, you may want to move to a RISC-based platform (like Alpha) to get an extra boost in performance. In other cases, you'll want to take advantage of your OS's support for the *clustering* of SMP machines.

Clusters make a group of interconnected SMP machines behave like a single system. Typically, the interconnection is via a high-speed LAN. Clustering has been around on mainframes and Unix systems for many years. In 1997, Microsoft (and others) brought clustering to NT. The first release of the Microsoft *NT Clustering Services*—also known as *Wolfpack*—does not scale. However, it provides some level of fault-tolerance via failovers.

Typically, clusters come in one of two flavors: *shared-disk* and *shared-nothing* (see Figure 5-5). In both cases, some form of high-speed LAN is used for intercluster communications; it can be a simple Ethernet connection or a specialized high-speed redundant bus such as Compaq/Tandem's *ServerNet*. Clusters provide high-availability because they do not share memory or synchronized caches. Consequently, failures are contained within a single node. Some

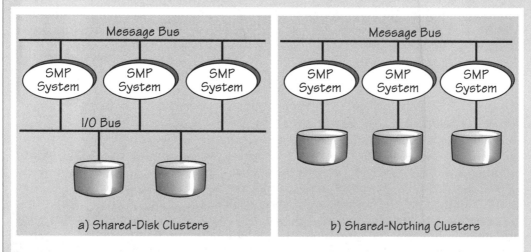

Figure 5-5 Clustering Architectures: Shared-Disk Versus Shared-Nothing.

clustering systems use "I'm alive" messages to determine the health of each node on the cluster. If a node dies, messages can be re-routed to an alternate node. Of course, the alternate must be capable of doing the job and must also have access to the shared data. Typically, all this messaging is transparently handled on behalf of your application by a TP Monitor or DBMS.

Shared-nothing clusters like Compaq/Tandem's *NonStop* systems, IBM's *SP2*, and Oracle's *NCube* provide very high levels of parallelism. Their "shared-nothing" architectures eliminate the bottlenecks found in SMP systems, thus allowing them to scale to hundreds or even thousands of processors—all working together. ❑

CLIENT ANATOMY 101

Client/server applications are *client-centric*. The client side provides the "look-and-feel" for the services a system provides. All client applications have this in common: they request the services of a server. What makes client applications different is what triggers the requests and what GUI, if any, is needed. Based on these differences, we can classify clients into three categories: *Non-GUI Clients*, *GUI Clients*, and *OOUI Clients* (see Figure 5-6).

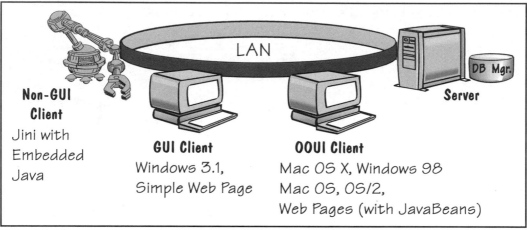

Figure 5-6. Three Client Types: Non-GUI, GUI, and OOUI.

Non-GUI Clients

Non-GUI client applications generate server requests with a minimal amount of human interaction (see Figure 5-7). Non-GUI clients fall into two sub-categories:

■ *Non-GUI clients that do not need multitasking.* Examples include automatic teller machines (ATMs), barcode readers, cellular phones, fax machines, smart gas pumps, and intelligent clipboards (coming soon). These clients may provide a simple human interface in the request generation loop.

■ *Non-GUI clients that need multitasking.* Examples include robots, testers, and daemon programs. These clients often require very granular, real-time, event-driven multitasking services.

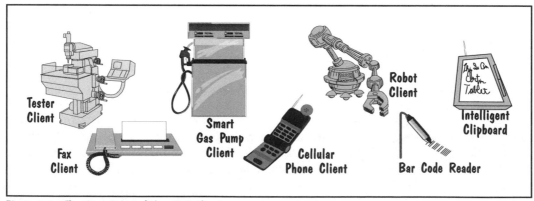

Figure 5-7. The Many Faces of Non-GUI Clients.

GUI Clients

Simple GUI Clients are applications where occasional requests to the server result from a human interacting with a GUI. The simple GUI interface is a good fit for mainstream, OLTP-type business applications with repetitive tasks and high volumes. They also make good front-end clients to database servers. Simple GUI client applications are graphical renditions of the dialogs that previously ran on dumb terminals. GUIs replace the "green-screen uglies" with graphic dialogs, color, menu bars, scroll boxes, and pull-down and pop-up windows (see Figure 5-8). Simple GUI dialogs use the object/action model where users can select objects and then select the actions to be performed on the chosen objects. Most dialogs are serial in nature. This model of user interaction is predominantly used in Windows 3.X, and OSF Motif applications, as well as most of today's form-based Web pages.

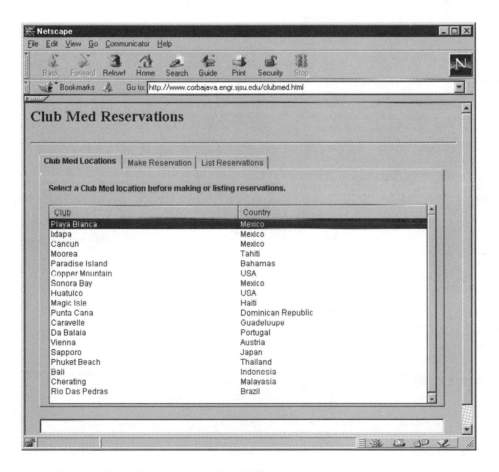

Figure 5-8. A Club Med GUI Application "Look-and-Feel."

Object-Oriented User Interface (OOUI) Clients

The *Object-Oriented User Interface (OOUI)* metaphor provides a highly iconic, object-oriented user interface that lets you directly manipulate objects on a screen (typically, via drag-and-drop). OOUIs are used by information workers doing multiple, variable tasks whose sequence cannot be predicted. Examples include executive and decision-support applications, multimedia-based training systems, system management consoles, and stockbroker workstations. OOUIs have an insatiable appetite for communications. OOUI desktop objects need to communicate among themselves and with external servers. The communications are, by necessity, real-time, interactive, and highly concurrent.

Examples of OOUIs are the OS/2 Workplace Shell, NextStep (now Mac OS X), Mac OS, and, to some extent, Windows 98. In addition, you will start seeing OOUI-like Web pages populated with Java 2 JavaBeans (these are beans that support direct manipulation via drag-and-drop).

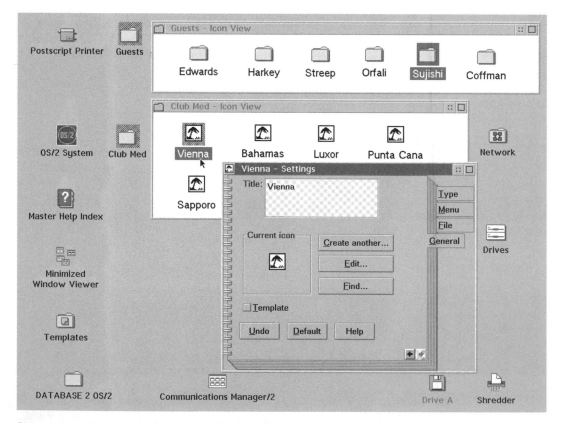

Figure 5-9. A Club Med OOUI Application "Look-and-Feel."

Current OOUIs provide a visual desktop metaphor (think of it as an arcade game) where you can bring together related objects and programs to perform a task. The desktop can contain multiple workplaces running concurrently (see Figure 5-9). Each workplace may be running parallel dialogs, also called *modeless dialogs*, over parallel sessions with the server. With advanced multimedia-type applications, you can use these parallel dialogs to display images, video, multiobject folders, and voice-annotated mail. Information is displayed to the user in the foreground windows, while background tasks are constantly moving information to and from servers. For example, the first page from a multimedia document is displayed in a window while a background task is busy prefetching the rest of the document from the server.

OOUIs focus on the objects required to accomplish a task. They provide folders, workareas, shadows (short cuts), and associations that allow users to personalize their desktops and manage their objects. OOUIs provide a common metaphor for creating, copying, moving, connecting, and deleting any object on the desktop. One of the major features of OOUIs is the concept of multiple views of objects.

In OOUI environments, the user interacts with objects rather than with the operating system or with separate programs. The interaction has the same look-and-feel across all tasks. The OOUI is a simulation of how users interact with objects in real life. It is a computer visual of the real-life situation.

Application Features: GUI Versus OOUI

The best way to compare GUIs and OOUIs is to put the two side-by-side and contrast some of their features. Let's go back to Figures 5-8 and 5-9, the GUI and OOUI vintages of our Club Med application.[1] By just looking at these two pictures, can you tell what the OOUI fuss is all about?

■ The OOUI Club Med is an extension of the operating system's user interface. You can't tell where the application starts and the OS desktop ends. They appear to be seamlessly integrated.

■ The OOUI Club Med invites the user to manipulate the visual Club Med objects through drag-and-drop. For example, a transaction may be triggered by drag-

---

[1] The GUI Club Med was developed in our book, **Client/Server Programming with Java and CORBA, Second Edition** (Wiley, 1998). We used pre-Java 2 JavaBeans that did not support OOUI-like features. The OOUI Club Med was developed in a previous life (in the mid-90s) using the OS/2 Workplace Shell. So the Web is more retro when it comes to user interfaces. The new generation of JavaBeans will help the Web catch up.

ging a guest object to the shredder to delete it. Or, if we want to be kind, we'll drop it on the fax machine icon to send a confirmation of the reservation.

■ The OOUI Club Med icon can be opened at any time to reveal a notebook view of the information inside it. The notebook control makes it possible to visually staple together many dialog windows and let the user find the information needed. This is a giant step forward for OLTP-type of applications.

■ The OOUI Club Med setup will reappear the way the user left it when the machine is turned on again. The desktop configuration is persistent.

■ The OOUI Club Med is very familiar, especially to kids. It feels like a video game. Kids feel quite at home with drag-and-drop, icons, and direct manipulation. The OOUI is a simulation of reality that they can easily recognize. Can we say the same about adults?

■ The OOUI Club Med can be extended to seamlessly work with any other OOUI object (with very little new code). We could easily think of mail-enabling it or allowing scanned pages to be dragged into the notebook view. The OLTP transaction is starting to look more like its real-world counterpart.

■ The GUI Club Med, on the other hand, is your typical Windows or Web interface. The icon is just there to represent the application to the desktop. You're not invited to play with it. You start the application by clicking on the icon (or on a URL link). From then on, you're in menu land. The user is quite aware that there is a running Club Med application.

Table 5-1 provides a detailed summary of the features that distinguish OOUIs from GUIs.

Table 5-1. GUI Versus OOUI.

Feature	Graphical User Interface (GUI)	Object-Oriented User Interface (OOUI)
Application Structure	A graphic application consists of an icon, a primary window with a menu bar, and one or more secondary windows. The focus is on the main task. Ancillary tasks are supported by secondary windows and pop-ups. Users must follow the rigid task structure (and may get trapped in a task). An application represents a task.	A graphic application consists of a collection of cooperating user objects. Everything that you see is an object. Each object is represented by an icon and has at least one view. Objects can be reused in many tasks. The application's boundaries are fuzzy. The user defines what's an application by assembling a collection of objects. These objects may come from one or more programs and are integrated with the desktop objects the system provides (like printers and shredders). The users can innovate and create their own "Lego-like" object collections.
Icons	Icons represent a running application.	Icons represent objects that may be directly manipulated.
Starting an Application	Users start applications before selecting an object to work with.	Users open the object on the desktop, which causes a window view of the object to be displayed.
Windows	Users open a primary window and then specify the objects they want to interact with. The same window can be used to display other objects.	A window is a view of what's inside an object. There is a one-to-one relationship between a window and an object.
Menus	Menus provide the primary method for navigating within an application.	Each object has a context menu. You navigate within an application or across applications by directly manipulating objects. The desktop functions as one big menu; icons represent the objects that you can manipulate.
Active Application Visual	Icons represent minimized windows of active applications.	Icons are augmented with the *in-use* emphasis to represent an active object.
Direct Manipulation	An application may provide direct manipulation on an ad hoc basis.	Objects are created, communicated with, moved, and manipulated through drag-and-drop manipulation.
Creating New Objects	Objects are created in an application-specific manner, usually through some form of copy mechanism or using the menu choices: new or open.	A templates folder contains a template for every object type. To create a new instance of an object, drag its template to where you want the new object to reside.

Table 5-1. GUI Versus OOUI. (Continued)

Feature	Graphical User Interface (GUI)	Object-Oriented User Interface (OOUI)
Actions	Choose object; then choose action from menu bar.	In addition to choosing actions from menus, a user can drag objects to icons to perform operations; for example, dragging a file to a printer icon.
Containers	Text-based list boxes provide the primary form of containment.	In addition to list boxes, OOUIs provide container objects, including folders and notebooks. These in turn can contain other objects. Actions performed on container objects affect all the objects inside them.
Focus	Focus is on the main task.	Focus is on active objects and tasks.
Who Is in Control?	Control alternates between the user and the application.	All the applications behave the same and the user acts as the conductor. Think of the user as the visual programmer of the desktop.
Product Examples	Windows 3.X, Motif, and simple Web pages.	NextStep/Mac OS X, Mac OS, Windows 98, OS/2 Workplace Shell, and Web pages that take advantage of Java 2 JavaBeans.

Compound Documents: OOUIs on Steroids

*Compound documents frameworks—like ActiveX and JavaBeans—*are the latest and greatest OOUI technology (see Figure 5-10). You can think of compound documents as OOUIs on steroids. Every visual object on the screen is a live component. Some components are also containers, which means that they can embed other components. You can edit the contents of any component "in-place," regardless of how deeply embedded it is within other components. A component is an independent piece of software that you can separately purchase on the market. Components can play together in visual suites that mimic applications.

In today's OOUIs, visual objects are typically rectangular icons with underlying views. Ideally, components can take any shape, and you can move them around and embed them at will. You can resize components, zoom in on their contents, and visually rearrange them within a visual container in any way you want. The components automatically share the document's menu, clipboard, and palette. Everything looks seamless—it's like a visual tapestry. So compound documents are a better simulation of reality than vintage OOUIs. 3-D compound documents will provide even more realistic simulations. The document becomes a virtual world populated with components. We cover components and compound documents in more detail in Parts 7 and 8.

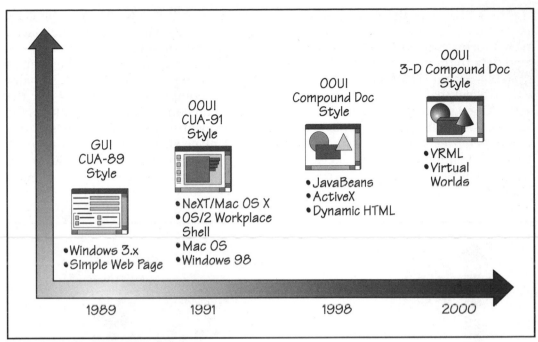

Figure 5-10. The GUI/OOUI Evolution.

Shippable Places

Imagine a world in which we assume that everyone is always a member of a network—not necessarily attached, but always belonging.

— Amy Wohl

A *place* is a visual ensemble of related components. A *shippable place* is a mobile container of components; it's a place that can be shipped over the Net. Today's user interfaces are centered around a primitive place that represents a desktop. In contrast, shippable places let you interact with multiple places that represent collaborative environments based on real-world models; it's like having multiple desktops.

So a place is a mini *virtual world* that servers can ship to their clients; it's a shippable front-end for all kinds of specialized Internet services and server objects. Places allow servers to automatically update their client's desktop. It also gives them a visual place on the client in which to display information in real time. So a place can be a dynamic assembly of ever-changing data, video feeds, and other live content.

Figure 5-11 shows the evolution of shippable client front-ends. Web technology made it possible for servers to ship HTML pages to clients where they are displayed in GUI format. The Web then evolved to support HTML-based forms that let clients send data to their servers. With Java, servers can now embed code—in the form of applets—within HTML pages; Java makes the Web page active and smart. Finally, we have shippable places. These are shippable compound documents—in the ActiveX or JavaBeans sense. Like a page, a place can contain Java components (or beans). But unlike a page, a place does not go away after you switch pages; it can live on your desktop for as long as you need it. A place also has its own storage, so it can remember your preferences and maintain active links to the outside world. Again, we will have a lot more to say about the objects, places, and the Web in Parts 7 and 8.

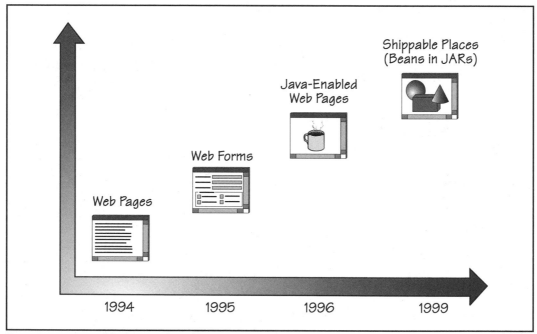

Figure 5-11. From Web Pages to Shippable Places.

WHAT DOES A CLIENT NEED FROM AN OS?

Each of the three types of clients described here places a different set of requirements on the operating system. These requirements are listed in Table 5-2. As you can see, all client applications need some mechanism to communicate service requests and files to a server. All three client categories will function best in a robust, multitasking environment. It is particularly important for the client environment to be robust because it is impossible for system providers to test the client software on all possible hardware/software combinations (you can't dictate what people run on their PCs). It is important to use an operating system that can protect programs from clashing and crashing. No client program should cause the system to hang (requiring a reboot).

GUI and OOUI clients work best with a thread-like mechanism for handling the background requests. By using separate threads for the user interface and background processing, the program can respond to user input while a separate thread handles the interaction with the server. This is how GUIs avoid the notorious "hourglass" icon, a sure sign that the computing environment is not keeping up with the human users. Threads also help clients respond to asynchronous calls from a server (i.e., they implement *callbacks*). Priority-based, preemptive multitasking is also required to respond to multimedia devices and to create client applications where multiple dialogs are displayed in parallel.

Increasingly, one of the most important requirements of a client operating system is to host mobile code in a secure fashion. In practice, this means the client OS must provide a Java VM. This lets servers ship mobile code to clients on an as-needed basis.

Table 5-2. What Does a Client Need From an OS?

Requirements From an OS	Non-GUI Client		Simple GUI Client	OOUI Client
	Without Multitasking	With Multitasking		
Request/reply mechanism (preferably with local/remote transparency)	Yes	Yes	Yes	Yes
File transfer mechanism to move pictures, text, and database snapshots	Yes	Yes	Yes	Yes
Preemptive multitasking	No	Yes	Desirable	Yes
Task priorities	No	Yes	Desirable	Yes
Interprocess communications	No	Yes	Desirable	Yes
Threads for background communications with server and receiving callbacks from servers	No	Yes	Yes (unless you like the hourglass icon)	Yes
OS robustness, including intertask protection and reentrant OS calls	No	Yes	Desirable	Yes

CLIENT/SERVER HYBRIDS

Another point to consider is that the industry is moving beyond the pure client/server model. This is because more intelligence (and data) is moving onto the client. Database clients keep snapshots of tables locally. TP Monitor clients coordinate multiserver transactions. Groupware clients maintain queues. Multimedia clients check-in and check-out folders. And distributed object clients accept requests from objects anywhere. These "New Age" clients must provide a *server lite* function—an interim step toward fulfilling the post-scarcity vision of a full client and server function on every machine. Note that even the thinnest of Network Computers should still be able to download shippable places, run Java applets, and receive calls from a server. For example, someday the dashboard on your car may receive a call from a server to display your location on a map.

A server lite provides a thread, queue, or background process on the client machine that can accept *unsolicited* network requests—usually from a server. For example, a server may call its clients to synchronize locks on a long-duration transaction, refresh a database snapshot, or recall a checked-out multimedia document. A server lite implementation (as opposed to a full-blown server) does not need to support concurrent access to shared resources, load balancing, or multithreaded communications. We call clients that provide a server lite function *hybrids* (as opposed to pure).

CONCLUSION

Looking at what's needed from a client/server platform is a good mental exercise. It helps sharpen our understanding of the issues and platform trade-offs. In the real world, things are not black and white. There are no hermetically sealed computer worlds at the intergalactic client/server level. And very few machines started life as green-field client/server systems—most of the world's computers, even the PCs, are "legacy systems." You'll typically be dealing with heavy doses of platform mixing. Luckily, client/server middleware is starting to become the *cross-platform unifier*. So, once you're fully proficient with one platform, you'll be able to work with the next one without too much sweat. In the meantime, diversity is what makes client/server so much fun.

Chapter 6

The OS Wars:
Meet the Players

> We love them all equally and we hate them all equally. Our strategy is operating system agnosticism.
>
> — Jim Manzi, Ex-CEO
> Lotus

Picking a client/server platform is not an easy task. New operating systems for the desktop seem to be sprouting like weeds, while older operating systems are fragmenting into mutant "sibling" variants. This is not necessarily bad news for the client/server architecture model, which thrives on diversity. However, it can be bad news if you're trying to develop a software product and you end up picking the wrong client/server platform.

The popular press has declared the OS wars to be over: Windows 95/98 won the desktop, and Windows NT is winning the server. So what is there left to write about? As it turns out, quite a bit. Microsoft may have won the standalone desktop, but it certainly does not control either the client or the server. The client environment is just too diversified for one winner to take it all—especially in the age of Java, the Internet, and smart appliances. And the battle for the server—at both the departmental and intergalactic levels—is just starting. NT happens to have finally joined the fray—it is just now considered to be a mainstream OS contender. This chapter starts by looking at some of the key client and server OS trends; yes, we enjoy danger. Then we introduce you to the key players.

CLIENT OS TRENDS

Very few computers will be on the desktop in 10 years. Today's workstation capacity will be in wristwatches, on the wall, off the wall, and so on.

— Ted Nelson, Guru
(November, 1995)

In the last chapter, we covered what clients require from their OSs. Here are some of the trends we see developing in the client industry:

■ ***The desktop is becoming more fragmented***. The move to 32-bit OSs is fragmenting the desktop. Unlike its predecessors—DOS and Windows 3.X— Windows 95 does not own the client. In fact, the Microsoft world has five competing client OSs to choose from: Windows CE, Windows 3.X, Windows for Workgroups, Windows 95/98, and NT Workstation—not to mention MS-DOS. In addition to Windows, OS/2 Warp is still alive on some corporate desktops, Mac OS has its dedicated following among the Internet crowd, and Linux is becoming more attractive every day. So diversity is in. Figure 6-1 shows the total client OS shipments in 1997. As you can see, there's quite a bit of diversity. Of course, the total installed base is even more diverse—especially on corporate desktops. According to IDC's Dan Kusnetzky, the desktop in large corporations

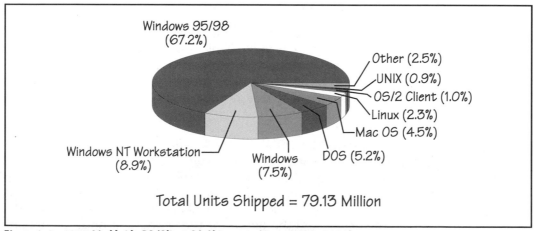

Figure 6-1. 1997 Worldwide PC/Client OS Shipments (Source: IDC, 1998).

is most likely running Windows 3.1, followed by a large jump down to Windows 95, and then a dumb terminal.

- **The universal client is really a Web browser.** If you think about it, Microsoft does not own the standards for the intergalactic client. The Internet community owns these evolving standards. In addition, the Java VM is an operating system for Web mobile code; it's an OS that lives on top of existing OSs. Of course, Microsoft does not control Java, either.

- **There will be a huge demand for super-fat PCs.** These are ordinary PCs that act as both clients and servers. These servers must be shrink-wrapped; you can't afford a system administrator with every server.

- **There will be a huge demand for ultra-thin PCs.** Typically, these minimalist PCs are centrally managed via a server. As we explained in Part 1, there's currently enough bandwidth behind corporate firewalls to effectively download applets and JavaBeans on demand. The idea here is that zero-footprint net-worked PCs may be easier to use, maintain, and upgrade than our current PCs. They can bring to the Web millions of new users—mostly people who can't afford, comprehend, or deal with the cost of ownership of a full-blown PC. These low-cost Web clients may become as ubiquitous as the telephone. Of course, our current PCs—as we know and love them—will continue to do very well.

- **Shippable places will become the new desktops.** Today, you mostly live within a Windows desktop. Soon, you will be living in your favorite *shippable places*. These are the virtual worlds that connect you with the network at large. For example, there will be places for lawyers, dentists, and 12-year olds. So you will spend your time in the virtual worlds that make you feel the most at home. The desktop is no longer a single monolithic place. Instead, you now have multiple places to choose from. You will be able to run these places either from your Web browser or from more specialized place viewers. *Internet Portals* will serve as "home places." They will also become dispensers of shippable places.

- **Embedded clients will be everywhere.** This is the old Novell vision of "the billion-node network by the year 2000." To get to this number, millions of little network nodes will be installed in fuel injectors, copy machines, crockpots, refrigerators, cash registers, televisions, telephony devices, automated teller machines, and pick-up trucks. Sun estimates that by 1999, the typical home will contain 100 microcontrollers. These nodes require an OS with a small footprint that can also run some form of client/server middleware. *Embedded Java* (with *Jini*) could be the perfect OS for these types of environments.

In summary, the client is transforming itself. The desktop OS will not be the absolute center of the client universe; it may even become irrelevant. Servers—via Web browsers and shippable places—will have more say over what gets displayed inside the client's visual space. Internet portals and shippable places will become the de facto Webtops where people live and work.

New clients—such as Internet PCs and intelligent appliances—will require network-savvy OSs with very small footprints; Java seems to be a good fit. At the high-end, the client must also be a full-function personal server. So can one client OS do it all? We wouldn't bet on it.

CLIENT OS: MEET THE PLAYERS

Windows 98 is a six-story building sitting on DOS's log-cabin foundation. The Leaning Tower of Redmond can't take much more expansion.

> — **Mark Schlack, Editor-in-Chief**
> **BYTE Magazine**
> **(June, 1998)**

As you can see in Figure 6-2, most of today's client platforms belong to Microsoft. The only other serious competition on the desktop comes from Mac OS and Linux. OS/2 is no longer a serious player (see the next Soapbox). Java OS may eventually become a formidable competitor—especially in the area of Internet appliances, Web TVs, and embedded clients. If we're lucky, Web browsers and Java VMs will provide a portability layer on top of whatever runs out there. In the future, the client OS (and the browser) will simply provide a player for running Web content. The real client is whatever you download from the Net—whether it's Web pages, simple forms, or shippable places packed with beans. The Web (and Java) will make us client-OS agnostic.

Though ubiquitous, *DOS* and *Windows 3.x* do not make very good client platforms. Their poor little computer brains are too weak to give us what it takes to build universal clients and fulfill the vision of post-scarcity client/server computing, where each machine is both a client and a server.

For client/server computing to unleash its potential, the industry is moving to 32-bit client platforms with full multithreaded support, robust memory management, and preemptive multitasking. Even Microsoft has finally decided to bite the bullet and discontinue its Windows line in favor of the more robust NT engine; *Windows 98* is the last of the 16-bit Windows line. Also, Apple is in the process of moving its user base from *Mac OS* to *Mac OS X* (née Rhapsody). Finally, there's Linux, which started life as a freeware 32-bit OS—it's Unix, but without the bloat.

Microsoft has declared NT to be the natural successor to Windows 98 on the desktop; it may well be. However, as part of their conversion to the next-generation

32-bit OS, many corporations may decide to reassess their client OS strategies. This means they will be evaluating Linux and Mac OS X as well as NT client. In addition, many may decide that all they need is a minimalist Java PC with a Webtop. In this section, we provide a super-brief synopsis of how these OSs compare.

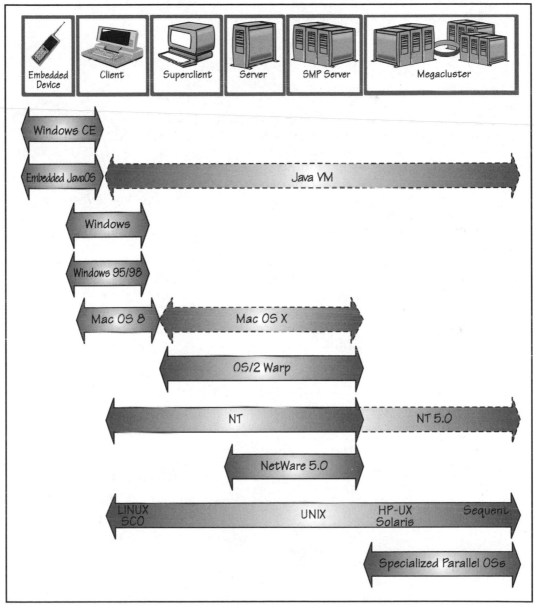

Figure 6-2. What the Different Operating Systems Cover.

What Happened to OS/2?

Soapbox

Millions of OS/2 users are bitterly disappointed at IBM's failure to promote and improve the OS/2 platform as an alternative to Microsoft Windows.

> — *Ralph Nader, Consumer Advocate*
> *Open Letter to Lou Gerstner*
> *(June, 1998)*

What happened to OS/2? Ralph Nader says it all—OS/2 as a client platform has been all but abandoned. IBM is repositioning OS/2 as a low-end server platform for Java and thin clients (more on this later). Warp OS/2, under IBM's tutelage, will go down in history as one of the biggest missed opportunities to stop the Microsoft juggernaut. *OS/2 Warp Connect* is a robust and proven 32-bit client OS. Its advanced OOUI, preemptive multitasking, and page-based virtual memory are ideal for multimedia-intensive client applications. Warp Connect is network-ready; it includes a complete TCP/IP stack, NetBEUI, IPX/SPX, PPP, SLIP, and an IP router. Warp Connect is also very laptop-friendly—it supports PC-card plug-and-play and provides advanced power management. OS/2 runs DOS and Windows 3.X applications seamlessly in a protected-mode environment.

But all this is now history. OS/2 as a client platform is not going anywhere, as long as IBM owns it. In his letter to IBM CEO Lou Gerstner, Ralph Nader also requests that IBM release the OS/2 code to the Open Source community. It's a good idea, but it may already be too little, too late. In any case, the Open Source community already has Linux, which may end up being the alternative to NT on the client as well as the server (more on this later). ❑

NT Client

We are not "write once, run anywhere" kind of guys.

> — *Steve Ballmer, President*
> *Microsoft*
> *(March, 1998)*

Windows is splintering: With every release, it leaves behind one more legacy platform.

> — *John Montgomery, Editor*
> *BYTE Magazine*
> *(June, 1998)*

Windows NT Workstation is a robust 32-bit client OS. It supports preemptive multitasking, multithreading, memory protection, and a transactional file system. Windows NT is network-ready; it supports TCP/IP, NetBEUI, IPX/SPX, PPP, and AppleTalk. NT as an advanced client platform—has very few system upper limits. It also provides C2-level security. Finally, NT's Windows 95 user interface is very familiar to millions of Windows users, which is also a big plus.

So what are the cons? First, NT is a resource hog, but this may not be a problem as the price of memory continues to drop (in addition, Microsoft is rumored to be working on an *NT Lite* version). Second, compared to Windows 95/98, NT's support for laptops is very poor; it has limited PC card support and power management. Third, NT provides poor emulation of DOS and 16-bit Windows applications; it does not support virtual device drivers (VxDs). In addition, NT does not support plug-and-play, which makes it harder to configure. Compared to Windows, NT has limited device driver support. Finally, NT Workstation is an expensive client platform. It sells for $250—Windows 98 is only $100 (or less). Because of all these limitations, NT Workstation does not get the same level of ISV support as the rest of the Windows platforms. Consequently, fewer applications run on it.

However, this may be changing. In 1997, NT Workstation shipped over 7 million copies—a very respectable number, even by client standards. Microsoft is also adding conversion features in NT 5.0 (now called *Windows 2000*) that will make it easier to migrate from Windows 98. For example, it is adding a utility that will let users convert their Windows 98 registry to NT.

Mac OS X

With 10-15 million users, the Mac is a key player on the desktop. Mac users also have a disproportionate presence on the Web. They may account for almost 20% of the Web client population. Apple views the Web as a key software and hardware initiative. The idea is to extend the Mac's friendliness to the Web. The Mac can then become the client platform of choice for the Internet and intranets.

Apple's weapon to win the client is *Mac OS X*—a modern OS (formerly code-named Rhapsody) that is a synthesis of *Mac OS 8.5* and NeXT's *OpenStep 4.2*. In other words, Mac OS X combines the Mac's user-friendliness with NeXT's no-compromise object-based frameworks. In addition to OpenStep applications, the new OS can run existing Mac applications (either unchanged in a compatibility environment, or natively as recompiled "Carbon" applications). Mac OS X also inherits from NeXT a modified Mach microkernel and BSD 4.4 Unix layer, allowing it to run most Unix applications (see Figure 6-3). Mach provides memory protection, threading, and preemptive multitasking. In addition, the new OS also comes with a fully compatible Java VM that supports 100% Pure Java and JavaBeans as well as some of the "less pure" Microsoft extensions, so it should run most Java programs.

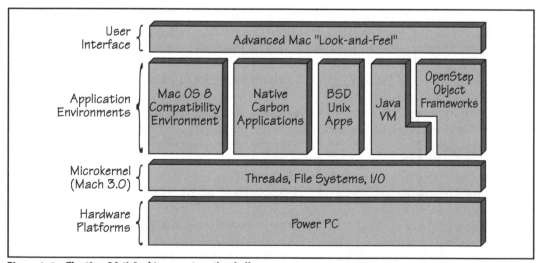

Figure 6-3. The Mac OS X Architecture in a Nutshell.

So what are the cons? First, Mac OS X is still under construction. Can Apple really deliver this time? Second, it requires new device drivers for most third-party hardware. Third, it remains to be seen how well Apple will integrate the different application personalities to provide a seamless Mac look-and-feel. Finally, it's not clear how Apple will continue to position Mac OS X versus Mac OS; eventually, it will have to put all its eggs in one basket.

Linux

Lest we forget the Internet was created by technologists...Consider this: over half of all the Web pages on the Internet today are produced by free Web software—mostly Apache—running on Linux operating systems.

> — **Doc Searls, President**
> **Searls Group**
> **(August, 1998)**

Release early and often, delegate everything you can, be open to the point of promiscuity.

> — **Linus Torvalds, Creator of Linux**

Linux is evolving naturally to do what an OS does best, while Windows is constantly adding non-OS functionalities as part of a vertical strategy to take over layer after layer above the OS.

> — **Marc Andreessen, Co-founder**
> **Netscape**
> **(August, 1998)**

Until recently, Linux—the wildcard of operating systems—ran mostly on servers: It's the "free Unix" that people use with their *Apache* Web servers. But now, Linux is also moving in a big way to the client side. According to IDC, Linux is one of the fastest-growing client operating systems—over 2 million desktop units shipped in 1997. This is an amazing feat for a piece of freeware that prides itself as "the technologists' OS." In fact, Linux is really the pride and joy of a very large diaspora of computer scientists that have lovingly enhanced it and supported it over the years. They call themselves the *Open Source* community. Some say it's a bad idea to bet against them. Today, the technologists control the code for the most popular Web server—*Apache*. In early 1998, Netscape bet on the technologists when it put the code for its browser in the public domain. As a result, the technologists now also own the Internet's most popular Web browser. So what's left? You guessed it— the operating system. The technologists want to have their very own OS, which is where Linux comes into the picture.

Linux is probably the most reliable version of Unix running on Intel. It's sometimes called "Unix-for-geeks-with-PCs." So how does this kind of operating system get packaged for the masses? This is where companies like Caldera and Red Hat come into the picture. These for-sale Linux distributors provide shrink-wrapped versions of the OS on CD-ROMs that include installation programs, GUI desktops, device drivers, and automatic hardware detection and configuration.

So where are the apps? In theory, any Intel-based Unix application will run on Linux without modification—including productivity suites like *StarOffice* and *Applix-Ware*. There are also suites of freeware apps that specifically target Linux. Finally, AOL/Netscape plans to bundle its free browser with Linux to create what Mark Andreessen calls the GUI of the future—"the user environment where people can live and work on the Net."

What about support? The community of Linux technologists provides excellent free support. However, corporations (and novice users) are still nervous about running what they perceive to be an "unsupported OS." So the for-sale Unix distributors also include support with their packages.

So what are the cons? First, Linux does not run popular Windows applications such as Microsoft Office. This could be a problem for corporations that have standardized on these packages. The Linux technologists must provide a Windows-emulation layer soon. Second, Linux does not provide a single desktop environment—although the *K Desktop* (a GUI that looks like a blend between Windows and Mac) comes close. Third, the for-sale vendors provide a very useful service, but they may also end up splintering the Linux community. Fourth, Linux needs to be bundled with client PCs—even an easy CD-ROM installation may be too hard for the mass market. Finally, Linux needs some marketing help from folks like AOL/Netscape, IBM, and Oracle.

SERVER OS TRENDS

Sorry Bill, none of the server operating system environments are dead.

> — *Dan Kusnetzky, Director*
> *IDC*
> *(March, 1998)*

According to IDC, server OS sales are going through the roof and will continue to do so over the next few years. The fastest growing category is what IDC calls *application servers*. These are your Web, DBMS, TP Monitor, object, and groupware servers. Figure 6-4, from Summit Strategies, shows where application servers fit in the scheme of things. They started out from the department and are now spreading in two directions: 1) downward into the space held by traditional NetWare LAN servers; and 2) upward into the space held by Unix servers running downsized mainframe applications. Of course, all server OSs—including NetWare, OS/2, NT, and all the Unixes—are going after this high-growth market.

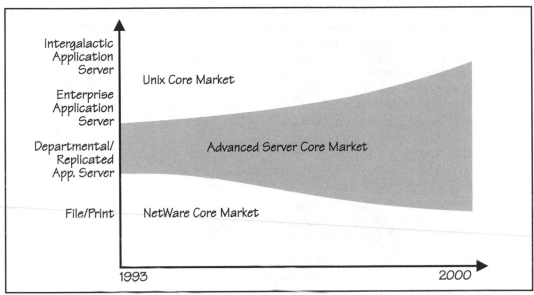

Figure 6-4. The Application Server Market (Source: Summit Strategies).

Figure 6-5, from IDC, shows the breakdown of worldwide server OS license shipments in 1997.[1] The numbers show that NT server unit shipments now outpace all Unix versions combined. NT sold over 1.2 million server licenses. The Unixes (and Linux) combined sold 962,000 server licenses. NetWare was a close third with 924,000 server licenses. Finally, OS/2 sold 218,000 server licenses.

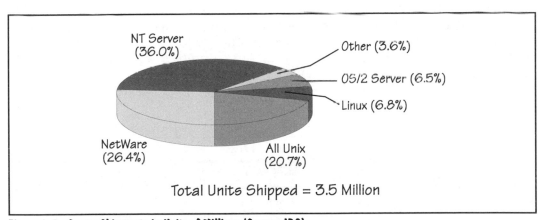

Figure 6-5. Server Shipments in Units of Millions (Source: IDC).

---

[1] Source: IDC, *Server Operating Environments: 1998 Worldwide Markets and Trends* (June, 1998).

However, these numbers do not tell the whole story. The majority of NT, OS/2, and NetWare shipments are for low-end server environments. Figure 6-6, also from IDC, paints a completely different picture of the server market—it shows hardware revenues by server OS platform. As you can see, Unix emerges as the clear winner; it sells three times more server hardware than NT. According to IDC, Unix also emerges as the winner when the server market is measured by the total number of clients supported by each platform. NetWare falls into second place; NT holds the number-three spot, followed by OS/2.

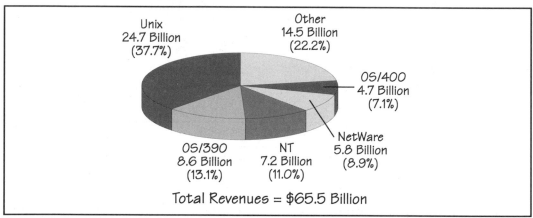

Figure 6-6. Server Hardware Platform Revenues by OS Environment in 1997 (Source: IDC, 1998).

Table 6-1 is also informative. It shows that Unix is primarily used as an application server platform. In contrast, over 50% of NT server licenses are used for departmental file/print servers. So NT is slugging it out with NetWare and OS/2 in the departmental trenches while also trying to encroach on the traditional Unix turf in the more lucrative application server market. In the last few years, NT made outstanding progress against both NetWare and OS/2 as a platform for database application software. But NT made very little progress against NetWare as a file/print server; it mostly grew there at the expense of OS/2. NT is currently battling Unix for the Web application server market; it also gearing up to go after the Unix enterprise server business with NT 5.0.

Table 6-1. Server OS Platform Functional Segmentation in 1997 (Source: IDC, 1998).

	Application or Mixed Server	File/Print Server
Unix	83.0%	17.0%
Windows NT	46.0%	54.0%
OS/2 Warp Server	31.8%	68.2%
NetWare	18.0%	82.0%

So the message is that the server market is highly heterogeneous. And we didn't even mention the significant players that fall into the "other" category—including Tandem/Compaq's NonStop Kernel, Digital's VMS, and IBM's OS/370 and OS/400. So how do you navigate through this crowded field? The answer is *very carefully*. But first let's meet some of the players.

SERVER OS: MEET THE PLAYERS

Well, it may be the devil, or it may be the Lord, but you're gonna have to serve somebody.

— *Bob Dylan*

As you can tell from the last section, the competition in the server market is intense. Again, Figure 6-2 on page 107 shows how the different server platforms are dividing the turf. The players in the low-to-medium end of the server market include NetWare, OS/2 Warp Server, NT Server, and Unixes on Intel such as SCO, Solaris, and Linux. The high-end currently belongs to Unix clusters and to any mainframe or supermini that can act as a server to PCs. The most formidable competitors at the very high-end are the RISC mainframe vendors that can provide massively parallel computing, scalability, and/or fault tolerance (for example, Tandem/Compaq, Sun, IBM, and Sequent). The parallel, MVS-based IBM mainframes—with their transaction engines, enterprise-based system management, and large databases—are also key players.

NetWare

This may come as a surprise: The largest server installed base (by far) belongs to Novell's NetWare. NetWare is a very fast, effective, well-supported file server that seamlessly supports OS/2, Mac, and Windows clients. The product also includes an

X.500-like global directory service and the tools that make it usable. NetWare is a well-managed server platform; its global directory provides a single point of network administration. Over 5,000 applications run on NetWare—including the major DBMSs. NetWare has a very large support and sales infrastructure—including over 200,000 *Certified NetWare Engineers (CNEs)* and 20,000 reseller partners across the world. In 1997, Novell introduced *IntranetWare* (a.k.a., *Netware 4.5*), which provided a built-in Web server.

So what are the cons? First, NetWare 4.X makes a poor application server. *NetWare Loadable Modules (NLMs)* are the Achilles' heel of NetWare. These are special namespaces set aside on the server that let programmers provide new system services (or write new applications). The NLM server modules you create get loaded by NetWare to manage these namespaces. Your NLMs, in effect, become part of the NetWare operating system kernel. There are many problems with NLMs that make it very difficult (if not impossible) to use NetWare 4.x as a general-purpose, modern, application server platform. The three worst culprits are: 1) limited memory protection; 2) lack of memory management—NetWare 4.x does not provide virtual memory; and 3) no support for preemptive multitasking.

The second issue with NetWare 4.X is that it is too closely tied to a proprietary networking protocol, IPX/SPX. The third issue raised against NetWare 4.X is that it does not take full advantage of SMP. The final criticism is that it does not provide an integrated suite of back-end applications (a la NT's BackOffice).

The good news is that *NetWare 5.0*—which shipped in October, 1998—fixes all these problems (and more). It's a modern OS whose kernel was rewritten to provide native support for SMP, preemptive multitasking, and virtual memory management. The other big news is that NetWare 5.0 provides pure IP support—no more encapsulation or tunneling of IPX inside IP packets. This means that standard IP products will interoperate better with NetWare. In addition, NDS is now LDAP-enabled, which should help it get more acceptance on the Internet.

On the application development front, Novell has embraced server-side Java with a passion. NetWare 5.0 provides one of the fastest and most secure Java VMs. In addition, it allows your Java programs to be directory-enabled. Novell will also provide native support for Enterprise JavaBeans and CORBA/IIOP. So developers will be able to use standard Java tools to create their server-side beans on the NetWare platform.

Finally, Novell is bundling a best-of-breed suite of integrated back-end products with NetWare 5.0. All these products are directory-enabled and have common administration facilities. The current suite includes Netscape's *FastTrack Server*, a five-user version of the *Oracle8*, a certificate server, and *Z.E.N.works*—an NDS-centric system management utility.

In summary, NetWare 5.0 is a great platform for writing server-side Java code. With NetWare 5.0, Novell may—for the first time—have created a winner in the application server space. Of course, this assumes that the product will prove to be both robust and scalable. Further on the horizon, Novell is working on a follow-up product code-named *Modesto*. It's a 64-bit version of NetWare for Intel's *Merced* chip; it will also provide advanced clustering support.

NT Server

NT Server provides the following additional features over *NT Workstation*: file/print server support, built-in Internet server, disk mirroring and striping, and SMP. NT Server code can be compiled to run on different microprocessor platforms—including Intel, Alpha, PowerPC, and MIPS. The turning point for NT Server came in September 1994 with the release of *NT 3.5* and the *MS BackOffice* server application suite. This release enhanced the TCP/IP stack, provided better support for NetWare, and improved the performance. In 1997, *NT 4.0* added support for the DCOM ORB, enhanced security, multiprotocol routing, better SMP support, and ISDN communications. *NT 5.0*—now in beta—introduces a network directory, enterprise-level security, enhanced clustering, a built-in Object Transaction Monitor called *MTS*, and a built-in message queue facility called *MSMQ*. Some of these products are already available as part of *NT Server Enterprise Edition* or as add-ons via the *NT Server Option Pack*.

NT is a good application, database, and file/print server platform. Its tight coupling with Windows, BackOffice, and DCOM makes it a natural server in Microsoft environments. NT comes from the PC LAN tradition, which means that it is easy to install, manage, and configure. The NT programming environment and tools are familiar to programmers versed in Microsoft tools.

So what are the cons? First, NT does not scale well. Its SMP engines seem to top out at four processors (it could also be an Intel bottleneck). In addition, Wolfpack clustering does not support load balancing in its current incarnation. So it doesn't help NT scale either. In contrast, Unix platforms have been pushing SMP and clustering technology into larger and larger configurations with almost linear scalability. For example, Solaris has demonstrated linear scalability of up to 64 processors using clusters. Even if NT solves its current scaling problem, it will always be around two years behind Unix in this area.

Second, NT 4.X does not provide an enterprise directory server; its domains-based flat directory does not even integrate with other BackOffice applications. Of course, this problem may be solved by either running NDS on top of NT or waiting for NT 5.0's *Active Directory*. Third, NT security is really a work-in-process; NT 5.0 promises to provide intergalactic security and fill many of the holes. Fourth, NT

add-ons—such as MTS, MSMQ, and Active Directory—are all based on Microsoft's *COM+* object model. Consequently, these services lock you into the Microsoft platform and server component model. This may be OK if you're an all-Microsoft shop. However, as we explained earlier, the enterprise and the Internet are very heterogeneous environments—especially when it comes to servers. Today, Microsoft does not own the server. So it's safer to stay with more open standards—such as CORBA and Enterprise JavaBeans—that are supported by multiple vendors on multiple platforms.

Finally, there are some skeptics who believe that with 40 million lines of code (50% of which are new), it will take some time before NT 5.0 shakes out and becomes enterprise ready. So even if NT 5.0 ships in 1999, it may take some time before you deploy it for mission-critical systems. According to IDC, today over 95% of the world's mission-critical systems run on either Unix or IBM mainframes.[2] So it may take some time for NT to join this exclusive club. Also note that an enterprise server platform requires a long sales cycle and a lot of customer hand-holding—which is not part of Microsoft's current business model. NT must also learn how to coexist with every form of legacy system if it is to play a role in the enterprise. It takes a lot more than a certified Microsoft Professional Engineer to support a mission-critical system. Microsoft's forte is still shrink-wrapped products.

---

[2] Source: IDC, *Transaction Processing Software: 1998 Worldwide Markets and Trends* (June, 1998).

OS/2 Warp Server

Like NT, OS/2 is also an excellent application server for departments. It is a seasoned, 32-bit operating system that has incubated some leading-edge server software—for example, Lotus Notes. In February 1996, IBM introduced *OS/2 Warp Server*, which combines OS/2 Warp's application server environment with LAN Server—a very fast file and print server. Warp Server provides an OOUI user interface for easy installation, configuration, and system management. You do everything via point-and-click. The installation autodetects hardware, which makes it easier to find and configure all these strange network adapters. Warp Server also provides disk mirroring, remote administration, remote software distribution, a backup server, and software metering.

In 1997, IBM introduced a set of back-office and middleware offerings for OS/2, NT, and AIX. These are integrated families of server offerings for database management, transaction processing, data warehousing, Web commerce, groupware, and system management. In 1998, IBM introduced the OS/2 Warp-based *WorkSpace on Demand*. This is a thin-client architecture that lets users remotely boot from an OS/2 server. The application software and the operating system reside on the server while keeping their unique desktop configurations. Clients can run OS/2, DOS, Windows 3.X, and Java applications. The system comes with a server management console.

In late 1998, IBM started to beta test a new release of OS/2 Warp Server code-named *Aurora*—due in the first half of 1999. Aurora's new features include a built-in SMP engine, a journaling file, support for a single European currency, full year-2000 compliance, a super-fast Java engine, and an improved Web server. Aurora will also provide a single logon capability that lets users log on to an OS/2 server and access files, printers, and applications on networked NT servers. It will also let OS/2 Warp Server administrators create and delete NT user accounts, passwords, and user groups.

OS/2's main shortcoming is that it appears to be going nowhere. It seems that IBM feels obliged to introduce—at a very slow pace—just enough features to keep OS/2's current customers happy. Note that OS/2 users are IBM's largest enterprise customers, so they must be kept happy with tiny incremental releases. Without turning this into another OS/2 Soapbox, it seems to us that OS/2—in the hands of IBM—is really dead. So if you need a server OS with a bright future, you're better off with Novell's made-for-Java NetWare 5.0, NT 5.0, or one of the popular Unix server platforms—such as Linux, Solaris, HP-UX, or SCO.

Unix

Unix provides a seasoned, function-rich operating system that is scalable from the desktop to the supercomputer. Unix is the melting pot of the computer industry.

Its close connection with universities makes it a great incubator of new ideas. Most of these ideas first appear on the commercial market as Unix extensions and variants. The Unix mainstream, on the other hand, moves a lot more cautiously. Unix can claim an army of trained programmers, integrators, and technicians.

The Unix server industry grew out of the downsizing of mainframe applications. In the last 16 years, Unix was able to successfully surround the mainframe. It then provided "a poor man's mainframe" alternative. However, in the PC LAN environment, Unix is viewed as a "rich man's server." Unix is now surrounded by low-cost PC alternatives such as NT, OS/2, and NetWare. But Unix continues to thrive. As you saw earlier in this chapter, the Unix server market alone was close to $25 billion in 1997—that's not counting workstations, software, or services. The latest high-growth area for Unix servers is the Internet. Unix standards have become Internet standards—including mail, FTP, TCP/IP, and the domain name service. In a sense, the Internet is a showcase for distributed Unix technology.

Unix vendors have always been at the forefront of client/server middleware. Now they are introducing Java and CORBA objects to the world, again by incorporating them into the Internet infrastructure. Unix is also a well-regarded choice for database servers, especially ones that scale. Unix vendors are focusing much of their efforts on scalability and high-availability. For example, HP-UX will be able to support a 64-processor cluster system with 99.999% availability. So Unix boxes are really the new mainframes. They are incredibly resilient and can automatically isolate and correct failures. Finally, all the key Unix vendors are already shipping 64-bit versions of their products—including Digital, Silicon Graphics, Solaris, and IBM's AIX. In addition, almost every Unix variant (except for AIX) will be ported to *Merced*—Intel's 64-bit processor. Of course, Intel must first ship Merced, which is now due in late 1999 (or 2000). In the meantime, you have 64-bit Unix running today on non-Intel RISC chips. So the Unix crowd is always at the forefront of the technology curve, leaving the competition—NT, OS/2, and NetWare—to always play catch-up.

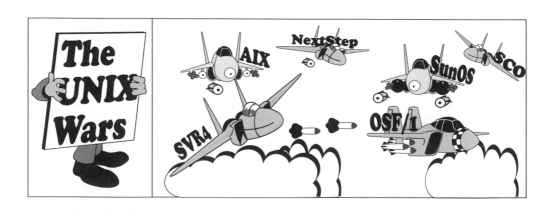

So what are the cons? The main problem with Unix has always been: Which Unix do you choose? At last count, there were still dozens of Unix variants on the market, but they appear to be consolidating. Because Unix is a hardware-independent operating system, an application should be able to run on any machine that supports Unix, from a PC to a supercomputer. This server scalability story is very attractive, but it is not realistic. In the real world, what keeps this from happening are two factors:

- ■ *Lack of binary compatibility*. The Unix world is different from the PC world, where software comes in low-cost, shrink-wrapped floppy packages that can run on any PC clone that runs MS-DOS, NT, Windows 95/98, or OS/2. Unlike these operating systems, Unixes vary widely. There is still no broadly supported binary standard. Unix applications, at a minimum, must be recompiled to be ported from platform to platform. This is a major headache and expense for software providers.

- ■ *Functional differences among the Unixes*. There will always be differences among the Unixes: Vendors like to sell products, and functional differences are required to avoid relentless, no-win price wars. However, most Unix vendors have fully implemented the *Unix 95* application interface formerly known as *Spec 1170*. It supports over 1,170 kernel APIs selected from the top 50 Unix applications. The Open Group—which owns the Unix name—uses it to "brand" Unixes as such. In June 1998, the Open Group introduced *Unix 98*. This latest spec standardizes many more Unix fundamentals—including support for real-time apps, DLL extensions, a common GUI, Internet profiles, and the year 2000. The Internet profiles will make every Unix box a full-function Web server. On the Intel side of Unix, vendors are also collaborating on a 64-bit *Unix for Merced*. So the situation is improving.

The NT threat is pushing Unix vendors toward some kind of unification. SCO has become the new guardian of the Unix standard, but not everyone is playing by its rules. It seems that for Unix to effectively compete, it must change its model. Instead of each vendor reinventing the wheel with their Unix extensions, they must learn to cross-license each other's technology.

CONCLUSION

Client/server is about "mix-and-match." It's also about how to make a set of independent networked computers behave like a single system. Taming diversity is the name of the game. Each of the computers may be running on different hardware and operating systems, but they must still provide the illusion of being a single system. Some of us may decide to tame diversity by standardizing on a single operating system for both clients and servers. Unfortunately, for most of us, there is no one-size-fits-all operating system. In addition, none of us live in a green field—

we must integrate with our existing systems. Finally, none of us can control what runs on the Internet. So the conclusion is that we must learn to live with both client and server diversity—and grow to love it. The operating system is just one more element of the mix-and-match puzzle. As you will see in later parts of this book, middleware is the glue that integrates the disparate pieces on the intergalactic network. So middleware is the operating system of the intergalactic network. Read on to get the scoop.

Part 3
Base Middleware:
Stacks and NOSs

An Introduction to Part 3

Multivendor systems have serious barriers to cooperation. An articulated aim of the industry is to increase the capacity of systems to cooperate.

— *Hal Lorin, Author*
Doing IT Right
(Prentice-Hall, 1996)

Congratulations, you're still alive after going through the OS wars. Wasn't that exciting? Yes, Earthlings are always fighting over one thing or another. That seems to be in their nature. But we're going to change the pace now and take you through some more secular terrain. Instead of fighting each other, the client/server vendors will now try to hide their differences behind a facade called the "single-system image."

Now don't get us wrong. The folks you met in Part 2 are far from burying the hatchet. Instead, they're all trying to make everybody else's system look like their own. If they can't get rid of the other systems, the next best thing is to make them disappear (the politically correct term is to "make them transparent"). So how do they do that disappearing trick? By throwing layer upon layer of middleware until everything becomes one. Now that's magic!

Part 3 is about the base middleware that is used to create the "single-system illusion" on an intergalactic level. We will start with a brief tutorial on *Network Operating System (NOS)* middleware. You'll discover the "bag of tricks" NOSs use to create illusions that would put to shame the great Houdini himself—that's one of our better magicians who lived on Earth not too long ago. There were no NOSs in Houdini's time.

After exploring the NOSs, we go into the *stacks* middleware, which introduce their own repertoire of tricks. Eventually, nothing is what it appears to be. Everything gets deconstructed, reconstructed, and then repackaged so that it "appears to work" with everything else. But you'll know better, of course.

You'll soon discover that each vendor will be glad to sell you a different set of middleware products. Unfortunately, middleware does not extend its disappearing act to make the products themselves transparent. This is because middleware is a lucrative business in its own right. Yes, when there's money to be made, nothing disappears. And we pay for the pleasure of seeing the heterogeneous world look like it's one happily integrated system. Yes, we pay for illusions on Earth. Look at our movie industry.

Finally, we will introduce you to some of the products you'll need to create the type of illusions that meet your fancy (or real needs). You can create almost any type of facade as long as you have the money to pay for it. Another important reason to look at products is to get a reality check of what's really there. The middleware

vendors are practitioners of magic who, like all magicians, sometimes forget what's real. So it's essential to go behind the stage and see what's really there, at least in terms of product. As you will soon see, the Internet is becoming the ultimate NOS. We hope you'll enjoy the show.

Chapter 7

NOS: Creating the Single-System Image

Single-system image creates an illusion in the minds of users that all the servers on the network are part of the same system or behave like a single computer.

— Andrew Tanenbaum, Author
Modern Operating Systems
(Prentice-Hall, 1992)

This chapter goes over the functions that the Network Operating System (NOS) middleware must provide to create a "single-system image" of all the services on the network. As we explained earlier, this is really a Houdini-sized illusion that makes all servers of the world—we're talking about a multiserver, multiservice, multivendor, and multinetwork world—appear to the client as one big happy family. In a sense, the NOS middleware provides the glue that recreates the single system out of the disparate elements. It's a thankless job, but without it there can be no client/server computing. By the end of this chapter, you'll get a better appreciation of the "bag of tricks" that are used by clients and servers to create the *grand illusion*.

NOS MIDDLEWARE: THE TRANSPARENT ILLUSION

NOSs are evolving from being a collection of independent workstations, able to communicate via a shared file system, to becoming real distributed computing environments that make the network *transparent* to users. The reach of the NOS now transcends its departmental origins. It now includes enterprise networks, intranets, extranets, and the Internet (see Figure 7-1). In all cases, NOS technology must provide the illusion of a single system. In departmental LANs, this shared illusion only extends to a few hundred users. But on the Internet, the illusion extends to hundreds of millions of users. In between, you have enterprise networks and extranets that may have thousands—or sometimes hundreds of thousands—of users. Of course, the complexity of the NOS is proportional to its reach. For example, the Internet encompasses many organizations and diverse communities. So the NOS must do more work to provide its single-system illusion.

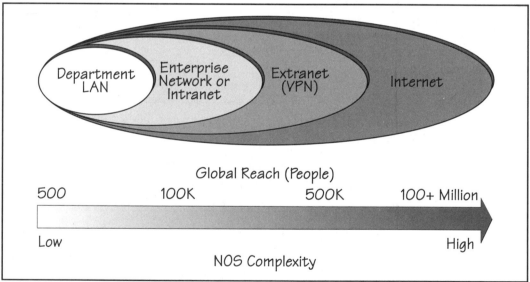

Figure 7-1. The Long Arm of the NOS: From Departmental LAN to Intergalactic Internet.

What Does Transparency Really Mean?

Transparency means fooling everyone into thinking the client/server system is totally seamless—the single-system illusion. It really means hiding the network and its servers from the users and even the application programmers. Here are some of the types of transparencies the NOS middleware is expected to provide as part of its "network disappearing act":

- *Location transparency*—You should not have to be aware of the location of a resource. Users should not have to include the location information in the resource's name. For example, *Machine**directory**file* surfaces the name of the server machine. This is a transparency violation.

- *Namespace transparency*—You should be able to use the same naming conventions (and namespace) to locate any resource on the network. The whole universe is one big tree (see Figure 7-2). This includes every type of resource on any vendor's product.

- *Logon transparency*—You should be able to provide a single password (or authentication) that works on all servers and for all services on the network.

- *Replication transparency*—You should not be able to tell how many copies of a resource exist. For example, if a naming directory is shadowed on many machines, it is up to the NOS to synchronize updates and take care of any locking issues.

- *Local/remote access transparency*—You should be able to work with any resource on the network as if it were on the local machine. The NOS must handle access controls and provide directory services.

- *Distributed time transparency*—You should not see any time differences across servers. The NOS must synchronize the clocks on all servers.

- *Failure transparency*—You must be shielded from network failures. The NOS must handle retries and session reconnects. It must also provide some levels of service redundancy for fault-tolerance.

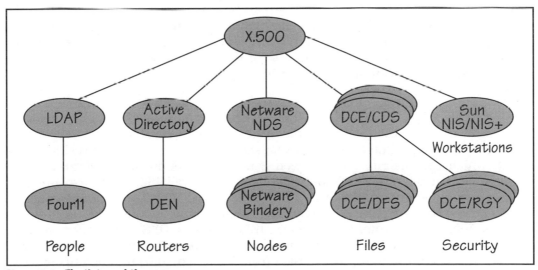

Figure 7-2. The Universal Namespace.

■ *Administration transparency*—You should only have to deal with a single-system management interface. The NOS must be integrated with the local management services.

The challenge for the NOS middleware is how to provide this high level of transparency *without sacrificing the autonomy of the local OS*.

NOS: Extending the Local OS's Reach

One of the functions of a NOS is to make the physical location of resources (over a network) transparent to an application. The early NOSs were in the business of virtualizing the file and printer resources and redirecting them to LAN-based file and print servers. These NOSs provided proxies on the local machines—the *requesters*—that intercepted calls for devices and *redirected* them to servers on the LAN. The only way an application (or user) could tell the difference between a local or remote resource was from a pathname, which included its machine name. But aliases could be used to even hide the pathnames from the users. The NOS thus extends the local OS's device support transparently across the network. Practically anything that can be done on a local OS can be done remotely and transparently. The NOS allows applications written for the local OS to become networked without changing a line of code. Most NOSs allow clients that run on different OSs (such as DOS, Windows 98, Mac, and Unix) to share files and other devices. For example, a Mac client sees DOS files in the Mac format.

A new generation of network file servers promises to introduce even more transparency into the file systems. For example, the DCE *Distributed File Service (DFS)* provides a single-image file system that can be distributed across a group of file servers (see Figure 7-3). The DFS file naming scheme is location-independent. Each file has a unique identifier that is consistent across the network. Files use the DCE global namespace just like the rest of the network resources. And the file system is integrated with the DCE security mechanisms.

DFS provides a *Local File System (LFS)* with many advanced features, including replication facilities that make the file system highly available. Fast response is achieved with a distributed cache. A snapshot of the file system can reside on the client, which can operate on files even if the server is down. Backups and file relocations can take place without making LFS unavailable. LFS also provides transactional log support. In case of a system crash, file records can be replayed to bring the system to a consistent state. DFS can work with other local file systems, such as NFS, or the Unix file system. IBM provides DFS servers for multiple platforms—including MVS, several Unixes, and NT. The NT version, which shipped in early 1998, lets you move shared data from NT to a mainframe (or Unix system) and back again; it's totally transparent to end users.

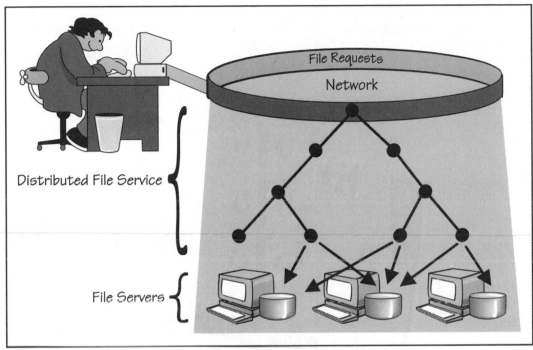

Figure 7-3. The New Generation: DCE's Distributed File Server.

Global Directory Services

The state of a client/server system is always in flux. Users join and leave the network. Services can be added and moved around at will. Data is always being created and moved around. So who keeps track of all this activity? How do clients find their servers in a constantly changing universe? Where is the single-system image kept? It's kept in the NOS directory service, of course (see Figure 7-4). This essential component tracks all the NOS's resources and knows where everything is. Without it, we would be lost. Ideally, a distributed directory should provide a single image that can be used by all network applications—including e-mail, system management, network inventory, file services, RPCs, distributed objects, databases, authentication, and security.

Directories and name servers solve the same problem: How to resolve human understandable names into machine addresses? In addition, a directory object can have *attributes*. For example, a person could have an e-mail address, various telephone numbers, a postal mail address, and a job title. A directory lets you search its objects by attribute. A *schema* describes the types of objects a directory may contain; it also describes the attributes—both mandatory and optional—associated with an object type.

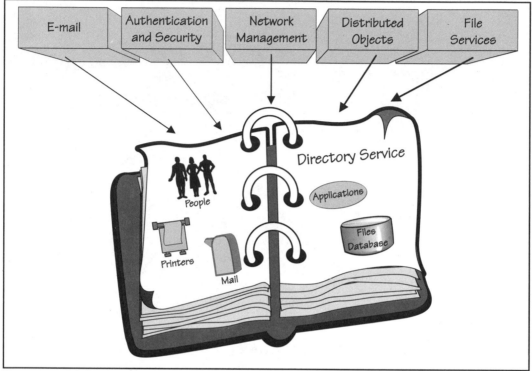

Figure 7-4. Global Directories: Keeping Track of NOS Resources.

A typical directory is implemented as a set of named entries and their associated attributes. For example, "MyServer" may be an instance of an application server type (or class). Its attributes can be: room number = 54, status = up, and CPU utilization = 54 percent. MyServer may also contain a list of the functions it exports and their interface definitions.

In a modern NOS, the directory server is implemented as a distributed, replicated, object database. It is *distributed* to allow different administration domains to control their environment. It is *replicated* to provide high availability and performance where needed. Remember, if the directory is down, all the network activity comes to a grinding halt. Nothing can be found. It's an *object database* in the sense that everything that is tracked is an instance of an object class. You can use inheritance to derive new object types.

Modern NOS directories have APIs and user interfaces that allow programs (or humans) to locate entities on the network by querying on the name or attributes. For example, a program can issue a query to locate all the 1200-dpi printers that are not busy. If you know the name of an entity, you can always obtain its attributes. The directory service itself is a well-known address known to all the trusted users on the network (and sometimes even intruders).

FYI

What's in a Name?

Briefing

In client/server systems, names must be unique within the context in which they are resolved (and used). You can think of a context as an autonomous naming authority. It's like the area code in the telephone system. A federated naming scheme (or *namespace*) is a conglomeration of independent naming authorities. In a federated namespace, each name must include its naming authority. For example, if you're within the U.S. telephone naming authority, you can only call somebody in Switzerland by including the country code for Switzerland along with the person's telephone number. It's a tree-like (or hierarchical) naming scheme. If you create enough layers of hierarchy, you'll end up with a namespace that includes every communicating entity in the universe. In summary, a local directory allows us to locate entities within our own network neighborhood; a federated— or global—directory allows us to find things outside the local neighborhood. ❑

How do directories maintain their autonomy in a global network environment? How do they let us create unique names on the network without bumping into each other? How do we accommodate legacy naming services? This is usually accomplished by introducing hierarchical namespaces like in a file system (see Figure 7-5). In each name, there is a *global component* and a *local component*. The global component is the name by which the local directory is known at the intergalactic level. The global component manages a federation of loosely-coupled local directories. You can name the local component according to local conventions. In addition, a gateway agent can reside on each local directory and can forward queries for non-local names to a global directory (or naming service).

How are directories replicated? Typically, a directory maintains a master copy and read-only shadow replicas. Two types of synchronization schemes are used to refresh the replicas:

■ *Immediate replication* causes any update to the master to be immediately shadowed on all replicas.

■ *Skulking* causes a periodic propagation (for example, once a day) to all the replicas of all changes made on the master.

Note that some directories—for example, the *NetWare Directory Service (NDS)*— now supports multi-master updates. In contrast, LDAP is currently a single-master technology (see the next Briefing box).

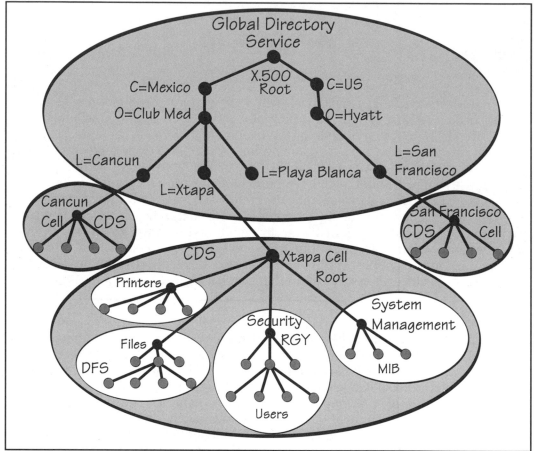

Figure 7-5. Federated Directories—Creating a Unified Namespace.

In summary, the new generation of NOS directory services uses some of the most advanced distributed database and object technology to keep track of distributed system resources. The directory is the critical element that extends your network neighborhood. The current directory technology is flexible enough to manage and track today's coarser network entities—such as printers, users, programs, and servers—and the more fine-grained entities that are beginning to appear—such as distributed objects and router bandwidth allocation.

How Do You Interface to These Directories?

So how do you talk to these directories? Most of us will use directory-enabled programs like e-mail, Web browsers, Four11, or system management consoles. However, a few of us will have to write code to create these types of programs. If you're one of the chosen few, you'll be happy to know that there are a ton of "standard" APIs to help you. Here's a sampling of what's available:

- **_Directory-specific APIs and class libraries._** These provide interfaces that are tightly-coupled to a product—for example, Novell and Banyan provide APIs to their respective directories.

- **_LDAP and X.500 APIs._** These are the standards-based interfaces defined by the IETF, X/Open, and the CCITT for the LDAP and X.500 directories (see the next Briefing box).

- **_Java classes._** The JavaSoft-defined _Java Naming and Directory Interface (JNDI)_ provides a set of generic Java classes that let you interface to a variety of directory services—such as LDAP, NDS, CORBA Naming, and NIS.

- **_Distributed object interfaces._** These are ORB-based interfaces that let you talk to directory servers across ORBs. Typically, these interfaces let you pick your language, directory service, and platform. For example, the CORBA _Naming Service_ is directory-neutral, language-neutral, and platform-neutral. In the COM parallel universe, Microsoft defines the _Active Directory Service Interface (ADSI)_. It is a directory-neutral and language-neutral interface for COM+ objects. Currently, this is a Windows-only interface. However, Cisco may be porting ADSI to Solaris as part of its joint initiative with Microsoft, called _Directory Enabled Networking (DEN)_.

- **_Meta-directory services and scripts._** Meta-directories are glue products— from companies like Zoomit, NetVision, and WorldTalk—that synchronize data in existing directories via scripts. You may find these scripts easier to use than standard programming languages.

So you have many choices. You'll find that all these APIs let you navigate the directory namespace, formulate your query, and iterate through the results.

X.500 and LDAP: A Tale of Two Directories

Briefing

Warning: This box is filled with TLAs (Three-Letter Acronyms).

In the old days, a directory service was tied to a single application such as e-mail or to a specific operating system, such as NT domains. In contrast, a _universal directory_ must be totally independent of both applications and NOSs. The original industry standard for universal directories was CCITT's *X.500*. However, X.500 proved to be too bulky and overly complicated. Today, the industry's new Esperanto for directories is *LDAP*—a downsized version of the original X.500. Here's a brief introduction to these two directories.

X.500

As you can guess, the X.500 architecture is based on a replicated distributed database (see Figure 7-6). Programs can access the directory services using the *X/Open Directory Service (XDS)* APIs. The XDS APIs allow programs to read, compare, update, add, and remove directory entries; list directories; and search for entries based on attributes. You use the *X/Open Management (XOM)* API for defining and navigating through the information objects that are in the directory. Think of XOM as an object meta-language. Each object in an X.500 directory belongs to a class. A class can be derived from other classes. XOM provides an API for defining object classes and their attributes. XOM APIs also define basic data types such as string.

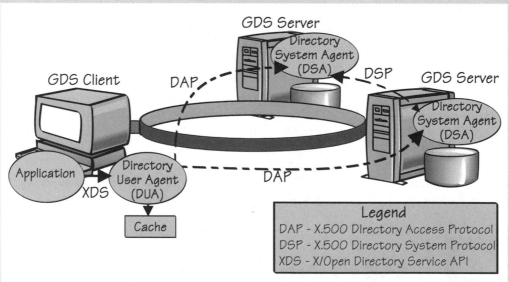

Figure 7-6. The X.500 Directory Components.

The X.500 client component—the *Directory User Agent (DUA)*—and server component—the *Directory System Agent (DSA)*—communicate using the *Directory Access Protocol (DAP)*. Servers talk to each other using the *Directory System Protocol (DSP)*. The DAP and DSP formats and protocols are defined in the X.500 standard and provide worldwide interoperability among directory services.

The X.500 standard was written to run on top of the OSI communication protocol. OSI is not very popular, so most implementations of X.500 cheat and use alternatives like TCP/IP or IPX/SPX. X.500 is implemented—fully or partially—in a number of products—including *DCE*, *Microsoft Exchange*, *Lotus Notes*, and the *NetWare Directory Service*. However, these partial implementations of X.500 did not interoperate, which was a big problem. Most vendors found the entire X.500 protocol too bulky to implement, so the *Lightweight Distributed Access Protocol (LDAP)* was born. The operative word here is "lightweight." Sorry for all the acronyms!

LDAP

LDAP was originally designed by Netscape with help from researchers at the University of Michigan to provide a simplified version of the X.500 DAP that could also run on TCP/IP networks. The idea was to provide a lightweight PC client implementation that could access X.500 directory servers over the Internet. LDAP became very popular and is now supported by all major directories—including Netscape, Lotus/IBM, NDS, and NT 5.0's Active Directory. In 1997, LDAP evolved to provide a fat-free version of the X.500 server. The design goal was to provide 90% of the X.500 functionality at 10% of the processing cost. In February 1998, Netscape began shipping *Directory Server 3.0*, which was designed from the ground up as a native LDAP server. In addition, IBM and Sun are creating their own native implementations. Netscape Navigator, Lotus Notes, and Microsoft Internet Explorer are examples of LDAP clients. Netscape even uses the LDAP API in its address book.

LDAP uses the X.500 naming scheme and namespace. LDAP *objects* are named collections of named attributes. Each object has a *distinguished name (dn)* and belongs to an *objectclass* that identifies its object *type* (or *schema*). Attributes have common mnemonics. Here are some examples:

objectclass = object type
dn = distinguished name
cn = common name
mail = e-mail
c = country
o = organization
ou= organization unit

Here's an example of a directory object of type employee:

objectclass = employee
dn = Jeri L. Edwards, o = BEA Systems, ou = strategy, c = US
mail = jledwards@beasys.com

LDAP lets you issue queries using a URL-like syntax. For example:

ldap://ldap.beasys.com /o = BEA Systems, ou =Java, c = US?

This hypothetical query returns all the Java programmers working for BEA Systems in the U.S. Here's a sampling of the kind of questions you could ask your LDAP directory:

- What is the telephone number of BEA Systems' strategy department?
- What is Jeri Edwards' fax number?
- What is Jeri Edwards' boss's e-mail?
- What is the beeper number for the network administrator?
- Is there a color printer on the second floor? Is it up?
- Is there an XYZ project?
- Who are the developers working on the XYZ project?

The *LDAP Data Interchange Format (LDIF)* lets you populate a directory using an ASCII text file containing entries and attributes. Of course, you can also export the contents of a directory to an LDIF file.

In early 1998, the IETF issued *LDAP v3*. This new version of the standard adds the following features:

- ***Schema discovery*** lets a client query an LDAP server to discover the object types it supports; it can also discover the attributes associated with a given type.

- ***Dynamically extensible schemas*** let a client define at run time new types of objects to be stored on a server. The client does this using LDAP v3's new *extensibleObject* class.

- ***Enhanced security*** includes LDAP over secure sockets and simple authentication.

- ***Intelligent referrals*** let a server refer a query to another server. This creates the illusion of a single directory, even if the data is scattered across multiple servers.

- ***Support for international character sets*** lets users deploy and search directories using their native language.

In August 1998, the IETF further enhanced LDAP's security arsenal by adding support for access control lists. This means that an authenticated user must now have the proper permissions to access different types of information within an LDAP directory. As you can tell from all this activity, LDAP is continuously being enhanced. It's well on its way to becoming a mission-critical directory standard.

So what's left? Currently, the IETF is working on an LDAP replication standard. Today, all LDAP directories perform replication in proprietary ways, which means their replication mechanisms do not interoperate. However, by the time you read this, the IETF should have completed two replication standards for LDAP: a *multi-master* standard that lets you update any directory in the system, and a *single-master* standard that only lets you update the master. In both cases, the changes are propagated to the rest of the directories. The other work in progress is to create standard schemas for entities like people, printers, routers, JavaBeans, digital certificates, and so on. But, don't hold your breath waiting for this work to complete. ❏

Distributed Time Services

Maintaining a single notion of time is important for ordering events that occur on distributed clients and servers. So how does a client/server system keep the clocks on different machines synchronized? How does it compensate for the unequal drift rates between synchronizations? How does it create a single-system illusion that makes all the different machine clocks tick to the same time? With the NOS's distributed time services, of course.

Typically, the NOS addresses the problem of distributed time using two complementary techniques:

■ *It periodically synchronizes the clocks on every machine in the network.* The NOS typically has an agent on each machine—DCE calls it a *Time Clerk*—that asks *Time Servers* for the correct time and adjusts the local time accordingly. The agents may consult more than one Time Server, and then calculate the probable correct time and its inaccuracy based on the responses it receives. The agent can upgrade the local time either gradually or abruptly. Typically, the universal time to which all machines must be synchronized is the *Universal Coordinated Time (UTC);* it keeps track of time elapsed since the beginning of the Gregorian calendar—October 15, 1582.

■ *It introduces an inaccuracy component to compensate for unequal clock drifts that occur between synchronizations.* The local time agents are configured to know the limits of their local hardware clock. They maintain a count of the inaccuracy factor and return it to an API call that asks for the time. The time agent requests a synchronization after the local clock drifts past an inaccuracy threshold.

As you can see, today's NOSs may have even surpassed the Swiss in their attention to intricate timing details. Today's most popular standard for keeping time on the

Internet is the *Network Time Protocol (NTP)*, as defined in *RFC's 958* and *1305*. NTP—long a publicly available tool—is now part of many Unix operating systems, including Digital Unix, HP-UX, and Solaris. The NTP protocol provides very accurate levels of time synchronization—in the order of milliseconds on LANs and tens of milliseconds on WANs. Note that most corporations have pools of time servers with which you can synchronize. If you don't work for a corporation, check with your ISP—many provide time servers, which they call *chimers*. There are also a number of publicly accessible time servers on the Internet (see *http://www. eecis.udel.edu/~ntp*).

Distributed Security Services

The client/server environment introduces new security threats beyond those found in traditional time-shared systems. In a client/server system, you can't trust any of the operating systems on the network to protect the server's resources from unauthorized access. And even if the client machines were totally secure, the network itself is highly accessible. Sniffer devices can easily record traffic between machines and introduce forgeries and Trojan horses into the system. This means the servers must find new ways to protect themselves without creating a fortress mentality that upsets users.

To maintain the single-system illusion, every trusted user must be given transparent access to all resources. How is that done when every PC poses a potential threat to

network security? Will system administrators be condemned to spend their working lives granting access level rights to users, one at a time, for each individual application on each server across the enterprise? Let's find out what the NOSs have to offer.

Can We Obtain C2-Level Security on the Intergalactic Net?

C2 is a U.S. government security standard for operating systems; it requires that users and applications be authenticated before gaining access to any operating system resource. To obtain C2 certification on a network, all clients must provide an authenticated user ID, all resources must be protected by access control lists, audit trails must be provided, and access rights must not be passed to other users that reuse the same items. Let's go over the security mechanisms a modern NOS can provide to meet (and even beat) C2 level security on the network.

■ *Authentication: Are you who you claim to be?* In time-shared systems, the authentication is done by the OS using passwords. NOSs must do better than that. Any hacker with a PC and network sniffer knows how to capture a password and reuse it. OK, so let's encrypt the password. Oh boy! Who is going to manage the secret keys and all that good stuff? Luckily, enterprise NOSs have an answer: *Kerberos*. Kerberos is the trusted third party that allows two processes to prove to each other that they are who they claim to be. It's a bit like two spies meeting on a street corner and whispering the magical code words that establish the "trust" relationship. Both parties obtain the magic words—called *secret keys*—separately from Kerberos (see the next Briefing box). These secret keys are used to create an authenticated communications session between two entities.

Unfortunately, Kerberos does not scale well in an unmanaged environment like the Internet. Currently, the Internet's best solution for authenticating both clients and servers is to use *digital certificates* on top of a *public/private key* infrastructure (see later section). Within a year, you may be carrying your digital certificate (and private key) inside a Java *smart card*. A bit further out on the horizon are *biometric* forms of identification—such as fingerprints and retina scans. In all cases, the best defense is to use two authentication methods together—such as a password and a certificate. The authentication server can then use the password to decrypt the digital certificate. This double gauntlet is called *two-factor authentication*.

■ *Authorization: Are you allowed to use this resource?* Once clients are authenticated, the server applications are responsible for verifying which operations the clients are permitted to perform on the information they try to access—for example, a payroll server may control access to salary data on a per-individual basis. Servers use *Access Control Lists (ACLs)* to control user access. ACLs can be associated with any computer resource. They contain the list of names (and group names) and the type of operations they are permitted to

Kerberos: "You Can't Trust Anyone"

Briefing

MIT's project Athena adopted the position that it is next to *impossible* to make sure each workstation on the network is secure. Instead, the MIT folks took it as a given that some "impersonation" would take place on the LAN and decided to protect themselves against it. The result was a software fortress called *Kerberos* that delivers a higher level of security than traditional passwords and access control lists. Kerberos automatically authenticates every user for every application. The Kerberos protocol, especially with the add-ons introduced by the OSF DCE, fulfills the authentication requirement of C2. It allows servers to trust their clients (mostly PCs), and vice versa. You must remember that we could always put a Trojan horse on the server side, so the servers also need to prove their identity. ❑

perform on each resource. NetWare's administration services, for example, make it easy for network managers to add new users to groups without having to specify access rights from scratch. NOSs can easily meet C2's ACL requirements.

■ *Audit Trails: Where have you been?* Audit services allow system managers to monitor user activities, including attempted logons and which servers or files are used. Audit services are a piece of the arsenal needed by system managers to detect intruders in their own organizations. For example, you should be able to monitor all the network activity associated with a suspect client workstation (or user). Knowing an audit trail exists usually discourages insiders from tampering with servers using their own logon, but they can do it under somebody else's logon. Most NOSs support audit trails, and that should make the C2 accreditation people happy.

In summary, it looks like C2 security on a LAN is within the reach of a modern NOS.

Can We Do Better Than C2 on the Intergalactic Net?

We really need better security than C2 when traffic moves over unsecured wide area networks. How can we guarantee that vital messages are not tampered with? You don't want the data in an electronic fund transfer to be intercepted and rerouted from your account to somebody else's. In addition, electronic commerce on the Internet is introducing the need for a new security feature called *non-repudiation*. This is the electronic equivalent of a notarized signature that can hold in court.

Integrity: Is My In-Transit Data Safe?

Modern NOSs provide at least two mechanisms for dealing with tampering and the confidentiality of in-transit data:

■ *Encryption* allows two principals to hold a secure communication. Each principal must obtain a copy of a *session key* from a trusted third party (for example, a Kerberos server). This session key can then be used for encoding and decoding messages. Another approach is to use a public/private key encryption technique. The advantage of the public/private key scheme is that it can also be used for electronic signatures and non-repudiation. However, public key algorithms—like DES—provide faster encryption.

■ *Cryptographic checksums*, a less extreme solution, ensure that data is not modified as it passes through the network. The sender calculates a checksum (or *message digest*) on the data, using a session key to encrypt it, and appends the result to the message. The receiver recalculates the checksum, decrypts the one received in the message using the session key, and then compares the two. If they don't match, the message is suspect. Without the session key, intruders will not be able to alter the data and update the checksum. Examples of message digest algorithms are *Message Digest 5 (MD5)* and *Secure Hashing Algorithm 1 (SHA-1)*.

Encryption may be an overkill in some situations because it introduces performance overheads and may be subject to governmental restrictions.

Non-Repudiation: Can You Prove It in Court?

A NOS must be able to provide irrefutable evidence that an action took place. For example, it must be able to prove that a message was really originated by you and only you. The NOS must also be able to prove that the recipient got your method invocation (or data). *Non-repudiation* has become a hot topic in electronic commerce circles. It means providing irrefutable evidence that two parties were involved in a client/server interaction. Neither party should be able to deny this evidence in a court of law.

To support non-repudiation, the NOS must provide safeguards that protect all parties from false claims that data was tampered with or not sent or received. In other words, the NOS must provide the electronic equivalent of a hermetically sealed envelope. The information must be protected against corruption or replay. To do this, the NOS must provide the sender with proof of delivery and the receiver with proof of a sender's identity.

The ISO non-repudiation model defines the following non-repudiation services (see Figure 7-7):

- **Evidence of message creation** proves that the originator created the message. The sender must create a *proof-of-origin* certificate using the non-repudiation service. It then sends the certificate along with the message using the non-repudiation *delivery authority* service. The receiver stores this evidence using the non-repudiation *storage* service. In the case of a dispute, it can later retrieve this evidence.

- **Evidence of message receipt** proves that the message was delivered. The recipient must create and send a *proof-of-receipt* certificate using the non-repudiation delivery authority service. The sender receives this evidence and stores it using the non-repudiation storage service; it can later retrieve it if there is a dispute.

- **An action timestamp** is generated by the non-repudiation service as part of the evidence. It records the date and time when an event or action took place.

- **The evidence long-term storage facility** is used to store the certificates of origin and receipt. If there is a dispute, the adjudicator uses this facility to retrieve the evidence.

- **The adjudicator** is used to settle disputes based on the stored evidence.

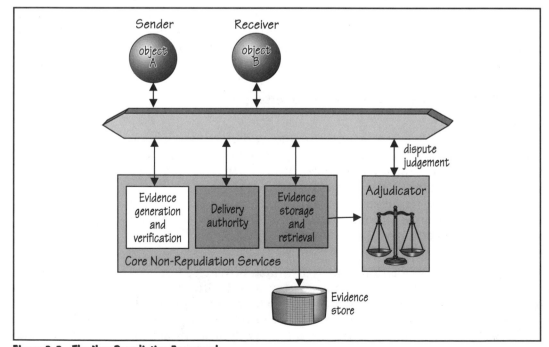

Figure 7-7. The Non-Repudiation Framework.

145

As you can see, a non-repudiation system must establish *who* executed an action and *when*. A very simple non-repudiation system can be provided using digital signatures, some form of trusted timestamps, and a secure log facility.

Single Logon Makes It Easier for the User

In today's enterprise, there is no Holy Grail more coveted than that of the single sign-on.

— *Jamie Lewis, President*
Burton Group
(August, 1998)

Users are always complaining about having to do multiple logons to different servers and resource managers. Modern NOSs provide the technology that allows a user to access any server resource from anywhere—including hotel rooms, offices, homes, and cellular phones—using a single sign-on. How's that done? It depends. If you're dealing with single-vendor backoffice products, you're probably in luck. Most ERP vendors provide single sign-on to all their modules and to any vendor product that supports their APIs. In addition, Microsoft provides a single sign-on for NT and BackOffice using the Registry (eventually, it will use the Active Directory). Likewise, Netscape provides a single sign-on to all its products by storing user credentials on its LDAP server. Novell does the same using NDS.

But, what if you're dealing with multi-vendor products? It gets a little harder. Here are your current choices:

■ *Use a proxy single-logon product*—such as IBM's *Global Sign-On*, Memco's *Proxima*, New Dimension's *Control-SA*, CKS's *MyNet*, CyberSafe's *TrustBroker*, and Axent's *OmniGuard/ERM*. For example, IBM's DCE-based *Global Sign-On* currently supports ODBC applications, Lotus Notes, PeopleSoft, and SAP. In its next release, it will also support fingerprint readers as well as smart cards. Typically, single-logon products maintain your credentials in a secure database or LDAP directory. To connect to server resources: 1) you first authenticate yourself to a local proxy client via a dialog-box, 2) the proxy client invokes the security server without transmitting your password on the net, and 3) the server then logs in to multiple systems on your behalf—using your credentials.

■ *Use an enterprise system management suite*—such as Bull's *AccessMaster*, CA's *Unicenter-TNG*, Platinum's *AutoSecure/SSO*, and IBM/Tivoli's *TME 10*. These products integrate single logon within the overall system management framework.

■ *Wait for standards.* The idea behind single logon is to provide a centralized authentication system. As you can imagine, there will be as many standards in this area as there are authentication systems. For example, IBM, Platinum, and Microsoft (with NT 5.0) build their single-logon systems on top of DCE and Kerberos. You simply log in once (see Figure 7-8), get authenticated, and then obtain a set of security tickets (also called tokens) for each server with which you want to communicate. All this activity is conducted under-the-cover by the NOS's security agents. No password is stored in the login script on the client, and no telephone callbacks are required. It doesn't get any easier, as long as you can remember your password.

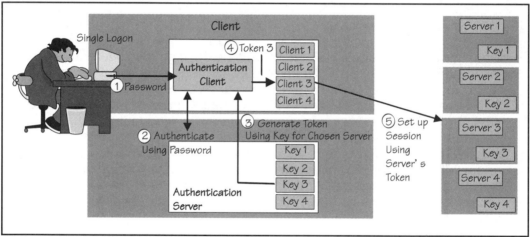

Figure 7-8. Log On Once and Get to Everything You Need.

For Internet-based single logons, the preferred method combines digital certificates with LDAP-stored credentials. Here's how it works: 1) you log in locally to your workstation, 2) special software unlocks your public key certificate and sends it to the single sign-on server, and 3) the server extracts your credentials from an LDAP database and logs in—on your behalf—to different services. An alternative to LDAP is to pass an *attribute certificate* that contains all your permissions. With these certificates, you can store credentials on the client and avoid going through the LDAP server. CORBA Security defines such a credential. In addition, the Open Group is working on a specification called the *Single Sign-On Standard (XSSO)*; it brings all these initiatives together (see *www.rdg.opengroup.org/public/tech/security/sso*).

In summary, single logon is still not as transparent as we would like it to be. It will take more work to realize the single-system illusion. Most of the technology is available today. It's now just a matter of getting some standards in place—as well as products that implement these standards.

THE INTERNET: IN CERTIFICATES WE TRUST

Part of the problem with the Internet is that nobody really knows who you are.

— *Peter Wayner, Author*
Digital Cash

In the previous sections, we briefly discussed keys and digital certificates. As you may already know, the Internet is developing a complete infrastructure to manage these keys and digital certificates. The SET standard from Visa and Mastercard for electronic payments on the Internet is completely dependent on this infrastructure. The whole idea is to make the Internet a little bit less anonymous—especially when you're conducting business. In the spirit of the grand illusion, the trick is to make the whole process transparent and painless to the people that live on the Net. In this section, we take a few moments to explain the magic behind these digital certificates.

How Do You Like Your Keys?

Encryption has been used to protect information for at least 4000 years. Today, the two predominant approaches to electronic encryption are based on *shared cypher keys* and *public cypher keys*. You may also have heard the terms *symmetric keys* versus *asymmetric keys*, or *secret keys* versus *public keys*. It's all the same thing. Here's what it all means.

Shared Private Keys

The *shared private key* approach uses a single key to encrypt or decrypt information (see Figure 7-9). Each pair of users who need to exchange messages must agree on a private key and use it as a cypher to encode and decode their messages. This method works well as long as both sides maintain the secrecy of the private key. It's their shared "little secret."

The *Data Encryption Standard (DES)* is based on this public key approach and has been the official U.S. national cryptographic standard since 1977. DES was originally proposed by IBM as a 128-bit cypher, but the NSA (the U.S. spy agency) insisted that it be trimmed to 56 bits before accepting it as the basis for the national cryptographic standard. The NSA didn't want an algorithm that they couldn't break. DES has been the encryption algorithm of choice for interbank electronic fund transfers.

Part 3. Base Middleware: Stacks and NOSs

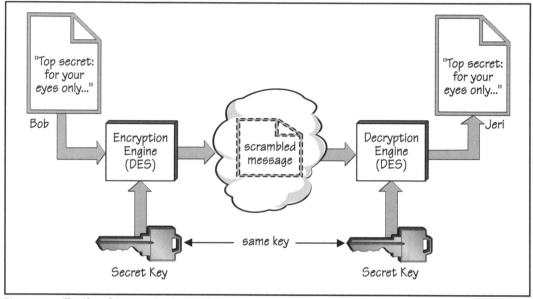

Figure 7-9. The Shared Private Key Approach to Encryption.

Until 1997, there was never a reported case of DES cracking. A machine performing one DES decryption per microsecond would take 2000 years to crack a given key. The DES algorithm enables 72 quadrillion possible keys. But in June 1997, fortress DES was finally cracked by an ad hoc team of tens of thousands of people using their PCs on the Internet. Together, their PCs were able to test up to 7 billion keys per second—at this rate, they could crack a new key every four months. For $600,000, you can build a DES-cracking machine that could crack a new key in 3.5 hours.

Triple-DES is slower than DES, but harder to crack. As we go to press, the *National Institute of Standards and Technology (NIST)* is soliciting a replacement for DES that can scale up to 256 bits. The winner will be selected in the year 2000. Note that Kerberos uses an encryption cypher based on DES. As far as keys go, Kerberos uses a shared, session-specific, private-key approach. There is also a public-key version of Kerberos.

Public Keys

The public-key approach uses two keys: a *public* key and a *private* key. The public key may be listed in directories and is available for all to see. Anyone can send you an encrypted message by using your public key as a cypher; you decode it with your private key (see Figure 7-10). In the figure, Bob uses Jeri's public key to send her an encrypted message. Jeri uses her private key to decrypt the message.

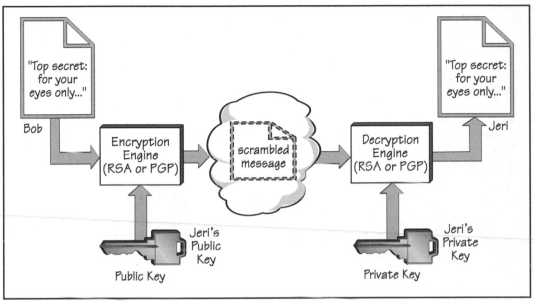

Figure 7-10. The Public/Private Key Approach to Encryption.

Public/private keys can also be used to sign messages and create electronically sealed contracts (see Figure 7-11). In this case, Bob used his private key to sign a contract to buy Dan's car. Dan opens the sealed document using Bob's public key—this way, he is sure the sender is really Bob. Note that for non-repudiation purposes, Dan would also need to time-stamp the message with a trusted-time source, and then store it in a secure log. Again, all this works well, as long as you keep your private key secret.

RSA is a public key algorithm invented at MIT. RSA stands for the initials of its three inventors. It is considered the public key algorithm of choice and is used mostly for authentication. RSA can also be used for encrypting very short messages. The problem is that RSA is too slow for encrypting longer messages and it requires DES to do that. If the encryption is done in software, DES is about 100 times faster than RSA. In hardware, DES is between 1000 and 10,000 times as fast, depending on the implementation.[1]

So why would anybody want RSA? Because it lets you encrypt messages without the prior exchange of secrets (or tokens), and it provides an unforgeable electronic signature. Only you can know your private key—there is no "trusted third party" like Kerberos. An RSA signature—with the proper non-repudiation techniques—can be binding in legal courts because there can be no fingerpointing. And if you lose control of your private key, you're the only one to blame. One of the problems

---

[1] Source: Stang and Moore, **Network Security Secrets** (IDC Books, 1993).

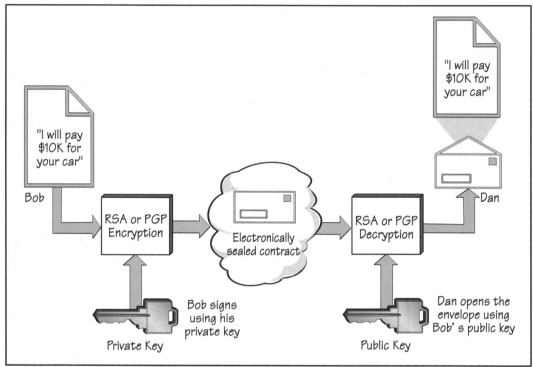

Figure 7-11. Using Public/Private Keys to Send Signed Documents and Contracts.

with RSA is that the private key part must be delivered to each node on the network without breaching security. So they need something like Kerberos to do that. An alternative is to use a *Certificate Authority (CA)* that authenticates the public key. The CA digitally signs the public key and distributes it via a public key infrastructure (more on this in the next few sections).

Finally, just how cracker-proof are these public key cyphers? According to security expert Bruce Schneier, in the year 2000 you will need a 1024-bit public key to adequately protect yourself against attacks from individuals, a 1280-bit key to protect yourself from corporations, and a 1536-bit key to protect yourself from governments.[2]

So What Exactly Is a Digital Certificate?

A *digital certificate* is an electronic file that serves as a container for a public key. It's the Internet's version of a driver's license—it's your electronic ID. There is even

---

[2] Bruce Schneier, *The Crypto Bomb is Ticking*, BYTE Magazine (May, 1998).

a standard way of encoding these digital certificates—it's called *X.509 V3*. Better yet, this standard is already supported by the major browsers, so there's a good chance that you're already using these certificates—you use them if you do *Secure Sockets Layer (SSL)* communications over the Internet or sign your e-mail.

An *X.509 certificate* (see Figure 7-12) contains a variety of information, including: 1) the owner's public key, 2) the owner's name, 3) some attributes associated with the owner (such as an e-mail address), 4) the name of the encryption algorithm, 5) the issuer (or signer) of the certificate, and 6) an expiration date. Of course, anyone can issue a digital certificate. But, any plain old certificate won't exactly open the gates of the Internet.

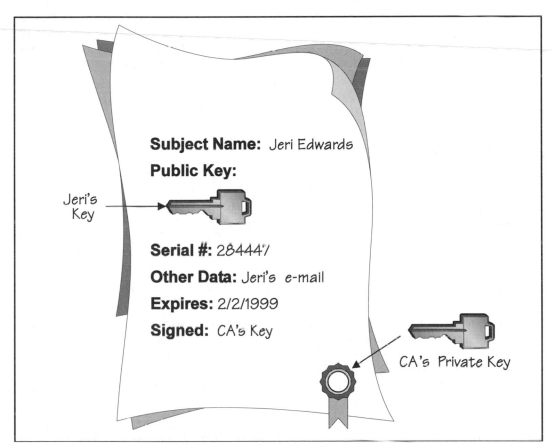

Figure 7-12. An X509 V3 Digital Certificate.

To be useful, some well-known trusted authority must guarantee the authenticity of the certificate; it must vouch that the public key does indeed belong to the named person, program, ActiveX, or JavaBean. To return to our analogy, we need the

Internet version of the Department of Motor Vehicles (or an agency that issues valid driver licenses). The people that do this kind of work for digital certificates are called *Certificate Authorities (CAs)*.

One of the services that CAs provide is to issue certificates and then sign them using their own private keys. Sometimes, a single trusted signer is not enough. So an X.509 certificate can contain a chain of signers. For example, BEA may sign Jeri's certificate and Verisign may also sign it at the next level to vouch for BEA. Eventually, the buck stops with a *root* signer—for example, a national bank or government. One day, the U.N. may even get into this business. The receivers of certificates have their work cut out. They must traverse the signature chain looking for the first signer they can trust. For example, your browser contains a list of trusted authorities—make sure you trust them too. When you click on a secure page that connects to a SSL-enabled server, the server will establish its identity by shipping its certificate. The browser validates the certificate by checking against its list of approved signers. If it finds a signer, the connection is established.

The Digital Certificate Infrastructure

A public key infrastructure must deal with the following issues: Where do you store these certificates? In what form? How do you revoke a certificate? Who keeps track of the *Certificate Revocation List (CRL)*? How do you check out an applicant for a certificate? How can certificates be used for single logon? All these issues must be resolved in a standard way to provide NOS transparency. The good news is that the *Internet Engineering Task Force (IETF)* is driving the standards in this area through its *Public Key Infrastructure for X.509 (PKIX)* working group. The bad news is that these standards won't be widely deployed until 2000. In the meantime, there are some interim solutions to these problems.

You may decide to create your own certificate infrastructure for use on an intranet or extranet. To do this, you'll need to provide CA-like services for your organization. You can do this in one of two ways: outsource the service to a CA firm like VeriSign, or purchase an X.509-based *certificate server* to do the job yourself. Today, you can purchase this type of server from several vendors—including Netscape, IBM, Microsoft, and GTE Cybertrust.

Now let's try to answer some of the questions we just raised. Where do you store these certificates? Today, the certificates are stored on the user's machine. The CAs will tell you to make sure the machine is secure. Eventually, the certificates will be stored on a smart card that you can take with you from machine to machine. Most people today don't have a clue about how to move their certificates across machines. A certificate can also be stored on a shared LDAP database. But in what form is this certificate stored on the database? Clearly, there's a need for a standard

LDAP schema for certificate storage. Check for this with the PKIX working group. In the meantime, Netscape provides a tightly-integrated solution that lets you safely export a certificate from its *Certificate Server* to its LDAP-based *Directory Server*; you can then track and distribute the certificates via LDAP.

How do you revoke a certificate? Who keeps track of the *Certificate Revocation List (CRL)?* Today, a CA—like VeriSign—provides both services. Vendors can even dial into a VeriSign server to verify a certificate and make sure it hasn't been revoked. How do you check out an applicant for a certificate? If you go back to the driver's license analogy, the DMV takes a picture of the applicant and creates the driver's license. In the CA world, there are multiple levels of checks. For example, VeriSign provides three different classes of certificates. You can get a *Class 1* certificate by simply filling out an application on the Web. A *Class 2* certificate requires some form of credit check. Finally, a *Class 3* certificate requires that you personally take your application to a notary who will check your identification.

The final question: How can certificates be used for single logon? We already alluded to the answer earlier in this chapter. In a nutshell, certificates are the only way to make single logon seamless. However, there is a need for a standards-based solution before this can work.

A Certificate Usage Scenario

Let's walk through a short scenario that shows how this infrastructure works today. In this scenario, Jeri needs a certificate to open an online shopping account. Here are the steps (see Figure 7-13):

1. ***Jeri must first obtain a certificate***. Jeri provides the CA with a copy of her public key and some personal data. She must also pay for the certificate. The CA wraps Jeri's public key in a signed X.509 certificate and returns it. Jeri stores her new certificate on her PC.

2. ***Jeri applies for a store account***. Jeri clicks on an electronic store's Web page and presents her certificate to open an account (perhaps via a separate e-mail).

3. ***Merchant determines if the certificate is OK***. In this scenario, the merchant transmits the certificate to the CA clearinghouse for verification. The CA verifies the signature and makes sure the certificate is not on a CRL list. If everything is OK, the certificate is approved.

4. ***Jeri's certificate is OK.*** This may be done via e-mail.

5. *Jeri can now shop, shop, shop*. Jeri and the merchant have now established a trust relationship. She can now shop until she drops.

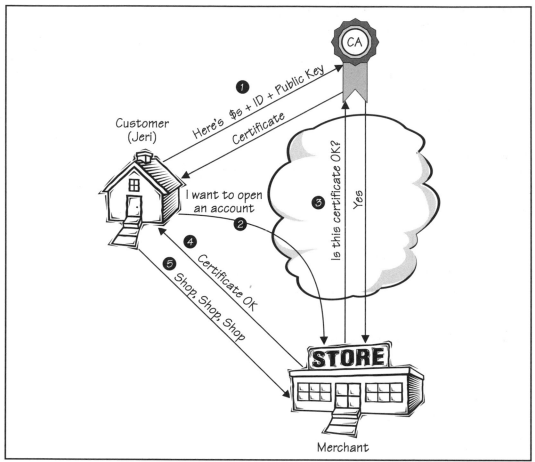

Figure 7-13. What a Certificate Authority Does Today.

In the next section, we will show you how SET applies more stringent controls on this type of scenario. After all, someone must mind the store.

Electronic Payments: The SET Protocol

Banks and merchants are not stampeding toward the Internet because it is so much fun; they're doing it because of economics. The cost of a teller-driven transaction is about $2. In contrast, the cost of an electronic transaction is less than 15 cents. Many banks now allow customers to use the Web to pay bills electronically, balance their checkbooks, and submit applications for loans. Banks are also in the process of creating a secure electronic payment infrastructure on top of the Internet's SSL.

Before you send payments or your credit card number all over the Web, you'll want someone to cover you in case of fraud. This is where Visa and Mastercard come into the picture. Originally, they were each supporting a different standard for electronic payment, which caused a lot of confusion. This changed in 1997 when they both coauthored a new protocol called *Secure Electronic Transactions (SET)*. The SET protocol automates all the steps that are currently associated with the processing of a credit card in a store—including the phone calls and transaction slips. It's now all done automatically over the Internet. SET uses digital certificates to authenticate every player—including the customer, merchant, bank, and credit card issuer. SET even checks the CRL list to determine that all the involved certificates are still valid.

Let's replay Jeri's previous shopping spree scenario, but this time we will use SET. We also assume that Jeri has both a valid certificate and credit card. Here are the steps (see Figure 7-14):

1. ***Jeri places an order.*** She fills up an electronic shopping cart, populates the form, electronically signs it, and encloses her encrypted credit card number. Eventually, all this will be done via drag-and-drop.

2. ***Merchant asks bank for authorization.*** The merchant's server program can't access Jeri's credit card number because it's encrypted. So it passes the authorization to the bank. The bank decrypts the credit card number and also checks Jeri's signature.

3. ***The bank asks the credit card issuer for authorization.*** The idea is to determine if the card is still OK and if Jeri has enough credit to cover the transaction.

4. ***The credit card company approves the transaction.*** The card company authorizes the transaction via an electronically signed message.

5. ***The bank says it's OK.*** The bank returns a signed OK to the merchant; it will also credit the merchant's account.

6. ***The merchant sends Jeri a receipt and ships goods.*** Now, Jeri must wait for the goods to show up at her door.

7. ***Jeri receives her monthly credit card bill.*** It's almost certain that this transaction will show up on this bill. There is very little room for error in this closely inter-locked system.

The SET standard is slowly being adopted by banks and merchants. When SET is fully deployed, it will have an insatiable appetite for digital certificates. This means that the two leading credit card companies may also become the world's largest CAs. VeriSign and IBM are also working very closely with Visa and Mastercard to make sure the entire system works end-to-end.

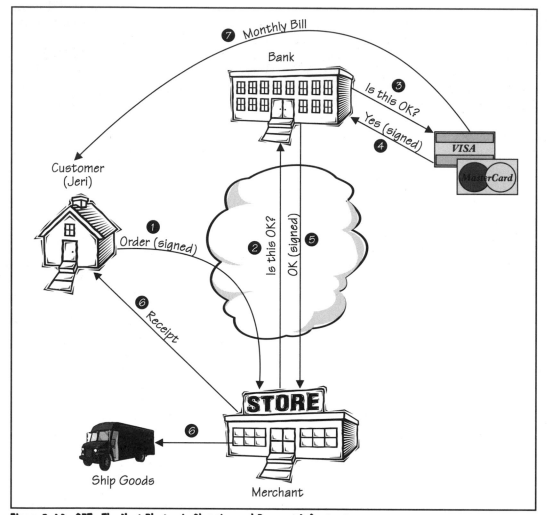

Figure 7-14. SET: The Next Electronic Shopping and Payment Infrastructure.

CONCLUSION

This was a long chapter. We explored some of the key technologies that provide transparency across LANs, enterprise WANs, and the Internet. We will continue our exploration of the modern NOS in the next two chapters. And, because the topics we covered in this chapter are so fundamental, you will run into them again in the context of application frameworks in future chapters.

Chapter 8

RPC, Messaging, and Peer-to-Peer

Therefore, ye soft pipes, play on.

— **Keats**

Client/server applications are split across address spaces, physical machines, networks, and operating systems. How do clients and servers talk to each other? How are the requests and responses synchronized? How are the dissimilar data representations on different computers handled? What happens if one of the parties is unavailable? You guessed it: The modern NOS is taking on a lot of these responsibilities. It comes with the territory. The purpose of the NOS is to make distributed computing transparent. This means it must create an environment that hides the nastiness of dealing with communication protocols, networks, and stacks.

All NOSs offer *peer-to-peer* interfaces that let applications communicate using close-to-the-wire send/receive semantics. Most NOSs provide some form of *Remote Procedure Call (RPC)* middleware that hides "the wire" and makes any server on the network appear to be one function call away. An alternative type of model—message queuing, or simply *Message-Oriented Middleware (MOM)*—is gaining new converts. It turns out that messaging is incredibly helpful in situations where you do not want the clients and servers to be tightly synchronized. With the exception of the forthcoming NT 5.0's *MSMQ*, the current NOSs don't include MOM

in their offerings. However, best-of-breed product offerings are available from companies that specialize in this field—including IBM's *MQSeries*, BEA's *MessageQ*, PeerLogic's *Pipes*, and TIBCO's *TIB/Rendezvous*. Let's take a closer look at what each type of interface has to offer (also see the next Briefing box).

FYI

What's a Stack Anyway?

Briefing

Like everything else on the network, RPCs, MOM, and peer-to-peer APIs sit on top of communications stacks (see Figure 8-1). So what exactly is a stack? Communications software vendors have tackled the problem of network complexity by breaking down complex protocols into layers. Each layer builds on top of the services provided by the layers below it. Eventually, you get a *stack* of layers that looks like a birthday cake. Vendors sell their communication products as stack offerings that are architected to work together. In theory, each stack layer has a well-defined set of APIs and protocols so that it should be possible to mix-and-match different vendor offerings within the same stack. In practice, this is not the case. You buy an entire stack from a single vendor and pray that it works with the hardware.

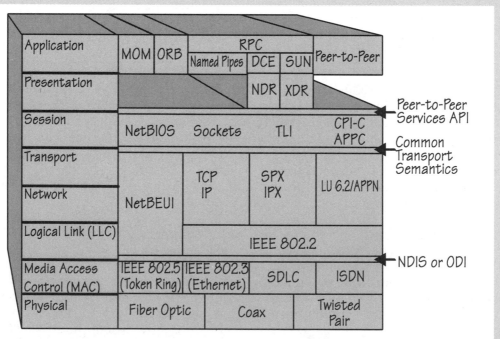

Figure 8-1. Where the Most Popular Stacks Fit in the OSI Reference Model.

The lowest layer of communication software belongs to the device drivers that provide an interface to several types of communication hardware adapters. The bottom of the stacks sits on top of the device drivers. The top of the stacks sits right below the NOS. The stacks and NOS are simply divisions that help us create a survival map. The *OSI Reference Model* defines seven layers of functions that a complete stack should ideally provide. To help you navigate through this chapter, we couldn't resist coming up with our own interpretation of where the most popular commercial stacks fit in the OSI Reference Model (see Figure 8-1). Remember, it's just a reference model. So take it in with a grain of salt. *Real* products don't have any notion of architectural boundaries or reference models—they just get a job done.

So what do stacks provide? At the lower layers, they interface to the hardware using the physical *Media Access Control (MAC)* protocols defined by the IEEE. The *Logical Link Control (LLC)* provides a common interface to the MACs and a reliable link service for transmitting communication packets between two nodes. The OSI *link* layer combines the LLC and MAC functions. On top of this layer is the *network* layer that allows packets to be routed across multiple networks. The *transport* layer sits on top of the network layer and provides some form of reliable end-to-end delivery service. The *session* layer deals with network etiquette—who goes first, who reconnects in case of failure, and synchronization points. On top of the session layer is a *presentation* layer that deals with data representation. Finally, the *application layer* provides network services and interfaces to an application.

The boundary between the stacks and NOS gets fuzzy at the upper layers. For example, is the peer-to-peer interface an application, presentation, or session layer service? Does it belong to the NOS or to the stacks? But, then, everything in client/server is a bit fuzzy. ❑

PEER-TO-PEER COMMUNICATIONS

Most early client/server applications were implemented using low-level, conversational, peer-to-peer protocols—such as sockets, TLI, CPIC/APPC, NetBIOS, and Named Pipes. There were very few alternatives then. These low-level protocols are hard to code and maintain, so they are loosing their popularity. Instead, programmers are now using RPCs, MOMs, and ORBs, which provide higher levels of abstraction. So the conversational protocols should only be used by very demanding user applications or system-level software.

The term "peer-to-peer" indicates that the two sides of a communication link use the same protocol interface to conduct a networked conversation. Any computer can initiate a conversation with any other computer. The protocol is symmetrical, and it is sometimes called "program-to-program." The peer-to-peer interface tends

to be "close to the wire" in the sense that it does not fully mask the underlying network from the programmer. For example, the interface will surface transmission timeouts, race conditions, and network errors, and then leave it to the programmer to handle. The peer-to-peer protocols started as stack-specific APIs. But as we explained in Part 1, most of these APIs now support multiple stacks. So their association with a particular stack is only of historical interest. Here's a brief description of the major peer-to-peer protocols and their associated stacks.

Sockets

Sockets were introduced in 1981 as the Unix BSD 4.2 generic interface that would provide Unix-to-Unix communications over networks. In 1985, SunOS introduced NFS and RPC over sockets. In 1986, AT&T introduced the *Transport Layer Interface (TLI)* that provides functionality similar to sockets but in a more network-independent fashion. Unix SVR4 incorporates both sockets and TLI. As it stands, sockets are far more prevalent than TLI. Sockets and TLI are very similar from a programmer's perspective. TLI is just a cleaner version of sockets. An application written to TLI is, in theory, stack independent. It should run on IPX/SPX or TCP/IP with very few modifications. The TLI API consists of about 25 API calls.

Sockets are supported on virtually every operating system. The Windows socket API, known colloquially as *WinSock*, is a multivendor specification that standardizes the use of TCP/IP under Windows. The WinSock API is based on the Berkeley sockets interface. In the BSD Unix system, sockets are part of the kernel and provide both a standalone and networked IPC service. Non-BSD Unix systems, MS-DOS, Windows, Mac OS, OS/2, NT 4.X, and NetWare 4.X provide sockets in the form of libraries. So it is safe to say that sockets provide the current *de facto* portable standard for network application providers on TCP/IP networks.

The three most popular socket types are *stream, datagram*, and *raw.* Stream and datagram sockets interface to the TCP and UDP protocols, and raw sockets interface to the IP protocol. The type of socket is specified at creation time. In theory, the socket interface can be extended, and you can define new socket types to provide additional services. A socket address on the TCP/IP Internet consists of two parts: an IP address and a port number (see Figure 8-2). So what's an IP address? And what's a port number?

Figure 8-2. Socket = IP Address + Port Address.

In today's IPv4 networks, an *IP address* is a 32-bit number, usually represented by four decimal numbers separated by dots, that must be unique for each TCP/IP network interface card within an administered AF_INET domain. A TCP/IP *host* (i.e., networked machine) may have as many IP addresses as it has network interfaces. The forthcoming *IPv6* introduces 128-bit addresses, which is effectively a limitless number. It's right on time because IPv4's 4.2 billion addresses will run out in about ten years.

A *port* is an entry point to an application that resides on a host. It is represented by a 16-bit integer. Ports are commonly used to define the entry points for services provided by server applications. Important commercial server programs—such as Oracle and Sybase DBMSs—have their own *well-known* ports.

The price you pay for this reliable class of service is the overhead associated with creating and managing the session. If a session is lost, one of the parties must reestablish it. This can be a problem for fault-tolerant servers that require automatic switchovers to a backup server if the primary server fails. The backup server needs to reestablish all the outstanding sessions with clients. In addition, sessions are inherently a two-party affair and don't lend themselves well to broadcasting (one-to-many exchanges).

Datagrams—also known as *connectionless* protocols or *transmit and pray* protocols—provide a simple but unreliable form of exchange. The more powerful datagram protocols such as NetBIOS provide broadcast capabilities. NetBIOS allows you to send datagrams to a named entity, to a select group of entities (*multicast*), or to all entities on a network (*broadcast*). Datagrams are unreliable in the sense that they are not acknowledged or tracked through a sequence number. You "send and pray" that your datagram gets received. The recipient may not be there or may not be expecting a datagram (you will never know). Novell literature estimates that about 5% of datagrams don't make it. You may, of course, design your own acknowledgment schemes on top of the datagram service. Some stacks provide an acknowledged datagram service.

Datagrams are very useful to have in "discovery" types of situations. These are situations where you discover things about your network environment by broadcasting queries and learning who is out there from the responses. Broadcast can be used to obtain bids for services or to advertise the availability of new services. Broadcast datagrams provide the capability of creating electronic "bazaars." They support the creation of very dynamic types of environments where things can happen spontaneously. In situations where the name of the recipient is not known, broadcast datagrams are the only way to get the message out. The cost of broadcast datagrams is that, in some cases, recipients may get overloaded with "junk mail." The multicast facility helps alleviate this problem because broadcast mail can then be sent only to "special interest" groups. The alternative to broadcast is to use a network directory service.

Datagrams are also very useful in situations where there is a need to send a quick message without the world coming to an end if the message is not received. The typical situation is sending control-like information, such as telling a network manager "I'm alive." It doesn't make sense to go through all the overhead of creating a session with the network manager just to say "I'm alive," and what if there are 500 nodes on the network? The manager will need 500 permanent sessions, an exorbitant cost in resources. This is where the datagram alternative comes in. With datagrams you can send your "I'm alive" message. And if the manager misses your message once, it will get another one when you send your next heartbeat (provided you're still alive). ❑

NetWare: IPX/SPX and TLI

Because Novell owns—depending on whose numbers you quote—between 40% and 50% of the network market, it follows that IPX/SPX, NetWare 4.X's native stack, must be the most widespread stack in the industry. IPX/SPX is also popular with network managers in large enterprises who are delighted with its internetworking capabilities. This means that IPX/SPX covers the entire spectrum, from PC LANs to enterprise LANs. IPX/SPX is an implementation of the *Xerox Network Services (XNS)* transport and network protocol. Banyan Vines is also an adaptation of XNS, but it uses a TCP/IP-like addressing scheme. XNS, developed by the Xerox PARC research institute, is a much cleaner architecture than the older TCP/IP protocol. It's ironic that XNS (in the form of IPX/SPX) is the world's most predominant stack. This is another example of a PARC technology that Xerox was not able to exploit.

The IPX/SPX network layer is provided by the *Internet Packet Exchange (IPX)* protocol. This is a "send and pray" datagram type of protocol with no guarantees. It is used as a foundation protocol by sophisticated network applications for sending and receiving low-overhead datagram packets. Novell's SPX builds a reliable protocol service on top of IPX. NetWare provides 12 API calls that you can use to obtain datagram services using IPX. The transport layer of IPX/SPX is provided by the *Sequenced Packet Exchange (SPX)* protocol—a reliable connection-oriented service over IPX. The service consists of 16 API calls. NetWare provides four peer-to-peer protocols on top of the IPX/SPX stack: NetBIOS, Named Pipes, TLI, and the IPX/SPX APIs. These protocols are supported in the DOS, Windows, NT, Windows 95/98, OS/2, Unixware, and NLM environments. Note that with NetWare 5.0, Novell is finally moving to TCP/IP in a big way. So what does this say about the future of IPX/SPX?

NetBIOS and NetBEUI

NetBIOS is the premier protocol for LAN-based, program-to-program communications. Introduced by IBM and Sytek in 1984 for the IBM PC Network, NetBIOS now runs with almost no changes on every LAN. NetBIOS is used as an interface to a variety of stacks—including IBM/Microsoft LANs (NetBEUI), TCP/IP, XNS, Vines, OSI, and IPX/SPX. Support for a NetBIOS platform exists on a multiplicity of operating system environments, including MS-DOS, Windows, Windows 95/98, OS/2, Windows NT, Unix, and some mainframe environments. One of the many reasons for NetBIOS's ubiquity on PC LANs is its intuitive simplicity.

NetBEUI is the protocol stack that comes with IBM and Microsoft LAN products—including Windows for Workgroups, NT, LAN Manager, Windows 95/98, and OS/2 Warp. It came to life as the original transport for NetBIOS commands. The literature often uses the term NetBIOS to refer to the combination of the NetBIOS

interface and the NetBEUI stack. This can be misleading. NetWare, for example, has nothing to do with NetBEUI, yet it uses NetBIOS as an interface to both IPX/SPX and TCP/IP.[1] IBM and Microsoft use NetBIOS as an interface to both TCP/IP and NetBEUI. So be careful, especially when you read our books; we've been known to use NetBIOS and NetBEUI interchangeably.

NetBEUI offers powerful datagram and connection-oriented services. It also offers a dynamic naming service based on discovery protocols. NetBEUI's main weakness is the lack of a network layer. Its other weakness is the lack of security. The broadcast mechanism, used to dynamically "discover" names, can be a liability on an unsecured network where it's not a good idea to expose names. Broadcasting names also causes unwanted traffic on the network. Luckily, most bridges and routers have ways to filter the discovery packets and block them from propagating to other networks.

The NetBIOS services are provided through a set of commands, specified in a structure called the *Network Control Block (NCB)*. The structure also contains the parameters associated with the command and the fields in which NetBIOS will return information to the program. A command can be issued in either wait or no-wait mode. In the *wait* mode, the requesting thread is blocked until the command completes. In the *no-wait* mode, control is returned to the calling thread at the earliest time possible, usually before the command completes. When the command completes, the NetBIOS DLL places a return code in the NCB.

Named Pipes

Named Pipes provide highly reliable, two-way communications between clients and a server. They provide a file-like programming API that abstracts a session-based two-way exchange of data. Using Named Pipes, processes can exchange data as if they were writing to, or reading from, a sequential file. Named Pipes are especially suitable for implementing server programs that require many-to-one pipelines. A server application can set up a pipeline where the receiving end of the pipe can exchange data with several client processes. Then it lets Named Pipes handle all the scheduling and synchronization issues.

A very important benefit of Named Pipes, at least for Windows, OS/2, and NT client/server programmers, is that they're part of the base interprocess communications service. The Named Pipes interface is identical, whether the processes are running on an individual machine or distributed across the network. Named Pipes run on NetBIOS, IPX/SPX, and TCP/IP stacks. Named Pipes are built-in networking

---

[1] The confusion may have started with Microsoft's naming of NetBEUI. It stands for *NetBIOS Extended User Interface (NetBEUI)*.

features in Windows NT, Windows for Workgroups, Windows 95/98, and Warp Server. Unix support for Named Pipes is provided by LAN Manager/X.

The "New" SNA: APPC, APPN, and CPI-C

IBM is continuing to evolve SNA into a true distributed operating system that supports cross-network directory services, transparent network access to resources (such as servers, applications, displays, printers, and data), common data streams, and integrated network management. *Advanced Peer-to-Peer Network (APPN)* is the network infrastructure responsible for this "true distribution."

APPN creates an SNA network without the mainframe-centric hierarchy of traditional SNA configurations. The mainframe is just another node on the network. APPN allows LU 6.2 SNA applications, using APPC or CPI-C APIs, to take full advantage of peer networks. It also greatly simplifies SNA configuration, provides better availability through dynamic routing, makes it easier to maintain SNA networks, and meets the flexibility requirements of modern networks.

Common Programming Interface for Communications (CPI-C) builds on top of APPC and masks its complexities and irregularities (see Figure 8-3). Every product that supports APPC has a slightly different API. CPI-C fixes that problem. Writing to the CPI-C API allows you to port your programs to all SNA platforms. The CPI-C API consists of about 40 calls; APPC consists of over 60 calls. Most of these calls deal with configuration and services. The X/Open consortium has licensed the CPI-C interface from IBM; several other companies (including Novell and Apple) have, too.

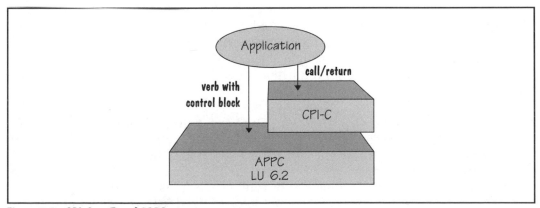

Figure 8-3. CPI-C on Top of APPC.

REMOTE PROCEDURE CALL (RPC)

An essential problem is that RPCs are not procedure calls at all; they are truly process invocations. The invoked program runs across the wire in a different resource domain.

> — Hal Lorin, Author
> *Doing IT Right*
> (Prentice-Hall, 1996)

RPCs hide the intricacies of the network by using the ordinary procedure call mechanism familiar to every programmer. A client process calls a function on a remote server and suspends itself until it gets back the results. Parameters are passed like in any ordinary procedure. The RPC, like an ordinary procedure, is synchronous. The process (or thread) that issues the call waits until it gets the results. Under the covers, the RPC run-time software collects values for the parameters, forms a message, and sends it to the remote server. The server receives the request, unpacks the parameters, calls the procedure, and sends the reply back to the client.

While RPCs make life easier for the programmer, they pose a challenge for the NOS designers who supply the development tools and run-time environments. Here's some of the issues they face:

■ *How are the server functions located and started?* At a minimum, somebody's got to provide a run-time environment that starts a server process when a remote invocation is received, passes it the parameters, and returns the response. But what happens when multiple clients go after the same function? Is each function packaged as a process? Pretty soon you discover that an entire environment is needed to start and stop servers, prioritize requests, perform security checks, and provide some form of load-balancing. It also becomes quickly obvious that threads are much better at handling these incoming requests than full-blown processes. And it is better to create a server loop that manages a pool of threads waiting for work rather than create a thread for each incoming request. What is really needed on the server side is a full-blown *TP Monitor.* This is, of course, a lot more function than what the current NOSs provide.

■ *How are parameters defined and passed between the client and the server?* This is something NOSs do quite well. The better NOSs provide an *Interface Definition Language (IDL)* for describing the functions and parameters that a server exports to its clients. An *IDL compiler* takes these descriptions and produces source code stubs (and header files) for both the client and server (Figure 8-4). These stubs can then be linked with the client and server code. The client stub packages the parameters in an RPC packet, converts the

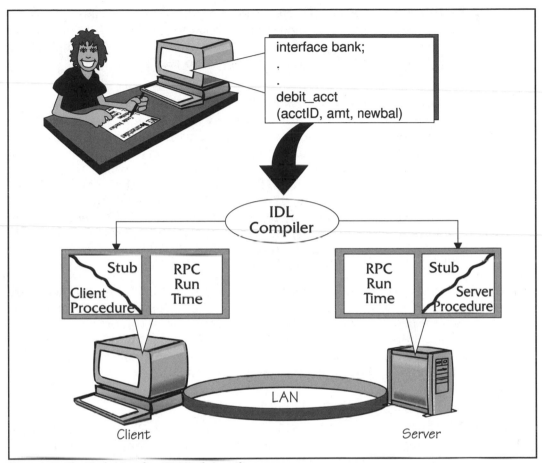

Figure 8-4. The Mechanics of an RPC Stub Compiler.

data, calls the *RPC run-time library,* and waits for the server's reply. On the server side, the server stub unpacks the parameters, calls the remote procedure, packages the results, and sends the reply to the client.

■ ***How are failures handled?*** Because both sides of the RPC can fail separately, it is important for the software to be able to handle all the possible failure combinations. If the server does not respond, the client side will normally block, time out, and retry the call. The server side must guarantee *only once semantics* to make sure that a duplicate request is not re-executed. If the client unexpectedly dies after issuing a request, the server must be able to undo the effects of that transaction. Most NOSs provide connection-oriented and connectionless versions of their RPCs. If you need a more robust environment, use the connection-oriented RPC.

■ *How is security handled by the RPC?* Modern NOSs make it easy to automatically incorporate their security features into the RPC. All you need to specify is the level of security required (authentication, encryption, and so on); then the RPC and security feature will cooperate to make it happen.

■ *How does the client find its server?* The association of a client with a server is called *binding*. The binding information may be hardcoded in the client (for example, some services are performed by servers with *well-known* addresses). Or a client can find its server by consulting a configuration file or an environment parameter. A client can also find its server at run time through the network directory services. The servers must, of course, advertise their services in the directory. The process of using the directory to find a server at run time is called *dynamic binding*. The easiest way to find a server is let the RPC do it for you. This is called *automatic binding*, meaning that the RPC client stub will locate a server from a list of servers that support the interface.

■ *How is data representation across systems handled?* The problem here is that different CPUs represent data structures differently (for example, *big-endian* versus *little-endian*). So how is data transparency achieved at the RPC level? To maintain machine independence, the RPC must provide some level of data format translation across systems. For example, the Sun RPC requires that clients convert their data to a neutral canonical format using the *External Data Representation (XDR)* APIs.

In contrast, DCE's *Network Data Representation (NDR)* service is multica-nonical, meaning that it supports multiple data format representations. The client chooses one of these formats (in most cases, its own native data repre-sentation), tags the data with the chosen format, and then leaves it up to the server to transform the data into a format it understands. In other words, the *server makes it right*. DCE assumes that in most cases, the client and server will be using the same data representation, so why go through the translation overhead? Sun assumes that client MIPs are cheap, so it lets the client do the translation, which makes life easy for the server. With Sun, all clients look the same to the server: *The client makes it right*.

Figure 8-5 shows how the RPC mechanism all comes together. The scenario shows a simple seat reservation application. The seating server first starts up, advertises its location and service in the network directory, and begins its continuous cycle of receiving and servicing requests. A ticketing client keeps in its cache the location of the server. When a customer is ready to buy a ticket for a Madonna concert, an RPC is issued to reserve a seat. Notice how the client and server stubs cooperate to make that happen. It takes a lot of work to make that reservation for the Madonna concert. RPCs take away some of that drudgery.

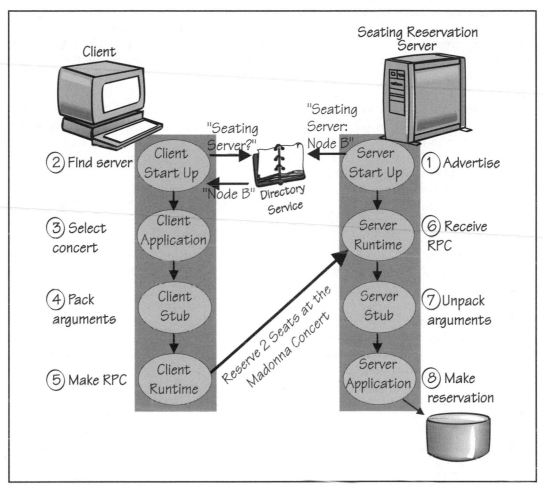

Figure 8-5. Getting a Seat for a Madonna Concert Using RPCs.

MESSAGING AND QUEUING: THE MOM MIDDLEWARE

Every DAD needs a MOM.

— *The Message-Oriented Middleware (MOM) Consortium*

"Every DAD needs a MOM" is the unofficial motto of the MOM Consortium. In this context, DAD stands for *Distributed Application Development* and MOM stands for *Message-Oriented Middleware*. We agree with the motto. MOM is a key piece of middleware that is absolutely essential for a class of client/server products. If your application can tolerate a certain level of time-independent responses, MOM provides the easiest path for creating inter-enterprise client/server systems. MOM also helps create nomadic client/server systems that can accumulate outgoing transactions in queues and do a bulk upload when a connection can be established with an office server.

MOM allows general-purpose messages to be exchanged in a client/server system using message queues. Applications communicate over networks by simply putting messages in queues and getting messages from queues. MOM hides all the nasty communications from applications and typically provides a very simple high-level API to its services. A MOM Consortium—called *MOMA*—was formed in mid-1993 with the goal of creating standards for messaging middleware. Members are product providers, including IBM (*MQSeries*), BEA (*MessageQ*), Level8/Momentum (*XIPC*), Talarian (*SmartSockets*), and Peerlogic (*PIPES*). In addition, the OMG has just finished specifying an object-based CORBA *Messaging* standard with the help of the major MOM vendors. According to IDC, the MOM market was $385 million in 1997; it is growing at the blistering rate of 61.7%.[2] So what can you do with MOM?

MOM's messaging and queuing allow clients and servers to communicate across a network without being linked by a private, dedicated, logical connection. The clients and servers can run at different times. Everybody communicates by putting messages on queues and by taking messages from queues (see Figure 8-6). Notice that the server sends back the reply via a message queue. Messaging does not impose any constraints on an application's structure: If no response is required, none is sent.

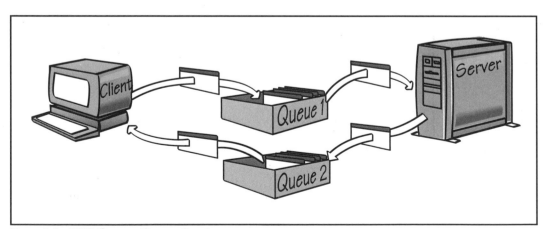

Figure 8-6. MOM: Two-way Message Queuing.

---

[2] Source: IDC, *Middleware: 1998 Worldwide Markets and Trends* (May, 1998).

MOM products provide their own NOS services—including hierarchical naming, security, and a layer that isolates applications from the network. They use virtual memory on the local OS to create their queues. Most messaging products allow the sender to specify the name of the reply queue. The products also include some type of *format field* that tells the recipient how to interpret the message data.

MOM-enabled programs do not talk to each other directly, so either program can be busy, unavailable, or simply not running at the same time. A program can decide when it wants to retrieve a message off its queue—there are no time constraints. The target program can even be started several hours later. Or, if you're using a laptop on the road, you can collect outgoing requests in a queue and submit them to the server when you get to a phone or to an office LAN. Messaging allows either the client or the server to be unavailable (see Figure 8-7).

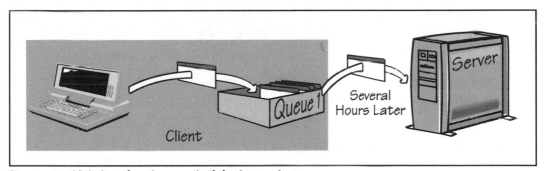

Figure 8-7. MOM: Save Your Messages Until You Get to a Server.

Messaging queues are very versatile. You can use them to create one-to-many or many-to-one relationships (see Figure 8-8). In the figure, many clients are sending requests to one server queue. The messages are picked off the queue by multiple instances of the server program that are concurrently servicing the clients. The server instances can take messages off the queue either on a first-in/first-out basis or according to some priority or load-balancing scheme. In all cases, a message queue can be concurrently accessed. The servers can also use messaging filters to throw away the messages they don't want to process, or they can pass them on to other servers.

Most MOM messaging products make available a simple API set that runs on multiple operating system platforms. Most also provide *persistent* (logged on disk) and *non-persistent* (in memory) message queues. Persistent messages are slower, but they can be recovered in case of power failures after a system restart. In both cases, messages can be either copied or removed from a queue. A message queue can be *local* to the machine or *remote*. System administrators can usually specify the number of messages a queue can hold and the maximum message size.

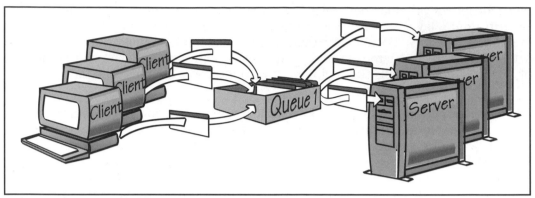

Figure 8-8. MOM: Many-to-Many Messaging via Queues.

Most messaging products provide a minimum level of fault-tolerance in the form of persistent queues. Some of the products provide some form of *transactional protection*, allowing the queue to participate in a two-phase commit synchronization protocol. And some may even reroute messages to alternate queues in case of a network failure.

MOM VERSUS RPC

Comparing the RPC and messaging paradigms is like doing business via a telephone call versus exchanging letters or faxes (see Figure 8-9). An interaction using a telephone call is immediate—both parties talk to each other directly to conduct their

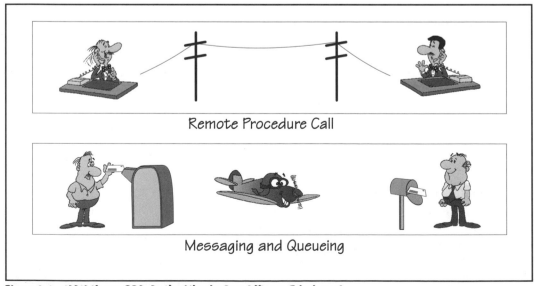

Figure 8-9. MOM Versus RPC: Do You Like the Post Office or Telephones?

business. At the end of the phone conversation, a unit of work is concluded. In contrast, conducting business via mail allows you to stage work, prioritize it, and do it when you're ready for it. You're in control of the workflow, not that ringing phone. On the other hand, it may be frustrating on the client side not to receive immediate feedback.

Table 8-1 compares the messaging and RPC architectures. Messaging is, of course, more flexible, loosely-coupled, and time-tolerant than RPC. However, messaging only skews things in time and may create its own level of complications. In the telephone analogy (RPC), you complete the work as it arrives; you don't have to manage stacks of incoming letters (or faxes). Your clients are happy to get immediate service. When you close shop at the end of the day, you're all done with your work. In the mail analogy, letters may start to pile up, and clients may be polling their incoming mailboxes continuously, waiting for a response. We may have made life easier for the server at the expense of the client. On the other hand, messaging does free clients from being synchronized to their servers; this can be very liberating for mobile and home users.

Table 8-1. Comparing MOM and RPC.

Feature	MOM: Messaging and Queuing	Remote Procedure Call (RPC)
Metaphor	Post office-like.	Telephone-like.
Client/Server time relationship	Asynchronous. Clients and servers may operate at different times and speeds.	Synchronous. Clients and servers must run concurrently. Servers must keep up with clients.
Client/Server sequencing	No fixed sequence.	Servers must first come up before clients can talk to them.
Style	Queued.	Call-Return.
Partner needs to be available	No.	Yes.
Load-balancing	Single queue can be used to implement FIFO or priority-based policy.	Requires a separate TP Monitor.
Transactional support	Yes (some products). Message queue can participate in the commit synchronization.	No. Requires a transactional RPC.
Message filtering	Yes.	No.
Performance	Slow. An intermediate hop is required.	Fast.
Asynchronous processing	Yes. Queues and triggers are required.	Limited. Requires threads and tricky code for managing threads.

Messaging encourages an event-driven model of communications. You can send off multiple requests to multiple servers and then accept the responses as they come back. Your application doesn't block waiting for the responses. Instead, responses are treated like events. They just happen. Of course, you must be prepared to deal with them when they happen. RPCs can mimic this type of asynchronous, loosely-coupled, event-driven behavior using threads.

So, Which One Do You Choose?

There's plenty of room for MOMs, RPCs, and peer-to-peer styles of communication on the modern NOS. Each distinctive style presents its own paradigm for conducting business. You'll end up choosing the style that provides the best fit for your particular needs.

If you really like the loosely-coupled, event-driven programming style, then MOM is made for you. Or, you may want to go all the way with a publish-and-subscribe solution (see the next Briefing box). MOMs are an especially good fit if you need to integrate existing applications in a loosely-coupled way. For example, it's a nice way to do business process automation using workflow. As you can imagine, MOMs have been touted by some analysts as the answer to IT's application integration problems. However, they are not a substitute for synchronizing important updates within or between applications.

Without turning this into a Soapbox, MOMs are like chocolate sundaes. They are great when used in moderation—overuse, however, leads to serious side effects. Here's why. Let's assume you want to notify several applications that Joe just opened a checking account. Queued messages will work well in this environment if the other applications can't veto Joe opening the account. But if one of these applications can veto the action—for example, if it doesn't like Joe's credit rating—you can have a messy situation. The application that opened the account must now implement a *compensating transaction* to close the account. Next, it must send a message to all the applications that received the original notice, informing them that Joe's account is no longer open. Then, each of the recipients must also perform a compensating transaction. In general, you will find that synchronous RPC-like transactions are better for applications that depend on each other for their actions. You are assured that everything is OK before the transaction is committed. You do not need to write compensating transactions to undo updates in case of failures.

In the world of components and objects, RPCs are being replaced by ORBs as the preferred inter-component communication method. ORBs that follow the CORBA 3.0 or COM+ models provide three styles of communications: 1) RPC-like request-reply, 2) MOM-like asynchronous messaging, and 3) publish-and-subscribe via events. So you can have it all (more on this in Part 7).

What About Publish-and-Subscribe?

Briefing

Call them business events, publish-and-subscribe middleware, or push, most of the folks who would benefit most from their use don't understand what they are, how they work, or what benefits they can provide.

— Mitchell I. Kramer, Analyst
Seybold Group
(January, 1998)

If you like the asynchronous, loosely-coupled, event-driven model of communications that MOMs introduce, then you owe it to yourself to look at a new generation of publish-and-subscribe middleware products. The currency of these new systems is *business events*. There are producers of events—called *publishers*—and consumers of events—called *subscribers*. The publish-and-subscribe middleware brokers the distribution of events; it mediates between the producers and consumers. Typically, an event is some occurrence that is of interest to a business—for example, an inventory level is too low, a loan gets approved, or a digital certificate just expired. The software that can do something about this event is then notified. Of course, the software must first register its interest by subscribing to an event or an event type.

An *event broker* establishes a *channel* between subscribers and publishers of events. The producers and consumers of events do not talk to each other directly—they go through their broker (see Figure 8-10). This level of indirec-

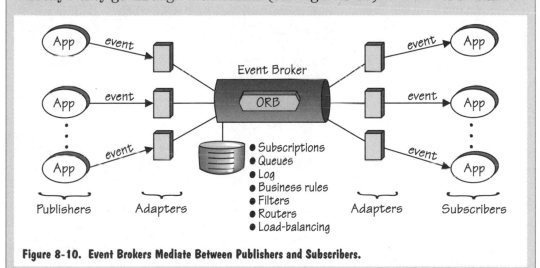

Figure 8-10. Event Brokers Mediate Between Publishers and Subscribers.

tion makes it possible for a broker to provide a ton of value-added services such as event filters, event logs, event queues, event-driven rules, priority event routing, subject-based event routing, event multicasting, and event load-balancing across multiple subscribers.

So who are the players in this market? And, what standards do they support? Here's our short list:

- **TIBCO** is one of the earliest pioneers in this field. According to IDC, TIBCO's 1997 publish-and-subscribe product revenues were a little over $59.9 million. TIBCO's *TIB/Rendezvous* event broker supports certified messaging, MOM, load-balancing, and fault-tolerance. In late 1997, TIBCO introduced *TIB/ObjectBus*—a CORBA-based event broker that uses IIOP as its transport protocol. TIBCO is now working with Cisco on an ambitious project to "event-enable the Internet." The two companies are implementing subject-based routing using IP multicast technology. This will allow routers to become super-fast event brokers. Note that Cisco has since made an equity investment in TIBCO. The two companies plan to submit their subject-based event routing protocols to the IETF for standardization.

- **Vitria** was created in 1994 by two of the founders of TIBCO. In 1997, Vitria introduced *Velociti*, an Internet-based event broker. Velociti is 100% CORBA-based. It implements the CORBA *Event Service* and uses CORBA IIOP as its pipe. Everything is object-based. In 1998, Vitria introduced *Agiliti*—a product that lets you visually create workflows by connecting events across business objects. Vitria provides event adapters for the major DBMSs, MOMs, and ERP systems.

- **BEA** *Tuxedo* was one of the first products to implement publish-and-subscribe functions; it was one of the new features Tuxedo introduced in 1995. In 1997, BEA added publish-and-subscribe to its *MessageQ* MOM. In July 1998, BEA shipped *M3*—a CORBA-based Object Transaction Monitor. In the next release of M3, BEA intends to provide a CORBA-based MOM that also supports publish-and-subscribe.

- **Iona** is a leading CORBA ORB vendor; it provides a full-implementation of the CORBA Event Service as an add-on product.

- **Inprise** (formerly Borland) is also a leading CORBA ORB vendor; it acquired the Visigenic ORB in 1997. Inprise also provides a full-implementation of the CORBA Event Service.

- **Active Software** is a start-up with a publish-and-subscribe product called *ActiveWeb*—now in its second release. The product provides a powerful set of agent-based event adapters for Web browsers, DBMSs, and ERP packages. You can also program these adapters via Java and C interfaces.

■ **Open Horizon** introduced *Ambrosia* in 1997—an all-Java publish-and-subscribe product. In 1998, it added C and CORBA interfaces. An Ambrosia business event has a subject and an associated message. The product implements a reliable (and secure) distribution system on top of TCP/IP; it supports both guaranteed delivery and non-repudiation.

In summary, publish-and-subscribe can be an attractive alternative to MOM. Or, it can be an added service on top of either a MOM or an ORB. As you can see from our list, there are some good products out there. Many support the CORBA distributed object standard, which is good. So you have a choice of standards-based, state-of-the-art products. Check it out. ❏

CONCLUSION

As you may have surmised by now, the NOS middleware pieces are of interest to all client/server apps. If you don't acquire the pieces "off-the-shelf," you'll have to recreate them in some shape or form. After all, a network is almost unusable without security, directory, and naming services. And everybody needs MOM, RPC, or peer-to-peer communications; you may also want publish-and-subscribe. The NOS creates a "gentle and civilized environment" on raw networks that hides the underlying nastiness and lets you focus on your client/server business. Eventually, you will access all the NOS services via a standard ORB. Both the Microsoft and CORBA/Java camps are building object interfaces to all the NOS services. So the ORB will become the NOS.

Chapter 9

NOS: Meet the Players

> Choosing a NOS can seem like part blind luck, part mysticism—just like the feeling when you step into a casino. The NOS newcomer must learn the rules of each network offering and discover which vendor requires the steep ante, which game is most likely to pay off at high odds, and which best suits the situation.
>
> — PC Magazine

In this chapter, we first look at NOS technology and market trends. Next, we briefly introduce you to the key players. Then, we go over the OSF's *Distributed Computing Environment (DCE)* in some detail. DCE is important because it provides a comprehensive NOS solution for integrating multivendor servers in enterprise client/server environments. In the mid-90's, DCE was the archetypal example of an intergalactic postmodern NOS; it represented the best-of-breed NOS technology of the time. DCE was designed from scratch to become the "mother of all NOSs." Today, elements of DCE can still be found in most Unixes. In addition, NT 5.0 is built on top of the DCE RPC and security services. IBM also uses DCE as the foundation for its directory and security services. However, today the "mother of all NOSs" is the Internet—not DCE. So we will conclude this chapter by looking at the remaining elements of the Internet's NOS technology. We cover the Internet as a client/server application platform in Part 8.

NOS TRENDS

We already discussed server OS trends in Part 2. Here's our take on where NOSs are heading:

- **_NOS functions are being subsumed by server OSs._** The early NOSs, like *NetWare 3.X* and *LAN Manager*, were mainly in the business of providing shared file and printer access to DOS client machines. However, the newer server OSs—such as *NT 5.0*, *NetWare 5.0*, and various *Unixes*—are now bundling the NOS functions in the OS. For example, most server OSs now bundle a Web server, global directory, proxy server, and support for Internet security— including SSL, IPSec, and digital certificates.

- **_NOSs are becoming intergalactic._** NOSs are transcending their LAN origins and are now extending their global reach to include the enterprise, intranets, extranets, and the Internet.

- **_Global directories are becoming strategic._** In the age of intergalactic networking, companies without a global directory will be at a disadvantage. We learned from the Internet just how painful life can be without one. The competing global directories include Novell's *NDS*, Banyan's *Universal Street-Talk*, DCE, Netscape's *Directory Server*, and NT 5.0's forthcoming *Active Directory*. The next big challenge is to get these directories to interoperate, which is where X.500 and LDAP will play a big role. It will help customers create federations of loosely-coupled directories.

- **_ORBs will subsume the NOS and expand their scope._** In a sense, ORBs are the new NOSs. It's not surprising that both CORBA 3.0 and COM+ are creating competing object interfaces on top of traditional NOS services— including directories, events, MOMs, publish-and-subscribe, RPCs, and system management. Of course, ORBs extend the reach of the NOS deep into the application space, so they're much more than just NOSs (we cover ORBs in Part 7).

- **_NOSs are becoming turn-key commodities._** NOSs are being delivered as "shrink-wrap" software in the form of commodity server OSs. They are becoming increasingly easier to install, use, and maintain.

- **_NOSs are becoming multiplatform and Internet-savvy._** As you will see in the next section, a NOS is more than just an extension of the local OS. In the age of the Internet, the NOS itself must be multiplatform. DCE started this trend. Next, Novell ported its best-of-breed NDS directory to other OS platforms— including Unix and NT. Netscape went even further when it introduced a whole suite of multiplatform Internet NOS offerings; Netscape doesn't even own an OS. Finally, there is Java; it provides a multiplatform OS on top of the OS. So the NOS is also becoming a vehicle for packaging turn-key Internet services and related middleware.

In summary, the NOS—which has been with us since the earliest days of client/server computing—is continuously reinventing itself. More on this in the next section.

THE PLAYERS

Figure 9-1 shows the three groups of vendors who are competing to provide next generation's intergalactic NOS. Figure 9-2 shows the technology each of these players bring to the party. Here's what these players have to offer:

1. ***The Unix/NOS vendors***. As we explained in Part 2, the Internet was originally built on top of Unix servers. Unix provided the core NOS technology that became the foundation for the Internet—including TCP/IP, IP routing, sockets, NFS, FTP, and the NIS-based domain name service. And, from the very start, Unix was built as a client/server enterprise NOS. It incubated new intergalactic technologies such as DCE and the Sun ONC+ alternative.

2. ***The PC LAN/NOS vendors***. The PC departmental NOS has been with us since the earliest days of client/server computing. NetWare, NT, and OS/2 are running millions of PC networks. They have almost become turn-key applications and are very familiar to millions of network specialists. So it shouldn't come as a surprise that the NOSs have set their sights on the intergalactic market. This is

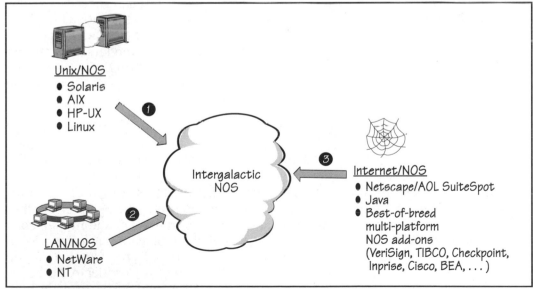

Figure 9-1. The Intergalactic NOS Players.

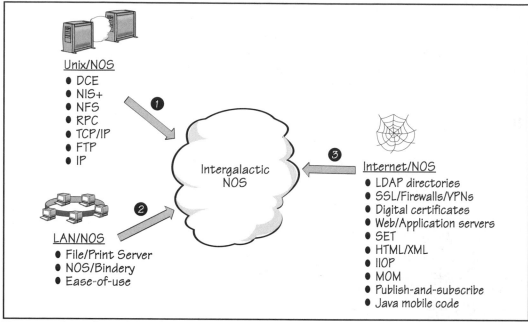

Figure 9-2. Intergalactic NOS: Where the Technology Comes From.

where the growth is. The LAN NOSs had to be completely re-architected to take on the Internet. The flat address spaces of the NetWare 3.X bindery and NT domains were replaced with *NDS* and the NT 5.0 *Active Directory*. The new PC NOSs now support TCP/IP natively and are starting to support Internet security protocols—like X.509 certificates, SSL, and firewalls. These NOSs now all come with a standard Web server. We don't want to turn this into a Soapbox. But, if you think about it, the LAN/NOS vendors are really playing catch-up. They are at least a year behind their competition—the Unix NOS vendors and Internet NOS providers. Instead of innovating, they are simply imitating. They are using their PC-friendly packaging technology to get their intergalactic NOSs to the mass market starting with their installed base.

3. *The Internet/NOS vendors.* These vendors provide multiplatform NOS products specifically designed for the Internet, intranets, and extranets. This is where most of the innovation is currently taking place. The premier vendor of Internet NOS products is Netscape (now AOL). This is the company that popularized Web browsers, HTTP servers, LDAP directories, SSL security, certificate servers, and CORBA IIOP for the Internet. JavaSoft is another company that is innovating in this space with its portable OS and mobile code system. Finally, there is a ton of Internet/NOS niche players that offer add-on products in this space. Typically, these are best-of-breed products that run on multiple OS platforms. For example, VeriSign offers a Certificate Authority framework, Check Point has firewalls, TIBCO, BEA, and Vitria provide pub-

lish-and-subscribe, Inprise provides a Java/IIOP ORB, and Cisco provides IPSec VPNs. At the end of the day, you have a very impressive set of OS-independent technologies. This is how the Internet is being developed.

In summary, the intergalactic NOS is still under construction. The good news is that all the NOS vendors (even Microsoft) seem to be converging on open Internet standards such as LDAP, X.509, and SSL. As you will see in later sections, the NOS is being encapsulated in a layer of ORB-based middleware; it promises to make you independent of the underlying OS and NOS. More on this in Part 8.

THE EVOLUTION OF THE NOS

Figure 9-3 brings together the ideas we've discussed so far. It shows how the NOS evolved from the departmental LAN, to the enterprise, and now the Internet. As you can see, the technology is continuously being improved. For example, the security and directory services that worked well for the department do not scale to the enterprise. In addition, the technology that works well for the enterprise—like DCE—is not cut out for the Internet. All this change is happening over a very short time span. It only took a few years for DCE to become legacy. So welcome to Internet time. In the next two sections, we will cover both DCE and the remaining Internet NOS technology (i.e., what we have not already covered).

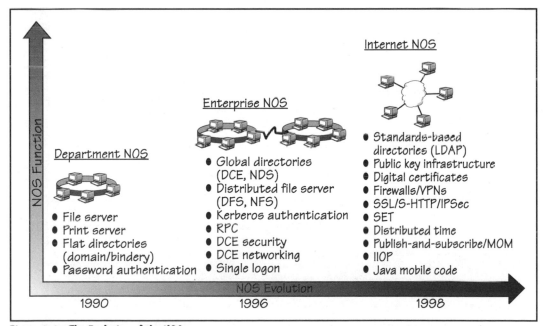

Figure 9-3. The Evolution of the NOS.

DCE: THE ENTERPRISE NOS

DCE is a big system, designed for solving big problems.

> — *Sandy Rockowitz*
> *Minaret Software*

The *Distributed Computing Environment (DCE)* from the Open Software Foundation (OSF)—and now the Open Group—creates an open Enterprise/NOS environment that spans multiple architectures, protocols, and operating systems. DCE provides key distributed technologies, including a remote procedure call, a distributed naming service, a time synchronization service, a distributed file system, a network security service, and a threads package (see Figure 9-4). The sections that follow contain a brief summary of the main DCE components, including their origins.

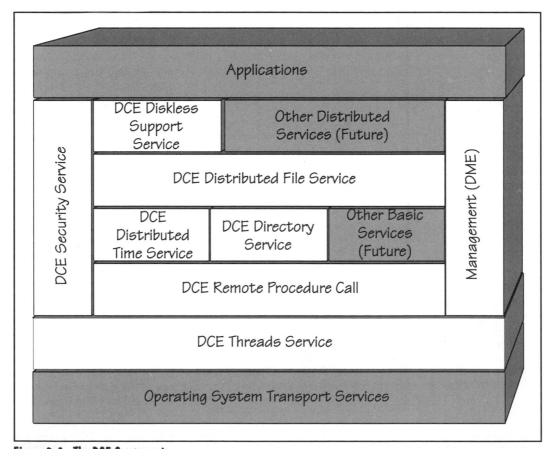

Figure 9-4. The DCE Components.

DCE allows a client to interoperate with one or more server processes on other computing platforms, even when they are from different vendors with different operating systems. In addition, DCE provides an integrated approach to security, naming, and interprocess communications. All these pieces are used to create a coherent heterogeneous client/server environment.

DCE RPC

The DCE RPC initially came from HP—it is an adaptation of the Apollo RPC. DCE provides an *Interface Definition Language (IDL)* and compiler that facilitate the creation of RPCs. The IDL compiler creates portable C code stubs for both the client and server sides of an application. The stubs are compiled and linked to the RPC run-time library, which is responsible for finding servers in a distributed system, performing the message exchanges, packing and unpacking message parameters, and processing any errors that occur.

The most powerful feature of the DCE RPC is that it can be integrated with the DCE security and naming services. This integration makes it possible to authenticate each procedure call and to dynamically locate servers at run time. Servers can concurrently service RPCs using threads. The RPC mechanism provides protocol and network independence.

DCE: Distributed Naming Services

OSF adopted the DCE distributed naming services from Digital's *DECdns* product and Siemens' *DIR-X X.500* services. The DCE naming services allow resources such as programs, servers, files, disks, or print queues to be identified by user-oriented names in a special-purpose distributed database that describes the objects of interest. Object names are independent of their location on the network.

DCE divides the distributed environment into administrative units (or domains) called *cells*. A DCE cell is a combination of client and server workstations. The cell's domain is defined by the customer. A cell usually consists of the set of machines used by one or more groups working on related tasks. The cell size is dictated only by how easy it is to administer. At a minimum, a DCE cell must have one cell directory server and one security server.

As shown in Figure 9-5, the DCE directory service consists of two elements: *Cell Directory Service (CDS)* and *Global Directory Service (GDS)*. This two-tier hierarchy provides local naming autonomy (at the cell level) and global interoperability (at the intercell level). Global access is provided using X.500's intergalactic naming system or with TCP/IP's Internet *Domain Name System (DNS)*. All the

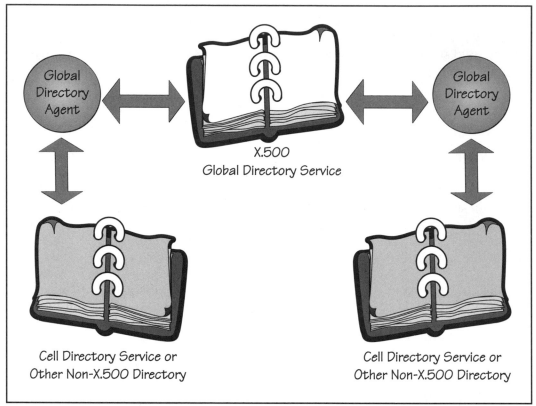

Figure 9-5. DCE's Directory Services.

names in the DCE system taken together make up the DCE *namespace*, which looks like a hierarchical file system. The DCE namespace is used by the different DCE services. For example, the security service uses a part of the namespace to maintain its information on user accounts and principals. The DFS file system uses another part of the namespace for the file system.

DCE: Distributed Time Service

OSF adopted the Distributed Time Service from Digital. This technology provides a mechanism for synchronizing each computer in the network to a recognized time standard. The DCE Time Service provides APIs for manipulating timestamps and for obtaining universal time from public sources such as the Traconex/PSTI radio clock. DCE requires at least three *Time Servers*; one (or more) must be connected to an *External Time Provider* (see Figure 9-6). The Time Servers periodically query one another to adjust their clocks. The External Time Provider may be a hardware device that receives time from a radio or a telephone source. DCE uses

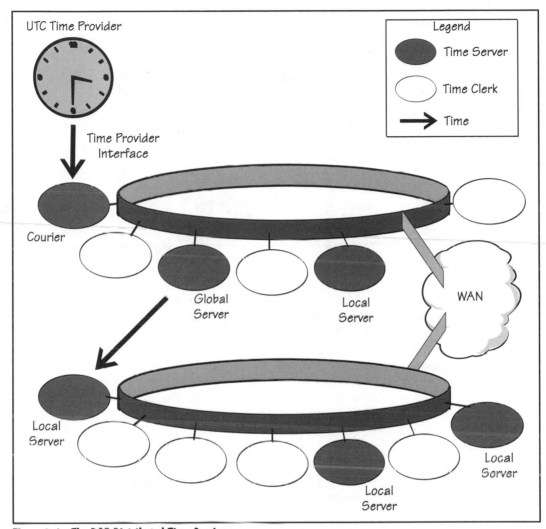

Figure 9-6. The DCE Distributed Time Service.

the UTC standard, which keeps track of time elapsed since the beginning of the Gregorian calendar—October 15, 1582.

DCE: Distributed Security Services

Kerberos—A three-headed dog that guarded the gates of Hades.

— Greek Mythology

OSF adopted MIT's Kerberos authentication system and enhanced it with some HP security features. Kerberos, a protocol that Machiavelli would have loved, is based on total mutual distrust. The MIT folks who built it named it after a three-headed mythological monster that guarded the gates of Hades (yes, hell). Why would anyone want to crash the gates of hell? We'll let security administrators answer that one. The Kerberos monster consists of three "heads," all residing on the same secured server: the *Authentication Server*, *Security Database*, and *Privilege Server*. The MIT three-headed monster gives network administrators the heavy-duty security they need to keep "intruding hackers" from crashing through their network's gates.

DCE's network security services provide authentication, authorization, and user account management. *Authentication* validates that a client, typically a user or program, is who or what it claims to be. This validation is accomplished through the secure communications capability provided by the RPC and the Kerberos ticketing mechanism. Each DCE machine must run a security agent.

The DCE *security server* is a physically secured server that stores security-related information such as names and associated passwords. Each DCE cell must have a security server; it is usually a dedicated machine. A cell may have replicated security servers for backup. The DCE *login facility* enables users (DCE calls them *principals* or *units of trust*) to establish their identity by authenticating themselves using a password. The DCE security system never sends a password in "clear text" across the network.

The security agent works with the authenticated RPC to provide secure access to all the DCE services—not just authentication. The RPC mechanism hides all the complexity of the security system from the user. It obtains the tickets, provides encryption when needed, and performs authenticated checksums if the policy requires it. Under-the-covers, both the RPC client and server must mutually authenticate one another by exchanging tickets (little secrets) with a trusted third party (the Kerberos server). Each party trusts the Kerberos server to identify the other party on the network. This is called *trusted third-party, secret-key encryption*. In addition, information is timestamped so that the usefulness of a ticket expires within a relatively short period of time, measured in hours.

Authorization comes after authentication; it determines whether the authenticated client has permission to access a resource. DCE supports authorization through *Access Control Lists (ACLs)*. Each DCE implementation that uses ACLs must implement an ACL manager that controls access to services and resources managed by it (DCE provides sample code that shows how to create an ACL manager). *Data integrity* is provided by DCE using cryptographic data checksums to determine whether a message was corrupted or tampered with while passing through the network. In addition, *data privacy* can be ensured by encrypting data that is transferred across a network.

 DCE and Access Control Lists

Briefing

Modern NOSs provide a set of APIs that allow servers to create and manage their ACLs. The DCE NOS also provides hooks that help the clients present their authorization credentials to the server applications. DCE calls it the *Privilege Attribute Certificate (PAC)*—a security-server issued ticket the client must present to the server. PACs contain authorization information specific to the client, such as its designated group. DCE provides a set of server APIs that can read the information contained in the PACs and match it with the information in the ACLs. ❑

In summary, DCE solves the problems associated with user authentication in enterprise networks. Passwords are never sent in the "clear text." The security database (DCE calls it the *registry*) can be propagated across trusted servers. DCE's Kerberos, in addition to solving the authentication problem, helps with the authorization issue. And better yet, the whole scheme can work on heterogeneous systems.

Distributed File System (DFS)

For its distributed file server, OSF chose the *Andrew File System (AFS)* from Transarc (and Carnegie Mellon University) and the diskless client from HP (also based on AFS protocols). The DCE *Distributed File System (DFS)* provides a uniform namespace, file location transparency, and high availability. DFS is log-based and thus offers the advantage of a fast restart and recovery after a server crash. Files and directories can be replicated (invisibly) on multiple servers for high availability. A cache-consistency protocol allows a file to be changed in a cache. The changes are automatically propagated to all other caches where the file is used, as well as on the disk that owns the file. The DFS file system APIs are based on the POSIX 1003.1a (portable OS interface). DFS is interoperable with Sun's NFS, giving NFS sites an easy migration path to the more function-rich DFS file server.

DFS provides a single-image file system that can be distributed across a group of file servers. The DFS file naming scheme is location independent. Each file has a unique identifier that is consistent across the network. Files use the DCE global namespace just like the rest of the network resources. And the file system is integrated with the DCE security and RPC mechanisms. Because DFS fully exploits the DCE services, you can administer it from any DCE node, which helps keep costs down in a widely distributed system. Note that you do not need DFS to use the rest of the DCE services.

Threads

For its thread package, OSF chose the *Concert Multithread Architecture (CMA)* from Digital. This portable thread package runs in the user space and includes small wrapper routines to translate calls to a native kernel-based thread package (like NT or Mach threads). Threads are an essential component of client/server applications and are used by the other DCE components. The DCE thread package provides granular levels of multitasking on operating systems that do not provide kernel-supported threads. The DCE thread APIs are based on the POSIX 1003.4a (Pthreads standard). The DCE threads also support multiprocessor environments using shared memory. DCE provides a semaphore service that helps threads synchronize their access to shared memory.

So Who Is Implementing DCE?

DCE has been out in some form or another since 1992. It began as a Unix facility, but it now exists on systems ranging in scale from PCs running Windows NT 5.0 to mainframes running MVS. DCE implementations are available on all the Unixes. Even Sun now provides DCE support on Solaris in addition to ONC+.

So where do you buy DCE? Typically, you won't go out and purchase a shrink-wrapped version of DCE. Instead, you will be using products that incorporate DCE under the hood. For example, DCE provides the foundation for Transarc's *Encina* TP Monitor and IBM's *Directory and Security* servers. Parts of DCE—security and RPC—are also being incorporated in *NT 5.0*.[1]

THE INTERNET AS A NOS

The Internet started out as the least common denominator of NOSs. It was a no-thrills textbook implementation of an IP backbone that grew to interconnect over 150,000 networks. Today, the Internet is evolving into a first-class intergalactic NOS—with global directories, system management, and extensive security. We already covered LDAP directories and some of the foundation technology for Internet security—including X.509 digital certificates, public and private keys, and the SET protocol for electronic payments. In this section, we will complete the Internet security picture by introducing the following technologies: firewalls, SSL, S-HTTP, and IPSec. All these technologies require a good understanding of the TCP/IP stack, which you now have. We will conclude this section with a discussion of VPNs (or extranets).

Web Security

The Internet has long fought a battle to maintain security of resources in the face of unlimited access from the outside world.

> — Michael Goulde
> Seybold Analyst

Security is a critical factor in the establishment and acceptance of commercial applications on the Web. For example, if you are using a home banking service, you want to be assured that your client/server interactions are both confidential and untampered with. In addition, both you and your bank must be able to verify each other's identity and to produce auditable records of your transactions.

Security on the Web is a two-sided affair that involves both the client (the browser) and the server. They each have a role to play. Currently, most of the Web security technology is focused on solving the four usual suspects that are standing in the way of widespread electronic commerce:

---

[1] Microsoft has reversed engineered the DCE RPC so as not to pay OSF licensing fees.

- **Encryption:** You don't want to send your password, credit card number, electronic cash, and other sensitive messages in the clear (i.e., plain text). Who knows what "sniffing" devices may be lurking on the wide-open intergalactic backbone?

- **Authentication:** On the Internet, the clients—and the servers—must prove their identity. The last thing you want is to send your credit card to a Trojan horse masquerading as the real server.

- **Firewalls:** How do you protect your private intranets from the Internet hordes? This typically involves creating some kind of gateway (or buffer) between the intranet and the Internet.

- **Non-repudiation:** Electronic commerce on the Internet requires some form of unforgeable *electronic signature* that can stand in a court of law.

Currently, the Web supports three wire-level security protocols: Netscape/IETF's *Secure Sockets Layer (SSL)*, EIT's *Secure HTTP (S-HTTP)*, and the IETF's *IPSec*. In addition, there are firewalls.

SSL (now TLS)

As the name implies, *Secure Sockets Layer (SSL)* is a secured socket connection. Today, all commercial browsers and Web servers support SSL; it is the standard for authentication and encryption between Web browsers and servers. SSL also verifies that the content of the message hasn't been altered.

SSL implements a security-enhanced version of sockets that provides transaction security at the transport level. You can think of SSL as providing an unobtrusive security layer between the TCP/IP transport and sockets. In other words, SSL provides a secured communications link without involving the applications that invoke it; for example, the existence of SSL is transparent to e-mail or HTTP. HTTP servers that implement SSL must run on socket port 443 instead of the standard 80; it has become a common practice for firewall vendors to leave this port open.

The SSL protocol provides: 1) private client/server interactions using encryption, 2) server authentication, and 3) reliable client/server exchanges via message integrity checks that detect tampering. When a client and server first start communicating, they agree on an SSL protocol version, select the cryptographic algorithms, optionally authenticate each other, and use public-key encryption techniques to generate shared secrets.

The SSL *handshake protocol* must first be completed before an application can transmit or receive its first byte of data. The handshake protocol is like a dance that allows the client and server to authenticate each other and to negotiate an encryption algorithm. Typically, the browser needs to ensure that the server is using a valid certificate. This is how you protect yourself against rogue server impersonators. Servers can also use SSL to verify a client's credentials (or certificate). An SSL session may include multiple secure connections; in addition, you can have multiple simultaneous sessions. The encryption established between a client and a server remains valid over the multiple connections.

SSL uses public key authentication and encryption technology developed by RSA Data Security, Inc. The export implementation of SSL—U.S. government approved—uses a 40-bit key RC4 stream encryption algorithm. The 128-bit domestic version provides many more orders of protection.

To enable SSL on the server, you must mark as secure either the entire server or a selected part of the namespace. On the browser side, you can tell whether a document comes from a secure server by looking at the URL. If the URL begins with *https://* then the document comes from a secure server. You'll always be warned if a secure URL is redirected to an insecure location or if you're submitting a secure form to an insecure location.

The second way you can verify the security of a document is via a security icon that is displayed by the browser. For example, Microsoft's Internet Explorer displays a lock to indicate an SSL session. In contrast, Netscape displays a closed lock for a secure session and an open lock for a insecure session (see Figure 9-7).

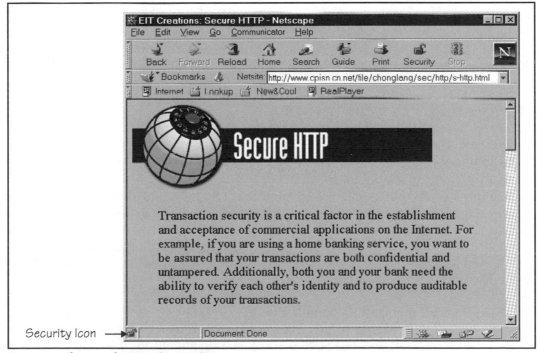

Figure 9-7. Netscape Navigator Security Cue.

The third way you can be made aware of security is through notification dialogs. For example, the Netscape browser informs you via notification dialog boxes when you: 1) enter or leave a secure space, 2) view a secure document that contains insecure information, or 3) use an insecure submission process. The dialog boxes typically display the encryption type that protects the document and also provide information about the certificate that backs the document. The certification request process requires that each server administrator supply an e-mail address and certain identifying information about the certifying authority (or CA).

In July 1998, Netscape handed over the ownership of SSL to the IETF, which then promptly renamed the protocol. SSL is now the *Transport Layer Security (TLS)* protocol—yes, the world needs another acronym like a hole in the head! TLS will offer additional options for authentication as well as support for the latest version of the X.509 digital certificate standard. So it will provide enhanced certificate management, improved authentication, and additional error-alerting capabilities. Future versions of the TLS specification will support Kerberos authentication.

S-HTTP

S-HTTP is a security-enhanced variant of the Internet's *Hypertext Transport Protocol (HTTP)* that was developed by EIT. A fully functional reference implementation of an S-HTTP client and server was released by EIT to members of CommerceNet in the fall of 1994. A commercial implementation of S-HTTP is available from Terisa Systems, which was co-founded by EIT and RSA Data Security in 1994. Terisa produces a security toolkit software product that allows software developers to integrate S-HTTP into their Web clients and servers.

S-HTTP adds application-level encryption and security on top of ordinary sockets-based communications. The client and server communicate over an ordinary HTTP session and then negotiate their security requirements; they use a MIME-like protocol to encrypt the contents of their messages.

S-HTTP provides the following security checks: 1) it authenticates both clients and servers, 2) it checks for server certificate revocations, 3) it supports certificate chaining and certificate hierarchies, 4) it supports digital signatures that attest to a message's authenticity, 5) it allows an application to negotiate the security levels it needs, and 6) it provides secured communications through existing corporate firewalls.

Like SSL, S-HTTP incorporates public key cryptography from RSA. In addition, it supports traditional shared-secret (password) and Kerberos-based security systems. Like SSL, HTTP also provides security at a document level—each document may be marked as private and/or signed by the sender.

In summary, S-HTTP provides many of the security services that are needed for electronic commerce—including encryption, authentication, message integrity, and non-repudiation (also see the next Briefing box).

Are SSL and S-HTTP Mutually Exclusive?

Briefing

S-HTTP and SSL approach the problem of security from two different perspectives. S-HTTP marks individual documents (or Web pages) as private or signed. In contrast, SSL ensures that the channel of communication between two parties is private and authenticated. SSL layers security beneath application protocols, while S-HTTP adds message-based security on top of HTTP.

An outstanding concern in the market has been the development of two different security approaches—S-HTTP and SSL—that were unable to interoperate with each other. The good news is that SSL and S-HTTP are not mutually exclusive. They can easily coexist in a very complementary fashion by layering S-HTTP on top of SSL (see Figure 9-8). Consequently, we can get much better security than either approach provides on its own. Is this overkill? Absolutely not. You can never have enough security on the Internet. ❏

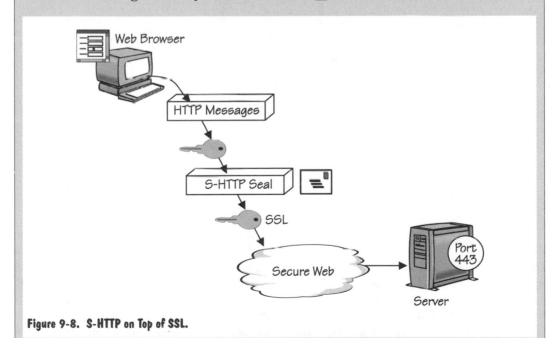

Figure 9-8. S-HTTP on Top of SSL.

IPSec

IP Security (IPSec) is the IETF's new IPv6 security protocol. It provides authentication and encryption at the IP layer—or Layer 3 (see Figure 9-9). In contrast, SSL operates at Layer 4. Consequently, IPSec provides an even less obtrusive security channel than SSL. And, because it's closer to the wire, it may be faster. For example, IP switches or routers could implement the protocol in their hardware. You don't have to wait for IPv6 to use IPSec; it's widely available today as an add-on to the existing IPv4 stack.

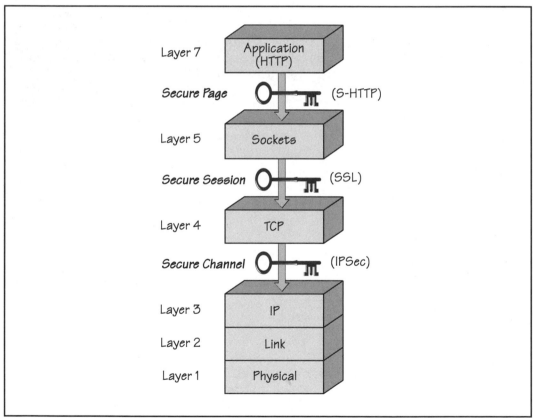

Figure 9-9. TCP/IP Encryption: The Choices.

IPSec requires the *Internet Key Exchange (IKE)* protocol to securely manage and exchange cryptographic keys between the two ends of a connection. The IKE protocol exchanges keys, while IPSec encrypts and signs packets. Currently, IPSec does not mandate a specific encryption algorithm because of U.S. export restrictions. However, most IPSec implementations currently support DES and Triple DES for encryption, and MD5 or SHA-1 for non-tampering and digital signatures.

In May 1998, the *International Computer Security Association (ISCA)* began a certification program for IPSec. This will help accelerate IPSec's market acceptance (we will have more to say about IPSec in the VPN section).

Firewalls: The Network Border Patrol

A firewall is a gatekeeper computer that sits between the Internet and your private network. It protects the private network by filtering traffic to and from the Internet based on policies that you define. You use the firewall to define who can get on to your network and when. A firewall typically provides two network interfaces—one connects to the internal protected network, and the other connects to the external, unprotected network (see Figure 9-10). The firewall provides a single chokepoint where you can impose access controls and audit network traffic. There are, generally speaking, two types of firewalls: *packet-filtering routers* and *proxy-based application gateways*.

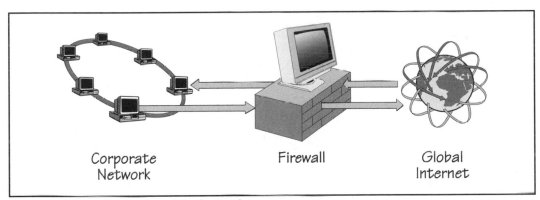

Corporate Network · Firewall · Global Internet

Figure 9-10. Firewalls: The Network Border Patrol.

Packet-Filtering Firewalls

A packet filter is a mechanism that provides a basic level of network security at the IP level. Packet filters are typically implemented in routers. They are configured using complex tables to indicate what communications protocols are allowed into and out of a particular network. Packet filters drop, reject, or permit packets based on destination IP address, source IP address, and application port numbers.

Packet filters do not maintain context or understand the application they're dealing with. They make their decisions purely by looking at the IP header of the current packet, and then interpreting the rules they were programmed to follow. Crackers can exploit this lack of general information to spoof IP packets past the router; for example, they can mimic the IP addresses of trusted machines. Networks that rely

solely on packet filtering technology are less secure from the outset than those guarded by proxy-based firewalls. And because packet-filtering solutions are more complex to maintain, they are also more susceptible to security breaches. It is difficult to tell what holes you may have left open.

Proxy Firewalls

Proxy firewalls—also known as *application* firewalls—are the most secure form of firewall. They run a small number of programs—called *proxies*—that can be secured and trusted. All incoming Internet traffic is funneled to the appropriate proxy gateway for mail, HTTP, FTP, Gopher, IIOP, and so on. The proxies then transfer the incoming information to the internal network, based on access rights of individual users. Because the proxy is an application, it makes its decisions based on context, authorization, and authentication rules instead of IP addresses. This means that the firewall operates at the highest level of the protocol stack. This lets you implement security policies based on a richer set of defensive measures.

Proxies are relays between the Internet and the private network. The proxy's firewall address is the only one visible to the outside world. Consequently, the IP addresses on your internal network are totally invisible to the outside world. Outsiders must authenticate themselves to the appropriate proxy application. The proxy will not forward any packets that contain a final destination address on the internal network. Many proxies require that end-users set up their application programs to point to the proxy. *Transparent proxies*, on the other hand, are completely transparent to end-users—they don't even realize that they're using a proxy.

Some firewalls combine router and proxy techniques to provide more security. Figure 9-11 shows a popular firewall combination that runs proxies on a "bastion host" and uses a router to block all traffic to and from the Internet, except for the

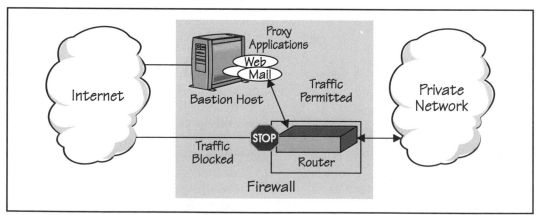

Figure 9-11. Firewall Combo: Proxies and Routers.

bastion host. The router is configured to only allow traffic from the bastion host's IP to get into the inner sanctum. This means that computers on both sides of the firewall can only communicate via the proxies on the bastion machine; all other traffic is blocked. It is very easy to configure such a router. So this is one way to sleep better at night.

Intranets and Extranets

A few short years ago, it seemed as if LANs would expand into intergalactic backbones. Now it seems that the Internet is the intergalactic backbone; LANs are just extensions of the Internet. In some circles, corporate LANs are seen as very fast private extensions of the Internet—in other words, they're just intranets. You can interconnect geographically distributed intranets via the Internet backbone (using firewalls).

Internet NOS technology is increasingly being used on private networks called *intranets*. These internal corporate networks are either standalone enterprise networks or they sit on the other side of a firewall. An intranet simply leverages the public technology on which the Web is built. Intranets may become the new corporate backbones. Netscape reports that intranets account for over 70% of its server sales.

So, What Exactly Is a VPN?

An *extranet* extends the corporate backbone to outsiders using standard Internet NOS technology and ISPs; it is also a way for corporate intranets to speak to one another. The idea is to create a *Virtual Private Network (VPN)* on top of the public Internet to tie a corporation with its suppliers, employees, and business partners anywhere in the world. The VPN creates a secure channel across public IP networks by securing the traffic between two end-points. Nodes on the VPN view geographically remote sites as if they were part of the same network, but the IP traffic is unintelligible to nodes located outside the VPN.

VPN technology must support intranets, extranets, and remote access. A VPN user will be able to dial into any *Internet Service Provider (ISP)* with a local call. As a result, a VPN can eliminate the costs of long-distance calls, modem banks, and remote-access servers. In addition, a VPN lets organizations connect their geographically dispersed LANs via the Internet. This means they can get rid of expensive leased lines and frame-relay connections. Figure 9-12 shows how a secure VPN is created over the public Internet.

However, allowing outsiders to access a corporate network opens a can of worms in two areas: security and interoperability. Today, IPSec appears to be the cure for

both problems. IPSec is the protocol with the largest following among VPN vendors. It is also the VPN protocol of choice of the *Automotive Network Exchange (ANX)*—a pilot for what could be the largest trading extranet in the world. Eventually, ANX will enable the major auto makers to electronically communicate with thousands of auto industry suppliers using an IPSec-based VPN. The ANX pilot has been pushing security vendors to ensure that their IPSec products interoperate. It is also enlisting ISPs worldwide to provide IPSec-compliant Internet access.

According to Infonetics Research Inc., the VPN market was an estimated $205 million in 1997—including products and services. However, it is expected to grow to $11.9 billion in 2001—a huge jump. Three groups of vendors are going after the

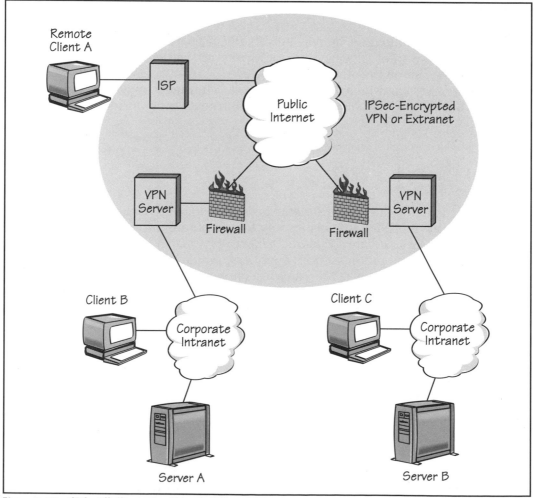

Figure 9-12. VPN: All Clients Can Securely Talk to All Servers.

VPN market: 1) the major router vendors—including Cisco, 3Com, Ascend, Nortel, and Bay Networks; 2) the major firewall vendors—including Check Point (*Fire-Wall-1*), Axent (*Raptor*), Network Associates (*Gauntlet*), and Secure Computing (*SecureZone*); and 3) pure VPN vendors—including RedCreek (*Ravlin*), TimeStep (*PERMIT*), VPNet (*VPNware*), Aventail (*Aventail VPN Server*), and Shiva (*Lan-Rover VPN*). In addition, Novell is playing in this market with its *BorderManager* product.

CONCLUSION

Intergalactic NOSs are creating brave new possibilities for client/server application developers. There are no limits to the possible system ensembles that can be built on top of these distributed NOS substrates. And the best is yet to come. Distributed objects are the ultimate NOS. They extend the distributed NOS all the way into the application space, and then meld it with the Internet (more on this in Parts 7 and 8). The winners in the software development game will be those who learn how to harness the extensive NOS power and use it to create exciting new software packages.

Part 4
SQL Database
Servers

An Introduction to Part 4

The relational model is over 25 years old, predicate logic and set theory are each over 100 years old, and propositional logic dates back to the ancient Greeks (4th century BC).

— Chris Date

Ah! You're still with us, so you must have enjoyed the "single-system illusion" in the last part. NOSs and stacks are great—there can be no client/server computing without them. But the real hot area in client/server today is in SQL databases. Have you Martians heard about Database Valley? That's a strip of highway south of San Francisco where database companies are creating a new California Gold Rush. But in the new Gold Rush, they mine SQL instead of gold.

So pack your luggage: We're heading west. What? You Martians don't have cowboy boots? No problem. They wear sneakers in Database Valley. You won't need mining gear either. All the modern mining is done on computer screens by looking at SQL tables and relational calculus. The guy who discovered the gold, a guru named Codd, is a mathematician. Yes, an abstract mathematician created a new gold rush with tables. No, the tables are not made of gold. They're computer creations that point to other tables and store and organize information. In this part, we're going to visit the gold country and understand how putting SQL databases on client/server networks could have created such a commotion.

Even though all these new database barons live within a few miles from each other, they all speak different SQL dialects. They can't understand each other. And the biggest barons are always charging ahead with new features that bring in more gold. So how do they ever work together? By throwing tons of middleware onto networks. These folks have agreed to create loosely coupled database federations fueled by middleware. The more ambitious are now proposing to pull all the world's data into warehouses that transform it into information. The warehouses could turn into perpetual gold-generating machines.

The plan for Part 4 is to first look at what this SQL stuff is all about: What standards are being created? What awesome new extensions are the barons concocting? We then look at the middleware needed to create the database federations. With all this preparation behind us, we can look at these fabulous warehouses—the new gold-mining machines. We close with an overview of some representative products that give us some form of reality check. When you deal with gold rushes and California dreams, you really need reality checks.

Chapter 10

SQL
Database
Servers

At present the majority of existing client/server-based software is to be found in the area of databases, and it is here that the greatest challenge to any corporation currently lies.

— **Richard Finkelstein, President**
Performance Computing

This chapter covers SQL databases from a client/server perspective. SQL servers are the dominant model for creating client/server applications. SQL server vendors—including Oracle, Sybase, Informix, IBM, and Microsoft—have become household names. Why is SQL so popular from a client/server connectivity perspective? Can relational databases hold the fort against newer models of client/server computing—including object databases, object request brokers, Web application servers, and groupware? Are TP Monitors and ORBs needed, or can we do just fine with the stored procedures provided by the database vendors? What does Java do for stored procedures? In this chapter, we give you a snapshot of where things are in database-centric client/server computing. This sets the stage for answering these questions later in the book.

Our plan for this chapter is to first look at the magic of SQL and the relational model from a client/server perspective. We go over the standards—including SQL-89, SQL-92, and SQL3. We conclude with the important SQL "extensions" that add active intelligence to tables—including stored procedures, rules, triggers, and server-side Java.

THE FUNDAMENTALS OF SQL AND RELATIONAL DATABASES

I believe that SQL will remain the "intergalactic dataspeak" far into the next century.

— *Paul Cotton, SQL3 Architect*
IBM
(March, 1998)

Perhaps the most important trend among database servers of any size is the emergence of SQL as the *lingua franca* for the manipulation, definition, and control of data. SQL, now an ISO standard, is a powerful set-oriented language consisting of a few commands; it was created as a language for databases that adhere to the *relational model*.

SQL's Relational Origins

The relational model of database management was developed at IBM's San Jose Research Lab in the early 1970s by E.F. Codd. SQL—pronounced "sequel"— originally stood for Structured Query Language; now the acronym is the name. It was also developed by IBM Research in the mid-1970s to serve as an "English-like" front-end query language to the *System R* relational database prototype. Even though the SQL language is English-like, it is firmly rooted in the solid mathematical foundation of set theory and predicate calculus. What this really means is that SQL consists of a short list of powerful, yet highly flexible, *commands* that can be used to manipulate information collected in tables. Through SQL, you manipulate and control *sets* of records at a time. You tell the SQL database server what data you need; then it figures out how to get to the data.

The relational model calls for a clear separation of the physical aspects of data from their logical representation. Data is made to appear as simple tables that mask the complexity of the storage access mechanisms. The model frees you from having to concern yourself with the details of how the data is stored and makes the access to data purely logical. Using SQL statements, you only need to specify the tables, columns, and row qualifiers to get to any data item.

Oracle Corporation was the first company to offer a commercial version of SQL with its *Oracle* database in 1979. In the early 1980s, IBM came out with its own SQL products: *SQL/DS* and *DB2*. Today, over 300 vendors offer SQL products on PCs, superminis, and mainframes. Most of these products incorporate the SQL-89 standard features, quite a few include SQL-92 features, and some have even implemented their proprietary versions of SQL3 functions.

SQL has become the predominant database language of mainframes, minicomputers, and LAN servers; it provides the focus for a market-share battleground. The emergence of SQL client tools that can work across servers is heating up the competition even more, making SQL a horizontal industry where you can "mix-and-match" front-end tools with back-end servers.

What Does SQL Do?

The SQL language is used to perform complex data operations with a few simple commands in situations that would have required hundreds of lines of conventional code. Physicists might call SQL "the grand unified theory of database" because of the multifaceted roles it plays. Here is a partial list of roles:

- *SQL is an interactive query language for ad hoc database queries.* SQL was originally designed as an end-user query language. However, modern graphical front-ends to SQL databases are much more intuitive to use. And, they do a good job of hiding the underlying SQL semantics from end-users.

- *SQL is a database programming language.* It can be embedded in languages such as C, C++, Pascal, PL/1, Java, and COBOL to access data, or it can be called using SQL/CLI callable interfaces. Vendors, like Sybase and Oracle, even offer SQL-specific programming languages. SQL provides a consistent language for programming with data. This raises programmer productivity and helps produce a more maintainable and flexible system.

- *SQL is a data definition and data administration language.* The data definition language is used to define simple tables, complex objects, indexes, views, referential integrity constraints, and security and access control. All the SQL-defined objects are automatically tracked (and maintained) in an active data dictionary (that is, system catalogs). The structure and organization of an SQL database is stored in the database itself.

- *SQL is the language of networked database servers.* It is being used as a universal language to access and manipulate all types of data. For example, the IBM data warehouse uses SQL as the network access standard for both relational and non-relational data (like IMS and Indexed files). Even the object database vendors have adopted a derivative of SQL as a query language for objects.

- *SQL helps protect the data in a multiuser networked environment.* It does that by providing good reliability features such as data validation, referential integrity, rollback (undo transaction), automatic locking, and deadlock detection and resolution in a multiuser LAN environment. SQL also enforces security and access control to database objects.

SQL provides a number of advantages to system builders because the same language that is used to define the database is also used to manipulate it. The SQL language makes it easy to specify product requirements in an unambiguous manner. This helps communications between customers, developers, and *Database Administrators (DBAs)*.

The ISO Standards: SQL-89, SQL-92, and SQL3

Although many commercial implementations of SQL have existed since 1979, there was no official standard until 1986, when one was published jointly by the American National Standard Institute (ANSI) and the International Standards Organization (ISO). The 1986 standard was revised in 1989 to introduce referential (and check constraints) integrity; it is now known as *SQL-89* or ANSI SQL. In late 1989, a separate ANSI addendum for Embedded SQL was added to SQL-89.

SQL-89

The SQL-89 standard was an "intersection" of the SQL implementations of that time, which made it easy for existing products to conform to it. SQL-89 was a "watered-down" SQL that made the term "SQL compliant" almost meaningless. The DBMSs of the time would usually add DB2 compliance to their checklist of compliances. And even that didn't mean too much, at least in terms of creating a unified SQL.

SQL-92

The ISO *SQL-92* (also called SQL2), ratified in late 1992, is over five times the length of the original SQL-89 standard. SQL-92 standardizes many of the features previously left to the implementor's discretion (i.e., the loopholes); it is essentially a superset of SQL-89. C.J. Date warned that it was going to take a big implementation effort to bring the current relational databases to SQL-92 standards. He was right. It took over five years to get there. To make it easier on the vendors, ISO defined three levels of compliance: entry, intermediate, and full. To help you understand where you're at, the SQL-92 standard introduces the concept of a *flagger*—a program that examines the source code and "flags" all SQL statements that do not conform to SQL-92.

What's New in SQL-92?

Details

Incidentally, the word "relation" does not appear anywhere in the standard. And the word "database" is used only informally (it is formally replaced by "SQL data"). This is a relational database standard?

— C.J. Date

This section provides a quick summary of what's new in SQL-92 for readers who are already familiar with SQL and the previous SQL-89 standard. If you're not familiar with SQL, first read this chapter and then come back to this box.

The previous SQL-89 standard supports the SQL *Data Definition Language (DDL)* for creating tables, indexes, views, and referential integrity constraints. The standard also supports GRANT/REVOKE security privileges. The SQL-89 *Data Manipulation Language (DML)* consists of the SELECT, INSERT, UPDATE, and DELETE commands. COMMIT and ROLLBACK are used for transaction management. A cursor mechanism provides row-at-a-time navigation. The SQL-89 Embedded SQL addendum defines the mechanism for embedding SQL statements in FORTRAN, COBOL, PL/I, and Pascal.

The "new" SQL-92 standard supports all the SQL-89 features and adds the following features:

- **SQL agents**—these are defined as programs or interactive users that produce SQL statements. In the previous standard, SQL statements were associated with Authorization IDs (an ambiguous concept).

- **SQL client/server connections**—before performing any database operations, an SQL agent must ask the SQL client code to CONNECT to some SQL server. A *connection* establishes an SQL session. SQL-92 supports concurrent connections (or sessions), but only one can be active at a given time. Agents can explicitly switch between connections using the SET CONNECTION command.

- **More granular transaction controls**—using the SET TRANSACTION command, we can specify a transaction as read-only or read/write. A read-only transaction cannot change the state of the database. In addition, we can set the *isolation level* (i.e., the level of automatic lock protection) for a given transaction to *read-uncommitted*, *read-committed*, *read-repeatable*, or *serializable*.

- **_Standardized catalogs for describing the structure of a database_**—a catalog, in the new standard, is a collection of _SQL-schemas_ describing "one database." The schemas are SQL tables that describe the structure of base tables, views, privileges, constraints, and so on. Each SQL-session has one _cluster_ of catalogs describing all the data available to that session.

- **_Embedded SQL support for new languages_**—including C, Ada, and MUMPS.

- **_Support for dynamic SQL_**—including dynamic cursors and the typical commands (with minor surprises) that have been used by most database vendors to generate SQL code at run time.

- **_Support for new data types_**—including BLOBs, VARCHAR, DATE, TIME, and TIMESTAMP.

- **_Support for temporary tables_**—including local and global tables. Temporary tables are used as working storage and are automatically dropped at the end of a session. Think of them as memory variables created using the SQL DDL statement with the TEMPORARY attribute.

- **_Support for join operators_**—including outer join, union join (no matching), cross join (all combinations), and inner join. All of these joins are supported with special operators in the FROM clauses of queries. SQL-89 did not specify mechanisms for creating the different types of joins.

- **_Standardized error codes and diagnostics_**—the use of SQLCODE is not recommended anymore; the preferred approach is to use SQLSTATE, which contains a five-character text string with standard values for the different error conditions. A GET DIAGNOSTICS statement was introduced to return more error information.

- **_Domain checks and constraints_**—including domain constraints (acceptable values), assertions, and base table constraints. _Constraints_ are rules that a user defines to restrict the values of what goes into the table columns. Any constraint can be defined to be immediate or deferred.

- **_Miscellaneous improvements_**—including new string functions, support for backward and forward scrollable cursors, commands for altering and dropping objects, refinements to the referential integrity model, support for data type conversions, improvements in revoking privileges, and a CASE statement.

Most of the SQL-92 features are already implemented in existing database products. However, be prepared for a few surprises in almost every area, regardless of how familiar they may seem. ❏

SQL3

There's a very real danger that SQL3 will be far less relevant than previous versions of the SQL standard... If the SQL standards process is to continue, we must find ways to make it both faster (no more than three years per cycle) and more relevant.

> — Jim Melton, SQL3 Architect
> Sybase
> (June, 1998)

So, what is happening with SQL3? It's almost here. As we go to press, the SQL3 specification—which now weighs-in at over 2,000 pages—is going through its final reviews. Jim Melton expects the standard to be published in mid-99 as *SQL-99*. In late 1998, SQL3 consists of nine parts:

- Part 1, **SQL/Framework**—provides basic definitions and explains the structure of the SQL3 specification.

- Part 2, **SQL/Foundation**—includes the bulk of the SQL3 effort. It covers triggers, roles, recursive queries, collections, and object SQL—including *User-Defined Types (UDTs)*. A UDT is like a C++ class—it consists of a set of properties and methods. The SQL3 UDT can be public, private, or protected. A UDT can also be inherited using the keyword *UNDER*—for example, *CREATE TYPE Dog UNDER Animal*. Your UDTs can appear in columns like any other built-in SQL data type.

  Recursive queries solve the SQL parts explosion problem. For example, you'll be able to discover all the descendants of a parent by issuing one SQL statement (instead of successively searching for the children of each intermediary parent in the family tree). *Roles* are permissions (and privileges) that you assign to groups, not to individuals; users are assigned to roles so that they inherit the permissions and privileges that come with a role. We cover triggers later in this chapter.

- Part 3, **SQL/CLI**—defines the *Callable Level Interface (CLI)*. It's an extension of the X/Open SQL Access Group (SAG) CLI that was started over nine years ago. The interest in the SQL CLI was so high that it was put on the fast track; it became the ISO standard 9075-3 in early 1996. We cover the SQL CLI, SAG, JDBC, ODBC, and OLE DB in the next chapter.

- Part 4, **SQL/PSM**—defines the SQL *Persistent Storage Modules (PSMs)*. This is a fancy name for procedural extensions to SQL using an Ada-like syntax; it also defines exception handlers for doing *undo*, *redo*, and *commit*. The PSM specification for SQL-92 was "fast-tracked" through the standards bodies; it was published in 1996 as the ISO *SQL/PSM-96* standard. The idea was that this

standard would be used as the common language for writing stored procedures in SQL. Unfortunately, this didn't happen. SQL guru and writer Joe Celko reports that "only the *Mimer* database from Sweden has implemented PSM-96 thus far."[1] We cover stored procedures later in this chapter.

■ Part 5, ***SQL/Bindings***—defines the mechanics of intermingling SQL with other languages via precompilers, embedded SQL, and dynamic SQL. We cover these topics in the next chapter.

■ Part 6, ***SQL/Transactions***—defines how SQL databases participate in global transactions. According to Jim Melton, "Part 6 may be cancelled due to lack of a need—the DBMS vendors seem to be interfacing SQL with the X/Open XA standard just fine."[2] We cover XA in Part 5.

■ Part 7, ***SQL/Temporal***—defines how SQL databases handle time-series data. The idea is for SQL databases to model time so that you are able to submit queries with time as a variable. An example of a query is, "What were Q4 sales in 1990?" The SQL3 committee was about to standardize on work done by Richard Snodgrass—a temporal database researcher from the University of Arizona. However, they put Part 7 on hiatus to complete the rest of SQL3. The committee will resume work on Part 7 in the Spring of 1999. So don't don't hold your breath waiting for a standard in this area.

■ Part 9, ***SQL/Med***—defines the management of external data—including datalink types, large BLOBs, abstract tables, and federated database support. The work in this area has just started. So don't expect a standard until late 2000 or early 2001.

■ Part 10, ***SQL/OLB***—defines object language bindings for SQL. The first binding is the Java embedded SQL standard developed by Oracle, IBM, Tandem, and JavaSoft—it is also known as *SQLJ*. By the time you read this, SQLJ should be an ANSI standard. SQLJ will then adopt it as is.

Did we forget Part 8? No, this isn't a typo. Originally, Part 8 was ***SQL/Object***—for extended object constructs. Most of these constructs have now folded into the core SQL object model. As a result, Part 8 is deleted.

The SQL3 draft also contains suggested SQL improvements—including persistent (or "held") cursors that remain open after a commit, new join types, temporary views, column specific privileges, and a better definition of how to update views. It also deals with esoteric topics—including syncpoints over sessions, subtables and supertables, and asynchronous SQL statement execution.

---

[1] Source: *BYTE Magazine* (March, 1998).
[2] Source: Private e-mail exchange with Jim Melton (September, 1998).

SQL3 may also include specifications for multimedia SQL, called *SQL/MM*. The ISO group commissioned to look at the implications of "full text" data for SQL expanded its charter to include the more general issue of multimedia data—including full text, digitized audio, video clips, spatial and seismic data, and other forms of real-life data structures. SQL/MM will use UDTs to define the operations supported on each multimedia object type. Unlike today's BLOBs, UDTs provide methods to manipulate each of the multimedia data types. Providing the storage is the easy part; the harder part is providing the methods and multimedia-specific data fields that allow us to do something meaningful with these BLOBs (like rotating or playing them). As Jim Melton puts it, "BLOBs and objects are two very different animals."

As you can see, SQL3 adds a ton of new features to an already bloated SQL-92 standard. We don't expect the DBMS vendors to fully implement the standard until sometime in the next century. However, it was important to get a cursory understanding of what's being proposed in the SQL3 standard to get an idea of where SQL is heading (see Figure 10-1).

Figure 10-1. The Evolution of the SQL Specification.

WHAT DOES A DATABASE SERVER DO?

In a database-centric client/server architecture, a client application usually requests data and data-related services (such as sorting and filtering) from a database server. The database server, also known as the SQL engine, responds to the client's requests and provides secured access to shared data. A client application can, with a single SQL statement, retrieve and modify a set of server database records. The SQL database engine can filter the query result sets, resulting in considerable data communication savings.

A generic SQL server manages the control and execution of SQL commands. It provides the logical and physical views of the data and generates optimized access plans for executing the SQL commands. In addition, most database servers provide server administration features and utilities that help manage the data. A database server also maintains dynamic catalog tables that contain information about the SQL objects housed within it.

Because an SQL server allows multiple applications to access the same database at the same time, it must provide an environment that protects the database against a variety of possible internal and external threats. The server manages the recovery, concurrency, security, and consistency aspects of a database. This includes controlling the execution of a transaction and undoing its effects if it fails. This also includes obtaining and releasing locks during the course of executing a transaction and protecting database objects from unauthorized access.

Most SQL servers provide, at a minimum, SQL-89 level functionality. Most servers also include some SQL-92 features. Quite a few servers offer proprietary versions of SQL3 stored procedures, triggers, and rules. Some server engines (for example, Oracle, Informix, and DB2) provide object-relational extensions for SQL.

So what is an SQL server? It's a strange mix of standard SQL and vendor-specific extensions. For a long time, it seemed like there was nothing an SQL server couldn't do. DBMS vendors were loading their servers with everything but the kitchen sink. Luckily, this craze is behind us. By 1998, all major DBMS vendors came to the realization that their SQL servers couldn't be all things to all people. Consequently, they are now supplementing their server engines with a broad mix of complementary products—including ODBMSs, Object Transaction Monitors, and Web application servers.

In this section, we briefly go over the architecture of database servers. We then review some of the major features they provide—including shared data access, transactional protection, referential and domain integrity, and database catalogs.

SQL Database Server Architectures

Figures 10-2, 10-3, and 10-4 show three server architectures that databases use to handle remote database clients: process-per-client, multithreaded, and hybrid. Here are the trade-offs of the three approaches:

- *Process-per-client architectures* provide maximum bullet-proofing by giving each database client its own process address space. The database runs in one or more separate background processes. The advantage of this architecture is that it protects the users from each other, and it protects the database manager from the users. In addition, the processes can easily be assigned to different processors on a multiprocessor SMP machine. Because the architecture relies on the local OS for its multitasking services, an OS that supports SMP can transparently assign server processes to a pool of available processors. The disadvantage of process-per-client is that it consumes more memory and CPU resources than the alternative schemes. It can be slower because of process context switches and interprocess communications overhead. However, these problems can easily be overcome with the use of a TP Monitor that manages a pool of reusable processes. Examples of database servers that implement this architecture include DB2, Informix, and Oracle6.

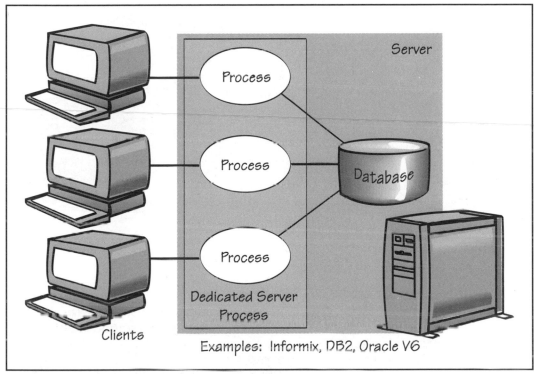

Figure 10-2. Process-per-Client Database Server Architecture.

■ *Multithreaded architectures* provide the best performance by running all the user connections, applications, and the database in the same address space. This architecture provides its own internal scheduler and docs not rely on the local OS's tasking and address protection schemes. The advantage is that it conserves memory and CPU cycles by not requiring frequent context switches. In addition, the server implementations tend to be more portable across platforms because they don't require as many local OS services. The disadvantage is that a misbehaved user application can bring down the entire database server and all its tasks. In addition, user programs that consist of long-duration tasks (for example, long queries) can hog all the server resources. Finally, the preemptive scheduling provided by the server tends to be inferior to the native OS's scheduler. Examples of database servers that implement this architecture include Sybase and MS SQL Server (SQL Server uses Windows NT's SMP scheduler).

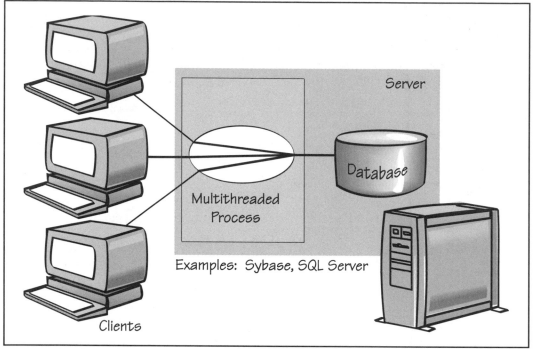

Figure 10-3. Multithreaded Database Server Architecture.

■ *Hybrid architectures* consist of three components: 1) multithreaded network listeners that participate in the initial connection task by assigning the client to a dispatcher; 2) dispatcher tasks that place messages on an internal message queue, and then dequeue the response and send it back to the client; and 3) reusable shared server worker processes that pick the work off the queue, execute it, and place the response on an out queue. The advantage of this architecture is that it provides a protected environment for running the user tasks without assigning a permanent process to each user. The disadvantages are queue latencies. The first database server to implement this architecture is Oracle7, and it did suffer from queue latencies. However, it seems that Oracle8 may have fixed this problem; it's a screamer when it comes to performance.

So which architecture is best for client/server? It's a tough choice. The process-per-client architectures perform poorly when a large number of users connect to a database, but they provide the best protection. The multithreaded architectures can support a large number of users running short transactions, but they do not perform well when large queries are involved. They also do not provide bullet-proof protection. Hybrid architectures may provide the best balance. However, are they better than using a TP Monitor with a process-per-client database server? As a rule of thumb, these architectures don't matter much if you're just doing simple

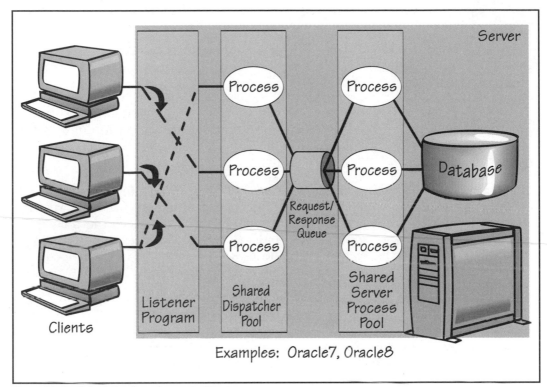

Figure 10-4. Hybrid Database Server Architecture.

LAN-based decision support. However, they do matter if you're planning to create a bullet-proof OLTP system. If you're planning the latter, we suggest that you check references carefully and go for the maximum amount of bullet-proofing. In addition, you should seriously consider using a 3-tier client/server architecture. Typically, your server-side application will run in the middle tier under the control of a TP Monitor or Object Transaction Monitor—the database server is the third tier (more on this in Part 5).

STORED PROCEDURES, TRIGGERS, AND RULES

Relational databases now have built-in procedural extensions—including stored procedures, triggers, and rules. These extensions are very useful but extremely non-standard. So why are database servers moving into the procedural turf? What are these extensions and what new services do they provide? We answer the first question with an opinionated Soapbox. The contents of this section attempt to answer the second question.

Soapbox

Look Who's Cheating

Relational database vendors are cheating big time. They're adding all sorts of procedural extensions to SQL that deviate from the original vision of a "pure declarative language for relational data." Database purists used to scoff at procedural languages for being "relationally incomplete and insecure."

So what are today's hottest SQL extensions? They are procedural constructs of all types—including stored procedures, triggers, rules, and proprietary scripting languages. Instead of keeping the data separate from the code, the relational vendors have simply brought the code to the database. Databases not only store procedures, they also have given them the keys to the data kingdom. Procedural constructs, as you will find out in this section, are simply taking over the database.

The message we're getting from the relational vendors is: "Procedures are OK as long as they're *ours* and we get to store them on *our* databases." But we believe database vendors are stepping out of their territory. They should stick to managing the data and leave the procedural extensions to the middle-tier application servers, TP Monitors, and OTMs (more on this later). ❑

What Is a Stored Procedure?

Stored procedures are trouble in the making...Not only do they violate the theoretical rules of databases, they can be inefficient and make portability difficult.

> — Joe Celko, SQL Guru
> (March, 1998)

The major database vendors are now offering an RPC-like mechanism for executing functions that are stored in their databases. This mechanism is sometimes referred to as "TP-Lite" or "stored procedures." A stored procedure is a named collection of SQL statements and procedural logic that is compiled, verified, and stored in the server database. A stored procedure is typically treated like any other database object and registered in the SQL catalog. Access to the stored procedure is controlled through the server's security mechanisms.

Stored procedures accept input parameters so that a single procedure can be used over the network by multiple clients using different input data. The client invokes a remote procedure and passes it the parameters required to do a job. A single remote message can trigger the execution of a collection of stored SQL statements. The result is a reduction of network traffic, which should provide better performance (see Figure 10-5).

The concept of stored procedures was pioneered by Sybase in 1986 to improve the performance of SQL on networks. Stored procedures are used to enforce business rules and data integrity; to perform system maintenance and administration functions; and to extend the database server's functions. However, the primary use of stored procedures (in all of its variations) is to create the server side of an application's logic. The encapsulation features of stored procedures are well suited for creating performance-critical applications known as *Online Transaction Processing*, or *OLTP*. These applications typically: 1) receive a fixed set of inputs from remote clients; 2) perform multiple precompiled SQL commands against a *local* database; 3) commit the work; and 4) return a fixed set of results.

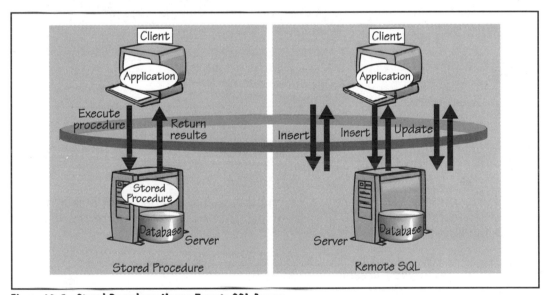

Figure 10-5. Stored Procedures Versus Remote SQL Access.

In other words, a stored procedure is a database-centric, RPC-like SQL entity that is persistent, shared, and has a name. It reduces network traffic, improves response times, and provides a service-oriented interface that is well suited for OLTP applications. Stored procedures also provide better *site autonomy* because the remote modification of tables can only occur through locally executing programs. If the tables change, you don't need to recompile all your remote applications. In general, stored procedures provide better distribution of intelligence than static or dynamic SQL.

FYI

Static and Dynamic SQL

Briefing

Static SQL statements are defined in your code and converted into an access plan at program preparation time. The SQL statement is known before your program is run. The database objects need to exist when precompiling static SQL statements. You can think of static SQL as being a compiled form of the SQL language. Static SQL is a performance enhancement feature.

Dynamic SQL statements are created and issued at run time. They offer maximum flexibility at the expense of execution speed. You can think of dynamic SQL as an interpretive form of the SQL language. The database objects need not exist when precompiling dynamic SQL statements. The compilation of dynamic SQL statements is done at run time and must be repeated every time the same statement gets executed again.

Static SQL is used for writing highly optimized transaction programs. Dynamic SQL is used for writing general database programming utilities and by GUI front-end tools that need to create ad hoc queries. ❑

Stored Procedures Versus Static and Dynamic SQL

Table 10-1 compares the client/server functional characteristics of stored procedures with other forms of SQL programming. You can see that stored procedures offer many advantages.

Table 10-1. Stored Procedures Versus Static and Dynamic SQL.

Feature	Stored Procedure	Remote SQL	
		Embedded Static	Dynamic
Named function	Yes	No	No
Persistently stored on server	Yes	Yes	No
Tracked in catalog	Yes	Yes	No
Procedural logic	Within object	External	External
Flexibility	Low	Low	High
Abstraction level	High	Low	Low

Table 10-1. Stored Procedures Versus Static and Dynamic SQL. (Continued)

Feature	Stored Procedure	Remote SQL	
		Embedded Static	Dynamic
Standard	Coming (with SQL3)	Yes	Yes
Performance	Fast	Medium	Slow
Tool-friendly	Medium	No	Yes
Client/server shrink-wrap friendly	Yes (call procedure)	No (messy)	Yes (CLI calls)
Network messages	One request/reply for many SQL commands	One request/reply per SQL command	One request/reply per SQL command

So, What's Wrong With Stored Procedures?

One drawback of stored procedures is that they provide less ad hoc flexibility than remote dynamic SQL. In addition, stored procedures may perform very poorly if their plans are not refreshed (rebound) to take advantage of the optimizer statistics—dynamic SQL creates a fresh plan with every execution. Another drawback is that there is no transactional synchronization—that is, two-phase commit—between stored procedures; each stored procedure is a separate transaction. Another problem is that stored procedures are slow—especially when compared to a compiled language. Also, many databases recompile their stored procedures every time they are invoked or whenever they get swapped out of memory.

However, the main drawback of stored procedures is that they're totally non-standard. This results in a number of problems. No two vendor implementations are alike. The language for describing the stored procedures and their functionality varies from server to server; stored procedures are not portable across vendor platforms. There is no standard way to pass or describe the parameters. It is difficult for database tools to create and manage stored procedures. Dealing with the parameters is very messy (there is no standard interface definition language or stub compiler tool).

Alternatives to Stored Procedures

Soapbox

OK, we'll admit it. Stored procedures are better than the embedded SQL alternative. But now that you've seen what these stored procedures are all about,

you may agree with us that they're not a panacea, and they're certainly not the only game in town. Stored procedures (or "TP-Lite") are facing some stiff competition from other types of RPC-like extensions that offer more sophisticated functions and are further along in their standardized implementations. For example, NOSs, Transaction Monitors, distributed objects, and Web application servers have their own architectures for implementing function that is equivalent to the database stored procedures. You've already encountered the NOS's in Part 3. In Part 5, we'll go over the "TP-Heavy" implementation of stored procedures. You'll discover that Transaction Monitors provide an OS-like environment for scheduling and managing transactions. Transaction Monitors execute stored procedures "in style" by providing message queuing, load balancing, routing, nesting, and two-phase commit synchronization. In addition, Object Transaction Monitors are defining their own versions of stored procedures (that is, method invocations) through the CORBA and DCOM standards. ❑

Which Stored Procedure?

The following examples illustrate some of the differences in vendor implementations of stored procedures:

■ **Sybase and MS SQL Server** stored procedures can return multiple rows, but they do not support cursors. They require the use of *Transact-SQL*, a proprietary procedural language, to create the stored procedures that are single-pass compiled and stored in the catalog. The procedures are invoked using the SQL EXECUTE command and passing it the name of the stored procedure and server on which it resides.

■ **Oracle** stored procedures only return a single row, but they support cursors. They require the use of *PL/SQL*—a proprietary procedural language. The procedures are invoked by following the procedure or function name with a database link that points to the remote server. With *Oracle8i*, you can also code your stored procedures in Java. Oracle8i provides a very efficient Java VM that runs inside the database server.

■ **IBM's DB2/UDB** family implements stored procedures as ordinary DLL functions (or shared libraries) written in standard programming languages. In addition, you can write your stored procedures as Java classes. The stored procedures reside on the same server as the database, but they are not stored within the database. Client applications calling DB2 stored procedures don't need to know what language was used to code the procedure. Note that, in addition to stored procedures, DB2/UDB supports SQL3-like user-defined data types called *extenders*. You can use these abstract data types to extend your database with new functions and data types. IBM currently offers extenders for text, image, audio, video, and fingerprints. DBAs and third parties can add their own extenders.

■ **Informix** provides a proprietary language called *Stored Procedure Language*. It won't let you share stored procedures between transactions. Informix will eventually support Java-based stored procedures; it also supports *DataBlades* that let you extend the database with your own object types.

The list of vendor differences goes on. The bad news is that the current SQL/PSM specification is not used by any of the DBMS vendors—they have too much invested in their proprietary languages. For this same reason, it's quite unlikely that they will adhere to the SQL3 stored procedure standard when it is released in 1999 (also see the next Soapbox).

Stored Procedures: Is Java the Answer?

Soapbox

The future of portable stored procedures appears to be bleak. The only good news we can report is that almost every SQL vendor claims they will support Java stored procedures in some form or another. So Java may become the common language for writing stored procedures. However, the environment for running these Java-based stored procedures may not be the same across different implementations. For example, Oracle had to completely rewrite the Java VM to tightly integrate it with its database.

However, let's assume—and this is a leap of faith—that the DBMS vendors rewrite the Java VM for their databases without introducing proprietary features. Then we must still answer the following questions: How are these Java procedures packaged to run across different vendor VMs? How are they invoked and executed in a standard way? How do off-the-shelf Java tools support them?

The bottom line is that true portability requires that we can: 1) use a variety of off-the-shelf tools to create and package our procedures, 2) import our procedures into any DBMS engine, 3) run the procedure within any of these engines without recompiling our code, and 4) allow a variety of clients—written in any language—to transparently invoke these procedures. So have we had one cup of espresso too much? Have we turned into science fiction writers? The answer to both of these questions is no.

Today, there is a common server-side Java component standard called *Enterprise JavaBeans (EJB)*, which we cover in Part 7. In theory, you should be able to write an SQLJ stored procedure as a single-method EJB. And, you should be

Part 4. SQL Database Servers

able to use any Java EJB tool to develop and package your procedure. The tool should let you declaratively set your EJB's transaction and security attributes. Based on information you provide, the tool packages the EJB inside a Java JAR. The JAR also includes a standard *deployment descriptor* that describes the quality-of-service your EJB requires from a container.

You should then be able to run your EJB in multiple containers—including database engines, Web application servers, TP Monitors, and Object Transaction Monitors. An added benefit is that the same EJB can run either in 2-tier mode inside a DBMS or in 3-tier mode inside an application or transaction server. With the exception of Microsoft, all the major DBMS vendors plan to support EJB in either a 2-tier or 3-tier mode (or both). As you will see in Chapter 14, Oracle is leading the pack. However, IBM, Sybase, and Informix are not too far behind.

So is Java/EJB the savior of stored procedures? Perhaps. However, the questions that you must now answer are: Why would you ever want to write a stored procedure in the first place? Why not move to objects and write first-class beans? We answer these questions throughout this book. ❑

Triggers and Rules

Triggers are special user-defined actions—usually in the form of stored procedures—that are automatically invoked by the server based on data-related events. Triggers can perform complex actions and can use the full power of a procedural language. A *rule* is a special type of trigger that is used to perform simple checks on data. Both triggers and rules are attached to specific operations on specific tables. In other words, an event tells you something happened to the database; a trigger or rule is an event handler you write to take the proper action in response to that event (see Figure 10-6).

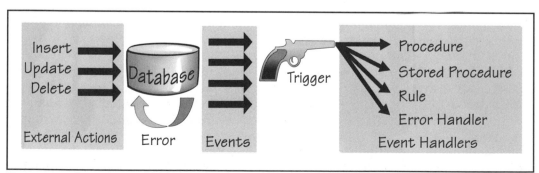

Figure 10-6. The Mechanics of SQL Triggers.

Triggers and rules are typically used to perform tasks related to changes in tables, such as auditing, looking for value thresholds, or setting column defaults. Enabled triggers or rules are executed whenever a table is updated by an SQL DELETE, INSERT, or UPDATE command. A separate trigger or rule can be defined for each of these commands, or a single trigger may be defined for any updates to a table. In general, triggers can call other triggers or stored procedures. So what makes a trigger different from a stored procedure? Triggers are called implicitly by database generated events, while stored procedures are called explicitly by client applications.

Server implementations of triggers are extremely non-standard and vendor-specific. Here are some examples of vendor implementation differences:

- **Sybase** supports only one trigger per INSERT/UPDATE/ DELETE operation.

- **MS SQL Server** supports a maximum of three triggers per table—for UPDATE, INSERT, and DELETE. Each trigger can call up to 16 stored procedures. SQL Server 7.0 allows recursive firing of triggers from within triggers. However, it does not support *before triggers*. All triggers are executed only *after* the data is modified (i.e., they are *after triggers*).

- **Ingres** supports multiple triggers, but the execution of the triggers is non-deterministic.

- **Oracle** supports up to 12 triggers per table. It does this by allowing you to specify for each INSERT/UPDATE/DELETE the following: a before trigger that fires before the SQL statement executes, and an after trigger that fires after the SQL statement executes. In addition, Oracle lets you specify the number of times a trigger fires. *Row-level triggers* fire once for each updated row. *Statement-level triggers* fire once for the entire SQL statement, even if no rows are inserted, updated, or deleted. Both can be defined to be active simultaneously. Oracle's implementation of triggers is close to the SQL3 draft standard (but it's not fully compliant).

- **Informix** supports before and after triggers and more than one trigger per operation; it uses the column numbers to determine the sequence of trigger firings.

- **DB2/UDB** supports multiple triggers for each INSERT/UPDATE/DELETE to a table. DB2 executes the triggers in the order that you create them. A DB2 trigger consists of one or more SQL INSERT, UPDATE, or DELETE functions. In addition, DB2 supports a special type of trigger called an *alert*; it has the ability to inform an external application of a database state change.

Triggers are written in proprietary SQL procedural extensions. Different implementations limit what triggers can do. For example, Oracle7 will not let you issue commits or rollbacks from within a trigger; DB2 does not let you write procedural code within a trigger or call a stored procedure. Triggers and rules are also used, in a very *non-standard* manner, by Sybase (prior to System 10) and by SQL Server to enforce referential integrity. For example, a trigger associated with a particular table is invoked when data in the table is modified or updated (see the next Warning box). In summary, triggers are extremely non-standard, and the situation will not improve until SQL3 becomes a standard.

The Pitfalls of Referential Integrity

Warning

Trigger-enforced referential integrity is non-standard, error-prone, and difficult to implement and maintain. Triggers require programming efforts to implement referential integrity; declarative integrity doesn't. Because a server has no way of knowing that a trigger is being used for referential integrity, it cannot do anything to help optimize it. For example, a transaction that adds 100 new parts to a trigger-enforced relationship between a supplier and parts table will cause the trigger to be executed 100 times. It will check the same key value each time; the execution of triggers is not deferrable. In contrast, a server-enforced referential implementation would check the value only once for the entire transaction.

In addition, referential triggers are hard to document (and query) because they consist of procedural code. In contrast, declarative integrity provides better documentation and clarity by using catalog-based standard DDL SQL statements. Finally, some trigger implementations only support three triggers (or fewer) per table, which may not be enough to exhaustively cover all the referential constraints and rules that need to be enforced. ❑

CONCLUSION

In this chapter, we covered SQL databases—the good, the bad, and the ugly. SQL has come a long way in a very short time. It went from being a theoretical model—the brainchild of mathematicians—to a multi-billion dollar industry that is now the cornerstone of modern application development. The two-tier SQL client/server model was very successful—it launched client/server computing. Now, as we move to Internet-based client/server, the database vendors are reinventing themselves as N-tier client/server providers. And they're moving their customer base to this new form of component-based computing. Of course, it's a big leap to go from proprietary stored procedures to N-tier Java-based components. So expect some turbulence in the database industry. It's not easy to depose yourself when you're king of the hill.

Chapter 11

SQL Middleware and Federated Databases

The issue of deciding how to handle an organization's real systems is like trying to remodel the bathroom without rebuilding the whole house. Perfect synchronization is only possible if the world stands still...Only stagnant companies are able to unify their environments.

— **Don Haderle**
IBM

How does an SQL database client access data that's on multivendor database servers? With database-specific middleware, of course. Why not use straight SQL? Because it's not that simple. A heavy dose of *middleware* is needed to smooth over the different SQL dialects and extensions, network messaging protocols, and vendor-specific "native" APIs. It's sad to report that after 12 years of intense standardization efforts, multivendor SQL clients cannot talk to SQL servers without layer upon layer of middleware. Fierce competition is driving vendors to build database engines and APIs that increasingly diverge from each other. Despite vendor efforts to conform to SQL-92, the complete set of SQL APIs from each vendor are further apart today than they were when we wrote the second edition of this book. The best we can do today is to allow a "federation" of loosely-coupled, autonomously-owned, multivendor database servers to communicate using a "least

common denominator" approach. The industry calls this compromise *federated database systems*.

This chapter looks at the middleware that's needed to make SQL clients and servers work across multivendor, heterogeneous, database networks—or more simply put, federated databases. How well does this middleware provide a "single database illusion" in a federated world?

To create the single database illusion, the middleware must make two sets of customers happy: 1) the developers of applications and front-end tools who need a single OS-independent SQL API to get to any database server; and 2) the MIS interoperation people who must make the disparate desktop clients talk to the "federated" database servers on their enterprise networks. The middleware must address difficult issues such as: How does a client program issue multivendor SQL calls? How do federated database desktops interoperate with federated database servers? Can all this be done transparently?

The good news is that there is middleware that you can use to glue together disparate systems. The bad news is that you cannot use this middleware to create production-strength, federated databases. It does, however, provide an adequate foundation for decision-support systems and data warehousing.

SQL MIDDLEWARE: THE OPTIONS

*T*rue database independence will not be possible without 3-tiered architectures.

— Meta Group

Based on our previous definition, middleware starts with the API on the client side that is used to invoke a service, and it covers the transmission of the request over the network and the resulting response. Middleware does not include the software that provides the actual service. So the questions we need to answer are: What APIs do SQL database servers provide to clients? And how is the request/reply exchanged with the server? As you will discover, there are too many answers to both of these questions.

Before going into detailed answers, let's first create a common mindset that will help us understand the solutions. We'll start with SQL "Nirvana"—these are the integrated single-vendor offerings. We then look at the problems created in a multivendor, federated SQL environment. Next, we give you a quick overview of the two leading architectures for smoothing over the federated database discrepancies. Finally, we give you our two cents worth on what *federated* SQL Nirvana should include.

SQL Nirvana: The Single Vendor Option

If a single vendor SQL solution can fulfill all your shared data needs, consider yourself *very* lucky. All you need to do is read this section and then move on to the next chapter. Figure 11-1 shows what a typical single-vendor middleware solution currently provides:

■ *A vendor-proprietary SQL API that works on a multiplicity of client platforms.* Most vendors support DOS, Windows, and OS/2 clients; quite a few also support Macintosh and some Unix variants. Most vendor APIs support SQL-92 with proprietary extensions. Some of the vendor APIs use *Embedded SQL (ESQL)*, and others support a call-level interface (CLI). This will be discussed in more detail later in this chapter.

■ *A vendor-proprietary SQL driver.* This is a thin client run-time element that accepts the API calls, formats an SQL message, and handles the exchanges with the server. The format of the SQL message and the handshake are known affectionately as the FAP, which stands for *Format and Protocols*. The SQL FAPs are typically vendor-defined.

■ *FAP support for multiple protocol stacks.* As a result of user pressures, most vendors now support multiple protocol stacks. Some vendors bundle the stacks with their drivers; others support a common transport interface (like Sockets or Named Pipes) and require that you provide your own stacks. At the server side, the vendor typically provides "listeners" for the different stacks. However, some vendors provide their own internal protocol gateways—for example, Oracle on Unix translates IPX/SPX packets to TCP/IP on the server side.

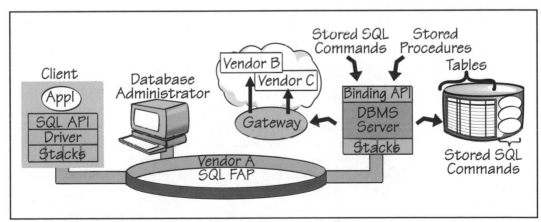

Figure 11-1. The Components of a Single-Vendor SQL Client/Server Offering.

■ *Gateways to other vendor databases.* Some vendors provide gateways that make other vendors' databases look like their own. For example, Oracle, Sybase, Informix, Centura, and XDB all provide gateways to DB2. Most vendor-supplied database gateways only provide an intersection of the features supported by the two databases—the least common denominator. This means that most vendor-supplied database gateways only support dynamic SQL. They are only good for simple data extracts and queries—not for transaction processing.

Most vendor-supplied gateways require two database engines: the vendor's own database, which acts as a middle tier on the gateway server, and the "foreign" database. The middle-tier database server provides a directory of connected databases, catalog services, and handles the shipping and routing of "foreign" requests.

■ *Client/Server database administration tools.* Most vendors will let you manage and administer the database from a remote workstation using a graphical user interface. You have a single point of management for the middleware, the clients, and the servers, as long as they're from the *same* vendor.

■ *Front-end graphical application development and query tools.* These help you create visual interfaces to the database server. Of course, each vendor supplies GUI tools for its own database servers. Most third-party tools do a good job for a particular database (see the following Warning box).

Tools: Not All Databases Are Equal

Warning

The SQL database server peculiarities and extensions create major headaches for the vendors of multiplatform client/server database tools. As a result, the support of server extensions tends to be highly uneven. Most tool vendors usually do an excellent job supporting their "preferred" server platform, they do a mediocre job on the second platform, and they do an atrocious job for the rest of the platforms (they provide almost no support for server-specific extensions). Let's face it: Front-end tool vendors have their plate full just trying to keep up with the graphical engines on which they run; they can only deal with so many server idiosyncrasies. You'll find that each database server has its own GUI tool specialists. With over 200 GUI tool vendors out there, many are trying to stay alive by becoming best-of-breed—or specialists—for a particular database server. ❑

SQL Nightmare: The Multivendor Option

Interoperability between N vendor databases ends up being an N^2 problem.

> — **Mohsen Al-Ghosein, TP Architect
> Microsoft**

Figure 11-2 shows what happens when you move into a multivendor database world. Here's the short list of obvious inconsistencies that you will immediately face:

- **Different SQL APIs** make it a nightmare to write a common set of applications. Even if common API semantics were magically to show up later in this chapter, we still need a way to deal with all the proprietary SQL extensions.

- **Multiple database drivers** eat up precious memory space on the client machines (especially for DOS). Can these drivers use the same protocol stacks or do we need duplicate stacks? If multiple stacks are needed, how will they share the LAN adapter? Who do we call when a problem occurs? How do we keep track of which driver (and which version) runs on which client?

- **Multiple FAPs and no interoperability** means that the database protocols from the different vendors are simply sharing the physical network; they cannot talk to one another.

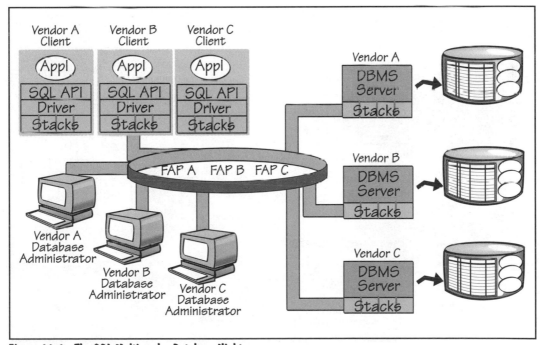

Figure 11-2. The SQL Multivendor Database Nightmare.

■ *Multiple administration tools* means that database administrators must familiarize themselves with a set of managing workstations, each of which have their own semantics and user interfaces.

We have not even addressed some of the thornier issues, such as federated database joins, federated commits, or concurrent access to federated data.

The federated middleware solutions concentrate on simple SQL access to a federated database—one connection at a time. More ambitious schemes, such as RDA and DRDA, aim at creating a federated environment that matches the power of a single-vendor distributed database approach. But they're far from accomplishing that goal. The best we can do today is focus on the issues of submitting simple SQL statements against one federated database at a time.

Middleware Solution #1: The Common SQL Interface

The first step toward regaining some level of sanity in a federated database environment is to *standardize on a common SQL Interface* (see Figure 11-3). The idea is to create a common SQL API that is used by all the applications, and then let the server differences be handled by the different database drivers. This is, of course, easier said than done. Here are the problems:

■ *Which SQL API do you standardize on?* You'll soon discover that there are many SQL "standard APIs" on the table. How are stored objects on the server defined and invoked (remember the stored procedures and static SQL)? Should

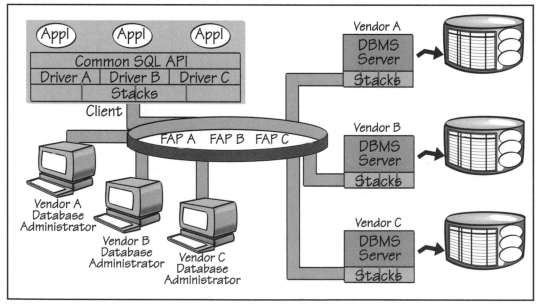

Figure 11-3. The First Convergence: A Common SQL API.

we use a call-level API or the ISO-defined embedded SQL? How do we deal with the non-standard SQL extensions? Will the common interface be slower than the native vendor implementation?

- ■ ***Multiple drivers are still required.*** Should the drivers reside on the client or on the server side? Who provides the drivers to the "common APIs"? What's the incentive for the vendors to support a "common" driver over their own "native" driver? Can the drivers coexist on the same stacks or on the same LAN adapters?

- ■ ***Multiple managing stations and multiple FAPs are still required.*** We haven't solved those problems; we've just made them invisible to the developer. So the system administration people are still not happy.

Later in this chapter, we will go over the contending schemes for creating a common SQL interface—including Embedded SQL, the X/Open SAG CLI, ODBC, JDBC, OLE DB, and EDA/SQL.

Middleware Solution #2: The Open SQL Gateway

Let's assume that we have all magically agreed on a common SQL interface. What is the next middleware improvement that can be *realistically* accomplished to better articulate the federated database environment? Figure 11-4 shows a middle-

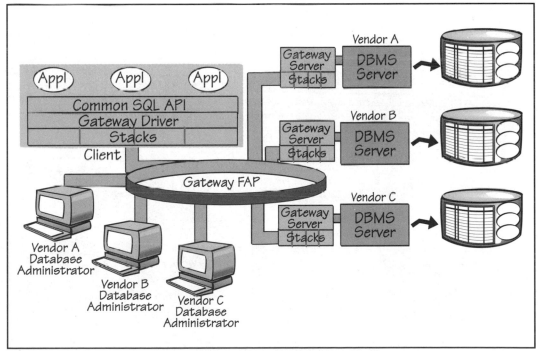

Figure 11-4. The Second Convergence: A Common FAP Using Gateways.

ware solution that's currently in vogue: *the open gateway.* The idea is to standard-ize on one (or most likely two) open industry FAPs, supply a common client driver for the FAP, and develop a gateway catcher for each server. The gateway catcher will "catch" the incoming FAP messages and translate them to the local server's native SQL interface. The good news is that the industry has at least two "common" FAPs to choose from—IBM's DRDA and the EDA/SQL—which are both non-stan-dard. The official ISO/RDA FAP has suffered from lack of vendor support. Later in this chapter, we will spend some time looking at the two de facto approaches.

Middleware Solution #3: Federated Nirvana

Let's assume that we have both the common FAP and the common API. What else is needed to create a federated SQL environment that provides the same level of completeness as the single vendor implementation? Figure 11-5 shows what this "ideal" would look like. Notice that we've removed the gateway catchers, which improves server performance, reduces cost, and simplifies maintenance. And, we've created a single database administration interface.

To eliminate the gateway catchers, the common FAP must either support a superset of all the SQL dialects or it must tolerate native SQL dialects (meaning that it must allow pass-throughs). The SQL vendors must also agree to replace their own private FAPs with the common FAP. Note: None of this is in the works.

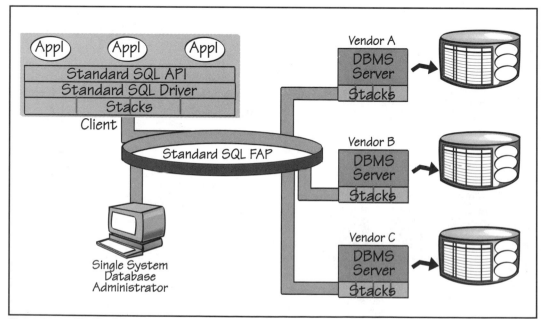

Figure 11-5. The Third Convergence: Direct Implementations of the Common FAP.

The database administration facility will be the last proprietary stronghold to fall. There is just too much variety in the database server implementations to create a common interface. Even if we solved the technological issues, there are still some thorny political issues to be resolved. For example, is there a single point of administration control in a federated database environment? Heterogeneous database management products—like Tivoli's *TME 10*, BMC's *Patrol*, and Platinum's *DBVision* and *Enterprise DBA*—are beginning to address these issues. Most of these tools let you administer users and monitor multi-vendor databases. Some even let you manage the schemas of multiple databases—for example, Platinum lets you create, alter, rename, and update database objects at an enterprise level. The good news is that database vendors have a DBMS MIB standard that defines database configuration and control parameters to SNMP management stations.

WILL THE REAL SQL API PLEASE STAND UP?

How do you access SQL data? Can an application transparently access a system of federated databases? Can an application built for one SQL database be deployed on another? What's the state of the SQL data access standards? The answers, as you will discover in this long section, are a fuzzy yes, no, and maybe.

The early SQL architects felt it was very important to keep SQL language-neutral. In fact, SQL was created as a higher-level declarative language that was to isolate us from low-level procedural constructs. Remember, it was designed as an end-user query language. But to create applications that use SQL, it became obvious that SQL constructs needed to be integrated within existing programming languages. Incidentally, "SQL first" people view this process as extending SQL with procedural capabilities, while programmers think of it as providing an interface to SQL services. Two competing approaches are currently in vogue for supporting SQL from within programming languages: *embedded SQL* and the SQL *Call-Level Interface (CLI)*. Figure 11-6 shows the two approaches.

This section looks at the SQL interface from the point of view of how it helps create a federated middleware solution. We will first look at embedded SQL because it is an ISO standard. We then look at the CLI alternatives, including the SAG CLI and some of its more famous mutants: ODBC, X/Open (and now ISO) CLI, and JDBC. We also briefly introduce Microsoft's OLE DB and its *ActiveX Data Objects (ADO)*. We will defer the discussion of the EDA/SQL CLI to the gateway section.

The SQL-92 Embedded SQL (ESQL)

Embedded SQL (ESQL) is an ISO SQL-92 defined standard for embedding SQL statements "as is" within ordinary programming languages. The SQL-92 standard

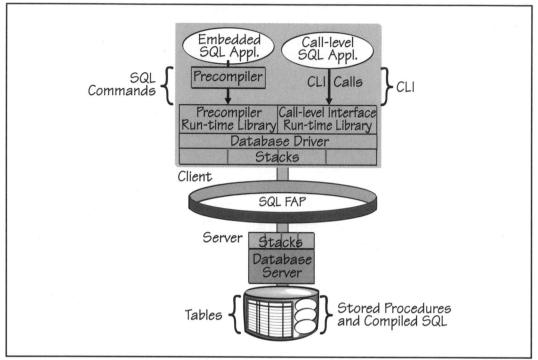

Figure 11-6. SQL APIs Come in Two Styles: CLI and ESQL.

specifies the syntax for embedding SQL within C, COBOL, FORTRAN, PL/I, Pascal, MUMPS, and Ada. Each SQL statement is flagged with language-specific identifiers that mark the beginning and end of the SQL statement. This approach requires running the SQL source through a *precompiler* to generate a source code file that the language compiler understands. As an example, for C, an embedded SQL statement must start with the **EXEC SQL** keyword pair and end with a semicolon (;). These bracketed statements will be processed by the precompiler and anything else in your source code will be passed through unchanged.

From a client/server packaging perspective, the biggest hurdle with ESQL is that the target database must be known (and available) when the program is being developed. This makes it hard to target a client program to a database at run time. In addition, the installation process involves binding applications to each server database they connect to—a process that may be too complicated for the "shrink-wrapped" client/server software market. Finally, precompilers have traditionally been tied to a particular database product; you must recompile your embedded SQL code for each vendor's database server. The same features that make precompilers so popular with IS shops and corporate developers have turned into liabilities for the providers of shrink-wrapped client/server software.

SQLJ—Java's Embedded SQL

In 1997, Oracle, Tandem, and IBM announced they were working together on an ESQL implementation for Java called *SQLJ* (née *JSQL*). In 1998, SQLJ became the basis for the ISO SQL3 object language bindings—remember, this is Part 10 of the SQL3 document. Like all ESQLs, SQLJ lets you directly insert SQL statements inside your Java programs. In many ways, SQLJ is easier to use than JDBC, and it is more amenable to compiler-time checking.

SQLJ is particularly important because it will be widely used to write Java-based stored procedures. Like all ESQLs, SQLJ lets you embed any valid SQL statement as well as transaction directives. Unlike other ESQLs, SQLJ also defines calls to stored procedures and user-defined types.

By the time you read this, many of the major database vendors—including Oracle, Informix, IBM, and Sybase—will provide SQLJ precompilers for their databases. Most of these SQLJ precompilers will generate embedded JDBC calls. IBM is also working on an optimized SQLJ precompiler that generates static SQL.

The SQL Call-Level Interfaces (CLIs)

The alternative to Embedded SQL is to use a callable SQL API for database access. An API does not require a precompiler to convert SQL statements into code, which is then compiled and bound to a database. Instead, an API allows you to create and execute SQL statements at run time. In theory, a standard API can help you write portable applications that are independent of any database product. Of course, in practice things are not that simple. In this section, we go over the SAG CLI and some of its more famous mutants: ODBC and the X/Open SQL CLI.

The X/Open SAG CLI

In 1988, 44 database vendors created a consortium called the *SQL Access Group (SAG)*, which was to provide a unified standard for remote database access. The original goal of the SAG charter founders—Tandem and Digital—was to accelerate the pace of remote SQL standard development and put in place a multivendor SQL solution that would allow any SQL client to talk to any SQL server. Tandem and Digital were very interested in an open set of multivendor front-end tools for enabling their SQL databases. So they drove the SAG effort, which resulted in one of the industry's most successful "open standards."[1]

---

[1] The early efforts of Jim Gray (then associated with Tandem Computers, and now with Microsoft) and of Jeri Edwards (your co-author) led to the formation of the SAG consortium.

In December 1994, SAG turned over its finished CLI to X/Open. So X/Open is now the official "guardian" of the SAG CLI, which is now called the *X/Open CLI*, to differentiate it from Microsoft's ODBC and other SAG variants. In early 1996, the X/Open CLI became an international standard—it's now the *ISO 9075-3 SQL/CLI*. The forthcoming SQL3 CLI is based on the X/Open CLI, with some extensions.

The SQL/CLI requires the use of intelligent database drivers that accept a CLI call and translate it into the native database server's access language. With the proper driver, any data source application can function as a CLI-server and can be accessed by the front-end tools and client programs that use the CLI. The CLI requires a driver for each database to which it connects. Each driver must be written for a specific server using the server's access methods and network transport stack. The CLI provides a *driver manager* that talks to a driver through a *Service Provider Interface (SPI)*.

Currently, the SQL/CLI only supports *dynamic SQL* and provides functions that correspond to the SQL-92 specification. The CLI provides common SQL semantics (and syntax), codifies the SQL data types, and provides common error handling and reporting. The API calls allow you to connect to a database through a local *driver* (3 calls), prepare SQL requests (5 calls), execute the requests (2 calls), retrieve the results (7 calls), terminate a statement (3 calls), and terminate a connection (3 calls).

You should note that a CLI is not a new query language. It is simply a procedural interface to SQL. Your applications use the CLI to submit SQL statements to a DBMS. You must write SQL to perform database queries and updates. So you can think of the CLI as just an SQL wrapper—it neither adds nor subtracts from the power of SQL. You should be warned that not all databases support all the APIs a CLI exposes. To write database-independent code, you must use the CLI's introspection calls to discover—at run time—the capabilities of the database you connect to and then adjust your calls accordingly. It can get quite tricky.

The Microsoft ODBC CLI

ODBC has started the process of commoditization of databases, and nine out of ten DBMS vendors don't like that.

> — *Kingsley Idehen, President*
> *OpenLink*

Microsoft's *Open Database Connectivity (ODBC)* Windows API standard for SQL is an extended version of the SAG CLI. In August 1992, Microsoft released the ODBC 1.0 SDK; it was to be the shrink-wrapped answer for database access under Windows. Since then, ODBC has gone cross-platform. Visigenic was the first vendor to receive a license from Microsoft to provide ODBC SDKs on non-Windows platforms. In addition to Visigenic, third parties—such as Intersolv (*Q+E Software*) and OpenLink—are offering ODBC driver suites on Windows, Windows 95/98, Windows NT, OS/2, Mac, and Unixes that run against a variety of database servers.

ODBC 1.0 was slow and buggy; it was limited to the Windows platform and lacked the documentation and code examples necessary to educate developers. In April 1994, Microsoft shipped the ODBC 2.0 SDK, which fixed many of the problems with the previous driver manager. In December 1994, the first 32-bit drivers were shipped. ODBC 2.0 defines about 61 API calls that fall into three conformance levels:

- *Core* provides 23 base calls that let you connect to a database, execute SQL statements, fetch results, commit and rollback transactions, handle exceptions, and terminate the connection.

- *Level 1* provides an additional 19 calls that let you retrieve information from a database catalog, fetch large objects (BLOBs), and deal with driver-specific functions.

- *Level 2* provides yet another additional 19 calls that let you retrieve data using cursors; it supports both forward and backward scrolling.

Applications are responsible for making sure that an ODBC driver supports a conformance level. Note that the X/Open CLI includes ODBC's Core and some of the Level 1 and Level 2 functions. It also includes SQL descriptors that are not in ODBC 2.0. The X/Open CLI does not include the ODBC functions that are specific to Microsoft applications—such as SQL Server, Access, and Excel.

Most database server vendors—including Microsoft, IBM, Oracle, Sybase, Tandem/Compaq, CA/Ingres, and Informix—now support the ODBC API in addition to their native SQL APIs. They also include ODBC drivers for their respective servers. The problem is that ODBC always seems to play second fiddle to the native interfaces on the client and server sides. For example, Oracle supports ODBC as an optional API, but its native CLI is the *Oracle Call-Level Interface (OCI)*. IBM's DB2 family supports ODBC (with extensions) and the X/Open CLI (with extensions), but its native protocol is ESQL/DRDA. Sybase supports ODBC as an optional API, but its native CLI is the *Sybase Open Client*. Informix has no native CLI; it plans to support an extension of ODBC. Microsoft's SQL Server is, of course, the exception; it uses ODBC as its native protocol.

The other problem is that server vendors add their own proprietary extensions to the server driver and to the ODBC CLI (for example, most vendors extend ODBC to support stored procedures). If you really must have a portable ODBC solution, your best bet is to require CLIs and drivers from a third party that specializes in ODBC. The other problem is that server vendors add their own proprietary extensions to the server driver and to the ODBC CLI (for example, most vendors extend ODBC to support stored procedures). If you really must have a portable ODBC solution, your best bet is to require CLIs and drivers from a third party that specializes in ODBC middleware—for example, Intersolv, OpenLink, and Visigenic (see the next Soapbox).

Is CLI Always the Least Common Denominator?

Soapbox

The average corporation has eight databases today, and I'd rather have one common client/server language everyone can speak.

> — *David Waller, Director*
> *Intersolv*

Use native (direct) APIs whenever possible. Standard APIs like ODBC should be considered as a last resort...not the first.

> — *Richard Finkelstein, President*
> *Performance Computing*

The reason Finkelstein doesn't like "standard" CLIs is that they require too many levels of translations before they reach the native APIs. Any type of layering scheme requires release-level synchronizations between the different components, which all come from different vendors. As can be expected, vendors will first support their native API sets and then worry about the "standard CLIs." This means the CLIs will not be synchronized with the latest releases of the database engines and drivers. In addition, the CLI approach on top of database drivers adds layers of complexity. For example, debug is far more complicated. You can expect a lot more fingerpointing between vendors when the protocol stacks, API libraries, database drivers, native OSs, and database engines all have to be in sync for things to work.

But the million-dollar question is: Why can't vendors—like Oracle, Informix Sybase, and IBM—make the ISO SQL/CLI the "native API" of their respective databases? The answer is that each database engine offers a unique set of extensions to native SQL; these extensions require a different set of APIs to invoke their services. Will vendors ever offer a non-extended version of SQL? Of course not—they're out there trying to differentiate their product! So by definition, the common CLI will always be a "least common denominator" approach that is not optimized for a particular database. Database vendors are not likely to reveal their future "extended plans" to standards bodies, so common CLIs will always trail behind the SQL engine's native API capabilities. And forget portability because even the "standard CLIs" have escape clauses (or pass-throughs) that defeat that goal. The bottom line is that any program that takes advantage of the advanced capabilities of a database engine will not be database-neutral. So much for standards! ☐

ODBC 3.5

In November 1996, Microsoft shipped *ODBC 3.0*, which introduces 20 new function calls and supports Unicode. ODBC 3.0 also returns more information on approximately 40 items. In mid-1998, Microsoft introduced ODBC 3.5—a unicode-enabled version of the ODBC driver manager. You should note that Microsoft fully controls the ODBC standard. So the million-dollar question is: Will the future ODBC align itself with the SQL3/CLI, or will it become a proprietary OLE-based standard? According to Microsoft, the answer is all of the above. Microsoft promises SQL3 support, yet it announced OLE DB as the future ODBC replacement (more on this later).

ODBC has many drawbacks. The most serious one is that the specification is controlled by Microsoft, and it is constantly evolving. Its future is also uncertain, given Microsoft's current commitment to OLE DB, which introduces a different programming paradigm—it is object-based rather than procedural. ODBC drivers are also difficult to build and maintain. The current drivers have different ODBC conformance levels, which are not well documented. The ODBC layers introduce a lot of overhead (especially for SQL updates and inserts), and they are seldom as fast as the native APIs. Note that for simple read-only functions, the current ODBC drivers can match native driver performance.

CLI Versus Embedded SQL

Table 11-1 compares the CLI with the more traditional ESQL style of programming.

Table 11-1. ISO SQL/CLI Versus ISO ESQL.

Feature	ISO SQL/CLI Call-Level Interface (CLI)	ISO SQL-92 Embedded SQL (ESQL)
Requires target database to be known ahead of time	No	Yes
Supports static SQL	No (future)	Yes
Supports dynamic SQL	Yes	Yes

Table 11-1. ISO SQL/CLI Versus ISO ESQL. (Continued)

Feature	ISO SQL/CLI Call-Level Interface (CLI)	ISO SQL-92 Embedded SQL (ESQL)
Compile-time type checking	No	Yes
Uses the SQL declarative model	No	Yes
Applications must be precompiled and bound to database server	No	Yes
Easy to program	No	Yes
Tool-friendly	Yes	No
Easy to debug	Yes	No
Easy to package	Yes	No
Supports database-independent catalog tables	Yes	No
Supports database-independent metadata	Yes	No

The Object CLIs: JDBC and OLE DB

The computer industry is moving to object-oriented languages and distributed objects. So it should come as no surprise that CLIs are also moving to object interfaces. Based on tool support, the two most popular object CLIs are *JDBC* and OLE DB's *ActiveX Data Objects (ADO)*. Both provide a CLI that you can access via object interfaces (and classes) instead of procedural APIs. In addition, they both support distributed data access via off-the-shelf ORBs. The following is a brief introduction to JDBC and OLE DB's ADO:

JDBC

JDBC represents the first time that all the major database vendors have agreed upon and supported a single native interface in any language.

> — *Mike Higgs, VP of Development*
> *I-Kinetics*
> *(July, 1998)*

JavaSoft's *Java Database Connection (JDBC)* is a portable SQL CLI written entirely in Java. It lets you write DBMS-independent Java code. Like ODBC and

ISO SQL/CLI, JDBC provides two major sets of interfaces: 1) an *application interface* that lets you access SQL services in a DBMS-independent manner, and 2) a *driver interface* that DBMS vendors must adapt to their particular databases. Like the other CLIs, JDBC uses a driver manager to automatically load the right JDBC driver to talk to a given database (see Figure 11-7).

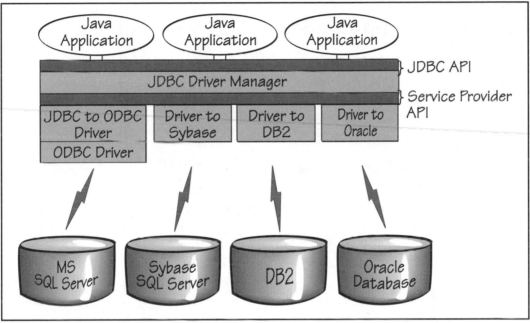

Figure 11-7. The Layers of JDBC.

JDBC Drivers

JDBC drivers are either *direct* or *ODBC-bridged*. A direct driver sits on top of the DBMS's native interface. For example, Symantec provides direct drivers for *Oracle* using OCI, *Sybase* using *DB-Lib*, and Microsoft *SQL Server* and *Access* using ODBC. In contrast to direct drivers, bridged drivers are built on top of existing ODBC drivers. JDBC is patterned after ODBC. Consequently, the translation between these two protocols should be minimal. JavaSoft and Intersolv provide a reference *JDBC-to-ODBC* bridge implementation that makes it easier to translate between JDBC and the various ODBC drivers.

To pass the JDBC compliance tests, a driver must provide at least ANSI SQL92 Entry Level functionality. This is currently the least common denominator among the SQL DBMSs on the market. As a result, the JDBC applications you write are guaranteed to be portable across multivendor DBMSs. Portability is a Java credo. JDBC

reinforces this credo and extends the portable Java core to include multivendor SQL database access. At the last count, there were over 50 different JDBC implementations available from a number of vendors.

JDBC URL Naming

So how does a JDBC application find its database? It does this using the following URL-based naming scheme:

```
jdbc:<subprotocol><domain name>
```

For example, the URL to access "MyJavaDB" via a JDBC-to-ODBC bridge might look like this:

```
jdbc:odbc://www.bob.com/MyJavaDB
```

In this example, the subprotocol is "odbc" and the hostname is "www.bob.com." You can also use this scheme to provide a level of indirection in database names. You do this by specifying a naming service as the subprotocol. Here's an example of a URL that does this:

```
jdbc:dcenaming:MyJavaDB
```

In this example, the URL specifies that the DCE naming service is used to resolve the database name "MyJavaDB" into a global name that connects to the database. JDBC recommends that you provide a pseudo-driver that looks up names via a networked name server. It then uses the information to locate the real driver and pass it the connection information.

The JDBC naming scheme makes it easy for different drivers to use a naming syntax that matches their needs. Each driver needs to understand just a single URL naming syntax; it can then reject any other URLs it encounters. JavaSoft is acting as an informal registry for JDBC subprotocol names.

JDBC is part of the Java core. Consequently, it must pay close attention to mobile code issues. For example, a JDBC driver must prevent an untrusted applet from accessing databases outside its home machine—meaning the machine from which the applet originates. Likewise, a driver that is downloaded as an applet can only be allowed to access its home database. Of course, applets and drivers can get around these limitations by convincing the Java loader that they are trustworthy—for example, by presenting certificates that authenticate them.

JDBC 2-Tier

Figure 11-8 shows a 2-tier JDBC client/server split. In this "fat client" approach, the client maintains JDBC drivers for every database engine it needs. In the pure 2-tier approach, the application logic runs on the client. In a less pure 2-tier approach, you can offload some of the application logic to stored procedures on the database engine. However, you should not use stored procedures if you want your JDBC applications to be portable across multivendor DBMSs.

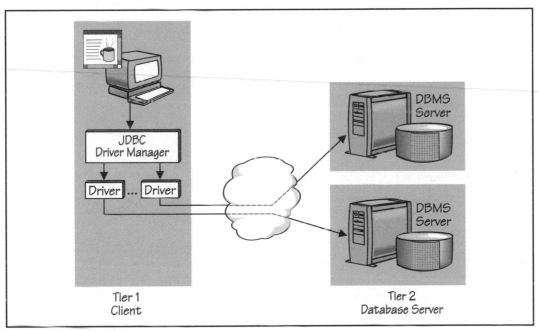

Figure 11-8. JDBC 2-Tier.

JDBC 2-Tier Plus

Figure 11-9 shows an innovative twist on the 2-tier architecture model; we'll call it *2-tier Plus*. The 2-tier Plus approach introduces a middle-tier "JDBC driver server" that sits between the client and the DBMS engines. Clients invoke normal JDBC calls that are then transmitted—via ORB or RPC—to the JDBC driver manager on the server. The driver manager hands the call to the appropriate JDBC driver. In 2-tier Plus, all the JDBC drivers reside on the server side. Examples of 2-tier Plus products include Symantec's *dbANYWHERE*, Visigenic's *VisiChannel*, and I-Kinetics' *OPENjdbc/DataBroker*. Symantec uses a sockets-based RPC to communicate calls between the client and the driver server; Visigenic and I-Kinetics use CORBA. In both cases, the underlying ORB is totally transparent to your clients; you simply invoke JDBC calls.

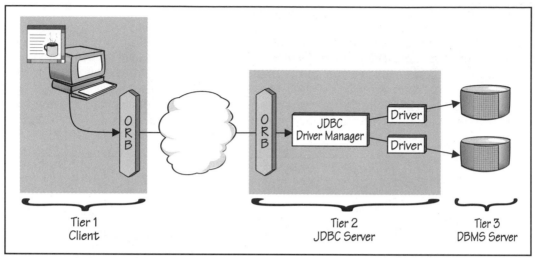

Figure 11-9. JDBC 2-Tier Plus.

The 2-tier Plus approach is a major improvement over simple 2-tier. Here are some of the benefits:

■ *A simpler client environment.* You have less software to install and maintain on the client. You don't need to be constantly deploying the "latest and greatest" JDBC drivers to each client. In addition, you don't have to deal with conflicting JDBC drivers on the client. In general, 2-tier Plus removes some of the administrative burdens associated with managing the 2-tier client.

■ *A mixed client environment.* For example, I-Kinetics provides CORBA IDL definitions of the JDBC interface. This allows clients written in any CORBA-compliant language (such as C++ and Smalltalk) to invoke its JDBC middle-tier server. If you think about it, this provides a language-independent data access solution based on the CORBA and JDBC standards; it's very similar to OLE DB.

■ *Standard client/server middleware.* Both I-Kinetics and Visigenic use CORBA IIOP as a standard client/server middleware for JDBC. The I-Kinetics middle-tier server—called *DataBroker*—supports any IIOP-compliant CORBA ORB—including VisiBroker and Orbix.

■ *A managed server environment.* All the drivers are on the server. This makes it easier to upgrade, maintain, and control the JDBC environment. It lets you easily add or replace third-party JDBC drivers. It also reduces your administrative overhead.

- *A more secure environment.* You can centralize all data access controls on the server. You're also dealing with a single point of management for security.

- *A better performing client/server environment.* The 2-tier Plus architecture could potentially improve the performance of a system by caching data on the server. For example, *dbANYWHERE* allows a server to satisfy requests for recently accessed data directly from its cache; it doesn't need to access the DBMS for every request. In addition, *dbANYWHERE* can cache the results of a large query; it then returns, on demand, subsets of the query results. In theory, caching can dramatically reduce bandwidth requirements. Consequently, it can improve performance.

You must remember that 2-tier Plus is still a fat client approach. The bulk of the application logic still runs on the client. On the plus side, the client can be a lot slimmer than its 2-tier counterpart; the drivers are now on the server.

JDBC 3-Tier

Figure 11-10 shows a 3-tier JDBC split using distributed objects. In this next step up in the evolutionary scale, a significant part of the application is offloaded from the client to server-side objects. Any function that deals with JDBC data should be on the server side. The idea is to make the application that handles the data reside on the server with the JDBC drivers and possibly the DBMS engine. You can always offload some of the processing by running the DBMS engines on their own server machines. It's all one big trade-off.

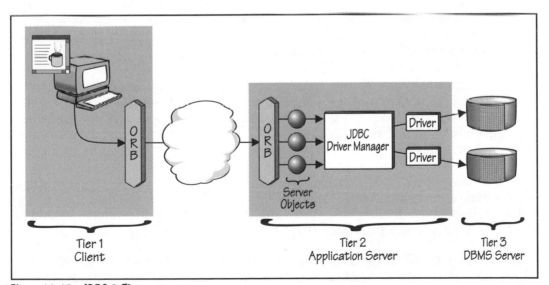

Figure 11-10. JDBC 3-Tier.

OLE DB and ADO

Everything that Microsoft does is COM- and Windows-related. Nobody, not even Microsoft's biggest adversaries, can blame Microsoft for being inarticulate about their strategy.

> — Max Dolgicer, Director
> International Systems Group
> (July, 1998)

The latest Microsoft strategy for data is simply called the *Universal Data Access (UDA)*. The goal of this strategy is to provide ORB-based access to any type of data on any system. The idea is that you should be able to access the data wherever it lives. Of course, the Microsoft ORB is COM+. *OLE DB* defines a set of COM objects and interfaces for data access. ADO provides a data access API on top of OLE DB; it's the CLI for this new type of system. Like JDBC, ADO is based on an object model.

OLE DB defines a set of interfaces (and classes) that mediate between *data providers* and *data consumers* (see Figure 11-11). Data providers are OLE DB components that represent a specific data source—SQL data, spreadsheets, file systems, directories, multi-dimensional data, e-mail messages, Web pages, and so on. Providers return data using an OLE DB abstraction called a *rowset;* it's a table that can also contain embedded tables in its columns—you can think of it as a multi-dimensional table. In contrast, an ODBC *result set* only returns two-dimensional tables. Data consumers are applications that access this data; OLE DB provides a set of classes that you can use to consume data. The *service* components act as both providers and consumers. They provide value-added data functions like joins, cursor manipulations, and transformations.

ADO is a higher-level programming model for OLE DB; it's a replacement for two Microsoft data access protocols—*Data Access Object (DAO)* and *Remote Data Objects (RDO)*. ADO supports a variety of front-end tools and programming languages—including Visual Basic, PowerBuilder, Delphi, Java, and JavaScript. It also provides a *Remote Data Service (RDS)* component that supports client-side caching (with updates) and data-aware controls. The ADO object model consists of: 1) *connection* objects that represent a connection to a data source, 2) *command* objects that represent a query (or command) to be executed on the data source, and 3) a *recordset* object that represents the results of the query. This model should be quite familiar if you program with JDBC (or ODBC).

So where does ODBC fit in this grand Microsoft strategy? It's now the SQL data source provider. ODBC vendors must provide OLE DB adapters for their data sources to play in this universal data access game. Today, you can buy these

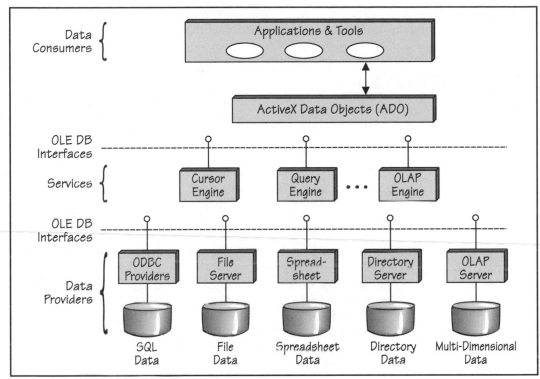

Figure 11-11 The Microsoft Universal Data Access Architecture.

adapters from Intersolv. In late 1997, Microsoft released a client ODBC bridge that acts as an ODBC consumer—it takes an ODBC request and converts it into an OLE DB invocation. The company also released an OLE DB driver adapter for ODBC—an ODBC producer. In the bigger scheme of things, Microsoft is positioning OLE DB as the successor to ODBC. It is adding new OLE DB features that aren't yet available in ODBC. Eventually, Microsoft will recommend that you use pure OLE DB drivers for SQL support. So, for Microsoft, ODBC appears to be just a short-term solution until OLE DB becomes ubiquitous.

Microsoft delivered the first pieces of the OLE DB infrastructure in October 1996. Two years later, there are some supporting products on the market—including OLE DB adapters for Lotus Notes, a variety of e-mail systems, and DBMSs. In addition, Microsoft ships OLE DB data providers for both MVS VSAM files and AS/400 files. It also intends to deliver data providers for both LDAP and Active Directory. Finally, Microsoft is bundling OLE DB and ADO with most of its products—including Internet Explorer 4.0, IIS 4.0, Windows 98, and NT 5.0.

Microsoft's universal data access strategy faces some stiff competition from Oracle's CORBA/Java data *Cartridges* as well as from data warehouses. We will have more to say about OLE DB (and its competitors) in later chapters—this brief introduction was just to introduce the CLI element in OLE DB.

OPEN SQL GATEWAYS

The average client/server site today runs 12 operating systems, 9 databases, and 17 development tools.

> — *Bob Breton, Product Manager*
> *Sybase*
> *(May, 1998)*

In this section, we look at "open SQL gateways" that translate the SQL calls into an industry-standard common *Format and Protocol (FAP)*. The FAP provides the common wire-level protocol between the client and the server. As we explained earlier in this chapter, the gateway acts as the broker that translates client API calls into the FAP format, transports them, and then maps them to the appropriate server calls (and vice versa). The open gateway must provide (or support) a standard SQL interface (CLI or ESQL). It must also be able to locate remote servers and provide catalog services without requiring an intermediary database server. Finally, it must provide tools for creating the server side of the gateway.

We will look at the three contending architectures (or products) for common FAPs: ISO/SAG *Remote Data Access (RDA)*, IBM's *Distributed Relational Data Access (DRDA)*, and IBI's *EDA/SQL*—an open gateway that currently supports more than 72 database server platforms. Gateways are a temporary fix until vendors agree on a common FAP and implement it *natively* on their servers—don't hold your breath waiting. So we will look at which of the contending FAPs has the best chance of becoming this common standard (see the next Briefing box).

 FYI

RDA and DRDA: More Than Just Gateways

Briefing

DRDA and RDA are more than just gateway protocols. They both provide end-to-end architectures for creating true federated distributed databases. Most gateways simply pass an SQL statement to a remote database system, generally treating each SQL statement as a separate transaction. DRDA and RDA aim at supporting multisite transactions (though RDA isn't quite there yet). Some gateways handle character conversions but don't have all the sophisticated fea-

> tures provided by DRDA and RDA for creating common data representations. Gateways typically link two locations; DRDA and RDA are built to support data backbones (with multiple entry and exit points). ❑

IBI EDA/SQL

Enterprise Data Access/SQL (EDA/SQL), from Information Builders Incorporated (IBI), is a family of open gateway products that uses SQL to access over 72 relational and non-relational database servers—an industry record. EDA/SQL is a continuation of IBI's twelve-year experience in developing gateway code primarily for read-only query access. According to IDC, IBI now owns over 10% of the data access middleware market; its 1997 data access revenues grew by 24% to $62 million. This puts IBI in the number-one spot in terms of marketshare.[2]

Figure 11-12 shows the EDA/SQL components. Here's what they do:

■ **API/SQL** is another "common" CLI that uses SQL-92 as the standard database access language. API/SQL will pass-through SQL calls that it does not recognize. The calls can be issued asynchronously—meaning the client application does not have to block waiting for the call to complete. Clients can query the status of any pending requests. API/SQL also provides an RPC call that can be used to invoke CICS transactions or user-written procedures. API/SQL is available on DOS, Windows, Windows 95/98, OS/2, OS/400, AIX, Solaris, VAX/VMS, HP-UX, MVS, VM, Wang/VS, and Mac OS.

■ **EDA/Extenders** are utilities that allow API/SQL calls to be issued from within existing products that support some form of dynamic SQL. You can think of the extenders as "redirectors" of SQL calls. Of course, the calls get redirected to API/SQL, which then routes them through the gateway network. Extenders are provided for many popular client applications, Web browsers, and database front-end tools that work with popular databases—relational or non-relational. In addition, IBI has developed, with Microsoft, an ODBC driver for EDA/SQL gateway servers. Today, many popular client tools—for example, Symantec—are being delivered "EDA-enabled" out of the box.

■ **EDA/Link** supports over 12 communication protocols—including NetBIOS, Named Pipes, SNA, TCP/IP, and DECnet. EDA/Link provides password verification and authentication; it also handles message format translations. And, it lets you create communications profiles using pop-up menus. The stacks it supports vary with different client/server configurations.

---

[2] Source: IDC, *Middleware: 1998 Worldwide Markets and Trends* (May, 1998).

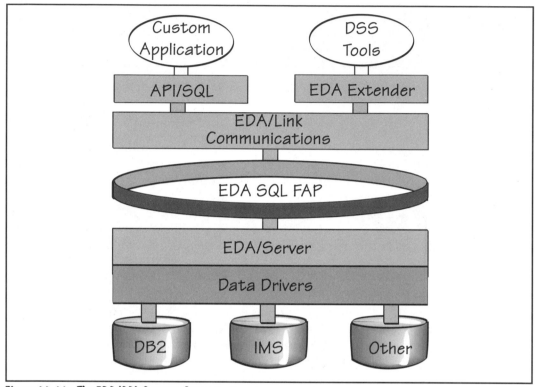

Figure 11-12. The EDA/SQL Gateway Components.

- **EDA/Server** is a multithreaded catcher that typically resides on the target database server machine. It receives client requests and translates them into server-specific commands. If the target database is relational, it passes the ANSI-compliant SQL directly to the *EDA/Data Driver*. If the target database is not relational, SQL requests are passed through the *Universal SQL Translator*, which maps the SQL syntax of the incoming request into the data manipulation language that is specific to that server's driver. EDA/Server also handles security, authentication, statistics gathering, and some system management. EDA/Servers are available for every known database server. In addition, IBI provides an EDA/SQL "Transaction Server" for CICS and IMS using EDA/SQL RPCs.

- **EDA/Data Drivers** provide access to data in over 72 different formats. These drivers take care of any variations in syntax, schema, data types, catalog naming conventions, and data representation. A specific data driver must be installed for each data source you need to access.

In early 1998, IBI extended its line with two Java-related products: a JDBC interface and a Java-based CORBA ORB called *Enterprise Component Broker (ECB)*. The

ORB extends EDA's middleware with a modern infrastructure (see Figure 11-13). It allows CORBA and Java clients to access data on the 72 database and file structures that EDA supports today. ECB provides a complete environment for developing and configuring distributed, data-aware Java beans. With ECB's built-in *Visual Configurator*, you develop a data-aware bean by: 1) dragging a generic JavaBean, 2) dropping it on a specialized, EDA-provided Enterprise JavaBean for accessing transaction systems (like IMS) or other specialized data types, and 3) deploying your newly-customized bean to the client or server.

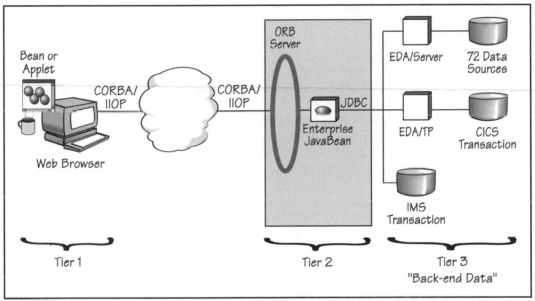

Figure 11-13. EDA Enterprise Component Broker Provides ORB-based Access to 72 Data Sources.

As a parting note, EDA/SQL is an excellent piece of middleware for decision support systems and data warehousing. Its greatest strength is that it can extract data from almost any data source in the universe. However, EDA/SQL does not provide the robust transactional support needed for OLTP and production-type database access. Its FAP is not a complete replacement for existing vendor-specific middleware. Let's look at the RDA and DRDA alternatives to understand why this is the case.

ISO/SAG RDA

ISO 9579 RDA is a standard for universal data access; it is based on the little-used OSI stack. One of SAG's original goals was to port (and extend) the RDA FAP to the TCP/IP protocol; SAG (or X/Open) realized this goal in late 1996. RDA provides functionality that is equivalent to the SQL-89 and SQL-92 (entry) specifications.

However, RDA is not very tolerant of SQL deviations and extensions. The server will reject any SQL command that does not conform to an RDA-defined SQL subset.

The current version of RDA only supports dynamic SQL. RDA allows a client to be connected to more than one database server at a time, but it does not support a two-phase commit protocol to synchronize updates on multiple databases. An RDA client may issue asynchronous requests to a server whenever it desires; it does not have to wait for pending requests to complete.

RDA defines a set of SQL catalog tables that are based on the SQL-92 standard. Again, it doesn't tolerate any catalog deviations. RDA returns error codes using the SQL-92 SQLSTATE return codes. It also supports the SQL-92 subset of SQLCODE return values. All other return codes are rejected. RDA supports a *repetition count* mechanism that lets any operation be repeated one or more times—for example, multirow fetches. Each repetition may use a different set of inputs.

RDA requires that all data exchanged between the client and the server be converted to a common "canonical" format. This means that all data is converted twice—once by the sender and once by the receiver. The benefit is that everybody needs to learn only one common conversion format. The disadvantage is that multiple conversions may result in the loss of data precision and can impact performance, especially when both the client and server use the same protocol.

RDA uses the ISO *Abstract Syntax Notation One (ASN.1)* to define the messages and then encodes (or tags) their contents using the ISO *Basic Encoding Rules (BER)*. BER uses a type/length/value tagging scheme to convey a value. Each data item must be tagged individually, so if a query generates a result set of 20,000 rows, you must tag each field in each of the 20,000 rows—that's a lot of tagging overhead.

In early 1997, the RDA committee was working on defining a two-phase commit protocol based on the *ISO Transaction Processing (ISO TP)* standard. It was also waiting on the final SQL3 specifications for stored procedures before it could incorporate them into RDA v3. In addition, the committee was looking at providing static SQL support along lines similar to DRDA packages (see the next section). By early 1999, ISO intends to publish a new version of the standard under the name *RDA for SQL;* it's not clear what features will be included in the new standard. Note that the U.S. has withdrawn from the ISO RDA effort. The standard is being driven by other countries.

So what's wrong with this picture? Not much, except that RDA is dying because of lack of vendor interest. The major database companies are not implementing it. RDA's only support appears to come from small middleware companies—like *ATI, Retix, Cycle Software,* and *Blue Star.* Consequently, there's very little hope for a standards-based SQL FAP. This means that SQL from different vendors will not interoperate "on-the-wire"—at least not in our lifetime.

IBM's DRDA

IBM's distributed database strategy is known as the *Distributed Relational Database Architecture*, or simply *DRDA*. IBM is promoting DRDA as the standard for federated database interoperability. A number of influential database and gateway vendors—including Oracle, Sybase, Micro Decisionware, IBI, Informix, XDB, Ingres, Inprise (i.e., Borland), Cincom, Progress, Novell, and Centura—now support DRDA. DRDA is the glue that ties the DB2 family together.

DRDA's goal is to provide an interoperability standard for fully distributed heterogeneous relational database environments. To do that, DRDA defines the protocols (or FAPs) for database client-to-server and server-to-server interactions. In DRDA terminology, a client is called an *Application Requester (AR)*, and a database server is an *Application Server (AS)*. The AR-to-AS protocol is used for the typical client/server interactions. The AR-to-AR protocol synchronizes transactions that span across multiple SQL servers; it is also used to route SQL commands from server to server.

Figure 11-14 shows the four levels of database transactions defined by DRDA:

- **Remote request** means one SQL command to one database. This is used mostly for issuing queries among dissimilar systems.

- **Remote unit of work** means many SQL commands to one database. This is your typical client-to-single-server transaction. The client can connect to one database server at a time, issue multiple SQL commands against that server's database, issue a commit to make the work permanent, and then switch over to another database server to start a subsequent unit of work.

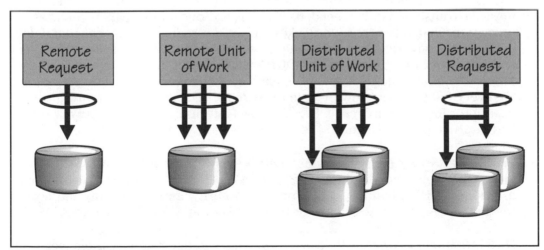

Figure 11-14. DRDA's Four Types of Database Transactions.

- ***Distributed unit of work*** means many SQL commands to many databases but each command goes to one database. This is your typical multiserver transaction. DRDA handles the multisite synchronization, security, and data integrity functions (two-phase commit). It locates remote data sites and coordinates requests (including the update of data) at several locations in a single transaction.

- ***Distributed request*** means many SQL commands to many databases, but each command can execute against multiple databases. With this capability, DRDA can service single requests that span multiple sites, such as a *multisite JOIN*. It can also distribute a single query across multiple servers to improve performance through parallelism.

DRDA Features

DRDA works great if everybody complies with the server's SQL syntax and semantics. But in a heterogeneous world, IS organizations might have to wait a very long time for such compliance.

— *David Stodder, Editor-in-chief*
Database Programming and Design

What type of additional functions does DRDA provide? It mainly handles the thorny network and code portability issues, including:

- ***SQL Message Content and Exchange Protocol:*** DRDA handles the negotiations between clients and servers for supported server attributes. It only does message translations when needed. There is no concept of a canonical message format; instead, it is a "receiver makes it right" protocol. This means that if data needs to be converted, it is only done once. And no conversion is done if a client and server use the same formats. DRDA takes care of dissimilar data representations, catalog structures, and command syntax conversions. DRDA does not tag every field in every row in a multirow result set. Instead, it creates a single descriptor for the entire result set. All these features help reduce network traffic and improve performance.

- ***Transport Stack Independence:*** DRDA supports the MPTN interface, which means that it can run on top of APPC/APPN or TCP/IP for client/server communications. DRDA handles data blocking, security, authentication, and server routing; it also generates alerts for both network and database failures.

- ***Multiplatform Program Preparation:*** DRDA supports under-the-cover, multiplatform program preparation. A program is created locally; its output can be distributed to multiple servers using a remote BIND utility. The BIND process produces executable SQL code (called *packages* or *plans*) on the servers.

- *Static or Dynamic SQL Support:* A DRDA client can invoke the SQL statements on the server one at a time by identifying a package and the statement within it. Packages make it possible to execute precompiled static SQL statements on the servers (including support for cursors).

- *Common Diagnostics:* DRDA returns status information upon completion of each SQL command. DRDA provides a standard set of return codes in the SQLSTATE field (based on the SQL-92 standard). Database-specific return codes are still provided in the SQLCODE field. IBM's DataHub and Tivoli products provide an integrated system management approach to DRDA databases. They perform database management tasks across multiple sites. And, they can trace a transaction through the database network and provide status.

- *Common SQL Syntax:* DRDA recommends using a subset of SQL-92 for application portability across platforms. DRDA also supports target-specific SQL commands for situations when it is more efficient to use SQL extensions. In other words, if the client knows that a server supports certain SQL commands, it can issue the calls and DRDA will convey them to the server. Who says you can't have your cake and eat it, too?

IBM is licensing both the DRDA specifications and the code to interested parties for a nominal fee. At least six major vendors have licensed the DRDA code. IBM also supports the ISO CLI on top of DRDA.

CONCLUSION

The success of SQL has opened up a plethora of interface and middleware "choices." You'll have to decide which one meets your needs best. As we see it, SQL (with its extensions) will remain vendor-specific for a long time to come. If you're using SQL databases for mission-critical applications, the "mix-and-match" of SQL database servers can only spell trouble. You might have to accept some form of vendor lock-in, in return for the convenience of getting more SQL power, better support, platform portability, and finding somebody to blame. The situation is better for decision-support systems and data warehouses. There, you have a much better chance of working with data from multivendor database platforms. The current SQL federated database middleware can easily support these kinds of "non-mission-critical" applications. We'll discuss this in more detail in the next chapter.

Chapter 12

Data Warehouses: Information Where You Want It

In a half-decade or so, data warehousing and its mutant forms have gone from theory derided by academics to conventional wisdom...Data warehousing has more than delivered on the hype made on its behalf.

— Bill Inmon
(January, 1998)

This chapter provides an overview of the technology used to create *data warehouses*—one of the most exciting new developments in client/server databases. "Warehouses" provide the foundation technology for creating intelligent clients that look like Danny DeVito's desktop in the movie *Other People's Money*. For those of you who haven't seen this movie, Danny's closest associate was an information-hungry PC that literally lived on real-time data, which it grabbed (or got fed) from multiple sources. Danny's PC would continuously grab data, massage it, and present it in dynamic formats—including trends, animations, simulations, and 3-D business graphics—that were relevant to Danny's interests. Danny, of course, was in love with that PC, which he used to make all his investment decisions and lots of money. The poor machine even had to wake him up every morning with an analysis of how his investment portfolio was doing.

WHERE IS THAT OLTP DATA KEPT?

In the year 2000 alone, users will install more storage capacity than the entire decade of the 1990s.

> — Jim Rothnie, Senior VP
> EMC
> (May, 1998)

Modern businesses live on data. The total quantity of data on computers currently doubles every five years. With the proliferation of client/server (and multimedia) technology, we expect data to double at least once a year in the future. So who is creating all this data? The answer is modern institutions in the course of conducting their everyday business. The computerized production systems that collect and consume this data are called OLTP systems—these are true data factories that run around the clock.

What Is OLTP?

Database-centered client/server applications fall into two categories: *Decision-Support Systems (DSS)* and *Online Transaction Processing (OLTP)*. These two client/server categories provide dramatically different types of business solutions. These differences need to be understood before we can appreciate what data warehouses have to offer.

OLTP systems are used to create applications in all walks of business. These include reservation systems, point-of-sale, tracking systems, inventory control, stockbroker workstations, and manufacturing shop floor control systems. These are typically mission-critical applications that require a 1-3 second response time 100% of the time. The number of clients supported by an OLTP system may vary dramatically throughout the day, week, or year, but the response time must be maintained. OLTP applications also require tight controls over the security and integrity of the database. The reliability and availability of the overall system must be very high. Data must be kept consistent and correct.

In OLTP systems, the client typically interacts with a Transaction Server instead of a Database Server. This interaction is necessary to provide the high performance these applications require. Transaction servers come in two flavors: *OLTP Lite*, provided by stored procedures, and *OLTP Heavy*, provided by TP Monitors. In either case, the client invokes *remote procedures* that reside on a server. These remote procedures execute as transactions against the server's database (more on this in Part 5). OLTP applications require code to be written both for the client component and for the server transactions. The communication overhead in OLTP applications is kept to a minimum. The client interaction with the transaction server is typically limited to short, structured exchanges. The exchange consists of a single request/reply as opposed to multiple SQL message exchanges.

Is Client/Server Creating New Islands of OLTP?

Today, even the smallest business can quickly build up large databases—by capturing transactions from cash registers and using Web servers that produce gigabytes of data after short operational periods.

> — *Usama Fayyad, Senior Researcher*
> *Microsoft*
> *(March, 1998)*

In the old days, OLTP applications ran on expensive mainframes that stored massive amounts of data, provided minimum downtime, and were the pride of the enterprise and the MIS shops. Today, the top-of-the-line OLTP applications—such as airline reservations, banking, stock markets, airport control towers, and hospitals—still run on expensive Unix superservers and mainframes; MIS shops still control them. However, today any department with enough budget to buy a few PCs, hook them on a client/server LAN, and hire a programmer (or consultant) can create its *own* OLTP application. In addition, almost anyone can open shop on the Internet by simply investing in a Web application server.

In other words, database-centric, client/server technology has lowered the barriers of entry for creating private or department-owned OLTP systems. These systems are giving departments (and individuals) total autonomy and control over the applications they create and the data they gather. At the extreme, an entire OLTP system can run on a Web application server; all the data collected can be kept private (in other words, outside the reach of the enterprise). We all know how easy it is to create ad hoc database systems on stand-alone PCs using spreadsheets and simple database tools.

In general, all the data collected by an OLTP system is of direct use to the application and people that are creating this data. They understand exactly what this data means. And they know how to use it to solve their immediate day-to-day production problems. The application typically provides a sophisticated graphical interface to view and manipulate the data with transactional controls. The members of the organization understand how the data is structured. They can create sophisticated built-in reports and manipulate the data for their production uses.

What happens if somebody outside the direct OLTP group needs this data? How do they know what data is available? Where do they find it? How do they access it?

What format will it be in? And, what will it mean? The last thing the OLTP people want is to give outsiders access to their precious production systems. These outsiders often don't really know what they want, and they may be issuing long ad hoc queries that can slow down the entire production system, corrupt the data, and create deadlocks.

In the old days, the outsiders could ask their MIS representatives to deal with their MIS counterparts that controlled production data to give them an indication of what data was available and how to get to it. With the proliferation of departmental OLTP (and individual) solutions, even MIS doesn't know what data is available anymore. The data in the enterprise is fragmented, and we've gone back to islands of data processing. Data ends up being all over the place: on the client that originates it, on the departmental server, Web server, one of many federated servers, or on the enterprise server. There is no integrated view.

One of the great attractions of client/server and PCs is the autonomy they provide. Most of us feel disassociated with enterprise data and would prefer local control of our resources. In many cases, our new-found freedom causes us to withdraw into our own little production turfs and ignore the needs of the larger community. We've created a dichotomy between the departmental (or personal) needs and the needs of the organization or larger community. We've also created a dichotomy between production data and informational data.

So who are these "outsiders" we're trying to keep off our turf? They're the people who comb through data looking for patterns, trends, and informational nuggets that can help them make better decisions. Creating barriers to data is like creating barriers to trade. If they can't get to our data and we can't get to theirs, then everybody loses. Precious data is kept out of the reach of those who may need it most.

INFORMATION AT YOUR FINGERTIPS

How do we preserve the local autonomy of production systems and yet allow access to outsiders? How do we make sure the outsiders don't impact the production systems? What data is made available to those outsiders? What data is kept private within the production system? Who owns the shared data? Who can update it? Should we allow direct access to production data or copy it to another database? How is extracted data maintained and refreshed? We'll answer all these questions in this chapter. But first, let's look at the informational needs of these outsiders and understand how decision-support systems differ from OLTP production systems.

Information Hounds

The road from raw data to knowledge is a long and arduous one.

> — **Usama Fayyad, Senior Researcher**
> **Microsoft**
> **(March, 1998)**

Let's give a name to these "outsiders" who want to consume our information. They range from those with compulsive appetites for data—like the character played by Danny DeVito in the movie *Other People's Money*—to those with occasional needs—such as a student researching a term paper. What shall we call them? How about *decision makers*? Or, would you prefer *information hounds*? Let's settle on *information hounds* because it captures the role millions of us will soon be able to play with database warehouse technology. Anyone with a PC connected to a data warehouse will be able do the same types of things the Danny DeVito character did.

Of course, the first ones to consume this technology are business people making strategic decisions—pricing and market analysis—that depend on the availability of timely and accurate data. The ability to access information and act on it quickly will become increasingly critical to any company's (or individual's) success. Raw data becomes information when it gets into the hands of someone who can put it in context and use it. The data is the raw ingredient, which makes all this possible. There are many parallels between the manufacturing and distribution of goods and the manufacturing and distribution of information. High-impact, high-value decision making involves risk. Making decisions using old, incomplete, inconsistent, or invalid data puts a business at a disadvantage versus the competition.

Information is becoming a key component of every product and service. For example, analysts use information to spot the trends and shifts in buying patterns of consumers. Information sleuthing is an iterative process. The sophistication of queries increases as the information hound grasps more of the nuances of the

business problem. The hound needs the ability to access information for multiple combinations of "what if" situations.

An example may help explain the value of timely information. An unnamed apparel manufacturer was having problems reconciling the fast-moving fashion season with a distribution system that replenished stock based on what was forecast. The manufacturer decided to adopt a different technique and put in a system that collected daily sales information from the point-of-sale registers. The company also invested in analysis tools for knowledge workers and executives who needed to watch the daily sales. As a result, the manufacturer was able to cut costs by $47 million, resulting in a profit increase of over 25%. So timely information is highly valuable to some people.

What Is a Decision-Support System?

Decision-Support Systems (DSS) are used to analyze data and create reports. They provide the business professional and information hounds with the means to obtain exactly the information they need. A successful decision-support system must provide the user with flexible access to data and the tools to manipulate and present that data in all kinds of report formats. Users should be able to construct elaborate queries, answer "what if" questions, search for correlations in the data,

plot the data, and move it into other applications such as spreadsheets and word processor documents. Decision-support systems are not generally time-critical and can tolerate slower response times. Client/server decision-support systems are typically not suitable for mission-critical production environments. They have poor integrity controls and limited multitable access capabilities. Finding information may involve large quantities of data, which means that the level of concurrency control is not very granular; for example, a user may want to view and update an entire table.

Decision-support systems are built using a new generation of screen-layout tools that allow non-programmers to build GUI front-ends and reports by painting, pointing, and clicking. Point-and-click query builders take the work out of formulating the question.

What Is an Executive Information System?

Executive Information Systems (EIS) are even more powerful, easy-to-use, and business-specific than DSS tools. And they're certainly more expensive, which may explain why the "executive" attribute is in the name. In any case, distinctions between EIS and DSS are becoming less clear. The EIS tools have recently expanded their scope and offer a broader range of functions at the enterprise level. Dick Lockert, an information guru, makes a case that the "E" in EIS stands for "Enterprise" instead of "Executive" because these systems now have hundreds of users with many roles such as executive, manager, and business analyst. Some vendors prefer to call them "Everyone's Information Systems" while still charging a small fortune for their tools. If this is not confusing enough, you may often hear these evolving EIS/DSS systems referred to as *Online Analytical Processing (OLAP)* or *Multidimensional Analysis (MDA)* tools. At the upper echelons, they're called *Data Mining* tools or *Intelligent Agents*. If you prefer, let's simply call them the Danny DeVito tools (see the next Briefing box).

Regardless of what they're called, these tools are creating a huge market. According to Dataquest, the low-end query and reporting tools and OLAP viewers accounted for $768 million in license revenue in 1997—up 19% from 1996. These new-breed tools allow information hounds to perform deeper levels of analysis on totally up-to-date, real-time data that is obtained from internal business systems—such as OLTP-driven financial, personnel, and customer information systems—and external data sources—such as Dow Jones, Reuters and the Web.

Because the Danny DeVito tools were originally designed for executives, all information is presented in highly visual forms. Extraneous details are filtered out to suit the user's needs. These tools offer unique features—including "hot spot" finders, "slice and dice," "goal seekers," and "drill-downs" to related information. They also provide more mundane features—including graphs, charts, statistical

analysis, trends, queries, reports, and project management. The tools specialize in presenting information using visual metaphors that make it easy to navigate and sift through tons of data. Some of the better tools are used to discover late-breaking news on competitors, suppliers, government legislation, market research, economic conditions, or the latest stock market quotes.

Comparing Decision-Support and OLTP Systems

As shown in Table 12-1, decision-support applications can be created directly by end-users. Network administrators are still needed to help set up the client/server system, and Database Administrators (DBAs) may help assemble collections of tables, views, and columns that are relevant to the user (the user should then be able to create decision-support applications without further DBA involvement). The design of client/server systems for OLTP is a lot more involved. In OLTP, performance and high availability are kings; if the OLTP system stops, your business stops. Consequently, OLTP systems require a large amount of custom programming effort. We discuss OLTP system requirements in Parts 5.

Table 12-1. Comparing the Programming Effort for Decision Support and OLTP.

Client/Server Application	Client	Server	Messages
Decision Support	Off-the-shelf decision-support tool with end-user scripting. Canned event handlers and communications with the server.	Off-the-shelf database server. Tables usually defined by DBAs as part of a data warehouse.	SQL queries and joins.
OLTP	Custom application. GUI tool lays out screen, but the event handlers and remote procedure calls require programming at the C or Java level.	Custom application. Transaction code must be programmed at the C or Java level. The database is off-the-shelf.	Custom function calls are optimized for performance and secure access.

Production Versus Informational Databases

By looking across multiple quarters, corporations can start to see the forest from the trees. They can start to understand the seasonality of their business across multiple years.

— Bill Inmon
(January, 1998)

Table 12-2 compares the database requirements of OLTP and decision-support systems. We need to understand the differences to get some better insights into what data warehousing can do for information hounds. The key point of difference is that decision-support data needs to be stable at a snapshot in time for reporting purposes. Production databases reflect the up-to-the-minute state of the business in real time. Information hounds typically don't want the data changed so frequently that they can't get the same answer twice in a row. So informational copies may be updated less frequently.

Decision-support data—or *informational data*—is collected from multiple sources; production data is collected by OLTP applications. The raw data that decision-support systems extract from production databases is not normally updated directly. However, information hounds have a high requirement to tailor the informational database to their specific needs. This process is called "derived data enhancement." The informational database may contain derived data that records changes over time and summaries. Information hounds are rarely interested in a specific past event. They're always looking at summaries and trends. They need to understand the larger picture before they zoom-in on interesting details.

Table 12-2. Database Needs: OLTP Versus DSS.

Feature	OLTP Database Needs	Decision-Support Database Needs
Who uses it?	Production workers.	Information hounds.
Timeliness of data	Needs current value of data. Reports cannot be reconstructed.	Needs stable snapshots of time-stamped data. Point in time refresh intervals are controlled by user. Reports can be reconstructed using stable data.
Frequency of data access	Continuous throughout workday. Work-related peaks may occur.	Sporadic.
Data format	Raw captured data. No derived data. Detailed and unsummarized transaction data.	Multiple levels of conversions, filtering, summarization, condensation, and extraction.
Data collection	From single application.	From multiple sources—internal and external.
Data source known?	Yes, most of it is generated by single application.	No, it comes from different applications, databases, the Web, and ERP systems.
Timed snapshots or multiple versions?	No, continuous data. Single version.	Yes, you can key off a snapshot's date/time. Each snapshot is a version unless you overwrite it during refresh.

Table 12-2. Database Needs: OLTP Versus DSS. (Continued)

Feature	OLTP Database Needs	Decision-Support Database Needs
Data access pattern	Multiple users updating production database.	Mostly single-user access. Intense usage on an occasional basis. For example, when a report is due.
Can data be updated?	Current value is continuously updated.	Read-only, unless you own the replica.
Flexibility of access	Inflexible, access to data via precompiled programs and stored procedures.	Very flexible via a query generator, multi-table joins, and OLAP.
Performance	Fast response time is a requirement. Highly automated, repetitive tasks.	Relatively slow.
Data requirements	Well understood. Known prior to construction.	Fuzzy and unstable. A lot of detective work and discovery. Subject-oriented data.
Information scope	Finite. Whatever is in the production database.	Data can come from anywhere.
Average number of records accessed	Less than 10 individual records.	100s to 1000s of records in sets.

THE DATA WAREHOUSE

The "data warehouse" in the client/server environment is the repository of data for decision-support processing.

— Bill Inmon (1993)[1]

Bill Inmon is credited as being the "father of the data warehouse," a concept he started writing about as far back as 1981. Inmon argues that "one cornerstone of client/server applications is the notion of the difference between and separation of operational and decision-support processing." In September 1991, IBM announced its *Information Warehouse* framework, an event that "sparked much interest in the industry." By the middle of 1994, hundreds of data warehouse products started to ship—including various decision-support tools, Sybase 10's replicated server, Oracle7's replication facility, Teradata, Ingres' Replica Manager, MDI Database Gateway, Red Brick, Prism Solutions' Warehouse Manager, Evolutionary Technologies Extract ToolSuite, Trinzic Corp's InfoPump, and Digital's Data Distributor.

---

[1] Source: W.H. Inmon, **Developing Client/Server Applications** (QED, 1993).

In early 1996, we counted over a dozen "integrating" *Data Warehouse Frameworks* from leading vendors—including HP's *OpenWarehouse*, Sybase's *Warehouse Works*, IBM's *Information Warehouse*, Software AG's *Open Data Warehouse Initiative*, Informix's *Data Warehouse*, AT&T's *Enterprise Information Factory*, Prism's *Warehouse Manager*, Red Brick's *PaVER Program*, SAS Institute's *SAS System*, Pyramid's *Smart Warehouse*, and Oracle's *Warehouse Technology Initiative*.

These "frameworks" are nothing more than loose coalitions of vendors that provide a data warehouse solution on a particular database platform (or tool). The framework, at most, defines common metadata and APIs. Of course, the coalitions are formed because no single vendor is able to provide the entire data warehouse solution on its own—large data warehouses are probably the most complex forms of client/server systems in existence. Each partner in the coalition provides one or more pieces of the data warehousing jigsaw—for example, data extraction, copy management, EIS/DSS tools, information directories, or parallel database engines.

By late 1998, over 95% of large corporations either had adopted or were planning to adopt data warehousing technology. Meta Group predicts that data warehouses will grow into an $8 billion market in 1998—a jump of 40% over 1997.[2] This is a lot more attractive than 1997's 7% growth for databases. Obviously, all the major database vendors want to own a piece of this huge market. They're being joined by hundreds of new niche players that are vying for smaller pieces of the action via their participation in the various coalitions. The smaller vendors are adeptly providing key pieces of technology such as multivendor replication, data cleansing and purification, multidimensional databases, information and metadata repositories, and tools of every stripe.

What's a Data Warehouse?

Bill Inmon and vendors like Teradata define a *warehouse* as a separate database for decision support, which typically contains vast amounts of information. Richard Hackathorn defines a *warehouse* as "a collection of data objects that have been inventoried for distribution to a business community."[3] In our own modest definition, a warehouse is an active intelligent store of data that can manage and aggregate information from many sources, distribute it where needed, and activate business policies. We hope that one of these definitions will ring a bell for you.

---

[2] Source: Meta Group, *Data Warehouse Corporate Scorecard* (April, 1998). These numbers include the sales of data warehouse hardware, software, and services.

[3] Source: Richard D. Hackathorn, **Enterprise Database Connectivity** (Wiley, 1993).

The Elements of Data Warehousing

A *warehouse is a place; warehousing is a process.*

> — *Richard Hackathorn*
> *(May, 1995)*

The first step on the road to data warehousing Nirvana is to understand the constituent elements that make up a solution. Almost all data warehousing systems provide the following four elements (see Figure 12-1):

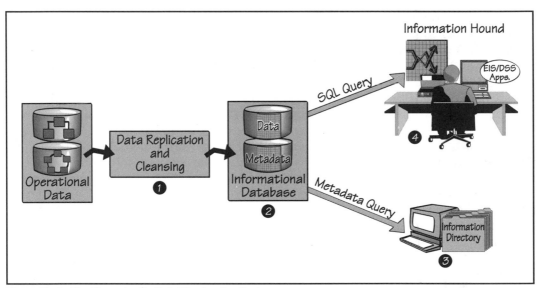

Figure 12-1. The Elements of a Data Warehousing System.

1. ***The data replication manager***—sometimes called "the *warehouse manager*"—manages the copying and distribution of data across databases as defined by the information hound. The hound defines the data that needs to be copied, the source and destination platforms, the frequency of updates, and the data transforms. *Refresh* involves copying over the entire data source; *update* only propagates the changes. Everything can be automated or done manually. Data can be obtained from relational or non-relational sources. Note that almost all external data is *transformed* and *cleansed* before it's brought into the warehouse. We will be covering data replication in detail in the next sections.

2. ***The informational database*** is a relational database that organizes and stores copies of data from multiple data sources in a format that meets the needs of information hounds. Think of it as the decision-support server that transforms, aggregates, and adds value to data from various production sources. It also stores *metadata* (or data about data) that describes the contents of the

informational database. *System-level metadata* describes the tables, indexes, and source extracts to a database administrator (DBA); *semantic-level metadata* describes the contents of the data to an information hound. The informational database can be a personal database on a PC, a medium-sized database on a local server, or a massively parallel database on an enterprise server. Most of the major SQL database engines can be now be used as informational databases. The new features they provide to improve query executions include *bitmap indexes*, *star query* optimizations, and *cost-based* parallel-aware optimizers. We will have more to say on information database engines in the next two chapters.

3. ***The information directory*** combines the functions of a technical directory, business directory, and information navigator. Its primary purpose is to help the information hound find out what data is available on the different databases, what format it's in, and how to access it. It also helps the DBAs manage the data warehouse. The information directory gets its metadata by discovering which databases are on the network and then querying their metadata repositories. It tries to keep everything up-to-date. Some estimates claim that information hounds in large enterprises spend 80% of their time gathering data and 20% of the time analyzing it. Sometimes the hounds don't even know the names of the objects they're looking for, where they're located, and how to access them. The information directory helps alleviate these problems by serving as a business directory.

DBAs use the information directory to access system-level metadata, keep track of data sources, data targets, cleanup rules, transformation rules, and details about predefined rules and reports.

Examples of information/metadata directories include Enterprise Solutions' *InfoCat*, Prism's *Warehouse Directory*, IBM's *DataGuide*, Logic Works' *Universal Directory*, Blue Angel's *MetaStar*, Cornerstone's *Information Catalog Guide*, One Meaning's *Marlow*, ETI's *Extract and Metadata Exchange*, and Apertus/Carleton's *Passport Relational Dictionary*. Many of these products comply with the Metadata Coalition's new *MetaData Interchange Specification v1.1 (MDIS)* adopted in mid-1997 (see *http://www.he.net/~metadata/standards/toc.html*).

4. ***EIS/DSS tool support*** is provided via SQL. Most vendors support ODBC and some other protocol. Some vendors—for example, Red Brick—provide extended SQL dialects for fast queries and joins. The tools are more interested in sequential access of large data quantities than access to a single record. This means that you must tune the table indexes for queries and sequential reads as opposed to updates. In addition, most data warehouse vendors have alliances with OLAP and data mining tool vendors. We cover these tools in the next chapter.

In summary, data warehousing is the process of automating EIS/DSS systems using the four elements we just described. You must be able to assemble data from different sources, replicate it, cleanse it, store it, catalog it, and then make it available to EIS/DSS tools. The trick is to be able to automate the process and have it run like clockwork.

What's Being Automated?

One major difference between an OLTP system and a data warehouse is the ability to accurately describe the past. OLTP systems are poor at correctly representing a business as of a month or year ago. A good OLTP system is always evolving.

> — *Ralph Kimball, Founder*
> *Red Brick*

Data warehousing is a framework for automating all aspects of the decision-support process. Instead of asking the database administrators (DBAs) what information is available, the information hounds can now directly consult the information directory. Of course, like all good DBAs, the information directory obtains its data definitions from the metadata stored on the various servers.

The hounds simply use the replication manager to perform copies of the data instead of asking the DBAs to do that. The replication manager keeps the informational databases automatically refreshed (or updated) with changes from the source database. If you really want to take automation to the extreme, you may consider using a *workflow manager* to orchestrate the multistep movement of data through the network. For each step of the process—and there can be many steps—the workflow manager knows which tool to invoke and what to do next.

Finally, the informational database is a normal SQL database that replaces all the private schemes that information hounds have used to store copies of their favorite data extracts. Data warehousing makes it easy for the hounds to get to their data and removes the overburdened DBAs from the loop (now they can focus their attention on the OLTP side of the house).

Warehouse Hierarchies: The Datamarts

Datamarts are a bit like children. Sometimes they come along whether those in charge of the warehouse program plan them or not.

> — *Richard Winter, President*
> *Winter Corporation*
> *(July, 1998)*

You can create almost any type of topology with data warehouses. Figure 12-2 shows a multilevel topology that's currently very popular. All data extracts—from production databases—are first applied against an enterprise data warehouse. Once the data gets into the enterprise warehouse, it can then be distributed, as needed, to departmental warehouses, also known as datamarts. These datamarts are organized by subjects that are of interest to a department—for example, sales data and customers for the West Coast region. According to Dataquest, the datamart sector of the data warehouse market grew by 205% in 1997. However, in that same year, datamarts accounted for less than 5% of total data warehouse sales. So it's a small but rapidly exploding market.

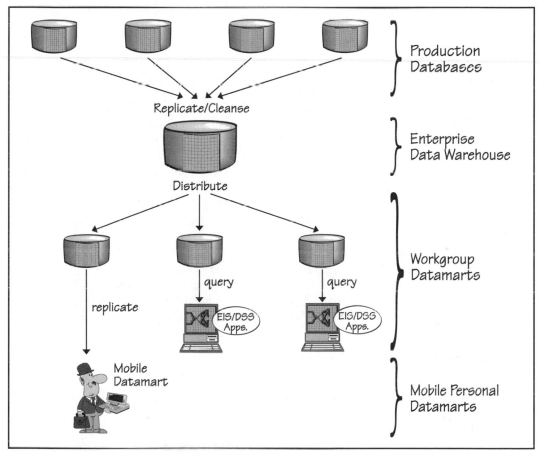

Figure 12-2. The Top-Down Approach to Data Warehousing.

There is also a growing interest in *mobile datamarts*. These are personal warehouses that you can load in a laptop and take with you on the road. For example, real-estate brokers could carry a multiple-listing catalog in their laptops. They could then show customers comparative listings during an open house. Mobile

datamarts are built on low-end desktop databases, such as Oracle's *Personal Oracle Lite*, Sybase's *Adaptive SQL Anywhere*, and CA's *OpenIngres/Desktop*. Companies like Synchrologic offer bidirectional replication solutions between desktop databases and a variety of enterprise data sources.

So the million-dollar questions for datamart designers are: Why not get the data directly from the production systems? Why go through all these intermediaries? The answer is that you don't want to slow down the production databases with too many data extracts. In addition, it is better to cleanse the data once rather than cleanse it at each datamart. If nothing else, the data will be consistent throughout the enterprise. Finally, there's talk of turning the enterprise data warehouse into an active information database. It's the place where you want to apply rules to data before you distribute it. On the downside, the centralized approach requires up-front planning and consensus across an organization. It's much easier to spend $20K on a "warehouse in the box" and create your own departmental datamart.

Unfortunately, the "real world" doesn't really work this way. Most organizations typically develop their data warehouses from the bottom up. They start with a small datamart that extracts its data directly from the production databases. If the project succeeds, more datamarts are added incrementally. Soon, you have many isolated datamarts, or the DBAs may try to form a loose federation of datamarts that is collectively called "the data warehouse." The easiest way to do this is to introduce a federated information directory. Finally, some DBAs may succeed in "creating order from chaos" by making a business case for an enterprise data warehouse—the best justification is that it's needed to keep the production people from going insane.

Here are some examples of datamarts with starting prices of under $50,000: Prism's *Prism Scalable Datamart*, IBI's *SmartMart*, Informatica's *PowerMart*, Sagant's *DataMart*, Oracle's *Express Server*, Sybase's *WarehouseNow*, IBM's *Visual Warehouse*, SAS's *Rapid Warehouse Assessment*, Oracle's *Datamart Suite*, Red Brick's *Red Brick Warehouse*, and Informix's *FastStart Datamart*.

Replication Versus Direct Access

> Applications that can tolerate data that is anywhere from a few hours to a day old are much better candidates for replication.
>
> — Glenn Froemming

With the spread of client/server technology and loosely-coupled federated databases, it becomes impractical from many perspectives—performance, security, availability, debt-to-history, and local control—to create a single centralized repository of data. Replicated data management is being increasingly used to remove the capacity, performance, and organizational roadblocks of centralized data access.

Automated copy management—or the management of replicated data—becomes a key technology for sharing data in a federated database environment. Decision-support applications using data warehouses are perfect candidates for replicated data technology. These applications usually tolerate a certain amount of obsolescence—the politically correct term is *volatility*—in their data. Data replication for decision support minimizes the disruption of production systems and allows you to tailor the informational databases to fit your needs.

On the other hand, *direct data access* is required by applications—mostly production OLTP—that cannot tolerate any "volatility" in their data. These applications require "live data" that reflects the state of the business. This type of live data is obtained in distributed situations using one of four approaches:

■ *Using federated databases that support synchronous (or continuous) replication of data*—the target databases must be synchronized within the same transaction boundary as the primary (or source) database. A target database that allows a user to directly update it is called a *replica*. To maintain a single-site update policy, the replica that gets updated becomes the new source database and must immediately propagate its updates. In general, synchronous replicated technology is a risky proposition in federated database environments. It requires support for two-phase commit protocols across heterogeneous databases.

■ *Using a centralized database server*—all the data is kept on one highly-scalable and fault-tolerant server. This solution, if it fits your organizational needs, will give you the least amount of headaches.

■ *Using a single vendor's distributed database multiserver offering*—notice that we did not say multivendor because this technology is still full of holes (see the following Briefing box).

■ *Using a TP Monitor to front-end multivendor database servers*—the database servers must support X/Open's XA protocol to be managed by a TP Monitor. As you will find out in Part 5, this technology can be very attractive in many situations.

In summary, there's a need for both kinds of data access: replicated and direct. The issues of direct access are well understood by the industry; many commercial solutions are available. On the other hand, the management of replicated data within a data warehouse framework is opening up exciting new opportunities. As more PCs become multimedia-enabled, we will start seeing federations of informational databases that include the desktop client, where local information is captured and viewed; the local server, which provides overflow storage; and global servers that collectively contain an infinite amount of information and storage. Efficient replication and copy management becomes the glue that ties these new federations of databases together.

FYI

The Distributed Database Model

Briefing

Replication is easier to understand and far easier to implement than two-phase commit protocols.

— *GartnerGroup*

Despite vendor claims and widespread wishful thinking among users, replication servers do not rigorously enforce data integrity; they tend to look the other way and patch up the problems later.

— **John Tibbetts and Barbara Bernstein**

Standard *off-the-shelf* commercial distributed database packages will provide, when they fully blossom, transparent access to data on a network. The distributed database keeps track of the location of data on the network, and it will route your requests to the right database nodes, making their location transparent. To be fully distributed, a database server must support multisite updates using a transactional two-phase commit discipline (see Figure 12-3). It should allow

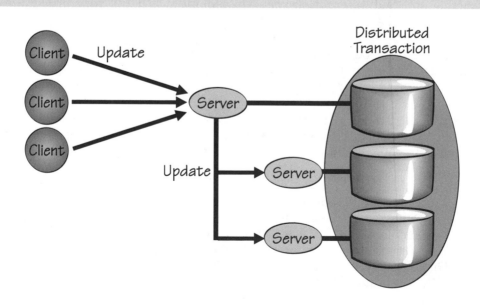

Figure 12-3. The Distributed Database Model.

you to join data from tables that reside on several machines. It should also *automatically* update data in tables that reside on several machines.

Distributed databases make it easy to write distributed applications without having to first decompose your applications. With *true* distributed databases, the location of the data is completely transparent to the application. The chief advantage of distributed databases is that they allow access to remote data transparently while keeping most of the data local to the applications that actually use it. The disadvantages of distributed databases are:

- They currently do not work in heterogeneous database environments. As a result, you're locked into a single-vendor solution.

- They poorly encapsulate data and services. You cannot change a local database table if it is being used by other sites.

- They require too many low-level message exchanges to get work done. Distributed databases exchange messages at the SQL level. This is not as efficient as using stored procedures or RPCs managed by a TP Monitor.

- They are very slow over long wide-area networks. Two-phase commits are very expensive in terms of messages sent, and it is difficult to join tables located on different computers and achieve good performance.

- They are very hard to administer. If one machine is not available, all the distributed transactions associated with it cannot execute. In contrast, with replicated databases, you can access data even if one server node is down.

The alternative to distributed databases are *federated* data warehouses, which are more easily adaptable to today's organizational realities. We also believe that eventually millions of desktop machines will come with a standard database. When you start dealing with millions of databases, you're much better off with loose federations that are synchronized using distributed object managers or a new breed of personal TP Monitors—but, now we're talking about the "post-scarcity" client/server scenario. ❑

The Mechanics of Data Replication

For users, replication means data at your service, but for IS, it means finding a solution to the difficult problem of reconciling different versions of the data.

— David Stodder

It's very common for business people to routinely populate their spreadsheets with data extracted from external sources. The process (see Figure 12-4) consists of the following manual steps: 1) Extract data using a query, 2) Copy the results to a diskette file, 3) Copy the diskette file to the machine with the spreadsheet program, and 4) Import the file into the local database (or spreadsheet). This technique, called *manual extract*, is primitive, labor intensive, and error prone.

Figure 12-4. Getting to the Data Manually.

In this section, we look at the mechanics for the total automation of this extract process (see Figure 12-5). The copy mechanics deal with the following issues: How is the extract specified? How is data from multiple sources blended? Can data be transformed as part of the copy? Who orchestrates the copy process? How is data copied into the informational databases? How are the copies refreshed? How tightly synchronized are the replicas (or extracts) with the source? When can the replicas be updated? What are the transactional boundaries of a copy?

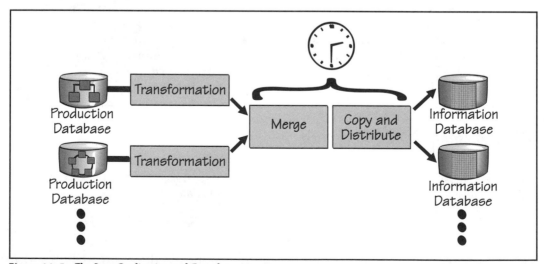

Figure 12-5. The Data Replication and Transformation Process.

Refresh and Updates

The informational databases are populated with data that originates from the various production databases. Typically, the data is copied or extracted using one of two techniques:

- *Refresh* replaces the entire target with data from the source (see Figure 12-6). This works well when you are moving small amounts of data, which have low requirements for frequency of update (that is, the data has low volatility). It is also used for doing initial bulk loads to the target database.

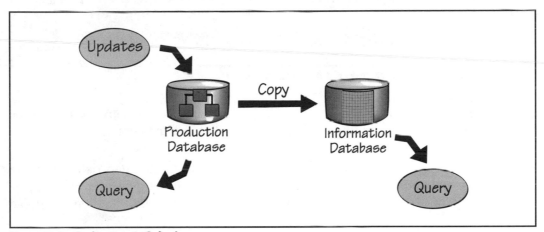

Figure 12-6. Replication via Refresh.

- *Update* only sends the changed data to the target (see Figure 12-7). Updates can be either *synchronous*, which means that the target copy is updated in the same commit scope as the source table, or they can be *asynchronous*, which means that the target table is updated in a separate transaction than the one updating the source. Synchronous updates are useful in production environments for creating replicated databases that provide high availability. Asynchronous updates are useful in data warehousing situations. You get to specify the level of synchronization that you want to maintain between the source and the target and the interval of updates. This means that you get to control the level of data obsolescence you can tolerate.

Staging the Updates

Some of the warehouse products allow you to finely control the frequency of updates. For example, you can specify the intervals at which you want *asynchronous update* data sent from the source to one or more targets. The changes to the source tables are captured in one or more *staging tables* for subsequent propaga-

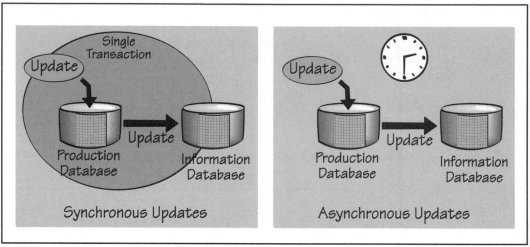

Figure 12-7. Replication via Synchronous and Asynchronous Updates.

tion to target tables (see Figure 12-8). At the intervals you specify, all the target databases in the system are updated simultaneously from the staging area.

To be more precise, the *data capture* component takes changed data from the database log and stores it in the *data staging tables* (see Figure 12-8). The *apply* component then takes the data from the staging tables and applies those changes to the target copies.

Staging provides users with a consistent view of the data across the copies. It reduces contention on the production database—the copy tool does not interfere with production applications.

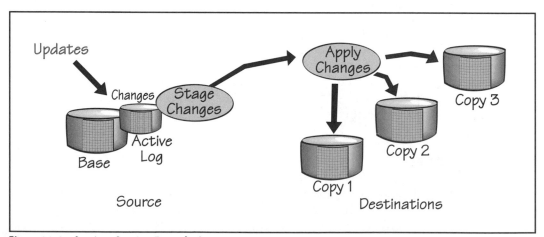

Figure 12-8. Staging: Copying From the Log.

Cleansing and Transforming the Raw Data

As you increase the number of data sources, the complexities involved with a data warehouse increase exponentially.

— **Judith Hurwitz, President**
Hurwitz Consulting

One of the attractive features of replicating data in warehouses is that you can control, enhance, and transform the "raw" data before storing it in the target databases. A well-designed warehouse lets you "filter and cleanse" raw data from production databases and store it in a form that's suitable for your informational needs. In other words, data warehouses are not simply passive collectors of data—they're also in the business of creating value-added data from raw data.

As part of the copy, a warehouse translates data from its original raw formats (which may vary widely) into a single common format that's consistent for the informational application. The related data from multiple sites is combined and merged so that the "copy" becomes a single logical database. During this process, data may also be *enhanced*; that is, empty fields may be filled in or records extended. The data may be timestamped and stored in snapshots that capture a moment in time for historical trend analysis. The copy process also takes care of any data format conversions for different targets.

Some of the more sophisticated warehouses may apply user-defined specialized functions to the data to forecast trends; that is, fill in future values or create "on-the-fly" video presentations. They will also be able to convert data into formats that are appropriate to the decision-support, spreadsheet, and multimedia-viewing tools on the client machines. The sky is the limit when it comes to value-added warehousing functions.

Figure 12-9 shows some of the more common functions that you can apply on data extracts:

- **Subsets** allow you to transmit only the rows and columns that are of interest to your informational applications. You use SQL once to define your subsets to the copy tool, and these subsets will be performed automatically as part of the copy. In addition, different views of the same source data can be delivered to different copy targets. Multitable joins can also be used to define the copy transforms.

- **Aggregates** allow you to transmit only the aggregations of data such as averages, sums, maximums, and so on. Again, you specify this once using SQL, and the copy tool will perform the aggregate every time a transfer takes place.

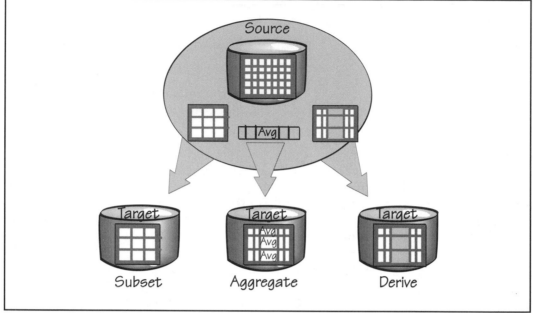

Figure 12-9. Upgrading the Raw Data: Subsets, Aggregates, and Derived Functions.

■ ***Derived functions*** allow you to specify data that does not exist but is the result of some calculation (or function) on data that does exist. For example, a new column of data may be defined on the target database that is the sum of two columns on the source database. The new column will automatically get created and updated as part of the automated copy process.

In addition to cleaning and merging the data, these functions can help you reduce the network traffic between the targets and the destinations because you only copy the data you want.

Some of the more sophisticated replication tools let you extract and copy data from non-relational sources such as Lotus Notes, Internet Web Servers, spreadsheets, news feeds, and CICS and IMS databases. Most data warehouses are SQL databases, so the majority of extract tools provide one-way transforms from the foreign data sources into SQL. As you can expect, this involves a significant amount of data cleansing. Most tools provide callbacks that let you apply customized cleansing functions to the data extracts. The data transformations are usually described in the information directory or in a warehouse management tool.

According to GartnerGroup, the market for tools that extract, cleanse, replicate, and load data is growing at 26% per year. Inmon estimates that, on average, 80% of the efforts of building a warehouse go into these tasks. In late 1998, we counted over 200 tools that partially automate these functions. Examples of data extraction and replication tools include Apertus/Carleton's *Passport*, Legent's *Data Mover*, Sybase's *Replication Server*, Oracle's *Replication Services*, Praxis's *OmniReplicator*, Ingres's *OpenIngres Replicator*, Prism's *Warehouse Manager*, ETI's *Extract*, Lotus' *NotesPump*, and IBM's *DataJoiner*, *DataPropagator*, and *DataRefresher* tools. Examples of transformation and cleansing tools include Applied Database Technology's *Data Mapper*, Trillium Software's *Trillium*, Reliant Data's *Data Conversion Engine*, Metadata Information Partners' *DataConvert*, Group 1 Software's *NADIS*, Platinum's *InfoPump*, Informatica's *PowerMart*, Sagant's *Data Mart*, and Torrent's *Orchestrate*.

In addition, there are all kinds of specialty data extraction tools. For example, there are now Web extraction tools—such as WebMethods' *Web Automation*, Roving Software's *Agent Studio*, and OnDisplay's *CenterStage*—that extract and load HTML information. And, there are warehousing tools that extract data from ERP packages—for example, Acta's *ActaLink for SAP*, and Oracle's *Warehouse Toolkit for SAP* and *Warehouse Toolkit for PeopleSoft*. Finally, there are tools—such as Prism's *Quality Manager*—that will analyze the quality of your data and identify defects. Yes, the data warehouse vendors have come a long way since the last edition of this book.

True Replicas

Time is a relative concept in replicated systems, and it is not a concept upon which I would recommend any sort of collision-detection or resolution scheme.

— *Glenn Froemming*

Replicas are *copies* of data that you can update (see Figure 12-10). When this happens, the updated replica must find a way to resynchronize its state with the original primary database. Normally, updates only take place on a single designated replica, and the primary server must abstain from doing any non-replica generated changes. So the site of update shifts from the primary to the replica.

As a result, the replica starts off with a full image of the primary database and sends all subsequent updates to the primary, either continuously or on a periodic basis. The primary database is then in charge of propagating the changes it receives to its target databases using the normal processes. The single-site update constraint may be relaxed by using *check-out* versions of replicated data—a technology that is widely used in Object Databases.

Ingres implements a database that allows both the master and the replicas to be separately updated and uses a *conflict resolver* to synchronize the data. When the changes in the replica are applied against the master, an *update collision detector* resolves conflicts using one of four user-specified policies: the oldest update has

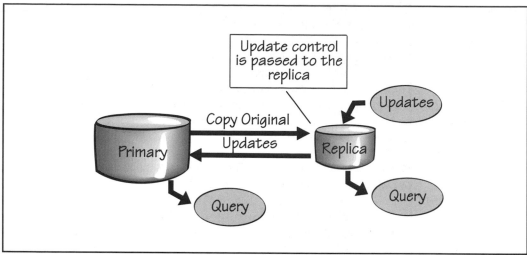

Figure 12-10. Replicas, or When the Copies Become the Master Data.

priority, the most recent update has priority, a user-specified action is applied, or all replication is halted. This last approach may be the right thing to do, but can you afford to stop the application completely until someone reconciles the data? You can also specify the winner by location or time interval. Other entrants in the "update anywhere" derby include ETI's *Extract*, Praxis's *OmniReplicator*, and Oracle's *Symmetric Replication* service. Be warned, though, that true replicas can corrupt data.

The Future Warehouses

We move snapshots of the OLTP systems over to the data warehouse as a series of data layers, much like geologic layers. Like geologists, we then dig down through the layers to understand what our business was like at previous points in time.[4]

— Ralph Kimball

Data warehouses will pop up everywhere. We expect most personal computer users to have private data warehouses with hot links to information sources all over the globe. We expect large data warehouses to play an important role as data stores for the Web. The replication technology that was presented in this chapter is an embryonic version of what can be done. In addition to moving tabular data, we'll soon be moving BLOBs of video and sound from the large data warehouses in the sky to our private and departmental warehouses (and vice versa). The EIS/DSS

---

[4] Source: Ralph Kimball, **The Data Warehouse Toolkit** (Wiley, 1996).

technology will help us distill massive amounts of data into a few visual pieces of information that we can quickly understand and use (see the next chapter). We expect to see personal versions of these currently expensive tools sell in the volume market for $50 (or less).

In addition to business information, we expect the warehouses to package tons of information related to personal, educational, and consumer topics. Finally, we expect that object request brokers—such as CORBA and DCOM—will increasingly be used to integrate the various functional components in a data warehouse; ORBs will let us create *active warehouses* using publish-and-subscribe, open middleware, and components.

Chapter 13

EIS/DSS: From Queries, To OLAP, To Data Mining

*T*he whole concept behind decision-support systems is to understand "what if?" rather than report on "what happened." To do this, you need a complex understanding of "what has happened."

— **Dennis Byron**
Application Development Trends

*T*here's gold in the data, but we just can't tell how much without exploration.

— **Don Haderle, Director of Database**
IBM

Executive Information Systems (EIS) and *Decision-Support Systems (DSS)* provide the human interface to data warehouses. The better the tools are, the more value we get from our investment in these warehouses. The tools literally bring the information to our fingertips. Not surprisingly, the EIS/DSS tools market is on a high-growth trajectory. According to the *OLAP Report*, the total OLAP software market—including services—was $1.4 billion in 1997 (see *www.olapreport.com*). This is a 40% increase over the previous year. This steep growth is, of course, creating a highly competitive market. Vendors compete by offering products with more functions and ease-of-use. EIS/DSS tools will eventually be priced for volume sales. When this happens, we expect them to become everyday tools—just like today's spreadsheets.

Growth in our business is almost always accompanied by conflicting vendor claims, counter-claims, and an explosion of new acronyms. EIS/DSS is no exception. Figure 13-1 shows the evolution of EIS/DSS tools. As you can see, we've introduced some strange new terminology; it comes with the new territory. The figure should give you the idea that EIS/DSS tools are getting smarter each day (at least they're not standing still). The holy grail of the EIS/DSS tools business is the "hands-off" query. This means that we should eventually be able to sit back and dispatch our personal information agents—armed with search algorithms—on data discovery missions. But we're not quite there, yet. This chapter is an overview of the state of EIS/DSS tools. We start with simple query and analysis tools. We then move to *OLAP*—an umbrella term for tools that let you view data from multiple perspectives (or dimensions). The next step in the evolutionary ladder is *data mining*, where the data tells you something about itself; it discovers hidden patterns. Ultimately, there are personal information agents that resemble Danny DeVito's data valet.

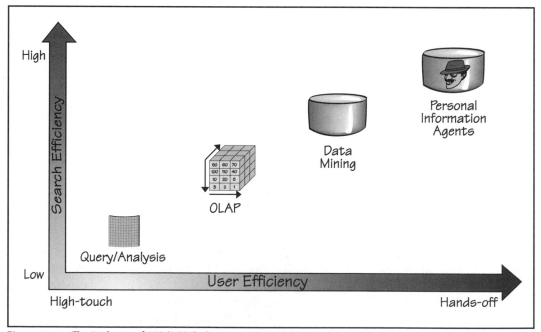

Figure 13-1. The Evolution of EIS/DSS Tools.

QUERY/REPORTING TOOLS

Your typical RDBMS query will tell you what, not why.

— **Christine Comaford**

Query and data analysis tools let you formulate a query without writing a program or learning SQL. You point-and-click to generate the SELECT statements and the search criteria (the WHERE clause). The tool then displays the results in some understandable form—usually a table. Most query tools provide common business graphics—including bar charts, pie charts, histograms, and line graphs—to let you chart the data that's pulled in by a query. Most tools let you run the query and fill in a form or spreadsheet from the output. Some tools let you run the query and then geographically map the output using a map package. Most tools provide scripting facilities that let you automatically schedule the execution of queries and reports.

The better query tools provide safeguards to prevent you from submitting "runaway queries." These queries return very large result sets. The most common safeguard is for the tool to provide a *query governor* that kills a query if it takes too long to execute or returns an excessive number of rows. Some governors cache large result sets on the server and return it to the client in fixed increments. Others display a dialog that shows you the number of rows that will be returned by a query—if the number is excessive, you should be able to click a "Cancel" button.

In late 1998, there are over 150 query and reporting tools on the market. Examples include Microsoft's *Access*, SAS Institute's *SAS System*, IBM's *Visualizer Query*, Brio's *BrioQuery*, IBI's *Focus/EIS*, Speedware's *Esperant*, Oracle's *Oracle Reports*, InfoSpace's *SpaceSQL*, Attachmate's *Select!*, Intersolv's *DataDirect Explorer*, Platinum's *Forest and Trees*, Business Objects' *Business Objects*, and Cognos' *Impromptu*.

OLAP AND MULTI-DIMENSIONAL DATA

Think of an OLAP data structure as a Rubik's Cube of data that users can twist and twirl in different ways to work through what-if and what-happened scenarios.

— **Lee Thé**

Online Analytical Processing (OLAP) tools create multi-dimensional data views on top of ordinary 2-D SQL databases (or using specialized multi-dimensional databases). OLAP's multi-dimensional access lets you formulate more sophisticated queries, and then look at the results accordingly. Think of OLAP as a

multi-dimensional spreadsheet with multiple axes. For example, you could have a product database that you access via multiple dimensions such as time, region, customer, store, price, and sales. The idea is to let you explore data using different dimensions. OLAP lets you ask the following question: What are the sales—by product, by store, and by month?

OLAP's multi-dimensional model makes it easier to visualize data. Instead of navigating through multiple tables and rows, you look at data through multi-dimensional views. *Relational OLAP (ROLAP)* provides this function by introducing a layer of abstraction on top of SQL databases that hides the physical structure of normalized relational tables. Instead, you get to see multi-dimensional views of that same data. It's like magic.

Figure 13-2 shows the difference between relational and multi-dimensional views. In the example, using OLAP you could analyze the Hawaii tourist industry by island, week, promotions, hotel category, car rentals, promotions, GNP, and so on. OLAP obviously provides a more intuitive way to look at data, especially if you used a spreadsheet's pivoting feature. The OLAP model comfortably handles data in ten

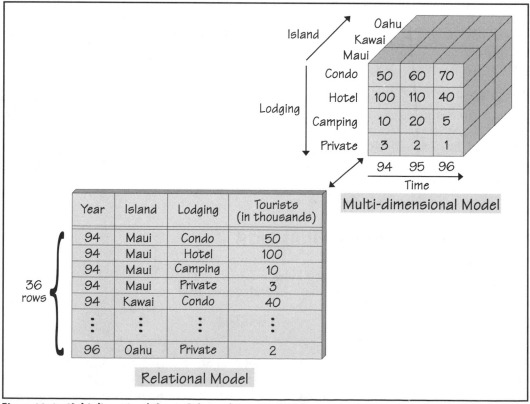

Figure 13-2. Multi-dimensional Versus Relational Data Visualizations.

or less dimensions. Beyond this, servers fail from index overload. In addition, our brains may also fail from n-dimensional visual overload.

How Do You Like Your OLAP?

The whole concept of OLAP has become somewhat less adhesive to the page, with each definition slipping away before the ink is dry.

> — Neil Raden, President
> Archer Decision Sciences
> (March, 1998)

From a technical perspective, OLAP is about how to tune the storage and calculation of multi-dimensional data to support client queries for a set of usage scenarios. An OLAP server must pre-aggregate fact data across multiple dimensions. Metadata tells the server how to aggregate the data and across what dimensions. The OLAP server uses this information to create a multi-dimensional cube—usually in a proprietary format. Note that data must be squeaky clean before it gets loaded into the cube. Typically, the source for OLAP data is a data warehouse.

As you can imagine, OLAP comes in multiple flavors. We found that the best way to classify the various OLAP products on the market is to ask two questions: Where and how is the bulk of the multi-dimensional data stored? And, where and how is the bulk of the OLAP server code executed? Figure 13-3 shows the resulting classification scheme and where some representative vendor products fit. As you can see, there are three choices for storing OLAP data: 1) on the local file system on the client machine, 2) on a specialized *Multi-Dimensional DBMS (MDBMS)*, and 3) on an ordinary RDBMS. In addition, there are three choices for running the OLAP server: 1) on the local client machine, 2) on the MDBMS server, and 3) on the SQL server using additional multi-pass SQL logic. Based on these choices, the OLAP vendors are split into four camps:

■ *Desktop OLAP.* These are standalone OLAP client tools. They create small OLAP cubes that can fit on the local file system. Most of these tools can be used with a spreadsheet like Excel. Some of these tools—for example Oracle's *Personal Express* and Arbor's *Personal Essbase*—are standalone versions of the vendor's multiuser server product.[1] So they can be used by mobile users on the road. Eventually, some of these products will be replaced by Java-based Web clients that can provide Internet-based access to remote users—*Web OLAP* is available today from companies like InfoSpace, Track Objects, Brio, and Business Objects.

---

[1] In August 1998, Arbor acquired Hyperion; the new company is now called Hyperion Solutions.

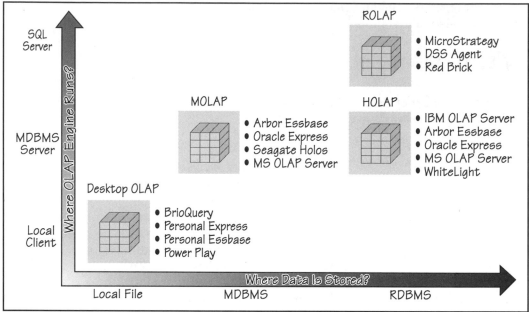

Figure 13-3. OLAP Comes in Multiple Flavors.

■ *Multi-dimensional OLAP (MOLAP).* Rather than storing data as keyed records in tables, MDBMSs provide specialized database engines to store data in arrays along related dimensions called *hypercubes*. Most MDBMSs use indexing-intensive schemes to optimize access to these cubes. MDBMS vendors typically provide OLAP client tools that are optimized for their engines. The good news is that there are at least two standards in the works for MDBMS data access (see the next section).

■ *Relational OLAP (ROLAP).* These tools provide multi-dimensional data access on top of relational databases. They do this by using a combination of indexing, caching, and metadata techniques. For example, they can create a cube using a *star schema*. In this scheme, a *fact table* is at the center of the star surrounded by *dimension tables*; each fact row contains a summary record as well as foreign keys that point to rows in the *dimension* tables (see Figure 13-4). So the fact table is the intersection of the axis of a cube; the dimension tables contain the details for each axis. Note that most RDBMS vendors now support star schemas in their query optimizers. Some DBMSs— for example, *Red Brick* and *MicroStrategy*—are optimized for running OLAP-savvy queries. These specialized SQL databases obtain performance gains by using special indexing techniques, parallel joins, OLAP-savvy SQL generators, parallel joining, and SQL query extensions (and metadata) that help the database engine optimize the query.

■ *Hybrid OLAP (HOLAP).* In this case, hybrid means combining ROLAP with an MDBMS engine in the same product. Typically, the data is stored in the

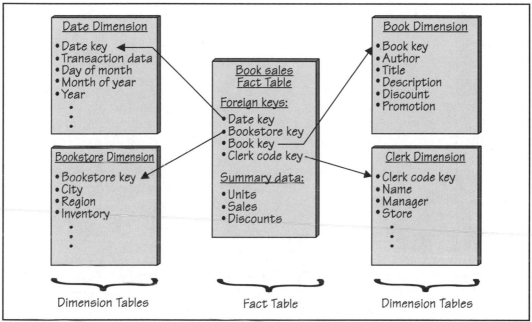

Figure 13-4. Star Schema: The Fact Table Surrounded by Dimension Tables.

RDBMS. However, a subset of the data can be loaded into a pre-aggregated MDBMS to obtain faster response. For example, Oracle lets you draw subsets of star-schema data from its *Oracle8* RDBMS engine into the *Oracle Express* MDBMS engine. IBM's *DB2 OLAP* lets you build an Essbase cube and physically store the data into DB2 star schema. By the time you read this, Microsoft will have integrated an MDBMS engine (from Panorama) inside the kernel of *SQL Server 7.0*. So hybrid can mean different things to different vendors.

As you can see, you're faced with quite a few OLAP implementation choices, which is normal at this stage for a hot new technology. In the next Soapbox, we speculate on how this technology may evolve.

OLAP: To RDBMS or to MDBMS?

Soapbox

The problem is that under the covers, most OLAP servers are extracting data from a two-dimensional DBMS and populating a multi-dimensional data cube.

— Christine Comaford

Everyone agrees that OLAP is wonderful. But the million-dollar questions are: Do you need an MDBMS to get the full benefits of OLAP? Or, can you get them with your trusty old RDBMS? The proponents of MDBMS make the case that you need a change. They make the following arguments:

- **MDBMS saves you money.** In theory, MDBMSs require less disk space because they use sparse matrices to store data in any number of dimensions, and they often relate the data using an embedded calculation language. Consequently, MDBMSs make better use of the underlying hardware by providing software that is fully optimized for OLAP. In contrast, the RDBMS vendors take the brute force approach by throwing costly massively parallel hardware at the problem—examples are Tandem/Compaq Himalaya, IBM SP2, and NCR Teradata.

- **MDBMS queries are an order of magnitude faster.** MDBMS vendors will show you benchmark results that will make you salivate.

- **Oracle cried uncle when it bought an MDBMS company.** In June 1995, Oracle purchased IRI—the maker of *Express MDB*—for $300 million. The proponents of MDBMS consider the purchase to be an admission—by the market leader—that MDBMSs are better suited for OLAP than RDBMSs.

Of course, none of these arguments carry much weight in the RDBMS camp. They will quickly point out that:

- **MDBMS data has to be loaded before you can do a query.** MDBMS queries slow down considerably if you first have to load a gigabyte of data from an RDBMS source (the warehouse).

- **MDBMSs are not standardized.** MDBMS standards are still under construction (see the next section).

- **MDBMSs are not suitable for ad hoc queries.** They only work with predefined hypercubes.

- **MDBMSs do not scale.** In contrast, today's RDBMSs do not have any problem scaling or handling terabytes of data. They are a proven technology.

- **RDBMSs are introducing new query smarts.** RDBMSs were traditionally tuned for OLTP, where the average transaction consists of a few database calls. However, because of the dramatic growth in warehousing, DBMS vendors are in a race to introduce better query capabilities. Their databases must now be able to handle queries that issue hundreds of database calls, some of which may need to scan many gigabytes of data.

So who is right? It's obviously not a black-and-white issue. In general, you are better off going with an RDBMS (or ROLAP) if you're dealing with tons of data and have very general query needs. MDBMSs (or MOLAP) make the opposite trade-off—better speeds on smaller quantities of pre-aggregated data (see Figure 13-5). And, of course, there is the proverbial compromise called HOLAP.

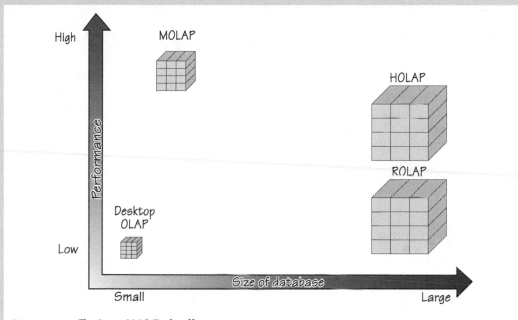

Figure 13-5. The Great OLAP Trade-off.

We believe that both the MDBMS and RDBMS vendors will plug the holes in their products and do whatever it takes to ride the OLAP wave. However, as the Object Database (ODBMS) vendors bitterly discovered, RDBMSs are "king of the hill," and they will not be easily displaced by superior technology alone. The next best thing is to co-opt them via coexistence. For example, an MDBMS can become nothing more than a new *multi-dimensional* data type within an RDBMS. □

OLAP Client/Server Interaction

Figure 13-6 shows the three tiers of an OLAP client/server solution. Here are the steps in a client/server interaction:

1. ***The client invokes the OLAP application and submits a command***. An OLAP application can be invoked from within a spreadsheet, Web page, or visual tool. The client application displays a user interface and submits commands to the OLAP engine on the server.

2. *The server executes the command*. Typically, the server performs the calculations on multi-dimensional data stored in an RDBMS, MDBMS, or both.

3. *The server returns the results to the client.* The results are then displayed inside the visual tool or in a spreadsheet.

4. *The client optionally caches the results*. The client may maintain a local hypercube with cached results.

As you can see, there are many interfaces in an OLAP client/server interaction—including the interface to a Web browser or spreadsheet, the client/server middleware, and the interface to an MDBMS (or the RDBMS extensions). So what is the equivalent of SQL and its CLIs in the OLAP world? Read on.

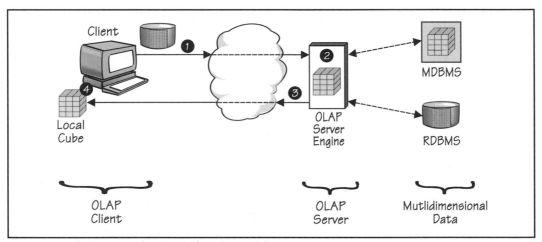

Figure 13-6. The Anatomy of an OLAP Client/Server Solution.

The Two Competing OLAP Standards

The OLAP community now has two competing standards. On one side is the *OLAP Council*—an industry consortium—with its *MD-API*. On the other side is Microsoft with its *OLE DB for OLAP (*also known as *Tensor)*. Each API has its supporters in the OLAP vendor community. The Microsoft camp includes many of the smaller OLAP tool vendors. They anticipate that the embedded OLAP engine in Microsoft's *SQL Server 7.0* will bring OLAP to the Windows masses. The OLAP Council's MD-API has the support of the OLAP market leader, Oracle—in 1997, Oracle had over 20% of the OLAP marketshare.

In January 1998, the OLAP Council published its long-awaited *MDAPI 2.0 specification* in the form of Java classes accessible via other languages. Unlike Microsoft's Tensor, the new MDAPI supports heterogeneous computing environments—

including Windows NT servers, any Windows client, Unix, OS/2, Macintosh, and any Java Virtual Machine. It also supports ORB-based client/server interactions using either CORBA/RMI or DCOM. In general, both competing standards provide some way to query a hypercube and its metadata. However, neither standard currently specifies a definition language for metadata. In addition, neither standard defines APIs for security, database loading, and multi-dimensional calculations.

DATA MINING

*D*ata mining lets the power of computers do the work of sifting through your vast data stores. Tireless and relentless searching can find the tiny nugget of gold in a mountain of data slag.

— Edmund X. DeJesus

Data-mining tools help you sift through vast quantities of information looking for valuable patterns in the data. A pattern may be as simple as the realization that 80% of male diaper buyers also buy beer. Data mining is the process of discovering unsuspected patterns. Some early data-mining pioneers are reporting immediate returns on investment. For example, a department store chain discovered that shoplifting of batteries, film, and midpriced pens was costing it $60,000 a month. Consequently, these items were moved to more visible store locations, thus saving the chain over $700,000 annually.

Data mining looks for patterns and groupings that you may have overlooked in your own analysis of a set of data. The tool typically performs a "fuzzy" search, with little or no guidance from an end user. In data mining, the tool does the discovery and tells you something instead of you asking it a question. In contrast, query tools and OLAP return records that satisfy a query that you must first formulate. Instead of responding to low-level queries, data-mining tools deal with fuzzy searches. They don't assume that you know exactly what you're seeking. Most tools use the following search methods:

- **Associations**—often called *market basket analysis*—look for patterns where the presence of something implies the presence of something else. For example, "Scuba gear buyers are good candidates for Australian vacations."

- **Sequential patterns** look for chronological occurrences. For example, "When the price of stock X goes up by 10%, the price of stock Y goes down by 15% a week later."

- **Clusterings** look for groupings and high-level classifications. For example, "Over 70% of undecided voters have incomes of over $60,000, age brackets between 40 and 50, and live in XYZ neighborhood." The idea is to group similar entities based on their affinities.

The output of the discovery process is often represented in the form of *if-then* rules; for example:

```
If
  Age = 42; and
  Car_Make = Volvo; and
  No_of_Children < 3
Then
  Mailorder_Response = 15%
```

Data-mining tools are beginning to be used in many industries. Health researchers use them to discover patterns affecting the success of back surgery. Banks use them to detect credit card fraud and predict which customers are likely to change their credit card affiliations. Attorneys use them to select juries and to analyze voting patterns of Supreme Court justices. Stockbrokers use them to identify stock movements and trading patterns. NASD uses them to monitor millions of NASDAQ stock trades per day, looking for unfair trading practices. Insurance companies use them to identify risky customers and behavior patterns. Resorts and hotels use them to identify return guests. As you can see from these examples, data mining is the ultimate "Big Brother" tool, but it can also be put to good uses.

In late 1998, there were over 15 data-mining tools on the market. Examples of these tools are IBM's *Intelligent Miner*, Thinking Machines' *Darwin*, Silicon Graphics' *MineSet*, Angoss Software's *KnowledgeStudio*, DataMind's *DataMind*, Integrated Solutions' *Clementine*, SAS's *Enterprise Miner*, Unica's *Pattern Recognition*, and NeoVista's *Decision Series*. In addition, we are now seeing packages that specialize for a particular industry. For example, IBM has a *Fraud and Abuse Management System* for the health care industry. Some vendors are also starting to embed data-mining calls as part of the processing of an electronic transaction.

PERSONAL INFORMATION AGENTS

Agents are mobile applications that are launched on data warehouses to perform specific queries or to search for patterns in data. Most agents are rules-based alerting programs that say, "If this happens, do that." Because agents are ad hoc and scripted, they should not be turned loose on production systems. You should use them to discover unsuspected occurrences within a data warehouse environment. The agents should alert you when something unusual happens. Agenting capabilities are finding their way in today's OLAP and query tools. The next step after this is agents that can understand data based on knowledge models. But we're not quite there yet.

Most of the agenting tools on the market allow you to specify subjects or events that interest you. Then, at time intervals you specify, the agents comb a variety of databases (and the Internet) to search for new mentions of a subject or changes to patterns of data. If a match is found, the tool typically notifies you via e-mail or a pager. One tool will even personalize the data with dynamically generated English sentences and deliver it to an output device of your choice. Examples of data agenting tools include MicroStrategy's *DSS Broadcaster*, Information Advantage's *DecisionSuite OLAP*, Autonomy's *Agentware Knowledge Server*, COM.sortium's *DocuMine*, Information Publishing's *Echo*, Hummingbird's *Pablo*, Amulet's *Info-Wizard*, Brio's *BrioQuery*, and Information Advantage's *DecisionSuite InfoAlert*.

CONCLUSION

With the increasing complexity of today's society, the information we can obtain through data mining can be dramatically more valuable than any other asset.

— Dr. Kamran Parsaye, CEO
Information Discovery

OLAP, data mining, and multi-dimensional databases are the hot new technologies of data warehousing. Startups are coming and going, and the market has yet to settle. The best we could do in this chapter was to provide you with a framework for looking at these new technologies; it's a good first step toward understanding what these technologies can do for you. It's still too early to pick winners—the fun is just starting.

Chapter 14

Database: Meet the Players

> *Database for most organizations today is practically in a pantheon with Mom and apple pie.*
>
> — *David Stodder*
> *(September, 1998)*

We've been dropping names of database products right and left in the last few chapters without formally introducing you to the players. We wanted to first give you a flavor for the technology before introducing the products. In this chapter, we provide a snapshot of the database market and discuss the current trends. Then we formally introduce the key players, most of whom are already household names.

THE DATABASE CLIENT/SERVER MARKET

According to Dataquest, the SQL database market revenues for 1997 were $6.6 billion. In addition, the database companies are major players in the data warehousing software market, which generated an additional $1.47 billion in 1997. Less than 10% of the world's data is stored in relational databases, so there's a lot of growth opportunity ahead. With their new support for BLOBs and object extensions,

relational databases are becoming suitable stores for faxes, images, fingerprints, HTML files, applets, spreadsheets, movies, soundclips, e-mail messages, and others.

TRENDS

Data warehousing is still very much relational: Everything is a row and a column.

> — *Mitch Kramer, Analyst*
> *Seybold Group*
> *(August, 1998)*

At age nineteen, the relational database industry is in its late teens. New developments in this rapid-growth industry are a way of life. The trend toward online data access is unstoppable. DBMSs can now store enormous quantities of online data; EIS/DSS tools make it easy to access this data. Here's a snapshot of the major movements that we're seeing in this industry:

■ ***SQL databases as portable operating systems***. SQL database engines are becoming portable server environments. They do much more than just manage data—they provide almost complete server environments. All the major SQL vendors, except Microsoft, provide portable server environments that run on multiple platforms—including Unixes, OS/2, NT, NetWare, and mainframes. In addition to managing ordinary data, the environments are now expanding into multimedia, fingerprints, images, sound, video, and multidimensional data. The environments come with their own procedural logic—including stored procedures, triggers, rules, alerts, assertions, user-defined data types, and Java VMs. The environments also include highly non-standard but fully portable crossplatform 4GLs and tools.

■ ***SQL databases from laptops to teraflops***. SQL database vendors are expanding beyond their departmental server niche and moving into two new areas: 1) Desktops and laptops, where they're replacing the Paradoxes, FoxPros, and XBase engines, thus becoming Trojan horses for production-strength SQL servers; and 2) Massively parallel databases, where they're competing head-on with traditional mainframes to become the new enterprise servers.

■ ***SQL databases as data warehouses***. SQL databases are expanding beyond their traditional OLTP and departmental decision-support functions to uncharted new territories such as the lucrative data warehousing market. The latest development is that SQL vendors are starting to embed full-MDBMS functionality inside the kernel of their database engines.

- **_SQL data replicated everywhere_**. For early SQL practitioners, redundant data was a sin. Elaborate normalization schemes were created to cut down on wasted duplication and to rationalize the data. Today, the new religion is called *replication*. With the cost of storage devices hitting new lows, you can now carry an entire data warehouse in your laptop. You simply replicate data to wherever you need it. For SQL databases, it's good-bye to the age of scarcity.

- **_SQL databases discover the Web_**. For SQL database vendors, the World Wide Web is potentially the land of milk and honey. They want to capitalize on the opportunity to make SQL data seamlessly available to millions of information-hungry Web surfers. The challenge is to create a commercial infrastructure to charge for these billions of new accesses.

- **_SQL databases pop up in all kinds of strange places._** SQL databases—with tiny footprints—are now being embedded inside intelligent devices. For example, the footprint for *Oracle Lite for PDAs* is about 150 KBytes of RAM. In late 1997, *Harmonia* became the first company to introduce a pure-Java relational database engine; it has a footprint of less than 800 KBytes. Harmonia was joined, in mid-1998, by *Cloudscape*, which shipped the world's first multi-user, all-Java DBMS. On another front, in 1998 *Times Ten* shipped the first all-memory relational database store; it claims to have ten times better performance than disk-based engines. Oracle now offers a similar feature as an add-on to Oracle8; it is called the *Very Large Memory* option.

Of course, the major database vendors can't cover every niche, which is why there are niche players. The biggest niche is *Object Databases (ODBMSs)*, with 1997 revenues of $210 million and growing at 69.5% per year.[1] Niche players also have a strong market in complex online information delivery, especially for the Web. Examples of these systems include document and image content searches, BLOB management, time series, knowledge inference engines, and anything that requires complex data types.

THE PLAYERS

Figure 14-1 shows how the database pie was divided in 1997.[2] Note that the Microsoft revenues include *Access*, *SQL Server*, and *Visual FoxPro*. Also note that the IBM numbers include both IMS and DB2 revenues—IMS is a hierarchical database.

GartnerGroup predicts that by the year 2000, the "Big Five" database vendors will still be Oracle, IBM, Informix, Microsoft, and Sybase. The second tier will include

---

[1] Source: IDC's Joshua Duhl (June, 1998).
[2] Source: Dataquest Research (August, 1998).

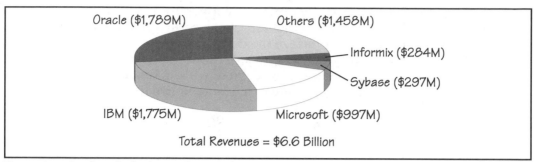

Oracle ($1,789M)   Others ($1,458M)

Informix ($284M)

Sybase ($297M)

IBM ($1,775M)   Microsoft ($997M)

Total Revenues = $6.6 Billion

Figure 14-1. Database Vendors' 1997 Revenues (Source: Dataquest, 1998).

Computer Associates, because of *Ingres* and *Jasmine*; Progress Software, because of its vertical market penetration; and Compaq/Tandem's *NonStop SQL*, because it has better than 99% scalability when moving from 16 to 64 processors.

In addition, hundreds of innovative products are seeking a place in the very lucrative online database market. The explosion of the new media types—especially on the Web—is creating a lot of new opportunity. Of course, the "Big Five" cannot overhaul their engines overnight to support every new data type—they must first meet the needs of their installed base. As a result, they're acquiring niche players left and right to fill the holes. In the race to be king of the database hill, anything goes.

Gartner's year 2000 predictions seem to indicate that the database market will consolidate around today's winners—the "Big Five." The remaining sections look at what these vendors offer today.

Oracle

Oracle continued to carve out mindshare in 1998 by offering its *Oracle8* database across more than 92 platforms (60 of which are Unixes). It provides a very consistent environment across all these platforms—from tools, to administration interfaces, to the Data Definition Language (DDL) and SQL directory. Oracle takes advantage of SMP on NetWare, NT, OS/2, AIX, and SCO. On the high-end, *Oracle8 Parallel Server* supports massively parallel databases on specialized hardware such as IBM's SP2 (loosely-coupled RS/6000s). On the low-end, it offers *Oracle Lite*.

Oracle8 supports a parallel query optimizer, bidirectional data replication, distributed database features, BLOBs, stored procedures, and triggers. It also supports object-relational extensions based on cartridges. *Oracle8* improves data warehousing performance via the very popular *Oracle Express* MDBMS; it also provides a new media add-on for text-mining called *Oracle ConText*. Other add-ons include a Web application server, an e-mail server, a component repository, and a video server.

Oracle8i—expected in early 1999—will have a built-in Java VM and will also support Cartridges in the form of CORBA-based *Enterprise JavaBeans (EJBs)*. In addition, Oracle's *Application Server 4.0*—which shipped in late-1998—already provides support for CORBA/EJB cartridges. So what's going on here? If you think about it, Oracle—the leader of the 2-tier client/server revolution—is moving to a 3-tier client/server architecture in a very big way. It's a no-compromise distributed object strategy based on CORBA and EJB.

Figure 14-2 shows how the pieces of this architecture play together. On the client side, you can have any type of client—including Web browsers, CORBA objects, ActiveXs, and JavaBeans. The clients communicate with the server via HTTP, DCOM, or CORBA IIOP.

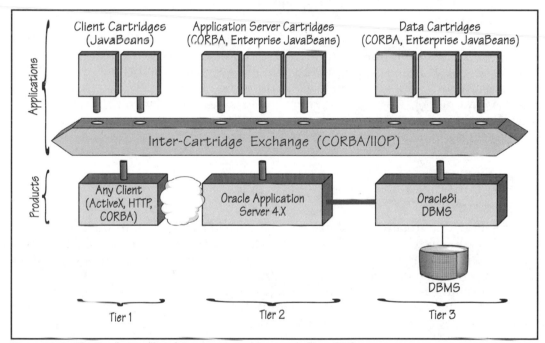

Figure 14-2. The Oracle Distributed Component Architecture (a.k.a., NCA).

In the middle-tier is the *Oracle Application Server 4.X*. It provides all kinds of services via CORBA-encapsulated cartridges—including *LiveHTML*, *ODBC*, *VRML*, *HTTP*, and wrappers for *PL/SQL* and *Perl*. The Application Server includes a Java VM that lets you run CORBA-based EJBs (Oracle also calls them *JavaCorba cartridges*). So you can write your middle-tier applications using any of these environments. Of course, all these applications sit on top of a common CORBA bus. Consequently, they can interoperate. In addition, the Application Server provides ORB-based security using SSL 3.0 and X.509 certificates. The ORB also supports CORBA transaction services, which means that you can make your EJBs (and

cartridges) transactional by simply setting attributes. Your transactions can span across multiple cartridges and any XA-compliant resource manager. Oracle also provides an *Application Server Enterprise Edition* that supports load-balancing and automatic failover.

The third tier is, of course, the Oracle database engine. *Oracle8i* includes a built-in Java VM and CORBA ORB. You can extend the DBMS's functionality by writing data cartridges for user-defined types. Oracle plans to provide a set of cartridges for the more common data types—such as text, video, XML, and time-series. In addition, you will be able to run your data-intensive EJBs inside the database engine. So the idea is that you write a CORBA/EJB once and then run it either inside the Application Server or Database Engine. You use the same Java tools—which Oracle also supplies—to develop your EJBs for either environment.[3]

To support this environment, Oracle provides a rich set of CORBA/Java tools, some of which it OEMs from Inprise/Borland and Rational. The tools are all driven from a common object-based repository. Eventually, everything in this environment will be wizard-based. Finally, Oracle is porting its entire ERP suite to this open CORBA/Java model. As we go to press, Oracle is the number-two ERP vendor after SAP. So this move should provide a shot in the arm to the nascent CORBA/EJB component industry.

IBM's DB2 Family

IBM revamped its relational database family in 1995 with the introduction of *DB2 2.1*—also known as "Common Server." This is the portable version of DB2 that runs on OS/2, NT, AIX, HP-UX, Solaris, SCO, and other Unixes. The *Common Server* DB2 supports object-relational extensions, ODBC, CLI, triggers, BLOBs, SMP (where available), replication, and an advanced cost-based query optimizer. In 1995, IBM also introduced *DB2 Parallel Edition for SP2*—a shared-nothing parallel database server. In late 1997, IBM introduced the *DB2 Universal Database 5.0 (UDB v.5)*—it's a morph between the Common Server and Parallel Edition. The mainframe and AS/400 versions of DB2—not currently part of the DB2 Universal Server code base—were also upgraded to support more parallelism, a smarter query optimizer, and stored procedures. At the low-end, IBM offers the *Lotus Approach 97* SQL database with its Basic-like scripting features, wizards, and easy-to-use front-end.

---

[3] Oracle8i includes a new client user interface called the *Internet File System*. It lets you easily store desktop files inside the Oracle8i DBMS. The database appears on the desktop like a network drive with folders that contain files—it's identical to your desktop file folders. You can drag files from the DBMS and then drop them on the local folders, and vice versa.

UDB v.5 provides an object-relational infrastructure via *extenders* that vaguely resemble SQL3 user-defined types. The product comes with built-in extenders for text, image, voice, audio clips, and video. UDB v.5 also provides better system administration via the *Control Center*—a GUI-based management tool. *Smart-Guides* provide wizard-like interfaces to assist you with the setup and configuration of databases. Even the setup of the parallel clusters is managed graphically. UDB v.5 is a lot more ROLAP-friendly than its successor. For example, it provides a built-in cube function to support multidimensional data as well as a *rollup* function for grouping the data. Note that the IBM *Visual Warehouse* is a separate product that combines the Essbase MDBMS with DB2. Finally, UDB v.5 includes a very useful component called *Net.Data*; it lets you access DB2 data via server-side JavaScripts.

Like Oracle, IBM is a strong supporter of EJB and CORBA. However, there is no built-in support for these technologies in UDB v.5. Currently, you can write stored procedures in Java that access DB2 via JDBC. IBM may eventually provide built-in support for both CORBA and EJB in the database kernel (a la Oracle). However, IBM's current strategy is to run CORBA/EJB on separate middle-tier application servers—including its *CICS*, *TXSeries*, *Component Broker*, *Domino 5.0*, *Project San Francisco*, and *WebSphere* products.

Informix

Informix started out as a department server for value-added resellers (VARs) with a low-end product called *Standard Edition*. In 1995, the company shifted its focus to the high-end of the database market by rearchitecting the core database for parallelism. They wrote 800,000 lines of new code. The result was *Informix 7.1*, which supports clustered SMP. In early 1996, Informix introduced a massively parallel database product—*Informix 8.0 XPS*.

On December 20, 1995 Informix acquired a leading-edge, object-relational company called *Illustra* for $385 million. Illustra pioneered object extensions on top of normal SQL database engines. Its claim to fame was an object-relational extension called *DataBlades*. They let you create new data types on top of SQL databases—for example, time series, text, image, 2D spatial, and 3D spatial. Illustra lets you store sets of objects in a single column and provides an extended SQL syntax to reference these objects.

Informix spent the next two years integrating Illustra's DataBlade technology into its DBMS engine. The result of this effort shipped in late 1997—it is called the *Informix Dynamic Server with the Universal Data Option (IDSUDO)*. The new Dynamic Server supports replication, stored procedures, triggers, BLOBs, and the typical SQL paraphernalia. Its forte appears to be high-performance OLTP and data warehousing (and Web) applications that require rich data types on top of a scalable RDBMS engine. Informix seems to be targeting the high-end of these markets.

Unlike its key competitors—Oracle, IBM, Sybase, and Microsoft—Informix does not have a middle-tier application server. So all the business logic must run directly inside its Dynamic Server (or you can use a third-party TP Monitor or OTM). Like Oracle, Informix plans to embed a Java VM in its DBMS. And, it also plans to run EJBs from within its engine. So the database engine becomes a container for the EJBs you write. Finally, Informix plans to also support both JDBC 2.0 and SQLJ in the next release of Dynamic Server.

Sybase

In the early 1990s, analysts were predicting that Sybase would topple Oracle and become the new king of the hill. The avant-garde company was well-known for its innovative technology. It pioneered important technologies such as stored procedures, triggers, data replication, multi-threaded servers, open servers, BLOBs, and SQL middleware. But, in the mid-90s, Sybase experienced a market failure with its *System 10*—the DBMS performed poorly and could not scale past four machines. Consequently, Sybase locked itself out of the lucrative SMP market. Its customers voted against the system by not upgrading to it. In late 1995, the company shipped its *System 11*, which fixed many of the previous problems. However, the product lagged its competitors in terms of core functionality. For example, it did not support row-level locking—a crucial requirement for highly-concurrent OLTP applications. In Sybase, the unit of locking was a page.

In late 1997, Sybase introduced *System 11.5*—a performance screamer. The product supports "new" features like record-level locking. Around the same time, Sybase renamed its DBMS product line to *Adaptive Server*. The top-of-the-line is now *Adaptive Server Enterprise 11.5* (previously *Sybase SQL Server*). In addition, there is *Adaptive Server/IQ* (previously *Sybase/IQ*); it adds very fast bitmap indexes for data warehousing. Finally, Sybase has a very small footprint SQL engine—called *Adaptive Server Anywhere* (previously *SQL Anywhere*). This low-entry database is now fully compatible with the rest of the Sybase DBMS family.

Like everyone else, Sybase has a server-side Java strategy. As we go to press, it's not clear if Sybase will embed a Java VM inside its DBMS. The main element of Sybase's server-side Java strategy is an application server—called the *Jaguar Component Transaction Server*. By the time you read this, Jaguar will support COM+, CORBA/EJB, and Sybase Open Server components. Sybase *PowerJ* will provide the premier visual construction tool for this new platform.

In summary, Sybase is extending the reach of its database to both the high-end and the low-end of the SQL market. In mid-1998, the company decided to focus on three markets: mobile computing, Internet applications, and data warehousing. If properly executed, this new strategy may help turn the tide for Sybase.

Microsoft

Microsoft is fast becoming a strategic player in the database market. The company fields its flagship *SQL Server* for the high-end and its mass-market *Access* product for the desktop. Microsoft's entry in the "serious" database market was a catalyst for driving down the prices of competitive products. Microsoft is the only database vendor that does not aspire to run its engine on every platform—they only do Windows 95/98 and Windows NT.

So what makes Microsoft—a relative latecomer—such a formidable player in the database market? We can think of four reasons: 1) High-volume desktop products like *Access* drag sales of SQL Server—the three million copies of Access can serve as client front-ends for SQL Server; 2) SQL Server is packaged with Microsoft's *BackOffice*—it is perceived to be the database server of choice for Microsoft's immensely popular "front-office" suite; 3) SQL Server is priced to kill; and 4) SQL Server is highly integrated with NT and perceived as being the database of choice for that platform.[4]

In 1994, Microsoft broke up with Sybase and took over the development of MS SQL Server. In September 1995, Microsoft introduced *SQL Server 6.0*—a low-cost, robust server that fixed many of the deficiencies of the previous product, *SQL Server 4.2*. Even though the product still had the Sybase look and feel, Microsoft changed about 60% of the original code. SQL Server 6.0 is tightly integrated with NT's SMP engine, system management, and administration. In addition, the Microsoft version of Sybase's Transact SQL is SQL-92 compliant and it supports scrollable cursors. SQL Server 6.0 also introduced a very basic but easy-to-use replication service. It is based on a publish-and-subscribe metaphor—the source database publishes rows and tables, and then holds them until SQL Server copies them to the subscribers.

In 1997, Microsoft introduced *SQL Server 6.5*, which extends data replication to include subscribers from Microsoft Access, Oracle, DB2, and other ODBC-compliant databases. The replication is one-way only. The product also introduced a partial *row-level locking* solution—it locks rows for SQL inserts only. The most important new feature in this release was the *Distributed Transaction Coordinator (DTC)*. It uses OLE TP to coordinate transactions, which can span across more than one SQL Server.

---

[4] As we go to press, Oracle is the best-selling DBMS engine on NT. Many corporations have standardized on Oracle for all their platforms.

As we go to press, *SQL Server 7.0* is in its third beta. If all goes well, the product will ship in early 1999. SQL Server 7.0 promises to be the most significant release of SQL Server since the product's introduction in 1989. It introduces new features that fall into four categories: 1) data warehousing enhancements, 2) ease-of-management, 3) upgraded existing features, and 4) Windows 98 support.

SQL Server 7.0's new data warehousing features include a built-in MDBMS engine, built-in data transformation, multi-master replication, parallel queries, and support for the OLE DB's OLAP APIs. These features will help Microsoft gain a foothold in the lucrative datamart market. However, SQL Server is still not a very scalable solution for data warehousing. It lacks competitive features such as high-end parallel server support, bitmap indexing, and proven support for very large databases.

SQL Server 7.0 introduces new self-managing features that fix some of the more annoying shortcomings found in the previous versions of the product. For example, SQL Server 7.0 now lets you back up databases online; it also supports incremental restores. In addition, the new version eliminates the need for manually pre-allocating system resources—gone are the logical database devices. Microsoft is also adding about 25 new wizards to *SQL Enterprise Manager* to help with typical day-to-day administration tasks.

SQL Server 7.0 fixes some of the problems found in previous releases. For example, the new lock manager now fully supports row-level locking. In addition, the table limits for joins is now 32 (up from 16). Microsoft has also increased the maximum limits on file size, database size, log file size, and memory addressing. The new release promises to provide better support for SMP scaling. Currently, SQL Server 6.5 cannot scale past four processors.

SQL Server 7.0 will also be able to run on Windows 98. However, Microsoft will continue to enhance Access; it is currently developing *Access 4.0*. Eventually, Access may be able to use SQL Server as its engine instead of its *Jet* database. Note that security is still a big problem on the Windows 98 platform. So you must use SQL Server's built-in security mechanism to protect resources.

Finally, what about Java? It should not come as a surprise that Microsoft is the only database vendor that does not have a server-side Java strategy based on EJBs. In Microsoft's parallel universe, you use COM objects. Period. Java is just another language for writing COM objects.

CONCLUSION

This concludes our coverage of SQL Database servers and data warehouses. It was a long tour, which is to be expected from a technology that accounts for the majority of client/server applications that are in production today. Database technology is still in its prime. SQL database servers are becoming commodity items and are now learning how to coexist in federated database arrangements. Mission-critical database systems will continue to be sold in packages that superbly integrate scalable fault-tolerant hardware with software. The new areas of growth will be in the mass markets for database-oriented products. What does it mean to put a data warehouse inside each desktop and mobile laptop? Who will keep these warehouses fed with continuous real-time information? How will data warehouses play on the Web? What tools will help us digest all this information in real time?

Yes, there are still fortunes to be made in database technology. Database companies—including Sybase, Oracle, Informix, Tandem, IBM San Jose, and Ingres—are transforming Silicon Valley (where your authors live) into "Database Valley." And they did it all with some relational and SQL technology from IBM research. Without turning this into a Soapbox, we predict that the marriage of "data warehouses" and "information highways" will create opportunities in database that dwarf anything we've seen so far. Java—especially, Enterprise JavaBeans—will play a key role in the next wave of database technology. So the best is yet to come. By the end of the decade, our valley may be called *Database Valley*—unless, of course, it's called *Java Valley*.

Part 5
Client/Server
Transaction
Processing

An Introduction to Part 5

TP Monitors, together with 3-tier client/server development, are one of the hottest IT technology items.

— *Jim Johnson, Chairman*
Standish Group

So what did you Martians think of the new California Gold Country? Oh, you want to start panning for SQL gold. Yes, it's a great business—but they do have earthquakes in California. And we have some other great opportunities to show you. For example, Part 5 is about transaction processing and TP Monitors, another important area of new client/server opportunity. Why? Because client/server computing can't live on shared data alone. The programs that operate on that data are just as important. To create effective client/server solutions, we need the software equivalent of a symphony conductor. That's the guy who waves the little wand to orchestrate all the musical instruments so that they play together.

So where is this client/server software conductor? What little wand can be used to orchestrate programs that don't even know about each other? How do we get these programs to act in unison when it takes tons of NOS and middleware just to get them to talk to each other? We've got news for you: The software conductor exists, and it is called a *TP Monitor*. The wand these software conductors use is called *transactions*. Using these transactions, a TP Monitor can get pieces of software that don't know anything about each other to act in total unison.

No, we're not selling snake oil. TP Monitors have solid credentials—they've been used for many years to keep the biggest of "Big Iron" running. In the mainframe world, a TP Monitor is sold with every database. The folks there discovered that without that conductor, they just had some very "inactive" data. If they needed TP Monitors on these single-vendor mainframes, we need them even more on client/server networks where every piece of software only knows how to play its own tune.

Without a conductor, don't expect any client/server music. Yes, an occasional Jazz ensemble may spontaneously create music, but it's becoming the exception. We're being deluged with new software every day, and we can't just depend on good luck and Jazz. We need to hire a software conductor for the network. And eventually, every desktop will have a personal software conductor.

So get your tuxedos out—we're going to the symphony. What? You didn't bring them? No problem. The TP Monitor people are not very formal these days; they, too, have discovered sneakers. The plan for Part 5 is to first explore *transactions*. Transactions are to TP Monitors what SQL is to relational databases—it's the commodity that brings it all together. You'll discover that transactions come in all types: flat, chained, nested, long-lived, and sagas. But all transactions have one

thing in common: They have ACID properties. What's that? We'll tell you soon. It's good stuff. Eventually, all our software will be ACID-ized.

With transactions in the bag, we're ready for TP Monitors. What do they do? What do the new client/server models look like? What kind of standards do they follow? We'll answer all these questions and more. You'll discover that the conductor may save you enough money to more than pay for itself. What a business! The SQL database servers are making gold—the TP Monitors help you save enough so that some of that gold gets diverted their way. Does this mean you don't move to California? We're not sure yet. The database people are making moves that suggest they may want to keep all the gold in their valley. They've invented something called *TP-Lite*—or "miniconductors"—for their databases. You've already encountered some elements of TP-Lite: stored procedures, triggers, and SQL transactions. We'll go over the TP-Lite versus TP-Heavy "miniwar." Do you still have your helmets from the OS wars?

Chapter 15

The Magic of Transactions

*T*he idea of distributed systems without transaction management is like a society without contract law. One does not necessarily want the laws, but one does need a way to resolve matters when disputes occur. Nowhere is this more applicable than in the PC and client/server worlds.

— Jim Gray

Transactions are more than just business events: They've become an application design philosophy that guarantees robustness in distributed systems. Under the control of a TP Monitor, a transaction can be managed from its point of origin— typically on the client—across one or more servers, and then back to the originating client. When a transaction ends, all the parties involved are in agreement as to whether it succeeded or failed. The transaction becomes the contract that binds the client to one or more servers.

In this chapter, we first go over the so-called ACID properties that make transactions such desirable commodities in client/server computing. We then explain the *flat transaction*, which is the workhorse of all the commercial transaction systems— including TP Monitors, Database Managers, transactional file systems, and message

queues. The flat transaction is not without its shortcomings; we look at these in some detail and suggest some workarounds. Finally, we go over some of the proposed alternatives to the flat transaction including sagas, chained transactions, and nested transactions.

THE ACID PROPERTIES

Transactions are a way to make ACID operations a general commodity.

— Gray and Reuter (1993)[1]

From a business point of view, a transaction is an action that changes the state of an enterprise—for example, a customer depositing money in a checking account constitutes a banking transaction. Technically speaking, a transaction is a collection of actions imbued with ACID properties. In this case, ACID—a term coined by Andreas Reuter in 1983—stands for Atomicity, Consistency, Isolation, and Durability. Here's what it means:

■ *Atomicity* means that a transaction is an indivisible unit of work: all of its actions succeed or they all fail. It's an all-or-nothing proposition. The actions under the transaction's umbrella may include the message queues, updates to a database, and the display of results on the client's screen. Atomicity is defined from the perspective of the consumer of the transaction.

■ *Consistency* means that after a transaction executes, it must leave the system in a correct state or it must abort. If the transaction cannot achieve a stable end state, it must return the system to its initial state.

■ *Isolation* means that a transaction's behavior is not affected by other transactions that execute concurrently. The transaction must serialize all accesses to shared resources and guarantee that concurrent programs will not corrupt each other's operations. A multiuser program running under transaction protection must behave exactly as it would in a single-user environment. The changes that a transaction makes to shared resources must not become visible outside the transaction until it commits.

■ *Durability* means that a transaction's effects are permanent after it commits. Its changes should survive system failures. The term "persistent" is a synonym for "durable."

---

[1] Source: Jim Gray and Andreas Reuter, **Transaction Processing Concepts and Techniques** (Morgan Kaufmann, 1993). This 1000-page book is the Bible of transaction processing. It gives some great insights into the motivation behind transaction processing, and it's written by two of the original gurus who pioneered this field.

A transaction becomes the fundamental unit of recovery, consistency, and concurrency in a client/server system. Why is that important? Take a simple debit-credit banking operation. You'd like to see all credit made to *your* account succeed. Any losses would be unacceptable (of course, any unexpected credits are always welcome). This means you're relying on the application to provide the integrity expected in a real-life business transaction. The application, in turn, relies on the underlying system—usually the TP Monitor—to help achieve this level of transactional integrity. The programmer should not have to develop tons of code that reinvents the transaction wheel.

A more subtle point is that all the participating programs must adhere to the transactional discipline because a single faulty program can corrupt an entire system. A transaction that unknowingly uses corrupted initial data—produced by a non-transactional program—builds on top of a corrupt foundation.

In an ideal world, *all* client/server programs are written as transactions. ACID is like motherhood and apple pie. It's necessary—and you can't have too much of it. OK, enough preaching. Let's take a look at how software transactions model their business counterparts.

TRANSACTION MODELS

When should a transaction start? When should it end and have its effects made accessible to the outside world? What are appropriate units of recovery in case of failures? Can computer transactions mirror their real-world counterparts? To answer these questions, we will look at the *flat transaction*, go over its shortcomings, and take a quick peek at the proposed extensions.

So What's a Flat Transaction?

Flat transactions are the workhorses of the current generation of transactional systems. They're called flat because all the work done within a transaction's boundaries is at the same level (see shaded area in Figure 15-1).

The transaction starts with *begin_transaction* and ends with either a *commit_transaction* or *abort_transaction*. It's an all-or-nothing proposition—there's no way to commit or abort *parts* of a flat transaction. All the actions are indivisible, which is what we wanted in the first place. Table 15-1 compares the commands used in different TP Monitors to delineate the transaction boundaries.

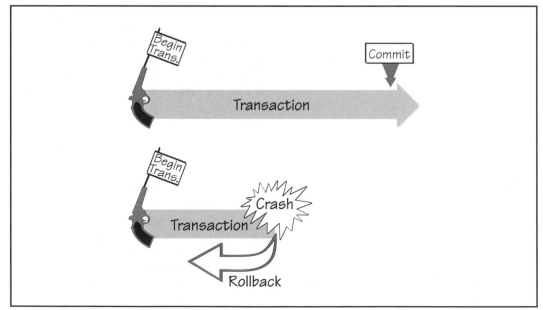

Figure 15-1. The Flat Transaction: An All-or-Nothing Proposition.

Table 15-1. Comparing Flat Transaction Delimiters for Major TP Monitors (Adapted from OTM Spectrum Reports).

System	Transaction Delimiter		
	Start	**Commit**	**Abort**
Tuxedo	TPBEGIN	TPCOMMIT	TPABORT
Top End	tx_begin	tx_commit	tx_rollback
Encina RPC	transaction	onCommit	onAbort
X/Open	tx_begin	tx_commit	tx_rollback
OSI TP	C-BEGIN	C-COMMIT	C-ROLLBACK
Tandem RSC	Begin_Transaction	End_Transaction	Abort_Transaction
CICS	SYNCPOINT	SYNCPOINT	SYNCPOINT or ROLLBACK

We Like Our Transactions Flat

Soapbox

The major virtue of the flat transaction is its *simplicity* and the ease with which it provides the ACID features. Thousands of commercial applications were created using the very simple concept of a flat transaction. Historically, the flat transaction was first developed for banking applications—it provides an excellent fit for modeling short activities.

But as the transactional discipline begins to permeate all facets of computing, we're discovering that the flat transaction model does not provide the best fit in all environments. Millions of lines of code have been written to compensate for its shortcomings. The model is particularly weak when it comes to handling business transactions that span over long periods of time—days or even months. It's somewhat weak in the area of batch jobs. And it's a nuisance in situations that require partial rollbacks without throwing away an entire transaction's work—the rigid "all-or-nothing" application of the ACID principle gets in the way.

For political reasons, flat transactions using two-phase commits are usually not allowed to cross intercorporate boundaries—asynchronous MOM may be the preferred approach in such situations. With MOMs, you lose end-to-end ACID protection in return for relaxing the strict lockstep synchronization imposed by a global two-phase commit protocol. We're also experiencing difficulties with the flat model in client/server environments where client "think time" is part of the transaction loop. There are workarounds for each of these problems, but they require writing some custom code. Wouldn't it be nice if we could extend the transaction model to automatically take care of all these situations for us?

It turns out that computer scientists everywhere are still frantically searching for a "unified theory" of transactions that covers all the complex real-life situations and yet still maintains the ACID properties and the simplicity of the flat model. As a result, the academic literature is flooded with proposed transaction models that have esoteric sounding names like Sagas, Chained, Promises, ConTracts, Check-Revalidate, Long-Lived, Multilevel, Migrating, Shopping Cart, and Anarchic and Non-Anarchic Nested Transactions.

With the exception of Non-Anarchic Nested Transactions—implemented in Transarc's *Encina*—none of these esoterics have found their way into commercial products. They make great reading and are always very clever. However, it's turning out not to be easy to extend the transactional model and still do ACID simply. And the jury is still out when it comes to nested transactions—they may be too difficult to manage in normal commercial applications.

At the risk of sounding too conservative, we still feel there's a lot of life left in venerable flat transactions. They can be used "as is" in over 90% of commercial client/server applications. And writing a *little* bit of code around them doesn't particularly bother us—at least we can get them to do exactly what's needed. We feel (remember, this is a Soapbox) it's more important to keep pushing the flat transaction discipline into every known program so that they can all participate in TP-Monitor coordinated transactions.

Transactions are here to help simplify our applications and give us better control over the environment in which they run. Some of the proposed extensions may create more problems than they solve. In any case, as Gray and Reuter point out, "No matter which extensions prove to be the most important and useful in the future, flat transactions will be at the core of all the mechanisms required to make these more powerful models work." Most of the commercial databases, MOMs, TP Monitors, and Object Transaction Monitors (OTMs) implement the flat transaction model. ❑

Baby Stepping With Flat Transactions

A typical flat transaction does not last more than two or three seconds to avoid monopolizing critical system resources such as database locks. As a result, OLTP client/server programs are divided into short transactions that execute back-to-back to produce results (see Figure 15-2). We call this effect transaction *baby stepping*—or getting work done by moving in "baby steps" from one stable state to the next.[2] For example, you could implement a complex multistep workflow as a sequence of flat transactions that are either conversational or queued.

---

[2] The term "baby step" is adapted from the movie, *What About Bob?* Richard Dreyfus played the role of a psychiatrist who advocated baby stepping as a cure-all.

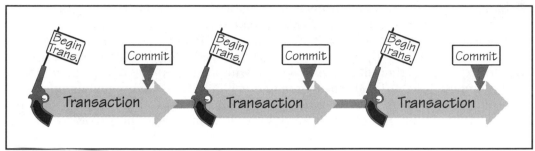

Figure 15-2. Back-to-Back Flat Transactions.

The Distributed Flat Transaction

Can a flat transaction run on multiple sites and update resources located within multiple resource managers? Yes. Even though a high level of parallelism may be involved, as far as the programmer is concerned, it's still just a flat transaction (see Figure 15-3). The programmer is not aware of the considerable amount of "under-the-cover" activity that's required to make the multisite transaction appear flat. The transaction must travel across multiple sites to get to the resources it needs. Each site's TP Monitor must manage its local piece of the transaction. Within a site, the

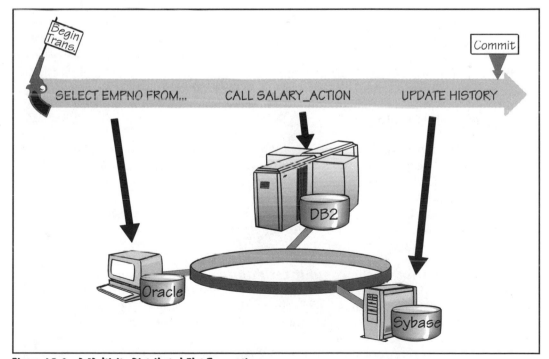

Figure 15-3. A Multisite Distributed Flat Transaction.

TP Monitor coordinates the transactions with the local ACID subsystems and *resource managers*—including database managers, queue managers, persistent objects, and message transports. For example, the TP Monitor will ensure that when a database gets updated, a message gets delivered, and an entry is made in a workflow queue. Either all of these actions will occur (exactly once) or none will. In addition, one of the TP Monitors must coordinate the actions of all its fellow TP Monitors. This is all done using a *two-phase commit* protocol, which coordinates the transaction's commit or abort across multiple sites (see the following Details box).

What's a Two-Phase Commit Protocol?

Details

The *two-phase commit* protocol is used to synchronize updates on different programs and machines so that they either all fail or all succeed. This is done by centralizing the decision to commit but giving each participant the right of veto. It's like a Christian marriage: You're given one last chance to back out of the transaction when you're at the altar. If none of the parties present object, the marriage takes place.

It should come as no surprise by now that each commercial implementation introduces its own variation of the two-phase commit protocol. As usual, they don't interoperate. And, of course, there are standards bodies that are trying to make it all work together. In December 1992—after a five-year development cycle—ISO published its *OSI TP* standard that defines very *rigidly* how a two-phase commit is to be implemented (see Figure 15-4). Let's go over the mechanics of this protocol:

1. ***In the first phase of a commit***, the *commit manager* node—also known as the *root node* or the *transaction coordinator*—sends *prepare-to-commit* commands to all the *subordinate* nodes that were directly asked to participate in the transaction. The subordinates may have spawned pieces of the transaction on other nodes (or resource managers) to which they must propagate the prepare-to-commit command. It becomes a transaction tree, with the coordinator at the root.

2. ***The first phase of the commit terminates*** when the root node receives *ready-to-commit* signals from all its direct subordinate nodes that participate in the transaction. This means that the transaction has executed successfully so far on all the nodes, and they're now ready to do a final commit. The root node logs that fact in a safe place (this information is used to recover from a root node failure).

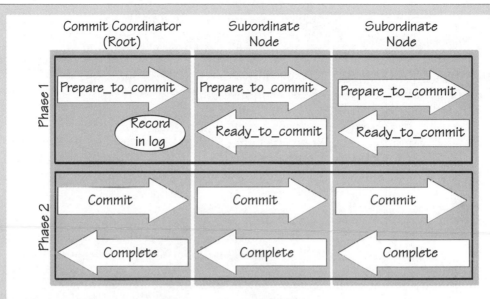

Figure 15-4. The Mechanics of the OSI TP Two-Phase Commit.

3. ***The second phase of the commit starts*** after the root node makes the decision to *commit* the transaction—based on the unanimous yes vote. It tells its subordinates to commit. They, in turn, tell their subordinates to do the same, and the order ripples down the tree.

4. ***The second phase of the commit terminates*** when all the nodes involved have safely committed their part of the transaction and made it durable. The root receives all the confirmations and can tell its client that the transaction completed. It can then relax until the next transaction.

5. ***The two-phase commit aborts*** if any of the participants return a *refuse* indication, meaning that their part of the transaction failed. In that case, the root node tells all its subordinates to perform a rollback. And they, in turn, do the same for their subordinates.

The X/Open XA specification defines a set of APIs that work with the underlying OSI TP protocol. To participate in an XA-defined two-phase commit, TP Monitors and resource managers (like databases and message queues) must map their private two-phase commit protocols to the XA commands. They must also be willing to let somebody else drive the transaction—something they're not accustomed to doing. The XA specification allows participants to withdraw from further participation in the global transaction during Phase 1 if they do not have to update resources. In XA, a TP Monitor can use a one-phase commit if it is dealing with a single resource manager. We'll have a lot more to say about XA in the next chapter.

Currently, most TP Monitors can easily handle transactions that span across one hundred two-phase commit engines. However, the two-phase commit protocol is by no means perfect. Here are some of its limitations:

■ **Performance overhead**, which is introduced by all the message exchanges. The protocol has no way of discerning valuable transactions that need this kind of protection from the more tolerant transactions that don't need protection. It generates messages for all transactions, even read-only ones. The workaround is to explicitly exclude calls that don't update data from a transaction's boundaries. For example, the CORBA *Object Transaction Service (OTS)* lets you explicitly control the propagation of a transaction via *suspend* and *resume* calls.

■ **Hazard windows**, where certain failures can be a problem. For example, if the root node crashes after the first phase of the commit, the subordinates may be left in disarray. Who cleans up this mess? There are always workarounds, but it's a tricky business. It helps if you have in your system some fault-tolerant hardware that is coordinating the transaction.

A number of suggestions were introduced on how to improve the two-phase commit protocol—including single-phase commits, read-only optimizations, overlapped transactions, implicit prepares, and delegated commits. The *delegated commit* proposal is a practical necessity in client/server and Internet environments. Delegated commit means a transaction originating from an unreliable platform—such as an Internet-connected personal computer—can delegate the commit coordination to an alternate node. Today, most TP Monitor vendors have implemented support for delegated commit in their products. ❑

The Limitations of the Flat Transaction

The "all-or-nothing" characteristic of flat transactions is both a virtue and a vice.

— *Gray and Reuter*

So when does the all-or-nothing nature of the flat transaction become a liability? Mostly in situations that require more flexibility than the all-or-nothing approach. The following are examples of business transactions that require a more flexible approach:

■ **Compound business transactions that need to be partially rolled back.** The classic example is a complex trip that includes travel arrangements, hotel reservations, and a car rental (see Figure 15-5). What happens if you simply want to cancel the car reservation but preserve the rest of the reservations? You can't do that within a flat transaction—the entire reservation is rolled back. It's

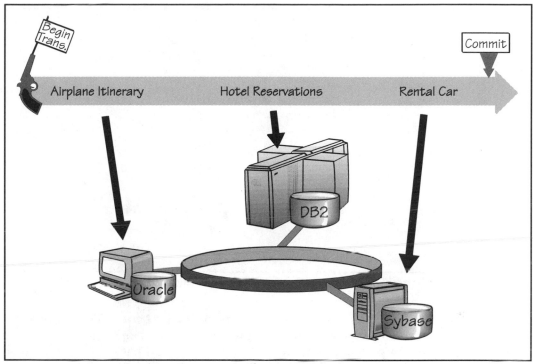

Figure 15-5. Flat Transactions: One Change and You Have to Start all Over.

an all-or-nothing proposition. This means you must give up the hotel and plane reservations just to get rid of the car—a real nuisance. The hotel/car reservation problem is used to justify the need for nested or chained transactions. But flat transaction advocates could make a case that the hotel/car transaction should be broken down into separate hotel and car transactions. In other words, use multiple flat transactions to simulate the compound one.

■ ***Business transactions with humans in the loop.*** This is a classic GUI client/server transaction where a set of choices are presented to the user on a screen, and the server must wait for the decision. In the meantime, locks are held for the records on the screen. What happens if an operator that's viewing some airline seats decides to go to lunch? How long are the seats locked out? If it's executed as a single flat transaction, the seats will be held as long as that user is thinking or eating. Nobody else can get to those seats. This is obviously not a very good way to run a business. The solution is to split the reservation into two transactions: a query transaction that displays the available seats, and a reservation transaction that performs the actual reservation (see Figure 15-6). Of course, the existence of the seats must be revalidated before the update. If the seat is gone, the user must be notified. These extra steps mean more work for the programmer.

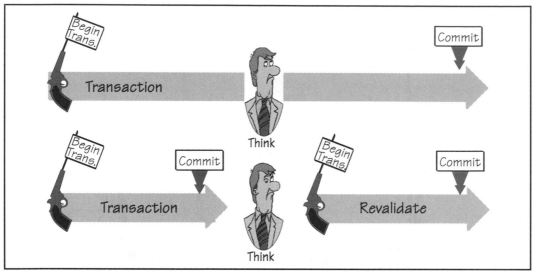

Figure 15-6. Keep the Human Out of the Loop by Creating Two Flat Transactions.

■ ***Business transactions that span long periods of time.*** These are your typical engineering Computer-Aided Design (CAD) transactions that may require CAD-managed components to be worked on for days and passed from engineer to engineer (see Figure 15-7). The CAD transaction must be able to suspend itself and resume after shutdowns, preserve ongoing work across shutdowns, and know where it left off and what needs to be done next. In essence, it becomes a workflow manager. Obviously, flat transactions must be augmented by a workflow program to handle such long-lived work. This is an area where alternative transactional models—including object database check-in check-out transactions, replica management, versioning, and workflow—look very promising.

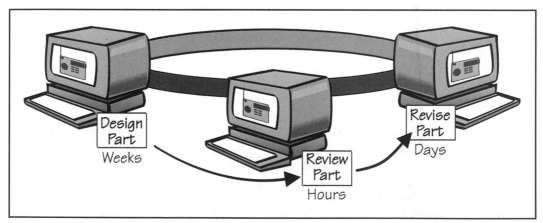

Figure 15-7. Long-Lived Transactions Spanning Days or Weeks.

■ ***Business transactions with a lot of bulk.*** The classic problem here is: How do you handle one million record updates under transactional control (see Figure 15-8)? Must the entire transaction be rolled back if a failure occurs after record 999,999 is updated? Yes, it's all-or-nothing if you're using a single flat transaction to do the million updates. On the other hand, if you make each update a separate transaction, it is much slower—a million separate commits are required—and where do you restart after the failure? This is an area where syncpoints or chained transactions have been proposed as a solution. But the solution may slow you down because it introduces more commits and maybe some restart code. We think you may be better off restarting an occasional flat transaction than going with the alternatives. After all, how often can a bulk transaction fail?

Figure 15-8. Flat Transaction: It Failed—Restart That Million Update Job.

■ ***Business transactions that span across companies or the Internet.*** The problem here is a political one. Very few companies will allow an external TP Monitor (or database) to synchronize in real time a transaction on their systems using a two-phase commit. The more politically correct solution may be to conduct an intercompany exchange using loosely coupled transactional message queues. A MOM solution allows organizations to split the unit of work into many transactions that can be executed asynchronously, processed on different machines, and coordinated by independent TP Monitors within each company (see Figure 15-9). You lose instantaneous consistency, but you're able to maintain arm's length controls between companies. From a software perspective, we ended up breaking a single two-phase commit flat transaction into three independent flat transactions that execute on company A's TP Monitor, MOM, and company B's TP Monitor. The MOM transaction ensures that the transaction has safely made it from company A's computer to company B's computer. We're assuming that MOM provides a durable queue that gives you the "D" in ACID at commit time.

In summary, most of the flat transaction's problems come from the rigidity (and interlock) imposed by the all-or-nothing discipline in situations that require more

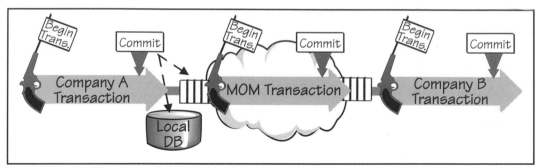

Figure 15-9. Flat Transactions: Using MOM for Intercompany Transactions.

flexibility. You can work around most of these problems by breaking down transactions into smaller units and developing the control code that synchronizes the several smaller transactions. It's a trade-off: You can write one long transaction that can fail in a big way, or several smaller ones that fail in smaller ways. The designer, as usual, must perform a balancing act.

The Alternatives: Chained and Nested Transactions

Most of the proposed alternatives to the flat transaction are based on mechanisms that extend the flow of control beyond the linear unit of work. Two of the most obvious ways to extend the flow of control are by chaining units of work in linear sequences of "mini" transactions—the chained transaction or Saga—or by creating some kind of nested hierarchy of work—the nested transaction. Each of these two basic approaches have many refinements.

The solution to the long-lived transaction requires some form of control flow language for describing activities that evolve in time. This is more or less the model proposed in some of the research literature under names such as *ConTracts*, *Migrating Transactions*, and *Shopping Cart Transactions*. None of these models are available in commercial applications. We feel that the best commercial solutions available today for long-lived transactions are in workflow managers and object databases, which we cover in Parts 6 and 7. So we will defer this discussion until then.

Syncpoints, Chained Transactions, and Sagas

The chained transaction, as the name implies, introduces some form of linear control for sequencing through transactions. The simplest form of chaining is to use *syncpoints*—also known as savepoints—within a flat transaction that allow periodic saves of accumulated work (see Figure 15-10). What makes a syncpoint different from a commit? The syncpoint lets you roll back work and still maintain

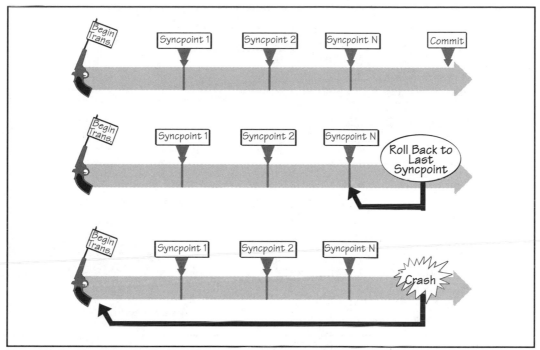

Figure 15-10. Syncpoints Are Not Durable.

a live transaction. In contrast, a commit ends a transaction. Syncpoints also give you better granularity of control over what you save and undo. You can divide the transaction into a series of activities that can be rolled back individually. But the big difference is that the commit is durable while the syncpoint is volatile. If the system crashes during a transaction, all data accumulated in syncpoints is lost.

Chained transactions are a variation of syncpoints that make the accumulated work durable. They allow you to commit work while staying within the transaction, so you don't have to give up your locks and resources. A commit gives you the "D" in ACID without terminating the transaction (see Figure 15-11). But what you lose is the ability to roll back an entire chain's worth of work. There's no free lunch.

Sagas extend the chained transactions to let you roll back the entire chain—if you require it (see Figure 15-12). They do that by maintaining a chain of compensating transactions. You still get the crash resistance of the intermediate commits, but you have the choice of rolling back the entire chain under program control. This lets you treat the entire chain as an atomic unit of work. You can now have your cake and eat it, too.[3]

---

[3] The term "Saga" was first suggested by Bruce Lindsay of IBM Almaden Research. The concept was fully developed by Hector Garcia-Molina and K. Salem in 1987.

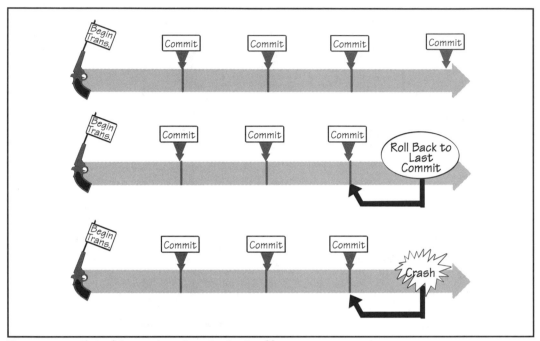

Figure 15-11. Chained Transactions: Commits Are Durable.

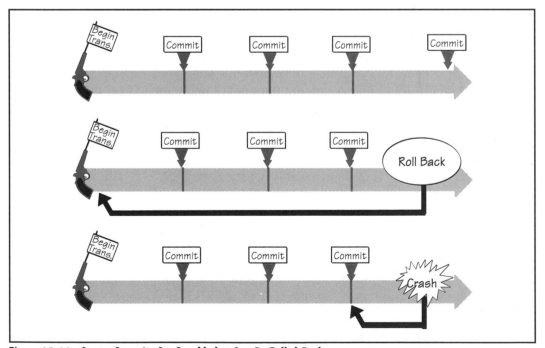

Figure 15-12. Sagas: Commits Are Durable but Can Be Rolled Back.

Nested Transactions

Nested Transactions provide the ability to define transactions within other transactions. They do that by breaking a transaction into hierarchies of "subtransactions" (very much like a program is made up of procedures). The main transaction starts the subtransactions, which behave as dependent transactions. A subtransaction can also start its own subtransactions, thus making the entire structure very recursive.

Figure 15-13 shows a main transaction that starts nested transactions, which behave as dependent transactions. Each subtransaction can issue a commit or rollback for its designated pieces of work. When a subtransaction commits, its results are accessible only to the parent that spawned it. A subtransaction's commit becomes permanent after it issues a local commit and all its ancestors commit. If a parent transaction does a rollback, all its descendent transactions are rolled back, regardless of whether they issued local commits.

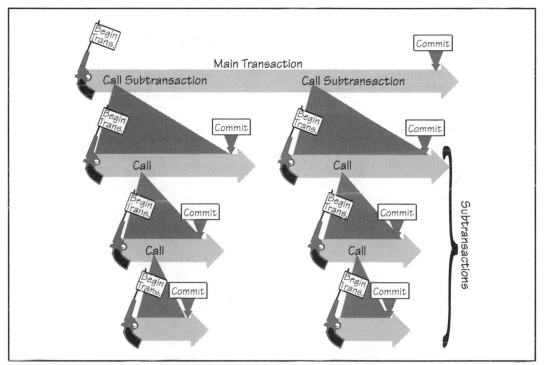

Figure 15-13. Nested Transactions: One Transaction and Many Dependent Subtransactions.

The main benefit of nesting is that a failure in a subtransaction can be trapped and retried using an alternative method, which still allows the main transaction to succeed. Nesting helps programmers write more granular transactions. The only commercial implementation of nested transactions we know of is the Encina TP Monitor. Encina's Transactional C (or C++) allows you to declare the nesting directly in your code where it starts resembling regular procedure invocations. In some cases, nesting may be overkill; it creates more problems than solutions. Of course, now that the Encina TP Monitor is on the market, you can decide for yourself.

CONCLUSION

Transactions are important because they give ordinary programs ACID qualities without writing a line of messy code. All you need to do is say begin and end transaction—and suddenly the magic appears. In the next chapter, we explain how the magic wand of TP Monitors provides the robust mechanisms that keep these transactions running under all sorts of conditions. We also noted that transactions are now being used to represent more complex business activities. Eventually, our transactions will be extended beyond their flat origins to cover some of these more complex business activities. The more pressing need is to permeate the simple flat transactions into all our client/server programs and "ACIDify" them. ACID is the best antidote to the inherent complexity in distributed systems.

Chapter 16

TP Monitors: Managing Client/Server Transactions

TP Monitors make a silk purse out of a sow's ear—they turn mundane operating systems into fast, highly reliable transaction engines.

— Jeri Edwards, VP of Strategy
BEA Systems

Transaction Processing Monitors (TP Monitors) specialize in managing transactions from their point of origin—typically on the client—across one or more servers, and then back to the originating client. When a transaction ends, the TP Monitor ensures that all the systems involved in the transaction are left in a consistent state. In addition, TP Monitors know how to run transactions, route them across systems, load-balance their execution, and restart them after failures.

One of the great appeals of a TP Monitor is that it is the overseer of all aspects of a distributed transaction, regardless of the systems or resource managers used. A TP Monitor can manage resources on a single server or multiple servers, and it can cooperate with other TP Monitors in federated arrangements. Future TP Monitors may reside on every client machine to bring desktop resources—such as the user interface, local data warehouses, or personal agents—within a distributed transaction's reach.

In this chapter, we explain in some detail what TP Monitors are and what functions they perform. We go over X/Open's model for how TP Monitors interact with other resource managers in an open environment. We conclude with a list of benefits that TP Monitors provide. We felt this list was needed because the benefits of TP Monitors are not well understood in the PC LAN and Unix worlds. TP Monitors are either treated with awe and left to the "High Priests" of computer science, or they are dismissed as antiques. Neither is true. TP Monitors are fun to program, and they create transactional magic on ordinary client/server networks. But enough talk; this isn't a Soapbox.

TP MONITORS

TP applications have once again become an important growth factor for the computer industry.

> — *IDC*
> *(June, 1998)* [1]

TP Monitors first appeared on mainframes to provide robust run-time environments that could support large-scale OLTP applications—airline and hotel reservations, banking, automatic teller machines, credit authorization systems, and stock-brokerage systems. Since then, OLTP has spread to almost every type of business application—including hospitals, manufacturing, point-of-sales retail systems, automated gas pumps, and telephone directory services. TP Monitors provide whatever services are required to keep these OLTP applications running in the style they're accustomed to: highly reactive, available, and well-managed. With OLTP moving to open client/server platforms, a new breed of TP Monitors is emerging to help make the new environment hospitable to mission-critical applications.

What's a TP Monitor?

It should come as no surprise that our industry has no commonly accepted definition of a TP Monitor. We'll use Jeri Edwards' definition of a TP Monitor as "an operating system for transaction processing." A TP Monitor also provides a framework for running middle-tier server applications and components. This definition captures the essence of a TP Monitor. So what does an operating system for transaction processing do in life? How does it interface with the rest of the world? What services does it provide? We'll answer all these questions. In a nutshell, a TP Monitor does three things extremely well:

---

[1] Source: IDC, *Transaction Processing Software: 1998 Worldwide Markets and Trends* (June, 1998).

- **Process management** includes starting server processes, funneling work to them, monitoring their execution, and balancing their workloads.

- **Transaction management** means that it guarantees the ACID properties to all programs that run under its protection.

- **Client/server communications management** allows clients (and services) to invoke an application component in a variety of ways—including request-response, conversations, queuing, publish-and-subscribe, or broadcast.

TP Monitors and OSs: The Great Funneling Act

TP Monitors were originally introduced to run classes of applications that could service hundreds and sometimes thousands of clients (think of an airline reservation application). If each of these thousands of clients were given all the resources it needed on a server—typically a communication connection, half a MByte of memory, one or two processes, and a dozen open file handles—even the largest mainframe server would fall on its knees (see Figure 16-1).

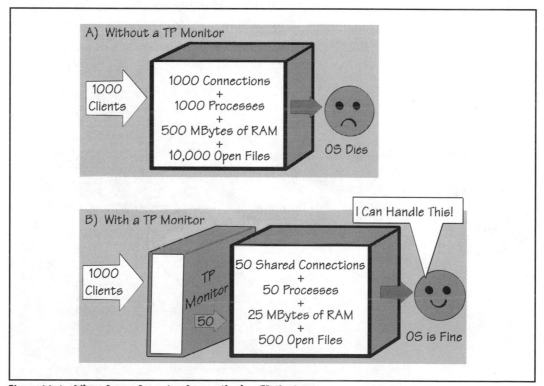

Figure 16-1. Why a Server Operating System Needs a TP Monitor.

Luckily, not all the clients require service at the same time. However, when they do require it, they want their service *immediately*. We're told that the humans on a client machine have a "tolerance for waiting" of two seconds or less. TP Monitors provide an operating system—on top of existing OSs—that connects in real time these thousands of impatient humans with a pool of shared server processes—this is called *funneling*.

How Is the Great Funneling Act Performed?

The "funneling act" is part of what a TP Monitor must do to efficiently manage OLTP applications. The server side of the OLTP application consists of *services*—typically packaged in DLLs or shared libraries—that contain a number of related functions. The TP Monitor assigns the execution of each service to *server classes*, which are pools of prestarted application processes or threads waiting for work. Each process or thread in a server class is capable of doing the work. The TP Monitor balances the workload between them. Each application can have one or more server classes. (Note: These are not classes in the object-oriented sense of the word.)

When a client sends a service request, the TP Monitor hands it to an available process in the server class pool (see Figure 16-2). The server process dynamically

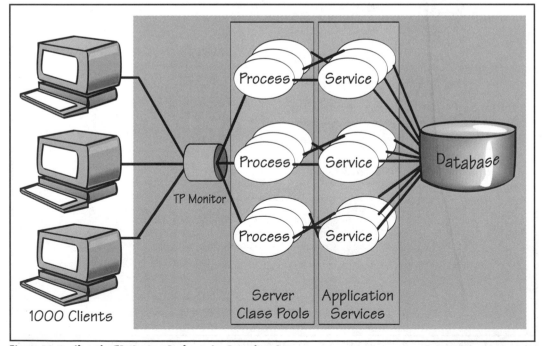

Figure 16-2. How the TP Monitor Performs Its Funneling Act.

links to the service called by the client, invokes it, oversees its execution, and returns the results to the client. After that completes, another client can reuse the server process. The operating system keeps the already loaded services in memory, where they can be shared across processes. It doesn't get better!

In essence, the TP Monitor removes the process-per-client requirement by funneling incoming client requests to shared server processes. If the number of incoming client requests exceeds the number of processes in a server class, the TP Monitor may dynamically start new ones—this is called *load balancing*. The more sophisticated TP Monitors can distribute the process load across multiple CPUs in SMP or MPP environments. Part of the load balancing act involves managing the priorities of the incoming requests. The TP Monitor does that by running some high-priority server classes and dynamically assigning them to the VIP clients.

Typically, short-running and high-priority functions are packaged in high-priority server classes. Batch and low-priority functions are assigned to low-priority server classes. You can also partition server classes by application type, desired response time, the resources they manage, fault-tolerance requirements, and client/server interaction modes—including queued, conversational, or RPC. In addition to providing dynamic load balancing, most TP Monitors let you manually control how many processes or threads are available to each process class.

In their load-balancing capacity, TP Monitors play the role of a client/server *traffic cop*. They route client requests to pools of application processes spread across multiple servers—some of which consist of multiple processors in SMP or MPP configurations.

TP Monitors and Transaction Management

*S*ystems involving thousands of clients and hundreds of services have lots of moving parts. Change is constant, and TP Monitors manage it "on-the-fly."

— *Jim Gray and Jeri Edwards*
BYTE Magazine
(April, 1995)[2]

The transaction discipline was introduced in the early TP Monitors to ensure the robustness of multiuser applications that ran on the servers. These applications had to be bulletproof and highly reliable if they were going to serve thousands of users in "bet-your-business" situations. TP Monitors were developed from the ground up as operating systems for transactions. The unit of management, execution, and

---

[2] Source: Jim Gray and Jeri Edwards, *Scale Up with TP Monitors*, BYTE (April, 1995).

recovery is an ordinary transaction. The job of a TP Monitor is to guarantee the ACID properties while maintaining high transaction throughput. To do that, it must manage the execution, distribution, and synchronization of transaction *workloads*.

As component-based middleware becomes dominant, transaction coordination becomes even more important. Clients mix-and-match several components to implement a single business transaction. Each of these components may make an update to a database. They become "mini-programs." As a result, their updates need to be coordinated. TP Monitors play this role by providing the ACID properties to the application. For example, components may update the same database or different databases—maybe even different types of databases. What happens if the business transaction is stopped or fails in the middle of all these updates? The TP Monitor ensures that all the updates associated with an aborted transaction are removed or "rolled back." It can even perform this trick when the components are on different servers and are updating databases from different vendors across networks. The TP Monitor synchronizes all the transaction's updates using a two-phase commit protocol.

With TP Monitors, the application programmers don't have to concern themselves with issues like concurrency, failures, broken connections, load balancing, and the synchronization of resources across multiple nodes. All this is made transparent to them—very much like an operating system makes the hardware transparent to ordinary programs. Simply put, TP Monitors provide the run-time engines for running transactions—they do that on top of ordinary hardware and operating systems. They also provide a framework for running your server applications.

TP Monitor Client/Server Interaction Types

Ordinary operating systems must understand the nature of the jobs and resources they manage. This is also true for TP Monitors—they must provide an optimized environment for the execution of the transactions that run under their control. This means they must load the server programs, dynamically assign incoming client requests to server processes, recover from failures, return the replies to the clients, and make sure high-priority traffic gets through first.

One of the jobs TP Monitors have is to provide communications between clients and servers—and between the servers. They need to do this while maintaining the ACID properties. So what kind of transactional communications do TP Monitors provide? They typically support one or all of these facilities: conversational, RPC, queued, publish-and-subscribe, and batch (see Figure 16-3). Conversational and RPC transactions usually involve a human user that requires immediate attention; they run in high-priority mode. Publish-and-subscribe transactions usually run as

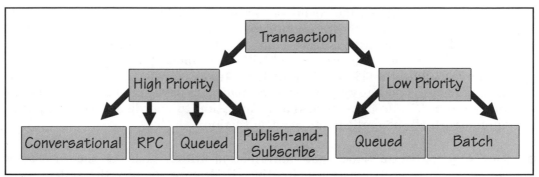

Figure 16-3. Client/Server Transaction Profiles.

high-priority messages too. Batch transactions typically run in low-priority mode. MOM-based queued transactions can be of either type.

TP Monitors complement Message Brokers (or MOMs) very well. Together, they can support long-lived transactions and workflow applications. TP Monitors can act as the transaction coordinator for work exchanged through transactional queues. The queued events can trigger server processes managed by the TP Monitor.

In addition, TP Monitors must be prepared to communicate with all the resource managers on which the transaction executes—whether they're on the same machine or across a network. When the resource managers are across networks, the TP Monitor synchronizes the transaction with the remote TP Monitors using a two-phase commit.

What Makes Transactional Communications Different?

On the surface, transactional client/server exchanges appear to use traditional communication models such as RPCs, queues, ORB invocations, publish-and-subscribe, and conversational peer-to-peer. This is not so. They're really using highly augmented versions of these traditional communication mechanisms. However, most of the value-added elements are made transparent to the programmer—they look like ordinary exchanges bracketed by start and end transaction calls. The transactional versions augment the familiar communications exchanges with the following value-added extensions:

■ They piggyback *transactional delimiters* that allow a client to specify the begin-transaction and end-transaction boundaries. The actual commit mechanics are usually *delegated* to one of the server TP Monitors—otherwise, each client would need to manage ACID properties and maintain transactional logs, which would be an unmanageable and unreliable situation.

- They introduce—under-the-cover—a three-way exchange between a client, server, and TP Monitor (the transaction manager). A new transaction is assigned a unique ID by the coordinating TP Monitor. All subsequent message exchanges between the participants are tagged with that transaction ID. The message exchanges allow the TP Monitor to keep track of what Jim Gray calls the "dynamically expanding web" of resource managers participating in a distributed transaction. TP Monitors need that information to coordinate the two-phase commit with all the participants in a transaction.

- They embed transactional state information within each of the messages exchanged. This information helps the TP Monitor identify the state of the distributed transaction and figure out what to do next.

- They allow a TP Monitor to enforce *exactly-once* semantics—this means that the message only gets executed once.

- They guarantee that a server process is at the receiving end of the message. Traditional RPCs and MOMs don't worry about this kind of stuff—they assume that a program will "automagically" appear on the receiving end.

- They provide server routing based on, for example, server classes, server loads, and automatic failover.

As you can see, there's a lot more going on here than a simple RPC, MOM, or ORB exchange. The literature calls these enhanced services *Transactional RPC (TRPC)*, *Transactional Queues*, *Transactional Publish-and-Subscribe*, *Transactional Conversations*, and *Transactional ORB Invocations*. The distinguishing factor is that all resource managers and processes invoked through these calls become part of the transaction. The TP Monitor is informed of any service calls; it uses that information to orchestrate the actions of all the participants, enforce their ACID behavior, and make them act as part of a transaction. In contrast, traditional RPCs, messages, and queue invocations are between separate programs that are not bound by a transaction discipline. Table 16-1 summarizes the differences between transactional communication mechanisms and their non-transactional equivalents.

Examples of commercial implementations of transactional RPCs include Transarc/IBM's *Encina Transactional RPC*, BEA's *Tuxedo TxRPC*, and IBM's *CICS External Call Interface (ECI)*. Examples of conversational transactional interfaces are found in *Tuxedo ATMI*, Tandem's *RSC*, and IBM's *APPC*. IBM's *MQSeries* and BEA's *MessageQ* are examples of a transactional implementation of an "open" MOM queue. Some TP Monitors also include their own bundled versions of recoverable queues. In Encina's case, it is *RQS*, and in Tuxedo, it is */Q*; CICS uses transient queues. In addition, Tuxedo has a transactional publish-and-subscribe subsystem called the *EventBroker*. Finally, commercial implementations of the CORBA *Object Transaction Service (OTS)* are beginning to appear in ORBs such as Iona's *Orbix*, BEA's *M3*, IBM's *Component Broker*, and Inprise/Borland's *VisiBroker*.

Table 16-1. Transactional Versus Non-Transactional Communications.

Feature	Ordinary Queues, RPCs, ORBs, Publish-and-Subscribe, and Conversational Communications	Transactional Queues, RPCs, ORBs, Publish-and-Subscribe, and Conversational Communications
Participants	Loosely-coupled client/server programs.	Transactionally bound client/server and server/server programs. The message invocation causes the recipient program to join the transaction.
Commit synchronization	No	Yes
Only-once semantics	No	Yes
Server management on the recipient node	No. It's just a delivery mechanism. (ORBs provide minimal server management.)	Yes. The process that receives the message is started, load balanced, monitored, and tracked as part of the transaction.
Load balancing	Using the directory services. The first server to register becomes a hotspot. No dynamic load balancing is provided.	Uses the TP Monitor's sophisticated load-balancing algorithms. Can spread work across multiple SMP machines and dynamically add more processes to cover hotspots of activity. Several servers can read from the same queue.
Supervised exchanges	No. Exchanges are simply between the client and the server. The exchanges are transient. No crash recovery or error management is provided. You're on your own.	The TP Monitor supervises the entire exchange, restarts communication links, redirects messages to an alternate server process if the first one gets hung, performs retries, and provides persistent queues and crash recovery.

TP Monitor Standards: XA, OTS, MTS/DTC, and EJB

TP Monitors need standards because they're the ultimate glue software. The applications they coordinate could be running on different platforms with access to different databases and resource managers. These applications are most likely developed using different tools. And they have absolutely no knowledge of each other. The only way to make these disparate pieces come together is through "open standards" that specify how a TP Monitor interfaces to resource managers, to other TP Monitors, and to its clients.

The X/Open standards body has defined a set of specifications that allows applications, *resource managers* (such as databases), and *transaction managers* to synchronize distributed transactions. This is called the X/Open *Distributed Transaction Processing (DTP)* standard (see Figure 16-4). Because there are multiple players involved in a transaction, multiple interfaces need to be defined. Here are the most important of these interfaces:

■ **RM API** is used by an application to query and update resources that are owned by a *Resource Manager (RM)*.

■ **TX API** is used by an application to signal the transaction manager that it is beginning a transaction, ready to commit it, or wants to abort it.

■ **XA API** is used by the transaction manager to coordinate transaction updates across resource managers. Through this interface, the transaction manager tells the resource managers when to *prepare to commit, commit,* or *rollback* transactions.

■ **OSI-TP** protocols allow heterogeneous transaction managers to work together to coordinate transactions.

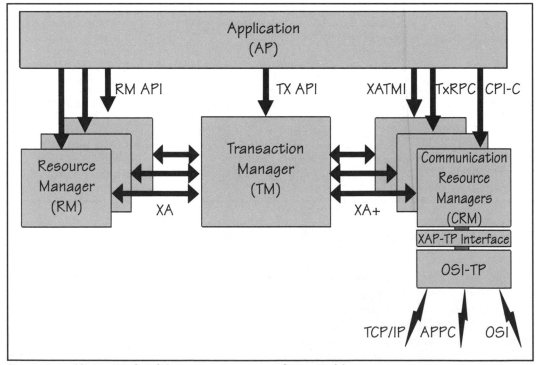

Figure 16-4. X/Open Distributed Transaction Processing Reference Model.

■ **XATMI, TxRPC, and CPI-C** are transactional communication programming interfaces. You have your choice of standards. XATMI is based on BEA Tuxedo's *Application-to-Transaction Monitor Interface (ATMI)*, a message-oriented interface; TxRPC is based on the *Distributed Computing Environment (DCE)* remote procedure call interface; and CPI-C is a peer-to-peer conversational interface based on IBM's CPI-C. There is a standard here to please every camp! Note that some transaction managers support more than one interface—for example, Tuxedo supports both XATMI and TxRPC.

The good news is that you, the programmer, only have to use TX and one of the remote communications interfaces. The rest are under-the-cover interfaces that each of your transaction managers and resource managers should support. The other good news is that CORBA ORBs have built-in transaction support. The CORBA *Object Transaction Service (OTS)* is patterned after XA. In addition, support for transactions is built directly into the ORB's communication service, which makes their propagation transparent to ordinary objects.[3] Finally, the *Java Transaction Service (JTS)* is an implementation of OTS in Java. The new Java Enterprise JavaBeans standard is based on OTS and JTS. EJB lets you write transactional beans by simply setting attributes. In the Microsoft parallel universe, COM+ provides a similar function; it uses OLE TP's DTC services to coordinate transactions (more on this in Part 7).

---

[3] Most of the architects that defined CORBA's *Object Transaction Service (OTS)* worked in TP Monitor development groups. So you can guess that OTS was designed to do two things: 1) be a really good implementation of the transaction processing principles collected from years of practice, and 2) allow TP Monitors and ORBs to be more easily integrated.

3-Tier Client/Server, TP Monitor Style

Soapbox

TP Monitors insulate the application from the RDBMS and make it easier to substitute one RDBMS for another. This will limit database vendors' ability to lock their customers. It effectively relegates their products to the status of interchangeable commodities.

— Summit Strategies

TP Monitors are an example (but not the only one) of a 3-tier client/server architecture. Remember, we belong to the school that defines a 3-tier distributed application as consisting of: 1) the GUI front-end, 2) the application logic, and 3) the back-end resource managers. Examples of resource managers include SQL databases, hierarchical databases, file systems, document stores, message queues, HTML stores, legacy applications, and other back-end services.

TP Monitors fit this 3-tier model because they manage the application processes independently from the database or the GUI front-end. TP Monitors provide an extra tier that separates client front-ends from the resource managers (see Figure 16-5).

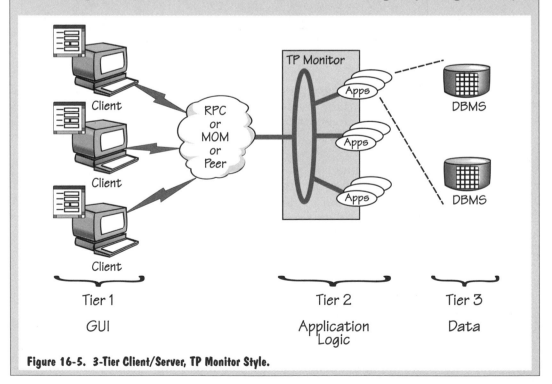

Figure 16-5. 3-Tier Client/Server, TP Monitor Style.

By breaking this direct connection, TP Monitors control all the traffic that links hundreds (or thousands) of clients with application programs and the back-end resources. TP Monitors ensure that the transactions are completed accurately, provide load balancing, and improve the overall system performance. More importantly, TP Monitors make your processes independent of any resource manager. They let you work with any back-end resource.

In a nutshell, TP Monitors treat processes as first-class citizens. They have a separate existence outside the database or GUI. This means that you can distribute processes across machines and networks to wherever it makes the most sense. In contrast, with database client/server, the application is either buried deep inside the bowels of a front-end tool (the fat client) or deep inside the bowels of a database in the form of stored procedures (the fat server). The database model does not treat processes as independent first-class citizens. So even though stored procedures have a 3-tier veneer, their packaging is the epitome of 2-tier.

As we explained in Part 1, the 3-tier approach is the only one that makes sense in an intergalactic, multiserver world. But keep in mind that TP Monitors are just one way to implement 3-tier client/server solutions. We will show you other approaches as we progress throughout the book. As usual, you get to pick the style that best suits your needs. ❑

TP MONITOR BENEFITS

A word of congratulations to the OLTP community is in order: We can now glue most any systems together.

— **Alfred Spector, VP**
IBM

Because TP Monitors may be unfamiliar to many of our readers, we will go over a list of benefits that TP Monitors offer to client/server applications. Even though TP Monitors were originally introduced to serve very large "mission-critical" applications, the new versions are well-suited for handling client/server applications that span from a few nodes to thousands of nodes. Eventually, we believe that a TP Monitor component will reside on every workstation that's connected to a network—not just servers.

Here's a list of benefits that can be obtained from using the current crop of client/server oriented TP Monitors:

- *Client/Server application development framework.* Increasingly, visual tool vendors are directly supporting RPCs and making the TP Monitor transparent to the developers. IDL-defined RPCs are easier to integrate with front-end tools than proprietary stored procedures. On the server side, TP Monitors provide general-purpose server shells (server classes) that run your RPCs. The TP Monitor introduces an event-driven programming style on servers by letting you associate RPCs (event handlers) with server events. In addition, the TP Monitor run-time environment enforces the ACID discipline without requiring any specialized code other than begin/end transaction. You can think of a TP Monitor as providing a pre-built *framework* that helps you build, run, and administer a client/server application (you don't start from ground zero). TP Monitors—augmented with open vendor GUI tools—provide an excellent platform for developing robust, high-performing, client/server applications quickly.

- *Firewalls of protection.* In a client/server world, it is important to protect yourself from everything that can go wrong in the distributed environment. TP Monitors implement "firewalls" between applications and resource managers and between applications themselves. TP Monitors support tightly-coupled firewalls such as two-phase commits or loosely-coupled firewalls such as those provided by transactional queues. The unit of protection is the ACID transaction.

- *High availability.* TP Monitors are designed to work around all types of failures. The permeation of ACID principles throughout all components helps create self-healing systems. TP Monitors are always aware of the status the client/server resources under their control. With ACID, you can detect a failure exactly where it happens. If a hardware failure occurs, the TP Monitor can then restart the failed process or switch over to a process on another node. Architectures with no single point of failure are achievable.

- *Load balancing.* TP Monitors specialize in process management and support both static and dynamic load-balancing techniques. TP Monitors support the prioritization of requests and can *dynamically* replicate server processes on the same server node or on different nodes. In the static case, a pool of server classes may be scheduled to handle certain peak loads (for example, between work shifts) and then scaled down to support other job mixes during the day. The TP Monitor's load balancing software is an excellent match for today's new breed of SMP (and MPP) server hardware.

- *MOM integration.* TP Monitors complement MOMs very well. Together, they can provide support for long-lived transactions and workflow type of applications. TP Monitors can act as the transaction coordinator for work that is exchanged through transactional queues. The queued events can trigger server processes managed by the TP Monitor.

- *Scalabilty of function.* TP Monitors encourage you to create modular reusable services that encapsulate resource managers. With a TP Monitor, you export the function call and not the data itself. This means that you can keep adding new function calls and let the TP Monitor distribute that function over multiple servers. TP Monitors allow you to create highly complex applications by just adding more services. The TP Monitor guarantees that services that know nothing about each other will work together in ACID unison. In addition, the TP Monitor lets you mix resource managers, so you can always start with one resource manager and then move to another one while preserving your investments in the function calls. All functions—even legacy ones—join the TP Monitor managed pool of reusable services. In other words, TP Monitors let you add heterogeneous server resources anywhere without altering the existing application architecture. The Standish Group calls this "matrix scalability."

■ **Reduced system cost.** With TP Monitors, you can save money. According to the Standish Group, TP Monitors may result in total system cost savings of greater than 30%—depending on system scale—over a more database-centric approach. In addition, the Standish Group research shows that significant "development time" savings—up to 40% or 50%—can be achieved. In addition, the funneling effect of TP Monitors can result in large savings in the acquisition of resource managers. This is because database vendors typically charge by the number of active users; funneling cuts down on that number, which equates to lower license fees. TP Monitors, with their load balancing, also provide better performance using the same system resources; this means that you can run your application on less expensive hardware. Finally, TP Monitors don't lock you into a vendor-specific database solution, which makes the acquisition process more competitive and adds to cost savings (instead, they lock you into a TP Monitor single-vendor solution).

OTMS: TP MONITORS MORPH WITH ORBS

TP Monitors are competing with distributed objects to become the application platform of choice for 3-tier client/server computing. So it should come as no surprise that the key TP Monitor vendors are introducing a new generation of TP Monitors built on ORBs. For example, the *Microsoft Transaction Server* is based on DCOM. IBM is introducing its *Component Broker* technology, which is based on CORBA business objects. Finally, BEA delivered its next-generation Tuxedo—called *M3*—on a CORBA distributed object foundation. GartnerGroup calls these morphs *Object Transaction Monitors (OTMs)*. An OTM is 70% TP Monitor and 30% ORB. In Part 7, we will have a lot more to say about OTMs—after we cover ORBs and Enterprise JavaBeans. However, here's a short preview.

What do ORBs do for TP Monitors? ORBs bring TP Monitors to the client/server mainstream. There, they will become the orchestrators of the *Object Web*—that is, the next-generation infrastructure that combines Web and object technologies to support Internet, intranet, and extranet applications. ORBs with built-in transactional middleware are being incorporated into commodity desktop operating sys-

tems, Web browsers, and Java VMs. For the first time, TP Monitor vendors will not have to provide transactional communications themselves. The ORBs will deliver the transaction context to the TP Monitors as part of a method invocation using CORBA OTS or COM+.

In addition, ORBs provide TP Monitors with a myriad of standard services—including metadata, dynamic invocations, persistence, relationships, events, naming, component factories, versioning, licensing, security, change management, and collections. And objects also make it easier for TP Monitors to create and manage rich transaction models—such as nested transactions and long-lived transactions (or workflow). TP Monitors will become frameworks for managing objects packaged as transaction-savvy components—for example, CORBA/EJBs or server-side ActiveXs.

So, what do TP Monitors do for ORBs? TP Monitors (OTMs really) offer these independently-developed components a broad array of mission-critical services—including transaction management, transactional workflow, load balancing, transactional queues, fault-tolerance, and lifecycle services. TP Monitors also make it possible for ORBs to manage millions of objects.

Pure CORBA and DCOM implementations are totally anarchistic. Objects can appear anywhere at any time. Once they do, they stick around—no one knows how to get rid of them. This is not a good scenario for applications that could have millions of run-time objects. In contrast, TP Monitors do not like to be surprised. They like to be in control of their environment. Under the supervision of an OTM, objects can be managed in a *predictable* manner. Instead of just loading and running an application, an OTM prestarts components, manages their lifecycle and persistent state, and coordinates their interactions across networks. OTMs make ORBs mission-critical.

Together, OTMs and a new generation of server-side components can literally perform magic. OTMs will become the coordinators of distributed components on the Internet and intranets. Instead of managing procedural services, OTMs manage Enterprise JavaBeans, CORBA Beans, and ActiveXs (see Figure 16-6).

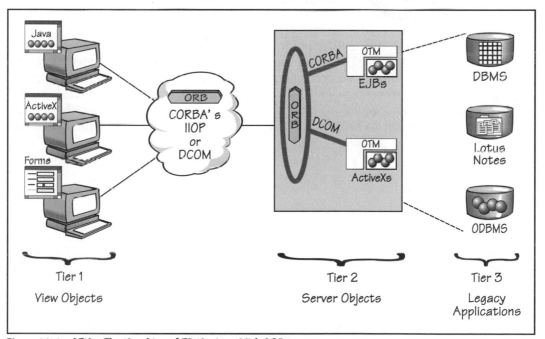

Figure 16-6. OTMs: The Morphing of TP Monitors With ORBs.

CONCLUSION

There is a strange dichotomy in how enterprise IT shops deal with the middle tier. The same organizations that would never dream of building a DBMS dive head first into building their own infrastructure for the middle tier. They tend to see it as a simple task—at least until the requirements start to grow exponentially. The result is that—according to Standish Group—IT shops spend 70% of their resources building infrastructure. These large, risk-prone projects probably contribute to the high rate of IT project failures—53% fail, according to Standish.

TP Monitors provide a rich infrastructure for 3-tier client/server applications that is difficult to duplicate. TP Monitor vendors spent hundreds of person-years building these systems in the first place. And they have had the added advantage of incorporating feedback from hundreds of production, mission-critical 3-tier applications.

So, when should you use a TP Monitor? Standish Group recommends that you use a TP Monitor for any client/server application that has over 100 clients, processes five or more TPC-C type transactions per minute, uses three or more physical servers, and/or uses two or more databases. We recommend that you use a TP Monitor for all of your client/server applications. Even though TP Monitors were originally introduced to serve very large mission-critical applications, the new versions are well-suited for handling client/server applications that span from a few to thousands of nodes.

TP Monitors put you in the healthy habit of writing 3-tier client/server applications. And—with the advent of OTMs—they prepare you for the final destination: the world of distributed objects where Internet, intranet, and extranet applications all use a common infrastructure—the *Object Web*. Now that some of the popular client/server tools have added support for TP Monitors, you can't use the excuse that they're too difficult to program. If you believe Standish Group, they save you money in the long run, so cost shouldn't be an issue.

300 - 354

Chapter 17

TP-Lite or
TP-Heavy?

The database companies want to control the application space through the use of their proprietary database stored procedures. By controlling the application space, they control the customer.

— **Jim Johnson, Standish Group**

TP Monitors are proprietary environments. It is a bit silly to suggest that their use provides independence.

— **Bobby Cameron, Forrester Research**

You may recall from Part 4 that the SQL database managers are also in the business of managing transactions across their own resources. Some database-centric advocates argue that database transactions with stored procedures is all that's needed in the area of transaction management. They call their approach *TP-Lite*.

In contrast to database managers, TP Monitors extend the notion of transactions to *all* resources, not just data-centric ones. TP Monitors track the execution of functions on a single server or across servers on the network—their approach is called *TP-Heavy*. We will go over the current industry debate between TP-Lite and TP-Heavy. As Jim Gray puts it, "Your problems aren't over by just embracing the concept of RPC or even TP-Lite."

And while these two TP camps are debating, the majority of the client/server world is *TP-Less*. There is very little awareness in the PC client/server world today of what transaction management is and why it's even needed. However, transaction management is second nature to most IS people who are "downsizing" from mainframe environments. These folks won't deploy an OLTP application on a client/server network without some kind of TP Monitor. As a result, they're creating demand for a new breed of open TP Monitors.

IDC reports that the total revenue from TP Monitors—hardware and software (but not services)—was $10.5 billion in 1997 and is expected to reach $16.1 billion in 2002.[1] These numbers say that the OLTP market represents a huge opportunity for client/server systems.

In this chapter, we cover the TP-Lite versus TP-Heavy debate. It's important to understand what's missing from database-centric transaction processing. And, of course, there will be a Soapbox that tells you our side of that debate. Again Jim Gray is right: "TP is where the money is: both literally (most banks are TP systems) and figuratively (CICS has generated more revenues than any other piece of software)." So it may be worth exploring which type of TP system—Lite or Heavy—is best for client/server needs.

THE ORIGINS OF TP-LITE

My transaction hopes are pinned on the impact of the distribution of processing—when it is realized that data is not everything and that process is just as important.

— Jim Gray

In the good old days of mainframes, the divisions were clear: Database servers focused on managing data, while TP Monitors focused on managing processes and applications. The two sides stayed out of each other's turf and kept improving on what they did best. It was a classic win/win situation where everybody prospered. This happy coexistence came to an end in 1986, when Sybase became the first database vendor to integrate components of the TP Monitor inside the database engine.

---

[1] Source: IDC, *Transaction Processing Software: 1998 Worldwide Markets and Trends* (June, 1998).

Sybase Breaks the Truce

How did Sybase do it? You may recall from Part 4 that Sybase funnels all client requests into a multithreaded, single-process server. It's an N-to-1 funnel. This may be called a case of *funnel overkill* because the database and user applications share the same address space—a sure invitation for disaster.

But Sybase did not stop with funneling; it also became the first database vendor to introduce stored procedures and triggers—two functions that definitely belong on the procedural side of the house. With its new architecture, Sybase became the uncontested champion of the database benchmarking wars. Of course, most database vendors were quick to follow suit. By now, most of them provide some level of funneling and support for stored procedures in their database engines. Application developers and tool vendors were quick to exploit the benefits of stored procedures, and the *TP-Lite* client/server architecture was born.

Given the popularity of database servers on PC LANs, does this mean TP Monitors are dead? Are they just an anachronism from the mainframe days? Is TP-Lite integrated with database the new platform of choice for application servers and OLTP? The answers to all these questions must, of course, be no; we didn't write an entire part on TP Monitors for nothing. So let's first review the facts in a cool, analytical manner. Then we'll jump on the Soapbox and throw in some opinions about where all this is heading.

What Is TP-Lite?

TP-Lite is simply the integration of TP Monitor functions in the database engines. Currently, only a few of the TP Monitor functions are integrated—including function shipping, some level of funneling, single-function transaction management, and RPC-like calls. It is not clear if the database vendors plan to reinvent the wheel and develop all the missing TP Monitor functions in TP-Lite. There's still a long list of unimplemented functions; the TP Monitor people have a ten-year headstart.

What Is TP-Heavy?

TP-Heavy is TP Monitors as defined in the last chapter. The new generation of TP-Heavy client/server products includes CICS, Encina, Tuxedo, Tandem's Pathway, Top End, and Digital's ACMS. All these TP Monitors support the client/server architecture and allow PCs to initiate some very complex multiserver transactions from the desktop. All these products are supported by open visual builder tools that let you create the front-end separately from the back-end. TP-Heavy includes all the

functions defined in the last chapter—including process management, load balancing, global transaction synchronization, interfaces to multiple resource managers, and error recovery.

TP-LITE VERSUS TP-HEAVY

TP-Lite systems may not solve all the world's problems, but they solve many simple ones. According to Ziph's law: most problems are simple.

— Jim Gray

We *won't have an OLTP environment manufactured by a single vendor (TP-Lite), but rather an OLTP environment that includes a mosaic of services (TP-Heavy). I think TP-Heavy will win.*

— Alfred Spector

A feature-by-feature comparison between TP-Lite and TP-Heavy is painfully unequal. It's like comparing a Harley-Davidson motorcycle with a bicycle. TP-Lite can best be defined by what it lacks, which is a long list of functions. In a nutshell, TP-Lite functions don't execute under global transaction control, there is no global supervisor, and the process management environment is very primitive. TP-Lite server functions only work with a single resource manager (the local database), and they don't support any form of ACID nesting. Like a bicycle, these functions are perfect fits for certain environments. Here are the biggest differences between these two technologies.

TP-Lite Versus TP-Heavy: Scope of the Commit

A *TP-Lite* stored procedure is written in a database-vendor proprietary procedural language—PL/SQL, Transact SQL, and so on—and is stored in the database. A stored procedure is a transactional unit, but it can't participate with other transactional units in a global transaction. It can't call another transaction and have it execute within the same transaction boundary. As shown in Figure 17-1, if stored procedure A dies after invoking stored procedure B, A's work will automatically get rolled back while B's work is committed for posterity. This is a violation of the ACID all-or-nothing proposition. This limitation causes you to write large transactions that put everything within the scope of the commit. It doesn't help the cause of modularization or writing reusable functions.

In contrast, *TP-Heavy* procedures are written using standard procedural languages. They can easily provide all-or-nothing protection in situations like the one shown in the right-hand side of Figure 17-1. For TP-Heavy, dealing with global transactions is second nature.

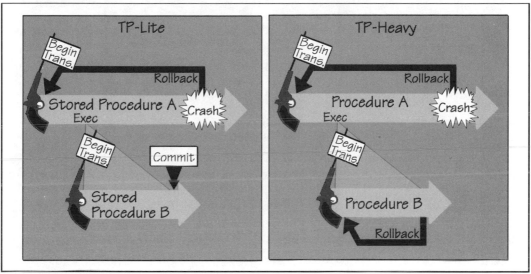

Figure 17-1. TP-Lite Versus TP-Heavy: Scope of the Commit.

TP-Lite Versus TP-Heavy: Managing Heterogeneous Resources

RDBMSs do not support the notion of a global transaction that encompasses more than one program.

— **Richard Finkelstein, President**
Performance Computing

A *TP-Lite* stored procedure can only commit transaction resources that are on the vendor's database or resource manager (see Figure 17-2). It cannot synchronize or commit work that is on a foreign database or resource manager—whether local or remote. In contrast, *TP-Heavy* procedures can easily handle ACID updates on multiple heterogeneous resource managers within the scope of a single transaction.

Note that some database vendors can extend two-phase commit to multiple databases—usually their own. Oracle's *Open Gateway* even lets you manage the two-phase commit across heterogeneous XA-compliant databases. However, the catch is that gateways are built on the assumption that a stored procedure within a

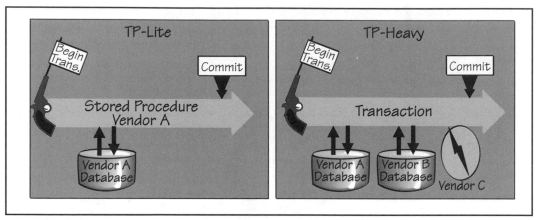

Figure 17-2. TP-Lite Versus TP-Heavy: Synchronizing Heterogeneous Resource Managers.

single database is the entire application (and also the point of origin of the transaction). Gateways do not allow multiple applications (or stored procedures) to participate in a transaction. Gateways also lock you into a database vendor's proprietary stored procedure environment. On the other hand, TP-Heavy really makes your applications resource-neutral. Of course, you're locked into your TP Monitor.

TP-Lite Versus TP-Heavy: Process Management

A *TP-Lite* stored procedure gets invoked, executed under ACID protection (within a single-phase commit), and *may* then be cached in memory for future reuse. That's about it. In contrast, *TP-Heavy* processes are prestarted and managed as server classes (see Figure 17-3). Server classes run copies of the application's

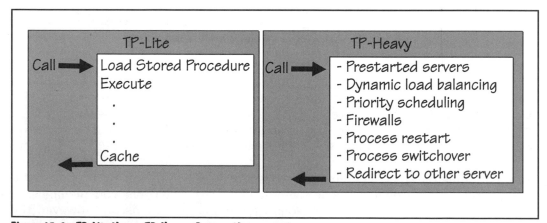

Figure 17-3. TP-Lite Versus TP-Heavy: Process Management.

business logic—so they are ready to act on incoming requests from clients. Loads are balanced across the server classes. If the load on a server class gets too heavy, more processes are automatically started. Server classes support priorities and other class-of-service attributes. Server processes have firewalls around them so that the programs that run within them don't interfere with each other. If a server class process dies, it is restarted or the transaction can be reassigned to another server process in that class. The entire environment runs under the constant supervision of the TP Monitor. The server class concept helps the TP Monitor understand what class of service is required by the user for a particular group of functions. It's an intelligently managed environment.

TP-Lite Versus TP-Heavy: Client/Server Invocations

The *TP-Lite* stored procedure invocation is extremely non-standard. Vendors provide their own proprietary RPC invocation mechanism. The RPCs are not defined using an IDL. And they're not integrated with global directory, security, and authentication services. The communications links are not automatically restarted, and they're not under transaction protection. In addition, TP-Lite does not support communications alternatives like conversations, queues, or publish-and-subscribe.

In contrast, the *TP-Heavy* environment is very open to different communication styles (see Figure 17-4). The RPC can use DCE as its base. You can easily integrate MOM transactional queues into the global transaction. Most TP Monitor vendors also support APPC/CPI-C for peer-to-peer communications. In addition, many TP Monitors now support ORB-based invocations.

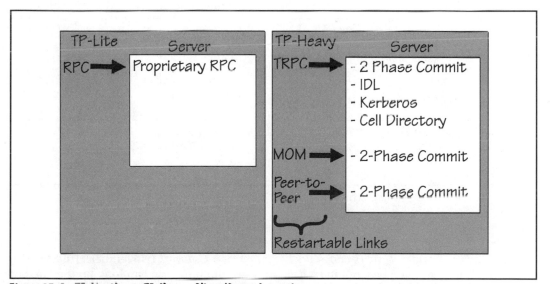

Figure 17-4. TP-Lite Versus TP-Heavy: Client/Server Invocation.

TP-Lite Versus TP-Heavy: Performance

Because they cut down on network traffic, *TP-Lite* stored procedures are much faster than networked static or dynamic SQL. However, they don't perform as well as TP-Heavy managed procedures, especially under heavy loads. Most stored procedures dynamically interpret each SQL statement for each transaction and then recreate the access plan. In addition, most stored procedures are written using interpreted 4GLs, which are slow. Virtually all standardized database benchmarks are executed with a TP Monitor managing the application services in front of a database.

In November 1998, 24 out of the top 25 TPC-C database benchmark scores were obtained using TP Monitors.[2] Table 17-1 shows the top-10 TPC-C results ranked by transactions per minute. Table 17-2 shows the top-10 TPC-C results ranked in dollars-per-transaction. In both cases, the hardware vendors used TP Monitors to get the best results.

Table 17-1. TPC-C Benchmarks Ranked by Performance.

Rank	Company	System	tpmC	$/tpmC	Database	TP Monitor	System Availability
1	Compaq	AlphaServer 8400 8 node 96 CPU Cluster	102,541	$139.49	Oracle8 Enterprise Edition 8.0	Digital TP Web	9/15/98
2	Sequent	NUMA Center 2000	86,252	$170.60	Oracle Enterprise Edition8.0.4	BEA Tuxedo	3/15/98
3	IBM	RISC System/6000 SP Model 309	57,053	$147.40	Oracle8 Enterprise Edition 8.0.4	IBM TX Series	4/30/98
4	Sun	Enterprise 6500 Server	53,049	$76.00	Sybase Adaptive Server Enterprise 11.9.3	BEA Tuxedo	1/31/98
5	Hewlett Packard	HP 9000 Model V2250 Enterprise Server	52,117	$81.17	Sybase Adaptive Server Enterprise 11.5	BEA Tuxedo	8/13/98

[2] Source: *The Transaction Processing Performance Council* (November, 1998). The TPC-C benchmark is measured in transactions per minute. You can look up the current numbers online at *http://www.tpc.org*.

Table 17-1. TPC-C Benchmarks Ranked by Performance. (Continued)

Rank	Company	System	tpmC	$/tpmC	Database	TP Monitor	System Availability
6	Sun	Enterprise 6000 Cluster	51,871	$134.46	Oracle8 Enterprise Edition 8.0.3	BEA Tuxedo	2/23/98
7	Sequent	NUMA Center 2000	48,793	$127.53	Oracle8 Enterprise Edition 8.0.4	BEA Tuxedo	3/15/99
8	IBM	AS/400e Server Model S40 2208	43,169	$128.91	IBM DB2 for AS/400 V4R3	CICS	9/11/98
9	Hewlett Packard	V2200 Enterprise Server	40,794	$103.43	Oracle8.1.5	BEA Tuxedo	2/28/98
10	Hewlett Packard	HP 9000 Model V2200 Enterprise Server	39,469	$94.18	Sybase Adaptive Server Enterprise 11.5	BEA Tuxedo	3/1/98

Table 17-2. TPC-C Benchmarks Ranked by Transaction Cost.

Rank	Company	System	$/tpmC	tpmC	Database	TP Monitor	System Availability
1	Compaq	Proliant 5500-6/400	$21.71	17,715	MS SQL Server Enterprise Edition 7.0	BEA Tuxedo	12/26/98
2	Unisys	Aquanta Server	$24.83	18,343	MS SQL Server Enterprise Edition 7.0	BEA Tuxedo	12/29/98
3	Unisys	Aquanta Server	$24.96	18,707	MS SQL Server Enterprise Edition 7.0	BEA Tuxedo	12/29/98
4	Unisys	Aquanta Server	$25.49	18,154	MS SQL Server Enterprise Edition 7.0	BEA Tuxedo	12/29/98
5	Compaq	ProLiant 7000-6/400-M1	$26.10	18,127	MS SQL Server Enterprise Edition 7.0	BEA Tuxedo	12/26/98
6	Unisys	Aquanta Server	$26.21	17,700	MS SQL Server Enterprise Edition 7.0	BEA Tuxedo	12/29/98

Table 17-2. TPC-C Benchmarks Ranked by Transaction Cost. (Continued)

Rank	Company	System	$/tpmC	tpmC	Database	TP Monitor	System Availability
7	Compaq	ProLiant 3000-6/450-512	$26.31	10,179	MS SQL Server Enterprise Edition 7.0	BEA Tuxedo	12/26/98
8	Compaq	ProLiant 5500 4P1M	$26.61	11,748	MS SQL Server Enterprise Edition 7.0	BEA Tuxedo	5/7/98
9	Acer	AcerAltos 19000Pro4	$27.25	11,072	MS SQL Server Enterprise Edition 6.5	BEA Tuxedo	2/16/98
10	IBM	Netfinity 7000 M10	$29.09	18,893	MS SQL Server Enterprise Edition 7.0	BEA Tuxedo	12/29/98

TP Monitors also save you money by being more efficient and requiring less hardware. Essentially, the TP Monitor offloads the database server by multiplexing client requests. It acts as a funnel on top of whatever funnel the database may have already put in place. In addition, the TP Monitor's precompiled (and prebound) application code runs more efficiently than the interpreted stored procedures.

Figure 17-5 shows you how dramatic some of these performance numbers can be—the benchmarks were run on the same hardware with an Informix database engine (with and without a TP Monitor). In addition, significant hardware cost savings can be achieved because fewer database resources are needed to support a given workload (the Informix example makes the point).

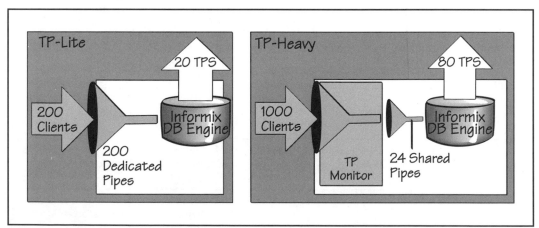

Figure 17-5. How TP-Heavy Helps the Performance of TP-Lite (Source: Unisys Corporation).

CONCLUSION

If I had to do an application that had a lot of processing, I'd use a distributed TP Monitor.

> — Ed Wood, VP of Interoperability
> Sybase

TP-Lite has turned out to be as complex as TP-Heavy once it is forced to move out from beneath the protection of the simple single server (with a small number of clients) environment where it originally took root.

> — Charles Brett, Senior Editor
> Middleware Spectrum

TP-Heavy products were created to meet the process management requirements of mission-critical OLTP environments. They tend to be very robust and have excellent system management facilities. TP-Lite products are newcomers in the area of process management and haven't had time to develop mature field-tested products. It takes years of product incubation to develop the right facilities in areas such as online distribution of new processes, remote debugging, built-in statistics, administration tools, and automatic switchovers during failures (and later reconciliations). However, for TP-Heavy vendors to win, they must make their products as ubiquitous and easy to use as TP-Lite. The OTM implementation of TP-Heavy could be the answer. Read the next Soapbox for a stronger opinion.

So Is It TP-Lite or TP-Heavy?

Soapbox

The attributes that made TP-Lite so profoundly dominant are about to become the same attributes that cause it to take a second seat to a rebirth of TP-Heavy, disguised as object systems.

> — Mohsen Al-Ghosein, MTS Architect
> Microsoft

Rome wasn't built overnight and neither were TP Monitors. And as far as we can see, TP Monitors have a huge head start over TP-Lite in the area of process management. TP-Lite doesn't even come close to managing environments where a transaction spans across machines or resource managers (the so-called multi-domain transactions). TP-Heavy provides global management and allows multivendor resource managers (including databases) to plug into the system; it gives us choice. You can then depend on TP-Heavy to make the "mosaic" whole. In contrast, TP-Lite provides an entry-level, single-domain, single-database solution for transaction processing.

So TP-Lite, like a bicycle, is quite useful in situations where you're dealing with a single vendor database and a small to medium number of users. And, as bicycles teach us the joy of being on wheels, TP-Lite will teach thousands of programmers the joy of transaction processing. TP-Lite is ideal in entry-level situations because it's less complex; you only have to deal with one server component: the database. The TP-Lite vendors also understand how to market to the client/server world—a very important advantage.

However, TP-Heavy technology is extremely important to the future of client/server computing. Think about what you could do with a Harley-Davidson instead of a bicycle. TP Monitors let us mix together components in all sorts of wild combinations; at the same time, they guarantee that everything comes together like clockwork. In other words, TP Monitors let us do the mix-and-match that is the forte of an open client/server world. Unfortunately, the TP Monitor vendors are having a very hard time selling this message to the client/server masses. They still use a lot of antique terminology— "CICS-speak"—that sounds very foreign to the PC client/server culture. People still wrongly believe that you have to be a high priest of computer science to deal with TP Monitors (and transactions in general).

Later in the book (after we explore a few more concepts), we will tell you why we believe that *Object Transaction Monitors (OTMs)* are the answer. In a nutshell, objects can subsume the functions provided by TP Monitors, groupware, and Internet application servers. And, they have the right shape to put a transaction manager into every PC. Yes, the future belongs to TP heavy, but the vision will be realized using OTMs, Enterprise JavaBeans, and CORBA/IIOP middleware (or COM+ if you subscribe to the Microsoft vision). Remember, this is a Soapbox, so you're getting a double dose of opinion at this early stage. ❑

Chapter 18

TP Monitors:
Meet the Players

> *TP Monitors are like the Rolling Stones—been around for a long time, but still drawing large crowds.*

> — **David Linthicum**

Like the Rolling Stones, TP Monitors are being rediscovered by a new generation of technologists. And like the Rolling Stones, TP Monitors are continuously reinventing themselves. This chapter gives you a snapshot of the TP Monitor market, goes over the current trends, and then introduces the key players. Of course, we will not be throwing reference manuals at you describing all the products. At this stage, it's more important for you to understand how commercial TP Monitors are lining up, where they are going, and what they can do for you. The good (and bad) news is that there are only a few major players to cover: BEA/NCR's *Top End*, Transarc/IBM's *Encina and TXSeries*, IBM's *CICS family*, and BEA's *Tuxedo*. We will briefly introduce Microsoft's *MTS*, which is really an OTM. We cover OTMs in Part 7, so you'll only be getting a foretaste here.

TP MONITOR MARKET OVERVIEW

The Standish Group estimates that the world electronically processes 68 million transactions every second. 53 million of the 68 million use a TP Monitor.

> — *Jim Johnson, Chairman*
> *Standish Group*
> *(October, 1998)*

According to IDC, TP Monitor software revenues for 1997 were $1.3 billion—growing at a rate of 19.9% per year.[1] According to Standish Group, in the same year the total TP Monitor-related systems sales—including hardware and tools—topped $20.6 billion. Today, over 70% of all TP Monitor applications are implemented on high-end systems such as IBM's *CICS on MVS*, IBM's *IMS/TP,* and Tandem Computer's *Pathway*. However, a new generation of "open" TP Monitors has entered the market—including *Encina* (now *TXSeries*), *Top End*, and *Tuxedo*. These products run on multiple operating systems and are client/server-based (as opposed to terminal-based). According to IDC, these Open TP Monitors grew at a very robust rate of 46.0% in 1997; BEA's above-average growth of 108.7% pulled up the entire market. IDC projects that Open TP Monitors will account for about 50% of all TP Monitor software sales by 2001—up from 26% in 1997 (see Figure 18-1).

TRENDS

OTMs combine the strengths of TP Monitors, MOMs, and ORBs. The result of this synergy is the ultimate middleware product.

> — *Karen Boucher, VP*
> *Standish Group*
> *(November, 1998)*

TP Monitors are competing with distributed objects to become the application server platform of choice for 3-tier client/server computing—the fastest growing segment of the client/server market. In addition, TP Monitors are going after new sources of transactions such as the Internet, intranets, and server-to-server electronic commerce. Again, they will face strong competition from object application servers in all these areas. Here's a snapshot of the major movements that we're seeing in the TP Monitor industry:

---

[1] Source: IDC, *Transaction Processing Software: 1998 Worldwide Markets and Trends* (June, 1998).

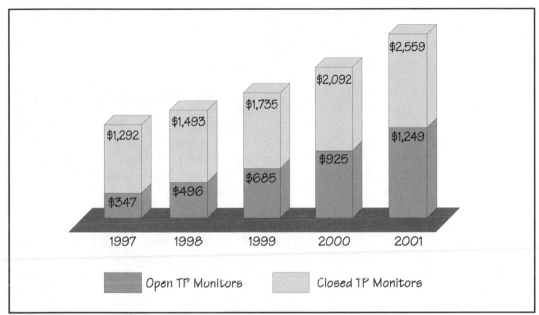

Figure 18-1. Estimated TP Monitor Yearly Revenues in Millions (Source: IDC, 1998).

■ ***TP Monitors become portable application server frameworks***. TP Monitors can now run across most major server operating systems. Consequently, they provide portable application server environments. You write your 3-tier application once and port it to the server environments of your choice.

■ ***TP Monitors become universal traffic cops***. In addition to supporting their traditional clients, TP Monitors now intercept and route calls from other types of clients—including Lotus Notes, CORBA/IIOP, COM, Java clients, the Internet (via HTTP/CGI), publish-and-subscribe, and MOM.

■ ***TP Monitors become universal resource brokers***. In addition to SQL databases, TP Monitors now support all kinds of back-end resource managers—including a variety of file systems, hierarchical databases, persistent queues, image stores, persistent objects, HTML repositories, and document databases (such as Lotus Notes).

■ ***TP Monitors discover client/server tools***. In addition to their venerable COBOL and C workbenches, TP Monitors are teaming up with popular client/server tools—including Sybase's *Powersoft*, Prolific's *JAM/TPi*, Borland/Inprise's *Delphi*, Gupta's *Centura*, Oracle *Developer/2000*, and IBM's *VisualAge*. It's getting to the point that you can access TP Monitor services from any tool that supports DLLs—for example, *Visual Basic*. A new generation of 3-tier client/server tools also support TP Monitors—including *Dynasty, Open Horizon, Magic*, Forte's *Advanced Application Development Environment*,

Magna's *Magna/X*, BEA's *Builder*, PlanetWorks' *InterSpace*, Seer's *HPS*, Inprise/Borland's *JBuilder*, and Symantec's *Visual Café*. TP Monitor vendors learned this lesson: Without equivalent tools, programmers will not convert from 2-tier to 3-tier development.

■ ***TP Monitors meet objects***. Most TP Monitors now provide C++ class libraries to access their services. Most TP Monitors—including Encina, CICS, Tuxedo, and Top End—let CORBA clients call their services using CORBA IDL-defined interfaces and IIOP. In addition, some TP Monitors are implementing interfaces to the CORBA-defined *Object Transaction Service (OTS)*. This will let TP Monitor-managed applications participate in global transactions with CORBA objects. We explain what this all means in Part 7.

■ ***TP Monitors morph into OTMs and Application Servers***. The Open TP Monitor vendors are transforming their TP Monitors into CORBA/Java OTMs; BEA shipped its *M3* OTM in July 1998, and IBM's *Component Broker* is in beta. Instead of coordinating procedural services, an OTM manages server-side components—such as CORBA Beans and Enterprise JavaBeans (EJBs). Microsoft has also entered the OTM market with MTS—an ActiveX-based component coordinator. OTMs provide an open and highly-toolable application platform for the middle-tier. Eventually, OTMs will subsume the functions of Web application servers, TP Monitors, and groupware servers. They will become the "universal application server."

In summary, the good news for classic TP Monitors is that they're very well situated to go after the fast-growing 3-tier client/server market—they are field-proven, robust, and highly scalable. The bad news is that the classic TP Monitor is being sandwiched between two very popular competing technologies: database stored procedures at the low end and CORBA/EJB distributed objects at the intergalactic level. TP Monitor vendors have responded to this challenge by introducing a new generation of OTMs that are a morph between an ORB and a TP Monitor. We will have more to say about this morphing in Part 7 after we introduce CORBA objects, COM+, and EJBs.

THE PLAYERS

Figure 18-2—from IDC—shows how the TP Monitor software pie was divided in 1997. Note that the mainframe monitors—CICS and IMS/TP—account for over 65% of TP Monitor sales. Figure 18-3—also from IDC—shows how the same pie may look in 2002. Notice that Open TP Monitors—like BEA Tuxedo—will account for a much larger share of the total TP pie. In addition, we expect Microsoft—with MTS—to become a major OTM player in 2002; it currently does not even show up on the IDC radar screen. Microsoft's approach is to bundle the OTM with NT 5.0 (see the next Soapbox). In this section, we will go over the BEA and IBM classic

TP Monitor offerings. We will also very briefly introduce the Microsoft OTM products to prepare you for Part 7.

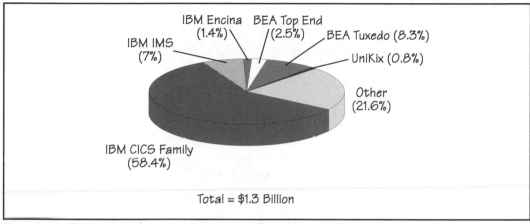

Figure 18-2. TP Monitor Vendors 1997 Revenues in Millions (Source: IDC, 1998).

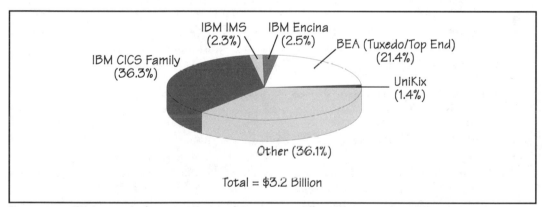

Figure 18-3. TP Monitor Vendors 2002 Projected Revenues in Millions (Source: IDC, 1998).

One of the challenges of writing this section is keeping track of who owns which TP Monitor. TP Monitor engines are like prime beach-front property. The engines are the same, but the owners keep changing. And with each new owner, the engines go through extensive remodeling, repackaging, and renaming. Like beach-front property, TP Monitors are very valuable—it takes many years for an engine to become industrial strength and shake out its bugs. The longer a TP Monitor engine has been in production the higher its value. Currently, two companies—IBM and BEA—control most of the TP Monitor engines on the market—they own all the hot properties.

The TP Wars: BEA Versus IBM

Soapbox

IBM does not intend to give up its dominant position in the TP market. It will take whatever means necessary, including joint technology ventures, technology purchases, blitzkrieg marketing, and aggressive merchandising to protect its lead in the TP market.

> — IDC
> (June, 1998)

BEA Systems continues to have all the trappings of a winner.

> — IDC
> (June, 1998)

As you can see from the IDC numbers, the market for "classic" TP Monitors will more than double over the next five years. And, the projected $3.2 billion in software license sales is just the tip of the iceberg—more than ten times this amount will be spent on TP services, tools, and hardware. Also, the IDC numbers do not include related TP technologies such as OTMs, Web application servers, and MOMs. The TP Monitor vendors—along with a raft of new competitors—are key players in these related middleware markets. The bottom line is that the TP market is already very large. And, soon, it may double in size.

The competition for this classic TP Monitor market is turning into a two-way race: It's IBM versus BEA. Over 20 years ago, IBM invented OLTP. Today, IBM's TP software handles over 20 billion mission-critical transactions per day. And its databases manage approximately 70% of the world's business information. In addition, TP Monitors are the enabling technology for IBM's all-out corporate thrust into e-commerce. So IBM will do whatever it can to protect its very large, lucrative, and mostly mainframe-based CICS business.

In the last year, BEA has emerged as the most formidable competitor IBM has ever faced in the OLTP market. Currently, BEA is by far the dominant player in the high-growth Open TP Monitor market. Just as importantly, BEA is now considered a secure bet for even the largest applications—Tuxedo and Top End are both mature products with solid mission-critical credentials. In addition, BEA has built a worldwide marketing and support infrastructure for mission-critical OLTP. This kind of hand-holding infrastructure is essential in the mission-critical market.

So is it BEA or IBM? One of your authors works for BEA, and another works for IBM, so we won't answer this question or speculate on the outcome (even in a Soapbox). However, you should note that IBM is also making a ton of money selling computer hardware for OLTP systems. Consequently, it also resells BEA software on its hardware platforms. So the competition can be friendly, sometimes.

What about Microsoft? In a sense, Microsoft is not really a player in the classic TP Monitor market. Technically speaking, MTS is really an OTM; and MSMQ is a MOM. So Microsoft doesn't even appear on the IDC TP Monitor pie chart. In addition, Microsoft is not a multiplatform middleware vendor. MTS's primary role in life is to help sell NT in the enterprise. So MTS—now part of COM+—is really an embedded application server for NT.

In a sense, this is very similar to how CICS is packaged on the mainframe. As you may already know, CICS started out life as IBM's application server for MVS. So history seems to be repeating itself here. The irony is IBM spent the last ten years porting CICS to multiple platforms; it had to do this to stay in the middleware business. History also tells us that it's very hard to transform a platform-specific product into an open middleware platform—IBM is still trying to get it right. Of course, a transactional middleware product that doesn't play on multiple platforms is severely handicapped in today's heterogeneous server environments. The Internet only makes it worse. So Microsoft's single-platform product is not really a big factor in this race. However, Microsoft will TP-enable almost all its software and operating systems. Consequently, Microsoft will contribute in a big way to the explosion in the number of transactions. ❑

IBM's TP Monitors

One of the biggest sources of confusion with IBM is keeping track of its various TP Monitors, their latest names, and how they are packaged. As we go to press, IBM has the following transactional application platforms: *CICS, IMS, Encina, Component Broker, WebSphere, Lotus Domino 5.0,* and *Project San Francisco*. To make matters worse, these platforms keep changing names. For example, CICS and Encina were part of the *Transaction Server* family—now they are called *TXSeries* on some platforms, but not others. On NT and some Unixes, TXSeries also includes the *MQSeries* MOM product and the *Lotus Go* Web Server. Finally, it is not clear whether the ORB for TXSeries is Iona's Orbix, Component Broker, or both.

To make matters worse, each of these environments provides a different programming personality, which can be very confusing to IBM customers. The application components you write are not interchangeable across the IBM TP platforms. In September 1998, IBM finally cleared up some of the smoke around its competing platforms by announcing that *Enterprise JavaBeans (EJB)* will become the

common denominator for all its server application platforms. So you will be able to write an EJB once and then run it on any of IBM's TP platforms. This is good news for IBM customers.

In the next two sections, we will introduce IBM's classic TP Monitors: *CICS* and *Encina*. We cover *Domino* in Part 6 as part of groupware. *Component Broker* and *San Francisco* are OTMs; we cover them in Part 7. Finally, *WebSphere* falls into the category of Web application server; we cover it in Part 8.

IBM's CICS and TXSeries

IBM CICS consists of different code bases (or products) that are all accessed via similar APIs. For example, there is a CICS for System/390, a CICS for OS/400, CICS for OS/2, and CICS for Unix and NT. The biggest difference is that the NT and Unix code bases run on Encina and DCE. In 1998, IBM repackaged the Unix and NT versions of CICS as the *TXSeries*. The other CICS products are still called *CICS Transaction Servers (TS)*. The TXSeries package includes CICS 4.0, Encina 2.2, MQSeries v5.0, Lotus Go, and DCE directory and security. TXSeries uses the Encina Transaction Manager, XA, and CORBA OTS. The RPC can either be on top of DCE or CORBA IIOP (via an Iona ORB). Finally, the Unix version of TXSeries supports SP2 MPP clusters.

CICS services are accessed via a variety of APIs. The *External Call Interface (ECI)* allows thin CICS clients to invoke services using a transactional RPC. The *External Presentation Interface (EPI)* lets clients call CICS services by emulating a 3270 terminal. Yes, terminals are still alive and well in many TP Monitor shops. There are a variety of CICS-to-CICS calls that require the full CICS environment on both clients and servers.

The *CICS Internet Gateway* lets Web users access CICS applications via the Internet's *Common Gateway Interface* (see Figure 18-4). We explain CGI in Part 8. IBM also provides a *Lotus Notes CICS Gateway* that lets Notes clients access CICS applications. We explain Lotus Notes in Part 6. The *CICS Java Gateway* lets you invoke CICS services from within Java; the gateway consists of downloadable Java classes that encapsulate the ECI/EPI interfaces. The TXSeries package includes all these gateways.

IBM/Transarc's Encina and TXSeries

Transarc's Encina was designed from the ground up as a postmodern TP Monitor based on OSF's DCE. In mid-1994, IBM acquired Transarc; it now owns two TP

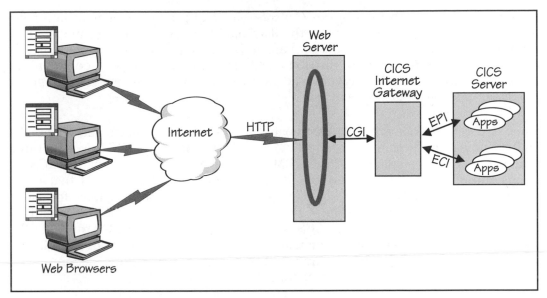

Figure 18-4. TP Monitor Meets Web: The CICS Internet Gateway.

Monitors: CICS and Encina. Encina 2.0 shipped in 1996 on top of DCE 1.1. It runs on nearly ten operating systems—including OS/2, NT, HP-UX, AIX, Solaris, and OSF/1. The servers support eight resource managers—including Oracle, Sybase, DB2, and Informix. Encina clients can talk to their servers using a "lightweight" DCE client that provides a transactional RPC on top of TCP/IP and APPC stacks. In 1997, Transarc introduced downloadable Java classes called the *DE-Light Web Client*. They let a Web client directly invoke Encina services via a protocol called *D-RPC*.

Transarc claims that performance improvements of up to 30% can be achieved using Encina 2.0—most of these improvements are attributed to DCE 1.1. Encina always used DCE as its underlying plumbing. DCE provides security and naming across networks as well as threads, distributed time, and a Distributed File System (DFS). Encina supports transactions across multiple resource managers—including SQL databases, ISAM, and Encina's own *Recoverable Queuing Service (RQS)* and *Structured File System (SFS)*. SFS extends DCE's DFS with support for nested transactions.

Encina 2.X includes C++ class libraries that let you build transaction processing applications using the *Encina++* development framework. *Encina++* masks some of DCE's complexities from the developer. For example, it automatically establishes DCE security mechanisms and object-location services without additional programming on your part. Encina 2.X also implements two versions of the CORBA *Object Transaction Service (OTS):* one works with CORBA ORBs, and the other works with Encina/DCE.

Encina 2.X comes with the *Encina Console*—a GUI-based management interface that lets you configure and monitor the distributed application environment. For example, you can use the console to manage Encina and non-Encina resources—including recoverable queues, distributed file systems, peer-to-peer communications gateways, application servers, and external databases. Encina also supports the SNMP management protocol.

Since it acquired Transarc, IBM has repackaged its CICS on Unixes and NT to run on the Encina transaction processing engine and its underlying DCE infrastructure. While some analysts speculated that IBM might give up either Encina or CICS, it seems the company is still developing both products. IBM believes that each product attracts a different kind of customer. Encina is the better choice for users that have an intimate knowledge of how distributed systems work and intend to build an application using DCE. CICS is a less complicated choice for the 300,000 application programmers (mostly on mainframes) that are familiar with its APIs. In early 1998, IBM repackaged Encina as *TXSeries* (see the previous section). So there is no longer a separate package for Encina.

BEA's: Tuxedo and Top End

BEA Systems has undoubtedly taken the distributed TP middleware industry by storm since its inception three years ago.

— *IDC*
(June, 1998)

BEA—founded in 1995—is not your ordinary start-up. Its goal from day one was to become the "transaction company." The company boot-strapped itself by acquiring *Tuxedo* from Novell; it also acquired the leading distributors of Tuxedo around the world. So the company created—almost overnight—a world-wide sales and support infrastructure for mission-critical OLTP.

In 1997, BEA acquired two key products from Digital: *Object Broker*—a mission-critical CORBA ORB, and *MessageQ*—a leading MOM product. In May 1998, BEA acquired *Top End* from NCR—the industry's second most important Open TP Monitor (after Tuxedo). Top End brings to BEA its substantial customer base, important transaction technology, TP developers, and more support people. In July 1998, BEA shipped *M3*—a CORBA OTM that combines the proven Tuxedo TP Monitor engine with the Object Broker CORBA/IIOP ORB. In September 1998, BEA announced it was acquiring *WebLogic*—the premier application server vendor for *Enterprise JavaBeans*. By the time you read this, BEA should have released an EJB version of M3. In addition, BEA is investing heavily in 3-tier TP tools—its own and those of third parties. BEA's strategy is to make TP systems as easy to build, deploy, and manage as 2-tier client/server.

This short introduction should give you an idea of how BEA became the fastest-growing transaction company in the industry. It's now in the number-two spot after IBM. And, BEA has already displaced IBM as the number-one company in the fast-growing Open TP Monitor market (see the previous Soapbox). In this section, we describe BEA's two classic TP Monitors: *Tuxedo* and *Top End*. We cover *M3* and *WebLogic* in Part 7.

BEA's Tuxedo

BEA's Tuxedo, originally from Unix Systems Lab (USL), provides a TP Monitor environment that runs on more than 50 platforms—including most Unixes, NT, OS/400, OS/390, and Tandem/Compaq's NonStop Kernel. Tuxedo provides a variety of communications options—including DCE RPCs, conversations, MOM-based queues, CORBA invocations, broadcast, and publish-and-subscribe. BEA provides an open tool environment for Tuxedo, which is now supported by more than 37 third-party tools. Tuxedo includes a very fast message switch that distributes loads across multiple servers. The messages are routed based on information Tuxedo maintains in its *bulletin board*. Tuxedo servers can be grouped into administrative domains that share a common namespace. This lets Tuxedo run applications across hundreds or even thousands of nodes.

In the last two years, BEA introduced two major Tuxedo releases and several add-ons. For example, *BEA Jolt* opens up Tuxedo services to Java clients; it also provides a downloadable JavaBean that lets you invoke Tuxedo from within a Web page. *BEA Connect* provides transparent access to MVS-based CICS and IMS services. *BEA Manager* provides a Web-based console for managing Tuxedo systems (and also M3). In addition, you can manage Tuxedo from any SNMP-based system-management console—including NetView, OpenView, Tivoli, CA Unicenter, and Solstice.

Tuxedo 6.3 supports dynamic data routing—which means that it transparently routes queries to appropriate data repositories and allows administrators to change routing rules "on-the-fly." It also provides new security features based on access control lists, SSL, and Kerberos-based authentication. You can control, at a very fine grain, the access to Tuxedo's queues, services, and RPCs. The security system is also integrated with the event manager. For example, an ACL violation can trigger an event that sends a message to your top security sleuth. Finally, Tuxedo fully supports XA-compliant databases—including DB2, Oracle, Sybase, SQL Server, and Informix.

BEA's Top End

Like all TP Monitor engines, Top End went through its share of owners. The technology was first developed at NCR, which was then acquired by AT&T. In January 1997, NCR became independent again. In December 1997, NCR released a new version of Top End, called *Release 2.05*. NCR announced that Top End was a key part of a new TP strategy centered on data warehousing and electronic commerce; it positioned Top End as an enterprise component manager.

According to NCR's marketing literature, "Top End 2.05 became the first middleware product to provide an all-in-one software package with the flexibility of MOM, the integrity and performance of a TP Monitor, and the ease-of-development of an ORB." In the first quarter of 1998, NCR won a major contract with the U.S. Postal Service. In May 1998, BEA acquired Top End. BEA is now merging its Top End and Tuxedo engines.

Like Tuxedo's bulletin board, Top End uses a distributed naming service that is self-replicating and self-registering. Typically, a new service registers itself with its *Node Manager*, which then notifies all other nodes with which it is connected. The Node Managers use heartbeats to detect that other nodes have failed, and will then update their respective directories accordingly. Top End's complementary *Life-Keeper* service provides automatic failover capabilities. The product includes pre-packaged recovery kits for the major DBMSs, MS Exchange, Lotus Notes, PeopleSoft, and SAP. The idea is that you should be able to recover your application as well as any system software it uses.

With Top End, BEA gets yet another MOM service. Top End provides very fast in-memory queues, which are also transactional and recoverable. Top End supports very large messages—up to 2 GBytes—that can be used to store and forward BLOBs via queues. This can be very useful in data warehousing situations. Top End supports its own procedural-style communications called CSI. In addition, it supports TxRPC, CORBA/IIOP, Java/RMI, and DCOM via an add-on called *Top ORB*. Top End supports Java-based Internet browsers via its *Java Remote Service (JRS)*. You can use JRS to invoke Top End services from within a browser. However, JRS also allows you to call back the Java client—so it acts as both a client and server.

In the past, AT&T (and NCR) rarely sold a Top End system directly to MIS. Instead, Top End was used in a number of vertical applications for different target markets— including retail, inventory management, branch banking, communications, and call centers. A large number of Top End monitors are embedded in AT&T's voice and phone message management systems. Of course, BEA now introduces new sales channels for Top End. Eventually, many of the Top End features will be integrated into BEA's TP engine, which is used by both Tuxedo and M3. So Top End may become just another TP personality on top of this engine.

Microsoft's MTS

We look at the world's most demanding transaction-processing systems and we ask ourselves: What does it take to make PCs or networks of PCs suitable for those tasks?

— Bill Gates

In 1997, Microsoft officially entered the world of TP with an OTM product called the *Microsoft Transaction Server (MTS)*. In a sense, Microsoft leap-frogged the industry by delivering the world's first OTM. However, this OTM only runs on Windows platforms. It is also based on Microsoft's proprietary *OLE Transactions*—a COM-based specification that is in direct competition with the CORBA *Object Transaction Service (OTS)*. MTS is the foundation for Microsoft's COM+ component model that will be embedded inside NT 5.0. MTS leaves no doubt that Microsoft believes that the future of software is with 3-tier architectures and COM-based objects. Transactions provide the glue that makes it all work in unison. We will cover MTS in Part 7 after we explain distributed objects, COM, and COM+.

Microsoft plans to become a major player in the transaction market by adopting a bottom-up approach to transaction processing. First, it plans to bundle COM-based transaction managers and logs with all its key software—including file systems, SQL Server, Excel, Access, Exchange, Active Directory, and the Internet Information Server (IIS). MTS becomes the *component coordinator* that combines the function of an enterprise ORB and a TP Monitor. MTS will coordinate COM+ objects and OLE DB resource managers across an enterprise using ACID principles. In NT 5.0, MTS will be fully-integrated with MSMQ to provide transactional MOM interactions as well as RPC-like object invocations.

CONCLUSION

The Standish Group estimates by the year 2000 that 30% of all transactions will be Web-based.

— Jim Johnson, Chairman
Standish Group
(October, 1998)

As you can see, TP Monitors have come a long way. TP Monitor vendors have successfully created a need for their products in the 3-tier client/server application space. In addition, TP Monitors are constantly reinventing themselves and finding new uses for their services. For example, TP Monitors are now starting to provide the backbone for Web-based electronic commerce. From a technology viewpoint,

TP Monitors are reinventing themselves as OTMs. Distributed object standards—like CORBA, Enterprise JavaBeans, and COM+—will help bring TP technology to the programming masses. You will be able to use any ordinary visual tool to set transaction attributes on beans that you can then run inside a TP Monitor, OTM, or database. Transactions become the glue that make independently developed components act in unison. But we're getting ahead of ourselves. You'll have to wait until Part 7 to get the full story. As you can see, we're trying to generate some suspense.

Part 6
Client/Server
Groupware

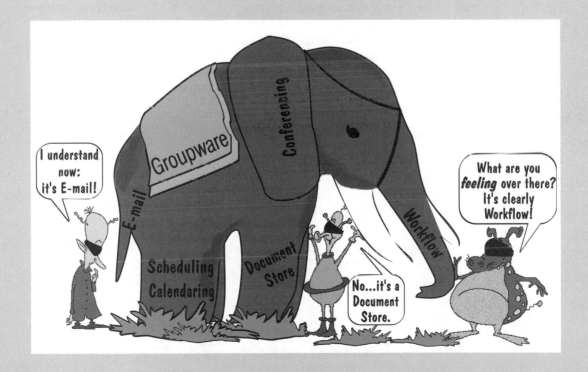

An Introduction to Part 6

If you buy into the motto that diversity is the spice of life, then groupware is for you.

— *Joe Paone, Internetwork*

Well, if you Martians think that ACID transactions and TP Monitors were fun, wait until you see groupware. Oh, by the way, we have an Earthling game for you to play—it's called the blind men and the elephant. We're going to put some blindfolds on you and let you guess what groupware is. The winner gets a night on the town. Are you ready?

OK, so what's groupware? Martian number one says "it's e-mail." Martian number two thinks it's a multimedia "document store." And Martian number three says they're both wrong: "It's clearly workflow." Do we have any more takers? Does anybody think it's got something to do with electronic conferencing? How about group calendaring and scheduling? As you can see from the cartoon, the groupware elephant is all of the above. OK, so you all won a night on the town. Do you need a party guide? We have a volunteer.

Part 6 is about this amorphous client/server category called groupware; it's amorphous because it's so new, and we don't yet fully understand its potential. The groupware proponents claim that their technology allows us to create new classes of client/server applications that are unlike anything we've seen on mainframes or minis. It does that by enabling the people-to-people elements in client/server communications. The PC revolution was built around *personal* computing; groupware may create an analogous software revolution around *interpersonal* computing. Yes, of course it includes Martians. Is groupware lucrative? IBM must think so—it paid $3.5 billion to acquire Lotus Notes, the premier groupware product. Anytime someone writes a $3.5 billion check for a technology, we should take notice. So where is Groupware Valley? You Martians are always one step ahead of us.

We'll start by defining groupware. (Don't laugh: We really *can* do it.) We then go over what makes groupware different from SQL databases and TP Monitors. Next, we explore the constituent technologies that make up groupware—including multimedia document processing, workflow, e-mail, conferencing, and group calendaring and scheduling. However, with groupware, the whole is more than the sum of the parts, so we need to explore where that synergy comes from. We conclude with Lotus *Notes/Domino* and its closest competitors—including Microsoft's *Exchange*, Novell's *GroupWise*, and Netscape/AOL's *SuiteSpot/Collabra*.

Chapter 19

Client/Server Groupware

Defining exactly what groupware does isn't easy, and its sudden love affair with Internet standards hasn't helped.

— **Internet Week**
(January, 1998)

Client/server groupware is a collection of technologies that allow us to represent complex processes that center around collaborative human activities. It builds on five foundation technologies: multimedia document management, workflow, e-mail, conferencing, and scheduling. Groupware is not another downsized mainframe technology; it's a genuinely new form of computing. It provides an excellent example of how you can use client/server technology to extend the computing envelope into uncharted territory. Of course, this also means that groupware doesn't neatly fit into predefined software categories. So we'll have some explaining to do.

Our plan for this chapter is to first define groupware and the problems it solves. We'll then place groupware in the client/server model we've been building throughout this book. This won't be easy—groupware is an elusive concept that's continuously redefining its role as well as its relationship to the more established

technologies. In addition, no single groupware product incorporates all the technology pieces—although the new Lotus *Notes/Domino 5.0* comes pretty close. After we get a working definition, we'll look at the foundation technologies and how groupware combines the pieces within a client/server setting.

WHY IS GROUPWARE IMPORTANT?

Groupware is what you make it.

— Karl Wong

According to IDC, the groupware software market was $1.7 billion in 1997.[1] In the first half of 1998, groupware seats were growing at a rate of over 3 million per month. In mid-1998, Lotus Notes—an amorphous groupware product that escapes definition—had an installed base of 21.9 million users.[2] Input Research estimates that for every dollar in groupware software license sales, resellers make another $7 or $8 in application design, systems administration, and training.

So what's causing all this sudden interest in groupware? According to groupware author David Coleman, the rapid growth is occurring because groupware can transform a company by changing the way people communicate with each other and, as a result, change the business processes. For example, you can use groupware to automate customer service and make a company more responsive. Groupware also has the potential to flatten organizations and remove layers of bureaucracy (see the following Soapbox).

Groupware allows direct contributors—wherever they may be—to collaborate on a job using client/server networks. We anticipate the growth of "virtual corporations" that get formed by unaffiliated groups of people to collaborate on a particular project. Groupware helps manage (and track) the product through its various phases; it also allows the contributors to exchange ideas and synchronize their work. It keeps track of the "collective memory" of the group.

Groupware, in many cases, allows departments to develop and deploy their own applications. Anyone who can create a simple spreadsheet can learn how to create a Lotus Notes, GroupWise, Exchange, or SuiteSpot application—few programming skills are required. The ability for departments to develop and create their own client/server groupware applications is leading to phenomenal returns on investment. For example, a study of 65 Notes users by IDC in 1994 revealed that return on investment ranged from 16% to 1,666% on a median investment of $100,000.

---

[1]   This number also includes e-mail and workflow licenses.
[2]   Source: IDC (September, 1998).

More than half showed returns greater than 100%, and a quarter showed returns of more than 200%. Because of these extraordinary numbers, IDC repeated the study with a different set of users and obtained similar results. The groupware phenomenon—like spreadsheets or word processors—is self-feeding. The difference is that groupware is a self-feeding client/server application; it is networked and interpersonal. Most groupware products also support open APIs that allow third parties (and IS shops) to add new functions on top of the foundation.

Groupware and Re-Engineering

Soapbox

Are we investing in groupware to infuse the organization with collaborative energy? Or are we investing primarily to staunch the bleeding?

— *Michael Schrage, Fellow*
MIT Sloan School

Bureaucracy in most organizations is very resilient; it will take a lot more than groupware to eliminate it. In fact, groupware can be misused to automate bureaucracy and make it more permanent. The "re-engineering" movement thinks it has found the problem: We've been applying Ford's assembly-line processes to business operations. We need to rethink the way we work—that is, re-engineer the process. We wish them luck. Hopefully, they'll leave a few jobs behind after the re-engineering.

The re-engineering movement asserts that throwing technology into a poorly performing process won't help. We agree; nobody can quarrel with the fact that it doesn't make sense to automate a process that shouldn't be there in the first place. However, groupware is a secular technology; it can automate any type of process, including bad ones. You can use it to automate inefficient processes and make them more "efficiently inefficient." Or you can automate the re-engineered structures and shoot to attain the order-of-magnitude improvements the Gurus promote. But we'll probably see a great deal of misuse of the technology until people learn this lesson. It's a lot more effort to rethink the way we work than to throw a shrink-wrapped package of groupware at it.

Groupware vendors will make the same amount of revenue either way, but the value of their products to the companies that buy them will be radically different. ❏

WHAT IS GROUPWARE?

If you were to put twelve groupware experts in a room, you would get twenty definitions.

— *David Coleman, Principal*
Collaborative Strategies

In a contest for the most fuzzily defined client/server software category, "groupware" would be the hands-down winner. Over 500 products call themselves groupware. So let's cut the suspense and propose the following working definition: "Groupware is software that supports the creation, flow, and tracking of non-structured information in direct support of collaborative group activity."

There are other terms used as synonyms for groupware—collaborative computing, workgroup computing, knowledge management, and the academic sounding "computer-supported cooperative working." Groupware is the easiest of these terms to remember; vendors like the way it sounds because of the "ware" attached to it. So groupware it is.

Our definition implies that groupware is involved in the management of both information and activities. The "million-dollar" question is: What makes groupware different from database managers and TP Monitors? For a change, we have some ready and straightforward answers.

How Is Groupware Different From SQL Databases?

Using an RDBMS to support documents is like teaching an elephant to fly.

— *Frank Ingari, VP of Marketing*
Lotus

The relational databases we covered in Part 4 deal with highly structured data that is accessed using SQL. They are excellent for managing applications that require high concurrency controls—including locking and isolation features—that are needed for immediate updates. They also provide excellent ad hoc query facilities. In contrast, groupware deals with highly unstructured data—including text, image, graphics, faxes, mail, and bulletin boards. Groupware provides the tools to capture this data at the point of entry and organize it in a nebulous thing called a *document*. You can think of a document as the container of diverse types of information. The document is to a workgroup what a table is to an SQL database: It's a basic unit of management. Groupware helps end users create document databases. It can move these documents via electronic mail and database replicas. And it provides everything you need to query, manage, distribute, and navigate through document databases. Documents are the currency of groupware.

Using Web browsers with plug-ins and JavaBeans, groupware lets you view the components of the documents by launching the tools that created them in the first place. This means that if the document contains an image, movie, or sound clip, the groupware software will find it for you and let you view it. But can't we do that kind of stuff using SQL database BLOBs? Not quite. (See the following Soapbox.) SQL databases are great for providing access to structured data that's organized in table formats, but when it comes to multimedia and non-structured data, they're not quite there yet. Objcct-rclational extensions are starting to fill this gap. In the meantime, groupware-style document management is the only game in town.

What About BLOBs?

Soapbox

In their current form, BLOBs are a lousy tool for handling advanced data types. They buy little or no leverage over storing data in a flat file. The RDBMS acts as little more than a very expensive flat file server.

— Wayne Duquaine
Sybase

A BLOB, at least in an SQL database, is nothing more than up to four GBytes of uninterpreted binary data. All the rich semantic information is buried in the binary headers that the SQL database ignores. The headers describe the various sub-types and components that make up the BLOB—including the data type (image, voice, text, and so on), thc comprcssion type, and the various indexes. The SQL database throws back at the application all the navigation tasks that are required to move through the BLOB's components.

SQL does not specify a self-describing data standard for BLOBs. Determining what's in the BLOB has to be reinvented by each application. GUI tools are left blind and clueless as to what each BLOB contains and how it should be processed. When it comes to BLOBs and multimedia, a SQL database is just a glorified and expensive file server with no value added. In contrast, the groupware documcnt scrvers havc made great strides toward providing some kind of a multimedia, client/server solution. Note that some SQL database vendors now provide proprietary object-relational extensions that let you manipulate BLOB-like data types—including images, fingerprints, files, and e-mail messages. As SQL databases become more object-oriented, they will give the document databases a run for their money. ❑

How Is Groupware Different From TP Monitors?

The TP Monitors we covered in Part 5 deal with management of transaction-aware applications across client/server networks. So how do they compare with groupware? When it comes to document stores, TP Monitors can complement groupware software very well. The TP Monitor treats the document store like any other resource manager. If it supports a two-phase commit, the TP Monitor will gladly coordinate a distributed transaction that includes the document store. However, TP Monitors and groupware compete in the area of workflow. We believe that the groupware workflow is a much more developed technology than the TP Monitor long-lived transaction (but it's less protected).

The current workflow model—and groupware in general—is not transaction-oriented in the ACID sense. Groupware is good at reflecting the changing states of information over time, but it does not do very well when it comes to reflecting the current state of the data in real time. For example, groupware does not use two-phase commits to synchronize distributed changes across resource managers. It would be nice if TP Monitors and groupware combined efforts to infuse workflow with ACID properties (if it can be done). We cover workflow later in this chapter.

THE COMPONENTS OF GROUPWARE

As we said earlier, groupware builds on five foundation technologies: multimedia document management, workflow, e-mail, group conferencing, and group scheduling (see Figure 19-1). Groupware achieves its magic by combining these technologies and creating new synergy. The technology for multimedia document management and workflow comes from electronic document imaging systems; e-mail and scheduling come from office automation; and conferencing is native to groupware. Before we get into groupware proper, let's quickly review what these component technologies have to offer.

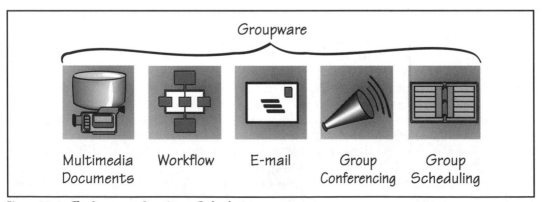

Figure 19-1. The Groupware Constituent Technologies.

From Electronic Imaging to Multimedia Document Management

Groupware document management technology has its roots in electronic imaging. If we want to be purists, electronic imaging is just another form of special-purpose groupware. Of course, electronic imaging people—who have created a huge multi-billion dollar industry—can make the claim that groupware is just an imaging spin-off. In either case, we need to look at electronic imaging because it's an important client/server industry that is a precursor to groupware.

Electronic imaging started small. In the 1960s, many businesses replaced large information paper warehouses with microfilm and computer-aided retrieval systems. By the mid-1980s, the appearance of PCs, LANs, scanners, compression boards, and optical disk juke-boxes allowed the automation of image storage as well as the data-centered tracking systems that locate those images. The new technologies made the online storage and display of images economical. In some applications, the cost savings associated with reduced staff and faster online access to documents (in seconds rather than days) justified the incremental expense for the new client/server systems. It costs $25,000 to fill a four-drawer paper file cabinet and $2,160 annually to maintain it. More importantly, 3 percent of paper is lost; the average cost to recover a document is $120. It is estimated that 3 billion paper documents are buried in U.S. businesses alone; it's those kind of numbers that gave birth to the electronic imaging industry.

Electronic Imaging Client/Server Architecture

Electronic imaging systems are inherently database-oriented, client/server applications (see Figure 19-2). The client PCs capture and manipulate the images; they serve as front-ends to the data stored in image servers. The client PC typically does the following:

■ The scanner attached to the client's PC digitizes the image through a process similar to that of a fax machine. (Not so coincidentally, fax machines sometimes serve as remote scanners.)

■ After being digitized, the image is displayed and checked for quality; it is rescanned if necessary.

■ While the image is displayed, information is extracted from it by an operator who enters the data in the fields of a GUI form. At a minimum, the document is assigned a simple index and identification code so that it can be retrieved later. More sophisticated (and costly) applications automate the extraction of information from the image into the GUI form using intelligent character recognition or bar-code readers.

■ A software or hardware coprocessor compresses the images and then sends them to the server where they get stored.

■ The client can always access the documents in the server and visually display them. An image can be reviewed, printed, faxed, annotated with red lines or electronic notes, and so on.

The server side of an imaging application manages a shared database of images. Image servers typically store all the structured information in an SQL database; the document itself (i.e., the BLOB) is stored in a file server. Large image servers can handle 400,000 documents or more per day. Images are big. The average compressed digitized image weighs in at about 75 to 100 KBytes, but images can be as large as 2.5 MBytes for medical X-rays and engineering drawings. Consequently, many imaging applications may require terabytes of online storage.

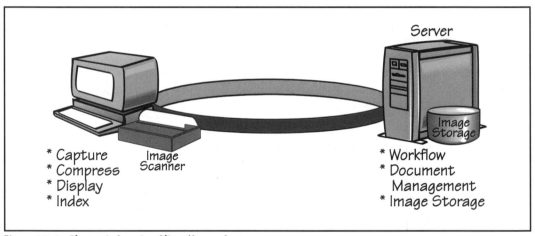

Figure 19-2. Electronic Imaging Client/Server Systems.

The image servers manage the workflow, security, image indexing (or metadata), and the pointers to the file systems where the BLOBs are physically stored. Here are some of their key functions:

■ Servers manage electronic renditions of file cabinets, which contain drawers and folders comprising documents. A document comprises a series of multimedia pages.

■ Workflow automates the movement of documents by moving them from one business operation to the next according to customer-defined rules and routes. The image server uses rules to control the routing, which may be based on document content, age, priority, workload balancing, external events, the day you need a document, database triggers, and other user-defined criteria.

■ User profiles and work queues are created and maintained on the server to specify the type of work users receive.

■ Reporting facilities allow managers to monitor the volume and types of work-in-process in the system, and to note its progress.

■ Documents are stored on various media; the server moves them around to optimize the delicate trade-off between storage cost and performance.

Groupware Multimedia Document Management

The groupware document management paradigm is a generalization of the electronic imaging file cabinet. For example, the basic unit of storage in groupware, such as Notes/Domino or Exchange, is the *document*. A Notes document has an extremely flexible structure; it can be tagged with properties such as *client*, *region*, and *subject*. A Notes document can have any number of BLOB-like *attachments* (or embedded objects). Notes supports a multimedia document architecture, which means that it can handle multiple data types—including text, images, graphics, voice clips, and video.

Related collections of Notes documents are stored in *databases* that can then be indexed and retrieved by any of the documents' properties, or by the actual contents of the documents. Notes also supports full-text indexing. In addition, Notes created its own document database technology from scratch; unlike the image vendors, it does not build on top of existing file and SQL database servers. We're dealing with a groupware-specific, document-centric, and multimedia-enabled database technology.

Workflow: What Is It? Where Does It Come From?

Imagine submitting a home mortgage application and having it go through in a matter of hours. Workflow is the "up and coming" client/server technology that can be used to automatically route events (and work) from one program to the next in structured or unstructured client/server environments (see Figure 19-3). The "classical" workflow paradigm is a river that carries the flow of work from port to port and along the way value gets added. Workflow defines the operations that must be visited along the way and what needs to be done when exceptions occur. The original work item may be merged with other work, transformed, or routed to another workflow. It's quite a dynamic environment. Some workflows may be fuzzy and not understood very well; others are deterministic and highly repetitive. In all cases, these workflows are there to help us collaborate in getting work done.

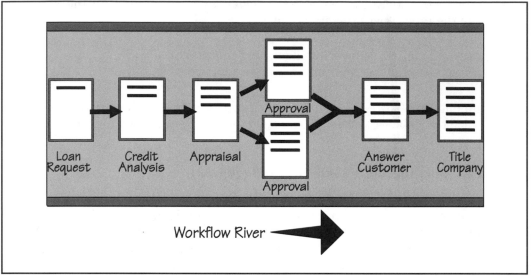

Figure 19-3. The Workflow River.

To appreciate what workflow is all about, you must understand its origins. Workflow technology has its historical roots firmly planted in the world of image management and computer-integrated manufacturing technology. FileNet Corporation—an imaging vendor—was a pioneer of this technology in 1984. FileNet and other electronic imaging companies—including ViewStar (now Mosaix), Plexus, Wang (now Eastman Software), and IBM's ImagePlus—discovered that workflow could be used to automate the high-volume, formerly paper-based processes (see Figure 19-4).

Workflow is especially applicable to "paper factories," meaning large offices that routinely process documents representing business transactions (for example, loans, claims processing, and tax returns). Paper to these factories is what raw material is to manufacturing: "grist for the mill" that produces the organization's product. When the paper became an electronic image, workflow automated the movement of documents from one image processing operation to the next. Both the workflow controller and the work are electronic renditions of real-life factory constructs.

The imaging workflow systems are costly, rigid, centralized, and typically require a highly skilled IS professional to do the design and integration. These systems tend to be proprietary and cannot interface well with other applications. On the positive side, they can handle very large workloads and have excellent built-in security and version controls. They are very good at scheduling document-related tasks and then tracking them to completion. The cost of such systems starts at $1,000 per seat.

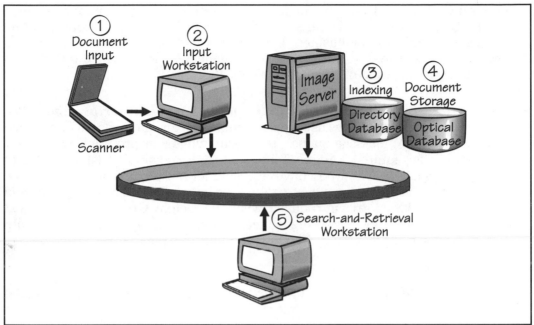

Figure 19-4. Workflow in Electronic Imaging Systems.

The New Workflow Systems

Groupware introduces a new breed of client/server workflow software for the masses. The new workflow packages go beyond their imaging counterparts in the following areas:

- **Support for ad hoc user needs.** The new workflow packages address both structured and unstructured process automation needs. They can automate well-understood processes as well as more nebulous ones.

- **Low cost.** The new workflow packages sell at PC software prices—expect to pay between $50 to $500 per seat.

- **Integration with other applications.** The new workflow packages can integrate with existing applications by either spawning a process or sending them some type of message-based event notification when their intervention is needed. Applications can also call the workflow manager to participate in or initiate a workflow process.

- **Programming with visual metaphors.** The new workflow packages support drag-and-drop iconic manipulations for creating workflows and defining busi-

ness rules. They typically provide tools for designing forms (or importing them from a GUI Builder), designing sequential or conditional routes, and scripting languages to specify the business logic. The routes and workflow definitions are sometimes stored in SQL databases. Templates are provided to help you jump-start the creation of a workflow application.

■ *Integration with e-mail, MOM, ORB, publish-and-subscribe, and RPC.* The new workflow packages use loosely coupled forms of communication, such as e-mail or MOM message queues, to inform humans or programs when their intervention is required. Action Technologies, for example, defines a set of message formats that can be conveyed using all the popular mail transports. These formats are used to convey, capture, or initiate workflow commands and actions. In 1998, Vitria introduced what the Delphi Group calls the "next generation workflow" by tying together existing applications via publish-and-subscribe messaging. The Vitria engine uses the CORBA Event Service to route events between applications.

■ *Provide facilities for tracking work-in-progress.* Most of the packages allow you to query the status of work-in-progress and what stage of the workflow it's in. Some of the better packages help you identify inefficiencies in the routes and bottlenecks.

■ *Provide users with tools to complete an action.* In addition to notifying users that an action is required, some of the better tools provide users with help panels that tell them how to complete an action and sometimes even the tools to perform the requested action. The user may also be able to obtain information about where the task fits in the overall process.

■ *Provide APIs that let developers customize workflow services.* This feature is currently very vendor-specific. However, the standards for workflow APIs are now being defined by the Workflow Coalition and the Object Management Group (see the next sections).

■ *Provide off-the-shelf component suites for assembling workflow.* For example, the *Novation* workflow server provides about 40 JavaBeans that you can use to visually wire together a workflow process. @Work Technologies' *Workout* provides a component-based document storage and routing solution based on CORBA/JavaBeans. Plexus' *FloWare 5.0* now includes JavaBeans and CORBA components that you can use to quickly model Internet-based, inter-company workflows. These Web-based beans are also used to allow disconnected participants to remain active in a workflow. Typically, you'll be able to use these components from within a visual tool to assemble about 90% of a workflow application. You must then write the remaining 10% using scripts or Java code.

■ ***Integration with LDAP directories.*** Some workflow vendors—for example, Plexus—now let you locate participants in a workflow (and their attributes) using LDAP directories.

The heart of a workflow system is the server that receives requests and events from the various client workstations and interprets them according to a user-defined workflow. The client agents are programmed to execute the repetitive parts of a user-defined script. The workflow server acts as a clearinghouse that determines what needs to be done next based on the global state of the system (and the rules). It usually maintains a database that dynamically tracks the work-in-progress and contains instructions (and rules) for what needs to be done at a given instance of a workflow process.

Workflow Models

The three R's of workflow are: Routes, Rules, and Roles.

— *Ronni T. Marshak*

The workflow software must create electronic renditions of real-world collaborative activity. The "real world," however, covers a wide spectrum of activities—from tax return processing to co-authoring a paper. These activities differ radically in their structure, number of users, flow of control, and process predictability. Almost any workflow can be represented using raw code; however, the trick is to minimize custom development using shrink-wrapped workflow models. The workflow packages must be able to visually define who does "what, when, and to what"; parallel routes; logic for dynamically determining routes at run time; and the exceptions to any rules. It must take into account Ronni Marshak's three R's: routes, rules, and roles.

■ ***Routes*** define the paths along which the object moves. They also include definitions of the objects—documents, forms, events, electronic containers and parts, messages, and so on—that are to be routed.

■ ***Rules*** define what information is routed and to whom. Rules define both the conditions the workflow must meet to traverse to the next step and how to handle exceptions: "If the loan is over $100,000, send it to the supervisor or else send it to the next hop."

■ ***Roles*** define job functions independently of the people who do it. For example, the "supervisor" role can be handled by users "Mary" and "Jeri." Any one of these people can do the job; just put the job on the next available supervisor's queue.

Groupware packages must provide the three R's for automating well-defined applications, which is called *process-oriented workflow*. And they must provide them for the more spontaneous type of applications, called *ad hoc workflow*. Here's the differences between the two models:

- **Process-oriented workflows** are used to automate business systems that have definable, repetitive, and well-understood policies and procedures. For example, a mortgage loan is an understood business process that goes through a prescribed set of procedures. Loans are processed in the same way every day. The routing of the work is automatic and requires very little user involvement. It's like taking a train. This type of workflow is a natural candidate for TP Monitor initiated Sagas or long-lived transactions.

- **Ad hoc workflow** deals with short-lived and unstructured work processes. They can involve task forces of people working on a common problem. Consider a short-duration project with a deadline. The workflow is used to assign roles, track and route work-in-progress, monitor deadlines, and track who got what and when. It's an excellent tool for tracking work among people who are physically dispersed. This type of workflow is like driving a car. The navigation is driver-centric, but you need road signs and a map to figure out where you're going. The driver also needs to know the set of options available at every turn. Ad hoc workflow is used for incremental automation—leaving anything the system can't handle to humans. It takes full advantage of desktop power to help humans navigate through the country roads.

Workflow Routes

Modern workflow packages support the same type of topologies that are common in human communications (see Figure 19-5). Typically, these packages let you specify a route that defines the set operations a unit-of-work traverses. They also let you define rules that specify acceptance conditions for moving from one operation to the next. You can create sequential routes, parallel routes (alternate paths), routes with feedback loops (for example, rework), circular routes, wheel-spoked routes, and fully interconnected routes. The first four routes are used in process-oriented workflows, while the last two are used in more ad hoc workflows.

Workflow Splits and Joins

Workflow objects can go off on different routes and then merge back into a single route at a "rendezvous" point. In addition, a workflow object can be split into multiple parts and merged back into a single part as it moves down the workflow river (see Figure 19-6). This is done using splits and joins, as explained in the following examples:

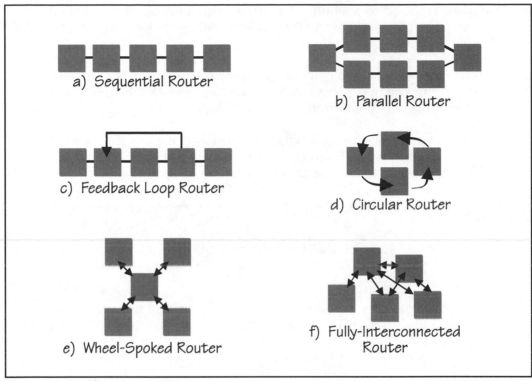

Figure 19-5. Workflows Come in All Patterns.

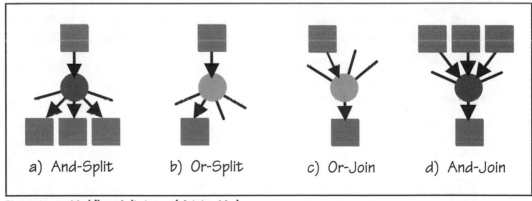

Figure 19-6. Workflow: Splitting and Joining Work.

■ *And-Splits* are used to explode an object into many parts. For example, a set of chips on a wafer is tracked as a group until the chips are split; each then goes its own way.

■ *Or-Splits* are used to peel off a few parts from a group. For example, a few chips may be split off the wafer for random testing; they rejoin the group later using an Or-Join.

■ *Or-Joins* allow certain members to rejoin the group. For example, in a manufacturing line, a defective part can go to a rework operation; it can then rejoin the group when it's fixed using an Or-Join.

■ *And-Joins* are rendezvous points that are used to group together objects so that they move in a route as a group. For example, you can use an And-Join to package many units into a container that can be shipped as a unit.

The Action Workflow Model

Briefing

Action Technologies' *Action Workflow*—an innovative ad hoc workflow product—is based on research by Terry Winograd and Fernando Flores on how people communicate to make an action happen. Action identifies for each unit of work in a workflow the *performer* who is doing the actual work for a *customer* (meaning the person for whom the work is being done). Each step in the workflow involves a negotiation loop between a customer and a performer (see Figure 19-7). At the end of each step, the conditions must be fulfilled to have a satisfied customer.

According to the Action Technologies methodology, every action in a workflow consists of four phases in which customers and performers coordinate with each other (see Figure 19-8):

1. *Preparation* is when the customer prepares to ask for something—often, for example, by filling out a form.

2. *Negotiation* is when the customer and performer agree on the work to be done and on the conditions of satisfaction—that is, they determine *exactly* what must be done to complete this job to the satisfaction of the customer.

3. *Performance* is the phase in which the actual job is done. After completion, the performer reports to the customer on how the mission was accomplished.

4. *Acceptance* of a job or task is not considered complete until the customer signs off and expresses satisfaction to the performer.

At any phase, there may be additional actions, such as clarifications, further negotiations, and changes of commitments by the participants.

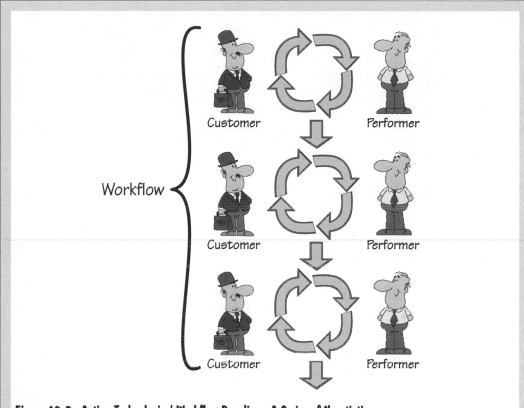

Figure 19-7. Action Technologies' Workflow Paradigm: A Series of Negotiations.

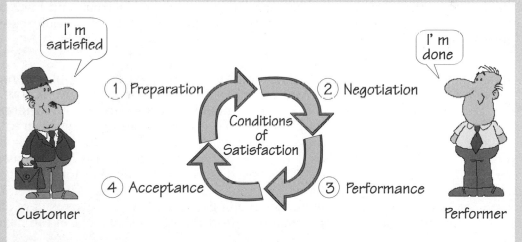

Figure 19-8. Action Technologies' Workflow: The Negotiation Details.

The Action Technologies approach does more than just coordinate between tasks: It helps specify the client/server contract and does it all very recursively. The entire application is a client/server task that gets broken down recursively into subtasks as defined by the workflow. The application is a series of "who is getting what done for whom" steps and the conditions of satisfaction. Action provides a set of visual tools to help capture the negotiation semantics and then automatically generates the scripts from them. ❑

Workflow: Meet the Players

We've literally built a whole business around the confusion and interest generated by workflow. Many users have no idea what the technology is.

— *Tom Koulopoulos, President*
Delphi Consulting

Workflow is still a growing market. Delphi Consulting estimates that spending on workflow software licenses will reach $578 million in 1998, up from $481 million in 1997—representing an overall growth rate of 20%.[3] According to the same Delphi study, over $1.9 billion was spent on workflow-related services in 1997. In 1998, over 50 vendors are competing in the workflow market, and they're frequent targets of acquisitions. For example, Mosaix acquired Viewstar; Wang acquired Sigma and was then acquired by Eastman; Jetform acquired Delrina; and FileNet bought Watermark. The workflow market is still in flux; there is no clear leader (see Figure 19-9).

Software vendors are now offering workflow as part of their packaged applications. For example, SAP built a workflow engine from scratch for *R/3*. In contrast, PeopleSoft is licensing its workflow engine from third parties. Groupware vendors are also workflow enabling their applications to create all-in-one offerings. You will be able to get workflow solutions at commodity prices from Lotus Notes, Microsoft Exchange, and Novell's GroupWise. In 1998, Netscape joined the fray by introducing *Process Manager*. This is a forms-based workflow application for building, managing, and deploying automated business processes—such as expense reimbursement, contract management and job bidding—over the Web. As a result of all this bundling, we expect the traditional workflow market to shake out in the next two years.

---

[3] Source: The Delphi Group, *Workflow Market Reference Point 97* (March, 1998).

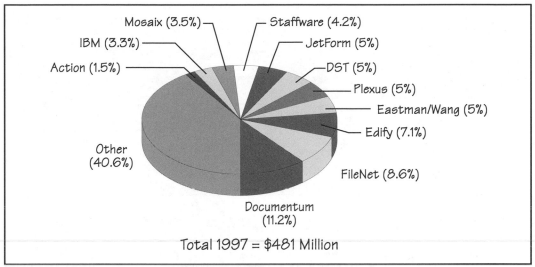

Figure 19-9. Workflow Vendors' 1997 Revenues in Millions (Source: Delphi, 1998).

The Workflow Coalition

The *Workflow Management Coalition (WfMC)* was founded in August 1993 as a non-profit international body for the development and promotion of workflow standards (you can visit them at *http://www.wfmc.org*). Its membership is open to all parties interested or involved in the creation, analysis, or deployment of workflow management systems. In 1998, WfMC had over 130 members—including all the key workflow vendors and leading system integrators.

In 1995, WfMC published a glossary of workflow-related terms—a first step toward creating a common vocabulary for the industry. The end goal is to create a language for specifying workflow *processes* that a variety of workflow *engines* can interpret and instantiate. According to WfMC, a workflow process consists of a collection of *activities*. An activity is a logical step that contributes toward the completion of a workflow process; it is executed by a *tool*, which is an application outside the workflow system. Figure 19-10 shows how the pieces of the workflow jigsaw come together in WfMC's conceptual framework.

The WfMC defines a reference model that consists of four areas: 1) workflow client interfaces, 2) workflow process definition, 3) system administration and monitoring, and 4) workflow inter-server interoperabilty (see Figure 19-11). The idea here is to define a set of APIs that client applications and tools can use to invoke and define workflow functions and to control a workflow engine. WfMC also wants to make sure that multivendor workflow engines can interoperate. In December 1995, WfMC published its first set of APIs called the *Workflow Client API (WAPI)*. In

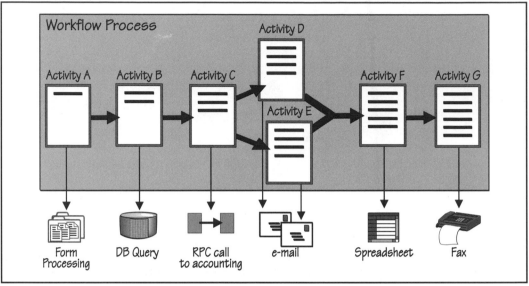

Figure 19-10. The Workflow Process as a Series of Activities Performed by Tools.

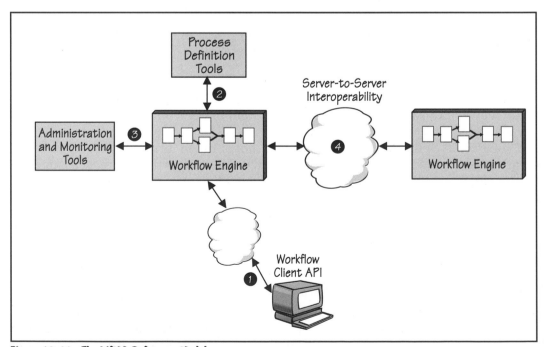

Figure 19-11. The WfMC Reference Model.

October 1996, it published the abstract interoperability specification. In 1998, it published an e-mail/MIME binding for this specification.

The Workflow Client API enables workflow clients to retrieve, perform, submit, and monitor work. An application can request work from a variety of workflow products and then construct a single worklist for the user. This means you don't have to deal with multiple desktop windows for each workflow product your organization uses. The APIs will help create standards-based workflow systems such as insurance claims or factory automation software.

The Workflow Client API consists of 56 function calls divided into four broad categories (see Figure 19-12):

■ *Connection functions* consist of 2 API calls that let you connect to a workflow engine and disconnect when you're done.

■ *Process control and status* consists of 23 API calls that let you query a process definition, read and update the current state, create a process instance, start the process, and obtain process status.

■ *Activity control and status* consists of 13 API calls that let you query an activity, read and update its attributes and state, and obtain its current status.

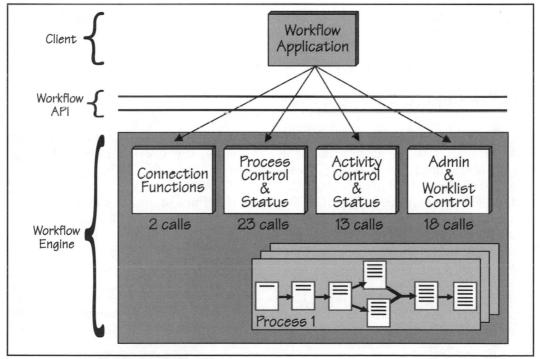

Figure 19-12. The Workflow Client API.

■ *Administration and worklist control* consists of 18 API calls that let you query a worklist, manipulate the work items it contains, and manage the execution of processes and activities.

The Workflow Client API does not address security, locking, process integrity, user interfaces, roles, and defining ad hoc activities. Despite these shortcomings, the Workflow Client API provides a giant first step toward standardizing diverse workflow engines that have their roots in imaging, e-mail, and ad hoc workflows.

The *Workflow interoperability specification* defines an abstract server-to-server workflow communication standard; it lets you execute a distributed process across multi-vendor workflow servers. The specification defines an abstract layer that can work on top of different communication channels (called *bindings*). In September 1998, WfMC published a binding for Internet e-mail with MIME protocols. In the next section, we describe two other bindings: one for CORBA/IIOP, and another for HTTP 1.1.

At the 1998 AIM show, WfMC members demonstrated two types of interoperability: 1) *simple chained processes*, where an activity is passed from one engine to another, and 2) *nested subprocesses*, where an activity is passed from one engine to another and then, when completed, it is passed back to the caller.

WfMC members that are implementing these workflow standards include Action Technologies, Computron, CSE Systems, Compaq/Digital, Fujitsu, IBM, ICL, Integrated Work, Lion GmbH, Recognition International, Microsoft, Oracle, Netscape, SAP, Siemens Nixdorf, Staffware, and Telstra Applied Technologies.

Workflow Objects: SWAP and jFlow

The WfMC provides CORBA *Interface Definition Language (IDL)* bindings for all its interfaces. At the urging of WfMC members, the OMG defined a CORBA workflow standard called *JFlow;* it was ratified in September 1998. The CORBA standard defines how distributed objects can participate in workflows using ORB-based invocations.[4] The CORBA standard defines an object-based workflow framework that consists of about 13 interfaces; it covers the WfMC standards for client invocations and workflow interoperability across servers. The OMG will continue to add new interfaces to its workflow framework as they are defined by WfMC.

In 1998, the *Simple Workflow Access Protocol (SWAP)* was introduced by Netscape, HP, and Sun to provide a simple protocol that complements WfMC and jFlow on HTTP networks. You can think of it as a lightweight version of WfMC and

---

[4] See *ftp://ftp.omg.org/pub/docs/bom/98-06-07.pdf*.

jFlow for HTTP. The supporters of SWAP intend to submit it to the IETF to become an Internet standard. If SWAP succeeds, it may be used to workflow-enable hundreds of Internet applications with straightforward requirements. You can get the latest information on SWAP by visiting their working group's homepage at *http://www.ics.uci.edu/~ietfswap/index.html.*

Workflow and the Internet

Together, Workflow and the Internet are set to provide us with some astonishing results.

— *WfMC White Paper*
(June, 1998)

Traditionally, workflow applications are executed within the confines of a single enterprise. However, the Web—with the new workflow standards—makes it possible to deploy workflow applications that span across multiple enterprises and servers. A workflow server on the Web can service any user with a browser. So the Web opens workflow applications to very large communities of new users. And by reducing deployment and maintenance costs, the Web drastically reduces the total cost of implementing a workflow process. Consequently, workflow applications become accessible to smaller enterprises as well as mobile users. They can now participate in workflows that span across multiple companies and home offices. For example, a Web-based workflow can track an order that involves a complex intercompany chain of supplies. Or a mobile worker can participate in a larger company project via a workflow-driven process.

Workflow: The Bottom Line

Workflow helps bring the information to the people who can act on it. It coordinates existing software and tracks the processes to make sure the work gets done by the right people. Workflow by itself cannot do too much; but with other software—such as e-mail, databases, and desktop productivity tools—it can create some dynamite combinations.

The Electronic Mail Component

The notion that a proprietary network can exist in the Internet era is gone.

— *Larry Moore, Lotus VP*

Part 6. Client/Server Groupware

For many organizations, all the groupware they need may be an e-mail package that's closely tied to group calendaring and scheduling features. Of course, groupware allows you to do much more with electronic mail; it uses it to extend the client/server reach. Why is e-mail so important to groupware? Because it matches the way people work. You can use e-mail to send something to others without making a real-time connection; the recipients don't have to respond to senders until they're ready to do so. In addition, it's one of the easiest ways for electronic processes to communicate with humans. And it's ubiquitous.

According to Eric Arnum, publisher of the *Electronic Mail & Messaging Systems (EMMS)* newsletter, in 1998, there are 153 million active e-mail users sending at least two messages per day. The number of e-mail users is expected to double by the year 2000. According to IDC, in 1997 purchases of Internet-based e-mail software grew by 726%—to 11 million users—compared with 16% growth for LAN-based or mainframe-based e-mail systems. Figure 19-13 shows how the e-mail pie was divided in mid-1998.

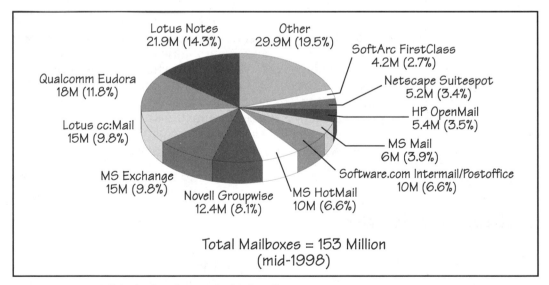

Figure 19-13. E-mail Vendors' Mid-1998 Marketshare.[5]

Mail-enabled groupware applications can take advantage of this very extensive mail infrastructure to send and receive information and communicate directly with users—electronic mail is one of the most hassle-free forms of distributed interactions. Most electronic mailboxes are now globally interconnected through mail backbones and gateways. E-mail front-ends are not the only way to send messages.

---

[5] We put together these numbers by combining the latest research from IDC, Dataquest, and EMMS.

Mail APIs—such as VIM, MAPI, and JavaMail—are designed to let any application work with the mail messaging infrastructure.

The Electronic Mail Infrastructure

The infrastructure required to create ubiquitous mail backbones is coming into place. There is a crucial distinction between the mail application—the front-end—and the mail infrastructure—the back-end. Ideally, the front-end and back-end should communicate along client/server lines—this is what Lotus Notes, Exchange, and GroupWise do today (see Figure 19-14). The older LAN-based e-mail packages bundle the front-end and the back-end in the same process and use a file server on the LAN for the mail store. This is the approach used by older protocols such as Lotus *cc:Mail* and *MS Mail*. In 1997, Lotus introduced cc:Mail *Release 8* based on a client/server architecture. Currently, both cc:Mail and Notes share the same back-end mail server—*Domino*.

However, it takes more than cc:Mail or Notes to create an intergalactic mail infrastructure. How do you connect cc:Mail or Notes to other mail networks? You need to hook into a server-to-server *mail backbone*. There are two ways to do that:

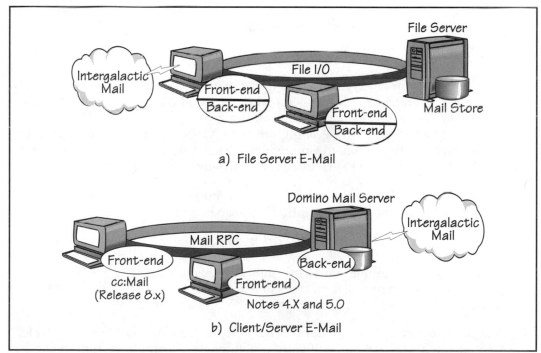

Figure 19-14. Client/Server E-Mail: Lotus Notes Versus cc:Mail.

■ *Gateways*—you'll need one gateway for each different e-mail system you need to access. But this could quickly turn into a management nightmare. Gateways also limit some functions like the capability to search for an address. They're also poor at providing synchronized directory management services, efficient message routing, global system management, and so on.

■ *Mail backbone*—you'll need one gateway to the backbone, period. But the question is: Which backbone? The contenders are the *X.400* international standard, Novell's *Message Handling Service (MHS)*, and the Internet's *Simple Message Transport Protocol (SMTP)* mail service. X.400 is much simpler and less expensive than it once was (see the following Details box). However, the pendulum seems to be swinging in SMTP's favor (more on this in the next section). Of course, MHS, SMTP, and X.400 backbones will most likely be interconnected via gateways. So all the backbones will survive.

The separation of mail functions along client/server lines facilitates the creation of front-end clients that are totally independent of the back-end mail engines. We'll now look at the mail API standards that will help make all of this happen.

X.400 Mail Backbones

Details

The X.400 mail protocol is finally hitting the critical mass as the common mail backbone for the industry. It has been adopted by all the major public service providers across the world. Most e-mail vendors—including Lotus, Microsoft, HP, IBM, and SoftSwitch—are coming out with X.400 products. Several large vendors—such as IBM, Tandem/Compaq, and Digital/Compaq—use X.400 as a way to link their messaging systems. X.400 provides the following features:

■ *Support for BLOB exchanges.* X.400 defines a way to exchange images, fax, and other binary attachments to messages.

■ *Support for Electronic Data Interchange (EDI).* EDI defines the contents and structures of messages that are used in electronic business exchanges (for example, invoices, billing forms, and so on). X.400 consolidates both e-mail and EDI on the same backbones. It maintains audit trails of EDI exchanges as required by the X.435 EDI standard.

■ *Support for distributed directories.* The X.500 standard, developed as part of the X.400 1988 specification, defines how a single system image is provided using directories that are distributed over multiple nodes.

■ **Security.** X.400 adheres to the X.509 security standard that specifies the mechanisms for password identification, digital signatures, encryption, and audit trails.

■ **Mail API.** The X.400 *Common Mail Calls (CMC)* API provides a simple way to access and manipulate e-mail.

Today, X.400 offers a secure, standards-based approach to creating electronic mail backbones. ❑

The Internet Mail Protocols: SMTP, IMAP, and POP

Internet mail is defined by a large number of standards and recommendations that are codified by the *Internet Engineering Task Force (IETF)*. Only a few of the protocols used in Internet mail are full IETF standards. However, the others are often useful and stable enough to be treated as standard by people writing Internet mail software. The key mail-related Internet protocols are SMTP/E, POP3, IMAP4, LDAP, and S/MIME. A mail client uses POP3 or IMAP4 to connect to a message server. It uses LDAP to access the e-mail address book (see Figure 19-15). MIME defines the mail message's data types; S/MIME is a secure version of MIME. Finally, SMTP provides the backbone that ties together e-mail servers. Here's a brief description of these protocols:

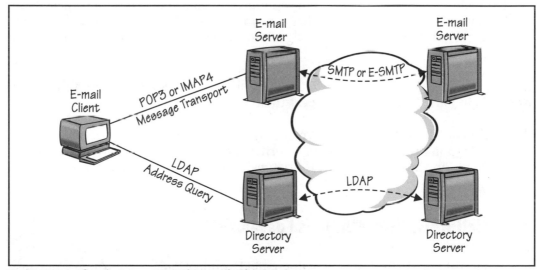

Figure 19-15. How the Internet E-Mail Protocols Play Together.

- **POP3**—or *Post Office Protocol Version 3*—allows a client to send and receive e-mail to and from mail servers. Here's how it works: 1) the client logs onto the server and sends any outgoing mail, 2) the server sends incoming mail to the client and deletes it from its store, and 3) the server sends the outgoing mail via the SMTP backbone.

- **IMAP4**—or *Internet Message Access Protocol Version 4*—allows a client to access and manipulate e-mail on a server. The client can remotely view the message subject lines and then selectively download incoming messages. IMAP4 also supports shared mail folders and folder hierarchies, while POP does not. Here's how this protocol works: 1) the client logs on to the server in either online or offline disconnected mode, 2) in offline mode, the client exchanges mail with the server, and 3) in online mode, the client selectively downloads the messages it wants to view or it can manipulate them directly on the server. Eventually, IMAP will become the primary client/server protocol for e-mail; it will replace POP as well as some of the proprietary e-mail protocols.

- **SMTP**—or *Simple Mail Transfer Protocol*—defines how messages are routed between e-mail servers. SMTP only defines the ASCII text; *MIME* defines non-text attachments and data types such as image, video, and audio. *Extended SMTP (E-SMTP)*—defined in *RFC 1651*—provides some of the sophisticated messaging features that are common in the proprietary protocols—including priorities, read receipts, message size negotiation, and error-tracing.

- **S/MIME**—or *Secure Multipurpose Internet Mail Extensions*—lets you sign an e-mail and also send it in a sealed envelope. S/MIME signs the message by first making a message digest of the content and then encrypting the digest using the sender's private key. To seal an envelope, S/MIME encrypts all the contents using the triple-DES secret key algorithm combined with an *ElGamal* public key scheme.

Internet mail also uses LDAP and X.509 digital certificates. We covered these two protocols in Part 3, so we won't repeat them here.

The bottom line here is that Internet mail is becoming ubiquitous. So it makes sense for organizations to standardize on Internet mail standards. It provides a more direct approach than relying on proprietary e-mail protocols that gateway to the Internet.

The E-Mail APIs: VIM, MAPI, and JavaMail

A new hot area in our industry is mail-enabled applications. The primary purpose of these applications is not mail, but they still need to access mail services. Most groupware products fall into that category. E-mail becomes just another form of client/server middleware. Electronic Data Interchange (EDI) is becoming an important source of mail-enabled business transactions (see previous Details box). Personal agents will be making extensive use of EDI to pay your bills and do your electronic shopping. And e-mail by itself supports the exchange of faxes, files, BLOBs, documents, and workflow events at an application-to-application level. It's a powerful form of middleware that may already be in place in an organization (in that case, it's free and ready to be exploited). One of the main advantages of using e-mail over lower-level APIs—like RPC—is the store-and-forward capability that's built into the mail system.

An application becomes mail-enabled by using e-mail APIs that allow programs to directly access mail transport services, mail directories, and message stores (see Figure 19-16). These used to be the *private domain* of mail vendors. The newly-exposed APIs are making it easy for developers to mail-enable their applications without becoming e-mail experts. What kind of functions can we expect from an open e-mail API that can work across multiple mail transports?

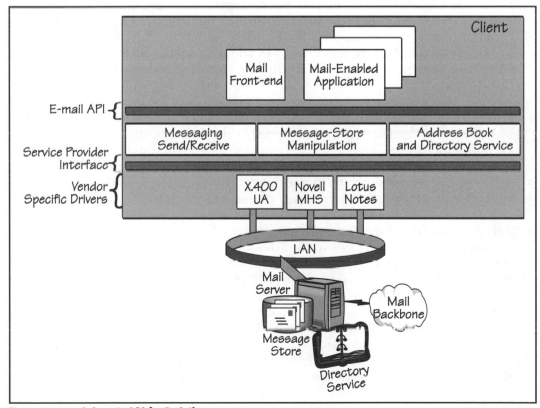

Figure 19-16. A Generic API for E-Mail.

The following is a composite of functions provided by the three leading contenders for the "common" mail API:

■ ***Simple messaging services.*** These are functions for addressing, sending, and receiving a mail message—including files and enclosures. An optional user interface is provided for logon, addressing the mail, and text entry.

■ ***Message store manipulation.*** This includes opening and reading messages delivered to a message store, saving messages, deleting messages, navigating through the contents of the store, searching for messages, and moving messages across containers. The message store can be external to the mail package. For example, a message store could be an SQL database, a Lotus Notes document database, or an Object Database. The same APIs should work across all stores. Message stores contain a wealth of information that is of interest to groupware applications. We expect to see a lot of exciting developments in this area.

■ ***Address book and directory services.*** An address book is a collection of individual or group recipients; it's really a bunch of distribution lists. Address books can be personal (cached on the local system) or part of a global directory. The API should let you read and write directory information as well as navigate through hierarchies of address books. You should be able to add or remove groups or members from address books and then search through them. Today, LDAP has become the common API for manipulating address books and global directories.

■ ***Mail object manipulation.*** The APIs should let you access the subcomponents of a mail object. For example, a message may consist of heading fields and various data items.

■ ***Authentication and security services.*** This includes APIs that let an application log on to the mail system and authenticate its users.

■ ***Service provider interface.*** This interface allows service providers to supply their own back-end services to the front-end mail APIs. For example, a Lotus Domino mail server is accessed through the proprietary Lotus RPC (note that Notes 5.0 and Domino also support CORBA/IIOP). We've already encountered the concept of the service provider interface in the ODBC section in Part 4. The service provider interface creates an open environment for the providers of mail services; it doesn't do much for the developers of mail-enabled applications.

The separation of the mail front-end from the back-end allows a single API set to work with multiple mail back-ends. In addition, different vendors can offer their own specialized plug-in services (for example, message stores). So what is the common API set that gives us access to all this mail server power?

Surprise! The e-mail industry has more than one common, open API set. Remember, we *always* get to choose from more than one standard. In the case of e-mail, here are some of your more popular choices: MAPI and Active Messaging from Microsoft, VIM from Lotus, CMC from X.400, and JavaMail from JavaSoft. Here's a brief overview of these APIs:

- **Vendor Independent Messaging (VIM)** was designed from the ground up as a cross-platform interface. It consists of about 55 API calls—10 are optional—that support simple mail, message store, and address book services. VIM also provides a *Simple Mail Interface (SMI)* that consists of two calls: SMISendMail and SMISendDocuments. The main strength of VIM is its cross-platform support and the vendors who are behind it. Its main weakness is that it does not provide a Service Provider Interface (SPI).

- **Messaging API (MAPI)** started out as a Windows-first client API—it's a Windows DLL that works primarily with Microsoft Mail back-ends. MAPI is now supported by virtually every e-mail vendor. The MAPI front-end APIs are written to the Windows *Mail Spooler*. Mail server providers can redirect the Mail Spooler calls to their back-end services using the MAPI SPI. Simple MAPI consists of 12 API calls that provide simple mail, message store, and address book services. *Extended MAPI*—a technology that is partially implemented in Windows 95—supports 100 API calls that allow applications to handle large numbers of messages, filter through mail, manage message stores, and access complex addressing information. Extended MAPI exposes the SPI to the application. There are three types of SPIs: Transport, Address Book, and Message Store. In 1997, Microsoft added a COM object layer—called the *Active Messaging* interface—on top of MAPI. Its main function is to provide a hierarchical navigation interface for the Microsoft Exchange Server mailbox. You start with a MAPI session and then navigate folders that contain message and address entries. With NT 5.0, Microsoft is introducing the *Active Directory* interface so there will be one more interface for directory entries.

- **Common Mail Calls (CMC)** is the X.400 API Association (XAPIA) interface. CMC only does simple mail. It is a poor man's e-mail API.

- **JavaMail 1.1**—released in August 1998—provides a set of abstract classes that model an e-mail system. Like MAPI, there is an open interface for e-mail service providers. The Java classes provide a platform-independent and protocol-independent framework to build Java-based mail and messaging applications. The JavaMail API is implemented as a Java standard extension. Sun provides a royalty-free reference implementation that developers can use and ship; it includes implementations of the *IMAP* and *SMTP* service providers.

So the good news is that you now have a choice of mail APIs to groupware-enable your applications. If you're in the Microsoft camp, Active Messaging may be your best bet. If you're in the Java parallel universe, then JavaMail may be the best choice.

Group Calendaring and Scheduling

Scheduling is a native groupware technology. There's extensive innovation behind the electronic scheduling of meetings, sharing calendars and "to do" lists, and all that good stuff. Scheduling was designed from the ground up on a solid client/server foundation. The client front-ends make excellent use of GUI facilities; the servers use background tasks, shared data, and triggers to manage and schedule group events. Now, imagine what could happen if we combine this scheduling and calendaring technology with workflow managers, e-mail, and multimedia document stores. This could result in some dynamite combinations of groupware. A workflow manager would be able to automatically add a meeting to the calendars of all the participants, schedule a meeting room, and send them reminder notices. Or, a workflow manager could consult group calendars to discover who is on vacation and route (or re-route) work accordingly.

So how do we get to the services provided by the scheduling and calendaring servers? Using APIs and client/server exchanges, of course. But which APIs? The good news is that the IETF has a *Calendaring and Scheduling Working Group* that is defining an entire framework for Internet-based group meetings and calendar access. The proposed standards include a new MIME content type—called *iCalendar*—for exchanging calendaring and scheduling information. This type lets you capture and exchange information normally stored within a calendaring and scheduling application—such as a Group Scheduling product. The standard also defines object methods for calendaring and scheduling operations—such as requesting, replying to, modifying, and canceling meetings or appointments. It also provides methods for obtaining free/busy time data.

In addition, the Internet Mail Consortium has defined an electronic business card format called *vCard;* it allows for the open exchange of information typically found on traditional paper business cards.[6] The format is independent of the particular method used to transport it. The ultimate destination for this information is often an electronic collection of business cards, a Rolodex file, or contact manager. The vCard and iCalendar APIs may become all-time favorites for personal agents.

---

[6] Note that the Internet Mail Consortium has also defined a calendaring object called *vCalendar*. Eventually *vCalendar* and *iCalendar* may merge.

Group Conferencing

Conferencing, or "electronic meetings," is another native groupware technology. Millions of PC users are now discovering the wonders of conferencing through electronic bulletin boards on CompuServe, America Online, Prodigy, and the Internet. We can divide client/server conferencing technology into two types: realtime and anytime.

- **Realtime conferences** allow groups to interactively collaborate on a joint project using instantly refreshed document replicas, electronic whiteboards, different colored cursors with the initials of each participant, and a designated chairperson that controls access to the shared document. Participants can speak on their microphones and see each other in video windows on their computer screens. Eventually—when we get the cheap bandwidth—we will be able to augment these conferences with movie clips. Lotus makes the *RealTime Notes* conferencing package available at no cost in Notes clients.

- **Anytime conferences** allow people to participate in group discussions when and where they want. You can join the discussion, add your own two cents, and leave at any time. And because you can jump into an ongoing discussion at any time, you can see the entire discussion in context. This flexible environment helps articulate spontaneous groups around a topic of interest—customer support, operating system advocacy, shared problems, and project tracking. The medium is open and democratic. Everyone gets the opportunity to express themselves—ideas are never lost.

  Using replicas, the system makes all the contributions available to all participants in close to realtime. The contributions then become part of the group memory—they are stored for posterity in the document databases that manage this wealth of shared information. As these conferences flourish and multiply, tools are provided for viewing and navigating through the mazes of information they contain. Conferences provide one more technology that helps articulate the "group" in groupware. Electronic meeting environments provide an almost bottomless set of opportunities for client/server technology. We're just seeing the tip of the iceberg.

The *Network News Transport Protocol (NNTP)*—defined in *RFC 977*—provides the ability to participate in discussion groups across the Internet. Here's how it works: 1) the client downloads the names of newly added groups hosted on an NNTP news server, 2) the client selects a group, 3) the server returns the message headings, 4) the user clicks on a subject line, and 5) the server returns the message text and attachments.

Groupware: Is It Just Hype?

Soapbox

In the future, any application that isn't groupware-enabled will run the risk of being an island in a sea of global communications. Groupware will bring together individuals, agents, processes, businesses, and corporations.

— Karl Wong

Like every new client/server technology, groupware is getting its share of high-decibel marketing hype. What makes it worse is that any multiuser piece of software can be called "groupware." All client/server software deals with group communications in some form or another. Even though we carefully defined the constituent technologies in groupware, there is still a tremendous amount of fuzziness associated with the term. You can't find two people—even from Lotus—that can give you a common definition of Lotus Notes; yet Notes is selling like hotcakes. So it must be fulfilling some need somewhere.

Groupware is a moving target. Groupware applications are constantly expanding into new territory as a result of changes in the technology. For example, groupware is now moving into two new areas: the Internet and telephony. We cover the Internet in Part 8. Telephony APIs—such as JavaSoft's *JTAPI*, Microsoft's *TAPI*, and Novell's *TSAPI*—let you telephone-enable groupware applications. This means that your groupware applications will be able to answer, place, screen, and route telephone calls; it's a key technology for Internet-enabled telephony, embedded phones, and call centers. The telephony APIs also let you route messages, manage voice-mail, and integrate voice, fax, and e-mail into one cohesive system. In a sense, a groupware application can now add to its repertoire of functions almost everything a modern PBX can do today. For example, in 1998, IBM introduced a suite of JavaBeans that third parties can use to develop call center applications that answer, conference, transfer, and associate data with customer calls.

We believe that any new technology will be fuzzy at first. The trick is to sort out reality from marketing hype, and then understand what we can do with the technology. In the case of groupware, the opportunity is in creating client/server applications—unlike any we've ever seen—using multimedia document databases, e-mail, workflow, conferencing, calendaring, and scheduling technology. The groupware industry is creating the common interfaces between these disparate pieces. All we need to do is learn how to use them and perhaps even integrate them with database warehouses, the Internet, and distributed object technology. ❑

CONCLUSION

Our groupware technology can serve to alienate and isolate people, or it can serve to forge a community. It is our choice.

> — Carol Anne Ogdin
> Deep Woods Technology

This chapter dealt with many of the emerging technologies that form a new genre of client/server software called "groupware." What's new is the synergy gained by bringing the pieces together on client/server networks. Groupware supports the asynchronous distribution of information to groups. It's a flexible technology that can adapt to the way people do business in both structured and ad hoc settings. The e-mail foundation helps bring humans into the loop. The information that is collected and distributed can be highly unstructured and rich with meaning. Workflow allows the creation of highly intelligent "routing clouds" that deliver information to the points where it can be processed. It also creates what Forrester calls "value-added rivers," as information moves from one point to the next along an intelligent route.

Chapter 20

Groupware: Meet the Players

Groupware is prehistoric by PC standards. Although the category is 20 years old, there have been few earth-shaking improvements since the release of Lotus Notes, the first commercially successful package, which appeared almost a decade ago.

> — John Taschek, Columnist
> PC Week
> (January, 1998)

Groupware is a fast-growing industry that's in a state of tremendous flux. For many years, groupware was synonymous with Lotus Notes. In late 1998, there's still no groupware product that's as comprehensive as Notes/Domino 5.0. However, Notes is no longer alone. It faces strong competition from three popular products: Novell's *GroupWise*, Netscape/AOL's *SuiteSpot*, and Microsoft's *Exchange*. These products are all backed by companies with strong mindshare and market presence. And all three products will soon match Notes' comprehensive, all-in-one groupware offering.

This chapter starts out by giving you a quick snapshot of the groupware market and the key trends within that industry. Next, we look at Notes/Domino 5.0 in some

detail—it's the product that sets the bar for all groupware vendors, so it's the product competitors must beat. We then briefly cover Lotus Notes' main competitors—GroupWise, SuiteSpot, and Exchange. We end with a Soapbox about where we think this is all going.

GROUPWARE MARKET OVERVIEW

Why, in this era of networked PCs, e-mail, and the Web, are business apps designed for individuals rather than groups?

> — *John Tibbets and Barbara Bernstein*
> *Kinexis Consulting*
> *(July, 1998)*

As we mentioned in the last chapter, groupware was a $1.7 billion software industry in 1997—not counting services. The lion's share of revenues went to the big four groupware vendors—Lotus/IBM, Microsoft, Netscape, and Novell. You may have noticed in the last chapter that these vendors are also the leading suppliers of e-mail. Lotus is the number one supplier of e-mail, with an installed base of 37 million users. It is followed by Microsoft, which has over 31 million users. Novell has over 12.4 million users. And, Netscape's mail servers service over 5.2 million users. Note that not everyone that uses a Netscape browser for mail also uses a Netscape server. The same is true for Microsoft. So in this case, giving away the razor does not necessarily sell the blades.

Excluding Netscape—which was an Internet company from the very start—we can say that the leading LAN-based e-mail vendors are turning into all-in-one groupware vendors. In addition, all these vendors have now adopted e-mail Internet standards. In 1998, groupware has become an Internet technology, and vice versa. Of course, Netscape was there first. However, the traditional groupware vendors were very quick to adopt their technologies to the Internet. So they successfully met the Netscape challenge. As we go to press, Netscape (or AOL) is de-emphasizing groupware and instead is concentrating on selling scalable Internet services to ISPs—some of these ISPs are IS shops that provide their own intranets and extranets.

TRENDS

Notes is still the product that's defining the groupware industry. And the competing vendors are still trying to field a credible alternative to Notes. The news is that the Notes competitors are finally starting to catch up. The other news is that the groupware industry is facing new challenges on many fronts—from SQL database vendors with their new multimedia data warehousing facilities, from object database vendors with their rich data types, and from the exploding Internet with its low-cost document-publishing and conferencing facilities. New standards such as XML may also have a big impact. Here's a snapshot of the major movements that we're seeing in the groupware industry:

- ■ ***Groupware vendors are embracing the Web***. The Web, with its open document standards—including document browsers, firewalls, the pervasive HTML/XML publishing standards, digital certificates, LDAP, and the SMTP/MIME e-mail backbone—is the most formidable competitor groupware vendors are currently facing. Just a few years ago, some pundits went so far as to proclaim the Web had made Lotus Notes irrelevant. This is obviously not true. Instead, groupware vendors were in the best position to provide industrial-strength technology for the Web—including scalable document databases, mission-critical mail backbones, security, server-to-server document replication, support for mobile users, workflow, and system management. Without exception, all the major groupware vendors have decided not to fight the Web; instead, they decided to "embrace it." Most of these vendors have successfully recreated their groupware offerings on top of open Web standards. In retrospect, it turned out to be easier to adapt existing groupware products to the Web than to create groupware products from scratch using Web standards.

- ■ ***Groupware is now mission-critical ready***. Lotus Domino 5.0 is the first product to provide a truly robust, scalable, and multiplatform groupware infrastructure. The product includes important backbone features such as dynamic routing, replication, pass-through servers, thread-based background routing, security, and global system management. Domino 5.0 is setting a new bar for the features you should expect from a groupware server. We expect that its "big three" competitors will follow suit with products that are just as reliable and mission-critical.

- ■ ***Groupware is expanding into new areas***. If they succeed in subsuming the Internet, the groupware vendors will be in a good position to subsume other forms of client/server—including database and NOS. Groupware is also moving into new areas such as telephony. Finally, groupware's workflow and agent-based mail systems are strong candidates for managing business processes across an enterprise.

- ■ ***Groupware is becoming tool-friendly***. Like TP Monitors and SQL databases, the groupware industry discovered that it takes great tools to win the hearts of client/server software developers. You can now create groupware applications that incorporate data from both document stores and SQL databases using popular client/server tools.

- ■ ***Groupware is discovering distributed objects and components***. Many of the newer groupware products are built on Java and CORBA. Even Domino 5.0

now includes a CORBA/IIOP ORB; it also supports JavaBeans. In the future, Domino will also support Enterprise JavaBeans. In the Microsoft parallel universe, Exchange supports ActiveX and COM technology.

Groupware has come a long way. However, the technology is still handicapped by its lack of support for ACID transactions. Groupware also suffers from being a monolithic technology that is not well-suited for dealing with distributed components. In other words, groupware lacks the component middleware foundation of a distributed object bus, such as CORBA or COM+. However, groupware technology is here today, and you can use it to create some very exciting client/server applications—especially on the Internet and intranets. The more avant-garde groupware products have already incorporated both ORBs and components.

LOTUS NOTES/DOMINO 5.0

Lotus Notes—now in its fifth major release—is the premier client/server groupware product in the industry. Even though Notes has been in the field for almost ten years and has sold over 21 million seats, it still remains a mystery to the vast majority of PC users. It's even a mystery to its competitors. Some call it a "cute bulletin board," others label it "glorified e-mail," and some SQL purists pooh-pooh it as—Heaven forbid—an "unstructured database." In reality, Notes/Domino is a multifaceted, client/server groupware product. And as we know from the last chapter, it is hard to define groupware in 25 words or less. The secret of a good groupware package is that it creates a whole that is *much* more than the sum of the parts. Notes does this very well.

So What Is Lotus Notes/Domino?

The first thing to understand is that *Lotus Notes* is the name of the groupware client—*Domino* is the server. Together, they allow groups of users to interact and share information that can be of a highly unstructured nature. The second thing to understand is that starting with *Notes/Domino Release 5* (or *R5*), the client and the server parts are separate. This means that the Notes client can access ordinary Web servers, POP3/IMAP Internet e-mail engines, and CORBA/IIOP distributed objects. It also means that the Domino server can service ordinary Internet e-mail clients, HTTP-based Web browsers, and CORBA/IIOP client invocations. In addition, Lotus provides a suite of JavaBeans—including views, forms, mail, navigator, calendar, and address book—that can invoke Domino services from within ordinary browsers. Of course, to get the most out of Notes, you need Domino—and vice versa. So Lotus Notes has the look and feel of a browser, only it provides a lot more information—especially when it's talking to Domino.

The combined Notes/Domino client/server application development and run-time environment provides the following functions (see Figure 20-1):

- *A document database server* stores and manages multiuser client access to semi-structured data—including text, images, audio, and video. Domino R4 supports up to 1000 concurrent Notes clients using 32-bit SMP server platforms (this is an order of magnitude greater than Release 3). Domino R5 adds support for load-balancing across servers in a cluster; it transparently synchronizes the databases within a cluster—as a result, they are all replicas. The load-balancer will direct a client request to a server in a cluster based on availability and workload. To the user, the cluster appears as a single database. Preliminary NotesBench performance tests show Domino R5 to be 3-5 times faster than the previous release.

- *An e-mail server* manages multiuser client access to mail. Domino 4.X comes with a proprietary mail backbone infrastructure that supports—via gateways—SMTP/MIME and X.400; it also includes a POP3 mail server. In contrast, Domino R5 natively supports SMTP, E-SMTP, MIME, and S/MIME—Notes mail is now Internet mail. In addition, Domino R5 supports IMAP4 and NNTP.

- *A global LDAP directory* supplements the messaging infrastructure. The *Public Address* book in R4 is now the *Domino Directory* in R5. Domino R5 also supports LDAPv3 with authenticated read and write. Clients access the Domino Directory via LDAP. The R5 directory can contain up to one million user entries per domain; in contrast, the previous release could only support 150,000 users.

- *An HTTP 1.1 Web server* that ties in directly to the Domino database. Starting with R4, Domino integrates ordinary HTML documents with Notes documents. Domino can also work with other HTTP servers such as Microsoft's IIS. In this case, IIS fields all the HTTP requests and then calls Domino to service URL requests for Domino pages—these are URLs with (.nsf) extensions.[1]

- *A CORBA-based Application Server* provides a modern distributed object application environment. Domino R5 now includes a built-in IIOP ORB as well as tools to create server-side CORBA objects with full access to the Domino services. The Notes client also includes a CORBA/Java ORB; it lets Java beans and applets invoke CORBA server objects as well as Domino services. In addition, Lotus provides a downloadable CORBA/Java ORB, which you can use in browsers that do not natively support CORBA—for example, Microsoft's Internet Explorer.

---

[1] NSF stands for *Notes Storage File*—it's the Domino database file format.

- *A backbone server/server infrastructure* supports both mail-routing and database replication. The replication mechanism synchronizes copies of the same database; these copies can reside on multiple server (or client) machines. Domino R4 introduced a *server passthrough* feature; it lets you dial into one Domino server and reach any other server to which you are authorized. Passthrough also lets you access multiple databases on multiple servers at the same time. Domino R5 introduces more router enhancements such as anti-spam controls to prevent unwanted mail from being forwarded through your domain. It also lets you configure who can route documents of a given size, and when they can do this.

- *The Notes client environment* presents views of the document databases and provides an electronic mail front-end. Users can navigate through the databases and their document contents. Views are stored queries that act as filters for the information in the databases. The e-mail front-end is just a specialized view of a mail database. Notes can attach GUI forms (private or public) to the various databases used for data entry. Notes R4 introduced a flexible three-pane user interface that integrates Mail, Web browsing, and the traditional Notes client. Notes R5 replaces it with a Webtop-like interface with bookmark folders, browser-like navigation buttons, and a headlines page with links to important information. You can also drag-and-drop objects.

  The new R5 user interface provides consistent access to your e-mail, browser, group calendar, documents, tasks, and favorite databases. You click to link to documents and information that can reside in any number of Notes/Domino databases, HTTP Web servers, CORBA application servers, relational databases, TP Monitors (Tuxedo and TXSeries), and MOM (MQSeries). The expanded Notes R5 search capabilities include Web-like support for searches that can range across all the documents in a single database (such as your mail folder) to searches across multiple Notes/Domino databases and the Internet.

- *Distributed services* include X509 digital certificates, SSL3 security, security and access control lists, database administration services, system management, and an X.500-based global namespace.

- *Application development tools* include: 1) a GUI forms and Web page designer; 2) tools and templates for creating databases; 3) two scripting languages—*LotusScript* and *JavaScript*; 4) an open API set—including the Notes API, VIM, MAPI, JDBC, and ODBC; and 5) support for CORBA/Java distributed objects. The new *Lotus Domino Designer R5* visual tool lets you create client and server applications using HTML 4, Java, JavaScript, and CORBA/IIOP. Domino also supports *Intelligent Agents*. These are scripted applications that you can use to automate repetitive tasks—including database replication, data-handling, the in-box actions, and messaging services. In addition, you can write Notes applications using many popular third-party client/server and Internet tools—such as Inprise/Borland *JBuilder*, Symantec *Visual Café*, IBM's *VisualAge for Java*, and NetObjects' *Fusion*.

Previously, all Notes/Domino communications—client/server and server/server—were done using a proprietary RPC. Now, Notes also supports IIOP and HTTP. Finally, Notes supports client/server drivers for NetBEUI, TPC/IP, IPX/SPX, and AppleTalk stacks. Optional APPC and X.25 drivers are available for server-to-server communications.

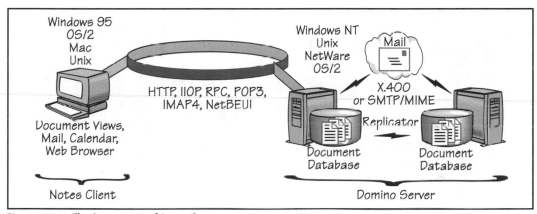

Figure 20-1. The Components of Lotus Notes.

The Multimedia Document Database

Ray Ozzie—founder of Iris Associates, the company that developed the original Notes under contract to Lotus—describes the foundation of the Notes/Domino architecture as a "database engine for semi-structured and unstructured information." Ozzie's model of a database is more akin to computer conferencing than Online Transaction Processing (OLTP). The Notes/Domino database was designed as a vehicle for gathering and disseminating all types of information; it was not meant to be a "database of record" that reflects the realtime state of the business. In this respect, Domino is more like a data warehouse, except that the data tends to be highly eclectic. Another way of putting it is that Ray Ozzie was more interested in adding and capturing real-time information than providing synchronized access to shared data for updates. You'll get a better feel for this after we explain the Domino replication model.

The primary commodity in a Domino system is a semi-structured, multimedia *document* that can contain a variety of data types—including voice, BLOBs, video, and multifont text (see Figure 20-2). A Notes/Domino system organizes, stores, replicates, and provides shared access to documents. Related collections of Notes/Domino documents are stored in a *database*. You can index and retrieve this database by any of the documents' properties or by the actual contents of the documents. Domino supports full-text indexing and searching. A Domino *document* consists of a set of fields, also known as *properties*; each has a name, type, and value. For example, you can tag a Domino document with properties such as *client*, *region*, and *subject*. The regions can contain any number of BLOB-like *attachments* (or embedded files). Embedded files are managed and organized as part of a Domino document.

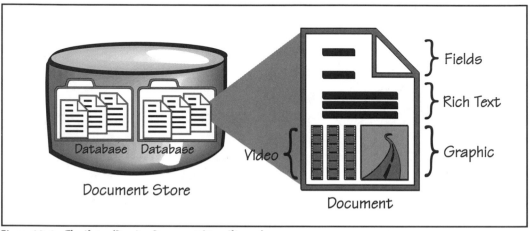

Figure 20-2. The Notes/Domino Document Store Hierarchy.

Domino R5 lets you create truly gigantic databases. Here are some of the new capabilities they advertise:

- **Object stores can be of unlimited size.** An administrator allocates maximum object store sizes in up to 32 GByte chunks—called *segments*. Domino will automatically span data across multiple segments and physical storage boundaries.

- **Databases can have an unlimited number of documents.** Domino stores an entire database in a single file (or object store). A Notes/Domino application typically consists of many databases that are organized by topic.

Again, the Notes/Domino concept of a database is more akin to conferencing (data is organized by topic) rather than relational DBMSs (all data is organized in a single database consisting of multiple tables).

Domino Database Replication

Like data warehouses, Domino allows you to replicate databases across servers (and clients). Unlike the warehouses we covered in Part 4, Domino has no notion of a master database—it uses replicas. The *replicator* is responsible for bidirectionally adding, deleting, or updating documents among all *replicas* of the database. Domino uses replication as a means to disseminate (or broadcast) information across geographically distributed locations.

The Domino replicator supports both full and partial replication, and it has a tunable level of consistency based on the desired frequency of replication. Domino time-stamps all new and edited (or updated) documents that are known to have replicas. Unattended servers can dial each other up, compare notes, and swap changes at times configured by an administrator. You can also store replicas on client worksta-tions and initiate swaps from there.

Many releases ago, Notes/Domino introduced *background replication*, which allows Notes laptop clients to continue working in Notes while replication is taking place in the background. Laptop users will find replication to be very helpful for on-the-road activity. You copy a Notes database, work on it, and then swap changes with the server when you can make a connection (see Figure 20-3). *Selective replication* limits the sections in documents that get replicated. You can choose not to replicate binary attachments to save on local disk space. You can also limit the size of each document to be replicated (for example, the first 200 characters). Finally, you can choose to only replicate unread messages from your boss or messages that are labeled urgent. Domino also provides *field-based replication* that gives you even more fine-grained control over the replication process. You can replicate selective fields within a document. This option lets you transmit only the updated fields within a changed document. With earlier versions, you had to wait for Domino to replicate all of a document's fields, even if only one field had been modified.

This loosely synchronized style of information update is adequate for most confer-encing applications, but it is a far cry from the synchronous two-phase commit updates used in OLTP applications. So how are concurrent updates handled? Prior to Notes Release 3, if two users simultaneously updated a server-based document, the first save was accepted and the next save was notified that it was overwriting someone else's changes. The decision of whether or not to overwrite the data was left to the user (not a very comforting thought if you were the first user). Notes R3 (and later) supports a versioning capability that lets an edited document become a response to the original document. Or, the last updated version can become the main document, with all previous versions displayed as responses.

Versioning does not guarantee that the last version is the most accurate, and it cannot merge changes into a single copy of the data. So Notes/Domino is not a suitable technology for OLTP database applications or applications that require high concurrency controls involving immediate updates. However, versioning eliminates the loss of data through concurrent updates or through replication. It's quite useful for its intended use: document-centric groupware applications—an area that OLTP doesn't even touch.

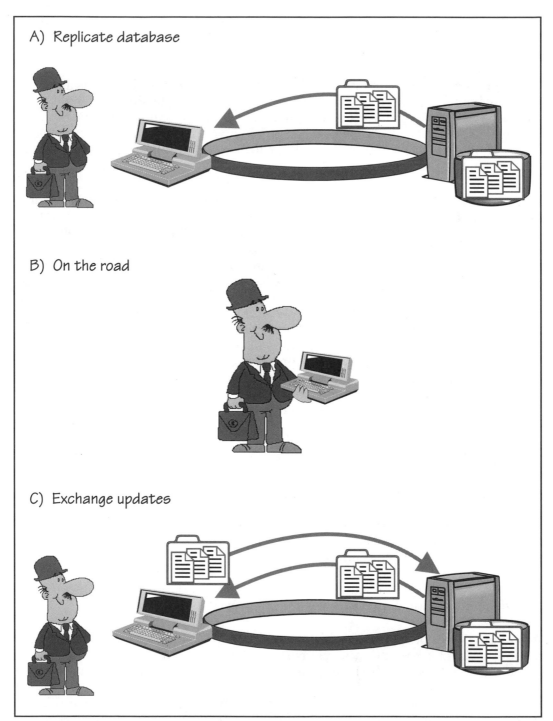

Figure 20-3. Replicated Databases Can Be Used on the Road.

How to Build a Notes Application

You typically create a new Notes/Domino *database* by using one of the Lotus-provided templates and then customizing it. A database is simply a new file; it can be given an identifying icon, a title, help panels, and a *policy document* that explains what it's all about. You use *forms* to define the data, enter new information, or view existing information in a database. To create a form, you can start with one of the pre-existing forms and then modify it using the GUI editor. Forms provide data entry fields, text fields, and graphic areas where pictures or other sources of multimedia data can be pasted (or attached). You can associate event handlers—written in Java, JavaScript, or LotusScript—with specific events and actions. The forms you create are associated with the database. You can designate them as either *public*, which means they're available to all client applications that have access to the database; or you can make them *private*, which means only the creator can use them.

Views are stored queries that display the contents of a database or of a particular document. You use them for navigation and for the filtering of information—for example, you can create a view that displays all documents less than one month old "by region" or "by salesperson." The view will display the list of documents in a tabular or outline format. Any database has one or more views that the designer creates for easy access to information. Users also can create *private* views to provide a listing or access criteria that the database designer didn't anticipate.

On the client side, the Notes *headlines page* displays bookmarked folders that let you organize databases by topics. Each folder can contain from zero to hundreds of databases. Each database is represented by a bookmark. You click on a bookmarked database to open it and then work with its views. Notes lets you open multiple databases and gives each its own window. The process of creating a new Notes client/server application and tailoring forms and views can take less than an hour. It's that simple.

The Lotus Notes API

Notes/Domino provides APIs that developers can use to store and retrieve Notes documents. It also gives you broad access to many of the features of the Notes user interface. Most of the Domino APIs are now remotely accessible via CORBA using multiple languages. The APIs allow you to:

■ Create or delete databases.

■ Read, write, and modify any document and any field in the document.

■ Create and use database views.

- Control database access with access control lists.

- Gather and report server performance statistics and register new workstations and servers.

- Write custom tasks that you can add to the Domino server software and specify the schedule under which the custom task executes.

- Perform full-text searches using the new search engine.

- Issue calls to restrict what documents get exchanged during replication.

- Obtain the list of names and address books in use locally or on a server.

- Issue mail API calls.

- Issue LDAP calls.

In addition, Notes supports both the VIM and MAPI e-mail client APIs. You can also access information on SQL databases, TP Monitors, and MOM using *Domino.Connect*.

Domino/Notes E-Mail

From a client workstation's perspective, e-mail is just another Notes/Domino database that contains a collection of mail documents. The procedures to read incoming mail, sort through mail, or create a mail document are the same ones used to create and read documents in any Notes/Domino database. You simply use forms and views that are tailored to your mail documents. Of course, one of the differences is that the mail documents you create will be sent to someone else's mailbox. Notes provides visual indicators to let you know that you have incoming mail. You then open the database and read it. Ray Ozzie's design seems to be very consistent.

Starting with Release 4, cc:Mail clients are able to use the Domino Mail server. With Release 5, any POP3-based Internet mail client can access the Domino Mail server. So what kind of services does a Domino Mail server provide? It provides mail backbone functions with the following features:

- ***Routing optimization.*** The techniques include outbound message prioritization and dynamic adaptive route selection based on link costs.

- ***Separate router threads.*** All server-to-server communications are handled by separate transfer threads. Threads allow multiple concurrent transfers to occur on different backbone routes. In addition, threads prevent large mail messages from delaying other server tasks.

- ***Delivery failure notification.*** Senders can be notified when delivery isn't possible (including the reasons).

■ **X.500/LDAP namespace support.** Domino supports the full X.500-compliant hierarchical naming as its native means of identifying *users* within the system. This makes it straightforward for Notes directories to interoperate at the naming level with other X.500/LDAP-compliant systems. Domino R5 also supports the Internet domain naming convention.

■ **Mail gateways and directory services.** Domino provides e-mail gateways to the most popular e-mail networks—including X.400, SMTP, cc:Mail, MHS, PROFS, Exchange, VinesMail, VAXmail, and SoftSwitch (see Figure 20-4). With R5, Domino natively supports SMTP/MIME—no gateways are required.

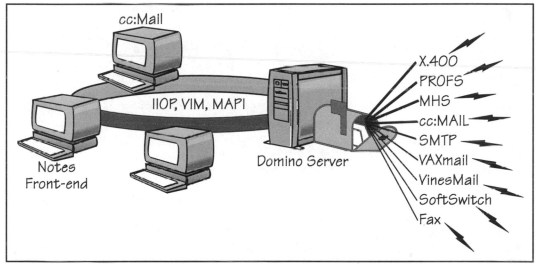

Figure 20-4. Notes/Domino's E-Mail Reach.

■ **Electronic signatures.** Notes/Domino uses the RSA public key cryptography for all aspects of Notes security, including encryption. It is also an X.509 certificate server.

The bottom line is that Domino provides a true client/server e-mail architecture. It supports a variety of e-mail clients—including cc:Mail, Lotus Notes, MAPI-based clients, and Internet mail clients. At the backbone level, Domino can route messages to almost any type of e-mail system.

Domino/Notes Systems Management

The new R5 *Domino Administrator* is a graphical management utility that lets you manage an enterprise-wide Domino environment from a single management station. The package lets you control any Domino Server and monitor the health of a Domino

backbone network. The utility displays an entire mail-routing topology, including routes to and from selected servers. It also shows you the replication topology, including the replication maps of specific databases. Domino Administrator provides real-time statistics on mail volume, number of pending or dead messages, replication time, low-level packet traffic, router loads, and so on. It can also serve as a proxy management station in an enterprise management hierarchy by supporting the SNMP management protocol and the *Mail And Directories MANagement (MADMAN)* MIB. We will have more to say on SNMP and MIBs in Part 9.

How Revolutionary Is Notes/Domino?

Soapbox

Notes is a very exciting product that makes you want to jump in and create client/server applications just for the fun of it. Notes/Domino databases tend to proliferate like rabbits. Once you get the hang of them, they're contagious. With R5, Notes/Domino addresses the client/server needs of mobile users, intergalactic enterprises, and the Internet. You can carry your Domino databases on a lap-

top or have them replicated to the far corners of the universe. Domino 5.0 even lets you carry around a compressed LDAP database. Lotus is also doing more to open up the Notes/Domino environment at the API level so that ISVs and IS programmers can jump in and provide add-ons. In addition, R5 now supports CORBA and Java, which makes Domino a serious application server platform. And soon, it will support Enterprise JavaBeans, which makes it a server-side component platform. So in many ways, Lotus Notes is a "killer app" that does for client/server what Lotus 1-2-3 did for PCs and DOS.

We like Notes/Domino and highly recommend it for certain classes of applications. But it's important to understand what it can and cannot do. Notes is a very good fit for applications that collect multimedia information, perform very few updates, and need to be integrated with e-mail. But Notes is not very good at handling applications that deal with structured data, are query intensive, and require multiuser updates with high levels of integrity. Notes does not handle transactions well; it does not even know how to spell ACID. These types of applications are best handled by TP Monitors, data warehouses, transactional MOMs, and SQL and object databases. In all fairness, Lotus now provides gateways to all these environments, so it's not trying to reinvent them. □

NOVELL'S GROUPWISE

Someone once remarked that Novell's *GroupWise* went through more name changes than an ex-con. It's true. The product—originally named *WordPerfect Office*—became *WordPerfect Symmetry* in May 1994 to avoid confusion with Microsoft Office. In July 1994, Novell acquired WordPerfect Inc. and renamed the product *GroupWise*. In 1996, the client/server version of the product was renamed *GroupWise XTD*. The current version—which shipped in September, 1998—is called *GroupWise 5.5*. So GroupWise it is.

In January 1996, Novell sold its WordPerfect division to Corel, but it kept the very successful GroupWise product. By mid-1998, the product had sold over 12.4 million copies, making it the third most popular groupware product after Lotus Notes and MS Exchange. The product is a key piece of infrastructure in Novell's push to make NetWare 5.0 ubiquitous. Novell's intent is to leverage the large installed base of NetWare networks and provide a common platform for administering both the network and groupware applications. GroupWise also integrates with the Novell Directory Services.

So what is GroupWise? Novell calls it "a messaging application." In its current incarnation, it is an e-mail product with a ton of groupware add-on functions. GroupWise is an integrated package that includes e-mail, calendaring, scheduling, task management, workflow, and faxes. It supports what Novell calls "rules-based messaging"—it lets you associate actions to incoming and outgoing e-mail messages. All of GroupWise's functions run under a common user interface.

GroupWise introduced many new messaging features that were later adopted by Lotus and Microsoft. For example, it lets you convert an item into a different type, such as changing an e-mail message into a calendar appointment or a to-do task. It was also the first groupware package to provide a single view to all information. In addition, GroupWise was the first of the "Big Four" to include a built-in workflow engine that allows users to construct workflows graphically.

GroupWise features a *universal in-box* that lets you access all types of incoming messages in one place—including e-mail, schedule requests, delegated tasks, voice mail, faxes, and electronic forms. The in-box profiles and manages information in the same way, regardless of data type. You should be able to sort, route, copy, and delegate a voice message exactly like you would with an e-mail message. It frees you from having to piece together information from separate applications or locations. In addition, GroupWise provides a *replicated folder* capability that lets teams share applications, information, and in-box items. You should be able to share information related to a particular topic or project. Unlike Domino, Group-Wise does message replication instead of database replication. The GroupWise *universal out-box* lets you track messages and retract them if they're unopened. You can see if your messages have been received, opened, deleted, or delegated.

GroupWise supports Internet protocols such as POP3, IMAP4, and LDAP; it supports SMTP/MIME via gateways. Novell also provides a Java add-on called *Web-Access* that lets you access your GroupWise in-box using any Web browser.

GroupWise 5.5 client software runs on Windows 16, Windows 95/98, and Macintosh. The server runs on NetWare and Windows NT. Novell intends to provide support for Unix—on the client and server—at a later date.

MICROSOFT'S EXCHANGE

Exchange is really the only enterprise application we sell...Mail will be a driving application that takes this infrastructure to the next level.

> — *Steve Ballmer, CEO*
> *Microsoft*
> *(March, 1998)*

Where Lotus views the world as one big business process, Microsoft sees it as one big mail system.

> — *David Marshak, VP*
> *Seybold Group*

Microsoft's *Exchange* is primarily a client/server messaging system. Exchange provides server-based e-mail, calendaring, and voicemail integration capabilities. Its primary client is Microsoft *Outlook 98*, which ships with both Exchange and Microsoft *Office98*. Outlook is an integrated messaging, mailing, and calendaring application; it can either operate standalone or in client/server mode via MAPI, POP3, or IMAP4. The built-in *Outlook Forms Designer* lets you create customized forms for accessing Exchange resources—including the databases for mail, discussion groups, calendaring, and contacts. You can add logic to these forms using VBScript and Visual Basic.

In addition to Outlook, Exchange can service any MAPI-compliant mail client. However, Exchange supports more than just Outlook and MAPI clients. It also supports most of the prerequisite Internet e-mail protocols—including POP3, IMAP4, LDAP, NNTP, X.509, and SMPTP/MIME (via gateways).[2] And, it provides facilities for translating its proprietary text format into HTML. Consequently, Exchange can also be used as a server for Internet mail clients. This means you can check your Exchange e-mail from within a browser on any platform. In addition, Web clients can retrieve HTML-formatted Exchange data by invoking *Active Server*

---

[2] *Exchange 5.5* uses X.400 for its mail backbone.

Pages (ASPs) on a Microsoft Web server. To do this, you must embed server-side scripts in the ASPs to dynamically generate the HTML. Typically, you will use the COM-based *Active Messaging API* to access the Exchange message and directory stores from your ASPs.

The Exchange database is a collection of hierarchical folders. A folder can either be public or private. A *private folder* contains personal data; *public folders* are shared resources that are accessed via a mail-centric system. Exchange replicates the data in the public folders across multiple servers; it is through these public folders that you selectively distribute information across an Exchange network. Clients that have access to these public folders can now post messages directly to the folder instead of sending them to a particular user or group of users. This means that you can use these public folders to create public forums where groups of users can create and respond to postings. Exchange keeps track of the message threads in the public folders and displays them in a tree-like configuration within the forum window.

With Exchange 5.5's *Collaborative Data Objects (CDOs)*, you can write event-handlers that take some action when a new message is received in a folder. You can think of this as a "publish and subscribe" service on top of public folders. For example, this lets you subscribe to a public folder and then receive automatic notifications whenever anyone posts a message to that folder. A built-in form designer lets you create custom forms for posting messages. You can also create forms using Visual Basic.

Exchange is an integral part of Microsoft's BackOffice family of products. Consequently, it builds on top of NT's common infrastructure for security, user authorization, and network administration. Exchange relies on Windows NT's security. You only need to log in once to an NT domain to access your Exchange account. The server code only runs on Windows NT. From an enterprise management perspective, Exchange 5.5 supports both SNMP and the MADMAN MIB.

Originally billed as a "Notes killer," Exchange—in its latest incarnation—is closer in function to Collabra than to Lotus Notes (we explain Collabra in the next section). Like Collabra, Exchange provides public folders for group discussions on top of a mail-centric system. In contrast, Notes provides a groupware application development environment on top of a shared document database. Exchange is now seen as primarily a way to synchronize e-mail communications. It is not seen as a groupware replacement for Notes. Think of it as Microsoft's strategic e-mail system. The next release of Exchange—code-named *Platinum*—may ship by the end of 1999. It will provide native support for SMTP/MIME, intercompany workflows, and OLE DB; it will also be integrated with NT 5.0's new directory and security services.

NETSCAPE/AOL'S SUITESPOT

I think we did a disservice to ourselves by positioning ourselves in the groupware space.

> — *John Paul, Senior VP*
> *Netscape*
> *(June, 1998)*

Netscape's next-generation hosting solution will enable the world's largest service providers to deploy value-added services such as web-based e-mail, unified messaging, hosted intranets, and business-to-business e-commerce.

> — *John Paul, Senior VP*
> *Netscape*
> *(September, 1998)*

So, has Netscape bowed out of the groupware business? Which of John Paul's statements should we believe? Is the company schizophrenic? To understand what's going on, we will first review Netscape's groupware products; then we will go over their new strategy. When Netscape acquired Collabra in November 1995, there was a perception that Web-based groupware was right around the corner. In reality, Collabra is not a full-featured groupware environment like Lotus Notes. It's more like a bulletin board add-on that works on top of existing e-mail systems. Collabra lets you create discussion groups—called forums—using ordinary e-mail instead of a document database.

In Collabra, if you want to start a new message thread or reply to an existing message, you simply click on the appropriate button in the toolbar to invoke a message form. You typically post a message to a forum. Collabra also provides a "Post and Notify" feature that lets you both post a message and send a copy of the posting as an e-mail message to specific users. You access all messages by viewing threads in individual conferences. Collabra lists conference topics in chronological order. It indents all responding messages directly underneath a topic, clearly marking messages that you haven't yet read.

Collabra provides powerful search and sort tools that let you quickly find the information you're after in the various forums. You can sort messages in a forum by author, title, date, size, or relevance. The *Search Assistant* lets you enter phrases, multiple terms, or wild cards. You can restrict searches to the body, title, or author of documents. In addition, you can combine search terms using boolean and proximity operators.

The Collabra *Replication Agent* lets you replicate entire forums across multiple servers, but it does not provide Lotus-like filters or field-based replication—all replication is done via e-mail. However, only the creators can edit forum postings. Consequently, it is easy to ensure that all servers have identical copies of a forum. Collabra lets you schedule replication times for each forum individually, but you're still constrained by your e-mail system's message propagation time. As you can see, Collabra is really an e-mail-based conferencing system that uses *Netscape Communicator* as its front-end. Collabra alone is not a Lotus replacement.

Of course, Netscape sells a lot more than just Collabra. In addition to Collabra Server, Netscape's *SuiteSpot 3.5* includes several other servers that provide Internet and groupware services. Here are the other SuiteSpot 3.5 servers that you can also use to create Web-based groupware solutions:

■ *Directory Server* provides the industry's fastest, most scalable, and most complete implementation of LDAP. It was designed to implement LDAP natively from the very start. Netscape's *Mission Control* management console uses the LDAP directory to access the other SuiteSpot servers to perform relevant directory-based management tasks from a single console.

■ *Messaging Server* provides the industry's fastest, most scalable, and most complete Internet mail server.[3] It was designed from day one for Internet mail. It natively supports IMAP4, POP3, SMTP, ESMTP, S/MIME, X.509 v3, and other Internet mail standards. It even supports *vCard*—the upcoming Internet standard for digital business cards. Plus, the Messaging Server includes facilities for filtering spam e-mail. Currently, any user with a browser or Internet e-mail can access the system; it is no longer tied to a Netscape browser.

■ *Certificate Server* lets you issue X.509 v3 certificates for SSL-based authentication, S/MIME messages, and for object signing; it uses the RSA digital signature algorithm. It also maintains a database of certificates that is tightly integrated with the LDAP Directory Server. So you can use this combination for single logons. It also maintains certification revocation lists. Certificate Server can be used to provide certificate security across all the SuiteSpot servers on an intranet; it can even extend that protection to extranet partners across the Internet.

■ *Calendar Server* provides group scheduling and calendaring. It lets you check on other people's schedules, create and post group schedules, manage to-do lists, and attach schedules to e-mail messages. Netscape *Communicator 4.5* provides the client to the Calendaring Server. It lets you schedule events in real time, view multiple schedules, and take advantage of the integration between Messenger and Calendar.

---

[3] The first version of this product was OEMed from *Software.com;* it's based on their *post.office* server engine. However, Netscape has subsequently evolved the product; it is now tightly integrated with the rest of the SuiteSpot family.

■ *Compass Server* offers intelligent agents and monitoring technologies. The agents can search for information on the Web, even if you're offline. When you reconnect, they deliver the information to you automatically. Compass Server has a built-in Web crawler that indexes data from intranets and the Internet. All the collected data—including HTML and non-HTML documents, e-mail messages, discussion group postings, and pushed information—is searchable.

■ *Enterprise Server* is Netscape's HTTP server; it also supports a built-in CORBA/IIOP ORB that lets you create server-side CORBA plug-ins called WAI; you can also directly invoke server-side CORBA objects from within a Netscape browser via IIOP. Enterprise Server is tightly integrated with the *Visual JavaScript* tool.

As we go to press, Netscape released an early beta of *Messaging Server 4.0 Hosting Edition*—its code name was *Toopers ISP*. The product works with the Directory Server to provide a unified messaging interface for e-mail, telephone, and fax. Netscape claims that the new Messaging Server can host up to half a million IMAP4 users on one server. Netscape will also deliver *Messenger Express 4.0* for roaming Web-based e-mail users. As you can see, Netscape has a very strong suite of groupware products which were designed from day one to work on top of Internet standards. With this background, we can now deal with the two sides of John Paul in the next Soapbox.

Netscape and Groupware: To Be or Not To Be

Soapbox

We won messaging and groupware business from customers that knew they needed highly scalable, highly centralized systems. They felt they needed a Mack truck and not a fleet of Hondas. Those are the ones we've been successful with, and so those are the ones we're focusing on now.

> — Marc Andreessen, Co-founder
> Netscape
> (July, 1998)

So is Netscape/AOL still a groupware vendor? Yes. The company is heavily involved in groupware—at least as we define it in this book. Just think of how many trees we just killed describing their current groupware products as well as those that are coming down the pike. So why the schizophrenic statements? It seems that Netscape's latest strategy is to sell scalable groupware infrastructure software to *Internet Service Providers (ISPs)* and also to large IT shops that provide ISP-like services for their companies (i.e., intranets and extranets). Netscape's ex-CEO Jim Barksdale has even coined a new name for these customers—*Enterprise Service Providers (ESPs)*.

This strategy makes a lot of sense because a large number of companies will outsource their e-mail (and other groupware services) to their ISPs. In fact, both Netscape and Sun make the claim that ISPs will be able to knock the total cost of ownership of an Internet e-mail system down to as little as $30 per user per year. ISPs will achieve these savings from directory-based administration and by loading tens of thousands of users on a single mail server. Note that the pricing of *SuiteSpot Hosting Edition* is based on an annual fee model, which is more appropriate for service providers.

In September 1998, Netscape announced that more than 75 ISPs and telcos worldwide are deploying hosted Internet and intranet services based on Netscape's server software. In addition, more than 15,000 ISPs and telcos globally have signed up to distribute 160 million copies of Netscape Navigator and Netscape Communicator client software to users this year through Netscape's free browser program.

So what are Netscape's unique advantages? How will it differentiate itself from Lotus, Novell, and Microsoft in the ESP/ISP market? Here are the two key advantages Netscape may have:

■ First, Netscape is typically about a year ahead of its main competitors in the development of pure Internet technologies; it almost always provides native Internet implementations of its products—no gateways here. In contrast, its competitors started with proprietary products and then added gateways to the Internet protocols—the native implementations came much later.

■ Second, Netscape provides cross-platform products that run on both Unixes and NT. In contrast, Novell's GroupWise currently runs on NetWare and NT only; Microsoft's Exchange is an NT-only solution. So why is this an advantage? Because ISPs need scalable solutions. Today, this means Unix.

Netscape must still deal with its archrival—Lotus. Domino 5.0 is a scalable, Internet-based groupware solution that also runs on Unixes (and many other platforms). So it may still be Netscape/Sun/AOL against Lotus/IBM. Netscape must be very agile and move very fast to shake off Lotus. In addition, Netscape may face some competition from niche vendors—like *software.com* and *ISO-COR*—who specialize in selling Internet mail engines to telcos and ISPs. Of course, all this competition is good for all of us. ❑

CONCLUSION

Now that Lotus has embraced the Web in a big way, the Internet is no longer a threat to Notes/Domino. On the contrary, the Internet and intranets may become important sources of new revenues for Lotus. Notes/Domino provides ideal technology for supporting document databases—the stuff the Internet is made from. Notes servers create a database paradigm on top of ordinary files. It is an order of magnitude better than dealing with billions of raw files. Of course, when it comes to the Internet, Netscape is still the company everyone must beat. In this case, Netscape's strategy of selling to ISVs is a brilliant move—especially if ISVs become the prime providers of Web-based groupware and mail.

With NetWare 5.0, Novell is recreating itself as a software company. GroupWise can become an important product for the new Novell—especially if its excellent technology is repackaged as Enterprise JavaBeans. Finally, Exchange will continue to prove irresistible to companies that standardize on Windows NT and Microsoft suites. The million-dollar question is: Will these companies use Exchange as their e-mail package and use Notes for groupware? Or, will they eventually use Exchange to provide their total groupware solution? Even if they make the latter choice, Lotus has a huge head start over Exchange, even on NT. It will take a long time for Microsoft to match Notes/Domino 5.0's mission-critical infrastructure.

Part 7
Client/Server With
Distributed Objects

An Introduction to Part 7

We expect that component-oriented, object transaction middleware will make all traditional styles of business-application middleware obsolete.

— *Roy Schulte and Yafim Natis*
GartnerGroup
(April, 1998)[1]

So did you all enjoy that night on the town? Oh, you want to play elephant and blind men again? We can't afford it—you Martians party too hard. But, we have a great new adventure ahead of us, and it's going to be fun. We're going to explore distributed objects and components. No, we're not talking about *Unidentified Flying Objects (UFOs)*—that's Martian stuff. Sorry, that was rude: Of course you Martians are not objects and, yes, you have identities. What we're dealing with here are software objects. Do they fly? Yes, some do over wireless networks. And, we know of roaming objects that live on networks and their brokers who organize communities of objects. Yes, it's another new frontier, and there may be a pot of gold there, too. Are you all packed and ready for another adventure?

Part 7 is about distributed objects. The word *distributed* is important because it means we're dealing with objects that participate in client/server relationships with other objects. More plumbing? Yes, but this is supposed to be the "mother of all plumbing." Objects can do everything we've covered in this book, and supposedly *they do it better*. Here's why:

- **Objects** themselves are an amazing combination of data and function, with magical properties like polymorphism, inheritance, and encapsulation. This magic works wonders in distributed environments.

- **Object brokers** provide the ultimate software bus. They allow objects to dynamically discover each other and interact across machines and operating systems.

- **Object services** allow us to create, manage, name, move, copy, store, and restore objects.

- **Object Transaction Monitors** may emerge as the most powerful and flexible transaction managers yet. Objects and transactions are a dynamite combination.

- **Object groupware** may change the way we interact. The new groupware will be built using roaming objects, mobile agents, publish-and-subscribe, trading services, intelligent event managers, and object replication services.

---

[1] Source: GartnerGroup Research Note, *There Is No Strategic OLTP Middleware in 1998* (April, l998).

■ **Object databases** provide the ultimate management system for BLOBs, documents, and almost any type of information—especially new information types that are appearing on the Web today.

■ **Object Web** technology provides the foundation for the next generation of the Internet and intranets, as described in Part 8. It's also the foundation technology for the new generation of Web application servers.

■ **Object linking** technology allows us to create highly flexible webs among programs that don't know about each other. The webs emanate out of ordinary-looking desktop documents.

■ **Object frameworks** promise to revolutionize the way we build our distributed systems. They provide flexible, customizable, prefabricated software subsystems.

Objects—packaged as *components*—may provide the ultimate infrastructure for building client/server systems. We say "may" because success depends on more

An Introduction to Part 7

than just great technology. What products are available? Are the major players lined up behind the technology? Are the key standards in place? Currently, most of the distributed object infrastructure is in place. We have two competing infrastructures for components: CORBA/JavaBeans and COM+. In 1998, some truly great products are starting to appear on the market. 1999 may go down in history as the "Year of the Server-Side Components."

We think you Martians will love this distributed object stuff. It has all the elements of a new gold rush. But first we must clearly understand what makes this 22-year-old technology finally ready for prime time. The answer is CORBA/JavaBeans—and COM+ for those of you in the Microsoft parallel universe. As usual, the competition will be quite exciting. Of course, you'll have to read the ORB chapters to discover what's behind this new magic.

Complementing ORBs are distributed object services, component technology, and object databases. So pack up; we have an interesting journey ahead of us. Pack lots of trail mix and energy bars—you'll need it all. And yes, it's new frontier country. So bring along all your exploration gear, and let's hope we don't lose any of you in those uncharted and potentially treacherous mountain passes and ravines.[2]

---

[2] Note: Much of Part 7 is derived from our 1000-page book, **Client/Server Programming with Java and CORBA, Second Edition** (Wiley, 1998). We include this material to make this Survival Guide stand on its own and to provide you with the background information you'll need for Part 8. These chapters were all updated to include the latest developments in distributed object technology—including *Enterprise JavaBeans*, *CORBA 3.0 Components*, and *COM+*.

Chapter 21

Distributed Objects and Components

An *object is a living, breathing blob of intelligence that knows how to act in a given situation.*

— Steve Jobs

By now, anybody associated with computers knows that objects are wonderful—we simply can't live without them. Objects are the foundation of GUI builders. OO languages—C++, Java, and Smalltalk—are the way to write code. Software engineering is now synonymous with object methodologies. Books on object patterns and anti-patterns are the current rage. And, the literature is full of articles on the wonders of components, encapsulation, inheritance, and polymorphism. But what can these things do on a client/server network? Where do objects fit in a world dominated by SQL databases, TP Monitors, Lotus Notes, and the Internet? What happens when we stray away from the cozy single-address space of a program and try to get objects to talk across a network? What happens to inheritance in a world of federated operating systems separated by networks? In a nutshell, we need to understand how object technology can be *extended* to deal with the complex issues that are inherent in creating robust, single-image, client/server systems.

The purpose of the next few chapters is to describe exactly what objects can do for client/server systems. The key word is *systems*—or how objects work together across machine and network boundaries to create client/server solutions. We're not going to rehash the marvels of *Object-Oriented Programming (OOP)* and methodologies because we assume you've heard about them all before. We're moving on to the next step: distributed objects.

We strongly believe that this is the area where objects will realize their greatest potential; in the process, they will become the new "mainstream computing model." We also believe that the Internet and intranets need distributed objects to fulfill their intergalactic promise—more on this in Part 8. Finally, we believe that without a strong distributed object foundation, the management of client/server systems is a lost cause—more on this in Part 9.

In this chapter, we cover distributed objects and components. This is the background information you'll need to understand the forthcoming chapters on CORBA, Enterprise JavaBeans (EJBs), COM+, and Object Database Management Systems (ODBMSs).

WHAT DISTRIBUTED OBJECTS PROMISE

Just as databases were at the center of the design of the applications of the '70s and '80s, components are at the center of design of the applications of the '90s and the next century.

— *David Vaskevitch, VP*
Microsoft

Object technology will radically alter the way we develop our client/server systems. The promise is compelling: We will be able to put together complex client/server information systems by simply assembling and extending reusable software components. Any of the objects may be modified or replaced without affecting the rest of the components in the system or how they interact. The components will be shipped in *suites* that run within *application frameworks*, where all the pieces are known to work together to perform domain-level applications.

Objects and components have already revolutionized the way we assemble our client systems. Now they are about to revolutionize the way we develop our server applications. They promise to provide the ultimate in mix-and-match capabilities across clients and servers. In addition, they allow server-side components to collaborate across multivendor platforms.

The Benefits of Distributed Objects

Distributed object technology is extremely well-suited for creating flexible client/server systems because the data and business logic are encapsulated within objects, allowing them to be located anywhere within a distributed system. The granularity of distribution is greatly improved. In addition, distributed objects—of the CORBA, Java, and COM+ variety—are highly *introspective*, which means they can tell you everything about themselves. This allows visual tools and other applications to discover an object's interfaces, events, and properties "on-the-fly." Consequently, distributed objects are very toolable.

So distributed objects have the inherent potential to allow granular components to be visually assembled via tools, interoperate across networks, run on different platforms, roam on networks, coexist with legacy applications through object wrappers, and manage themselves and the resources they control. Objects are inherently self-managing entities. Objects should allow us to manage very complex systems by broadcasting instructions and alarms. Each receiving object will react differently to the message based on its object type. In addition, objects can maintain management information as part of their state.

Object-oriented client/server applications can afford to be much more flexible than traditional vertical applications. Application frameworks allow end-users to mix-and-match components without making the distributed application *less* robust. In addition, distributed objects—of the CORBA, Java, and COM+ variety—have this unique property of separating their interfaces from the implementation. This means that you can use object interfaces to wrapper your existing applications and make them look like ordinary objects. So you don't have to toss away these old applications as you would have to do with 2-tier client/server. Figure 21-1 shows some of these benefits. What more could we want?

Why This Sudden Interest in Distributed Objects?

The transition to component-based software will change the way we buy and build systems and what it means to be a software engineer.

> — **Dave Thomas, President**
> **Object Technology International**

We still need to answer this question: Why is there a renewed interest in the 23-year-old object technology? The technology is now ripe. And we can't build the type of applications we need with any other technology. Also, our industry now has two competing distributed object infrastructures—CORBA/JavaBeans and

A) Component Assembly

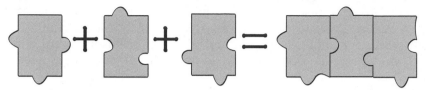

B) Interoperability

C) Portability/Mobility

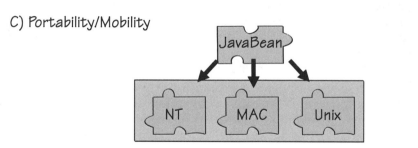

D) Coexistence

E) Self-managing Entities

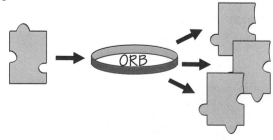

Figure 21-1. The Benefits of Distributed Objects.

COM+—that provide a *software bus* for components. Monolithic applications are monolithic because they're built as a whole. The object bus and component infrastructure make it unnecessary to build information systems from scratch. They let us create whole applications from parts.

However, distributed objects by themselves are not enough to get us there. They need to be packaged as components that can play together in *suites*. These suites combine the best in client/server and distributed object technology. They allow us to "build to order" entire information systems by assembling off-the-shelf object components. We will be able to assemble—in record time—highly flexible client/server applications tailored to a customer's needs. The components may be shipped in preassembled suites, where all the pieces are known to work together to perform a specific task. We anticipate that components and the client/server suites that integrate them will create vast new opportunities for ISVs, system integrators, ERP vendors, and in-house IS developers.

FROM DISTRIBUTED OBJECTS TO COMPONENTS

Everybody can resonate with objects—managers, 3 year olds, and superprogrammers. Object-oriented technology appeals to all these different camps.

— *Jim Gray*

A classical object—of the C++, Java, or Smalltalk variety—is a blob of intelligence that encapsulates code and data. Classical objects provide wonderful code reuse facilities via inheritance and encapsulation. However, these classical objects only live within a single program. Only the language compiler that creates the objects knows of their existence. The outside world doesn't know about these objects and has no way to access them. They're literally buried in the bowels of a program.

In contrast, a *distributed object* is a blob of intelligence that can live anywhere on a network. Distributed objects are packaged as independent pieces of code that can be accessed by remote clients via method invocations. The language and compiler used to create distributed server objects are totally transparent to their clients. Clients don't need to know where the distributed object resides or what operating system it executes on; it can be on the same machine or on a machine that sits across an intergalactic network.

Distributed objects are smart pieces of software that can message each other transparently anywhere in the world. Distributed objects can interrogate each other—"tell me what you do." Distributed objects are very dynamic—they come and go and may occasionally move around.

Components: The Grand Prize of Objects

When we talk about distributed objects, we're really talking about independent software *components*. These are smart pieces of software that can play in different networks, operating systems, and tool palettes. A component is an object that's not bound to a particular program, computer language, or implementation. A component is also a toolable. Objects built as components provide the right "shapes" for distributed applications. They are the optimal building blocks for creating the next generation of distributed systems.

Distributed objects are, by definition, components because of the way they are packaged. In distributed object systems, the unit of work and distribution is a component. The distributed object infrastructure makes it easier for components to be more autonomous, self-managing, and collaborative.[1]

Component technology—in all its forms—promises to radically alter the way software systems are developed. For example, distributed objects allow us to put together complex client/server information systems by simply assembling and reusing components. The goal of object-based components is to provide software users and developers the same levels of plug-and-play application interoperability that are available to consumers and manufacturers of electronic parts or custom integrated circuits.

The Driving Force Behind Components

Objects have been freed from the shackles of a particular language or platform. Programmers have been liberated from the confines of one compiler or family of class libraries. Objects can be everywhere, working together and delivering a new world of opportunity to the next generation of systems architectures.

— *Martin Anderson, Chairman*
Integrated Objects

ORBs provide the pipes that enable components to interoperate. However, ORBs by themselves are not enough. ORBs must be augmented by a high-level component infrastructure that defines the rules of engagement for distributed objects. More specifically, the component infrastructure defines how these objects live within

---

[1] Note that a distributed object of the CORBA or DCOM variety is a raw, system-level component. Standards like COM+, CORBA Beans, and EJB add mixin classes and callback objects to these raw objects to make them toolable. These standards also allow the objects to be deployed within server-side application servers or frameworks.

different *containers* (or frameworks). For example, you should be able to run your objects (or components) inside containers provided by visual tools, DBMSs, Object Transaction Monitors, and Web application servers. A component infrastructure defines the interfaces between objects and their containers.

ActiveX and *JavaBeans* are the competing component standards for the desktop. On the server-side, the component standards are *COM+*, *Enterprise JavaBeans (EJBs)*, and *CORBA Beans*—also known as *CORBA 3.0 Components*. CORBA and EJB complement each other; CORBA IIOP provides a transactional pipe for EJBs. In addition, CORBA lets you implement server-side beans in languages other than Java. These new component standards will change the economics of software development. Monolithic applications—both on the desktop and in the enterprise—will be replaced with component suites. Here's how this new technology could affect you:

■ **Power users** will find it second nature to assemble their own personalized applications using off-the-shelf components. They will use scripts to tie the parts together and customize their behavior.

■ **Small developers and ISVs** will find that components reduce expenses and lower the barriers to entry in the software market. They can create individual components with the knowledge that they will integrate smoothly with existing software created by larger development shops—they do not have to reinvent all the functions around them. They can get fine-grained integration instead of today's "Band-Aid" integration. In addition, they get faster time to market because the bulk of an application is already there.

■ **Large developers, ERP vendors, IS shops, and system integrators** will use suites of components to create (or assemble) enterprise-wide client/server applications in record time. Typically, about 80% of the function they need will be available as off-the-shelf components. The remaining 20% is the value-added they provide. The resulting client/server systems may be less complex to test because of the high reliability of the pretested components. The fact that many components are black boxes reduces the overall complexity of the development process. Components will be instrumented to work together in intergalactic client/server networks.

■ **Marketing people** will use components to assemble applications that target specific markets. Instead of selling monster suites—packed with everything but the kitchen sink—they will be able to provide their consumers with what they really need. Increased customization and more malleable products will create new market segments. Consumers will not be at the mercy of the long product release cycles to get new functions. They can buy add-on functions—in the form of components—when they need it.

In summary, components reduce application complexity, development cost, and time-to-market. They also improve software reusability, maintainability, platform independence, and client/server distribution. Finally, components provide more freedom of choice and flexibility.

When Can We Expect These Components?

Our take is that component/object software will be the dominant software by 1999. By 2001, 98% of all new applications will be distributed objects.

> — *Roy Schulte*
> *GartnerGroup*
> *(May, 1997)*

Today, most client software is being developed (or assembled) using components. And, according to Gartner, most of us will soon be using components for our server-side applications. If this forecast is correct, then the software industry is now at the same point where the hardware industry was about 25 years ago. At that time, the first integrated circuits (ICs) were developed to package discrete functions into hardware. ICs were wired together on boards to provide more complex functions. These boards were eventually miniaturized into ICs. These new and more powerful ICs were wired together on new boards, and so on. We should experience the same spiral with software. A component is what Brad Cox calls a *software IC*. *Application frameworks* are the boards—or containers—into which we plug these components. The object bus provides the backplane.

Families of software ICs that play together are called *suites*. You should be able to purchase your software ICs—or components—through standard part catalogs. According to GartnerGroup, components will foster the emergence of three new markets: 1) the component market itself, 2) a market for component assembly tools, and 3) a market for custom applications developed using components.

So, the million-dollar question is: Why didn't this happen any sooner? Why did we have to wait 25 years to follow the footsteps of our cousins, the hardware engineers? Yes, it's true that for almost 25 years, the software industry has been talking about reuse, objects, and methodologies that would get us out of the crises of the day. The difference this time is that we have two standards to choose from: CORBA/Java-Beans and COM/ActiveX. Without standards, you cannot have components. So, it didn't happen sooner because our industry did not have the right component infrastructure or standards. We now have both.

In addition, we have an infrastructure (and standards) for building scalable server-side objects that run inside a new breed of application server called *Object*

Transaction Monitors (OTMs). We also have great tools that support the creation of both client and server-side objects. Finally, we have a standard methodology for specifying distributed objects based on the *Unified Modeling Language (UML)*; you can now define objects in a visual tool—like *Rational Rose* or *Select*—and then let the tool automatically generate all the distributed object support classes. In summary, most of the pieces have finally come together to make distributed objects a mainstream software discipline. And we have the right tools to bring distributed objects to the programming masses.

So, What Exactly Is a Component?

A component is a piece of software small enough to create and maintain, big enough to deploy and support, and with standard interfaces for interoperability.

— Jed Harris

Components interoperate using language-neutral, client/server interaction models. Unlike traditional objects, components can interoperate across languages, tools, operating systems, and networks. But components are also object-like in the sense that they support interface inheritance, polymorphism, and encapsulation. Unlike classical objects, today's components cannot be extended using implementation inheritance. Ivar Jacobson calls them *black box* components.

Because components mean different things to different people, we will define the functions a *minimal* component must provide. In the next section, we expand our definition to include the additional features that server-side components must provide. Our definition of a component is a composite of what CORBA/EJB and ActiveX/COM+ provide. Most of the earlier definitions of components were based on wish lists. Now that we have standards, we can use them to derive a definition. So, a minimalist component has the following properties:

■ *It is a marketable entity*. A component is a self-contained, shrink-wrapped, binary piece of software that you can typically purchase in the open market.

■ *It is not a complete application*. A component can be combined with other components to form a complete application. It is designed to perform a limited set of tasks within an application domain. Components can be fine-grained objects such as a C++ size object; medium-grained objects such as a GUI control or EJB; or a coarse-grained object such as an ERP module.

■ *It can be used in unpredictable combinations*. Like real-world objects, a component can be used in ways that were totally unanticipated by the original developer. Typically, components can be combined with other components of the same family—called suites—using plug-and-play.

■ *It has a well-specified interface*. Like a classical object, a component can only be manipulated through its *interface*. However, the component's interface is separate from its implementation. The interface is the contract the component exposes to the outside world. How the component implements this contract is its own business—especially if it's a black box component. You can implement a component using objects, procedural code, or by encapsulating existing code. CORBA and COM also provide a language-independent *Interface Definition Language (IDL)* that you can use to specify a component's interfaces; Java supports interfaces as part of the language.

■ *Toolability*—a component must be toolable to encourage its widespread reuse. In practice, this means a component must allow itself to be imported within a standard tool palette from where it can be reused and also customized. Most visual tools now support ActiveX or JavaBeans. The palette is simply a container for components. In addition, most tools provide canvasses (or forms) that you can use to wire together components using drag-and-drop and other visual assembly techniques. The form is also a visual container of components.

■ *Event notification*—a component must be able to tell the world at large when something of interest happens to it. A component does this by posting an event. Other components that have an interest in this event can subscribe to it. They

will be notified when the event "fires." This loosely-coupled arrangement is ideal for wiring components together using a visual tool.

■ *Configuration and property management*—components have state. Properties can identify and surface this state information; they define the characteristics of a component. A *property* is a discrete named attribute that you can use to read and modify the state of a component—typically using a property editor within a visual tool. Some components may include full-blown wizards (or *customizers*). The idea is that you should configure components by setting their attributes. Occasionally, you may write some scripts or Java code.

■ *Scripting*—a component must permit its interface to be controlled via scripting languages. This means the interface must be self-describing and must support late-binding.

■ *Metadata and introspection*—a component must provide, on request, information about itself. This includes a description of its interfaces, properties, events, quality-of-service, and the suites it supports.

■ *Interoperability*—a component can be invoked as an object across address spaces, networks, languages, operating systems, and tools. It is a system-independent software entity.

■ *Ease of use*—a component must provide a limited number of operations to encourage use and reuse. In other words, the level of abstraction must be as high as possible to make the component inviting to use.

In summary, a component is a reusable, self-contained piece of software that is independent of any application. Components are *bona fide* objects in the sense that they support encapsulation, interface inheritance, and polymorphism. However, server-side components must also provide all the features associated with a shrink-wrapped standalone object. These features will be discussed in the next section. The next Details box shows the black-box component model for a JavaBean.

The JavaBeans Component Model

Details

Figure 21-2 shows a programmer's view of a JavaBean. As you can see, a bean exposes to the world its methods, properties, and the events it emits. Another bean or tool can dynamically discover this information. The bean saves its state in a (.ser) file that you can package inside a JAR. A bean is introspective; it can tell you quite a bit about itself via the **BeanInfo** class. A bean may provide a **Customizer** class to help you customize its behavior at design time—this is a custom wizard that you invoke from within a tool. In most cases, you will be able to customize a bean by setting its properties via property editors.

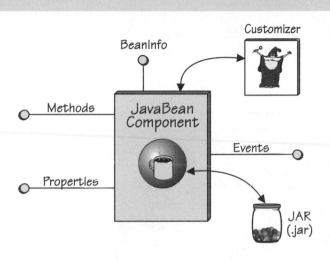

Figure 21-2. The Black-Box View of a JavaBean Component.

There is no IDL—or component definition language—that describes a bean. So how does a bean reveal its interfaces to the outside world? The JavaBean specification defines a set of naming conventions (JavaBeans calls them *design patterns*) that you use to identify the methods, events, and properties of your bean.

A visual assembly tool can pass your bean to an **Introspector** class to generate the **BeanInfo** metadata. The **Introspector** is part of the JavaBeans runtime; it knows exactly how to interpret the naming conventions. So it's important that you follow these naming rules. Alternatively, you can explicitly specify a bean's metadata by providing your own **BeanInfo** class; it lets you define—via descriptors—all (or parts of) the introspection information for your bean.

JavaBeans: The JDK as a Component Framework

So where is the component infrastructure for running these beans? In a sense, the *Java Developers Kit (JDK)* provides a giant framework for running your JavaBeans. In this JDK-as-a-framework view, beans are the end product of all Java development—this means that almost everything in Java is there only to support your components. Your job as a developer is to either: 1) create new beans from scratch, or 2) customize and assemble applications as well as bean subassemblies from existing beans. This is the software version of an assembly line.

JavaSoft designed the JavaBeans framework from day one to satisfy two groups of customers: bean developers and bean visual assembly tool vendors. It's very important that you note this distinction because there are different classes in the JDK to satisfy each of these two constituencies. Figure 21-3 shows the JDK as a framework for running beans. In this view, the JDK is simply a giant set of component services to satisfy the needs of JavaBeans.

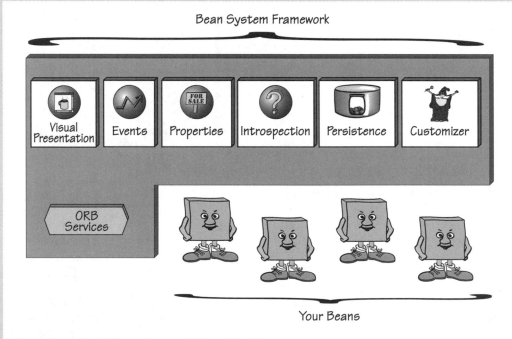

Figure 21-3. The JDK as a Framework View of JavaBeans.

The JDK provides the following infrastructure-type services to JavaBeans:

- **_Visual layout and presentation_**. A component infrastructure must support the visual layout of components in containers—for example, a form or an HTML page. It must also provide services that let components visually interact with each other and with their containers. In the case of JavaBeans, these services are provided by the _Java Foundation Classes (JFC)_, which include AWT, the 2-D graphics, and the new _Swing_ components.

- **_Events_**. The JavaBeans event model—also known as the _event-delegation_ model—is the same one JDK 1.1 introduced for AWT. It requires that interested beans explicitly register for events in which they have an interest.

■ **Properties**. JavaBeans abide by object encapsulation principles. Consequently, a bean does not let outsiders directly manipulate its properties. Instead, you must invoke get/set accessor (and mutator) methods for each variable. JavaBeans support both *single-value* and *indexed* properties. In addition, properties can be *bound* and *constrained*. There's nothing sinister going on here. A bound property will notify interested parties—via events—when its value changes. A constrained property allows the interested parties to veto the modification. Of course, the bean is responsible for specifying the behavior of its properties and for posting the events they generate.

■ **Introspection**. JavaBeans provide a higher-level *introspector* facility that makes it easy for a visual tool to discover a bean's incoming and outgoing interfaces. This facility is built on top of the JDK's lower-level *reflection* classes. Developers can define the behavior of their beans by either using the JavaBeans naming conventions or by providing an explicit **BeanInfo** class.

■ **Persistence**. You should be able to store away a component instance and then recreate it at a later time. In addition, visual tools require components that support some form of persistence. For example, a tool lets you customize a component by changing its properties; it must then be able to tell the component to save its newly modified state. Beans take advantage of the JDK serialization service to automatically save and restore their states. Your beans can be made to be implicitly persistent—you don't have to do any extra work unless you want to customize how a bean is stored. The serialization service also supports a simple form of *versioning*, which is an important requirement in component environments. It enforces simple rules that let newer beans load state written by their older versions; it also lets newer beans store state in a format that's consistent with older versions. Finally, beans can be packaged and distributed using *JAR* files, another built-in facility of the JDK.

■ **Customization**. Toolability is an important part of the JavaBeans component model. This is the area where you will find most of the new JavaBeans classes. They encourage you to provide as many hooks as possible to allow your beans to be used by non-programmers (and also programmers, but we won't admit it). *Property editor* classes provide the first level of support for tools. They let you visually edit a particular type of property—for example, a font, color, or integer. *Property sheets* are visual interfaces that group all the property editors you need to edit a bean (see Figure 21-4).

Finally, bean *customizers* provide wizard-like dialogs that let you edit a bean as a whole. In this case, JavaBeans only specifies a **Customizer** interface and leaves the implementation of the wizard as an exercise for the programmer. In most situations, property sheets provide all the customization your users will ever need.

Figure 21-4. A Property Sheet.

■ **ORB services**. You should be able to invoke a JavaBean across languages, operating systems, and networks. Java 2 (or JDK 1.2) now includes a built-in CORBA ORB that lets you invoke methods on beans across all these boundaries. We will show you how CORBA and JavaBeans play together in later chapters. Note that you can also use RMI for Java-to-Java bean communications. The JavaBeans component model simply builds on the JDK's distributed object facilities. The *Enterprise JavaBeans* further extends this model to support distributed transactions.

JavaBeans: Design-Time Versus Run-Time

Beans must be able to operate in a running application as well as inside a builder. So the next piece of the bean puzzle is to understand the difference between design-time versus run-time beans. Figure 21-5 says it all. To be toolable, the bean must carry a lot of extra baggage. Your bean must provide the design information necessary to edit its properties and customize its behavior. This includes metadata, property editors, customizers, icons, and any other paraphernalia a builder tool requires.

However, this is precisely the type of baggage you don't want your bean to carry around at run time—especially over low-bandwidth networks. The run-time beans must be compact. You can create compact beans by packaging the customization support classes separately. You typically include these classes in a helper package. So you should ship your beans in design-time or run-time JARs, depending on how they will be used. ❑

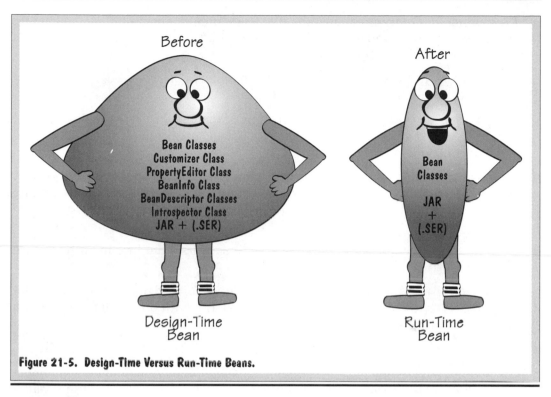

Before

Design-Time
Bean

Bean Classes
Customizer Class
PropertyEditor Class
BeanInfo Class
BeanDescriptor Classes
Introspector Class
JAR + (.SER)

After

Run-Time
Bean

Bean
Classes

JAR
+
(.SER)

Figure 21-5. Design-Time Versus Run-Time Beans.

So, What Is a Server-Side Component?

If the components come with a bad reputation, no one will use them. Therefore, components must be of an extraordinary quality. They need to be well-tested, efficient, and well-documented...The component should invite reuse.

> — Ivar Jacobson, Author
> Object-Oriented Software Engineering
> (Addison-Wesley, 1993)

Server-side components are components with added smarts. The smarts are needed for creating autonomous, loosely-coupled, shrink-wrapped objects that can service multiple clients across networks. Consequently, components need to provide the type of facilities that you associate with independent networked entities, including:

■ *Security*—a component must protect itself and its resources from outside threats. It must authenticate itself to its clients, and vice versa. It must provide access controls. And it must keep audit trails of its use.

- *Licensing*—a component must be able to enforce licensing policies including per-usage licensing and metering. It is important to reward component vendors for the use of their components.

- *Versioning*—a component must provide some form of version control. It must make sure its clients are using the right version.

- *Life cycle management*—a component must manage its creation, destruction, and archival. It must also be able to clone itself, externalize its contents, and move from one location to the next.

- *Transaction control and locking*—a component must transactionally protect its resources and cooperate with other components to provide all-or-nothing integrity. In addition, it must provide locks to serialize access to shared resources.

- *Persistence*—a component must be able to save its state in a persistent store and later restore it.

- *Relationships*—a component must be able to form dynamic or permanent associations with other components. For example, a component can contain other components.

- *Self-testing*—a component must be self-testing. You should be able to run component-provided diagnostics to do problem determination.

- *Semantic messaging*—a component must be able to understand the vocabulary of the particular suites and domain-specific extensions it supports.

- *Self-installing*—a component must be able to install itself and automatically register its factory with the operating system or component registry. The component must also be able to remove itself from disk when asked to do so.

This list should give you a pretty good idea of the level of quality and functionality we expect from our server-side components. The good news is that both the COM+ and CORBA/EJB products provide quite a few of these functions today. In both environments, the server-side container of choice is an *Object Transaction Monitor (OTM)*.

OTMs: The Server-Side Component Coordinators

An OTM is like an iceberg. Your application only sees the visible 10%. The other 90% provides functions that are beneath the water-line. OTMs imbue your applications with these invisible functions.

> — Jeri Edwards, VP of Strategy
> BEA Systems
> (February, 1998)

Object Transaction Monitors (OTMs) are top-of-the-line application servers for distributed objects. OTMs are a morph between a TP Monitor and an ORB. An OTM manages a set of containers that in turn run your server-side components. You declaratively define and administer the properties of your server-side components by setting their attributes—typically, using a visual tool. The container then provides the callback objects that implement the required functionality (or quality of service). You simply write your business logic. At run time, the OTM intercepts all incoming calls, invokes the appropriate callback objects within a container, and then passes the request to your object. In terms of the middleware model we introduced in Part 1, ORBs provide the pipes for distributed objects; OTMs provide the platform.

An ORB is simply an object bus. With an object bus, anything goes. This means your objects must determine when and how to call the ORB's services—for example, naming, security, transactions, and lifecycle. Your objects must explicitly provide all the calls to these services. Consequently, your objects will end up with a ton of system-specific code. This makes them hard to port across containers. In addition, each object must orchestrate the calls to the different services, which is also a difficult and error-prone process. It requires highly-skilled programmers who understand the workings of an ORB and its related middleware services. In contrast, an OTM provides a *framework*—or organized environment—for running server-side components (see Figure 21-6). With an OTM, you get organized anarchy: Everything goes, as long as you play by the framework's rules.

Like all good application frameworks, OTMs follow the *Hollywood Principle*: "Don't call us; we'll call you." The OTM framework is the primary orchestrator of

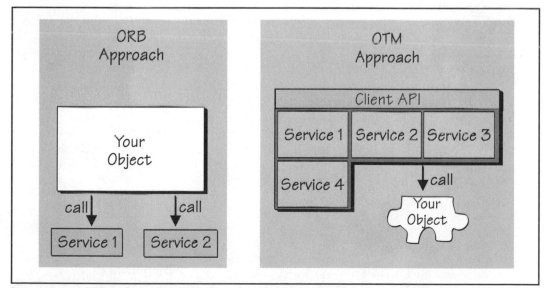

Figure 21-6. ORB-Based Versus OTM/Framework Approaches to Developing Objects.

your server-side components. It calls your components at the right time, and in the right sequence. It also calls the system services on behalf of your components based on the attributes you set. If you play by the OTM's rules, your objects become managed, transactional, robust, persistent, secure, and high-performing. The OTM automatically "makes it so." In addition, an OTM maximizes the reuse of scarce system resources by your components. It prestarts pools of objects, distributes their loads, provides fault-tolerance, and coordinates multi-component transactions.

In summary, OTMs have what it takes to fulfill the promise of scalable server-side objects. Without this new breed of component coordinators, you cannot manage millions of server-side objects—a key requirement of the Object Web. We will have more to say about OTMs in the next few chapters (also see the next Details Box).

Enterprise JavaBeans

Details

In a multitier application architecture, most of an application's logic is moved from the client to one or more servers. A server component model simplifies the process of moving the logic to the server. The component model implements a set of automatic services to manage the component.

— *Ann Thomas, Analyst*
Seybold Group
(February, 1998)

Enterprise JavaBeans (EJB) provides the first formalized component-to-OTM contract for the CORBA/Java world; it starts out where CORBA/POA leaves off. EJB defines the callback interfaces a server-side bean must expose to its OTM, and vice versa. In addition, EJB specifies a packaging mechanism for server-side components. So you should be able to set the quality-of-service attributes of an EJB via a visual tool, package the EJB inside a JAR, and then run it within any EJB-compliant container. Figure 21-7 shows the major functions a server-side container (or OTM) provides to the EJBs that run within it. Let's go over the pieces:

■ ***Distributed object infrastructure***—EJB does not concern itself with the distributed object infrastructure; it assumes an underlying ORB that understands the CORBA RMI/IDL semantics. The ORB transport must also be able to propagate CORBA OTS transactions; IIOP ORBs are designed to provide this type of service. We cover CORBA ORBs in the next chapter.

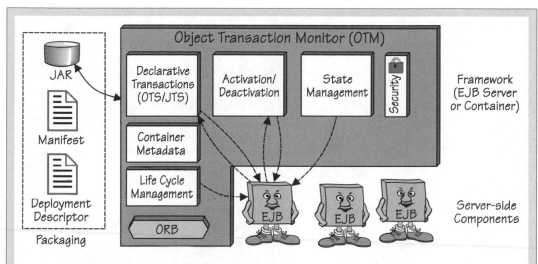

Figure 21-7. What EJBs Can Expect From Their Containers.

■ *Component packaging and deployment*—EJB defines a packaging mechanism for server-side components based on JARs, manifests, and deployment descriptors. The container un-JARs the EJB and then runs it based on the instructions it gets from the manifest and the deployment descriptors. We cover the Java basics in Part 8.

■ *Declarative transaction management*—EJB supports implicit transactions built on the CORBA OTS/JTS service. Your bean does not need to make explicit calls to OTS/JTS to participate in a distributed transaction. The EJB container automatically manages the start, commit, and rollback of a transaction. You define the transactional attributes of a bean at design time (or during deployment) using declarative statements in the deployment descriptor. Optionally, a bean can explicitly control the boundaries of a transaction using explicit CORBA OTS/JTS semantics.

■ *Life cycle management*—EJB containers manage the entire life cycle of an enterprise bean. As a bean provider, you are responsible for defining one or more *create* methods in your **Home** interface, one for each way you create an EJB object. Your bean must implement an *ejbCreate* method for each *create* method you defined in the Home interface. Your Home interface also defines *find* methods to help clients locate existing entity beans. As a last step, you must register your Home interface with a Naming Service so that clients can create new beans.

■ *Bean activation and passivation*—as part of managing the life cycle of an enterprise bean, the container calls your bean when it is loaded into memory (or *activated*); it also calls it when it is *deactivated* from memory (or *passivated*).

- *Bean state management*—EJB containers can manage both transient and persistent beans. Persistent (or *entity*) beans encapsulate in their object reference a unique ID that points to their state. An entity bean manages its own persistence by implementing the persistence operations directly. The container simply hands it a unique key and tells it to load its state. In a future release of EJB, the entity bean will be able to delegate the management of its persistence to its container. In the simplest case, the container will serialize the bean's state and store it in some persistent store. The more sophisticated containers will be able to map the bean's persistent fields to columns in an RDBMS. Finally, the container may choose to implement persistence using an embedded ODBMS.

- *Container metadata*—EJB containers can provide metadata about the beans they contain. For example, the container can return the class name of the enterprise bean that is associated with this Home interface.

- *Security*—EJB containers automate the management of some of the security aspects of your beans. You get to declaratively define the security rules for your enterprise bean in an **AccessControlEntry** object; you must then serialize this object and put it in your bean's JAR. The EJB container uses this object to perform all security checks on behalf of your bean.

This short list should give you a good idea of what an EJB container does for its beans. The beauty of the EJB framework is that it lets you declaratively define most of your server-side run-time attributes. So you can use visual tools to administer and set the properties of your server-side components—including their transactional, security, and state management policies.

EJB and CORBA

EJBs were a big hit with the CORBA camp. Perhaps it's because they were designed from ground zero to be 100% CORBA-compatible. The document that describes the EJB-to-CORBA mapping is a mere 20 pages. We can attribute this lack of "impedance mismatch" to the fact that EJBs use the RMI/IDL CORBA subset for their distributed object model. In addition, they use the *Java Transaction Service (JTS)*—a Java implementation of the CORBA *Object Transaction Service (OTS)*—for their distributed transaction model. EJB also requires CORBA IIOP to: 1) interoperate across multivendor servers, 2) propagate transaction and security contexts, 3) service multilingual clients, and 4) support ActiveX clients via DCOM-to-CORBA bridges.

EJB augments CORBA by defining the interfaces between a server-side component (or bean) and its container. Server-side components are managed beans that run on a server. The *container* acts as a component coordinator. It uses a standard JAR package to import EJBs from tools and other containers. Once an EJB is inside its container, it can then be managed in a scalable way using transactions, state management, and automatic activation and deactivation.

Sorry for using all these new acronyms. If you had trouble with them, make sure to return to this box after you read the CORBA and Java chapters. ☐

Business Objects: The Ultimate Components

Components will help users focus on tasks, not tools, just as a well-stocked kitchen lets you focus on preparing and enjoying great food and not on the brand of your ingredients.

— Dave LeFevre

In general, it is easy to get two components to collaborate if you write code for the two sides of the collaboration. The trick, however, is to get components that have no previous knowledge of each other to do the same. To get to this point, you need standards that set the rules of engagement for different component interaction boundaries. Together, these different interaction boundaries define a distributed component *infrastructure*.

At the most basic level, a component infrastructure provides an object bus—the *Object Request Broker (ORB)*—that lets components interoperate across address spaces, languages, operating systems, and networks. The bus also provides mechanisms that let components exchange metadata and discover each other. At the next level, the infrastructure augments the bus with add-on *system-level services* that help you create supersmart components. Examples of these services include licensing, security, version control, persistence, suite negotiation, semantic messaging, scripting, and transactions.

The ultimate goal is to let you create components that behave like *business objects*. These are components that model their real-world counterparts in some application-level domain. They typically perform specific business functions—for example, a customer, car, or hotel. You can group these business objects into visual suites that resemble real-world places on a desktop but have underlying client/server webs.

So the ultimate Nirvana in the client/server components business are supersmart business object components that do more than just interoperate—they collaborate at the semantic level to get a job done. For example, we could have component suites for hotels, airlines, and car rental agencies. Your travel agent component could collaborate with these suites to book a vacation or business trip. These components must be able to collaborate to conduct negotiations with their fellow components. To enable these types of interactions, the component infrastructure must define domain-specific collaboration standards in the form of *application frameworks*. These frameworks enforce the rules of engagement between independent components for a particular domain and allow them to collaborate in suites.

Figure 21-8 shows the evolution of components from interoperability to collaboration. This evolution corresponds to the service boundaries of the component infrastructure. The component bus gives you simple interoperability; the system services give you supersmart components; and the application frameworks provide the application-level semantics for components to collaborate in suites.

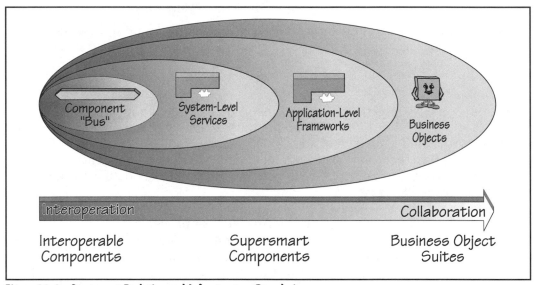

Figure 21-8. Component Evolution and Infrastructure Boundaries.

3-TIER CLIENT/SERVER, OBJECT-STYLE

Cooperative Business Objects (CBOs) are real things. Like other real things, they can be mixed and matched to suit user requirements—with no developer intervention necessary. You take an entity-like thing such as a customer and that's what you deliver—a customer object all by itself. You get a whole customer and nothing but the customer ready to run and use!

> — **Oliver Sims, Author**
> ***Building Business Objects***
> **(Wiley, 1998)**

Business objects are ideal for creating scalable 3-tier client/server solutions because they are inherently decomposable. A business object is not a monolithic piece of code. Instead, it is more like a Lego of cooperating parts that you break apart and then reassemble along 3-tier client/server lines (see Figure 21-9). The first tier represents the visual aspects of the business object—one or more visual objects may each provide a different view. These visual objects typically live on the client. In the middle tier are server objects that represent the persistent data and the business logic functions. Typically, these objects work in ensembles. In the third tier are existing databases, legacy server applications, and ERP systems. The partitioning of business objects is very dynamic. You should be able to decide where to host the different parts at run time.

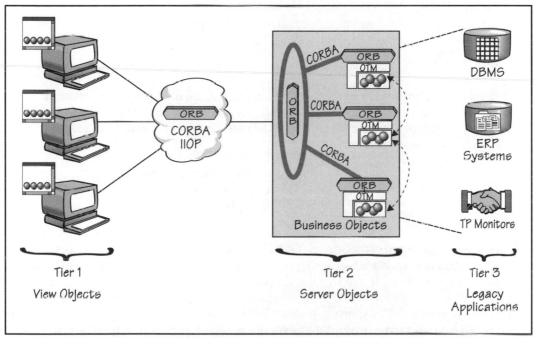

Figure 21-9. 3-Tiered Client/Server, Object-Style.

Middle-tier server objects interact with their clients (the view objects) and implement the logic of the business object. They can extract their persistent state from multiple data sources—for example, SQL databases, HTML files, LDAP directories, Lotus Notes, and TP Monitors. The server object provides an integrated model of the disparate data sources and back-end applications. Clients interact with business objects that naturally correspond to domain entities. They do not have to concern themselves with the hodgepodge of functions, stored procedures, and databases that live in the third tier. The business object hides all this nastiness.

The server object can cache the data it extracts on a local object database for fast subsequent access; or it may choose to directly update the third-tier data sources with fresh views from the object state. Clients must never directly interact with third-tier data sources. These sources must be totally encapsulated and abstracted by the middle-tier server objects. For example, you should be able to swap a database for another without impacting the clients.

The clients typically interact with the middle-tier server objects via an ORB. In addition, middle-tier objects can communicate with each other via an OTM-enabled server ORB that they can use to balance loads, orchestrate distributed transactions, and exchange business events. In general, you'll find OTM-hosted business objects to be very scalable. Finally, server objects communicate with the third tier using traditional middleware. We will have a lot more to say about business objects in the next few chapters.

CONCLUSION

Compared to the complexity of coordinating a modern distributed component-oriented system, managing a busy airport is child's play. As long as we are using components to build complex systems, we are going to be relying on component-oriented middleware to make these systems work.

> — *Roger Sessions, President*
> *ObjectWatch*
> *(October, 1998)*

Distributed components—modeled as business objects—are an excellent fit for 3-tier client/server architectures. They provide scalable and flexible solutions for intergalactic client/server environments and for the Internet and intranets. Business objects can be naturally decomposed and split across multiple tiers to meet an application's needs. They are self-describing and self-managing blobs of intelligence that you can move around and execute where it makes the most sense. Most importantly, business objects are evolutionary—they don't force you to throw away your existing server applications and start from scratch. You can encapsulate what you already have and incrementally add new intelligence, one component at a time. OTMs provide the application platforms for running these business objects in a scalable way. They make distributed objects mission critical. The next few chapters describe the CORBA/EJB and COM/ActiveX distributed component infrastructures that enable much of this magic.

Chapter 22

CORBA: From ORBs To Enterprise Beans

Orb—A jeweled globe surmounted by a cross that is part of a sovereign's regalia and that symbolizes monarchical power and justice.

> — **American Heritage Dictionary**

ORB—Putting down some pavement on the dirt road called distributed computing.

> — **Chris Stone, VP**
> *Novell*

The *Common Object Request Broker Architecture (CORBA)* is the most important (and ambitious) middleware project ever undertaken by our industry. It is the product of world's largest software consortium—called the Object Management Group (OMG)—which includes over 800 companies representing the entire spectrum of the computer industry. The notable exception is Microsoft, which has its own competing object bus called the *Distributed Component Object Model (DCOM)*. For the rest of our industry, the distributed object middleware is CORBA. The CORBA object bus defines the shape of the components that live within it and how they interoperate. Consequently, by choosing an open bus, the industry is also choosing to create an open playing field for components.

What makes CORBA so important is that it defines middleware that has the potential of subsuming every other form of existing client/server middleware—especially when it is combined with Java. In other words, CORBA uses objects as a unifying metaphor for bringing existing applications to the bus. At the same time, it provides a solid foundation for a component-based future. The magic of CORBA is that the entire system is self-describing. In addition, the specification of a service is always separated from the implementation. This lets you incorporate existing systems within the bus.

CORBA was designed to allow intelligent components to discover each other and interoperate on an object bus. However, CORBA goes beyond just interoperability. It also specifies an extensive set of bus-related services for creating and deleting objects, accessing them by name, storing them in persistent stores, externalizing their states, and defining ad hoc relationships between them.

CORBA OTMs—like BEA's *M3*, Oracle's *Application Server 4.0*, and IBM's *Component Broker*—let you create an ordinary object and then make it transactional, secure, lockable, and persistent by simply setting attributes. This means that you can design an ordinary component to provide its regular business function, and then insert the right middleware mix when you build it or create it at run time. So, welcome to the age of flexible "made to order" middleware. There is nothing like it for any other form of client/server computing.

This chapter is about the CORBA object bus and the object system services that extend the bus. We start with an overview of CORBA and what it does for intelligent components. Next, we cover the CORBA object model and the architecture that ties it all together. Finally, we look at CORBA 3.0's new component model and explain how the CORBA and Java EJB component models are coming together.

DISTRIBUTED OBJECTS, CORBA-STYLE

Standards are more important for distributed objects than for any other technology in any other industry. Objects from one company must be able to communicate and cooperate with objects from other companies.

> — *Roger Sessions, Author*
> *COM and DCOM*
> *(Wiley, 1998)*

Perhaps the secret to OMG's success is that it creates interface specifications, not code. The interfaces it specifies are always derived from demonstrated technology submitted by member companies. The specifications are written in a neutral

Interface Definition Language (IDL) that defines a component's boundaries—that is, its contractual interfaces with potential clients. You can access IDL-defined components—via a CORBA *Object Request Broker (ORB)*—across languages, tools, operating systems, and networks. And with the adoption of the CORBA 2.0 IIOP specification, these components can now interoperate across multivendor CORBA ORBs.

What Is a CORBA Distributed Object?

CORBA objects are blobs of intelligence that can live anywhere on a network. They are packaged as binary components that remote clients can access via method invocations. Both the language and compiler used to create server objects are totally transparent to clients. Clients don't need to know where the distributed object resides or what operating system it executes on. It can be in the same process or on a machine that sits across an intergalactic network. In addition, clients don't need to know how the server object is implemented. For example, a server object could be implemented as a set of C++ classes, or it could be implemented with a million lines of existing COBOL code—the client doesn't know the difference. What the client needs to know is the interface its server object publishes. This interface serves as a binding contract between clients and servers.

Everything Is in IDL

> OMG IDL is the best standard notation language available for defining component boundaries. It provides a universal notation for specifying APIs. IDL supports library function interfaces just as well as distributed objects across a network.
>
> — *Tom Mowbray et al., Authors*
> *The Essential CORBA*
> *(Wiley, 1995)*

As we said earlier, OMG uses IDL contracts to specify a component's boundaries and its contractual interfaces with potential clients. The OMG IDL is purely declarative. This means that it provides no implementation details. You can use IDL to define APIs concisely, and it covers important issues such as error handling. IDL-specified methods can be written in and invoked from any language that provides CORBA bindings—currently, C, C++, Ada, Smalltalk, and Java (Perl, Objective C, and JavaScript are in the works). Programmers deal with CORBA objects using native language constructs. IDL provides operating system and programming language independent interfaces to all the services and components that reside on a CORBA bus. It allows client and server objects written in different languages to interoperate (see Figure 22-1).

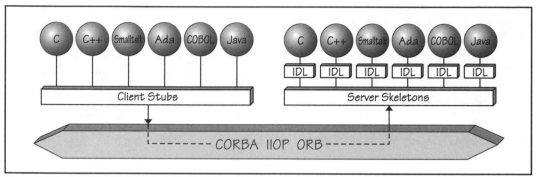

Figure 22-1. CORBA IDL Language Bindings Provide Client/Server Interoperability.

You can use the OMG IDL to specify a component's attributes, the parent classes it inherits from, the exceptions it raises, the typed events it emits, and the methods its interface supports—including the input and output parameters and their data types. The IDL grammar is a subset of C++ with additional keywords to support distributed concepts; it also fully supports standard C++ preprocessing features and pragmas.

The ambitious goal of CORBA is to "IDL-ize" all client/server middleware and all components that live on an ORB. OMG hopes to achieve this goal by following two steps: 1) it will turn everything into nails, and 2) it will give everyone a hammer.

■ The "nail" is the CORBA IDL. It allows component providers to specify in a standard definition language the interface and structure of the objects they provide. An IDL-defined contract binds the providers of distributed object services to their clients. For one object to request something from another object, it must know the target object's interface and object reference. The CORBA *Interface Repository* contains the definitions of all these interfaces. It contains the metadata that lets components discover each other dynamically at run time. This makes CORBA a self-describing system.

■ The "hammer" includes the set of distributed services OMG providers will supply. These services will determine which objects are on the network, which methods they provide, and which object interface adapters they support. The location of the object should be transparent to the client. It should not matter whether the object is in the same process or across the world.

Does this all sound familiar? It should. We're describing the "object wave" of client/server computing; this time it's between cooperating objects as opposed to cooperating processes. The goal of this new wave is to create multivendor, multiOS, multilanguage "Legoware" using objects. Vendors such as Oracle, Sun, HP, IBM, BEA, Netscape/AOL, Novell, Sybase, and Inprise are all using CORBA as their

standard IDL-defined interface into the object highway. The IDL is the contract that brings it all together.

CORBA Components: From System Objects To Business Objects

Objects can vary tremendously in size and number. They can represent everything down to the hardware or all the way up to entire design applications. How can we decide what should be an object?

— Erich Gamma et al., Authors
Design Patterns
(Addison Wesley, 1994)

Notice that we've been using the terms "components" and "distributed objects" interchangeably. CORBA distributed objects are, by definition, components because of the way they are packaged. In distributed object systems, the unit of work and distribution is a component. The CORBA distributed object infrastructure makes it easier for components to be more autonomous, self-managing, and collab-

orative. This undertaking is much more ambitious than anything attempted by competing forms of middleware. CORBA's distributed object technology allows us to put together complex client/server information systems by simply assembling and extending components. You can modify objects without affecting the rest of the components in the system or how they interact. A client/server application becomes a collection of collaborating components. In addition, CORBA is incorporating many elements of the Enterprise JavaBeans component model, which should help make CORBA components more toolable.

CORBA 2.0: THE INTERGALACTIC ORB

In the fall of 1990, the OMG first published the *Object Management Architecture Guide (OMA Guide)*. It was revised in September 1992. The details of the Common Facilities were added in January 1995. Finally, the CORBA 3.0 component support infrastructure was added in 1998. Figure 22-2 shows the four main elements of the architecture: 1) *Object Request Broker (ORB)* defines the CORBA object bus; 2) *CORBAservices* define the system-level object frameworks that extend the bus; 3) *CORBAfacilities* define horizontal and vertical application frameworks that are used directly by business objects; and 4) *Application Objects* are the business objects and applications—they are the ultimate consumers of the CORBA infra-

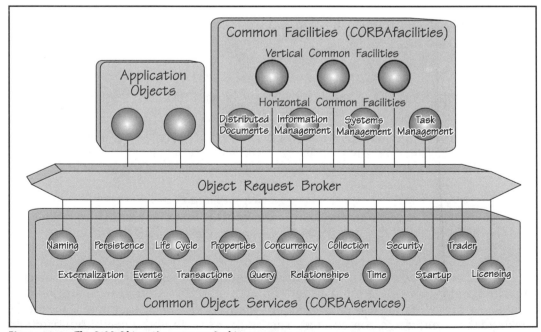

Figure 22-2. The OMG Object Management Architecture.

structure. This section provides a top-level view of the four elements that make up the CORBA infrastructure.

The Object Request Broker (ORB)

The *Object Request Broker (ORB)* is the object bus. It lets objects transparently make requests to—and receive responses from—other objects located locally or remotely. The client is not aware of the mechanisms used to communicate with, activate, or store the server objects. The CORBA 1.1 specifications—introduced in 1991—only specified the IDL, language bindings, and APIs for interfacing to the ORB. So, you could write interoperable programs that could run on top of the nearly dozen CORBA-compliant ORBs on the market. CORBA 2.0 specifies interoperability across vendor ORBs.

A CORBA ORB provides a very rich set of distributed middleware services. The ORB lets objects discover each other at run time and invoke each other's services. An ORB is much more sophisticated than alternative forms of client/server middleware—including traditional Remote Procedure Calls (RPCs), Message-Oriented Middleware (MOM), database stored procedures, and peer-to-peer services. In theory, CORBA is the best client/server middleware pipe ever defined. In practice, CORBA is only as good as the products that implement it.

To give you an idea of why CORBA ORBs make such great client/server middleware pipes, we offer the following "short" list of benefits that every CORBA ORB provides:

- *Static and dynamic method invocations.* A CORBA ORB either lets you statically define your method invocations at compile time, or it lets you dynamically discover them at run time. So you get either strong type checking at compile time or maximum flexibility associated with late (or run-time) binding. Most other forms of middleware only support static bindings.

- *High-level language bindings.* A CORBA ORB lets you invoke methods on server objects using your high-level language of choice. It doesn't matter what language the server objects are written in. You interface to the middleware using regular language constructs—no low-level communication buffer management is required. CORBA separates interface from implementation and provides language-neutral data types that make it possible to call objects across language and operating system boundaries. In contrast, other types of middleware typically provide low-level, language-specific, API libraries. And they don't separate implementation from specification—the API is tightly bound to the implementation, which makes it very sensitive to changes.

- *Self-describing system.* CORBA provides run-time metadata for describing every server interface known to the system. Every CORBA ORB must support an *Interface Repository* that contains real-time information describing the functions a server provides and their parameters. The clients use metadata to discover how to invoke services at run time. It also helps tools generate code "on-the-fly." The metadata is generated automatically either by an IDL-language precompiler or by compilers that know how to generate IDL directly from an OO language. For example, Visigenic/Netscape's *Caffeine* generates CORBA IDL, stubs, and skeletons directly from Java bytecodes. To the best of our knowledge, no other form of client/server middleware provides this type of run-time metadata and language-independent definitions of all its services. As you will discover later in this chapter, business objects and components require all the late binding flexibility they can get.

- *Local/remote transparency.* An ORB can run in standalone mode on a laptop, or it can be interconnected to every other ORB in the universe using CORBA 2.0's *Internet Inter-ORB Protocol (IIOP)* services. An ORB can broker interobject calls within a single process, multiple processes running within the same machine, or multiple processes running across networks and operating systems. This is completely transparent to your objects. Note that the ORB can broker among fine-grained objects—like C++ classes—as well as more coarse-grained objects—like JavaBeans. In general, a CORBA client/server programmer does not have to be concerned with transports, server locations, object activation, byte ordering across dissimilar platforms, or target operating systems—CORBA makes it all transparent.

- *Built-in security and transactions.* The ORB includes context information in its messages to handle security and transactions across machine and ORB boundaries.

- *Polymorphic messaging.* In contrast to other forms of middleware, an ORB does not simply invoke a remote function—it invokes a function on a target object. This means that the same function call will have different effects, depending on the object that receives it. For example, a *configure_yourself* method invocation behaves differently when applied to a database object versus a printer object (also see following Briefing box).

- *Coexistence with existing systems.* CORBA's separation of an object's definition from its implementation is perfect for encapsulating existing applications. Using CORBA IDL, you can make your existing code look like an object on the ORB, even if it's implemented in stored procedures, CICS, IMS, or COBOL. This makes CORBA an evolutionary solution. You can write your new applications as pure objects and encapsulate existing applications with IDL wrappers.

ORB Versus RPC

Briefing

So how are ORB method invocations different from RPCs? The mechanisms are very similar, but there are some important differences. With an RPC, you call a specific function (the data is separate). In contrast, with an ORB, you're calling a method within a *specific* object. Different object types may respond to the same method invocation differently through the magic of polymorphism. Because each object manages its own private instance data, the method is implemented on that *specific* instance data (see Figure 22-3).

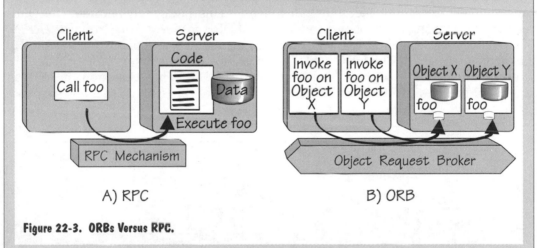

Figure 22-3. ORBs Versus RPC.

ORB method invocations have "scalpel-like" precision. The call gets to a *specific* object that controls *specific* data, and then implements the function in its own *class-specific* way. In contrast, RPC calls have no specificity—all the functions with the same name get implemented the same way. There's no differentiated service here. ❑

The Anatomy of a CORBA 2.0 ORB

A request broker mediates interactions between client applications needing services and server applications capable of providing them.

— *Richard Adler*

A CORBA 2.0 *Object Request Broker (ORB)* is the middleware that establishes the client/server relationships between objects. Using an ORB, a client object can transparently invoke a method on a server object, which can be on the same machine or across a network. The ORB intercepts the call and is responsible for finding an object that can implement the request, pass it the parameters, invoke its method, and return the results. The client does not have to be aware of where the object is located, its programming language, its operating system, or any other system aspects that are not part of an object's interface. It is very important to note that the client/server roles are only used to coordinate the interactions between two objects. Objects on the ORB can act as either client or server, depending on the occasion.

Figure 22-4 shows the client and server sides of a CORBA ORB. The light areas were introduced by CORBA 2.0. Even though there are many boxes, it's not as complicated as it appears to be. The key is to understand that CORBA, like SQL, provides both static and dynamic interfaces to its services. This happened because the OMG received two strong submissions to its original ORB *Request For Proposal (RFP)*: one from HyperDesk and Digital based on a dynamic API, and one from Sun and HP based on static APIs. The OMG told the two groups to come back with a single RFP that combined both features. The result was CORBA. The "Common" in CORBA stands for this two-API proposal, which makes a lot of sense because it gives us both static and dynamic APIs.

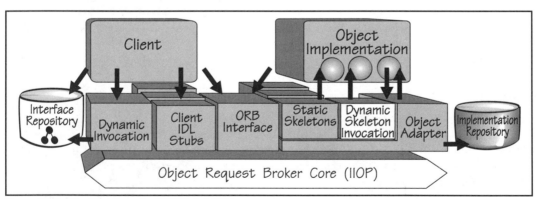

Figure 22-4. The Structure of a CORBA 2.0 ORB.

Let's first go over what CORBA does on the client side:

■ **The client IDL stubs** provide the static interfaces to object services. These precompiled stubs define how clients invoke corresponding services on the servers. From a client's perspective, the stub acts like a local call—it is a local *proxy* for a remote server object. The services are defined using IDL, and both client and server stubs are generated by the IDL compiler. A client must have an IDL stub for each interface it uses on the server. The stub includes code to perform *marshaling*. This means that it encodes and decodes the operation and its parameters into flattened message formats that it can send to the server. It also includes header files (or regular classes) that enable you to invoke the method on the server from a higher-level language (like C, C++, Java, or Smalltalk) without worrying about the underlying protocols or issues such as data marshaling. You simply invoke a method from within your program to obtain a remote service.

■ *The Dynamic Invocation Interface (DII)* lets you discover methods to be invoked at run time. CORBA defines standard APIs for looking up the metadata that defines the server interface. It also provides APIs to help you dynamically generate the parameters, issue the remote call, and get back the results.

■ *The Interface Repository APIs* allow you to obtain and modify the descriptions of all the registered component interfaces, the methods they support, and the parameters they require. CORBA calls these descriptions *method signatures*. The *Interface Repository* is a run-time distributed database that contains machine-readable versions of the IDL-defined interfaces. Think of it as a dynamic metadata repository for ORBs. The APIs allow components to dynamically access, store, and update metadata information. This pervasive use of metadata allows every component that lives on the ORB to have self-describing interfaces. The ORB itself is a self-describing bus (see the next Briefing box).

■ *The ORB Interface* consists of a few APIs to local services that may be of interest to an application. For example, CORBA provides APIs to convert an object reference to a string, and vice versa. These calls can be very useful if you need to store and communicate object references.

FYI

CORBA 2.0 Global Repository IDs

Briefing

With CORBA 2.0, ORBs provide global identifiers—called *Repository IDs*—to uniquely and globally identify a component and its interface across multivendor ORBs and repositories. The Repository IDs are system-generated, unique strings that are used to maintain consistency in the naming conventions used across repositories—no name collisions are allowed. Repository IDs are generated via *pragmas* in IDL. The pragma specifies whether to generate them via DCE *Universal Unique Identifiers (UUIDs)* or via a user-supplied unique prefix appended to IDL-scoped names. The Repository ID itself is a string consisting of a three-level name hierarchy. ❑

The support for both static and dynamic client/server invocations—as well as the Interface Repository—gives CORBA a leg up over competing middleware. Static invocations are easier to program, faster, and self-documenting. Dynamic invocations provide maximum flexibility, but they are difficult to program; they are very useful for tools that discover services at run time.

The server side cannot tell the difference between a static or dynamic invocation; they both have the same message semantics. In both cases, the ORB locates a server object adapter, transmits the parameters, and transfers control to the object implementation through the server IDL stub (or skeleton). Here's what CORBA elements do on the server side of Figure 22-4:

- The ***Server IDL Stubs*** (OMG calls them *skeletons*) provide static interfaces to each service exported by the server. These stubs, like the ones on the client, are created using an IDL compiler.

- The ***Dynamic Skeleton Interface (DSI)***—introduced in CORBA 2.0—provides a run-time binding mechanism for servers that need to handle incoming method calls for components that do not have IDL-based compiled skeletons (or stubs). The Dynamic Skeleton looks at parameter values in an incoming message to figure out who it's for—that is, the target object and method. In contrast, normal compiled skeletons are defined for a particular object class and expect a method implementation for each IDL-defined method. Dynamic Skeletons are very useful for implementing generic bridges between ORBs. They can also be used by interpreters and scripting languages to dynamically generate object implementations. The DSI is the server equivalent of a DII. It can receive either static or dynamic client invocations.

- The ***Object Adapter*** sits on top of the ORB's core communication services and accepts requests for service on behalf of the server's objects. It provides the run-time environment for instantiating server objects, passing requests to them, and assigning them object IDs—CORBA calls the IDs *object references*. The Object Adapter also registers the classes it supports and their run-time instances (i.e., objects) with the *Implementation Repository*. CORBA specifies that each ORB must support a standard adapter called the *Basic Object Adapter (BOA)*. Servers may support more than one object adapter. CORBA 3.0 introduces a portable version of BOA called the *Portable Object Adapter (POA)*. Among other things, the POA knows how to instantiate objects that are not active in memory.

- The ***Implementation Repository*** provides a run-time repository of information about the classes a server supports, the objects that are instantiated, and their IDs. It also serves as a common place to store additional information associated with the implementation of ORBs. Examples include trace information, audit trails, security, and other administrative data.

■ The ***ORB Interface*** consists of a few APIs to local services that are identical to those provided on the client side.

This concludes our panoramic overview of the ORB components and their interfaces.

IIOP: The Intergalactic Bus

CORBA 1.1 was only concerned with creating interoperable object applications; the implementation of the ORB core was left as an "exercise for the vendors." The result was some level of component portability, but not interoperability. CORBA 2.0 added interoperability by specifying a mandatory *Internet Inter-ORB Protocol (IIOP)*. The IIOP is basically TCP/IP with some CORBA-defined message exchanges that serve as a common backbone protocol. Every ORB that calls itself CORBA-compliant must either implement IIOP natively or provide a "half-bridge" to it. Note that it's called a half-bridge because IIOP is the "standard" CORBA backbone. So any proprietary ORB can connect with the universe of ORBs by translating requests to and from the IIOP backbone.

In addition to IIOP, CORBA supports *Environment-Specific Inter-ORB Protocols (ESIOPs)* for "out-of-the-box" interoperation over specific networks. CORBA 2.0 specifies DCE as the first of many optional ESIOPs (pronounced "E-SOPs"). The DCE ESIOP provides a robust environment for mission-critical ORBs (see the next Details box).

You can use inter-ORB bridges and IIOP to create very flexible topologies via federations of ORBs. Figure 22-5 shows an IIOP backbone with various proprietary

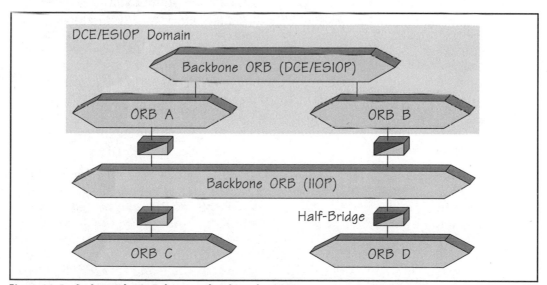

Figure 22-5. An Intergalactic Federation of Multivendor ORBs.

ORBs feeding into it via half-bridges. Note the presence of the DCE ESIOP. You can segment ORBs into domains based on administrative needs, vendor ORB implementations, network protocols, traffic loads, types of service, and security concerns. Policies on either side of the fence may conflict, so you can create firewalls around the backbone ORB via half-bridges. CORBA 2.0 promotes diversity and gives you total mix-and-match flexibility, as long as you use IIOP for your global backbone.

CORBA 2.0: The Inter-ORB Architecture

Details

The choice of ORB interoperability solutions does not impact application software. Interoperability is an issue between ORB vendors, not between vendors and users. Few, if any, developers will ever be involved in programming with GIOPs and ESIOPs.

— Tom Mowbray

Even though few application developers need to worry about how ORBs interoperate, it is interesting to understand the mechanics. So despite what Mowbray says, we'll dive into CORBA 2.0 interoperability. Figure 22-6 shows the elements of the CORBA 2.0 inter-ORB architecture. Here's a description of what each of these elements provides:

■ The ***General Inter-ORB Protocol (GIOP)*** specifies a set of message formats and common data representations for communications between ORBs. The GIOP was specifically built for ORB-to-ORB interactions. It is designed to work directly over any connection-oriented transport protocol. GIOP defines seven message formats that cover all the ORB request/reply semantics. No format negotiations are needed. In most cases, clients send a request to objects immediately after they open a connection. The *Common Data Representation (CDR)* maps data types defined in OMG IDL into a flat, networked message representation. The CDR also takes care of inter-platform issues such as byte ordering (no byte swapping is needed) and memory alignments.

■ The ***Internet Inter-ORB Protocol (IIOP)*** specifies how GIOP messages are exchanged over a TCP/IP network. IIOP makes it possible to use the Internet itself as a backbone through which other ORBs can bridge. It was designed to be simple and provide "out-of-the-box" interoperation for TCP/IP based ORBs. The GIOP may eventually be mapped to different transports. To be CORBA 2.0 compatible, an ORB must support GIOP over TCP/IP (or connect to it via a half-bridge). Note that both the IIOP and DCE/ESIOP have built-in mechanisms for implicitly transmitting context data that is associated with the transaction or security services. The ORB takes care of passing these requests without your application's involvement. Better yet, this information can also be passed across heterogeneous CORBA ORBs via bridges. The CORBA 2.0 standard does a good job specifying the location of this context data in an ORB-generated message.

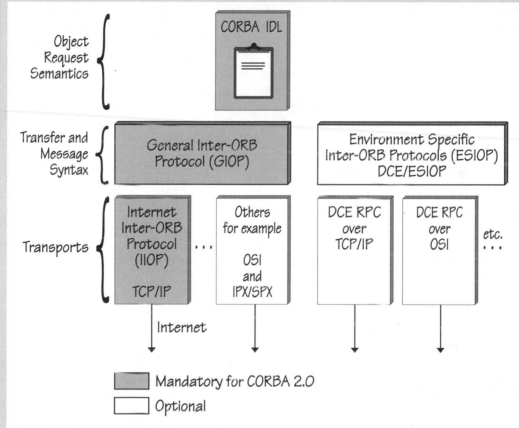

Figure 22-6. The CORBA 2.0 Inter-ORB Architecture.

■ The *Environment-Specific Inter-ORB Protocols (ESIOPs)* are used for "out-of-the-box" interoperation over specific networks. CORBA 2.0 specifies DCE as the first of many optional ESIOPs. Like GIOP, DCE/ESIOP supports IORs using a DCE tagged profile (we explain IORs later in this box). The DCE/ESIOP uses the GIOP CDR to represent OMG IDL data types over the DCE RPC. This means that DCE IDL is not required. Instead, OMG IDL and CDR types are mapped directly into DCE's native *Network Data Representation (NDR)*. The DCE ESIOP currently provides a robust environment for mission-critical ORBs. It includes advanced features such as Kerberos security, cell and global directories, distributed time, and authenticated RPC.

DCE also lets you transmit large amounts of data efficiently, and it supports multiple underlying transport protocols, including TCP/IP. Finally, with DCE you can use both connection and connectionless protocols for your ORB communications.

GIOP also defines a format for *Interoperable Object References (IORs)*. An ORB must create an IOR (from an object reference) whenever an object reference is passed across ORBs. IORs associate a collection of *tagged profiles* with object references. The profiles describe the same object, but they each describe how to contact the object using a particular ORB's mechanism. An IOR also specifies the location of the object and an ID field that serves as a key to its persistent data. So you can always reactivate a CORBA object and obtain its most current state. ❑

CORBA OBJECT SERVICES

CORBAservices are collections of system-level services packaged with IDL-specified interfaces. You can think of object services as augmenting and complementing the functionality of the ORB. You use them to create a component, name it, and introduce it into the environment. OMG has published standards for fifteen object services:

■ The **Life Cycle Service** defines operations for creating, copying, moving, and deleting components on the bus.

■ The **Persistence Service** provides a single interface for storing components persistently on a variety of storage servers—including Object Databases (ODBMSs), Relational Databases (RDBMSs), and simple files.

■ The **Naming Service** allows components on the bus to locate other components by name; it also supports federated naming contexts. The service also allows objects to be bound to existing network directories or naming contexts—including ISO's *X.500*, OSF's *DCE*, Sun's *NIS+*, Novell's *NDS*, and the Internet's *LDAP*.

■ The **Event Service** allows components on the bus to dynamically register or unregister their interest in specific events. The service defines a well-known object called an *event channel* that collects and distributes events among components that know nothing of each other.

■ The **Concurrency Control Service** provides a lock manager that can obtain locks on behalf of either transactions or threads.

■ The *Transaction Service* provides two-phase commit coordination among recoverable components using either flat or nested transactions.

■ The *Relationship Service* provides a way to create dynamic associations (or links) between components that know nothing of each other. It also provides mechanisms for traversing the links that group these components. You can use the service to enforce referential integrity constraints, track containment relationships, and for any type of linkage among components.

■ The *Externalization Service* provides a standard way for getting data into and out of a component using a stream-like mechanism.

■ The *Query Service* provides query operations for objects. It's a superset of SQL. It is based on the upcoming SQL3 specification and the Object Database Management Group's (ODMG) *Object Query Language (OQL)*.

■ The *Licensing Service* provides operations for metering the use of components to ensure fair compensation for their use. The service supports any model of usage control at any point in a component's life cycle. It supports charging per session, per node, per instance creation, and per site.

■ The *Properties Service* provides operations that let you associate named values (or properties) with any component. Using this service, you can dynamically associate properties with a component's state—for example, a title or a date.

■ The *Time Service* provides interfaces for synchronizing time in a distributed object environment. It also provides operations for defining and managing time-triggered events.

■ The *Security Service* provides a complete framework for distributed object security. It supports authentication, access control lists, confidentiality, and non-repudiation. It also manages the delegation of credentials between objects (also see the next Briefing box).

■ The *Trader Service* provides a "Yellow Pages" for objects; it allows objects to publicize their services and bid for jobs.

■ The *Collection Service* provides CORBA interfaces to generically create and manipulate the most common collections.

All these services enrich a distributed component's behavior and provide the robust environment in which it can safely live and play.

Figure 22-7 shows the *Request For Proposal (RFP)* schedules that OMG is using to develop the object service specifications. OMG RFPs are requests for a technology. They result in responses from members on how to implement a particular standard. Members must base their responses on existing products or products that are in development (some proof of concept is needed). Usually an RFP is met by merging the responses obtained from several organizations. From the time the OMG issues an RFP, it takes about 12 to 16 months to obtain a working standard. As you can see, the OMG has almost completed the work on its object services and ORB specifications.[1] With the release of CORBA 3.0, the action has now shifted to CORBA Beans, CORBA domains, and Business Objects (more on this later in the chapter).

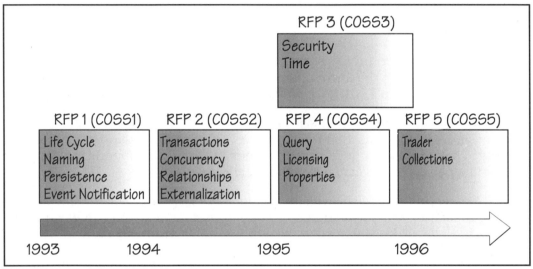

Figure 22-7. The OMG Road Map for Delivering Object Services.

CORBA COMMON FACILITIES

CORBAfacilities are collections of IDL-defined frameworks that provide services of direct use to application objects. Think of them as the next step up in the semantic hierarchy. The two categories of common facilities—*horizontal* and *vertical*—define rules of engagement that business components need to effectively collaborate.

The Common Facilities that are currently under construction include mobile agents, data interchange, workflow, firewalls, business object frameworks, and internationalization. Like the highway system, Common Facilities are an unending project. The work will continue until CORBA defines IDL interfaces for every distributed service

---

[1] The one exception is the *Persistence Object Service (POS)*. In early 1997, OMG issued an RFP for a POS2. In November 1998, it received a joint submission that is based on an automatic persistence model. It is similar to the model used in ODBMSs and Object-to-Relational mappers.

we know of today, as well as ones that are yet to be invented. When this happens, CORBA will provide IDL-interfaces for virtually every networked service (many will be IDL-ized versions of existing middleware).[2]

FYI

Are Distributed Objects Less Secure?

Briefing

Distributed objects face all the security problems of traditional client/server systems—and more. As we explained in Part 3, the client/server environment introduces new security threats beyond those found in traditional time-shared systems. In a client/server system, you can't trust any of the client operating systems on the network to protect the server's resources from unauthorized access. And even if the client machines were totally secure, the network itself is highly accessible. You can never trust information in transit. Sniffer devices can easily record traffic between machines and introduce forgeries and Trojan horses into the system. This means the servers must find new ways to protect themselves without creating a fortress mentality that upsets users. In addition to these threats, distributed objects must also be concerned with the following added complications:

■ ***Distributed objects can play both client and server roles***. In a traditional client/server architecture, it is clear who is a client and who is a server. Typically, you can trust servers, but not clients. For example, a client trusts its database server, but the reverse is not true. In distributed object systems, you cannot clearly distinguish between clients and servers. These are just alternate roles that a single object can play.

■ ***Distributed objects evolve continually.*** When you interact with an object, you're only seeing the tip of the iceberg. You may be seeing a "facade" object that delegates parts of its implementation to other objects; these delegates may be dynamically composed at run time. Also, because of subclassing, the implementations of an object may change over time without the original programmer ever knowing or caring.

■ ***Distributed objects interactions are not well understood***. Because of encapsulation, you cannot fully understand all the interactions that take place between the objects you invoke. There is too much "behind the scenes" activity.

---

2 The Common Facilities work is now being done by the *ORB Services Task Force*; it seems they've moved up the food chain. Some of this work is also being done by the *Business Object Domain Task Force*. Yes, it's hard to keep up with OMG's reorganizations.

■ ***Distributed object interactions are less predictable***. Because distributed objects are more flexible and granular than other forms of client/server systems, they may interact in more ad hoc ways. This is a strength of the distributed object model, but it's also a security risk.

■ ***Distributed objects are polymorphic***. Objects are flexible; it is easy to replace one object on the ORB with another that abides by the same interfaces. This makes it a dream situation for Trojan horses; they can impersonate legitimate objects and thus cause all kinds of havoc.

■ ***Distributed objects can scale without limit.*** Because every object can be a server, we may end up with millions of servers on the ORB. How do we manage access rights for millions of servers?

■ ***Distributed objects are very dynamic.*** A distributed object environment is inherently anarchistic. Objects come and go. They get created dynamically and self-destruct when they're no longer being used. This dynamism is, of course, a great strength of objects, but it could also be a security nightmare.

To maintain a single-system illusion, every trusted user (and object) must be given transparent access to all other objects. How is this done when every PC poses a potential threat to network security? Will system administrators be condemned to spend their working lives granting access level rights to objects—one at a time—for each individual object on each server across the enterprise? The good news is that many of these problems can be solved by moving the security implementation into the CORBA ORB itself.

The ORB can manage security for a range of systems—from trusted domains (within a single process or machine) to intergalactic inter-ORB situations. Components that are not responsible for enforcing their own security are easier to develop, administer, and port across environments. In addition, moving security inside the ORB can minimize the performance overhead. The CORBA Security Service—adopted by OMG in March, 1996—addresses *all* of these requirements; it's probably the most comprehensive client/server security standard in existence. ❑

CORBA BUSINESS OBJECTS

A business object is a representation of a thing active in the business domain, including at least its business name and definition, attributes, behavior, relationship, and constraints. A business object may represent, for example, a person, place, or concept.

— OMG, Business Object Task Force

Business objects provide a natural way for describing application-independent concepts such as customer, order, competitor, money, payment, car, and patient. They encourage a view of software that transcends tools, applications, databases, and other system concepts. The ultimate promise of object technology and components is to provide these medium-grained components that behave more like "the real world does." Of course, somebody must first define the rules of engagement for these components to play, which is where the OMG comes into the picture.

According to OMG's *Business Object Task Force*, a business object is an application-level component you can use in unpredictable combinations. A business object is, by definition, independent of any single application. Post-monolithic applica-

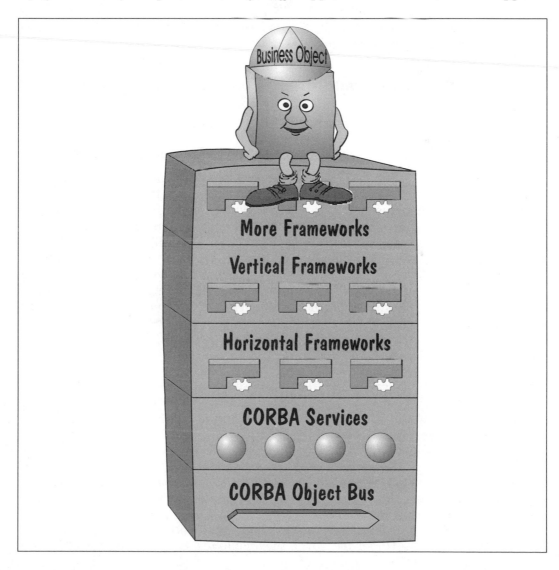

tions will consist of suites of business objects—the application simply provides the environment to execute these business objects. In other words, a business object is a component that represents a "recognizable" everyday life entity. In contrast, system-level objects represent entities that make sense only to information systems and programmers—they're not something an end-user recognizes.

In a high-rise building, everyone's ceiling is someone else's floor until you get to the penthouse. Then the sky is your ceiling. You may think of the business object as the penthouse of components. According to the OMG definition, these top-level objects are recognizable to the end-user of a system. The size of the object maps to "business" things like cars or tax forms. The word "business" is used in a very loose sense. A business object is a self-contained *deliverable* that has a user interface, state, and knows how to cooperate with other separately developed business objects to perform a desired task.

Cooperating Business Objects

A *group of business objects can form an information system only if they become a system and interact with each other.*

— *Rob Prins*

Business objects will be used to design systems that mimic the business processes they support. In the real world, business events are seldom isolated to a single business object. Instead, they typically involve clusters of objects. To mimic their real-world counterparts, business objects must be able to communicate with each other at a semantic level. You can capture and describe these object interactions using most of the popular design methodology tools—including Ivar Jacobson's *use cases*, Ian Graham's *task scripts*, Grady Booch's *interaction diagrams*, and Jim Rumbaugh's *event traces*. All these methodologies use some form of scenario diagrams to show who does what to whom and when. These scenarios can document the full impact of specific business events.

Business objects must have late and flexible binding—and well-defined interfaces—so that they can be implemented independently. A business object must be capable of recognizing events in its environment, changing its attributes, and interacting with other business objects. Like any CORBA object, a business object exposes its interfaces to its clients via IDL and communicates with other objects using the ORB.

Figure 22-8 shows a suite of four business objects that are part of a car reservation system: *customer*, *invoice*, *car*, and *car lot*. Note that *car lot* is a business object that contains other business objects—cars. Clearly, these four business objects have some agreed-upon semantics for communicating with each other to perform business transactions. Under the cover, they could use the CORBA *Object Trans-*

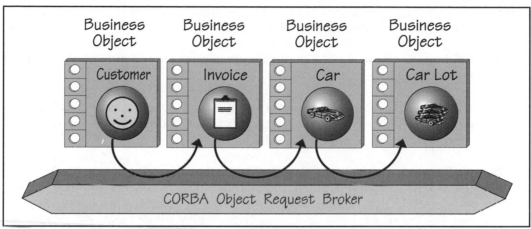

Figure 22-8. A Car Reservation System Using Cooperating Business Objects.

action Service to synchronize their actions. They also know how to share a single window to display their views seamlessly.

So how is this different from a traditional application? With very little work, you can reuse some of these business objects in another application context. For example, a car sales program could reuse most of these objects, especially if they were designed to work with more than one semantic suite. For example, the car, customer, and invoice objects could support multiple views to handle different business situations. In the extreme, the business objects could be specialized through inheritance to take into account the particularities of the car sales business. As you'll see in the next section, a business object is not a monolithic entity. It is factored internally into a set of cooperating objects that can react to different business situations. Business objects are highly flexible.

The Anatomy of a CORBA Business Object

Business objects directly represent the model of the enterprise, and this model becomes part of the information system. Every person, place, thing, event, transaction, or process in the business can be represented by an active object in the information system.

— **Cory Casanave**

A CORBA business object is a variation of the *Model/View/Controller (MVC)* paradigm. MVC is an object design pattern used to build interfaces in Smalltalk and in almost every GUI class library. MVC consists of three kinds of objects. The *model* represents the application object and its encapsulated data. The *view* represents the object visually on the screen. And the *controller* defines the way the user interface reacts to user input and GUI events.

In the CORBA model, a business object also consists of three kinds of objects (see Figure 22-9):

- **Business objects** encapsulate the storage, metadata, concurrency, and business rules associated with an active business entity. They also define how the object reacts to changes in the views or model.

- **Business process objects** encapsulate the business logic at the enterprise level. In traditional *Model-View-Controller* systems, the controller is in charge of the process. In the CORBA model, short-lived process functions are handled by the business object. Long-lived processes that involve other business objects are handled by the business process object—it's a specialization of the business object that handles long-lived processes and the environment at large. For example, it knows how to handle a workflow or long-lived transaction. The process object typically acts as the glue that unites the other objects. For example, it defines how the object reacts to a change in the environment. This type of change may be caused by the execution of a business transaction or by an incoming message from another business object. Note that some business objects may be entirely process-oriented and not associated with specific data or presentations.

- **Presentation objects** represent the object visually to the user. Each business object can have multiple presentations for multiple purposes. The presentations communicate directly with the business object to display data on the screen. And sometimes they communicate directly with the process object. The OMG also recognizes that there are non-visual interfaces to business objects.

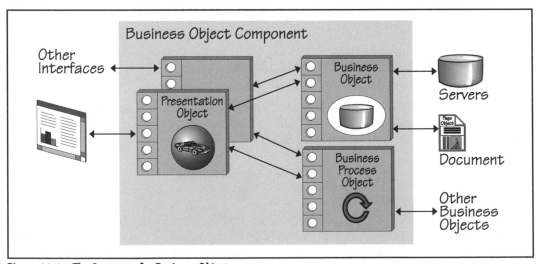

Figure 22-9. The Anatomy of a Business Object.

A typical business object component consists of a business object, one or more presentation objects, and a process object. Note that these entities act as a body. The underlying division of labor between the various objects is transparent to the users and clients of the business object. A business object also interacts with other servers and system-level objects but, again, in a totally encapsulated manner. The user only sees the *aggregate* business object. And clients of the object only deal with IDL-defined interfaces that are exposed by the aggregate business object.

The Anatomy of a Client/Server Business Object

Typically, a business object—like a car—may have different presentation objects spread across multiple clients. The business object and the process object may reside in one or more servers. The beauty of a CORBA-based architecture is that all the constituent objects have IDL-defined interfaces and can run on ORBs (see Figure 22-10). So it does not matter if the constituent objects run on the same machine or on different machines (ORBs provide local/remote transparency). As far as clients are concerned, they're still dealing with a single business object component, even though it may be factored into objects running in different machines. A well-designed business object builds on the CORBA services. For example, you can use the concurrency and transaction services to maintain the integrity of the business object's state. The ORB gives you these services for free, so you might as well use them.

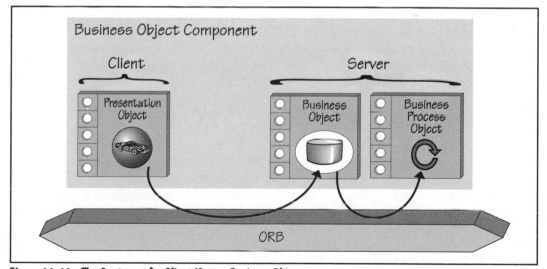

Figure 22-10. The Anatomy of a Client/Server Business Object.

CORBA Enterprise Beans

EJBs were designed to work with CORBA, which was designed to work in a multiplatform, distributed environment.

> — *Paul Harmon, Editor*
> *Component Development Strategies*
> *(September, 1998)*

In May 1997, the *Gang of Four (G4)*—Netscape, Oracle, IBM, and Sun—published a white paper called the *CORBA Component Imperatives*.[3] This influential paper was a call for action to marry the CORBA and Enterprise JavaBeans component models. It caused the OMG to issue, one month later, an RFP to solicit technology for a CORBA/JavaBeans component model. In general, this is a very good thing—the world doesn't need more component models.

However, you may ask: Why do we need CORBA Beans when we have Enterprise JavaBeans? What is the added value? The answer is that JavaBeans and EJB are language-specific component models—they lock you into using Java exclusively for your components. In contrast, CORBA components are a multi-language superset of EJBs. So they don't lock you into using a single language for your components. However, CORBA bean containers (or OTMs) will be able to host EJBs. And you will be able to play a Java-written CORBA Bean inside an EJB container. Of course, a CORBA container will also be able to host beans written in other languages—like C++, Smalltalk, JavaScript, or COBOL. In addition, CORBA containers and beans provide some advanced technology that won't be available until EJB 2.0. However, CORBA Beans will map to existing EJB 1.0 features. In addition, the EJB 1.0 specification includes a CORBA mapping layer.

As we go to press, OMG is still working on *CORBA 3.0 Components* (or *CORBA Beans*).[4] Figure 22-11 shows the anatomy of a CORBA Bean. To conform to the Java component model, a CORBA Bean supports multiple interfaces, single inheritance, attributes (or properties), and customizers. In addition, a CORBA bean can be both a producer or consumer of events (i.e., a publisher and subscriber).[5] A CORBA bean is packaged in a zipped (*.car*) file, which stands for *component archive*. Like an EJB, a CORBA Bean has a *deployment descriptor*. Unlike EJB 1.0, CORBA uses XML to specify the deployment descriptor, which makes it easier to support across multiple languages.[6] Like EJB, CORBA supports *entity* and

---

[3] See OMG Document *orbos/97-05-25*.
[4] See OMG Document *orbos/98-11-08*.
[5] Note that EJB 1.0 does not support events. However, events may be supported in EJB 2.0.
[6] We understand that EJB 2.0 may also support XML. Currently, EJB 1.0 uses Java serialized classes for its deployment descriptors, which is too Java specific.

session beans (i.e., persistent and non-persistent components). In addition, CORBA supports a *process* bean to represent an application.

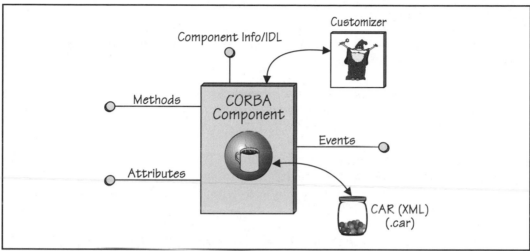

Figure 22-11. The Anatomy of a CORBA Bean.

You can fully-describe your CORBA beans using a new IDL construct called *component*. You can introspect a CORBA component via the Interface Repository. Like EJB, a CORBA container provides component metadata, factories, and finders. In addition, the container also manages events, transactions, activation/deactivation, persistence, and security on behalf of its beans (see Figure 22-12). CORBA

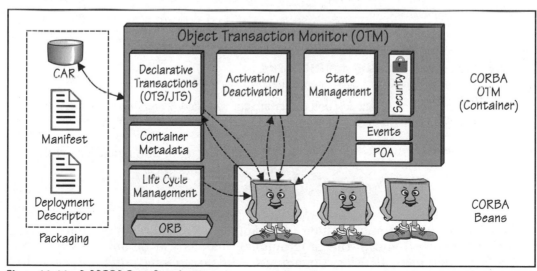

Figure 22-12. A CORBA Bean Container.

containers are built on top of the POA. So they are very consistent. In addition, they can incorporate standard CORBA services such as security, events, notifications, MOM, persistence, naming, traders, and transactions. So CORBA vendors will have some of the best server-side bean containers on the market.

For example, here are some of the activities a CORBA-based OTM can orchestrate on behalf of your CORBA components:

■ *Activates and deactivates your components.* In the CORBA world, the OTM works with the ORB's *Portable Object Adapter (POA)* to activate and deactivate objects when requests arrive and when they complete.

■ *Coordinates distributed transactions.* The OTM lets you declaratively define your transactional objects. It starts transactions if none exist. It will then manage the completion of a transaction using the underlying CORBA *Object Transaction Service (OTS)*.

■ *Notifies your component of key events during its life cycle.* The OTM notifies a component when it is created, activated, deactivated, and destroyed. Your component can then use these calls to explicitly manage its state, and to grab or release system resources.

■ *Automatically manages the state of your persistent component.* The more advanced OTMs can automatically load the state of a component from a persistent store and then later save it on transactional boundaries.

In summary, CORBA 3.0 Components and their containers are a superset of Enterprise JavaBeans.

CORBA Business Domain Frameworks

Without a common object model, you can crank out so-called "components" all day long without the slightest assurance that they can be used together in a new application.

> — Michael Guttman and David Frankel
> Genesis Corporation
> (May, 1998)

CORBA Beans will be able to hide from application programmers most of the CORBA system-level stuff. The programming masses will be able to write their intergalactic components using a minimal *surface area*—meaning the number of things they must understand to write a CORBA component.

In addition, instead of turning everyone into a CORBA Bean programmer, it may make more sense to embed CORBA within industry-specific frameworks that expose domain-level objects. To get there, OMG members are currently specifying domain frameworks for Manufacturing, Electronic Commerce, Transportation, Telecom, Healthcare, Insurance, Finance, and others. But, what do these frameworks build on? You may have guessed it: They build on the CORBA Beans framework. To be more exact, all domain-specific business objects inherit their system smarts from a generic CORBA Bean (see Figure 22-13). Domain-specific business objects are derived from this base object (or component). It's the root of all business objects.

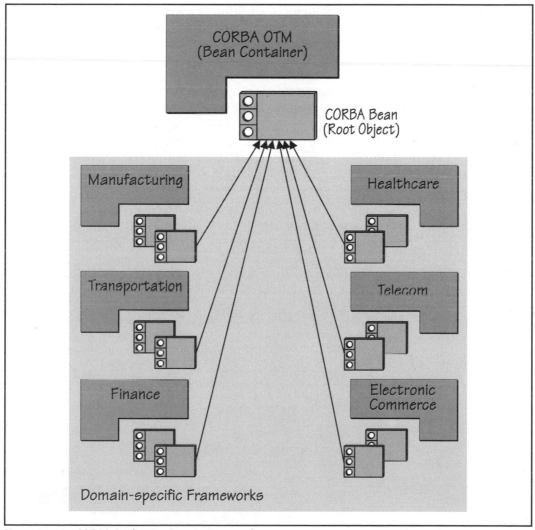

Figure 22-13. CORBA Application Domain Frameworks.

CORBA 3.0: THE NEXT GENERATION

CORBA seems to be perpetually under construction. It is moving at bullet-train speeds just to keep up with the requirements of the *Object Web* (see Part 8). CORBA must also maintain its headstart over COM—the ORB alternative from Microsoft. So there's no slowing down. In September 1998, OMG announced CORBA 3.0—the umbrella name for the next-generation ORB technology.

The ORB itself will be enhanced with several new features—including *Messaging*, *IIOP Proxy* for firewall support, and *CORBA/DCOM Interoperability*. The server side of CORBA is being enhanced with a *Portable Object Adapter (POA)* that lets you write portable server applications. In addition, we expect to see a new CORBA *Persistence Service* that supports automatic persistence. Many of these features have been under construction for several years now.

CORBA 3.0 is also much more integrated with the Java object model. CORBA now has an *IDL-to-Java* mapping as well as a reverse *Java-to-IDL* mapping—it lets you start with Java RMI semantics and produce CORBA stubs and skeletons. In addition, JavaSoft is co-developing—with IBM—*RMI-over-IIOP*, which it will include in the next JDK. CORBA is also becoming more Java-like with its support for *Multiple Interfaces* and *Objects-by-Value*. Finally, CORBA has adopted the EJB component model with extensions for multiple-language support.

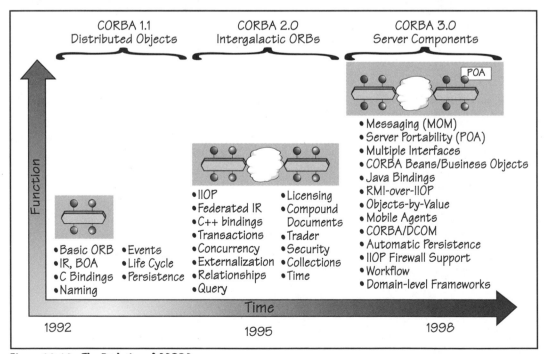

Figure 22-14. The Evolution of CORBA.

At a higher level, CORBA is being augmented with a Common Facility for *Mobile Agents*, a *Scripting Engine* specification, and a *Workflow Facility*. At the domain level, we expect to see industry-specific frameworks for Manufacturing, Electronic Commerce, Transportation, Telecom, Healthcare, Finance, and Electronic Commerce.

Figure 22-14 shows how CORBA is evolving. Yes, it's a moving target. There's a ton of new stuff coming down the object pipe. Some ORB vendors (and book authors) are complaining that they can't keep up with the pace of innovation. But there's no stopping in this fast-moving industry. For vendors, it's either stay ahead of this fast-moving train or get out of this business. For developers, it's good news because CORBA components are becoming more toolable, Java-like, and Internet-friendly. In addition, a new generation of OTMs is making CORBA ready for mission-critical prime time.

CONCLUSION

CORBA offers an integration-oriented viewpoint, where design efforts focus on the boundaries between elements of the system. The underlying interface technologies—IDL, IIOP, Interface Repository, CORBA components, and so on—are designed to make these boundaries as flexible, adaptive, and programming technology-independent as possible. Interface technologies such as CORBA are the best prophylactic against the aging and death of applications...

— *Dave Curtis, CORBA Guru*
Inprise
(January, 1998)

Distributed CORBA components—modeled as business objects—are an excellent fit for 3-tier client/server architectures. They provide scalable and flexible solutions for intergalactic client/server environments and for the Internet and intranets. Business objects—packaged as CORBA Beans—can be naturally decomposed and split across multiple tiers to meet an application's needs. They are self-describing and self-managing blobs of intelligence that you can move around and execute where it makes the most sense. Most importantly, business objects are evolutionary—they don't force you to throw away your existing server applications and start from scratch. You can encapsulate what you already have and incrementally add new intelligence, one component at a time.

Chapter 23

COM+:
The Other
Component Bus

---

*M*any years from now, a Charles Darwin of computerdom might look back and wonder how the Microsoft Windows APIs evolved into an object-oriented operating system.

— Kraig Brockschmidt, Author
Inside OLE 2, Second Edition
(Microsoft Press, 1995)

If CORBA is the industry's leading standard for distributed objects, then Microsoft's *Component Object Model (COM)* is the de facto "other standard." What makes COM so important? Microsoft. Everything Microsoft is doing and will do is based on DCOM. Today, COM is shipping with NT 4.0 and Windows 98. COM+—the next version of COM—will soon become the foundation of NT 5.0 (or *Windows 2000*). COM is also the foundation for Microsoft's Internet and enterprise component strategies. An *ActiveX* is simply a COM object. In early 1997, the *Microsoft Transaction Server (MTS)*—née *Viper*—shipped on the NT platform; it's an OTM for transactional COM objects. MTS appears to be the COM kingpin for the enterprise; it could eventually provide the scalability and robust intercomponent coordination that COM sorely lacks. The COM+ component model is based on MTS.

So what does this all have to do with client/server? Everything! COM is the ORB that CORBA/Java must beat—or learn to coexist with. COM+ is the Microsoft alternative to EJB and CORBA Beans. In this chapter, we start with a very brief history of COM. Then we explain the COM object model and its DCOM ORB. Next we cover MTS and MSMQ—the two server-side component foundation technologies of COM+. Finally, we look at the COM+ elements that will be included in Windows 2000.

COM: A SHORT HISTORY

The integration of COM into the operating system is just the first step. Making operating system functions available as COM objects is the next step.

> — *Michael Stal, Editor*
> *Java Spektrum*
> *(May, 1998)*

In 1990, Microsoft introduced the OLE 1 technology as its basic strategy for integrating multiple applications and multimedia data types within a compound document framework. OLE 1 was a clumsy and slow protocol built on top of DDE. When an application was launched from within a compound document, it was given its own window, and the data it needed was copied into its address space. There was no way for the application to directly access the document.

OLE 2, introduced in 1993, fixed many of these shortcomings with a new object-encapsulation technology called the *Component Object Model (COM)*. All of OLE 2 is built on top of COM—it's the heart of OLE. The lion's share of OLE still belongs to compound documents. In late 1994, Microsoft added a new custom control architecture—also known as *OCX*—to the compound document model. An OCX is the OLE version of a generic part that plugs into the compound document framework.

In early 1996, Microsoft announced *ActiveXs*, which are minimalist OLE objects for the Internet. Later in 1996, Microsoft released the first distributed version of COM—called the *Distributed Component Object Model (DCOM)*—as part of NT 4.0. In 1997, Microsoft announced COM+ as the next generation COM; it also introduced a new marketing architecture called the *Distributed interNet Application Architecture (DNA)*. According to Microsoft, all of DNA will ultimately be built on top of COM+.

COM 101

If you come from a classical object background (or from the world of CORBA), be prepared for some culture shock. COM looks and feels like classical objects, yet it is very different. COM provides some of the same functions as CORBA, but it is done very differently. COM introduces its own terminology and object jargon. We first explain in this section the COM ORB in CORBA terms. Then we explore each function using COM terms. This should help ease you into the new culture.

Looking at COM Through CORBA Eyes

Like CORBA, COM separates the object interface from its implementation and requires that all interfaces be declared using an *Interface Definition Language (IDL)*. Microsoft's IDL is based on DCE—it is, of course, not CORBA-compliant. A COM object is not an object in the OO sense. Unlike CORBA, COM objects do not have a persistent identity. A COM object reference is simply an interface pointer to an object in memory. If the object is released from memory, you cannot use the reference to access it again at a later time. To be precise, COM clients are given a pointer to access the functions in an interface—this pointer is not related to state information. A COM client cannot reconnect to exactly the same object instance with the same state at a later time. It can only reconnect to an interface pointer of the same class. In other words, COM objects do not maintain state between connections (see the next Briefing box). This can be a big problem in environments where you have faulty connections—for example, the Internet.

Like CORBA, COM provides both static and dynamic interfaces for method invocations. The *Type Library* is the DCOM version of an Interface Repository. COM precompilers can populate the Type Library with descriptions of IDL-defined objects—including their interfaces and parameters. Clients can query the Type Library to discover what interfaces an object supports and what parameters are needed to invoke a particular method. COM also provides a registry and some object look-up services that are similar to a CORBA Implementation Repository.

COM Monikers

Briefing

CORBA has persistent objects that also have persistent object references. COM has transient stateless objects that you can associate with a context via a *moniker*. A COM moniker is an object that acts as a persistent alias name for another object. Monikers can provide aliases for distributed filenames, database queries, a paragraph in a document, a range of spreadsheet cells, a remote computer, and so on. The intelligence of how to work with a particular name is encapsulated inside the name itself. The name becomes a "moniker object" that implements name-related interfaces. A moniker is really a patch for COM's lack of support for object identifiers. ❑

COM Style Interfaces

A COM *interface* is a collection of function calls—also known as methods or member functions. Like its CORBA equivalent, a COM interface serves as a client/server contract. It defines functions independently from their implementation. Like CORBA, a COM interface is language-independent, and you can use it to call functions across address spaces and networks. Microsoft provides COM language bindings for all of its development environments—including Visual C++, Visual Basic, and Visual J++. Borland/Inprise's Delphi provides DCOM bindings for Pascal.

A COM interface is defined as a low-level binary API based on a table of pointers. To access an interface, COM clients use pointers to an array of function pointers— also known as a *virtual table* (or *vtable*). The functions that are pointed to by the vtable are the server object's implementation methods (see Figure 23-1). Each COM object has one or more vtables that define the contract between the object implementation and its clients.

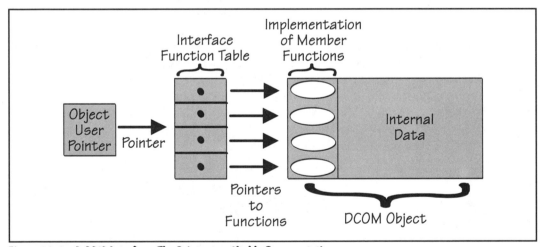

Figure 23-1. A COM Interface: The Pointer to a Vtable Representation.

The convention in COM is to represent an interface with a plug-in jack extending from an object (see Figure 23-2). These drawings are also called "bullet-and-stick" diagrams. Here, each bullet or plug-in jack represents an interface—meaning a group of semantically-related functions. It seems vtables make objects look rather intimidating. Plug-in jacks are more user-friendly; they use the metaphor of stereo system components that plug into each other.

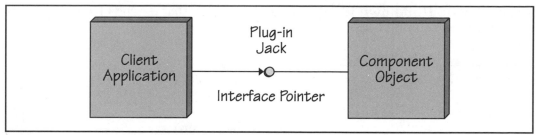

Figure 23-2. A COM Interface: The Plug-In Jack Representation.

An interface is, by convention, given a name starting with a capital "I"—for example, **IUnknown**. However, this name only has symbolic meaning (usually to a source-level programming tool). At run time, each interface is really known by its unique *Interface Identifier (IID)*. An IID is a COM-generated *globally-unique identifier (GUID)* for interfaces.

GUIDs—pronounced goo-ids—are unique 128-bit IDs you generate by calling the DCOM API function *CoCreateGuid*. This function executes an algorithm specified by the OSF DCE. If you really must know, this algorithm calculates a globally unique number using the current date and time, a network card ID, and a high-frequency counter. There's almost no chance for this algorithm to create duplicate GUIDs. The IID allows a client to unambiguously ask an object if it supports the interface. Clients ask questions using a *QueryInterface* function that all objects support through a ubiquitous interface called **IUnknown** (we cover this interface in a later section). Interfaces are meant to be small contracts that are independent of each other—they're the smallest contractual unit in COM.

So, What's a DCOM Object?

A COM object—also known as an *ActiveX* object—is a component that supports one or more interfaces, as defined by that object's class. A COM interface refers to a predefined group of related functions. A COM class implements one or more interfaces and is identified by a unique 128-bit *Class ID (CLSID)*. A COM object is a run-time instantiation of a class. A particular object will provide implementations of the functions for all the interfaces its class supports. For convenience, the word "object" is used to refer to both an object class and an individual instantiation of a class (see the next Details Box).

All COM objects must implement the **IUnknown** interface through which the client can control the lifetime of an object. Clients also use it for interface negotiations— a client can ask an object what interfaces it supports and obtain pointers to them. To use the stereo system analogy, the client must have the right kind of plug to fit into an interface jack so that it can talk to an object through that particular interface.

By convention, **IUnknown** is shown as a plug-in jack that extends from the top of an object (see Figure 23-3).

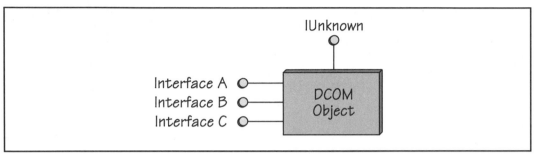

Figure 23-3. A DCOM Object Implements All the Interfaces Its Class Supports.

What? An Object With No ID?

Details

In a classical object system—like CORBA—each instantiated object has a unique identification (ID) that's a fundamental property of an object. The object ID—called an *object reference* in CORBA—is used by naming and trading services to locate a unique object. The ID is also used to track an object throughout its lifetime. Persistent services use it to save an object's state so that it can be reactivated at a later time. As we explained in the last chapter, the object reference of a persistent CORBA object encapsulates an identifier (or unique key); it can be used to reload the state of an object when it is reactivated. CORBA provides a set of APIs for converting an object ID to a string and vice versa. This lets you pass object IDs to other objects. Clients use the object ID to connect to a particular object. So, the concept of a unique object ID is fundamental to the classical object model.

In contrast, COM does not support the concept of an object ID. With COM, clients obtain a pointer to an interface and not a pointer to an object with state. DCOM clients cannot reconnect to that exact same object instance with the same state at a later time. Instead, clients have transient pointers to particular interfaces of an object. COM objects with the same set of interfaces and the same implementations for each are often loosely called instances of the same class. However, all access to the instances of the class by clients will only be through these transient interfaces; clients know nothing about an object other than that it supports certain interfaces. As a result, object instances play a much less significant role in COM than they do in classical object systems. ❑

What Is a COM Server?

A COM *server* is a piece of code—a DLL, an EXE, or a Java class—that houses one or more object classes each with its own CLSID. When a client asks for an object of a given CLSID, DCOM loads the server code and asks it to create an object of that class. The server must provide a *class factory* for creating a new object. Once an object is created, a pointer to its primary interface is returned to the client. The server is not the object itself. The word "server" in DCOM is used to emphasize the serving agent. The phrase "server object" is used specifically to identify an object that is implemented in a server.

So a COM server provides the necessary structure around an object to make it available to clients (see Figure 23-4). More specifically a COM server must:

- ■ ***Implement a class factory interface***. The server must implement a class factory with the **IClassFactory** interface for each supported CLSID. The class factory creates instances of a class. If a class supports licensing, then it must implement the **IClassFactory2** interface. This interface creates an object only if a valid license file is present or a license key is provided.

- ■ ***Register the classes it supports***. The server must register a CLSID for each class it supports with the *NT Registry*. For each CLSID, it must create one or more entries that provide the pathname to the server DLL or EXE (or to both). This information is recorded using the NT Registry APIs. Typically, the classes are registered at installation time.

- ■ ***Initialize the COM library***. The server issues a call to the COM API *CoInitialize* to initialize DCOM.[1] The COM library provides run-time services and APIs. These are functions with the *Co* prefix, which stands for component.

- ■ ***Verify that the library is of a compatible version***. The server does this by calling the API *CoBuildVersion*.

- ■ ***Provide an unloading mechanism***. The server must provide a way to terminate itself when there are no active clients for its objects.

- ■ ***Uninitialize the COM library***. The server calls the COM API *CoUninitialize* when it is no longer in use.

The implementation of the server—including registration, the class factory, and the unloading mechanism—will differ depending on whether the server is packaged as a DLL, EXE, or (.class) file.

---

[1] If you are ready to guarantee the thread safety of your objects, you can issue *CoInitializeEx*, instead of *CoInitialize*.

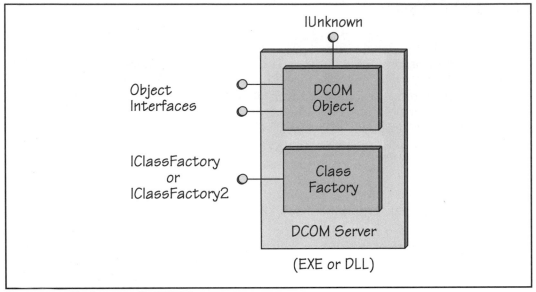

Figure 23-4. The Structure of a DCOM Server.

DCOM: Local/Remote Transparency

You can implement a COM server in one of many flavors. The actual flavor depends on the structure of the code module and its relationship to the client processes that will be using it. DCOM defines three flavors of servers (see Figure 23-5):

■ *In-process servers* execute in the same process space as their clients. Under Microsoft Windows and Windows NT, these are implemented as *Dynamic Link Libraries (DLLs)* that are loaded directly into the client's process.

■ *Local servers* execute in a separate process from their clients on the same machine (and operating system). Clients use DCOM's *Lightweight RPC (LRPC)* mechanism to communicate with a local server. Local servers execute in their own (.EXE) file.

■ *Remote servers* execute in a separate process on a remote machine and possibly on a different operating system. Clients will use a DCE-like RPC mechanism to communicate with remote servers.

In theory, DCOM enables clients to transparently communicate with server objects, regardless of where these objects are running. From a client's point of view, all server objects are accessed through interface pointers. A pointer must be in-process. In fact, any call to an interface function always reaches some piece of in-process code first. If the object is in-process, the call reaches it directly; there is no intervening system-infrastructure code. If the object is out-of-process, then the

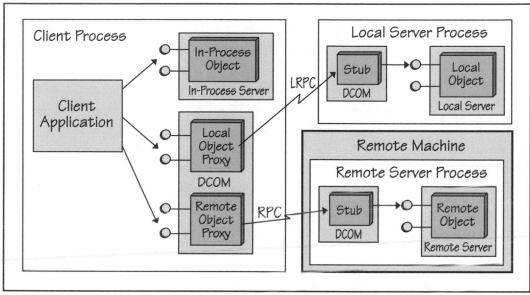

Figure 23-5. DCOM's Client/Server Boundaries.

call first reaches what is called a *proxy* object provided by DCOM itself. This object generates the appropriate remote procedure call to the other process or the other machine. The DCOM element that locates servers and gets involved with RPC invocations between clients and servers is called the *Service Control Manager (SCM)*—better known as "Scum."

From a server's point of view, all calls to an object's interface functions are made through a pointer to that interface. Again, a pointer only has context in a single process, so the caller must always be some piece of in-process code. If the object is in-process, the caller is the client itself. Otherwise, the caller is a *stub object* provided by DCOM that picks up the remote procedure call from the *proxy* in the client process and turns it into an interface call to the server object. Clients and servers always communicate using some in-process or local code (again, see Figure 23-5). The DCOM proxy and stub mechanism is very similar to the way CORBA implements local/remote transparency using static stubs on the client side and interface skeletons on the server side.

The Ubiquitous IUnknown Interface

The **IUnknown** interface is the heart of COM. It is used for run-time interface negotiations, life cycle management, and aggregation. Every COM interface must implement the three **IUnknown** member functions: *QueryInterface*, *AddRef*, and *Release* (see Figure 23-6).

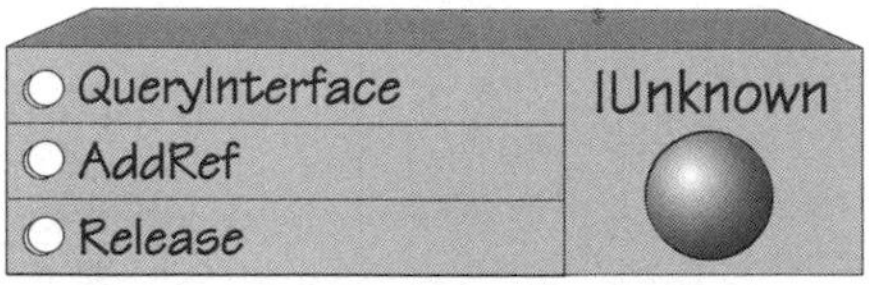

Figure 23-6.   DCOM's Ubiquitous IUnknown Interface.

IUnknown supports interface negotiations through *QueryInterface*. And it supports the life cycle management of an interface instance through *AddRef* and *Release*.   Because all DCOM interfaces derive from **IUnknown**, you can call *QueryInterface*, *AddRef*, and *Release* using any interface pointer. In other words, **IUnknown** is a base interface from which all other interfaces inherit these three functions and implement them in a polymorphic manner.

Interface Negotiations Using QueryInterface

When a client initially gains access to a COM object, by whatever means, it is given one—and only one—interface pointer in return. The client obtains the rest of the interfaces by calling *QueryInterface*, which forms the basis for interface negotiations. The *QueryInterface* function allows clients to discover at run time whether an interface—specified by an IID—is supported by an object. If the object supports this interface, the function returns the appropriate interface pointer to the client. After the client obtains an interface pointer, COM gets out of the way and lets the client directly interact with the server by invoking member functions of its interface.

So the unit of client/server negotiation is an interface, not an individual function. All clients must first obtain a pointer to an interface before they can interact with an object's services. The object can refuse service to a client by not returning a pointer. The *QueryInterface* function returns a failure code if the interface is not supported or if the server refuses to service a client.

QueryInterface supports the capability of returning pointers to the other interfaces a COM object supports, which is key to making aggregation work. COM requires that a *QueryInterface* call for a specific interface always return the same actual pointer value, no matter through which interface derived from **IUnknown** it is called. As a result, a client can perform an identity test to determine whether two pointers point to the same interface.

QueryInterface also lets components add new interfaces and lets clients discover them. This allows new interfaces to be added to an object's class as its function evolves. A client can ask an object: "Do you support Interface X?" An old object can answer the question with a "No," while a newer object can answer "Yes." This test allows clients to invoke the function only if an object supports it. In this manner, the client maintains compatibility with objects written before and after Interface X was available. This run-time negotiation is the cornerstone of COM's version control.

Life Cycle Management With Reference Counts

Briefing

In non-distributed object systems, the life cycle of objects—meaning the issues surrounding the creation and deletion of objects—is handled implicitly by the language or explicitly by application programmers. In a single program, there's always something—for example, the startup and shutdown code of a language runtime—that knows when objects must be created and when they should be deleted.

However, in distributed object systems, it is no longer true that someone or something always knows how to deal with the life cycle of objects. Object creation is still relatively easy—an object is created whenever a client with the right privileges requests it. But object deletion is another story: How do you know when an object is no longer needed? Even when the original client is done with the object, it can't simply shut the object down because it could have passed a reference to the object to some other client in the system. So who's in charge of garbage-collection in a distributed object system?

There are different approaches for dealing with the distributed object garbage-collection issue. The first approach is to ignore garbage collection and rely on the operating system to kill objects during system shutdown. This approach may be acceptable to clients, but it is not workable on servers. The second approach is to let the ORB (or OTM) keep track of outstanding connections. This approach may work, especially if it is combined with transactions and ORB-mediated object caching and load-balancing. The third approach is to let an object keep track of its usage using *reference counts*; the clients must cooperate by telling an object when they are using it and when they are done. This solution is based on having all objects maintain reference counts and having objects delete themselves when they are no longer in-use. In a strange twist, the Java version of COM uses the first approach—it depends on Java for its garbage collection. The C++ version of COM uses the third approach. CORBA ORBs and COM+ use the second approach.

The current C++ version of COM makes reference counting ubiquitous by adding that function to **IUnknown** through the member functions *AddRef* and *Release*. An interface's *AddRef* function is called when a client requests a pointer to that interface or passes a reference to it. An interface's *Release* func-

tion is called when the client no longer uses that interface. The internal implementation of the interface must increment the reference count every time *AddRef* is called and decrement it every time *Release* is called. C++ COM implementations are required to support at least a 32-bit counter to keep track of reference counts.

The reference-counting mechanism equates the lifetime of an object with references to it. It makes the following existential statement: "I'm being used; therefore, I exist." On the positive side, reference counting allows independently developed components to obtain and release access to a single object without having to coordinate with one another on life cycle management issues. On the negative side, it places an extra burden on every object implementation and assumes that clients are well-behaved—they must play by the rules. Reference counting is a cooperative client/server effort. ☐

IClassFactory2: Object Creation and Licensing

Every COM class must implement a class factory that a COM server can invoke to create instances of that class. A COM class factory is an implementation of either the **IClassFactory** or **IClassFactory2** interfaces. **IClassFactory2** is an extension of **IClassFactory** that enforces licensing at object creation time (see Figure 23-7). It was introduced in late 1994 with OLE custom controls to enforce the licensing of OCXs. In addition to the ubiquitous **IUnknown** functions, **IClassFactory2** provides two member functions of the old **IClassFactory** interface and three new member functions that enforce licensing. When a COM server is initially loaded, it must instantiate a class factory for each of its classes and register them with DCOM by invoking the *CoRegisterClassObject* API call.

Although the class factory is an interface, it is not the root interface of the component. Every instance of a class factory is associated with a single CLSID and exists strictly to facilitate the creation of an object of that CLSID. As shown in

IUnknown Functions	IClassFactory2	New Licensing Functions
○ QueryInterface		○ GetLicInfo
○ AddRef		○ RequestLicKey
○ Release		○ CreateInstanceLic
IClassFactory Functions		
○ CreateInstance		
○ LockServer		

Figure 23-7. The IClassFactory2 Interface.

Figure 23-7, the **IClassFactory2** interface implements two functions for creating a new instance of a class: *CreateInstance* and *CreateInstanceLic*. These two functions are like the C++ *new* operator. They both create an uninitialized instance of the object associated with the class factory and return an interface pointer of a requested IID. The *LockServer* function allows a client to keep a server object resident in memory even when it is not being used by clients—it keeps the object from getting automatically unloaded from memory when its reference count reaches zero.

COM considers a machine to be fully licensed when a *license file* is installed on that machine. Otherwise, the client must supply a special *license key* when it instantiates the component. If the license key is not provided, the server will not instantiate the component. You can think of a license file as providing global permission to use a component on a machine, while the license key is a specific permission to use the component on another machine. License keys are used by applications that are assembled with third-party components. The development machine is fully licensed because we assume the components were purchased in the first place. The license key makes it possible to use these components on other machines. It's a piece of information that must be extracted from a component in the development environment and then provided at run time on the target machine.

The *GetLicInfo* function returns the type of licensing a component supports. It answers the questions: Is a license key required and, if so, is it available? The *RequestLicKey* function is used by a client to request a license key to use the component on a different machine. The client can use *CreateInstance* if a global license file is installed on a target machine. Otherwise, the client must invoke *CreateInstanceLic*, passing it the license key as one of its arguments. To repeat, a licensed component can only be created if a license key is provided by the client or if a global license file is available on the machine. The **IClassFactory2** implementation will validate the key or the license file before creating an instance of a component.

The COM licensing implementation is very primitive. The license file is simply a text file installed with the component itself, and a license key is, typically, the first line of that text file. There's no protection against forgeries, and there's no way to meter the use of licenses. In addition, it's a system management nightmare to keep track of license files for thousands of disparate components.

Note that in addition to licensing, Windows NT 4.0 lets you control access to CLSIDs using the NT Registry. You can configure the registry to: 1) disallow the launching of servers of a given CLSID based on the client's access token, 2) disallow client connections to running objects based on their access token, and 3) configure a given CLSID to always run as a specific user.

Here's how it works. You invoke *CoCreateInstance* with a CLSID. This results in a call to "scum," which verifies that you have the proper access rights for this class.

Scum will impersonate you in a call to the NT Registry's *RegQueryValue* method; it will pass it your access rights. If the call succeeds, you will be able to instantiate an instance of this class.

COM-Style Inheritance: Aggregation and Containment

Like JavaBeans—and now CORBA—a COM component can support multiple interfaces. By issuing *QueryInterface* calls, COM clients can determine at run time which group of interfaces a component supports. These two mechanisms allow developers to create outer components that encapsulate the services of inner components and represent them to a client. COM supports two methods of encapsulation: *containment/delegation* and *aggregation* (see Figure 23-8). In both cases, the outer object controls the lifetimes of the inner objects, and its **IUnknown** represents the inner object's interfaces.

In *containment/delegation*, the outer object must reissue the method invocations it receives on behalf of its inner objects. In Figure 23-8, the outer object A contains the inner objects B and C. A's **IUnknown** knows about interfaces A, B, and C. When a client wants to talk to B or C, the outer object calls on the methods these inner objects provide—this is called *delegation*.

In *aggregation* mode, instead of re-issuing each call, the outer component's **IUnknown** directly exposes the inner object's interface pointers to its clients. In other words, the outer object exposes the inner object's interfaces as its own. So

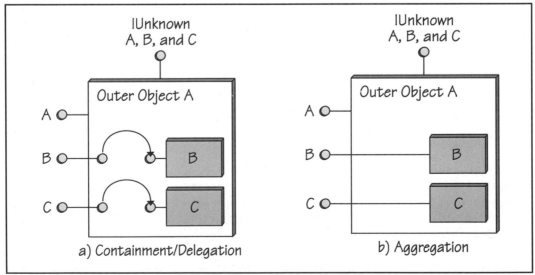

Figure 23-8. DCOM's Delegation Versus Aggregation.

the inner object directly talks to the client, but it delegates its **IUnknown** to the outer object. In Figure 23-8, inner objects B and C are part of A's **IUnknown**. However, the client directly talks to B and C without A's intervention.

What all this means is that the COM environment is inherently flat. "Inheritance" is achieved through a web of pointers that link or aggregate different interfaces. Microsoft believes that aggregation and containment provide all the reuse that's needed in a distributed object environment.

The COM IDL

To develop a COM interface, you need to create a file that describes the interface's methods and their arguments using COM's version of IDL. You must then run this file through the *Microsoft IDL (MIDL)* compiler to create the client proxies, the server stubs, and the code that marshals arguments between them.

The MIDL is more accurately a precompiler that turns text descriptions of an interface into code for both proxies and stubs. The MIDL compiler also creates header files that contain the interface definition. To finish the job, you must implement, compile, link, and register the server code.

COM's Dynamic Invocation Facilities

COM—like CORBA—provides dynamic invocation and metadata facilities. These facilities provide the foundation for OLE automation—now simply called *automation*. It allows client programs to dynamically invoke methods that manipulate the contents of scriptable objects. The COM *Type Library*, like the CORBA Interface Repository, allows clients to dynamically discover the methods and properties a COM automation server exposes. You must describe these interfaces using the COM *Object Definition Language (ODL)*. COM ODL is a subset of the Microsoft IDL; you use it to define class metadata.

COM programmers must describe their automation objects—including their method names and parameter types, as well as object properties—using ODL. They can use either the *MIDL* or *MKTYPLIB* utilities to compile the ODL file into a type library. Also tools—like *Visual Basic* and *Visual J++*—can automatically emit type libraries.

Figure 23-9 shows how the COM automation pieces come together. An automation server is a COM object that implements a specific interface called **IDispatch**. This interface provides the late-binding mechanism through which an object exposes its functions—including its incoming and outgoing methods and properties. These late-bound functions are called *dispatch interfaces*, or more simply, *dispinterfaces*. If you come from the world of CORBA, a *dispinterface* is the equivalent of a CORBA *dynamic skeleton interface*. The COM server decides at run time which method to invoke based on an identifier (the dispID) that it reads from the incoming message. In contrast, COM's static interfaces export their functions through vtable pointers that are compiled into the client source code. This means the client must be early-bound to a function based on its location in the vtable.

A *property* is like a CORBA *attribute*. The server's interfaces, methods, and properties are maintained in the type libraries, which act as a run-time repository. Automation controllers—meaning clients—can learn the names of the methods and properties an object supports using the **ITypeLib** interface. The type library, like the CORBA Interface Repository, lets you access this information without having to run the object. Finally, using the *IDispatch::Invoke* method, clients can create or obtain automation objects, get and set the properties they expose, and execute their methods.

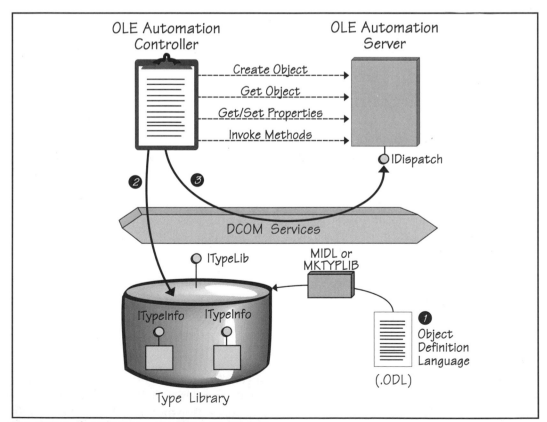

Figure 23-9. How OLE Automation Clients Find Their Servers.

Building and Registering Type Libraries

You create a type library by running your ODL through the *MIDL 3.0* compiler. You can also use the older *MKTYPLIB* compiler. The MIDL compiler reads your ODL and compiles it. The end result is a type library (.TLB) file.

You can ship the (.TLB) file with an object or attach it as a resource in a COM server's EXE or DLL. You can also store it inside a compound file's stream, or make it available through a shared file on a network server. Regardless of how it gets there, the information in these type libraries must be made available to automation objects and COM clients. In addition to creating registry entries for a COM server, an installation program must also create entries for the corresponding type libraries using the API function *RegisterTypeLib*. If you use automation-compatible interfaces, then COM uses type libraries to do on-the-fly marshaling. This is called *type library driven* marshaling.

Finding and Loading a Type Library

To obtain the metadata they need, automation clients must first be able to locate a type library and load its contents into memory. So how does the client find the type library in the first place? By looking for it in the registry. The client invokes the COM API *QueryPathOfRegTypeLib* and passes it the ID of the type library it wants. The API returns the path of a registered type library. Now that the client has the library's file name, it can load it by invoking the COM API *LoadRegTypeLib*. This function uses the registry information to load the type library. COM also provides the function *LoadTypeLibFromResource* to extract a type library from a resource attached to a DLL or EXE. Both load functions return a **ITypeLib** interface pointer through which a client can navigate the entire library.

COM+: "COM WITHOUT THE GUNK"

The primary purpose of COM+ is to provide a single object model across languages, enforced metadata, and, more importantly, common support for services provided by the operating system and by applications...COM's viability outside of Microsoft's operating systems remains an open question.

> — Max Dolgicer
> Component Strategies
> (June, 1998)

As you can see, programming in COM is not for the faint of heart. Like CORBA, COM is a complete object system. This tutorial only covered the COM core. So we only scratched the surface. At this point, you may be wishing for something that

makes COM more programmer-friendly and more consistent across languages.[2] This is where COM+ comes into the picture. According to Microsoft's Charlie Kindel, "COM+ is COM without the gunk." Eventually, COM+ will provide "a shared common run time" that hides most of COM's nastiness from developers—including the IDL, class factories, reference counting, **IUnknown** negotiations, class registration, and type libraries.

Most importantly, COM+ will follow the MTS model of programming, which means you will be using declarative attributes to specify a component's required services—including transactions, security, threading, and data binding. In a future COM+, you will use *metadata* directives—defined by a *coclass*—inside the programming language itself to specify the remote interfaces, quality-of-service, and other attributes of a component. The compiler—with help from the OS—will generate all the system "gunk." MTS-like *interceptors* will be placed in the call path—between the client and the server-side object—to automatically provide the required quality-of-service. At least this is the vision. Note that MTS is now part of the forthcoming NT 5.0; it provides the run-time environment for running COM+ components.

If you think about it, COM+ is Microsoft's answer to CORBA/EJB. The difference is that it is OS-specific. The DCOM pipe is being ported across platforms by Microsoft, Software AG, HP, Digital, and others. However, COM+—the platform—will be bundled deep inside NT 5.0. So the application server environment for server-side COM+ components is NT 5.0. At best, components on other platforms—including Unix, NetWare, and mainframes—will be able to interoperate as clients. In the next few sections, we will first introduce MTS and MSMQ. Then we will look at the elements of COM+ that will be included in NT 5.0.

MTS: COM's OTM

MTS is very similar to the CORBA/EJB OTMs we covered in the last two chapters. It lets you use attribute-based programming techniques on COM objects to control their transaction boundaries, resource management, and security. As with EJB, you do it all by setting attributes on a *package* that contains COM components. An MTS package groups a set of components that run together in an MTS process. MTS packages can either be *system* or *library*. System packages run as in-process servers inside an MTS process. In contrast, library packages can be hosted inside other containers—for example, a Microsoft *Internet Information Server (IIS)* process.

---

[2] Currently, every Microsoft language has its own way of dealing with COM. Visual C++ exposes every feature of COM, while Visual J++ makes COM almost transparent. In addition, Visual Basic's OLE automation uses a subset of the COM types. So it's typically the least common denominator COM environment.

Like EJB, MTS provides automatic transaction management. MTS components are managed by the *MTS executive* (i.e., the COM+ OTM). MTS maintains a wrapper—called the *context object*—for each component it manages. When it finishes its work, your component either invokes *SetComplete* or *SetAbort* on its context object to vote on the outcome of a transaction. If every object participating in the transaction agrees to commit, then MTS tells the OLE-TP *Distributed Transaction Coordinator* to commit the transaction.

At the end of each transaction, MTS deactivates the object and destroys its in-memory state. If a client tries to reconnect to that object—via a reference it holds—MTS will create a new instance of the object. It leaves it as an exercise for the object to recreate its prior state. And, because MTS uses COM, there is no persistent ID in the object reference to help the object recreate its state. So the client must explicitly help the server "regain its memory" by passing it some extra parameters or by creating a moniker. In EJB terms, all MTS objects are *session* beans. MTS does not have the equivalent of an *entity* bean, which means a classical object with state (also see the next Soapbox).

MTS: Great Idea, Poor Foundation

Soapbox

*U*nderstanding the MTS model is a challenge, even for COM devotees. At the heart of the difficulty is the typical conception of object identity.

> — Tim Ewald, "The COM Guy"
> Distributed Computing
> (April, 1998)

MTS is one of the few real technical innovations to come from Microsoft. It was the first commercial OTM to appear on the market. Yes, MTS came before EJB and CORBA Beans. Your authors have a very high respect for the MTS team. We know the current MTS engine does not scale, but we have faith that the MTS people will eventually get it right. In any case, it takes at least five years to make a TP engine mission-critical ready; MTS has only been shipping for two. So why are we writing this Soapbox? Despite its originality and elegance, MTS suffers from two serious architectural flaws:

1. ***It is built on top of COM.*** The underlying MTS object model is COM. As a result, MTS suffers from some of COM's problems. For example, COM does not support objects with persistent identities. Consequently, MTS cannot provide the equivalent of EJB session beans. However, you may have read in

the Microsoft marketing literature that this shortcoming is really a feature—only stateless objects scale. In reality, this is just marketing blah-blah. BEA's *M3* is a commercial example of a CORBA-based OTM that also supports state. And, M3 scales. In some cases, the performance of M3 is equivalent to (or better than) *Tuxedo*—the world's fastest open TP Monitor. So we don't buy this argument. Let's face it—if COM had CORBA-like objects, MTS would have entity beans today.

2. *It is built on top of Windows NT.* MTS is a single-platform OTM. Consequently, it is limited by NT's scalability. In contrast, CORBA/EJB components can run on NT as well as other platforms—including Unix megaclusters and mainframes. So they will always be faster than their NT-only MTS counterparts. In addition, the mix of servers in the enterprise and on the Internet is extremely heterogeneous. This means that server-side components will most likely be running on heterogeneous platforms. Because of its NT-only limitation, MTS is seriously handicapped—it cannot directly orchestrate components that run on multiple platforms. The role of OTM-like middleware is to hide the multi-platform diversity by providing a single-system image of components wherever they run. MTS can only do this if NT is the only server platform for components. Everything else—including Unix machines and mainframes—can only be a client.

In summary, MTS is a great idea. It has helped popularize transactions, which is a good thing. However, EJB has leap-frogged MTS and subsumed most of its good ideas. And EJB does not suffer from MTS's single-platform limitation. Of course, EJB has a single-language limitation, but this is where CORBA Beans come to the rescue. In general, we believe that EJB and CORBA Beans give you all the benefits of MTS (and more) without limiting you to a single platform or a single vendor. ❑

MSMQ: COM's MOM

Queued Components—a key feature of COM+—is based on the *Microsoft Message Queue Server (MSMQ)*. It's the COM+ equivalent of CORBA Messaging. Like CORBA, MSMQ provides a way to invoke and execute components asynchronously. It lets you queue regular method invocations if the receiver is not online. You can then access the message data as object properties. In addition, MSMQ is an OLE TP transactional resource manager. So it can protect the data in a queue on transaction boundaries. Consequently, COM+ components can write data to a queue and then let MTS roll it back if a transaction fails (as part of a two-phase commit). An MTS queue can also be persistent, which means it can survive system crashes. In summary, MSMQ enriches the COM+ communication model. Like CORBA Messaging, it brings MOM semantics to distributed objects.

How Much of COM+ Is in NT 5.0?

It looks as though for the next year or two COM+ will consist of something quite different from what we were originally told it would.

> — *David Chappell*
> *COM Guru and Author*
> *(July, 1998)*

As we go to press, Microsoft has released the beta 2 version of NT 5.0 (or Windows 2000). As David Chappell points out, very little of the original COM+ vision made it into NT 5.0. Instead, this version of COM+ is simply a more unified repackaging of MTS, COM, and MSMQ. These products are now more integrated with each other and with the operating system. MTS as a distinct technology is gone. An improved MTS is now the centerpiece of COM+. In addition, MSMQ now supports IDL-defined messages, which is an improvement over BLOB-based messaging; it is also better integrated with COM. However, it's MTS that gets the lion's share of improvements. Here's what's new in the NT 5.0 version of MTS:

- *Load balancing and server clustering.* In NT 5.0, you can mark an MTS component class as being load-balanced via attributes. MTS for the first time will support the load balancing of components across a cluster of application servers. An object is assigned to a server at creation time (not at activation). MTS does not recognize affinity between classes. When it receives a client request, MTS routes it to a server based on an average *response-time* balancing scheme. An MTS router will be able to handle cluster sizes of up to eight application servers.

- *Object pooling.* MTS will support pools of reusable pre-started server objects of a particular class. This avoids the extra time it takes to create a new instance of a class.

- *In-memory database.* MTS will provide a transient database-style transaction cache for fast access to data. You can access this database using OLE DB APIs or *ActiveX Data Objects (ADOs)*. You can load in-memory tables from SQL Server or create them dynamically at run time.

- *Publish-and-subscribe via event channels.* MTS will support channel-based events as well as publish and subscribe. This is very similar to the CORBA Beans event channel and notification services. It allows producers and subscribers of events to be decoupled via event channels.

In summary, COM+ is still under construction. The next release—NT 5.0—significantly improves the MTS run time. However, it does not deliver the unified

COM+ object model that Microsoft originally outlined. Consequently, the current COM model—with all its inconsistencies—will continue to live well into the next millennium.

CONCLUSION

If you still had doubts, this chapter should have helped convince you that Microsoft is really serious about distributed objects and OTMs. As you can see, the company is developing its own distributed object parallel universe, which is a complete mirror of the CORBA/EJB world. For better or for worse, COM+ is now our industry's other component model. And, it's here to stay. So, the bad news is that we have two component standards to choose from. The good news is that these parallel universes can be connected via COM/CORBA bridges. The other good news is that the competition from Microsoft is forcing the CORBA/Java world to abide by standards, which means they will provide a consistent component platform for the rest of us.

Chapter 24

Object Databases

We define an ODBMS to be a DBMS that integrates database capabilities with
object-oriented programming language capabilities. An ODBMS makes database objects
appear as programming language objects in one or more existing programming languages.

— Rick Cattell, Chairman
ODMG Committee

An *Object Database Management System (ODBMS)* provides a persistent store
for objects in a multiuser client/server environment. The ODBMS handles concurrent access to objects, provides locks and transaction protection, protects the object
store from all types of threats, and takes care of traditional tasks such as backup
and restore. What makes DBMSs different from their relational counterparts is that
they store the persistent state of an object rather than just data in tables. Objects
are referenced through *Persistent Identifiers (PIDs)*, which uniquely identify
objects, and are used to create referential and containment relationships between
them. ODBMSs also enforce encapsulation and support inheritance. The ODBMS
combines object properties with traditional DBMS functions such as locking, protection, transactions, querying, versioning, concurrency, and persistence.

WHAT IS AN ODBMS?

Rather than trying to mangle the data or tear it apart and put it into relational tables, obviously it was best to store those objects in their natural form.

> — **Jonathan Cassell, IS Manager**
> **Granite Construction**

Instead of using a separate language like SQL to define, retrieve, and manipulate data, ODBMSs use class definitions and traditional OO language (usually C++, Smalltalk, and Java) constructs to define and access data. The ODBMS is simply a multiuser, persistent extension of in-memory language data structures (see Figure 24-1). In other words, the client is the C++ or Java program; the server is the ODBMS—there are no visible intermediaries like RPCs or SQL. The ODBMS integrates database capabilities directly into the language.

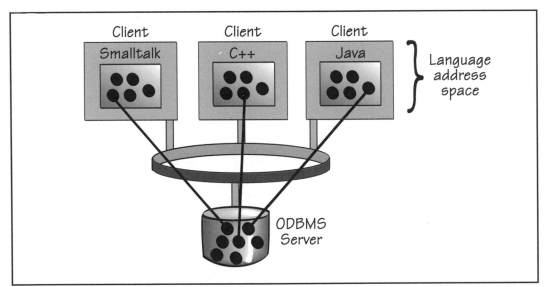

Figure 24-1. ODBMS: An Extension to OO Language Data Structures.

Of course, not everything is transparent to the language. By necessity, the ODBMS introduces extensions to the OO language such as container classes and operations that help you navigate through the containers. The *Object Database Management Group (ODMG)* specification includes a full-blown *Object Manipulation Language (OML)* that supports queries and transactions. In an attempt to make the data definition language neutral, ODMG specifies a generic *Object Definition Language (ODL)*. As a result, the ODBMS, like SQL, requires a precompiler to process the object definitions, language extensions, and queries. The output of the compiler, like SQL plans, must also be linked to the ODBMS runtime. So we've come full circle.

What's an ODBMS Good For?

ODBMSs are perfect fits for users whose data isn't simple enough to line up in relational tables. For a long time, ODBMSs were an area of great interest to academicians and OO researchers. The earliest commercial ODBMSs made their appearance in 1986 with the introduction of Servio (now GemStone) and Ontos. These two pioneers were joined (in the 1990s) by Object Design (ODI), Versant, Objectivity, O2 Technology (now Unidata), Poet, Ibex, UniSQL, and ADB MATISSE. The ODBMS vendors first targeted applications that dealt with complex data structures and long-lived transactions—including computer-aided design, CASE, and intelligent offices. With the emergence of multimedia, groupware, distributed objects, and the Web, the esoteric features of ODBMSs are now becoming mainstream client/server requirements. ODBMS technology fills the gap in the areas where relational databases are at their weakest—complex data, versioning, long-lived transactions, nested transactions, persistent object stores, inheritance, and user-defined data types.

Here's a list of the features that were pioneered by the ODBMS vendors (see Figure 24-2):

1. ***Freedom to create new types of information***. ODBMSs give you the freedom to create and store any data type using standard object descriptions. The data type is part of the object class definition. You can easily store arbitrarily complex data structures in an ODBMS (like XML container hierarchies). In contrast, traditional databases offer a limited number of hard-wired data types; complex structures must be converted into artificially "flattened" table representations.

2. ***Fast access***. ODBMSs keep track of objects through their unique IDs. A search can move directly from object to object without the need for tedious search-and-compare operations using foreign keys and other associative techniques.

3. ***Flexible views of composite structures***. ODBMSs allow individual objects to participate in a multiplicity of containment relationships, creating multiple views of the same objects. Objects can maintain pointers to other objects in a very recursive manner; there's no limit to the different container relationships that you can create. A container typically maintains references to object IDs as opposed to the objects themselves—it's a form of *linking* as opposed to *embedding*.

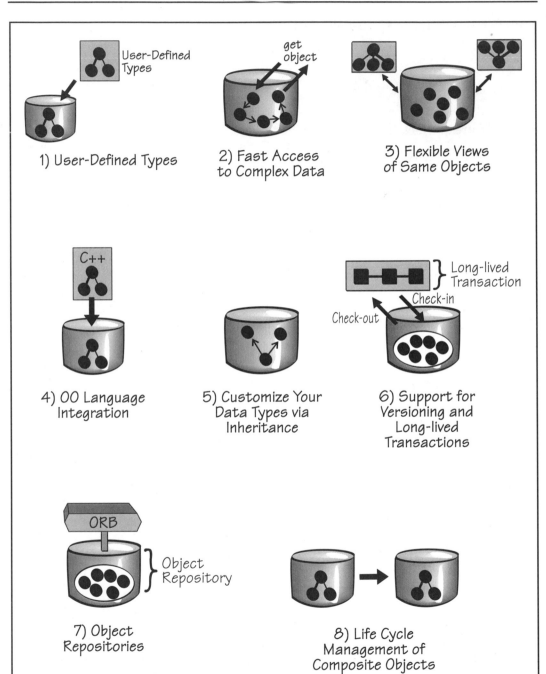

Figure 24-2. The Eight Wonders of ODBMS.

4. ***Tight integration with object-oriented languages.*** ODBMSs present themselves as persistent extensions of the OO languages' in-memory data structures. This allows them to minimize the impedance mismatch between programs and data while maintaining the strong encapsulation features that are inherent in OO languages. OO programmers should find an ODBMS to be a natural extension of their paradigm. ODBMSs provide the fastest and most direct access to objects they store; they also do a good job of preserving the characteristics of these objects. In contrast, RDBMSs require multiple transformations to represent the complex in-memory data structures of an OO language in tabular form. Relational systems can store objects, but they must first break them down into chunks and flatten them into structures that can fit in tables. SQL people, of course, may think that chasing corporate data via in-memory C++ pointers is a travesty. (We'll resume this discussion in the next Soapbox.)

5. ***Support for customizable information structures using multiple inheritance.*** The ODBMS data types are defined using object classes. This means that any class can be subclassed to create custom structures that meet exceptional data needs. In addition, the ODBMS lets you mix desirable characteristics from different classes and combine them using multiple inheritance. So the ODBMS extends the concept of object reuse through inheritance to the database.

6. ***Support for versioning, nesting, and long-lived transactions.*** Many commercial ODBMSs (including ObjectStore, Ontos, Versant, GemStone, and Objectivity) support nested transactions and versioning for long-duration transactions. Objects can be grouped in configurations and managed as one transaction. ODBMSs are most popular in engineering design applications that require the management of complex documents. A typical Computer Aided Design (CAD) system also depends on version control to track the progressively more enhanced versions of an engineering design. Because of their long involvement with CAD, ODBMSs have perfected the art of versioning and long-lived transactions. ODBMSs have introduced the concept of *configurations*—meaning a collection of objects that are managed as a locking and versioning unit. CAD users typically *check out* a configuration of objects from the ODBMS, work on it, and *check in* their configuration as a new version.

7. ***Repositories for distributed objects.*** ODBMSs provide natural multiuser repositories for run-time objects. We believe the ODBMS vendors have a huge lead in providing solutions for concurrent access to large numbers (in the millions) of fine-grained objects with ACID protection. ODBMSs also provide true stores for *mobile components* such as Java applets and Beans; they serve as object servers for roaming objects—think of them as object Hilton hotels.

8. ***Support for life cycle management of composite objects.*** ODBMSs have also perfected the art of managing composite objects as a unit. For example, you can assemble, disassemble, copy, store, restore, move, and destroy compos-

ite objects. The ODBMS automatically maintains the relationships between the parts and treats the aggregate as a single component. This is also a result of their long involvement with CAD. This technology is now used to create very scalable Web servers. The ODBMS becomes a replacement for the file system; it provides a very efficient database for the rich multimedia data types that are starting to proliferate on the World Wide Web.

In summary, ODBMS vendors have had the luxury of being able to create pure object databases without being encumbered by a debt to history. As a result, they were able to provide some missing pieces of technology needed to create the new generation of multimedia-intensive databases with flexible data types. An ODBMS has the advantage over a relational database of knowing the overall structure of a complex object (like a document) and sometimes its behavior (or methods) as well; it can refer to any constituent object by its ID. In contrast, RDBMS vendors are attempting to provide object technology (with SQL3) by using an object-relational hybrid approach that decomposes the data from the object and then stores it in tables. This is an area where relational databases are at a disadvantage, but we'll defer that discussion to the Soapbox.

THE ODMG 2.1 STANDARD

There is no object database life left outside the ODMG standard.

> — *Francois Bancilhon, CTO*
> *Unidata*

The *ODMG* standard is the ODBMS answer to SQL. The standard is the result of work done by the *Object Database Management Group (ODMG)*—a consortium that includes all the major ODBMS vendors. The ODMG is a working subgroup of the OMG, and it intends to submit its standard to both ISO and ANSI. In theory, the adoption of ODMG should allow applications to work with ODBMSs from any of the major vendors. Version 1.0 of the standard was published in 1993 (it was called *ODMG-93*). Revision 1.1 was published in 1994. Revision 1.2 was published in December 1995. The ODMG Java bindings were published in December 1996. Each revision strengthened the standard both in scope and depth. The most current major release, *ODMG 2.0*, was published in 1997—it includes the new Java bindings. In 1998, the ODMG broadened its charter to encompass any storage mechanism that uses the ODMG specification. So it changed its name to the *Object Data Management Group*. Sun now uses the ODMG interface on top of its *Java Blend* object-to-relational mapper.

ODMG 2.0 builds on the OMG object model. In addition, the new OMG persistent service is built on the ODMG 2.0 model. CORBA uses ODMG ODL semantics to define persistent object state—called value objects—in IDL. So there is a very strong synergy between these two efforts. The ODBMS's role in an ORB environment is to provide concurrent access to persistent stores capable of handling millions of fine-grained objects. To do this, the ODBMSs supplement the IDL-defined invocations with direct API calls (or library APIs) to the objectstore for faster access to data. Typically, a server object will use these APIs to store its state. Alternatively, an OTM—or application server—could provide automatic object persistence by directly invoking these APIs.

The ODBMS vendors are also actively promoting within the CORBA ORB task force a *Library Object Adapter (LOA)* that provides direct access via the ORB to specialized high-speed APIs. ODMG states that the ODBMS vendors would like CORBA to standardize on a specialized version of LOA called the *Object Database Adapter (ODA)*. Figure 24-3, adapted from the ODMG specification, shows the differences among POA, LOA, and ODA—yes, more TLAs (three-letter acronyms) you can use to impress the folks back home.

The ODA should provide the ability to register subspaces of object identifiers with the ORB instead of all the millions of objects that are stored in the ODBMS. From the client's point of view, the objects in the registered subspace appear just as any other ORB-accessible objects. The ODA should allow for the use of direct access—as in the LOA—to improve the performance of ORB/ODBMS applications. To summarize, the ODBMS vendors are pushing CORBA to be more flexible when it

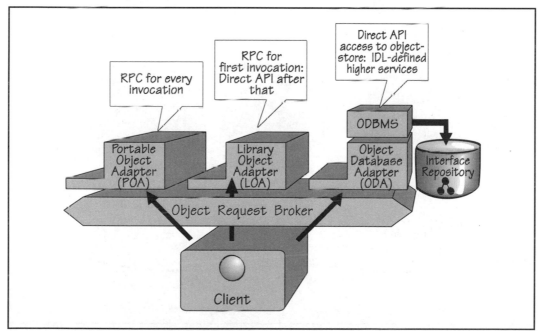

Figure 24-3. ODMG-Compliant ODBMS as Object Manager on an OMG ORB.

comes to dealing with applications that manage millions of fine-grained objects. The
OMG is responding to this issue with its new persistence standard.

The Elements of ODMG

*Developers can store objects directly from Java, C++, or Smalltalk into ODMG
2.0-compliant relational, object/relational, or object databases without having to manage
the actual storage process.*

> — **Douglas Barry, Executive Director**
> **ODMG**
> **(July, 1998)**

The ODMG standard consists of three major components (see Figure 24-4):

■ ***Object Definition Language (ODL)***—ODMG uses the OMG IDL as its data
definition language. ODL is a "clean" superset of IDL in the sense that it defines
elements that are not in IDL, such as collection classes and referential relationships. The ODL lets you describe metadata independently of the programming
language. The ODL is processed through a precompiler, which generates stubs
that get linked to the ODBMS and the client language (C++, Java, or Smalltalk).
The ODL provides interface and data definition portability across languages and
ODBMS vendor platforms.

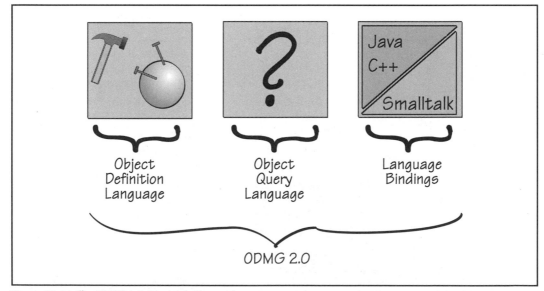

Figure 24-4. The ODMG 2.0 Components.

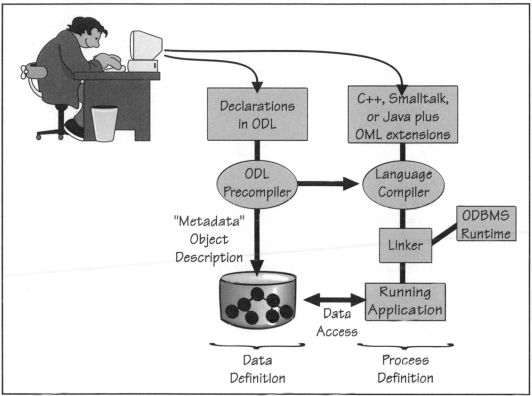

Figure 24-5. The ODMG 2.0 Development Process.

- *Object Query Language (OQL)*—ODMG defines an SQL-like declarative language for querying and updating database objects. It supports the most commonly used SQL SELECT structures, including joins; it does not support SQL INSERT, UPDATE, or DELETE (it uses C++, Java, or Smalltalk extensions for this). ODMG purposely did not use the SQL3 semantics for defining or manipulating objects because of "limitations in its data model and because of its historical baggage." OQL provides high-level primitives to query different collections of objects—including *sets*, which means unordered collections with no duplicates; *bags*, which means unordered collections with duplicates; and *lists*, which are ordered collections. OQL also supports structures in queries—a very powerful construct.Note that OQL is also part of the CORBA *Query Service*. In addition, ODMG 2.0's collections are identical to both the CORBA *Collection Service* and to the new Java 2 *Collection Classes*.

- *C++, Smalltalk, and Java language bindings*—ODMG defines how to write portable C++, Java, or Smalltalk code that manipulates persistent objects. The standard defines *Object Manipulation Language (OML)* extensions. The OML includes language extensions for OQL, iterations for navigating through containers, and transaction support. The ODMG people do not believe exclusively in a "universal" Data Manipulation Language (a la SQL). Instead, they propose "a unified object model for sharing data across programming languages, as well as a common query language." According to ODI's Tom Atwood, "The OML should respect the syntax of the base language into which it is being inserted. This enables programmers to feel they are writing in a single integrated programming language that supports persistence." In theory, it should be possible to read and write the same ODBMS from Smalltalk, Java, and C++, as long as the programmer stays within the common subset of supported data types.

Figure 24-5 shows the steps involved in using an ODMG-compliant ODBMS. The process is very similar to the CORBA IDL, except that the stub bindings are for an ODBMS and the OO language application that manipulates persistent objects. Your C++, Java, or Smalltalk applications can directly manipulate data that is either *persistent* or *transient*. The ODBMS updates the persistent data on transaction boundaries. Generally, every object that is reachable from a persistent object is also made persistent. This is called persistence by *reachability*. ODMG also lets you name any object or collection. You can then retrieve a named object, operate on it, or navigate to other objects by following a relationship link. You do all this from within your familiar language environment.

The Future of Database: Object or Relational?

Soapbox

Object Mania has taken over the industry. Proponents of object orientation are heralding object databases and ODBMSs as a cure for the purported weakness of relational technology. Poppycock...Applying object orientation directly and indiscriminately at the database level reintroduces problems that took the relational approach two decades to get rid of.

> — Fabian Pascal, Author
> Understanding Relational Databases
> (Wiley, 1994)

Among users, few doubts remain that ODBMS will ultimately be the successor to RDBMS...In the imagery of the poet William Blake, the young god of revolution Orc has begun to age into the icy tyrant Urizen—keeper of the law and standards.

> — Thomas Atwood, Chairman
> Object Design

We can have our cake and eat it, too! The point is to marry the two technologies instead of throwing mud at each other...It would be a great shame to walk away from the experience gained from more than 20 years of solid relational research and development.

— Chris Date

Date and Pascal both acknowledge that current SQL database implementations have weaknesses; however, they both feel the relational model per se can handle the problems that ODBMSs solve. The power of ODBMS can be approximated in the relational world using nested relations, domains (or user-defined encapsulated data types), and a more powerful set-oriented language than SQL. These features can do the job without chasing after object pointers or manipulating low-level, language-specific record structures. We don't have to mitigate the associative powers of relational theory. Developers won't have to resort to manual methods to maximize and reoptimize application performance—setting the clock back. Date believes that a domain and an object type are the same; the solution is for relational vendors to extend their systems to include "proper domain support."

Stonebraker notes that pure ODBMSs still lack functionality in the areas of complex search, query optimizers, and server scalability. Furthermore, many ODBMSs run their products in the same address space as user programs. This means that there is no protection barrier between a client application and the ODBMS. In addition, ODBMSs have a minuscule market penetration when compared to relational DBMSs. Finally, object/relational and SQL data-type extenders are filling some of the object needs within an RDBMS context.

The ODBMS people feel that there's more to this than just extending the relational model. In fact, they've rejected the SQL3 extensions as being insufficient. ODBMS diehards believe that they're creating better plumbing for a world where information systems will be *totally* object-based. Relational databases are an impedance mismatch in a plumbing consisting of ORBs, object services, OO languages, and the Object Web. A pure ODBMS is exactly what's needed. Why keep extending a legacy foundation like SQL with BLOBs, stored procedures, and user-defined types? They prefer to stick to objects all the way and sometimes borrow a few things from SQL (such as queries). They're also recreating the multiuser robust foundation that includes locking, transactions, recovery, and tools.

Of course, we're talking about David and Goliath here. SQL databases are the current kings of the hill. They have the big development budgets and wide commercial acceptance that ranges from MIS shops to the low end of the client/server market. Will the king of the hill be deposed because ODBMSs do objects better? It remains to be seen. But as Esther Dyson puts it, "Using tables to store objects is like driving your car home and then disassembling it to put it in the garage. It can be assembled again in the morning, but one eventually asks whether this is the most efficient way to park a car." ❑

Chapter 25

Distributed Objects: Meet the Players

Since Sun's EJB initiative incorporates CORBA and the OMG's new component standard is surely going to look very similar to EJB, the contest, for all practical purposes, comes down to two competing approaches: COM+ and EJB.

— *Paul Harmon, Editor*
Component Development Strategies
(September, 1998)

As you know by now, the Object Web is the next big thing. Distributed objects built as components are the foundation for 3-tier client/server computing and also for the next-generation Web (more on this in Part 8). In this chapter, we will look at the market for distributed objects and introduce you to the players. Of course, it's not going to be a clear-cut story. The complication is that distributed objects are becoming a pervasive technology. For example, they're used to create the next-generation operating systems, DBMSs, data warehouses, ERP applications, TP Monitors, groupware, and now the Web itself. So, are distributed objects a technology or a market? The answer is both. The plan for this chapter is to give you the best numbers (or guesses) various analysts have come up with. Then we

will go over the major trends. Next, we will introduce the players in a very general way. Finally, we conclude with a Soapbox.

THE DISTRIBUTED OBJECT AND COMPONENT MARKET

In general, there are four types of vendors in the distributing object space: 1) the middleware vendors who provide the ORBs and OTMs for running distributed objects (or components), 2) the component providers, 3) solution providers—including turn-key application providers, component assemblers, and system integrators, and 4) tool vendors who provide the tools to help you create and assemble these components. In addition, the object market can be segmented based on the two competing component models—CORBA/EJB and COM+. They each create their own market for tools, components, OTMs, and integration services. However, this can get even more complicated—many vendors may end up straddling the fence and supporting both component models.

Today, the object market is synonymous with ORBs, ODBMSs, client-side components, and tools. The huge market for server-side middleware platforms, tools, and components is just starting to materialize. As we go to press, COM+—as incarnated in NT 5.0—is still in beta. The competing camp completed its EJB 1.0 specification in March 1998. Consequently, EJB-compliant application servers and OTMs are just starting to ship. The tools will come next. The components and applications will follow.

What the Analysts Say

Corporations must nail down the choice between two competing platform technology initiatives: Microsoft's COM/DCOM and a federated JavaBeans/CORBA. This is a matter of some urgency in 1988, as many companies risk backing into unintended investments across multiple component platforms.

> — *Forrester Research*
> *(January, 1988)*

In this section, we summarize the more pertinent analyst research on distributed objects and components. Some of the findings are based on fearless forecasts. Others are based on detailed survey and market research. Here's a sampling of these findings by topic:

■ ***CORBA versus COM penetration.*** Forrester Research conducts a yearly survey of IT executives responsible for object-oriented development strategies in Fortune 1000 firms. In its 1998 study, Forrester reports that, "while 44% of respondents lack an object strategy today, only 4% expect to be without one in two years. As they project these outcomes to the year 2000, the number of uncommitted who expect to choose CORBA well outnumbers the contingent leaning toward Microsoft's COM/DCOM."[1] Figure 25-1 shows the results of the Forrester survey.

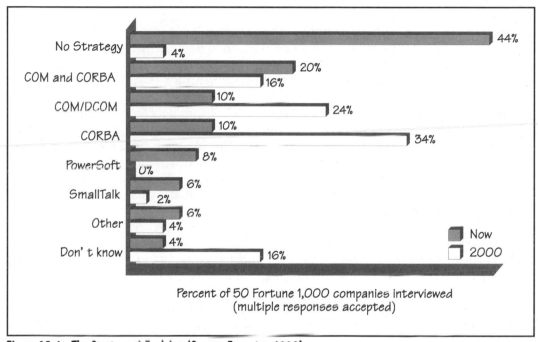

Figure 25-1. The Component Decision (Source: Forrester, 1998).

- **COM+ market size.** According to the Giga Group, the market for third-party components based on COM was $410 million in 1997. Giga projects this market will grow by 65% yearly to reach $3 billion by 2001. (Source: *http://www.microsoft.com/com/comintro.asp*). According to Microsoft, COM is in use on 150 million client machines world-wide.

- **OTM and application server market sizes.** According to a new study by Gartner/Dataquest's Larry Perlstein, the size of the application server market for components was $360 million in 1997 increasing to $1.7 billion in 2002.[2]

---

[1] Source: Forrester Research, *Software Strategies: The Component Decision* (January, 1998).

[2] Source: Dataquest, *Not Just Change, Structural Change* (October, 1998).

■ *Tool market size.* According to Dataquest's Perlstein, "development tools product licenses was $5.4 billion in 1997 and is forecast to grow to $10.3 billion in 2002, a 16% CAGR." Note that most development tools now follow an object/component paradigm. Most tools will support Java/CORBA, COM+, or both. Most server-side tools will accept input from or interoperate with Rational Rose. UML is now a CORBA standard, so it will help articulate the object tools industry.

■ *Server-side component market acceptance.* According to GartnerGroup's Roy Schulte, "OTMs will make components increasingly practical for the server side of mission-critical applications during the next four years...By 2002, components will be used in nearly all new applications (0.8 probability)."[3]

■ *ORB market size.* According to the Standish Group's Karen Boucher, "in 1997, CORBA ORBs generated $116 million in software licenses. We project this number to grow to $727 million by 2001—this shows a 58% CAGR." Ed Acly from IDC projects a more conservative 34% growth rate for the same period.[4] Note that these numbers only include ORBs as pipes. They do not include ORBs in OTMs—meaning the server-side middleware platforms. They also don't include services and tools.

■ *ODBMS market size.* According to IDC's Joshua Duhl, ODBMS license revenues were at $210 million in 1997 and are growing at 69.5% per year. IDC forecasts that the market will reach $1.2 billion by 2001.

These numbers should give you some idea on how the leading analysts are forecasting the distributed object and component markets. As you can see, the market is growing fast.

Distributed Objects Trends

A component revolution is reaching the enterprise. Microsoft, IBM, Oracle, Sun, BEA, Netscape, Iona, and Inprise are all rebuilding and repositioning their middleware technologies to attack the emerging component-based enterprise application market. This is a battle for the architectural control over the next generation of enterprise systems, a multibillion dollar market that has been dominated for the last 20 years by IBM's CICS and IMS, and other mainframe OLTP middleware.

> — *Yafim Natis*
> *GartnerGroup*
> *(April, 1998)*

---

[3] Source: GartnerGroup, *Enterprise Components* (July, 1997).
[4] Source: IDC, Middleware: *1998 Worldwide Markets and Trends* (May, 1998).

As we go to press, all the pieces are finally lining up for distributed objects and server-side components to take off in a big way. Here's a snapshot of the major movements that we're seeing in this industry:

- **ORBs—as pipes—are ubiquitous and practically free.** Microsoft includes the DCOM ORB in Windows 98 and NT. On the CORBA side, Netscape embeds the Visigenic CORBA/Java ORB with all its browsers. JavaSoft also includes a free CORBA/Java ORB with Java 2. If your browser does not support Java 2, you can freely download it from Sun as a Java plug-in. CORBA ORBs are also being bundled in various operating systems—including Linux, Solaris, HP-UX, Silicon Graphics, NetWare 5.X, OS/400, and OS/370. In addition, there are a ton of "Open Source" free CORBA ORBs—including *ORBit, OmniORB2, MICO* (for *Mico Is COrba*), *OAK, ORBacus, COOL ORB, ILU, TAO, Electra, JacORB*, and *CORBAPlus* (check *http://linas.org/linux/corba.html* for the latest information on CORBA Open Source). Note that many of the free CORBA ORBs also come with support.

- **Distributed objects are toolable.** In the Microsoft world, tools always come first. Consequently, COM objects were always highly toolable. The news is that the CORBA/EJB world also has first-class tools. Over 30 vendors provide visual builders for JavaBeans. In addition, there are now first-class tools for creating server-side CORBA objects—including Borland/Inprise's *JBuilder* and *Delphi*, Sybase's *PowerJ*, Rational's *Rose*, Symantec's *Visual Café*, IBM's *VisualAge for Java*, Netscape/AOL's *Visual JavaScript*, and Oracle's *JDeveloper*. There are also excellent high-end CORBA tools from *Dynasty, Forte*, and *Select*. By the time you read this, most of the CORBA tool vendors will also support EJB. So the good news is that support for world-class tools is no longer a Microsoft monopoly. There are now great CORBA/Java tools for the programming masses. It's no longer a closed club for the high-priests of computer science.

- **OTMs are becoming the scalable server-side of the ORB.** Typically, a raw ORB pipe—like DCOM or CORBA 2.0—will max out with a few hundred server-side objects. In contrast, OTMs allow you to manage millions of objects in a very scalable and robust manner. As we explained in previous chapters, OTMs also simplify the server-side programming model and let you create toolable objects. Gartner anticipates that most ORB vendors will also become OTM vendors by the year 2001, or they will be out of business (0.8 probability).

- **CORBA distributed objects are now mission-critical.** In 1998, the CORBA world saw the introduction of the first mission-critical OTM—BEA's M3. With M3, you can use CORBA for the first time to support the stringent demands of OLTP applications. Previously, you could only run these types of applications on TP Monitors—like BEA's *Tuxedo*, Transarc's *Encina*, and IBM's *CICS*. The COM+ world must wait for Windows 2000—or later—to get this type of scale. Gartner believes Windows 2000 will ship by the year 2000 and won't be usable

until 2001. With 35 million lines of code, will it scale? We don't know. At best, it may be 2002 before you get CORBA's M3-like scale on a COM+ platform.

■ ***Distributed objects are server-side components.*** In the past, distributed objects—of the CORBA 2.0 and DCOM variety—were raw server-side components that simply exposed distributed interfaces. The new server-side component standards—COM+, EJB, and CORBA 3.0 Beans—have elevated the component boundary to include automatic transaction support, state management, declarative security, and toolability.

■ ***Distributed objects are everywhere.*** Components are already ubiquitous on the client in the form of ActiveX and JavaBeans. They are now moving on to the server—in the form of COM+ and CORBA/EJB—where they will be used for everything from stored procedures to ERP suites. Distributed objects and components are also the foundation technology for the next-generation Web application servers and e-commerce platforms.

To summarize, components are expanding beyond their traditional role on the client—they are moving on to the server with a vengeance. Their next target is the Internet (more on this in Part 8). In the mid-90s, Sun coined the slogan "distributed objects everywhere." Today, this is becoming a reality.

MEET THE PLAYERS

There are two groups of players in the distributed object space: Microsoft and the CORBA/EJB camp. We already covered the Microsoft product line in the COM+ chapter. So there are no surprises left. On the CORBA side, ORBs—as pipes—have become commodity items. The three main suppliers of CORBA ORBs are: Inprise/Visigenic, Iona, and ICL (with DAIS). There's also a ton of free CORBA ORB providers. However, the center of the action in the CORBA camp is now on the server—that is, with OTMs. Some of the biggest names in the computer business are now competing to provide the next-generation OTMs and application servers based on CORBA/EJB technology. The larger players seem to be on a feeding frenzy, acquiring smaller players as fast as they can find them. So the CORBA/EJB OTM market is hot and also very competitive—the stakes are sky-high.

The Microsoft Camp

The Microsoft camp consists of a single player—Microsoft. In the past, Microsoft partnered with Software AG to port the COM pipe—not including MTS—to other platforms. Several years later, Software AG finally delivered its *EntireX* port on Unix and other platforms. Clearly, this effort took too long. In early 1998, Microsoft decided to bring the COM porting effort in-house. So it appears to be goodbye, Software AG.

In a strange twist, Microsoft decided—in mid-1998—to extend an olive branch to the CORBA vendors; it licensed the COM source to both Iona and Visual Edge to help them with their COM/CORBA bridges. Microsoft even threw in a simplified COM transaction protocol—called *TIP*—to allow transaction contexts to propagate across the COM/CORBA bridges. So, what's going on here? It appears Microsoft decided that these CORBA/COM bridges were the most expedient way to extend MTS's reach across platforms. Of course, MTS on NT still remains at the center of the Microsoft universe. However, MTS can now coordinate transactions with beans that run on other platforms. In general, this is a good thing. It will help customers create more integrated distributed object systems, which is a good thing. But make sure to read the next Soapbox before you declare victory.

The CORBA/EJB Camp

CORBA ORBs are available today for virtually every computer platform. In addition, there are many all-Java CORBA ORBs—including JavaSoft's *JavaIDL*, Visigenic/Inprise's *VisiBroker for Java*, and Iona's *OrbixWeb*—that run on any platform that supports a Java VM. The main CORBA ORB vendors are Visigenic/Inprise (*VisiBroker*), Iona (*Orbix*), and ICL (*DAIS*). You can also get CORBA ORBs from OTM vendors such as BEA (*ObjectBroker*) and IBM (*SOM*). CORBA ORBs are also getting bundled with a variety of operating systems and popular software packages.

As we explained earlier, a number of CORBA/EJB-based OTMs are currently either shipping or under construction. They come from four groups of vendors (see Figure 25-2):

1. ***TP Monitor vendors moving to ORB-based middleware***. The two examples from this camp are IBM's *Component Broker* and BEA System's *M3*. The IBM *Component Broker* builds on the SOM CORBA ORB and borrows elements from the Encina and CICS TP Monitors. The result is a framework for managed components that lets you mix in over nine CORBA services. In addition, Component Broker provides *instance managers* that let you automatically manage an object's state and map it to data in an RDBMS. Component Broker is still in beta. However, some elements of it have shipped with IBM's *Web-Sphere*—a Web application server. BEA's *M3*—née *Iceberg*—shipped in July 1998. It's a mission-critical OTM that combines the field-proven *Tuxedo* TP Monitor engine with the BEA *ObjectBroker* CORBA ORB; it also provides a higher-level framework for managing EJB-like C++ components—BEA calls them C++ Enterprise Beans. M3 will run Java EJBs in its next release, which is now in beta.

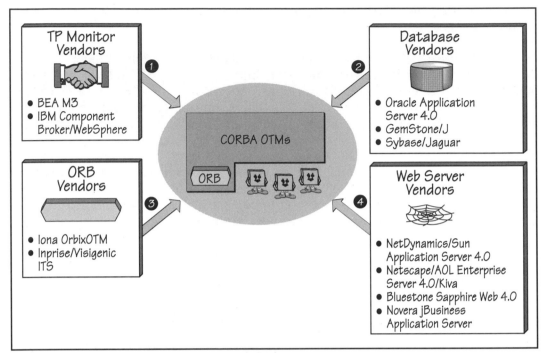

Figure 25-2. CORBA Object Transaction Monitors (OTMs).

2. **DBMS vendors moving from 2-tier to 3-tier.** The textbook example of a CORBA OTM from this camp is Oracle's *Application Server 4.0,* which shipped in late 1998; it provides an application server for CORBA/EJB components on top of the Borland/Visigenic ORB (and an Oracle server-side IIOP ORB). *GemStone/J* is a CORBA application server that uses an ODBMS-enabled Java VM to manage an EJB's state. Persistence just shipped its *PowerTier for EJB* application server; it uses an object-to-relational mapper to map an EJB's state into almost any RDBMS. Finally, Sybase is getting ready to ship a CORBA/EJB version of its *Jaguar CTS* application server.

3. **ORB vendors moving up from pipes to TP-based application servers.** The two examples of CORBA OTMs from this camp are Iona's *OrbixOTM* and Inprise/Visigenic's forthcoming CORBA/EJB-based *Application Server.*

4. **Web server vendors moving to TP-based application servers.** BEA/WebLogic's *Tengah* was the first application server to support the full EJB specification; it shipped in the summer of 1998. The other CORBA/Java Web application servers are: Sun/NetDynamics' *Application Server 4.0,* Sun/AOL/Netscape/Kiva's *Application Server,* Bluestone's *Sapphire Web,* SilverStream's *SilverStream Application Server 2.0,* Novera's *jBusiness Application Server,* and HAHT's *HAHTsite 4.0.* IBM/Lotus' forthcoming IIOP-based *Domino 5.0* may also be included in this category. Most of these application

servers intend to support EJB in their next release. Note that the products without slashes in their company's names have yet to be acquired.

All these OTMs support the CORBA object model with extensions. And, they all strive to provide robust object application platforms that can scale to support millions of server-side objects. The more advanced OTMs build on the CORBA *Object Transaction Service (OTS)* and its Java implementation called *JTS*. Some even provide transaction connectivity to existing products such as *CICS*, *IMS*, *Tuxedo*, and *MQSeries*. In addition, they can coordinate CORBA transactions with RDBMSs (and other resource managers) via the X/Open DTP standard and its XA interfaces. This means that an advanced OTM can coordinate—as part of a single transaction—CORBA objects, TP Monitor applications, and resource managers such as RDBMSs, ODBMSs, and Message Queues.

Some of these products already support the EJB component model. Most will support EJB by the time you read this. So this means that the same component model will run on a very wide variety of server-side platforms with different qualities of service. In addition, tools from IBM, Sybase, Symantec, Borland/Inprise, Dynasty, and Rational will also support EJB. So you'll be able to develop your components using a variety of tools and then run them on a variety of OTMs and application servers. It doesn't get better. Of course, we're assuming that it will all work as advertised, which takes a big leap in faith (make sure to read the next Soapbox).

Finally, the CORBA/EJB OTM landscape is going through a tremendous amount of consolidation. In late 1997, Netscape acquired Kiva and was then acquired by AOL/Sun—an even bigger fish. Inprise—formerly Borland—acquired Visigenics. In 1998, BEA acquired both WebLogic and Top End. During that same year Sun acquired NetDynamics and now Netscape's server technology. The big fish are paying top-dollar for all these acquisitions, so these application servers and OTMs must be worth a lot to them.

The Great Component War

Soapbox

Even as Microsoft is relentlessly integrating more and more features into its software, the Internet is just as relentlessly breaking the delivery of code down into Java-style objects. Component software will do in Microsoft, just as surely as smaller hardware—the PC— brought down DEC and IBM.

— George Gilder, Internet Prophet
(December, 1998)

The CORBA/Java and Microsoft camps share a common vision of "distributed objects everywhere." Unfortunately, the two sides are promoting different component standards. If you read the last few chapters, you may agree that a convergence is not in the cards. Some interoperability is possible, but ultimately developers will have to choose between COM+ and CORBA/EJB. The war over the component standard is really about who controls the next-generation client/server platform and the Object Web.

In the past, there was a green line—as in Bosnia—between the CORBA and COM camps that coincided with the client/server boundary. The previous consensus was that you ran COM on the client and CORBA on the server. COM clients could invoke CORBA servers via COM/CORBA bridges. Today, there's no longer a green line. COM+ is going after the server using NT as its Trojan Horse. And the CORBA/Java camp is going after the client with down-loadable JavaBeans and CORBA-enabled browsers. Of course, the CORBA/EJB backers—like IBM, Novell, Oracle, Netscape, Sybase, and BEA—already control the server. So they are defending their traditional turf against Microsoft's encroachment.

If you read the last few chapters, it may appear that choosing CORBA/EJB is a no-brainer. You get a component model today that can run on any platform including NT. So why wait for COM+ to mature in 2001? Why limit yourself to a single platform when you can have them all today with CORBA/EJB? Of course, tools are no longer an issue—the CORBA/Java camp has the backing of the best visual-tool vendors. In some cases, even price is no longer an issue— you can get the best client/server bargain in town using CORBA/EJB on Linux along with Apache and a Netscape browser. So how is Microsoft reacting to this challenge?

Microsoft's counter to all this is that NT is going to win the server. COM+ is to NT what CICS was to MVS—it's a built-in OTM. You already pay for MTS when you purchase NT Server, so why would you ever need anything else? In addition, Microsoft likes to claim that CORBA/EJB is a specification—which can be implemented in different ways. In contrast, COM+ is a real product—an implementation. So the word Microsoft is putting out on the street is that EJBs will never port across containers because each vendor will extend the specification to gain a competitive advantage.

In addition, Microsoft likes to point out that CORBA ORBs still don't interoperate—especially when you add transactions and security. EJB is built on CORBA, which only exacerbates its portability problems. Microsoft also points out that the OMG and JavaSoft have a fragile alliance, which could break down any time—for example, JavaSoft may not support some of the required multi-language features in the CORBA version of EJB. So you may end up with two different component models—CORBA Beans and EJB.

As a result, Microsoft claims that EJB will lock you into a single vendor. Consequently, this negates its main advantage—portability. If you're going to get locked into a single vendor, then why not make that vendor Microsoft—a safe bet? By going the COM+ route you will be able to seamlessly integrate with all the Microsoft products on NT—another great advantage.

Of course, there's definitely some grain of truth in these Microsoft arguments or else they wouldn't be effective. However, most of these arguments are meant to create FUD—which stands for *Fear, Uncertainty, and Doubt*—an old IBM marketing tactic. Microsoft's main point is that multivendor and multiplatform doesn't work. The counter-point is that turning your IT strategy over to a single vendor (on a single platform) is not too smart. You lose control, spend more money, and increase your risks. Now, let's deal—in more detail—with the points Microsoft makes.

As we explained earlier, the CORBA/EJB OTM landscape is experiencing a tremendous amount of consolidation. By the time the dust settles, Gartner anticipates that four or five key players will dominate the CORBA/EJB landscape. Their top candidates are: IBM, Oracle, BEA, Sun/AOL/Netscape, Iona, and Inprise. Of course, further acquisitions are also possible. As a result, Microsoft will be facing some very Internet-savvy competitors with long track records in the enterprise middleware market. These competitors will make sure their CORBA/EJBs interoperate. If they don't, they will hear from their customers. In addition, they will make sure the CORBA/Java coalition stays on course. If it doesn't, they will lose their sizeable investments. These vendors will also make sure the tools interoperate with their beans and they will fix—in their products—whatever interoperability problems still remain.

The bottom line is that CORBA/EJB is now controlled by a very small "gang" of fast-moving software giants—think of them as OMG's steering committee. These software companies will provide the reference middleware products—think of them as the anchor products—for CORBA/EJB. The smaller software companies will provide niche products that either complement or interoperate with the anchors. The rest of us will have a stable component infrastructure on which to build and deploy our components. If this scenario works out, we will eventually have a mass market for CORBA/EJB components. Because of the delays in shipping NT 2000, the CORBA/EJB coalition has a 2-year head start to establish this market.

If CORBA/EJB fails to interoperate across multivendor containers, then the worse that can happen is that you are locked into a single vendor's container—for example, IBM's *WebSphere*, Oracle's *Application Server*, or BEA's *M3/WebLogic*—that runs on multiple OSs. Or, you may have to do some minor tweaking to get your components to run within each vendor's container. If CORBA/EJB works as advertised, then you have a choice of vendor containers as well as OS platforms. With the Microsoft approach, you lock yourself from the very start into a single-OS, single-vendor solution.

Before we step down from this Soapbox, we'd like to address one of the technical points Microsoft is making about EJB's reliance on CORBA. It's important to note that JavaSoft does not have an alternative to CORBA on which to build the EJB infrastructure. CORBA IIOP—with its built-in transaction and security propagation mechanisms—is the best heterogeneous middleware pipe in the industry. And, it works. It's well-known that one of the key CORBA vendors has a defective IIOP product that causes an interoperation problem. But, they're fixing it. We could easily point to the rest of the IIOP products that successfully interoperate. The OMG—via the Open Group—is creating a CORBA compatibility test suite that should prevent such problems from occurring in the future. If a product doesn't pass the test suite, then it can't call itself CORBA. Hopefully, JavaSoft will do the same for EJB.

CORBA also solves another of EJB's shortcomings—the lack of multi-language support. Eventually, we hope everyone will move to Java. In the meantime, we have CORBA Beans to hold the fort. Microsoft's COM+ forces everyone to use a single platform—Windows. JavaSoft's EJB forces everyone to use a single language—Java. Unfortunately for both Microsoft and JavaSoft, the Internet and the enterprise are still very heterogeneous—both in terms of languages and computer platforms. CORBA supplements Java very well by providing interoperation in a heterogeneous world. Without its CORBA foundation, EJB would have a much harder time competing against COM+. The EJB architects understand this well, which is why they provided a CORBA mapping with the first release of EJB. The CORBA architects also understand this, which is why they made CORBA Beans a multi-language superset of EJB. So today it's CORBA/EJB against COM+.

This Soapbox concludes Part 7. As you can see, distributed objects have become mainstream. In practice, this means that objects are not just of interest to academicians, OO programmers, and methodologists. Some very large players now have very large stakes in distributed objects as the new middleware and component foundation. In addition, everyone in the computer industry has to deal with Microsoft. The component models have become the most visible part of the war between Microsoft and its largest competitors. Yes, "we are condemned to live in interesting times." ❑

Part 8

Client/Server

and the Internet

An Introduction to Part 8

The Web may be sparking the last gold rush of the millennium.

— Tom Halfhill

For the Internet specifically, we were quite aware that something very significant was going on, but I don't think anyone expected it to become so popular so quickly.

— Bill Gates

Do you Martians still have gold rush fever? This part is about client/server with the World Wide Web, which promises to be "the last gold rush of the millennium." If nothing else, it's the last gold rush we cover in this book. In case you haven't noticed yet, the Web is the hottest topic on our planet. There's no place to hide from it. It's everywhere—in the movies, on the billboards, in the tabloids, and on late-night TV. It's our planet's last, great technological frontier and our brightest hope for the future. It's a virtual world—free of hunger and disease. It's the fastest way to make a billion dollars.

So what does this all have to do with client/server? Everything. For starters, the Web is the world's largest client/server application. It's the first application that brings client/server to the masses. And it is the first client/server application of intergalactic proportions. Yes, you will be able to interact with Michael Jackson's avatar. What's an avatar? It's your electronic persona on the Web. The Web is creating *habitats* inhabited by avatars. Welcome to the brave new *virtual worlds*.

But the Web is more than fun, games, and avatars; it's also big business. The patrons of the Web—meaning those who are paying for the free goodies—are the stock market and our largest corporations. These patrons look at the Web and see intranets and electronic commerce. *Intranets* allow them to rebuild their private corporate networks using Web client/server technology. *Electronic commerce* is about turning the Web into the world's largest shopping mall; it's a new frontier for commerce of all sorts. The stock market looks at the Web and sees one thing—money. So it keeps the stocks going up. It's a self-feeding frenzy.

So when will this bubble burst? It won't, if the Web fulfills its promises. Right now, all we're getting are "cool" Web pages and lots of hype and noise. To become the world's largest shopping mall, the Web needs to build on a solid client/server foundation. We will make the case that the Web infrastructure needs to blend with distributed objects to fulfill its intergalactic destiny. Objects let us create more realistic virtual worlds called *shippable places*. Places are containers of components that can be shipped from the server to the clients to create a new generation of mobile, Web-based client/server applications.

An Introduction to Part 8

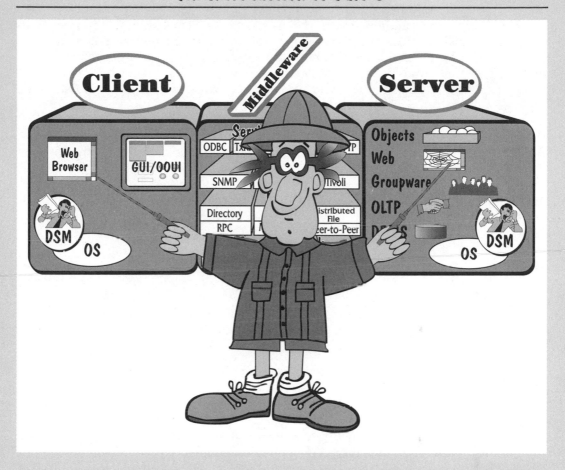

Part 8 covers the Web from a client/server perspective. We start with the hyper-linked Web—the world's largest file server. We look at the client/server technology behind the Web pages and the hypertext links. Then we go over the extensions that are being used to make the Web more interactive—that is, to make it behave more like a 3-tier client/server system. These extensions include HTML forms and tables on the client side and the CGI protocol on the server side. CGI is being used to attach any type of server to the Web, but it's just a Band-Aid; it does not provide a long-term solution. We look at some of the more popular CGI replacements—NSAPI, ISAPI, Servlets, WAI, ASPs, JSPs, and Dynamic HTML. These acronyms will become perfectly clear by the time you finish reading this part.

The heart of Part 8 is the *Object Web*. We believe that the Web is moving to objects in a big way. Java is just the first step in this progression. The Object Web chapters cover Java as a mobile code system in depth. We describe how HTML pages can be used as containers of JavaBeans that can be directly manipulated in-place. The containers can also be used to ship places (or virtual worlds) from the servers to the clients. Next, we explain how ORBs—such as CORBA, DCOM, and RMI—allow

An Introduction to Part 8

these beans to communicate over the Internet. We also explain how new W3C standards—such as XML and DOM—are transforming Web pages and their contents into first-class objects. In a nutshell, the Object Web is a 3-tier client/server architecture that combines the best of two worlds—the component-based distributed objects we covered in Part 7 and the Web. It provides a robust foundation for the next-generation of Web-based electronic commerce systems.

We conclude Part 8 with a market and product overview. It's your guide to the gold. Before you start on this trek, it's important to understand that life on the Internet is measured in dog years, not human years. This means that Internet technology moves very rapidly. The Internet seems to transform itself every two years. We're currently entering the Java phase of the Internet moving to the Object Web. So wear your seat belts tight because this will be a fast-moving ride with lots of bumps. We hope you'll have fun.

Chapter 26

Web Client/Server: The Hypertext Era

---

*T*he Web will drive the client/server reengineering revolution. This will be an industrial revolution whose scope makes the PC industry of the early 1980s seem like a small family business by comparison.

— Charles Ferguson

Over the last seven years, the Internet grew from a private sandbox for university researchers to a client/server application of intergalactic proportions. The "killer application" that brought the Internet into the public consciousness is the *World Wide Web*—the Web, for short. It's the world's most widely deployed client/server application. The Web consists of over a million online servers supporting 97 million users (growing at the rate of 2 million users per month). In late 1998, the Alexa Web crawler was able to catalog 20 million Web content areas—or home pages (see *http://www.alexa.com*). According to Alexa, the top 100,000 servers account for 90% of all Web traffic; 50% of this traffic goes to the top 900 Web sites. The total size of the Web is doubling every eight months, with 1.5 million new pages added daily. Instead of dealing with thousands of individual servers, users experience the Net as a huge virtual disk crammed with every form of information—all available at the click of a mouse. The world becomes one big *hyperlinked* document.

THE EVOLUTION OF THE WEB

For the most part, what we call Internet, e-commerce, extranet, and intranet applications are nothing more than new types of OLTP systems.

— *Richard Finkelstein, President*
Performance Computing
(December, 1998)

In late 1993, the Mosaic graphical Web browser introduced the first true client/server application environment on top of the Internet. This was the birth of Web-style client/server. This new model of client/server consists of thin, portable, "universal" clients that talk to superfat servers. The Web was built on open, cross-platform, intergalactic client/server standards. To be *intergalactic*, the technology must run across multiple networks, OSs, languages, and computer platforms.

Figure 26-1 shows the progression of Web technologies. The Web first started out as a giant—and very trendy—unidirectional medium for publishing and broadcasting static electronic documents. The predominant HTTP client/server middleware was primarily designed to serve documents. Consequently, the Web became a giant URL-based file server. It was a huge 2-tier client/server application that did certain things very well—such as electronic publishing, personal bulletin boards, document sharing, and discussion groups.

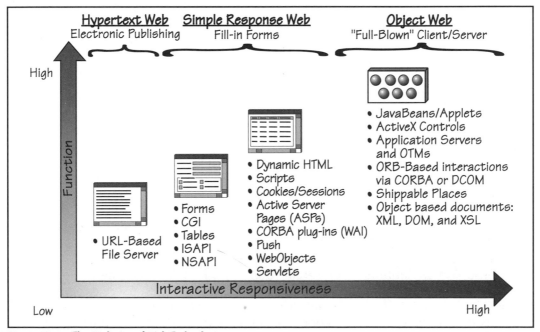

Figure 26-1. The Evolution of Web Technologies.

In late 1995, the Web evolved into a more interactive medium with the introduction of 3-tier client/server, CGI-style. The *Common Gateway Interface (CGI)* protocol lets Web servers route the content of your HTML forms to back-end server applications. CGI is now used to access every known server environment. However—as we explain later in this chapter—HTTP with CGI is a slow, cumbersome, and stateless protocol; it is not suitable for writing modern client/server applications. CGI is not a good match for object-oriented Java clients. In a sense, the Web server lives in the middle ages, while some of its clients are postmodern. Web server vendors have gone through contortions to work around the limitations of HTTP/CGI. Their solutions are usually in the form of proprietary server frameworks and APIs. Examples of such frameworks include Netscape's *NSAPI*, Microsoft's *ISAPI* and *ASP,* NeXT/Apple's *WebObjects*, JavaSoft's *Servlets*, and *Fast CGI*.

To get around HTTP's statelessness, some of these frameworks may require that clients pass *cookies* (meaning server data held on the client) to identify their state. Others, like Microsoft's *Active Server Pages (ASPs)*, extend cookies with session objects on the servers to represent their clients. These extensions are mostly proprietary and have serious flaws.

In addition, CGI is slow; it launches a new process to service each incoming client request. To get around this limitation, many of the vendor extensions provide memory-resident workarounds—such as in-process DLLs, server plug-ins, Java servlets, and even ORB-based objects. In general, the server side will do almost anything it can to keep the services in memory across invocations. As a result, they introduce another slew of non-standard—and sometimes platform-specific—extensions.

Recently, Microsoft's ASP, Netscape's WAI, and JavaSoft's *Java Server Pages (JSP)* introduced server-side scripts within HTML pages that can invoke objects. You invoke these pages via HTTP using the infamous submit button. The server page typically executes a server-side script that knows how to instantiate and invoke objects. In addition, the client side now has enough intelligence to interact with the user without going to the server every time. You do this using either applets or scripts—for example, with *Dynamic HTML,* every element in an HTML page is a scriptable object.

The main problem with these approaches is that they require HTTP and the Web server to mediate between objects running on the client and objects running on the server. There is no way for a client object to directly invoke a server object. The HTTP form you submit is still the basic unit of client/server interaction. This clumsy workaround is not suitable for full-blown client/server applications that require highly interactive conversations between components. It also does not scale well.

In 1996, the Web finally discovered objects in the form of Java applets and Java-enabled Web browsers. In June 1997, Netscape shipped *Communicator* with an embedded CORBA/Java ORB. On the server side, Netscape shipped both a

CORBA/C++ and CORBA/Java ORB with every copy of the *Enterprise Server*. In December 1998, there were over a dozen Web application servers that support CORBA/IIOP and server-side Java. In the Microsoft parallel universe, IIS and MTS support COM+ objects. 1998 was also a good year for the W3C Web consortium; it recommended two important object-based Web standards—*XML 1.0* and *DOM Level 1*. In addition, *HTML 4.0* now provides a consistent way to embed components within Web pages. As you can see, the Object Web is starting to take shape.

Is there anything left unsaid about the Internet? Could the computer press, tabloids, local dailies, and national magazines have missed anything? We think so, which is why we're about to embark on a four-chapter tour that covers the Web from a client/server perspective.

This chapter starts the tour by covering the hypertext era of the Web. It introduces the foundation client/server technologies on which the Web is built—including HTML, HTTP, and Web browsers. Chapter 27, "Web Client/Server: The Interactive Era," introduces the interactive Web technologies—including forms, CGI, Dynamic HTML, Servlets, and ASPs. Chapter 28, "Web Client/Server: The Distributed Object Era," covers the Object Web; it's about the marriage between distributed component technologies and the Web. Finally, Chapter 29, "Web Client/Server: Meet the Players," concludes the tour with an overview of the Web client/server market.

CLIENT/SERVER, WEB STYLE

The Internet is the world's largest experiment in anarchy.

— *Eric Schmidt, CEO*
Novell

The Web builds client/server order on top of what Novell's Eric Schmidt calls "the world's largest experiment in anarchy." In its enormously popular first incarnation, the Web is simply a global hypertext system. *Hypertext* is a software mechanism that links documents to other related documents on the same machine or across networks. The linked document can itself contain links to other documents, and this can go on forever. A link can also point to other external resources such as image files, sound clips, or executable programs. The Web could eventually link every document produced on this planet.

The beauty of the Web is in its simplicity. The Web client/server model achieves its intergalactic reach by using highly portable protocols on top of TCP/IP. Portability, platform-independence, and content-independence are emphasized at every level— they're the mantras of the Web architects. So what makes hundreds of thousands of distributed servers behave like a single application? This magic is created by introducing four new technologies on top of the existing Internet infrastructure: graphical

Web browsers, the HTTP RPC, HTML-tagged documents, and the URL global naming convention. We explain what all this means in the next sections.

The Web Protocols: How They Play Together

In many ways, the Web is the mother of all data warehouses.

> — *Richard Hackathorn*
> *(October, 1997)*

The first-generation Web applications were mostly read-only and static, which means that they were simple. By dealing with read-only documents, Web designers were able to avoid the thorny issues of distributed multiserver application design—such as security, transactions, and synchronized updates. A Web server simply returns documents when clients ask for them by name.

Because it is so simple and useful, the Web was able to mushroom. Although most of us don't think of the Web in this way, it has become the most visible demonstration of the power of intergalactic client/server computing today. The first-generation Web applications are built on the following technologies and protocols:

■ **The Internet is the global backbone**. The Web achieves its global reach by using the Internet as its backbone. The Internet is the world's largest public network. It consists of over 100,000 interconnected networks that span across 70 countries. These networks extend deep inside corporations as well as people's homes. The number of networks is expected to double each year. The beauty of the Web is that its application protocols are Internet-ready—they run on top of TCP/IP. In less than five years, the Web has become the graphical user interface of the Internet. Today, most people that access the Internet use the Web as their front-end. The Web subsumes most of the existing Internet application protocols—including the *Simple Mail Transfer Protocol (SMTP)*, *Telnet*, *File Transfer Protocol (FTP)*, *Network News Transfer Protocol (NNTP)*, and *Gopher*.

■ **The Internet is the private backbone**. The Web model of client/server is also the foundation for private corporate *intranets*. In many cases, intranets are becoming the new enterprise networks.

■ **URLs are used to globally name and access all Web resources**. The *Unified Resource Locator (URL)* protocol provides a consistent intergalactic naming scheme to identify all Web resources—including documents, images, sound clips, and programs. URLs fully describe where a resource lives and how to get to it. URLs support the newer Web protocols—such as HTTP—as well as older Internet protocols such as FTP, Gopher, WAIS, and News.

- **_HTTP is used to retrieve URL-named resources_**. The Web provides an RPC-like protocol—called the _Hypertext Transfer Protocol (HTTP)_—for accessing resources that live in URL space. HTTP is a stateless RPC that 1) establishes a client/server connection, 2) transmits and receives parameters including a returned file, and 3) breaks the client/server connection. HTTP clients and servers use the Internet's MIME data representations to describe (and negotiate) the contents of messages.

- **_HTML is used to embed hyperlinks and to describe the logical structure of Web documents._** The _Hypertext Markup Language (HTML)_ is the lingua franca of Web documents. The Web is a gigantic collection of HTML documents linked together to form the world's largest file server. A Web document—or _page_—is a plain ASCII text file with embedded HTML commands. The HTML commands—also known as _tags_—are used to describe the structure of a document, provide font and graphics information, and define hyperlinks to other Web pages and Internet resources. HTML documents live in HTTP servers—also known as _Web servers_. The beauty of HTML is that it is simple and portable. In addition, server programs can easily generate HTML-tagged text files in response to client requests.

- **_Web browsers are universal clients_**. A Web browser is a minimalist client that interprets information it receives from a server, and displays it graphically to a user. The client is simply there to interpret the server's commands and render the contents of an HTML page to a user. The browser executes the HTML commands to properly display text and images on a specific GUI platform; it also navigates from one page to another using the embedded hypertext links. HTTP servers produce platform-independent content that clients can then request. A server does not know a PC client from a Mac client—all Web clients are created equal in the eyes of their Web servers. Browsers are there to take care of all the platform-specific details.

So this is the Web client/server story in a nutshell. The devil is in the details, which we cover next. If you don't care about the details then just read the next section and move on. You'll at least know the names of the key protocols and client/server pieces. This alone should make you quite dangerous.

Your First Web Client/Server Interaction

The model we see emerging is a universal client, able to navigate the local network or the Internet and to go to any application at any point in time.

— Marc Andreessen

Figure 26-2 shows how the Web client and server pieces play together:

1. **You select a target URL.** A Web client/server interaction starts when you specify a target URL from within your Web browser. You do this either by clicking on a hypertext link, picking a URL off a list, or by explicitly typing in the URL (this is typically your last resort).

2. **Browser sends an HTTP request to server.** The browser takes the URL you specified, embeds it inside an HTTP request, and then sends it to the target server.

3. **Server comes to life and processes the request.** On the receiving side, the HTTP server spins in a loop, waiting for requests to arrive on its well-known port (the default port is 80 for HTTP). The incoming request causes a socket connection to be established between the client and the server. The server receives the client's message, finds the requested HTML file, ships it back to the client along with some status information, and then closes the connection.

4. **Browser interprets the HTML commands and displays the page contents.** The browser displays a status indicator while waiting to receive the requested URL. When it finally receives the URL, the browser looks at the type. If it's an HTML file, it interprets the tags and displays the contents in its window. Otherwise, it invokes a plug-in application that's associated with a particular resource type and hands it the returned file. The helper displays the contents in its own window or in an agreed-upon area within the browser's window. For example, most browsers don't know what to do with a video file, so they hand it to a video player—the helper—which then plays the movie in a separate window.

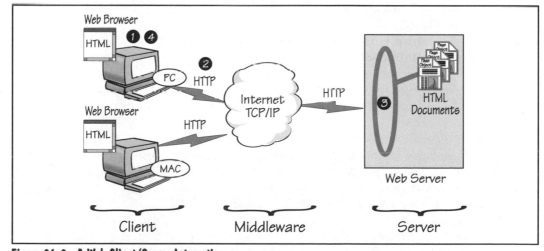

Figure 26-2. A Web Client/Server Interaction.

This primitive client/server interaction accounts for over 90% of today's Web transactions. In the next chapter, we go over the CGI protocols and browser forms and explain how they extend the basic model. But before moving to the next chapter, we must first cover the details of the URL, HTTP, and HTML protocols. You must understand how these protocols work before you tackle CGI, forms, and Web objects.

SO WHAT EXACTLY IS A URL?

Information wants to be free—free of platform, output destination, formatting instructions, proprietary file formats, and physical location.

— Art Fuller

A *URL* provides a general-purpose naming scheme for specifying Internet resources using a string of printable ASCII characters. The printable characters enable you to send URLs in mail messages, print them on your business card, or display them on billboards. A typical URL consists of four parts (see Figure 26-3):

■ ***The protocol scheme*** tells the Web browser which Internet protocol to use when accessing a resource on a server. In addition to HTTP, URL supports all major Internet protocols—including Gopher, FTP, News, Mailto, and WAIS. *HTTP* is the Web's native protocol; it points to Web pages and server programs. *Gopher* is a precursor to the Web; it displays information on servers as a hierarchy of menus. *FTP* is the oldest Internet protocol for retrieving files. *News* is a discussion-group protocol that lets you specify a newsgroup or article. *Mailto* lets you send mail to a designated e-mail address. *WAIS* lets you specify the domain name of a target database to be searched as well as a list of search criteria. Of course, the protocol scheme that you choose will directly affect the interpretation of path information within the URL.

■ ***The server name*** is usually an Internet-host domain name that identifies the site on which the server is running. Note that you can also use numeric IP addresses and include an optional user name or password. However, numeric IP addresses are hard to remember. Also, putting a password in a URL is not a secure way to access a resource.

■ ***The port number*** identifies a program that runs on a particular server. You explicitly specify a port number after a server name using a colon (:) as the separator. If you do not specify a port number, the browser will direct the call to a well-known port. For example, HTTP resources are on port 80, Gopher uses port 70, FTP files are on port 21, and so on.

■ ***The path to a target resource*** starts with the forward slash (/) after the host and port number. The interpretation of this field varies depending on the resource you access. The most common representation consists of a set of directory paths that lead to a particular file.

As you will see in the next chapter, you can also use URLs to specify specialized server functions. For example, you can specify a search by appending to the end of a URL a question mark followed by a query string. You can only do this with servers that support this function; currently, this means HTTP, Gopher, and WAIS.

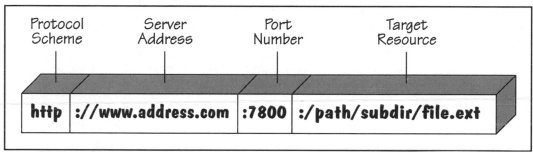

Figure 26-3. The URL Structure.

THE WORLD'S SHORTEST HTML TUTORIAL

*P*ersonal Web pages are the '90s equivalent of home video, except that you don't have to visit someone else's house to fall asleep—you can do so in the comfort of your own home.

— *Ray Valdes*

HTML is an elaborate protocol, and we can't possibly cover it completely in the next few pages. Instead, we will hit on some of the highlights of HTML to give you a feeling for what it does. We also cover some of HTML's more advanced features in the next two chapters. These include forms for data entry, tables, dynamic HTML, and the new OBJECT tag.

If you get a sinking feeling in the next few sections that HTML—to quote from Yogi Berra—is "like deja vu all over again," you're probably right. The technology is definitely late-70s retro. HTML is rooted in the ISO SGML standard, which has been around for quite some time. However, bear in mind that retro is a small price to pay to achieve universality. HTML was designed to be fully portable across every conceivable GUI, operating system, CPU architecture, and file system. You can print and view HTML documents on machines that have barebones displays; it's truly a minimalist protocol.

How To Mark Up Text in HTML

An HTML document is an ordinary text file whose appearance is controlled by magical tags that are embedded within the text. Whenever you want to highlight some text—for example, an italicized word or a link to another page—you place either a single tag or a pair of tags around it. *Tags* are non-case-sensitive commands surrounded by angle brackets. A tag pair consists of a command, then some text, and finally the inverse command—represented as the command with a slash in front of it. The first tag in the command pair applies the command while the second tag turns it off. This means that the command only applies to the text enclosed within tag pairs.

Figure 26-4 shows some of the more common HTML text markup tags and the output they produce on a typical Web browser. Note that we use the <BR> tag to force line breaks.

```
<H3>HTML Visual Markup Examples</H3>       HTML Visual Markup Examples

<B>Bold</B>                    <BR>        Bold
<I>Italic</I>                  <BR>        Italic
<U>Underlined</U>              <BR>        Underlined
<TT>Fixed-width</TT>           <BR>        Fixed-width
<STRIKE>Strike out</STRIKE>                Strike out
```

Figure 26-4. HTML: Visual Markup Examples.

The General Structure of an HTML Document

Right now, people just want to connect easily. Once that's accomplished, they'll see that content is what it's about.

— *Christine Comaford*

Figure 26-5 shows the structure of an HTML document. The structure primarily is there to help a browser understand how a document is organized. A well-structured HTML document begins with <HTML> and ends with </HTML>. In addition, every HTML document should have a header section at the top, bracketed by <HEAD> and </HEAD> tags, and a body section bracketed by <BODY> and </BODY> tags. The header contains information that describes the contents of the body, its title, URL, and whether the document is searchable. A Web browser displays the text marked off by <TITLE> and </TITLE> tags in the title bar of its window. This is also the text that describes the document in a user's hotlist (or *bookmark* list).

The <BODY> and </BODY> tags contain the portion of the document that you see displayed within the client area of a Web browser's window. This is where you view an HTML document's contents. HTML lets you further structure a document's body using a hierarchy of headings that can be nested up to six levels deep. You specify the headings in descending order using the tags <H1> through <H6>. When a Web browser encounters a heading tag, it terminates the current paragraph and displays the heading text using a left-aligned visually distinct font. Figure 26-6 shows a screen capture of a particular Web browser's rendition of the HTML in Figure 26-5.

```
<HTML>
  <HEAD>
    <TITLE>My Document</TITLE>
  </HEAD>
  <BODY>
    <H1>This is an H1 Heading</H1>
    <H2>This is an H2 Heading</H2>
    <H3>This is an H3 Heading</H3>
    <H4>This is an H4 Heading</H4>
    <H5>This is an H5 Heading</H5>
    <H6>This is an H6 Heading</H6>
  </BODY>
</HTML>
```

Figure 26-5. HTML for My Document.

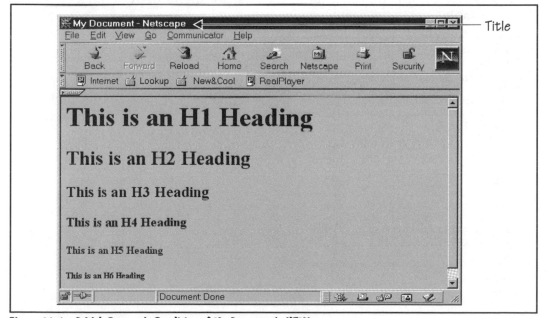

Figure 26-6. A Web Browser's Rendition of My Document's HTML.

How To Structure the Flow of Text in an HTML Document

You typically break the text within a document into paragraphs that you place under various headings. You use the <P> tag to indicate a new paragraph; <HR> to draw a horizontal line; and <PRE> to introduce a block of preformatted style text—such as a program listing or a table. Note that <P> and <HR> are singleton tags—they do not require </P> or </HR> pairs.

Figure 26-7 is an example of an HTML document that uses the <P>, <HR>, and <PRE> tags. Figure 26-8 shows how this document is rendered by a typical Web browser. Notice that all the text between <P> tags is reflowed by the Web browser to fit the window size, fonts, and general shape of the document. Most Web browsers use one line height's worth of white space to set each paragraph apart from the next. The horizontal rule is drawn with some amount of white space above and below it. You should use horizontal rules whenever possible. They help create a uniform appearance and are also much more efficient to transfer over the network than a bitmap or a line's worth of underscore characters.

Finally, note that the text marked off by <PRE> and </PRE> is not very attractive, but it respects the layout we specified in the HTML. We basically told the browser that the <PRE> text is off limits. Consequently, the browser can't reflow the text, make it pretty, or use an attractive proportional font to display it. Instead, it displays the text "as is," using a nonproportional font that maintains the white space, tabs, carriage returns, and strings of ASCII spaces. <PRE> tags are the only way to present tabular information on browsers that do not support HTML 3.2's table tags. We cover table tags in the next chapter.

```
<HTML>
<HEAD>
<TITLE>The Essential Distributed Objects Survival Guide</title>
<BODY>
<H1>Zog is Back</H1>
<P>Zog, the lovable, green, perpetually perplexed Martian, has returned,
this time to explore the world of distributed objects.  This new Survival
Guide by Bob Orfali, Dan Harkey, and Jeri Edwards provides a
comprehensive coverage of the big three object/component technologies:
CORBA, COM/OLE, and OpenDoc.  Here's a snapshot of the Table of Contents:

<PRE>
Part 1. Client/Server With Distributed Objects            42 pages
Part 2. CORBA: The Distributed Object Bus                 174 pages
Part 3. Frameworks for Business Objects and Components    122 pages
Part 4. OpenDoc Under the Hood                             86 pages
Part 5. OLE/COM Under the Hood                            108 pages
Part 6. Component Nirvana: Client/Server With Parts        72 pages
<HR>
</PRE>
</BODY>
</HTML>
```

Figure 26-7. HTML for "The Essential Distributed Objects."

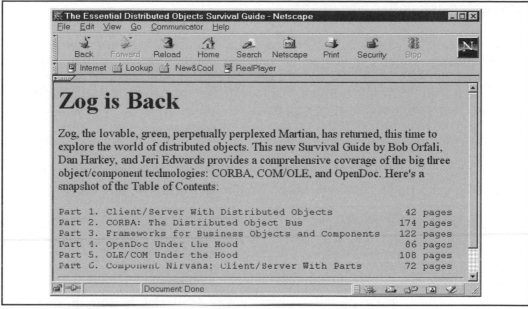

Figure 26-8. A Web Browser's Rendition of "The Essential Distributed Objects" HTML.

HTML Lists

HTML lets you specify a variety of list format types in your text—including unordered lists using the <UL> tag; ordered lists using the <OL> tag; definition lists using the <DL> tag; directory lists using the <DIR> tag; and menus using the <MENU> tag. You can also nest lists within lists. Most Web browsers display unordered lists using a hierarchy of differently shaped and colored bullets. Figure 26-9 shows the HTML for ordered and unordered lists and how they are displayed by a typical Web browser.

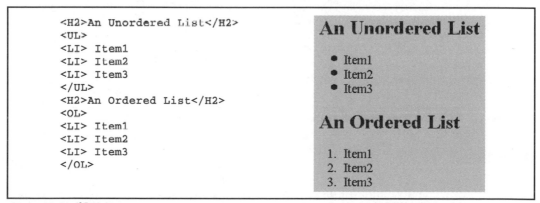

Figure 26-9. HTML Lists.

Embedding Images in Documents

Today, you can't have a "cool" Web page without embedding one or more in-line images within your text. In fact, some say that cool graphics is probably the main reason why the Web exploded out of nowhere in 1994 and eclipsed its text-only predecessors—for example, Gophers. You embed an image in your documents with the <IMG> tag. This tag includes an attribute—called SRC—that contains the URL of the external picture file or the name of a local file. For example, <IMG SRC= "zog.gif">. Attributes only appear in the first tag of tag-pair; they provide additional directives to the browser. Most Web browsers support the 8-bit GIF format that displays images in 256 colors. A few support the "true color" 24-bit JPEG format. JPEG can display up to 16 million colors, if your hardware supports it.

Second-generation Web browsers—such as Netscape Navigator—use background threads to retrieve graphics. This lets you scroll through the text of a document or jump to another document before the browser fully downloads the graphic elements. The browser must merge the images into the displayed text using the layout rules that you specify with the optional ALIGN parameter. The default alignment is BOTTOM, which means that the image aligns with the bottom of the text. Figure 26-10 shows the "cool" version of the Distributed Objects page. All we did is insert <IMG SRC= "zog.gif" ALIGN=RIGHT> after the <P> tag. This tells the Web browser to flow the text around Zog's image, on the left-hand side.

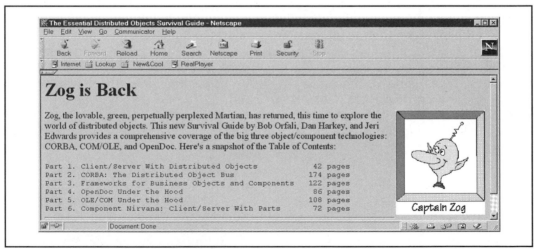

Figure 26-10. A Web Browser's Rendition of Zog's Picture.

Hyperlinks

In our opinion, what really made the Web explode out of nowhere are hyperlinks. They provide the hooks that let you transparently navigate from server to server by simply clicking the mouse. You hyperlink your document to other documents or to other locations in the same document using a pair of *anchor* tags that look like this: <A HREF="Target URL"> This is a hot link</A>.

Between the <A> and </A> tags, you insert the text that the user can click on to jump to the linked page. Most browsers highlight and underline the text to make it stand out. In addition to text, you can also place an <IMG> tag to hotspot an in-line graphic. The "very cool" hotspots—or visual links—combine text with graphics.

The HREF—or reference attribute—specifies the target document. You can specify the URL in one of three ways: 1) *Absolute*, which means it contains the full hostname and filename of the target document; 2) *Relative*, which means that the target's hostname and starting directory for the path are the same as the document containing the anchor tag; and 3) *Local*, which means that the file resides on the client machine, not on the Web server.

HTML links also let you point to other anchors within an HTML file. This means that you can hotlink not just to a file, but also to a specific point within a file. You do this by adding the name of the anchor after the filename separated by a pound sign "#". For example, the tag <A HREF="HTTP://host/target.html#mymarker> will transfer you to mymarker. Of course, you must first create mymarker in the target file by using an anchor tag with a NAME attribute—for example, <A NAME=mymarker">Text</A>. Figure 26-11 shows such a link.

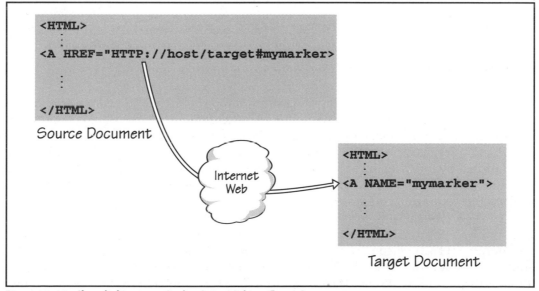

Figure 26-11. Hyperlinking to an Anchor Point Within a Target Document.

Cascading Style Sheets

Cascading style sheets (CSS) give you almost total control of the layout and formatting of HTML documents. As the term "cascading" implies, more than one style sheet can be used on the same document. For example, you can embed a style sheet in each document or as an attribute for a particular element. Or, you can use a common style sheet for standardizing the look-and-feel of all the documents on your Web site. You do this by referencing the standard style sheet from within each document. The styling rules within the document override the external style sheets. So "cascading" means resolving the sequence of styling rules that apply to a document or elements of a document. The rules are resolved from the inside out.

You can use style sheets to specify the font, size, color, and location of any HTML element on a Web page. In addition, you can specify the exact x, y, and z position of each HTML element. The z positioning lets you create overlapping layers within a document. Figure 26-12 shows an example of an embedded style sheet that redefines the H2 tag.

```
<HEAD>                                   Pablo Picasso's H2 Header
 <STYLE type="text/css">
  H2 { margin-left: 9%;
       font-family: "Comic Sans MS";
       font-style: italic;
       color: blue; font-size:24 pt}
 </STYLE>
</HEAD>
<BODY>
 <H2>Pablo Picasso's H2 Header</H2>
</BODY>
```

Figure 26-12. An Embedded Style Sheet.

You can also use style sheets to layer a document. A *layer* is like a piece of cellophane that you place on top of a Web page's real estate. You can write any HTML element inside a layer. A layer can be opaque or transparent. You can create animations by moving layers around a page using JavaScript. You can place multiple layers over, above, and beside each other. You can even nest layers within layers.

The W3C *CSS1* and *CSS2* recommendations define the *z-dimension* syntax for positioning HTML within cascading style sheets. As we go to press, there are still some differences between the Netscape and Microsoft browser implementations of style sheets and dynamic HTML. Some of the controversy centers around Netscape's LAYER tag; it provides a convenient way to create layers from within

HTML without using a style sheet. Unfortunately, the LAYER tag is not part of the CSS 1 standard. Netscape will continue to support both the LAYER tag and the CSS z-ordering in its browsers. You can check the latest differences in CSS implementations by pointing to *http://webreview.com/wr/pub/guides/style/style.html*.

HTML Versions

There are several different versions of HTML, and you should know a little bit about them. HTML is defined by a working group of the *Internet Engineering Task Force (IETF)* and by an industry consortium called *W3C*.[1] The first version—called *HTML 1.0*—was introduced in 1992. It was followed by *HTML 2.0*, which offers minor improvements over HTML 1.0. In January 1997, W3C issued its recommendation for *HTML 3.2*; it standardizes widely-deployed features such as tables, applets, text-flow around images, frames, and subscripts.

In December 1997, W3C issued its recommendation for *HTML 4.0*—the current version of the standard. It includes important new features—such as support for cascading style sheets (CSS), internationalization, and the new OBJECT tag. It also improves on existing features. For example, you can now add rich HTML on a button, create read-only controls, group together form controls, and provide keyboard shortcuts on controls. There are also minor improvements for tables and frames. We cover forms and tables in the next chapter. As we go to press, the two popular browsers mostly comply with HTML 3.2. We hope to get full HTML 4.0 compliance in Versions 5 of Netscape *Navigator* and Microsoft *Internet Explorer*.

HTTP

The *Hypertext Transfer Protocol (HTTP)* has been in use on the Web since 1990. The first version of HTTP—referred to as HTTP/0.9—was a simple protocol for raw data transfer across the Internet. HTTP/1.0—now the Internet's most ubiquitous protocol—introduced self-describing messages using a variant of the Internet Mail's MIME encoding. In late 1998, the W3C is getting ready to introduce HTTP/1.1— an upward-compatible version of HTTP, which took over four years to hatch. HTTP/1.1 introduces more efficient ways of using TCP, which makes it a better network citizen. Further on the horizon is HTTP-NG, which promises to evolve HTTP into a more ORB-like protocol. This chapter covers the HTTP basics. We cover some of the more advanced features in the next chapter.

---

[1] The *World Wide Web Consortium (W3C)* is headed by Tim Berners-Lee. It includes over 280 Web vendor companies. The purpose of the W3C is to accelerate the production of Web standards.

So What Exactly Is HTTP?

As we mentioned earlier, HTTP is the Web's RPC on top of TCP/IP. It is used to access and retrieve URL-named resources. The HTTP RPC is stateless. The client establishes a connection to the remote server, then issues a request. The server then processes the request, returns a response, and closes the connection. A client—typically a Web browser—requests a hypertext page, then issues a sequence of separate requests to retrieve any images referenced in the document. Once the client has retrieved the images, the user will typically click on a hypertext link and move to another document. Note that HTTP/1.0 sets up a new connection for each request. The client must wait for a response before sending out a new request. In contrast, HTTP/1.1 leaves the TCP connection open between consecutive downloads—a feature it calls *persistent connections* (see the next Briefing box).

HTTP 1.1: A More Efficient HTTP

Briefing

HTTP 1.0 was designed to deal with simple Web documents. It creates a separate TCP connection to download each URL. The client establishes a connection before sending a request; the server closes it after sending the response. This works well when you're dealing with a single file. However, most Web pages that you access today contain a ton of small images. So what happens if you download a modest document that contains six embedded images? It will cost you seven connections—one to retrieve the document, and six to retrieve the individual images. Clearly, this is not a very efficient protocol for today's image-crazy Web; each connection increases the load on HTTP servers and causes congestion on the Internet.

HTTP 1.1 introduces three new mechanisms to make the downloading of documents more efficient:

- **Persistent connections** allow multiple request/response interactions to take place before the connection is closed. Either the client or server can close the TCP connection for whatever reason. Persistent connections are the default in HTTP 1.1. However, clients and servers cannot assume that a connection is maintained for previous HTTP versions.

- **Pipelining** lets a client send multiple requests without waiting for a response. A server must send its responses to these requests in the same order it receives them. Of course, clients must also be prepared to resend their requests if the server closes the connection before sending all the corresponding responses.

■ *Cache validation commands* can reduce the overall network traffic and make the protocol more efficient. HTTP 1.1 provides a number of commands that help a client (or proxy server) maintain a consistent local cache of documents. For example, a proxy can determine the expiration date of a cached document and avoid making a request to the home server.

In summary, it looks like HTTP 1.1 will help reduce some of the Web's traffic load. Check out *http://www.w3.org/Protocols/HTTP/Performance* for an excellent study that documents HTTP 1.1's performance improvements. ❏

HTTP Data Representations

An important feature of HTTP is that it lets you pass self-describing data—using MIME—over the RPC. The protocol allows Web browsers to inform their server about the data representations they can understand. Clients and servers must negotiate their data representations every time a connection is made. This adds to the connection overhead. Why don't the servers keep track of their clients' attributes? Remember, HTTP servers are stateless, which means they have no recollection of previous client connections. HTTP's statelessness works well in simple client/server environments. It allows servers to function very efficiently. They pick up connections, fulfill the request, and quickly drop the connection. Note, however, that state is needed in all but the simplest client/server interactions. So this can be a problem with the current HTTP protocol. There are some clumsy workarounds to this problem that we cover in the next chapters.

So What Does an HTTP Request Look Like?

An HTTP client/server interaction consists of a single request/reply interchange. Figure 26-13 shows the syntax of an HTTP request. It consists of a *request line*, one or more optional *request header fields*, and an optional *entity body*. The lines are separated by a carriage-return/line-feed (crlf). The entity body is preceded by a blank line. Here are the details:

■ *The request line* consists of three text fields, separated by white spaces. The first field specifies the method—or command—to be applied to a server resource. The two most common methods are: GET, which asks the server to send a copy of the resource to the client and POST, which lets a client send a form's data to the specified URL. The second field specifies the name of the target resource; it's the URL stripped of the protocol and server domain name. The third field identifies the protocol version used by the client; for example, HTTP/1.0.

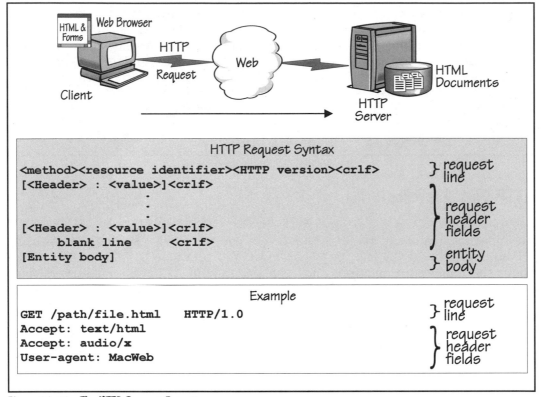

Figure 26-13. The HTTP Request Format.

■ *The request header fields* pass additional information about the request, and about the client itself, to the server. The fields act like RPC parameters. Each header field consists of a name, followed by a colon (:) and the field value. The order in which you transmit the header fields is not significant.

■ *The entity body* is sometimes used by clients to pass bulk information to the server.

The bottom of Figure 26-13 is an example of an archetypical HTTP GET request—the client requests a file called file.html from the server. The first *accept* header field tells the server that the client knows how to handle text HTML files. The second accept field tells the server that the client can also handle all audio formats. Finally, the *user-agent* field lets the server know that the client is a MacWeb browser. So, the various accepts tell the server which data types the client can handle; user-agent gives the implementation name of the client.

So What Does an HTTP Response Look Like?

Figure 26-14 shows the syntax of an HTTP response. It consists of a *response header line*, one or more optional *response header fields*, and an optional *entity body*. The lines are separated by a carriage-return/line-feed (crlf). The entity body must be preceded by a blank line. Here are the details:

- *The response header line* returns the HTTP version, the status of the response, and an explanation of the returned status.

- *The response header fields* return information that describe the server's attributes and the returned HTML document to the client. Each header field consists of a name, followed by a colon (:) and the field value. The order in which the server returns the header fields is not significant.

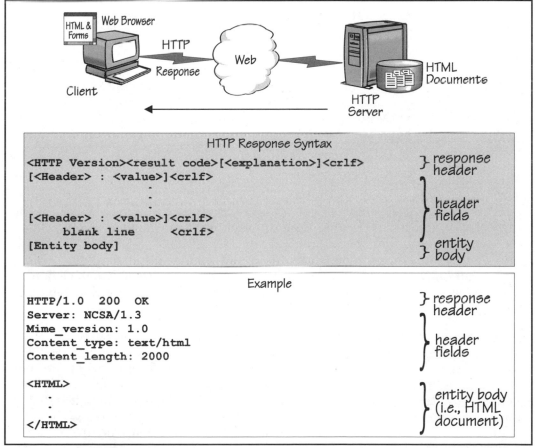

Figure 26-14. The HTTP Response Format.

■ *The entity body* typically contains an HTML document that a client has requested.

The bottom of Figure 26-14 shows a typical server's response to a GET request. The result code 200 indicates that the request was successful. The *server* header field identifies the server as an NCSA/1.3. The *MIME-version* field indicates that the server supports MIME 1.0 (see the next Details box). The *content-type* field describes the returned object as being a text/HTML document. The *content-length* field indicates the document length. This is followed by the HTML document itself—the object of the request. The server sends the requested data and then drops the TCP/IP connection. That's all there is to it. Congratulations, you're now a bona fide HTTP expert.

HTTP and MIME

Details

HTTP borrows heavily from the *Internet Mail* (RFC 822) and the *Multipurpose Internet Mail Extensions (MIME)* (RFC 1521), which provides extensible mechanisms for transmitting multimedia e-mail. In case you're interested, RFC 822 deals mostly with the headers that appear at the top of your Internet Mail, but it does very little to describe the contents of the mail.

MIME supplements RFC 822 by specifying additional headers that describe what sorts of data the message body contains. For example, MIME defines several headers that are used to specify if a message consists of multiple parts and how these parts are separated. A MIME header uses the familiar format "content-type: type/subtype" as in "content-type: text/html." MIME currently supports seven data types—including plain text; audio; video; still images; message, which can point to an external message; multipart messages in which each part can have a different type; and application-specific data. Each MIME type can also have subtypes.

It should come as no surprise that HTTP's content-type headers are very MIME-like. However, HTTP itself is not a MIME-compliant application. HTTP's RPC-like performance requirements differ substantially from those of Internet Mail. Consequently, the HTTP architects chose not to obey the constraints imposed by RFC 822 and MIME for mail transport. But even though HTTP is not MIME-compliant, you can include a *MIME-version* header field in a message to indicate what version of the MIME protocol was used to construct the message content-type headers. ❑

CONCLUSION

In five minutes on the Web, you suddenly understand Marshall McLuhan. The Web implodes the planet and places it on your desk. In a stroke, all the world is hypertext.

— Art Fuller

This concludes our whirlwind tour of the technologies that form the basis for the hypertext era of Web client/server. This relatively simple technology lets us very effectively construct interconnected webs of hyperlinked nodes that mirror the distributed nature of information. The webs are malleable, easy to restructure, and can support arbitrary complex collections of documents. In the next chapter, we explore how the Web technology—HTTP and HTML—is being extended to provide better client/server interactivity.

Chapter 27

Web Client/Server: The Interactive Era

Web technology isn't just a way to publish electronic documents. It's also a way to build networked applications that work within and across corporate boundaries. But it isn't yet a client/server developer's dream.

— Jon Udell

In the hypertext era, the only way you could interact with Web servers was by clicking on hyperlinks to surf between documents. However, in the middle of 1995, the Web began to go through a subtle transformation from a passive browsing medium into a more interactive client/server medium. So what triggered this transformation? The usual suspects, of course—market demand and the availability of new technology. We will spare you the "Web market explosion" story because you can get it from the headline stories in your local paper, the six o'clock news, or from your neighborhood barber. Instead, we will focus on the less-glamorous extensions of HTML and HTTP that have made all this possible, including everything you ever wanted to know about forms, tables, CGI, and "cgi-bin" programs. With CGI and forms, the Web became a 3-tier client/server medium. As you will see, it's a poor man's version of 3-tier client/server.

3-TIER CLIENT/SERVER, WEB-STYLE

The Navigator is more like a 3270 terminal than anything else, with a big difference being that you don't just use that terminal to access one mainframe.

— Marc Andreessen

Web browsers are the modern renditions of yesterday's 3270 terminals. Yes, we're going back into the future. But where are the 3270 "fill-out forms?" These are the computer equivalents of the paper forms that we fill out every day of our life. It so happens that the Web is teeming with forms. They're everywhere. In case you haven't seen one, a *Web form* is an HTML page with one or more data entry fields and a mandatory "Submit" button. You click on the Submit button to send the form's data contents to a Web server. This causes the browser to collect all the inputs from the form, stuff them inside an HTTP message, and then invoke either an HTTP GET or POST method on the server side.

On the receiving end, the typical Web server does not know what to do with a form—it's not your ordinary HTML document. So the server simply turns around and invokes the program or resource named in the URL and tells it to take care of the request. The server passes the method request and its parameters to the back-end program using a protocol called the *Common Gateway Interface (CGI)*.

The back-end program executes the request and returns the results in HTML format to the Web server using the CGI protocol. The Web server treats the results like a normal document that it returns to the client. So, in a sense, the Web server acts as a conduit between the Web client and a back-end program that does the actual work. Figure 27-1 shows the elements of this new 3-tier client/server architecture, Web-style. The first tier is a Web browser that supports interactive forms; the second tier is a vanilla HTTP server augmented with CGI programs; and the third tier consists of traditional back-end servers.

In addition to forms, Netscape pioneered the concept of HTML *tables*. These are HTML 3.2 (and above) tags that let a browser display multirow information—for example, query results received from a server—inside a graphic table widget.

CGI technology makes it possible for Internet clients to update databases on back-end servers. In fact, updates and inserts are at the heart of online electronic commerce. However, most online service providers will not let you update their databases without some form of iron-clad client/server security. This is where protocols like *Secure Sockets Layer (SSL)*, *Secure HTTP (S-HTTP)*, *IPSec*, and Internet firewalls come into the picture (see Part 3). They provide one more technology that's needed to turn the Internet into the world's largest shopping mall.

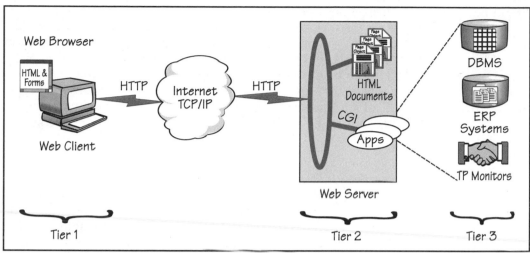

Figure 27-1. 3-Tier Client/Server, Web-Style.

Software vendors are using the technology we just described to connect Web browsers to virtually every form of client/server system—including SQL databases, TP Monitors, groupware servers, ERP systems, MOM queues, e-mail backbones, and ORBs. All these systems now provide gateways that accept CGI requests. And they all provide *transformers* to dynamically map their data into HTML so that it can be displayed within Web browsers. In other words, the servers build a Web page "on-the-fly" to display their results.

As they said in the movie *Field of Dreams*, "If you build it they will come." In the case of the Web, they built the universal client and then the servers all came. Unfortunately, as you will soon discover, these servers live on the other side of a bottleneck called CGI.

HTML'S WEB-BASED FORMS

*T*hink about it—a browser, a Web server, a server-based application, and a database. With this handful of potent tools, organizations can deploy applications that anyone in the world can access.

> — **Richard Finkelstein, President**
> **Performance Computing**
> **(December, 1998)**

In January 1997, W3C published the HTML 3.2 specification, which includes *forms* that let you embed within your documents text-entry fields, radio boxes, selection lists, check boxes, and buttons. Forms are used to gather information for a CGI-based server application. You can use forms for surveys, data entry, placing and tracking orders, database queries, and every imaginable Web transaction.

Creating a form is a three-step process. First, you must create the HTML for the input form. Second, you must write the server CGI application that acts on the data from the input form. Finally, you must design the reply document a user sees after submitting the form; the HTML for the reply document is dynamically generated by the CGI program. A reply document can be very simple or quite elaborate. A simple reply may say, "We received your request; thank you very much." An elaborate reply may return thousands of table rows from an SQL database; you may have to generate an HTML table "on-the-fly" to display the results in a row-column format.

The Form Tag

A form begins with <FORM> and ends with </FORM>. By convention, you visually separate the FORM contents from the rest of an HTML document with a horizontal line (or HR tag). A document can contain one or more forms, but they can't be nested within each other.

The <FORM> tag has two mandatory attributes: METHOD and ACTION. The METHOD can be either an HTTP GET or POST; it specifies how the data entered in the various fields of the form is transmitted to the CGI server application. The ACTION attribute specifies the URL to which you send the form's contents; it must be the name of a server CGI program (or script) that can process the form's data. Here's an example of a FORM tag:

```
<FORM METHOD="POST" ACTION="HTTP://www.mylab.org/cgi-bin/sampleform">
```

So what is *cgi-bin*? It's the name of a special executable directory where CGI programs reside. This directory is usually under the direct control of a Webmaster—you don't want the average user tampering with programs on your server. The /cgi-bin/ directory in a URL indicates to a Web server that the incoming HTTP request is for a CGI program. In this example, the URL causes the server to invoke—via the CGI protocol—an external program called *sampleform*.

The Form Interface Elements

You can have anything inside a form except another form. HTML defines tags for creating interface elements that you can place anywhere within a form to interact with a user. Figure 27-2 is a screen shot of a form that uses most of these interface elements; Figure 27-3 shows the HTML tags we used to generate this form. HTML defines three types of interface elements: input fields, text areas, and selection fields. Let's go over the details of what they each do.

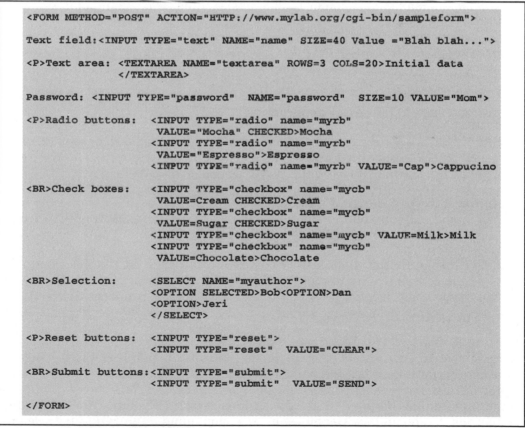

Figure 27-2. Sample Form: The Major Interface Elements.

```
<FORM METHOD="POST" ACTION="HTTP://www.mylab.org/cgi-bin/sampleform">

Text field:<INPUT TYPE="text" NAME="name" SIZE=40 Value ="Blah blah...">

<P>Text area: <TEXTAREA NAME="textarea" ROWS=3 COLS=20>Initial data
          </TEXTAREA>

Password: <INPUT TYPE="password"  NAME="password"  SIZE=10 VALUE="Mom">

<P>Radio buttons:    <INPUT TYPE="radio" name="myrb"
                  VALUE="Mocha" CHECKED>Mocha
                  <INPUT TYPE="radio" name="myrb"
                  VALUE="Espresso">Espresso
                  <INPUT TYPE="radio" name="myrb" VALUE="Cap">Cappucino

<BR>Check boxes:     <INPUT TYPE="checkbox" name="mycb"
                  VALUE=Cream CHECKED>Cream
                  <INPUT TYPE="checkbox" name="mycb"
                  VALUE=Sugar CHECKED>Sugar
                  <INPUT TYPE="checkbox" name="mycb" VALUE=Milk>Milk
                  <INPUT TYPE="checkbox" name="mycb"
                  VALUE=Chocolate>Chocolate

<BR>Selection:       <SELECT NAME="myauthor">
                  <OPTION SELECTED>Bob<OPTION>Dan
                  <OPTION>Jeri
                  </SELECT>

<P>Reset buttons:    <INPUT TYPE="reset">
                  <INPUT TYPE="reset"  VALUE="CLEAR">

<BR>Submit buttons:<INPUT TYPE="submit">
                  <INPUT TYPE="submit"  VALUE="SEND">

</FORM>
```

Figure 27-3. The HTML for the Sample Form.

INPUT Fields

You use input fields to enter and capture data. You can specify eight types of inputs with the HTML tag:

```
<INPUT TYPE="field-type" NAME="Name of field" VALUE="default value">
```

The TYPE property lets you specify an input type, which can be either text, password, hidden, checkbox, radio, reset, submit, or image. The NAME and VALUE properties create the name/value pairs that you submit to the server application. NAME specifies the symbolic name of the variable; it is not the displayed name. VALUE contains the actual data. In our example, most of the fields have default values. You can override these defaults while interacting with the form. Let's go over the details:

■ **Text** is the default input field; it lets you enter a single line of text data. You can specify the maximum number of characters in the field via the optional MAX-LENGTH attribute.

■ **Password** is a text entry field that echoes asterisks (*) when you type a value into it.

■ **Hidden** is a field that does not appear on the form; it may contain a default value that you send to the server application.

■ **Checkbox** is a toggle field that is either checked or unchecked. You can have a set of checkboxes with the same name. The browser ignores unchecked boxes; it sends the checked items to the server as name/value pairs.

■ **Radio** displays a group of radio buttons. All the radio buttons have the same name, and only one button can be checked. This means that a group of radio buttons only returns a single value to the server.

■ **Reset** displays a pushbutton of type "reset." You click on the reset button to clear the contents of a form and restore its default values. You can display any words you want inside a reset button using the VALUE property. If you do not specify a NAME property, the value will not be returned to the server application.

■ **Submit** displays a pushbutton of type "submit." When you click on submit, the browser collects the data from all the fields in a form, pairs each data item with a name, and then posts the name/value pairs to the server application. Each form must have exactly one field of type submit. HTML does not support multiple submit buttons—that is, one for each task. If you put multiple submit buttons in a form, they will all return the same thing. The FORM tag can only post the form's contents to a single server application. You can display any words you want inside a submit button using the VALUE property. If you do not specify a NAME property, the VALUE will not be returned to the server.

■ *Image* is a special submit type; it displays a picture instead of a button. You submit the form by clicking on the image.

Now that you know what these input fields do, you may want to review the HTML in Figure 27-3. Hopefully, it will make more sense this time around.

The SELECT Field

A SELECT tag lets you create a dropdown list box from which a user picks one or more items (or options). The selected items become the values associated with the SELECT tag's NAME attribute. If you pick more than one item, the browser will generate a "name/value" pair for each item you pick. The syntax for the SELECT tag is:

```
<SELECT NAME="Name of field" SIZE ="N" MULTIPLE>
<Option>choice 1
<Option>choice 2
     .
<Option>choice N
</SELECT>
```

You include the optional attribute MULTIPLE after the NAME string to specify multiple selections. The optional SIZE attribute lets you specify the number of visible items. In general, option menus are a good substitute for radio buttons. You can recover some space on a form by replacing radio buttons with option menus; it's a much more efficient use of space within a form's real estate.

The TEXTAREA Field

The TEXTAREA tag lets you create multiline data entry fields. In contrast, the INPUT type allows for only single-line text input. So a text area is simply a two-dimensional text box. The syntax for the TEXTAREA tag is:

```
<TEXTAREA NAME= "Name of field" ROWS="Visible rows" COLS="Visible columns">
 Default Text goes here
     .
     .
</TEXTAREA>
```

The TEXTAREA attributes, ROWS and COLS, let you specify the number of visible rows and columns in the text area. This is the field's visible dimension specified in character units. Most Web browsers let you scroll the text beyond these limits; they typically render the field's contents in a fixed-width font. You can optionally place some initial text between the TEXTAREA start and end tags. This lets you put some words in your user's mouth when the form is first displayed.

HTML Tables

The table tag is a very useful HTML extension that is now supported in most browsers. With the exception of a few enhancements, the tables these browsers implement are as described in the HTML 3.2 (and above) specification. In a Web client/server context, tables allow a CGI program to dynamically format the result of searches in a row/column grid format. So it is useful to give you a quick overview of how to create these tables in HTML.

A table begins with the <TABLE> tag and ends with </TABLE>. You must enclose the table elements with the surrounding <TABLE> tag pairs. HTML defines four main tags for creating table elements:

- *<TR>..</TR>* defines a single table row. The number of rows in a table is exactly specified by how many of these tags it contains.

- *<TD>..</TD>* defines a single *data cell* within a table row. A cell may contain any of the HTML tags normally present in the body of an HTML document.

- *<TH>..</TH>* defines a header cell within a table row. A header cell is identical to a data cell in all respects, except that the text it contains is bold and centered (the default).

- *<CAPTION>..</CAPTION>* lets you add captions to your tables. A caption can either appear at the bottom or at the top of a table; the default is top. Captions are always horizontally centered with respect to the table.

A picture is worth a thousand words, so let's put together some HTML to demonstrate tables in action. Figure 27-4 shows the HTML for a table layout; Figure 27-5 shows how this table is rendered by a Web browser. Note how easy it is to give the table a new look by simply playing with the layout of the headers. The COLSPAN attribute can appear in any table cell; it specifies the number of table columns this cell should span.

```
<TABLE BORDER>
 <TR><TH></TH><TH COLSPAN=4>Hawaii Hotel Occupancy: <B>Q4, 1998</B></TH>
 </TR>
 <TR><TH></TH><TH>Maui</TH><TH>Kawai</TH>
    <TH>Big Island</TH><TH>Wakiki</TH>
 </TR>
 <TR><TH>January</TH><TD>9,400</TD><TD>2,100</TD>
    <TD>3,200</TD><TD>30,900</TD>
 </TR>
 <TR><TH>February</TH><TD>8,210</TD><TD>1,450</TD>
    <TD>2,640</TD><TD>24,550</TD>
 </TR>
 <TR><TH>March</TH><TD>11,234</TD><TD>2,410</TD>
    <TD>3,560</TD><TD>31,100</TD>
 </TR>
</TABLE>
```

Figure 27-4. HTML Table 2 Example.

	Hawaii Hotel Occupancy: Q4, 1998			
	Maui	Kawai	Big Island	Wakiki
January	9,400	2,100	3,200	30,900
February	8,210	1,450	2,640	24,550
March	11,234	2,410	3,560	31,100

Figure 27-5. How a Typical Web Browser Renders the Table 2 Example.

CGI: THE SERVER SIDE OF THE WEB

So how is a form's data passed to a program that hangs off an HTTP server? It gets passed using an end-to-end client/server protocol that includes both HTTP and CGI. The best way to explain the dynamics of the protocol is to walk you through a POST method invocation.

A CGI Scenario

Figure 27-6 shows how the client and server programs play together to process a form's request. Here's the step-by-step explanation of this interaction:

1. *User clicks on the form's "submit" button*. This causes the Web browser to collect the data within the form, and then assemble it into one long string of *name/value* pairs each separated by an ampersand (&). The browser translates spaces within the data into plus (+) symbols. No, it's not very pretty.

2. ***The Web Browser invokes a POST HTTP method***. This is an ordinary HTTP request that specifies a POST method, the URL of the target program in the "cgi-bin" directory, and the typical HTTP headers. The message body—HTTP calls it the "entity"—contains the form's data. This is the string: *name=value &name=value&...*

3. ***The HTTP server receives the method invocation via a socket connection***. The server parses the message and discovers that it's a POST for the "cgi-bin" program. So it starts a CGI interaction.

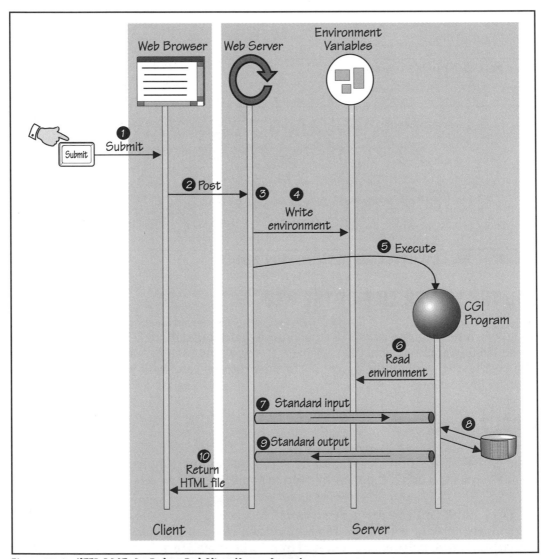

Figure 27-6. HTTP POST: An End-to-End Client/Server Scenario.

4. *The HTTP server sets up the environment variables*. The CGI protocol uses *environment variables* as a shared bulletin board for communicating information between the HTTP server and the CGI program. The server typically provides the following environmental information: *server_name, request_method, path_info, script_name, content_type*, and *content_length*.

5. *The HTTP server starts a CGI program*. The HTTP server executes an instance of the CGI program specified in the URL; it's typically in the "cgi-bin" directory.

6. *The CGI program reads the environment variables*. In this case, the program discovers by reading the environment variables that it is responding to a POST.

7. *The CGI program receives the message body via the standard input pipe (stdin)*. Remember, the message body contains the famous string of *name=value* items separated by ampersands (&). The *content_length* environment variable tells the program how much data is in the string. The CGI program parses the string contents to retrieve the form data. It uses the *content_length* environment variable to determine how many characters to read in from the standard input pipe. Cheer up, we're half way there.

8. *The CGI program does some work*. Typically, a CGI program interacts with some back-end resource—like a DBMS or transaction program—to service the form's request. The CGI program must then format the results in HTML or some other acceptable MIME type. This information goes into the HTTP response entity, which really is the body of the message. Your program can also choose to provide all the information that goes into the HTTP response headers. The HTTP server will then send the reply "as is" to the client. Why would you do this? Because it removes the extra overhead of having the HTTP server parse the output to create the response headers. Programs whose names begin with "nph-" indicate that they do not require HTTP server assistance; CGI calls them *nonparsed header programs (nph)*.

9. *The CGI program returns the results via the standard output pipe (stdout)*. The program pipes back the results to the HTTP server via its standard output. The HTTP server receives the results on its standard input. This concludes the CGI interaction.

10. *The HTTP server returns the results to the Web browser*. The HTTP server can either append some response headers to the information it receives from the CGI program, or it sends it "as is" if it's an nph program.

As you can see, a CGI program is executed in real time; it gets the information and then builds a dynamic Web page to satisfy a client's request. CGI makes the Web more dynamic. In contrast, a plain HTML document is static, which means the text file does not change. CGI may be clumsy, but it does allow us to interface Web clients to general-purpose back-end services—such as *Amazon.com*—as well as to Internet search utilities such as *Yahoo!* and *Excite*. You can even stretch CGI to its limits to create general-purpose client/server programs like the Federal Express package-tracking Web page. However, Federal Express uses CGI to connect to a TP Monitor in the backend.

CGI AND STATE

So how does CGI maintain information from one form to the next? Well, it doesn't. As we explained earlier, the protocol is totally stateless. The server forgets everything after it hands over a reply to the client. However, the nice thing about the Internet is that there is always some "kludge" that you can use to work around problems. In this case, the kludges are to use either *hidden* fields within a form or *cookies* to maintain state on the client side.

Hidden Fields

Hidden fields are basically invisible; they contain values that are not displayed within a form. They are used to store information a user enters and resubmit that information in subsequent forms without having the user reenter it or even be aware that the information is being passed around. In other words, the hidden fields act as variables that maintain state between form submissions. So how does this information get passed from one form to another? It gets passed through the CGI program.

Figure 27-7 shows an electronic transaction that requires multiple form submissions, which lead to an electronic payment. The first set of forms lets you pick the merchandise that you place on your electronic shopping cart. The next form requests a delivery address and time. The last form presents you with the bill and requests some form of payment.

How is the state of this transaction maintained across form invocations? Here's how: The CGI program processes a form and then presents you with the next form; this continues until you make your final payment or abort the transaction. The trick here is that the CGI program uses invisible fields to store information from the previous forms in the next form. For example, it writes inside the invisible fields the goods you selected in the previous forms. You never see the contents of these hidden fields. You never know they're there, unless you view the document's HTML. However, when you submit the form, all these hidden fields are passed right back to the CGI program along with any new data.

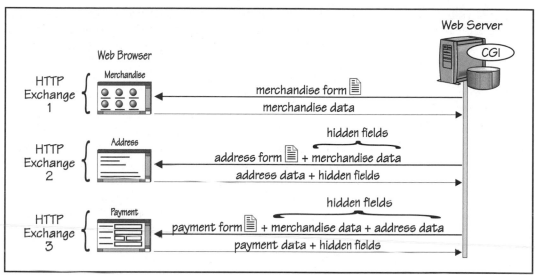

Figure 27-7. How Hidden Fields Maintain State Across Web Invocations.

So, in essence, the CGI program stores the state of the transaction in the forms it sends back to the client instead of storing it in its own memory. What do you think of this workaround? We did warn you that it was going to be a real work of art (also see the next Warning box).

Hidden Fields Are Not Really Hidden

Warning

A hidden field is an ordinary INPUT field inside a form that is marked with the attribute HIDDEN. Consequently, it can be viewed by any user via a browser's *View Source* command. This means that any good cracker can easily modify the field's information to trick the server. There is nothing to stop her from hijacking a session, impersonating a different user, or feeding the server false information. In the hands of a cracker, cookies can be just as bad. ❏

Cookies

Cookies provide another variation of this hidden field approach. A cookie is a small piece of data that is stored in the client on behalf of a server. In essence, a cookie is an invisible field that is stored on the client for a specified time. Typically, servers

use cookies to store user IDs or basic configuration information. The cookie is sent back to the server in subsequent page requests from this client. By default, cookies are only returned to the server that creates them. Of course, there are ways to change this default.

CONCLUSION

In this chapter, we covered the fundamentals of the Web's interactive client/server technology—including CGI, HTTP, tables, and forms. This fast-paced overview should give you an appreciation of what limits exist in the current Web model, at least from a client/server perspective. The HTTP/CGI Web is truly a minimalist client/server architecture; it can be used to create very portable solutions. It's great for serving documents. And it works well for very simple interactive client/server applications.

However, HTTP/CGI is not the right middleware for developing the next-generation Web. From a middleware perspective, HTTP is really a very primitive pipe; CGI is an even more primitive platform. HTTP as a pipe provides a bare-bones RPC; it was designed to serve Web pages. HTTP as an RPC does not support an IDL, typed parameters, or callbacks. And, it certainly lacks the distributed component infrastructure that today's ORBs provide.

CGI as an application platform has two serious shortcomings: 1) it does not maintain state between connections, and 2) the target program must be loaded into memory for each invocation. Of course, CGI was never meant to be a platform for running scalable server-side components. It was designed to be a simple gateway that could spawn an application and then pass it a request. As you will see in the next chapter, the HTTP Web is being augmented with all types of object-based middleware—including ORBs, application servers, OTMs, ODBMSs, client-side components, server-side components, and an XML-based object document model.

Chapter 28

Web Client/Server: The Distributed Object Era

---

*W*eb technology and distributed object technology are naturally complementary. We want to ensure that OMG and W3C work together to define a common future.

> — **Tim Berners-Lee, Director**
> **W3C**

*T*he Internet is the killer application that will accelerate object usage; it has transformed objects into a mass-market opportunity that is attracting the best and brightest developers from around the world.

> — **Donald DePalma, Forrester Research**

The next-generation Web—in its Internet, intranet, and extranet incarnations—must be able to deal with the complex requirements of multistep business-to-business and consumer-to-business transactions. To do this, the Web must evolve into a highly-interactive medium that can run your line-of-business applications. The current HTTP/CGI paradigm is flawed and is running out of steam. The various CGI extensions—such as cookies, ISAPI, NSAPI, Servlets, and ASP—are simply

Band-aids. To move to the next step, the Web needs distributed objects. We call this next wave of Internet innovation the *Object Web*.

In this chapter, we explain how this Object Web is coming together. We start with client/server, Java-style—or how the Java *mobile code system* is changing the nature of client/server interactions on the Web. Next we explain how CORBA extends Java, HTTP, and CGI. We also explain how CORBA and Enterprise JavaBeans are redefining what it means to be a Web application server. Then we introduce the new XML-based *Document Object Model;* it has the potential to turn every document on the Web—including its style sheets, structure, and contents—into a container of distributed objects that you can manipulate from anywhere. Finally, we explain how these pieces play together in a 3-tier CORBA/Java Object Web. We also describe the Object Web in the Microsoft COM+ parallel universe.

JAVA: THE MOBILE CODE SYSTEM

Java blows Bill Gates's lock and destroys his model of a shrink-wrapped software program that runs only on his platform.

— Scott McNealy, CEO
Sun Microsystems

Unless you've spent the last few years hiding in a cave, chances are you've heard of Java—the new object-oriented programming language from Sun. Java is more than a C++ derived language; it's also a portable operating system environment. In addition, Java lets you write portable components that can be distributed on the Web. In Part 7, we introduced the Java component model—including JavaBeans, and Enterprise JavaBeans (EJB). In this chapter, we focus on Java as a mobile code system for the Web.

Web Client/Server, Java-Style

If you build the client side of an application in Java, then launching a client app becomes just switching to a page. Installing is trivial—just put it on a Web server. And there are no ports, just one version of the application.

— James Gosling, Java Creator

Applets are what made Java famous. They are now literally changing the dynamics of client/server computing. What makes these applets so irresistible? They let you create component-sized applications that servers can ship to clients via ordinary

HTML pages. Once an applet lands in a Web browser, it becomes an instant front-end to the remote services you provide. So, in a sense, applets are "just-in-time" shippable clients. The server downloads the client application when and where it's needed. Typically, an applet consists of one or more *JavaBeans* that are stored in a *JAR* (or *Java Archive* file).

Applets allow us to distribute executable content across the Web along with data. Figure 28-1 shows a Web client/server interaction scenario that includes a Java applet. Here are the steps:

1. ***Request the applet***. A Web browser requests a Java applet when it encounters the new HTML 4.0 <OBJECT> tag.[1] The tag's attributes include the name of the program—the *class* filename. The program typically resides on the same server from which the HTML page originates.

2. ***Receive the applet***. The browser downloads each applet it encounters within a Web page. You can improve the download time by placing your objects inside a JAR. The HTML 4.0 *Archive* property lets you tell the browser where to find the JAR.

3. ***Load and execute the applet***. The browser loads the applet into the client's memory, and then executes it. Typically, the applet will display its contents (or create some kind of dynamic visual effect) within the area of the page that you assign to it. The <OBJECT> tag attributes let you specify the size of the region the applet will own. This is the piece of real estate within a page that belongs to the applet. The applet paints the contents of its region, chooses the background color and fonts, and handles all the keyboard and mouse events.

4. ***Discard the applet***. The browser deletes the applet from memory when it exits the Web page.

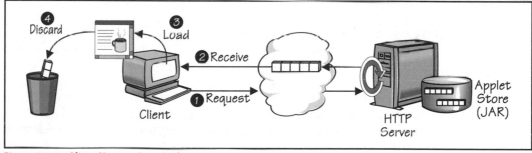

Figure 28-1. Client/Server, Java-Style.

---

[1] Note that the APPLET tag was deprecated in HTML 4.0. However, only the newer browsers—IE 4.0 and Netscape 4.0—understand OBJECT. So you may want to include both tags in your HTML pages.

As you can see from this scenario, Java applets—and their embedded JavaBeans—allow us to create highly interactive Web pages that have locally executable content. These applets introduce an unparalleled degree of flexibility. They allow the client to execute snippets of code (the beans), while the server becomes a warehouse of programs, data, and HTML pages.

What Is a Mobile Code System?

There are a lot of mechanisms in Java to let you sort of transparently move behavior around; it's about building applications that can rove around the network in a safe way.

— *James Gosling*

In addition to exchanging traditional content—such as text, graphics, audio, and video—Java lets Web applications exchange *mobile code*. Java is a mobile code system. Other examples of mobile code systems are *Safe-Tcl*, Colusa's *Omniware*, and General Magic's *Telescript*.[2] Mobile code systems also provide the foundation technology for *mobile agents*. They let you distribute code (and data) across clients and servers. Mobile objects—like Java *applets* and *beans*—are self-contained pieces of executable code. Like traditional software, mobile code consists of a sequence of executable instructions. Unlike traditional software, mobile code is dynamically loaded and executed by standalone programs such as Web browsers and servers.

At a minimum, mobile code must be portable and safe. As users browse the Web, they will be downloading and executing hundreds of these executable code modules, so it is crucial that you should be able to precisely control each module's access to host resources. Here's a short list of the services you should expect from a mobile code system:

- *A safe environment for executing mobile code*. You should be able to precisely control an applet's environment—including its access to memory, system calls, and server function calls.

- *Platform-independent services*. The system must provide cross-platform memory management, threads, synchronization, communications, GUI services, and a component framework. The applets must execute on top of a variety of operating systems and hardware platforms.

- *Life cycle control*. The system must provide a run-time environment for loading, unloading, and executing the code.

---

[2] Microsoft acquired Colusa in March, 1996.

■ *Applet distribution*. The system must provide facilities for moving applets across the network. It must guarantee that the code is not tampered with when in transit. It must also certify the applet and authenticate the identities of both clients and servers. In other words, you must do whatever you can to prevent mobile code from becoming a conduit for viruses.

In essence, mobile code systems let you write an application once and then run it anywhere. The network becomes the distribution vehicle for software applications. Mobile code systems slash software distribution costs and allow you to reach millions of customers instantly via global networks. Mobile code means that you do not have to deal with issues like porting and end-user installation.

The Magic of Bytecodes

Java delivers the goods right into the heart of Microsoft territory and breaks their lock on the desktop.

— **Dr. Jeff Sutherland, Homepage.Journal**

Like all mobile code systems, Java delivers both portability and safety. A Java *applet* is a portable unit of mobile code. Java achieves portability by compiling applets to the *Java Virtual Machine*, which is modeled after a virtual RISC processor's instructions. These primitive instructions are called *bytecodes*. Bytecodes bring the compiled instructions to the lowest level possible without making them machine dependent. The Java language puts a stake in the ground by specifying the size of its basic data types and the behavior of its arithmetic operators. Your programs are the same on every platform—there are no data type incompatibilities across hardware and software architectures.

Bytecodes make Java a partially compiled language. Creating the bytecodes is about 80% of the compilation work; the last 20% is performed by the Java run time. So you can think of Java as being 80% compiled and 20% interpreted. This 80/20 mix seems to provide excellent code portability; the bytecode abstraction was designed to transport code efficiently across multiple hardware and software platforms.

Of course, there's no free lunch. In this case, you're trading off performance for portability—the Java interpreted code is about fifteen times slower than native compiled code. Java also supports regular compilers as well as *just-in-time* compilers, which generate code that can almost match C++ native speeds.

The Java Verifier

Figure 28-2 shows the steps you must follow to create and execute a Java applet. First, you run your applet through a Java virtual machine compiler to create the bytecodes and store them on a server. Your bytecodes will be copied to a target client machine when a browser requests your applet. As soon as the bytecodes reach the target machine, they're run through a Java *verifier*, which is highly suspicious of any code it receives.

The verifier runs the bytecodes through a gauntlet of tests. It looks for things like forged pointers, access violations, parameter type mismatches, and stack overflows. In a sense, the verifier acts as a gatekeeper; it ensures that the code it receives from both local and remote sources is safe. No code is allowed to execute without passing the verifier's tests. If the verifier is satisfied that everything's OK, it hands over the bytecodes to the class loader.

The *class loader* typically hands the bytecodes to an *interpreter*. This is the run-time element that executes the Java instructions on the target machine. The

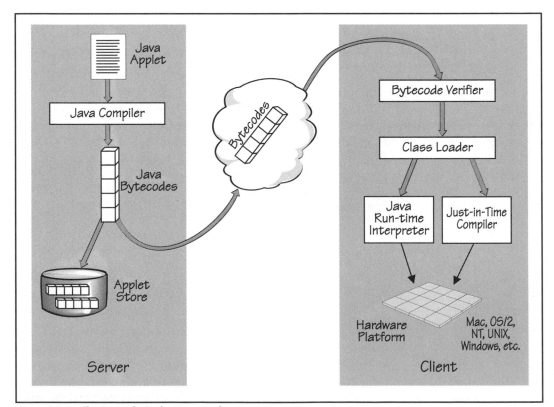

Figure 28-2. The Bytecode Cycle: From Production to Execution.

interpreter can proceed with the execution without checking anything because it knows that the code it received was sanitized. It can run at full speed without compromising reliability.

However, even at "full speed," an interpreter is still an order of magnitude slower than native compiled code. So the Java designers are now trying to improve the situation with *just-in-time* compiler techniques, which means storing the translation of your program's bytecodes into native code for subsequent execution. In addition, JavaSoft is preparing to introduce a technology called *Hotspot*. Note that Javasoft promises to achieve C++ speeds.

Java's Defense System

> *Microsoft has always had a very casual attitude about security and viruses. All their systems are just designed to host viruses. I mean, it's like a petri dish with the best culture you could buy.*
>
> — **James Gosling**

Importing code across the network is potentially an open invitation to all sorts of problems. Without the proper checks, Java applets can become a breeding ground for computer viruses. Java starts with the assumption that you can't trust anything, and proceeds accordingly. The environment provides five interlocking defense mechanisms or defense perimeters: 1) the Java language itself, 2) the verifier, 3) the Java bytecode loader, 4) the Java 2 access control lists and digital signatures, and 5) the Java browser. Here's a quick overview of Java's defense perimeters:

■ *The Java language defense perimeter.* One of Java's primary lines of defense is its memory allocation and reference model. The *memory layout* decisions are not made by the Java language compiler, as they are in C and C++. Instead, memory layout is deferred to run time. In addition, Java does not support "pointers" in the traditional C and C++ sense—meaning memory cells that contain the addresses of other memory cells. Instead, the Java compiled code references memory via symbolic "names" that are resolved to real memory addresses at run time by the Java interpreter. Together, these two late-binding mechanisms ensure that crackers can't infer the physical memory layout of a class by looking at its declaration. Java's memory allocation and referencing model is completely opaque to them. There's no way for them to go behind the scenes and forge pointers to memory.

■ *The verifier's defense perimeter.* As we described in the previous section, imported Java code fragments are subjected to a battery of checks by the verifier before they're allowed to run on the target platform. The verifier protects the

Java run-time environment from a range of external threats—including hostile compilers, code tamperers, and faulty bytecodes.

- *The class loader's defense perimeter.* The loader partitions the set of Java classes into separate *namespaces*. A class can only access objects that are within its namespace. Java creates one namespace for classes that come from the local file system, and a separate namespace for each network source. When a class is imported from across the network, it is placed into the private namespace associated with its origin. When a class references another class, Java first searches the namespace of the local system (built-in classes), and then it searches the namespace of the referencing class. Note that Java resolves all symbols at load time. Each class referenced by an applet is loaded in the browser, and all the symbolic references and class inheritance relationships are resolved at this time.

- *The access control lists' defense perimeter.* Java 2's new permission-based security uses access control lists to provide additional levels of security on top of its already secured language and run-time base. For example, the file access primitives implement access control lists. This lets you control read and write access to files by imported code (or code invoked by imported code). The defaults for these access control lists are very restrictive. If an attempt is made by a piece of imported code to access a file to which you did not grant access, a dialog box pops up to let the user decide if this specific access can proceed.

- *The Java browser's defense perimeter.* Java-enabled browsers let you set the security mode using a properties dialog box. The strictest level of security is *none*—meaning the applets cannot access the network. *Applet host* mode allows applets to access data only on the home server from which they originate (see Figure 28-3). *Firewall* mode allows applets from outside the firewall to only access resources that are outside the firewall. Finally, *unrestricted* mode allows applets to connect to any host on the Internet.

Java also supports digital certificates and public key technology to certify that a bean within a signed JAR comes from a reputed source. The idea is to place fewer restrictions on these "certified" bytecode fragments—especially if they have the right security credentials or permissions.

In summary, Java surrounds its mobile applets and beans with various levels of protection. It creates a "sandbox" that controls all access to client resources and remote server processes. In theory, Java lets you construct applications that can't be invaded from outside and are secure from intrusion by unauthorized code attempting to get behind the scenes and create viruses or invade file systems. Of course, it is still too early to declare victory.

Figure 28-3. Applet Visibility with "Host Mode" Restriction.

The Life Cycle of an Applet

In the pre-Java world, a Web page is essentially a piece of paper. In the Java world, a browser becomes a framework.

— James Gosling

You can run Java applications as standalone programs or as applets invoked by a browser. Technically, an applet is a piece of code that inherits its behavior from the Java *Applet* class, which it then extends with new function. An applet is not a complete application. It's really a component that runs within a browser's environment. In this case, the browser acts as a framework for running Java components— or applets.

So what type of component framework services do browsers provide? A Web browser provides three useful services to its applets. First, it fully controls the applet's life cycle. Second, it supplies the applet with attribute information from the OBJECT tag. And third, it serves as the *main* program or process within which the applet executes. Let's quickly go over these services.

A Web browser manages all phases of an applet's life cycle. Remember, the browser first downloads the applet and then runs it within its environment. The browser is also kind enough to inform the applet of key events that happen during its life cycle.

The Java *Applet* class and the *Runnable* interface define the methods that a browser invokes on an applet (see Figure 28-4). Most Java applets implement code that reacts to these method invocations.

The browser invokes *init* when it loads your applet for the first time. The browser calls *start* whenever a user enters or returns to the page containing your applet. This lets your applet do whatever it has to do before running. The browser calls *stop* whenever the user moves off the page. Finally, the browser calls *destroy* before it shuts down normally. The last two calls should cause your applet to kill all its threads, stop executing, and release all resources.

To be highly interactive, your applet should implement a *run* method that executes inside a thread. Here's how you manage the lifecycle of the thread within your applet: 1) create the thread when your applet receives an *init*, 2) *run* the thread when your applet receives a *start*, and 3) destroy the thread when your applet receives a *stop* or *destroy* (see Figure 28-4). In summary, the browser owns the applet; it provides it with a running environment that includes life cycle management.

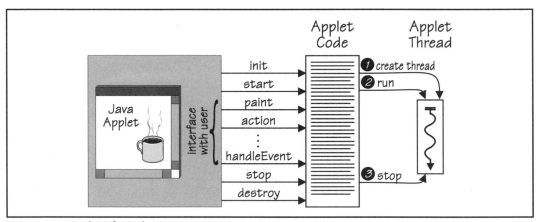

Figure 28-4. Applet Life-Cycle Management.

The HTML 4.0 Object Tag

*L*ive objects is our term for things like Java applets and inlined viewers embedded in HTML documents.

— *Marc Andreessen*

A Java applet's main role in life is to provide live content to Web pages displayed in a Java-enabled browser. In contrast, a Java application can run without a Web browser. You use the OBJECT HTML tag to place an applet in a Web page and describe its attributes and environment (also see the next Background box). The tag tells the browser where to find the applet to download. Java provides a set of methods that an applet uses to obtain information about its environment—including the embedded tag attributes and their values.

The OBJECT tag provides the essential information that connects the Web browser to the embedded applet. It also lets you specify key attribute information; you can use these attributes to configure an applet and control its behavior without having to write a line of code. A well-designed applet will provide as many attributes as is needed to let you control its behavior via HTML. Here's an example:

```
<OBJECT
CLASSID="Hello.class"
CODEBASE="applets/myapps" ARCHIVE="MyArchive.jar"
WIDTH=300 HEIGHT=200  ALIGN=Left>
<PARAM NAME=Parm1  VALUE="Java is cool">
<PARAM NAME=Parm2  VALUE="Is there life without Java?">
</OBJECT>
```

The CLASSID attribute specifies the file that contains the applet's bytecode. This file is normally in the same directory as the document-URL. However, you can use the optional CODEBASE attribute to specify a different location. The WIDTH and HEIGHT attributes specify the area within an HTML page that belongs to the applet. You can use the optional ALIGN attribute to tell the browser where you want it to place the applet (it's a relative placement). The PARAM attributes are specific to each applet. Each applet can define as many parameters as it needs. You must provide a PARAM tag for each parameter you want to pass to the applet via HTML; each tag contains a name/value pair. An applet can access any parameter—by name—by invoking the Java method *getParameter*. Finally, the ARCHIVE tag tells the browser to download a zipped file that contains the code for this applet. Typically, you use it to download a JAR full of beans. In this example, it's an overkill.

 Active Objects: OBJECT Tag Magic

Briefing

In December 1995, W3C Director Tim Berners-Lee announced a convergence agreement for "active objects" that—incredibly—had the support of Sun, Netscape, Microsoft, Spyglass, and IBM. These companies agreed to support a new active object tag called INSERT. Later, it was renamed OBJECT; it is now part of the HTML 4.0 standard. You can use this universal tag to insert almost any object within HTML—including HTML images, Java applets, JavaBeans, ActiveXs, media handlers, and a wide range of plug-ins. OBJECT was designed to replace a variety of HTML insertion tags—including APPLET, EMBED, DYN-SRC, and IMG.

The OBJECT tag lets you embed component code as well as data. Examples of data are image files, database result sets, and persistent data associated with code—such as an ActiveX object that requires a data source. You specify the data objects (and images) using the tag's DATA attribute. Here's an example:

```
<OBJECT data = "MyWedding.mpeg">
  <OBJECT data = "MyWedding.gif">
  </OBJECT>
</OBJECT>
```

In this example, the browser first tries to load the MPEG video; if it fails, it will instead try to render the GIF image. As you can see, the OBJECT tags can be used to load images and video. In addition, they can be nested.

When you embed components, OBJECT lets you specify persistent data as well as the properties and parameters that you use to initialize active objects placed within HTML documents. You can specify the location of the code for the object in several ways: by using the object's unique ID (UUID) via a URL, or by specifying the combination of class name and a network address. We already demonstrated how OBJECT can be used to embed a Java applet. This next example shows how it is used to specify an ActiveX control for a clock:

```
<OBJECT
 ID="clock1"
 CLASSID="clsid:{663C8FEF-1EF9-11CF-A3DB-080036F12502}"
 TYPE="application/x-oleobject"
 CODEBASE="http://www.foo.bar/test.stm"
 DATA="http://www.acme.com/ole/clock.stm"
 WIDTH=300  HEIGHT=200  ALIGN=Left>
</OBJECT>
```

The ID attribute allows other controls on the same page to locate the clock. The DATA attribute points to a persistent stream that you can use to initialize the object's state. The CODEBASE attribute points to a file that contains the code for this object. Note that if a global ActiveX directory is present, then the CLASSID may be all you need to locate the code. ❑

CORBA/JAVA AND THE OBJECT WEB

Java is the first step toward creating an Object Web, but it is still not enough. Java needs to be augmented with a distributed object infrastructure, which is where OMG's CORBA comes into the picture. The CORBA/Java story is really about the Object Web. Without the Object Web, CORBA and Java would just be esoteric technologies—mostly of interest to the enterprise client/server market and to object aficionados. As it turns out, CORBA and Java are having a shotgun wedding. Their marriage must be consummated for the higher good of the Object Web. The anxious parents—the ones with the shotguns—are a broad coalition of vendors that include almost everyone in the software industry but Microsoft. In this case, Microsoft is building its own Object Web—based on its COM+ component technology. This may explain the sense of urgency behind the CORBA/Java wedding.

Why the Shotguns?

The bottom line is that CORBA and Java complement each other well. Java starts where CORBA leaves off. CORBA deals with network transparency, while Java deals with implementation transparency. CORBA provides the missing link between the Java portable application environment and the world of intergalactic objects. So why isn't this marriage made in Heaven? Why were there so many shotguns at the wedding?

Until recently, the problem was one of establishing clean divisions between the work of OMG and JavaSoft—both of these organizations believe they are in the business of defining object standards, which can sometimes lead to overlaps. For example, JavaSoft started to get into the ORB business when it defined its *Remote Method Invocation (RMI)* for Java-to-Java communications across Virtual Machines. It really stepped squarely on OMG's toes with that one—the 800-plus members of the OMG gave it the mission to develop distributed object standards. So, we're talking about really big toes.

The good news is that this turf war appears to be over. JavaSoft adopted CORBA as its distributed object model; it will run the RMI APIs on top of CORBA/IIOP with help from IBM. This June 1997 agreement has done a lot to heal the rift between the CORBA and Java camps. Here's how JavaSoft has made CORBA part of the Java core:

- *A CORBA/IIOP ORB is now part of the Java 2 core*. This is an all-Java ORB called *Java IDL*. It also includes a development environment for generating CORBA stubs and skeletons from IDL. Java 2 also includes an all-Java version of the CORBA *Naming Service*. Note that pure Java ORBs are also available from other vendors—including Inprise/Visigenic and Iona (see Part 7).

- *Java RMI runs on top of CORBA IIOP.* JavaSoft worked with OMG to define an RMI/IDL subset that allows RMI applications to talk to CORBA objects written in different languages, and vice versa. The idea is that you write Java code with RMI semantics to generate CORBA objects. In mid-1998, OMG published this work as its new *Java-to-IDL* standard. JavaSoft is including an implementation of this standard in the JDK. Note that Java-to-IDL implementations are also available from other vendors—including Netscape, Inprise/Visigenic, and IBM (see Part 7).

- *Enterprise JavaBeans*. Enterprise JavaBeans uses the CORBA Java/IDL subset for its distributed object model. In addition, Enterprise JavaBeans is built on top of the *Java Transaction Service (JTS)*—the Java implementation of the CORBA *Object Transaction Service (OTS)*. Again, see Part 7 for a description of EJB.

These developments are very significant for both the low-end and the high-end of the CORBA/Java market. At the low-end, you will be able to get from your JDK providers—perhaps, even from Microsoft—a free CORBA/Java ORB as well as an IDL development environment.[3] At the high-end, you will be able to get transactional JavaBeans. Transactions provide ACID protection for beans. They also serve as the glue that you can use to synchronize independently developed beans. As a result of all this, what started as a shotgun wedding may be turning into a love affair.

The Other CGI Alternatives

As you may recall from the last chapter, CGI is a slow, cumbersome, and stateless protocol. It is not a good match for object-oriented Java clients. Some server vendors are trying to extend CGI with proprietary server APIs. Examples of such

---

[3] In November 1998, Microsoft was forced by a court ruling to comply with Sun's version of the JDK. So we assume that Microsoft will also comply with Java 2, which Sun shipped in December, 1998.

attempts include Netscape's *NSAPI*, Microsoft's *ISAPI*, Apple's *WebObjects*, Java-Soft's *Servlets*, Allaire's *Cold Fusion*, and many others. Most of these solutions require running some plug-in code in the same address space as the Web server. Some Web servers—for example, the IBM *Go Server*—will even run your server-side code on the same thread as the incoming TCP/IP request.

Most of the CGI workarounds improve performance by running server-side scripts in the same address space as the server. Some use proprietary protocols to off-load the application code from the Web server and then load-balance it across several application servers. Others use an ORB to invoke server-side plug-ins—for example Netscape uses a CORBA plug-in called *WAI* in its *Enterprise Server*; Microsoft uses COM+ to allow ASP scripts to call MTS objects. In general, all these servers use cookies as well as proprietary server-side objects to maintain state. And, as a rule, they will do almost anything to keep services in memory across invocations. As a result, they introduce many non-standard extensions. If this trend continues, we may end up with a totally non-standard server Web.

The good news is that we see some light at the end of this tunnel. In the non-Microsoft world, almost all the Web application servers are standardizing on the CORBA/EJB server-side component model; in the Microsoft parallel universe, the standard for server-side components is COM+ (see Part 7). This brings us back to the question: What does CORBA/Java do for the Web?

CORBA/Java and the Web: Look Ma, No Cookies

Java applets were the first step toward creating a client/server Object Web. To get the full benefits of object-to-object interactions, the Web is being augmented with a distributed object infrastructure. ORBs specialize in intercomponent communications across all kinds of boundaries—including client-to-client, client-to-server, server-to-client, and server-to-server. Figure 28-5 shows how a typical Web-based client interacts with its server on the Object Web:

1. ***Web browser downloads HTML page***. In this case, the page includes references to embedded Java applets.

2. ***Web browser retrieves Java applet from HTTP server***. The HTTP server retrieves the applet and downloads it to the browser in the form of bytecodes.

3. ***Web browser loads applet***. The applet is first run through the Java run-time security gauntlet and then loaded into memory.

4. ***Applet invokes CORBA server objects***. The Java applet can include IDL-generated client stubs, which let it invoke objects on the ORB server. The session between the Java applet and the CORBA server objects—including EJBs—will

persist until either side decides to disconnect. Later, you can reconnect to the same object if you know its CORBA IOR. Note that you will need an IIOP-savvy firewall to make this work. Today, you can use either Iona's *WonderWall* or Visigenic/Borland's *IIOP Gatekeeper*. By the time you read this, Netscape may have shipped its own IIOP firewall.

5. ***Dynamically generate the next page.*** Server objects can optionally generate the next HTML page for this client. This dynamic HTML generation on the server side is needed less frequently with the Object Web. In this new environment, a client application is typically packaged as a single HTML page with embedded components such as applets (or JavaBeans via the OBJECT tag). CORBA then lets you interact with the server by clicking on any of the components embedded in the HTML layers without switching out of the page's context to obtain each response. So you don't have to dynamically generate an HTML page for each response.

The technology we just described performs surprisingly well today. However, the Object Web is still under construction. Some key pieces of technology must become available before we can declare it ready for mission-critical prime time. We explain some of these key pieces later in this chapter.

Augmenting the Web infrastructure with CORBA/Java provides two immediate benefits: 1) it gets rid of the CGI bottleneck on the server, and 2) it provides a scalable and robust server-to-server Web infrastructure. We briefly explain what this means.

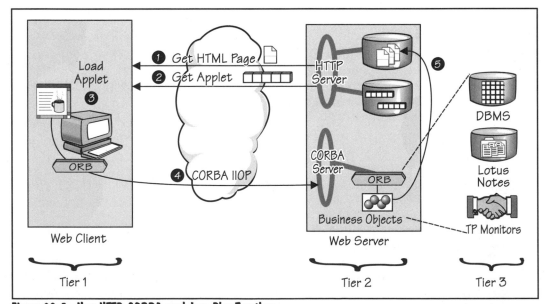

Figure 28-5. How HTTP, CORBA, and Java Play Together.

CORBA/Java: Life Without CGI

CORBA/IIOP bypasses the CGI bottleneck and replaces it with ORB-based object-to-object interactions. In the client/server interaction we just described, clients (applets or beans) directly invoke methods on a server. The client passes the parameters directly using precompiled stubs, or it generates them on-the-fly using CORBA's dynamic invocation services. In either case, the server receives the call directly via a precompiled skeleton.

With CORBA, you can invoke any IDL-defined method on the server. In addition, you can pass any typed parameter instead of just strings. This means there's very little client/server overhead, especially when compared with HTTP/CGI. With CGI, you must start a new instance of a program every time an applet invokes a method on a server; with CORBA, you don't.

CGI does not maintain state between client invocations; CORBA does. With CORBA, Java clients and applets can invoke a wide variety of IDL-defined operations on the server. In contrast, HTTP clients are restricted to a limited set of operations. Server-side applications are regular CORBA objects that are managed by an EJB container—such as an OTM or Web application server—based on the policies we described in Part 7. There is no need to go through the overhead of spawning a CGI script for every invocation.

Scalable Servers

CORBA provides a scalable server-to-server infrastructure. Pools of server business objects can communicate using the CORBA ORB. These objects can run on multiple servers to provide load-balancing for incoming client requests. The ORB can dispatch the request to the first available object and add more objects as the demand increases. CORBA allows the server objects—or EJBs—to act in unison using transaction boundaries and related CORBA services. In contrast, a CGI application is a bottleneck because it must respond to thousands of incoming requests; it has no way to distribute the load across multiple processes or processors.

What CORBA Brings to Java and the Web

Table 28-1 summarizes the differences between today's Java-to-CGI client/server approach and a solution based on CORBA's IIOP protocol. CORBA was designed from the start to provide powerful 3-tier client/server solutions. In contrast, client/server interactions were wedged into HTTP and CGI; it's more of an after-thought. CORBA naturally extends Java's object model for distributed environments.

Table 28-1. Java Clients With CORBA IIOP Versus HTTP-CGI.

Feature	Java With CORBA ORB	Java With HTTP-CGI
State preservation across invocations	Yes	No
IDL and Interface Repository	Yes	No
Metadata support	Yes	No
Dynamic invocations	Yes	No
Transactions	Yes	No
Security	Yes	Yes
Rich object services	Yes	No
Callbacks	Yes	No
Server/server infrastructure	Yes	No
Server scalability	Yes	No
IDL-defined methods	Yes	No

CORBA also makes it easier to split Java applets and beans into components that can be distributed along client/server lines. This means that the client side of the bean can remain small, which reduces the download time.

Without CORBA, Java on the Web is simply a competitor to Dynamic HTML; it's just a way to create a fancy page. With CORBA, the Java client becomes a rich object front-end to a mission-critical client/server system. It doesn't make much sense to use Dynamic HTML to invoke methods on server objects; it makes a lot more sense to use JavaBeans.

This highly uneven comparison clearly demonstrates why the Java Web needs CORBA. However, CORBA is not the only distributed object model to extend the Web. The other serious contender is Microsoft's DCOM (more on this later).

To further illustrate the benefits of ORBs on the Internet, we present the results of a simple Ping benchmark.[4] In our programming book, we developed code to measure the average response time of a client/server invocation—a JavaBean client calls a server-side Java object and then gets back a response (see Figure 28-6). We

---

[4] Source: Orfali and Harkey, **Client/Server Programming with Java and CORBA, Second Edition** (Wiley, 1998).

wrote the same Ping using the following protocols: TCP/IP Sockets, HTTP/CGI, Servlets, RMI, CORBA/IIOP, and DCOM. Table 28-2 shows the results.

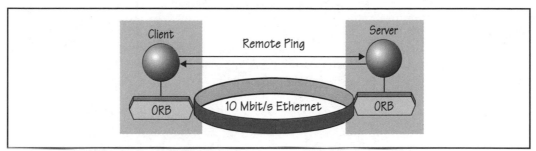

Figure 28-6. The Client/Server Ping Test Environment.

Table 28-2. A Comparison of Client/Server Pings.

Feature	CORBA/IIOP	DCOM	RMI/RMP	HTTP/CGI	Servlets	Sockets
Performance (remote Pings)	★★★	★★★	★★★	☆	★	★★★★
	3.5	3.8	3.3	827.9	55.6	2.1
	msecs	msecs	msecs	msecs	msecs	msecs

As you can see from the results, Sockets provide the best performance. So they provide a baseline for our benchmark. Of course, you shouldn't be programming directly to Sockets. It's like writing in assembler when you have high-level languages (see Part 3). As the numbers dramatically illustrate, HTTP/CGI is about 200 times slower than the three ORB alternatives—CORBA/IIOP, RMI, and DCOM. Servlets are one of the better and more recent CGI extensions. As you can see, they are over 10 times faster than HTTP/CGI. But, they are also about 15 times slower than the three ORB alternatives.

In summary, Java solves many thorny problems that have stood in the way of creating a truly portable distributed object market. Java lets you run portable applications that will one day be able to run on any machine in the galaxy. CORBA provides an intergalactic distributed object infrastructure over the Internet. Currently, most Java applications have been standalone demos, but the real value of Java is when you build portable clients to much larger transactional systems. This is where CORBA comes into the picture. On the Web, HTTP is great for serving documents and downloading HTML containers full of beans. However, once the beans land in the browser they should use an ORB to communicate with server-side objects. ORBs provide a modern distributed component infrastructure with all the benefits that come with it (also see the next Soapbox).

Soapbox

Is Java Dead on the Client?

The discovery that Web developers need to think in cosmic architectural terms for even relatively small projects comes as something of a shock.

— *Nelson King, Software Developer*
(March, 1998)

In the last year, quite a few industry pundits—mostly restating the Microsoft party line—have declared Java dead on the client. In their view, Java's real place isn't on the Web client; its place is on the server. Java is just another language that you use to write server code. Of course, there's also another group of pundits who say that Java is not robust enough for the server either. So where does this leave Java? In this Soapbox, we will look at the case against Java on the client. We will present the top ten reasons anti-Java pundits give for keeping the client Java free. We will also provide counterpoints (this is a Soapbox, after all):

- ■ *Client front-ends created with JavaBeans are far too fat to download.* In the early days of JavaBeans, each GUI builder tool provided its own widget libraries. The code libraries for these support widgets was huge. And they were included with your application's beans. So the downloads could be slow. *Counterpoint:* In mid-1998, JavaSoft released the *Java Foundation Classes (JFC)* also known as *Swing.* JFC provides a complete set of foundation beans that you can now use—via a visual tool—to assemble your beans. The JFC classes are part of the Java 2 runtime. Consequently, they are not downloaded with your beans. This should help slim down your applications. In addition, HTML 4.0 now lets you point to JAR packages as part of the OBJECT tag. A visual tool should be able to compress your beans and package them in a JAR; it should make your downloads even faster.

- ■ *Dynamic HTML removes the need for Java on the client.* You will hear that Java is overkill; Dynamic HTML scripts can do it all. *Counterpoint:* Dynamic HTML is not evenly supported on today's browsers. But, this will eventually get fixed. Yes, Dynamic HTML scripting may be all you need for simple animations. However, the book you're reading is about client/server applications—not animations. We highly recommend that you use a robust programming environment for your clients. You will need an object-oriented language that supports error handling, threads, and automatic garbage collection. For OLTP applications—like Web-based electronic commerce— you need all the protection you can get. Java is ideal for these kind of situations—especially on the client. The new W3C DOM defines a Java API for manipulating Dynamic HTML objects. So you can use Java for both your client-side invocations and your Dynamic HTML manipulations.

■ ***"Write once, run everywhere" is really "write once, debug everywhere."*** The idea here is that Java VMs are not consistent—especially on the client. So you will spend your time debugging Java code for different VMs on each platform. ***Counterpoint:*** This issue is now being settled in court. The Java VMs can become a lot more consistent, if Microsoft complies with the court's edict. Of course, the JavaSoft hype machine did quite a bit of harm by over-selling "write once, run anywhere." Lately, JavaSoft has made a real effort to make this slogan a reality. Their free *Java Plugin* can be used to equalize the Java experience on different platforms and browsers. In addition, JFC provides an all-Java rendering engine; it should make your Java GUI applications much more portable. With the law on its side, there is now a very real chance that Java may become the most consistent common platform on the Web—for both clients and servers.

■ ***Programming in Java is hard for scripters and VB programmers.*** Java is a professional programmer's language. However, early hype from JavaSoft made it sound like anyone could write Java code; it was the "cool thing to do." Needless to say, many people were disappointed. So now Java is perceived to be hard. ***Counterpoint:*** Yes, Java is a lot harder to master than JavaScript. However, today you can use visual tools to assemble very sophisticated front-ends using pre-built beans. The tools will automatically generate a good part of the Java code. Some tools can make Java transparent to scripters. So JavaBeans may eventually make Java accessible to the masses. Unfortunately, the "Java is easy" hype was started a bit too prematurely.

■ ***Browsers do not support the latest versions of Java.*** The move from JDK 1.02 to JDK 1.1 was a mess. It took forever to bring Java VMs and browsers in sync. ***Counterpoint:*** Yes, this particular transition was a horrible mess. However, you can now use JavaSoft's *Java Plugin* to get around these problems. You may also want to join the *Java Lobby* (check them out at *http://www.javalobby.org*). They can put pressure on JavaSoft to make sure that these plug-ins are delivered on time for all platforms and on all browsers.

■ ***Java is too slow.*** Java is a resource hog—especially on older platforms like Windows/DOS. ***Counterpoint:*** Yes, Java is particularly slow on 16-bit platforms. However, it's fast enough on most Windows 95/98 machines. Just-in-time compilers have helped a lot; Java 2 should further boost the performance. If nothing works, try Sun's new *Java PC*; it is optimized for DOS and Windows 3.X.

■ ***The universal client is Windows—you don't need Java.*** With Windows owning the desktop there is no longer a need for "write once, run everywhere." ***Counterpoint:*** There is a lot more than just Windows on the client (see Part 2). In any case, the mobile code infrastructure is the real benefit Java brings to the client. It lets you can download an entire client application—or an HTML container full of beans—by simply clicking on a URL.

■ *JavaSoft doesn't know how to write code.* Microsoft produced the world's fastest VM because it's a software company. Sun is really a hardware company; it shouldn't be in the software business. In Sun's hands, Java is just a resource hog; it helps sell Sun hardware. *Counterpoint:* We would love to see JavaSoft make Java Open Source. We could then get the world's best programmers to work on it. But even today Sun is not the only company working on Java. Thousands of programmers are working on the Java core in companies like IBM, Oracle, Gemstone, Novell, and BEA. The Java licensees are required to feed back their improvements to JavaSoft. Of course, Open Source would even be better. Yes, the Java Lobby is thinking about this one too.

■ *Java is always changing.* JavaSoft is all over the place. They've become a real API machine. Instead, they should focus on delivering a stable Java platform. *Counterpoint:* There's some truth here. However, it seems JavaSoft has got the message. Java 2 is the proof; it provides an orderly migration path. In all fairness, JavaSoft had to re-invent the Java equivalent of the Microsoft Windows APIs. So you should pressure both sides to declare an API freeze. Until then it's tit for tat.

■ *Java GUIs are real ugly.* The previous JDK's AWT was the ugly duckling of GUI frameworks. Consequently, client applications that were created in Java were bland compared to their equivalents for the Mac or Windows GUIs. *Counterpoint:* JavaBeans and JFC have changed all this. Java 2 even supports drag-and-drop. So you can download some very attractive-looking applications. Also, there are now world-class tools from Inprise, Symantec, Sybase, and IBM to help you create Web pages using JavaBeans. These tools rival their Windows counterparts. In fact, Java has become the favorite platform for visual tool vendors. Figure 28-7 shows a screen capture of our Club Med Web-based reservation system. Everything you see on this Web page is a JavaBean. We assembled these beans for our programming book using Symantec's *Visual Café* and Inprise's *JBuilder*. We used their beans to assemble ours.

To understand why Java is not universally accepted on the client, it's also very important to note the distinction between Web content providers and Web client/server programmers. The first group builds HTML content pages. Occasionally, they enhance these pages with scripts or pre-built applets. These people are really Web authors, not professional programmers. They're mostly interested in providing visually appealing Web pages.

The second group uses Web technology to develop 3-tier client/server applications. HTML pages are primarily containers of components; they use Java to download just-in-time clients. This second group consists of professional programmers. CORBA/EJB and COM+ are helping them create libraries of reusable components. However, when it comes to writing client/server systems, there are no silver bullets. You must write some business logic somewhere. Component-based tools can now help you create 80% of an application on both the client and the server. But you must still write that remaining 20%. For all but the simplest Web-based client/server applications, we recommend that you write new code in Java on both the client and the server. You can also use CORBA to encapsulate existing code on the server. ☐

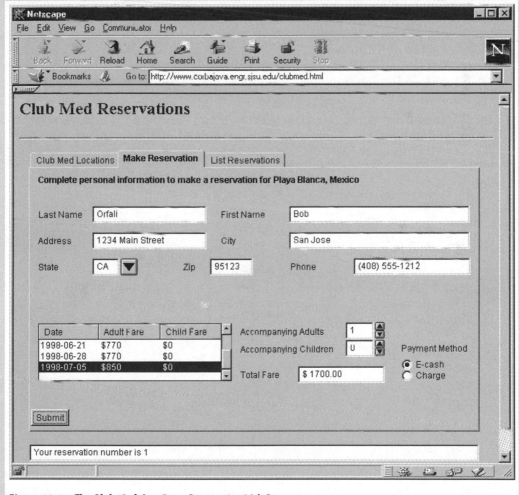

Figure 28-7. The Club Med JavaBean Reservation Web Page.

The CORBA/Java Object Web

Now let's go over the 3-tier client/server architecture of this emerging Object Web (see Figure 28-8).

■   *Tier 1* belongs to traditional Web browsers and the new Web-centric desktops. As opposed to today's static Web pages, the new content will have more the look-and-feel of real objects—for example, you'll be seeing places that contain people, things, and other places. This very dynamic content is provided by ensembles of JavaBeans embedded in mobile containers such as HTML pages or JARs that contain *shippable places*. You will interact with these objects via drag-and-drop and other forms of direct manipulation. Client beans will be able to interact with other client beans in the container as well as with server beans. In addition, server beans will be able invoke methods on client beans using CORBA events and callbacks. Note that both IIOP and HTTP can run on the same networks. HTTP is used to download Web pages, JARs, and images; CORBA is used for Java client-to-server and server-to-client communications.

■   *Tier 2* runs on any server that can service both HTTP and CORBA clients. This CORBA/HTTP combination is supported on almost every server OS platform—

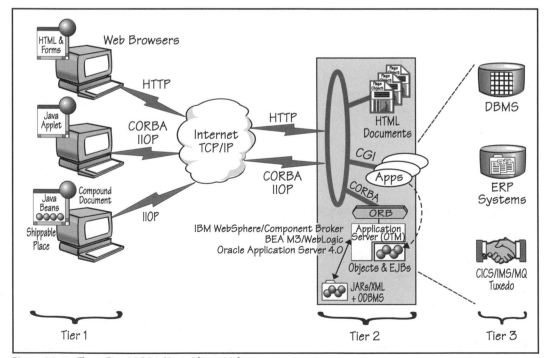

Figure 28-8. The 3-Tier CORBA/Java Object Web.

including Unixes, NT, OS/2, NetWare, Mac OS, OS/400, MVS, and Tandem NonStop Kernel. CORBA objects—packaged as Enterprise JavaBeans and CORBA Beans—act as middle-tier application servers; they encapsulate the business logic. These objects interact with client JavaBeans via CORBA/IIOP. Less-scalable applications can also call these objects via scripts that run in HTML server pages or via Servlets (see the next Briefing Box).

The CORBA Beans on the server interact with each other using a CORBA ORB. They can also talk to existing server applications in the third tier using JDBC or any other form of database middleware. You can even use the CORBA/IIOP server backbone as a general-purpose data bus. This is the technology Oracle is building for its data plug-ins. JDBC-on-IIOP data backbones are available today from I-Kinetics, Oracle, and Inprise/Visigenic.

The second tier must also provide a server-side application server or *Object Transaction Monitor (OTM)*. The application server prestarts pools of objects, distributes loads, provides fault tolerance, and coordinates multi-component transactions. Without these application servers, you cannot manage millions of server-side objects—a key requirement of the Object Web. Examples of CORBA-based Web application servers are IBM's *WebSphere/Component Broker*, BEA's *WebLogic/M3*, Oracle's *Application Server 4.0*, Netscape/ Kiva/AOL's *Application Server*, and Sun's *NetDynamics*. We provide a much longer list of CORBA application server vendors in Part 7.

But, what is a Web server component? In this case, it's an EJB or CORBA Bean. As we explained in Part 7, these are CORBA objects augmented with component features such as declarative transactions and security. In a CORBA/Java Object Web, the second tier also acts as a store of components, HTML pages, and shippable places. These can be stored in XML documents, HTML pages, and Java JARs. These stores can be managed by an ODBMS or DBMS. ODBMSs are better suited for the task. An ODBMS can treat a compound XML document as just another user-defined data type; an SQL database must support object extenders to provide the same kind of service. An ODBMS can transparently cache active XML documents in memory. So when a client requests a shippable place or component Web page, the ODBMS can service the request almost instantaneously. You will be able to get this technology on a CORBA/Java platform from vendors such as ODI, Gemstone, and Versant. We cover XML compound documents and their DOM interfaces later in this chapter.

- ■ *Tier 3* is almost anything a CORBA object can access. This includes procedural TP Monitors, MOMs, DBMSs, ODBMSs, ERP systems, mainframe applications, Lotus Notes, and e-mail. So the CORBA bus replaces CGI in the middle tier, which is good. Eventually, you will use off-the-shelf CORBA/EJBs that encapsulate most of the third-tier functions. For example, MDI currently provides a suite of CORBA/EJBs that encapsulate almost every existing data source. You should also look at the I-Kinetics work to understand what you can do today with these back-end components.[5]

FYI

What Is a Servlet?

Briefing

In mid-1997, JavaSoft shipped the *Java Web Server* (previously known as *Jeeves*). This product had two claims to fame: 1) it was the first implementation ever of a Java-based Web server, and 2) it introduced *Servlets*—a new all-Java plug-in architecture for servers. JavaSoft also provides a *Java Servlet Development Kit*, which lets you run Servlets on the more popular Web servers—including *Apache*, Netscape *Enterprise Server*, and Microsoft *IIS*. This kit includes a set of classes and interfaces that define exactly how a Web server must interact with a Servlet.

A Servlet is a small piece of Java code that a Web server loads to handle client requests. Unlike a CGI application, the Servlet code stays resident in memory when the request terminates. In addition, a Servlet can connect to a database when it is initialized and then retain its connection across requests. A Servlet can also pass a client request to another Servlet. This is called Servlet *chaining*. All these features make Servlets an excellent workaround for many of CGI's limitations.

Even though you can implement Servlets as CORBA or RMI objects, they still don't provide the full power of distributed objects. You can only interact with a Servlet using a generic API—meaning a set of predefined methods. Like CGI and sockets, Servlets provide a very primitive form of middleware. You must do your own marshaling and unmarshaling of parameters. Servlets do not support typed interfaces. Consequently, you must create your own command formats.

However, it's precisely this constraint that makes Servlets convenient for simple applications. For example, Servlets make good replacements for CGI-bin scripts. They are good at accepting form input, interacting with a single database, and then dynamically generating an HTML response page. They provide a simple callback API to a Web server. In addition, they include useful helper functions that let you extract HTTP name/value pairs and compose a dynamic HTTP response. So there may still be a place for Servlets in your Java server-side arsenal.

---

[5] See *http://www.i-kinetics.com/wp/cwvision/CWVision.htm*.

Without turning this into a Soapbox, Servlets are just one notch better than CGI (or Sockets) in the Web middleware hierarchy. Their simplistic API is a two-edged sword. It's a good fit for a CGI-like request/response paradigm. However, it's also a crippled distributed object solution; it does not take advantage of object interfaces to provide higher levels of abstractions to the services your write. Servlets also lack many of the important features you would expect from a scalable server-side component infrastructure. For example, they do not support transactions, which are now a standard feature of the CORBA/EJB and COM+ server-side component models. In addition, Servlets do not support a dynamic deactivation mechanism. ❑

Meet the CORBA/Java Object Web Players

A new vendor coalition is building around the CORBA/Java Object Web. The Web transforms CORBA/Java from a set of standards to a set of products that fulfill an intergalactic need. To use a shopping mall analogy, the anchor stores of the CORBA/Java Object Web are Netscape/AOL, Oracle, Sun/JavaSoft, and IBM/Lotus (the press calls them the "Gang of Four"). This mall is also populated with hundreds of software vendors that provide the boutiques and specialty stores—including specialized ORBs, tools, OTMs, application servers, components, ERP systems, and services. There should be enough critical mass to attract the shoppers with the dollars—ISVs, IT shops, and consumers of software. Let's take a quick look at what each of these players provides:

- **Netscape/AOL** is making CORBA ubiquitous on the client. It is bundling the Inprise *VisiBroker for Java* ORB with every browser. Netscape is also using CORBA for its server-to-server infrastructure. Potentially, Netscape can distribute over 60 million CORBA ORBs on the client and over a million CORBA ORBs on the server. CORBA also allows Netscape servers to play with other servers on the enterprise.

- **Oracle** has adopted CORBA/Java as the platform for its *Network Computing Architecture*. Oracle's entire software line—from the *Oracle8i* database engine to stored procedures, tools, and the Internet—is built on a CORBA object bus. For example, the database engine is being componentized using CORBA. Third parties can extend the database using CORBA components, called *Cartridges*. Oracle is building most of the CORBA Services on top of the Borland/Visigenic VisiBroker ORB; it also has its own server-side IIOP ORB. The first Oracle product to ship with this technology is *Application Server 4.0;* it supports both CORBA Beans and EJBs.

- **JavaSoft/Sun** is making CORBA a core Java technology. We explained what JavaSoft is doing in this area earlier in the chapter. Sun recently adopted

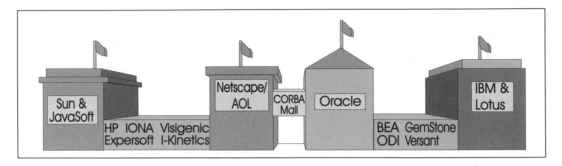

VisiBroker as its ORB technology for Solaris. In mid-1998, Sun acquired the *NetDynamics* CORBA-based Web application server. In December 1998, AOL announced a partnership with Sun to distribute the Netscape server line.

■ **IBM/Lotus** is building its cross-platform network computing infrastructure on CORBA/Java. IBM is bundling Java VMs in all its OS platforms. The IBM *VisualAge* tool lets you create CORBA/Java objects on both clients and servers across all the IBM platforms. The IBM *Component Broker* is a scalable server-side component coordinator for managing middle-tier CORBA/Java objects; IBM *WebSphere* is a Web application server that also supports CORBA/EJB. Finally, the next Lotus Notes—*Domino 5.0*—is being built on an IIOP foundation.

■ **The boutiques** come in all shapes. They include long-standing CORBA players like HP, Iona, Visigenic/Borland, Tandem, Novell, I-Kinetics, and Expersoft. This camp also includes the ODBMS vendors—for example, ODI, GemStone, Persistence, and Versant. In addition, TP Monitor vendors are now morphing ORBs with traditional TP Monitors. For example, BEA delivered *M3*, a scalable CORBA-based TP Monitor on top of Tuxedo. The boutiques also include tool vendors—such as Symantec, ParcPlace, Borland/Inprise, Penumbra, and Sybase. The latest arrivals are Web server vendors that are moving to scalable application servers—examples include NetDynamics, Kiva/Netscape, WebLogic/BEA, and BlueStone. Finally, the boutiques include the major ISVs (and ERP vendors) that gravitate in the Netscape/AOL, IBM, JavaSoft, BEA, Novell, and Oracle orbits. So there will be quite a crowd.

In summary, this new CORBA/Java coalition is building around a killer app called the Object Web. CORBA and Enterprise JavaBeans provide the architectural glue that connects the products on this Object Web. For example, ORBs running in Netscape browsers can talk to middle-tier Oracle Cartridges that also happen to be Enterprise JavaBeans. Object Transaction Monitors—from IBM, BEA, Netscape, GemStone, Oracle, and Sun—will synchronize and coordinate these server-side business objects because they all use CORBA OTS. Beans from thousands of vendors will play on both the client and server sides. The CORBA bus is the foundation technology that brings together all these disparate pieces of software from multiple vendors.

The CORBA/Java Object Web will eventually draw in thousands of smaller software developers that will create specialized components that service this huge market. This is our industry's first attempt to provide plug-and-play at the software product level, which is the ultimate open system dream.

The Microsoft Object Web

If we hadn't come along, Microsoft wouldn't be doing any of this client software to support any of the Internet standards. Instead of HTML you'd have Blackbird. Instead of IMAP you'd have MAPI. Instead of MIME you'd have Microsoft proprietary messaging formats.

> — **Marc Andreessen, Founder**
> **Netscape**
> **(March, 1998)**

In parallel, Microsoft is building its own rendition of the Object Web; it is based on COM+ and ActiveX. We described the Microsoft products in Part 7. So there should be no surprises. Currently, the Microsoft Web appears to be a single-anchor mall with tons of boutiques. Figure 28-9 is a rendition of the Microsoft Object Web. It is, of course, a 3-tier client/server architecture. Let's go over the tiers:

■ **Tier 1** belongs to the client. In this case, the client is the Windows desktop. COM provides the object bus that ties everything together. ActiveX as a mobile code system was a market flop; it did not have the right security model. So to fill its need for a mobile code system Microsoft supports Dynamic HTML and XML. Of course, Microsoft does not support the JavaBeans component model. However, the good news on the client is that Microsoft appears to be committed to Dynamic HTML and XML. It is investing a lot of resources into these two technologies.

■ **Tier 2** consists of Microsoft's *Internet Information Server (IIS)*. IIS is bundled with NT Server; it is also tightly integrated with MTS and the rest of the COM+ platform. IIS tracks a document (or title) by assigning it a globally unique ID (or GUID); it maps GUIDs to URLs using COM *monikers*.

IIS runs *Active Server Pages (ASPs)*, which provide an application server environment to run server-side scripts. ASPs supports both VB Script and JavaScript. Microsoft also lets you instantiate and invoke COM objects from within these scripts. For example, you can invoke a server-side transactional

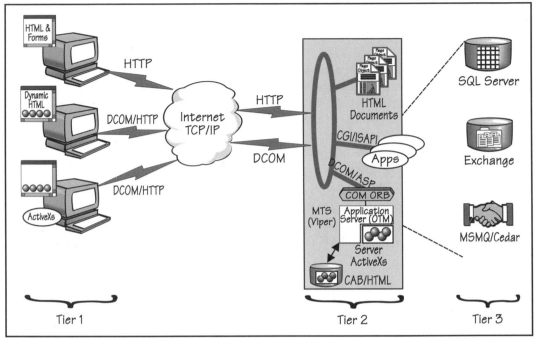

Figure 28-9. The Microsoft Object Web.

ActiveX that runs under MTS. Or you can invoke OLE DB objects via the ADO interface. So in the Microsoft Object Web the OTM is MTS, the ORB is DCOM, and the data bus is OLE DB.

■ *Tier 3* consists of Microsoft's BackOffice, and any server application that can be accessed using COM, ISAPI, or ODBC. Microsoft also provides gateways to CICS and IMS.

In summary, Microsoft has put together a compelling Object Web story. Are there any caveats? Yes, it's an NT-only solution; also see our criticism of COM+ in Part 7. Microsoft is again creating its own parallel universe on the Web. Like the enterprise, the Web is a very heterogeneous environment. So Microsoft faces some very strong competition from the heterogeneous CORBA/Java Object Web. In addition, Microsoft must contend with the Web Open Source movement—these are the people who created the Web in the first place. The Open Source movement now controls the three most popular Web platforms—Linux, Apache, and the Netscape browser. And, they're all free. We will have more to say about all this in the next chapter.

THE DOCUMENT IS THE OBJECT

In some sort of cosmic sense, XML could be the first true medium of data interchange over the world's first all-encompassing network...It provides us the handles for discovering meaning and structure that the vast flood of information on the Internet must have if we're not going to be inundated.

— *Nelson King*
(May, 1998)

Imagine a Web page where every element is an IDL-defined CORBA object—including its tags, attributes, style sheets, embedded scripts, and so on. Then imagine a Web page where you are not limited by the tags that Netscape, Microsoft, or, W3C define for you. The page can contain any tag you define. For example, you could create a tag called DOG or CUSTOMER and then define your own attributes. And, what if we told you that this document was smart enough to return metadata for every tag it contains?

In addition, this incredible document comes with style sheets that allow it to be rendered on different media and devices. Even better, the style sheet itself consists of first-class objects that you can navigate, query, and then invoke on-the-fly to create your own renderings. To top it off, this intelligent document can emit events that it uses to let you know when something of interest happens to it.

So have we had one espresso too much? Or, are we starting to get Object Web hallucinations? No, is the answer to both these questions. We are describing three key standards from W3C that together are radically changing what it means to be a Web document. The good news is that Web documents are being reborn as first-class objects. Today, the Web is the world's largest file server. With this new technology, it could turn into the world's largest Object Database. The documents—now objects—can be rendered, exchanged, and distributed in ways we haven't even dreamed of.

Before we explore these new possibilities, we must first explain this new technology. In this section, we describe three technologies that play together to provide the magic we described. And, it takes all three to get the magic. The first technology is XML; you use it to 1) describe the structure of a document, 2) define new tags, and 3) specify the metadata that lets programs discover "on-the-fly" this structure and understand your new tags. The second standard is DOM; it defines in CORBA IDL the interfaces that let you access—using a variety of languages—the structure of XML and HTML documents. The last standard is XSL; it's the XML version of style sheets.

XML: Stretching the Concept of Document

Yes, XML is forcing some pretty extreme elasticity on our notion of what a document is, and what it means to work with one...It will force document weenies (sometimes) to think like database geeks, and engineers (sometimes) to think like editors.

> — *Tim Gray, XML Architect*
> *W3C*
> *(December, 1998)*

In February 1998, W3C issued a recommendation for a new Web document standard called the *Extensible Markup Language (XML)*. Like HTML, XML has its roots in SGML. So it has the look and feel of HTML. Unlike HTML, XML does not define any tags. Instead, it lets you create your own tags and define your own document structures. XML simply defines standard ways to manage and exchange complex documents. You can think of XML as a language for creating document structures. For example, you could use XML to recreate all the HTML tags. However, why stop with HTML? You now have the flexibility of creating your own tags. The next step is to agree on tag vocabularies for different industries. For example, the medical community could agree on a suite of tags called: PATIENT, PRESCRIPTION, HOSPITAL, CLAIM, NURSE, and so on. They could then use these tags in their documents and e-mail; it's just like using HTML tags. Of course, a browser must also be able to decipher these new tags, but we're getting ahead of our story.

Unlike classical objects, these XML tags only define the data structure. They don't define the behavior of the object. So you'll still need your Beans to provide the behavior; XML is just a way for Beans to agree on the semantics of the data they exchange. It's the new data interchange medium for the Web. You define new XML tags (or object types) using a schema language called *DTD* (for *Document Type Definition*). So you need to create DTDs for PATIENT, DOCTOR, and so on. A tag in a document is just an instance of a DTD.

The best way to get a feel for XML is by example. Here's how you would use the new DOCTOR tag in an XML document:

```
<?XML version= "1.0"   standalone="no"?>
<!DOCTYPE DOCTOR   SYSTEM "http://www.medical.com/doctor.dtd">
<DOCTOR
    name="Doolittle"
    specialty = "Veterinarian"
    hobbies = "Long conversations with monkeys"  />
```

Here's the DTD that defines the DOCTOR tag:

```
<?XML version= "1.0"    encoding = "UTF-8" ?>
<!ELEMENT DOCTOR EMPTY>
<!ATTLIST   DOCTOR
      name CDATA #REQUIRED
      specialty CDATA #REQUIRED
      hobbies CDATA #IMPLIED>
```

Like HTML, an XML document can contain one or more *elements* bracketed by start and end tags. Each element has a tag name (or *type*). The text between the start and end tags is the element's *contents;* it can be empty. An element can also have *attributes*. Each attribute has a name and value. In our example, DOCTOR had three attributes: name, specialty, and hobbies. These attributes are of type CDATA, which stands for string. You can also tell the XML parser that the attribute is *required*, which means the value must be filled; *implied* means it's optional.

You can use XML to represent containment models. For example, a DOCTOR tag can contain one or more NURSE tags. Here's an example:

```
<?XML version= "1.0"    standalone="no"?>
<!DOCTYPE DOCTOR    SYSTEM "http://www.medical.com/doctor.dtd">
<DOCTOR
      name="Doolittle"
      specialty = "Veterinarian"
      hobbies = "Long conversations with monkeys"  />
<NURSE>Florence Nightingale</NURSE>
<NURSE>Sammy Happyface</NURSE>
</DOCTOR>
```

In this example, Doctor Doolittle has two nurses: Florence and Sammy. This means that a DTD can contain other DTDs. So you can use XML to represent tree-like nested data—for example, an invoice or book. For more information on XML, you owe it to yourself to look at the specification itself; it's only 31 pages long (see: *http://www.w3.org/TR/1998/REC-xml-19980210*).

Still in the works is an XML linking language called *XLink;* it will let you construct links between XML documents and elements (or tags). *Xlink* is a lot richer than HTML's simple links. Also under construction is *XPointer*; it provides constructs for navigating an XML document.

To conclude, XML lets you encode new tags and their metadata. It also lets you define complex structures within documents. With XML the imagination is at the controls. Here's our top-ten list of what XML will be able to do for the Object Web: 1) exchange data between clients and servers on the Web, 2) provide a common data exchange medium among the Web's various data stores, 3) provide common tags (or data vocabularies) for different industries and domains, 4) serve as the *Electronic Data Interchange (EDI)* language for Web commerce, 5) serve as a packaging technology for Web components—for example CORBA Beans use XML as their component interchange medium, 6) enable Web bots, crawlers, and agents to act more intelligently in their search for information, 7) serve as the lingua franca for Web-based workflow, 8) provide a common mechanism for objects to exchange state information, 9) provide common data vocabularies for component suites, and 10) provides a channel definition format for push technology.

We could go on with this list. By now you should get the idea that XML is an important addition to the Object Web; it augments it with a consistent data interchange medium.

DOM: Turning XML and HTML Into Objects

XML gives Java something to do.

> — *Jon Bosak, Chair*
> *XML Committee*

An XML document is not too useful if you can't process it. So the million-dollar questions are: How do you access the contents and rich structure of an XML document? What is the data manipulation language for XML documents? What is the SQL-equivalent for XML data? The answer to all these questions is DOM. In October 1998, W3C issued a recommendation for a sister standard to XML called the *Document Object Model (DOM)*. This standard provides an object model for both HTML and XML.

So what does this object model do? For starters, it defines—in CORBA IDL—interfaces that let you control every tag and structure within an XML or HTML document. It's the ultimate interface for generating dynamic Web documents on-the-fly; it's also a great tool for navigating the Web. DOM enables programs—like bots, beans, agents, and crawlers—to navigate the Web on your behalf. DOM also allows client and server programs to generate interchange data and manipulate the results. So what language do these programs use to access the DOM interfaces? You can use any CORBA-supported language. The specification also includes explicit language bindings for Java and ECMAScript—a standardized version of JavaScript.

You can use DOM on both clients and servers. On the client side, a browser parses an XML (or HTML 4.0) document and then generates a tree-representation in memory. Your programs use DOM invocations to navigate the tree and manipulate different elements within the document. On the server side, the document is parsed by an application server. You can then use the same DOM interfaces to manipulate the document. Eventually, DOM will become the SQL of the Web. All you need is a CORBA ORB to invoke any DOM object over the network. Clients will be able to remotely access Web document servers using DOM-over-IIOP. In other words, Web documents become distributed CORBA objects. In addition, ODBMSs appear to be the ideal store for XML's nested data. Together, these pieces provide an end-to-end object solution. Yes, all the elements of a killer application are here.

XSL: Or, How to Render XML

By now, you must be asking: How do I view an XML document? What happens after I click on a URL that points to an XML document? How does that new DOCTOR tag get rendered? After all, a browser doesn't know a DOCTOR from bowl of cereal. The answer to all these questions is XSL; it provides the third piece of this puzzle. In August 1998, the W3C issued the first public draft of a standard called the *Extensible Style Language (XSL)*.

XSL defines CSS-like style sheets for XML (and also HTML 4.0). An XML style sheet consists of *style rules* that define the presentation of a document. You can access and manipulate these rules using DOM. XSL lets you assign names to styles. You can then apply a named style to as many elements as you want. You can also nest XSL style sheets using an *import* tag. Like CSS, XSL separates the user interface from the structured data. This is a good thing. XSL appears to be CSS done right. And, this time it also has an object model.

Web Pages, Object Web Style

Together, Java 2, JavaBeans, and XSL/XML can provide an integrated visual experience for the Web unlike anything you've seen to date. With Java 2, you can now drag-and-drop beans. XSL allows beans to seamlessly share the visual real estate within a browser's window. You will also be able to drag and drop components within the browser. In today's browsers, components own a static rectangular area within a page. In an XSL-enabled browser, you should be able to move around components, resize them within a page, zoom in on their contents, and visually rearrange the contents of the page in any way you want. The components will automatically share the document's menu, clipboard, and palette. Everything will look very seamless.

Unlike today's browser experience, the visual components will be able to interact with each other in many unanticipated ways. For example, you'll be able to drag a URL and drop it on a button to create an active pushbutton. You'll be able to shop by dragging merchandise and dropping it in an electronic shopping cart. You'll pay with e-cash that you pull out of an electronic wallet and drop on an invoice. And you will be able to drag an electronic signature and drop it on a message to seal a deal. The imagination is really at the controls in terms of what you can do with this marriage of XSL/XML technology with JavaBeans.

Intelligent Containers, Object Web Style

In addition to Web pages, you'll be able to download containers of components called *shippable places*. XML provides the portable containers to store and distribute components. It provides a "file system within a file" that lets components store their data in self-describing, navigable data streams. So what can these *structured containers* do for the Object Web?

Simply put, structured containers allow us to store multiple components in a single document, move them as a single unit across networks, cache them where it makes most sense, and store them in document databases. The component store also becomes a unit of defense for an entire set of components. For example, you should be able to selectively encrypt a set of components. Finally, the containers can also persistently store a document's context and act accordingly. For example, you can store in an XML file—along with a set of components—a user's preferences, login state, and the most current visual layout of the document.

In summary, components need component stores so that you can move them around the Web at will. Structured containers are lightweight, shippable, object databases that were designed specifically to store, manage, and transport components. We can think of dozens of ways these structured component containers can be used to create a smarter Object Web. The next section looks at one such example— *shippable places*.

So, What Is a Shippable Place?

*U*sers will live in their browsers? Ridiculous. Browsers will live inside our applications. We won't even realize they are there.

— Jesse Berst, PC Week

A *place* is a visual ensemble of related components. A *shippable place* is a mobile container of components; it's a place that can be shipped over the Net. Today's user interfaces are centered around a primitive place that represents a desktop. In contrast, shippable places let you interact with multiple places that represent collaborative environments based on real-world models. A place is a *mini-virtual world*. For example, we can have places for 12-year olds, lawyers, or accountants. A place is typically used to display components that represent people and things. For example, places can represent meeting rooms, libraries, offices, homes, stadiums, shopping malls, museums, parks, and auditoriums. *People* live, work, shop, and visit these places. *Things* are tools that help us communicate, interact, and work within these places.

A place is implemented as a collection of components stored in a structured file container. You assemble a place by dragging components and dropping them within a visual container, which you then store in a structured file. You should be able to connect to a place via its URL and then download it just like any ordinary Web page. Of course, a place will have a digital signature that guarantees it came from a trusted server. The client will also have to authenticate itself before it can use the downloaded place.

Once the place is secured on your desktop, it will serve as a visual front-end for all kinds of specialized Internet services and business objects. The components within a place will typically communicate with their back-end counterparts using an ORB. A place is a dynamic assembly of ever-changing data, video feeds, and other live content.

You will probably keep the place on your desktop for weeks or months at a time, occasionally refreshing it with a newer version. The place is really one of many alternate desktops. You can also customize a place to reflect your preferences and needs. So, a place is a mobile document that you will store and access over time. In contrast, a Web page is more transient; it comes and then goes. With Web pages screen updates are wholesale page replacements, which destroy a user's context. In addition, there is no easy way for servers to tell clients that something has changed. Places fix these problems; they provide an anchor on the client that servers can call.

The Future Web Client

The operating system shell and the Internet browser will be one and the same.

> — Bill Gates, Chairman
> Microsoft

Figure 28-10 shows three client models for the Web. In the first model, the browser is the Webtop; it assumes that people live within their browsers. All you need is a browser and a good *portal* site where you store your Web environment. This is the current Netscape/AOL model of the world. In the second model, everything on the desktop is Web enabled; the idea is that you will be able to access the Web from within any application or component without starting a browser. This is the Microsoft Windows 98 model of the world. The third model is shippable places; it lets you access the Web from within your places. A place can have multiple concurrent sessions with Web object servers. In addition, multiple places can be concurrently active on the same desktop. The Object Web may end up supporting all three models.

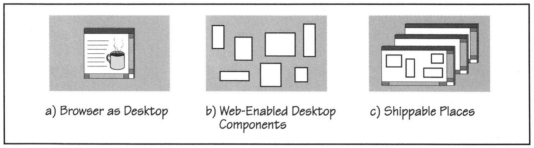

a) Browser as Desktop   b) Web-Enabled Desktop Components   c) Shippable Places

Figure 28-10. The Evolving Web Client Model.

CONCLUSION

I think people are only beginning to understand what networks really mean.

— *James Gosling*

The bottom line is that Java provides a simpler and newer way to develop, manage, and deploy client/server applications. You can access the latest version of an application by simply clicking on the mouse. You can distribute an application to millions of clients by putting it on a Web server. Distribution is immediate. And you don't have to concern yourself with installation and updates.

Java is also good for servers. It lets you write mobile server code that you can use in very flexible arrangements. For example, servers can transmit EJBs to other servers to look for information. Executable software can move to where it's needed most. Java provides a flexible, just-in-time execution environment on servers as well as on clients.

As we explained in this long chapter, CORBA complements Java; it provides the distributed object infrastructure—or the component object bus for the Web. Enterprise JavaBeans is the child of the Java/CORBA marriage. As we go to press, almost every Web application server vendor has standardized on the CORBA/EJB component model. The exception is Microsoft; it is promoting its competing COM+ component model.

The Object Web also needs an object document model, which is where XML and DOM come into the picture. They provide the intelligent containers for *shippable places*. A place is an ensemble of visual components; it's a shippable container filled with JavaBeans. You will typically store places on servers. You will be able to download your favorite places using ordinary HTTP commands. XSL and the Java Foundation Classes provide the rendering technology to seamlessly display these beans within Web pages. You can then interact with a place by simply clicking on the visual components it contains. The contents of a place are dynamic—you can edit everything "in-place." The beans invoke CORBA/IIOP—from within the context of a Web page or place—to obtain services anywhere in the intergalactic universe. Everything on the Web is an object invocation away; IIOP proxies augment the Web with object-based security.

The good news is that once this Object Web technology takes off, it will subsume all other forms of client/server computing—including TP Monitors, Database, and Groupware. Distributed objects and the Web can do it all, and better. Objects will help us break large monolithic applications into more manageable multivendor components that can live and coexist on intergalactic networks. They are also our only hope for managing and distributing the millions of software entities that will live on these intergalactic networks.

Chapter 29

Web Client/Server: Meet the Players

Two years ago the Internet was an emerging fad. Now it's a tsunami and vendors are scrambling to accommodate it.

— Jamie Lewis, President
Burton Group

The computer industry is once again recreating itself. The Internet is a giant tsunami that will not leave anything untouched in its path. It is redefining the client/server envelope and reshuffling the cards. As you can imagine, the Internet is creating more than its fair share of new instant winners and losers in the computer industry. And nobody knows for sure where the Internet market will lead.

It would be sheer lunacy for us to predict what the Internet client/server landscape will look like in the next two years. For example, server companies—like Sun, IBM, and Oracle—may use JavaBeans and XML to regain the desktop from Microsoft. Or, Microsoft may use the COM+ Object Web to become the new enterprise server company; it may then wipe the existing server companies from the face of the Earth. Or, the Open Source movement—Linux, Apache, and Mozilla—may use its solid Internet base to wipe out NT 5.0. In between, there are fortunes to be made in

Internet commerce, multimedia databases, security, firewalls, authoring tools, mobile agents, avatars, and virtual worlds. Beyond the basic plumbing, there are even greater fortunes to be made by providers of online content and goods—including entertainment, education, and commercial services.

One thing we can say for sure is that the Internet client/server race is turning out to be quite complex, with lots of contestants all vying for a lead within numerous market niches. This chapter starts out by giving you a quick snapshot of the Internet client/server market. We then bravely forecast some of the key trends. How big is the prize? What markets are emerging? Next, we pick our favorites in the Web client/server sweepstakes. Where is Jimmy the Greek when we need him? Note that this chapter focuses only on the client/server aspects of the Internet; extending the coverage beyond this limit would be too suicidal—even for us.

INTERNET MARKET OVERVIEW

*T*he Internet is basically a stack, and there are different amounts of opportunity at each level in the stack.

> — Bill Gates, Chairman
> Microsoft

The Internet means different things to different folks; it's become the umbrella name for multiple emerging subindustries. Figure 29-1 divides the Internet industry into six major segments:

1. ***Internet equipment providers.*** This includes the manufacturers of backbone routers, Internet access equipment, and server computers.

2. ***Internet service providers (ISPs).*** This includes traditional bandwidth providers such as PSI Net, UUNet, NetCom, BBN Planet, and @Home. It also includes providers of consumer online services such as America Online (AOL), Microsoft Network (MSN), Prodigy, MindSpring, GoSite, and CompuServe; these vendors are fiercely counterattacking the traditional ISPs to get their share of the Internet market. Finally, the telephone and cable-TV companies have also entered the fray; they are vying for a share of the high-bandwidth sweepstakes.

3. ***Internet client/server software.*** This includes browsers, HTTP servers, Web application servers, security, and tools; the software we covered in the last three chapters. It includes software used for both the Internet and intranets. Note that we do not include in this list related server software—including ORBs, RDBMSs, ODBMSs, Data Warehouses, TP Monitors, and groupware. These related server markets were covered in previous parts of this book; to include them here would be double-counting.

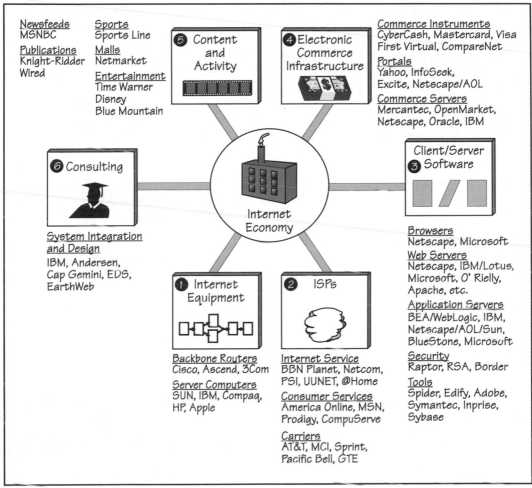

Figure 29-1. The Internet Industry Segments.

4. *Internet electronic commerce infrastructure.* This includes e-cash, electronic credit and debit cards, online banks, and anything that helps facilitate electronic commerce. This category also includes directory services and *search engines* that help you find things; for example, Yahoo!, Excite, and InfoSeek. We also include electronic shopping frameworks—like Broadvision, Electric Communities, and Open Market. Web *portals* also fall into this category; they are the cyberlandlords who control the entrances to the shopping malls. We include a new breed of *electronic brokers*—for example, CompareNet (*www.compare.com*) helps you compare products feature for feature and dollar for dollar; Bankrate.com lets you shop for the best mortgage rates. Finally, we include a new generation of Web *auctioneers*—like Priceline.com and eBay.com; they let potential buyers bid against each other. Auctions are very

big on the Web. For example, EBay claims to have one million items for sale; it receives 20 million page hits per day.

5. ***Internet content, online shopping, and business-to-business activity.*** This includes electronic newsfeeds, sports, malls, publications, entertainment, and other forms of content. It also includes consumer-to-business online sales— such as Amazon.com, Egghead.com, Dell.com, Gap.com, WellsFargo.com, Schwab.com, and E*Trade.com. Finally, there is the invisible network of business-to-business transactions. Ultimately, this is what Internet client/server is all about—fun, games, education, shopping, and business.

6. ***Internet consulting.*** This includes traditional systems integrators that are called in to create corporate intranets. It also includes a new breed of Internet consultant; such as Web-page graphic designers and online advertisement and Internet presence-building agencies.

There is nothing sacred about the six categories we just described. We use them to give you an idea about the different facets of what is now called the *Internet Economy*. As you can see, the Internet covers quite a broad territory. To borrow from Bill Gates, it's a big stack with a wide range of players.

How Large Is the Internet Economy?

So, how large is this Internet Economy? It appears to be gigantic. According to IDC, the Internet Economy now totals $200 billion worldwide. By 2002, it will total upwards of $950 billion. This is larger than the current economy of Greece or Portugal.[1] The IDC numbers include the combination of spending to build Web businesses and applications and the revenues of products and services sold over the Internet. This may come as a surprise: IDC's numbers are in the mid-range of the projections scale. For example, analyst Nicholas Lippis—of Strategic Networks— projects that Internet online sales alone will reach $1.5 trillion by 2002; John Chambers—CEO of Cisco—reckons that it will be around $1 trillion.[2]

Here are some more numbers that you may find interesting:

■ ***Internet hardware servers:*** According to Dataquest, the market for Internet servers grew at a rate of 114% in 1998; sales reached $13.7 billion, up from $6.21 billion in 1997. In 1997, Sun accounted for 22.3% of Internet server revenues followed by HP with 19.6% market share.[3]

---

[1] Source: IDC, *Internet Executive Forum* (September, 1998).

[2] Source: GartnerGroup, *Paradigm Shift* (November, 1998). Note that Cisco generates over 65% of its sales via the Web—well over $5 billion in 1998.

[3] Source: Dataquest, *1997 Internet Server Market Share and Forecast* (July, 1998).

- *Internet applications, tools, and Java:* According to Nationsbanc Montgomery Securities, the market for Web applications will mushroom from $400 million in 1997 to $7.4 billion in 2001, with Java becoming the main language of the Web. The total market for Java applications will grow from $180 million in 1997 to $5.5 billion in 2001. The Java development tool market is expected to grow from $145 million in 1997 to $700 million in 2001, or 37% per year. According to this same report, Web application servers will grow from $67 million in 1997 to $754 million in 2001—a compound growth rate of 62%. [4]

- *Internet services and consulting:* According to IDC, Internet services will grow from $4.5 billion in 1997 to $43.6 billion by 2002. Because of the shortage of IT resources, companies are turning to external service providers to help them deploy some or all parts of their e-commerce projects.[5]

- *Internet users:* According to IDC, the Internet will have one billion online users in the next 10 years, up from 100 million in 1998.[6]

- *Internet software and services:* According to INPUT Research, the Internet and intranet software and services expenditure will increase by 50% per year from 1997 to 2002—reaching $300 billion by 2002.[7]

- *Internet access, ISP, and hosting services:* According to INPUT Research, the worldwide market for ISP Internet access, hosting, and extranet services will increase from $18 billion in 1998 to $95 billion in 2003.[8]

- *Internet portals:* According to Forrester Research, in 1998 portals attracted 15% of Web traffic and 59% (or $520 million) of the online ad spending. By 2002, they are projected to grab 20% of Web traffic and 30% of online ad spending (or $2.4 billion). On the average, users spend about an hour per month visiting their portal. The top four portal sites are: Yahoo!, AOL, Netscape, and Excite.

These numbers explain why the investment community is so strongly behind the Internet; the projected growth rates are astronomical. The numbers seem to match the extraordinary valuation the stock market places on anything that has to do with the Internet.

---

[4] Source: Nationsbanc Montgomery Securities (June, 1998).

[5] Source: IDC, *WorldWide Internet and E-Commerce Services Market and Trends Forecast, 1998-2002* (November, 1998).

[6] Source: IDC, *European IT Forum for 1998* (September, 1998).

[7] Source: INPUT Research, *Internet and Intranet Market Forecast, Worldwide 1997-2002* (July, 1998).

[8] Source: INPUT Research, *Evaluation of Internet Access Services for Business* (August, 1998).

Is the bubble going to burst? We don't know. Pundits have been predicting the "death of the Internet" almost every year since the mid-70s. It certainly hasn't happened yet. We feel quite comfortable with the assumptions behind these forecasts. We also believe that many of today's Internet superstars may not be around in the year 2000. Revolutions tend to eat their own children; the Internet is no exception.

TRENDS

We are just beginning to grasp what the impact of the Internet is.

> — *Charles Schwab, CEO*
> *Schwab*
> *(December, 1998)*

Three years ago Schwab had no Web presence. Now, more than half the company's business is conducted over the Internet; more than $4 billion in securities are traded every week at Schwab's Website. As you can read from the quote above, Charles Schwab has just started to grasp the impact of the Internet on his business. The Internet is changing everything. In a sense, Schwab has just started to scratch the surface.

IDC forecasted that the Web will have one billion users in ten years. We believe we'll see this number a lot sooner—perhaps, by the year 2002. Why? Because the Internet forecasts are too conservative. The Web has its own pace. Every new user is also a new evangelist. So the network keeps expanding. And its value increases with every new user. So the real questions are: How will the Web expand to one billion users? What will a Web with one billion users look like? Who will get us there? And, how will it happen?

There are no sure answers to these questions. The Web seems to recreate itself every two years. At this rate, by the year 2008, the Web will have gone through five more transformations. An Object Web could quite possibly subsume every other form of client/server computing. So here's a snapshot of the major movements that we anticipate in the near-term evolution of the Web:

■ ***Distributed objects and components will be everywhere***. The Web will recreate itself on top of a distributed object bus; the two top contenders for the bus are CORBA/IIOP and DCOM. The next-generation HTTP—HTTP-NG—may end up supporting both COM and CORBA. HTML will morph into a true compound document container; the only contender for this role is XML/DOM. Web pages will simply become containers of live components; JavaBeans is the main contender for this role. Finally, the two contending server-side component models—CORBA/EJB and COM+—will battle for the Web application server. In summary, the component world war is just starting; the grand prize is the Internet.

■ ***Web application servers will become OTMs.*** Web application servers will evolve into EJB or COM+ containers. The most scalable and mission-critical containers are OTMs. So every application server will either become an OTM or cease to exist.

■ ***All Web services will be built as components.*** Today, each Web server vendor tries to sell you a server suite—for example, Netscape's SuiteSpot. So you have mail servers, commerce servers, merchant servers, payment servers, application servers, HTTP servers, LDAP servers, certificate servers, and so on. These servers hardly work together—even on a single vendor's suite. The next-generation Web server will be an OTM that runs different services as EJB or COM+ components. So you will be able to mix-and-match services by using a common component infrastructure. You will be able to customize servers to meet your needs.

■ ***All Web applications will also be built as components.*** Today, you have HTTP/CGI gateways to the major ERP suites and back-end enterprise applications. The next step is to encapsulate these applications with object wrappers. Eventually, the more successful of these applications will be repackaged as EJBs or COM+ components that run natively within an OTM-based Web application server. So you will have ERP components and applications that are native to the Web.

■ ***Intranets will extend the reach of corporate networks.*** Corporations are migrating from private networks to intranets. This means that private networks will layer on top of Internet technology. The intranets are the first step toward opening up the corporate network. We anticipate that corporations will take advantage of the common Internet technology to link up with their suppliers, customers, and business partners. Instead of hiding behind firewalls, corporations will increasingly use the Internet's wide-area security mechanisms—including SSL, S-HTTP, IPSec, and public keys—to reach out to the world at large. In contrast, most of today's corporate networks are primarily closed systems.

■ ***Web transactions will create vast new markets.*** The Web lowers barriers to entry and stimulates new forms of competition; you don't have to be a giant retail chain to compete on the Web. The irrelevance of size will recreate many of our existing distribution channels. Retailers will become wholesalers, and manufacturers will become distributors. The Internet will restructure the way industries deliver service; for example, what does it mean to be a bank in an online world? In addition, the Web will generate new types of online goods and services; examples include travel guides, shopping brokers, publish-and-subscribe auctioneers, consumer protection bots, interactive education, art exhibits, and multi-user games. It's just a matter of time before the Web turns into the world's largest shopping mall and games arcade. We expect the Web to generate trillions of new electronic transactions each year. In addition, the Web is becoming your *information utility*—just as important to you as electricity and the telephone. You won't be able to function in the modern world without it.

■ **The Web will generate demand for millions of Internet appliances.** Yes, there will be a huge demand for lightweight Java machines and Jini-like clients. These $200 Web appliances—which we covered in Part 2—will download beans and mobile objects on demand to perform a task. And, of course, they will be easier to use, maintain, and upgrade than current PCs. They will be used by millions of users who can't afford, comprehend, or deal with the cost of ownership of a full-blown PC. Web appliances could become as ubiquitous as the telephone. Components and shippable places will become the primary software distribution mechanisms in this new environment.

Java machines can potentially outflank Microsoft Windows in many new environments. Remember, the magic number was one billion users by the year 2008; 95 million of us are already on the Web. We will soon be joined by 100 million people with PCs today that are not yet on the Web. But where will the next 800 million come from? This is where the $200 Web appliance—or Java device—comes into the picture; it's the low-priced "volkscomputer" that will open up the Web to the masses. If we build it, they will hopefully come.

■ **The Web will also generate demand for millions of fat client/server machines.** Yes, there will also be demand for millions of ordinary PCs that act as both clients and personal Web servers. You will be able to publish Web pages faster than you can send electronic mail today. So your Web server will act as your electronic proxy (or avatar) to the world at large. You will existentially define yourself by your Web presence: "I'm on the Web; therefore, I am."

■ **The Web will expand into new client/server areas**. In the client/server technology world, you either subsume other technologies or get subsumed. We believe that an Object Web is an ideal architecture for subsuming all existing forms of client/server computing—including databases, TP Monitors, and groupware. Of course, if the Web does not evolve beyond CGI, it will simply become one more client type for the existing client/server models.

■ **Mobile containers will be everywhere.** The Web is about to create an explosion in mobile BLOBs, applets, and components that run within "containers." If you think about it, our current file systems and databases will not be able to deal with this new explosion of interlinked BLOBs. The trick is to use scalable Object Databases (ODBMSs) to track relationships between objects and the relationships between objects and their containers. Mobile containers— JARs and XML structured files—will be used to ship groups of related objects and BLOBs to any destination on the World Wide Web. A shippable place is an example of a visual container of components.

- ***Portals will evolve into the new desktops.*** Today, a portal provides a few basic services like search engines, e-mail, news, and pointers to various categories of Web information. In addition, portals serve as billboards for advertisers. In the future, portals will become dispensers of places where you live, play, work, and shop. Portals will make the desktop irrelevant.

- ***ISPs will become more than Web access providers.*** ISPs will evolve into one-stop-shops for Web services. They will host personal Web pages, dispense shippable places, provide VPNs to enterprises, host Web Commerce sites, and provide Web consulting services.

The Web promises to unleash a wellspring of entrepreneurial activity around client/server components. This new software distribution model will accelerate the shift toward components and beans; it will attract millions of small developers. It's only a matter of time before these developers supply the "killer beans" that will bring the masses to the Web. We will see killer beans for home shopping, electronic banking, electronic voting, online auctions, entertainment, education, and many activities yet to be invented.

So where are the showstoppers in this rosy picture? Three immediately come to mind: bandwidth, more bandwidth, and a million beans. It's obvious that the Web cannot become an information utility for the masses without low-cost abundant bandwidth. The ultimate fate of the client/server Web may depend on the adoption rate of technologies like ADSL, ATM, and cable modems. In addition to bandwidth, the Web must recreate all of client/server computing using mobile components. This is obviously a very tall order; it will take millions of Java-programmer-years to get us there. In summary, the Web needs abundant bandwidth and tons of new beans to maintain its current feeding frenzy.

MEET THE PLAYERS

Creating value in the Internet economy isn't rocket science. But it is different. You have to move faster, build momentum quickly, and find ways to get customers to literally stick to you.

— *Patricia Seybold, CEO*
Seybold Group
(December, 1998)

Thousands of small start-ups will make their fortunes by providing new Web content, special-purpose software, infobases, and innovative services. In addition,

a few million of us will make a good living on the Web selling wares, components, information, and services; it's a giant online flea market. So there are fortunes to be made at the application level. There are also fortunes to be made in each layer of the stack. In this section, we will focus on the client/server software layer. We anticipate that the lion's share of the Web client/server middleware revenues will end up in the pockets of the usual suspects—Netscape/AOL/Sun, Microsoft, Lotus/IBM, Oracle, and BEA/WebLogic.

Most of these players have deep pockets as well as a strong client/server technology base on which to build. Deep pockets are very important because much of the Web client/server infrastructure is given away. Even though the Web crowd expects everything to be free, we all know that there is no such thing as a perpetual "free lunch." Someone must eventually pay for all these goodies. In the case of the Web, money comes from two sources: 1) the stock market, and 2) corporations that buy intranet and Internet technology. The stock market is fickle; it will continue investing in the Web only if it sees revenues at the end of the tunnel. So that leaves us with the corporate intranets. In the short term, large corporations will pay for the Web infrastructure. In the long run, the Web will pay for itself by becoming the world's largest shopping mall.

Being Cool Just Isn't Enough

The good news is that corporations are now spending a ton of money rebuilding their computing infrastructures using intranet and Internet technology (see the previous section). Many are starting to use the Internet for mission-critical applications. Most corporations are, of course, not starting from ground zero with client/server technology, which means they will expect the Web to fit within their existing infrastructures. Web technology must be able to seamlessly interface with existing databases, TP Monitors, NOSs, groupware, and system management platforms. Corporations also expect their systems to be robust and mission-critical. This means that the Web players with the most mature client/server technologies are in the best position to win. Just being "cool" won't be good enough.

A client/server Web platform must support activities such as browsing, purchasing, billing, and payments. In addition, the platform must provide new middleware services such as transactions and workflow. Finally, it must be able to interact with existing systems—for example, ERP applications, DBMSs, and mainframes. Ideally, all these services are implemented as components—of the EJB or COM+ variety—that run within a standard container—such as an OTM or Web application server. This means that you can always extend the platform by purchasing best-of-breed components or by creating application-specific beans. It's like having a CD player to play the CDs you like. This plug-and-play capability is very important because no single vendor can provide all the pieces of a Web commerce solution.

Someone once said that sorting through Internet client/server product offerings is a bit like trying to describe a passing bullet train. It's an intensively competitive market in which vendor strategies and alliances change almost daily. To get the latest information, turn to the six o'clock news or read about it in the tabloids. In the next few sections, we give you a snapshot of what the top transactional e-commerce vendors are offering today.

AOL/Netscape/Sun

IDC believes that the AOL/Netscape alliance with Sun is one of the most significant server announcements to date regarding Internet server hardware and software.

> — *IDC Opinion*
> *(December, 1998)*

The AOL/Netscape/Sun axis is setting a new bar for what it means to provide an end-to-end Internet solution. Here are some of the highlights:

■ *A ubiquitous Web client base.* The combined Netscape and AOL portals challenge Microsoft's domination of the client desktop. Netscape's Mozilla browser is now in the good hands of the Open Source movement—the people who helped create the Internet. We believe that this combination of browser and portal provides a very attractive entry point to the Internet; it weakens Microsoft's grip on the client market by minimizing the importance of the operating system.

■ *A strong server hardware base.* Sun helped create the Internet, but now the Internet is redefining Sun. Almost all of Sun servers in operation are now intranet or Internet servers. In other words, the Internet has become Sun's core business. Sun is the leading hardware vendor for Internet servers. Sun also has a very strong presence in the ISP community where its servers own a large share of the fast-growing hosting business.

■ *A strong Internet NOS suite.* Netscape brings to the alliance its SuiteSpot server software; it supports all the popular Internet standards—including LDAP, IMAP, X509, S-MIME, IIOP, HTTP, and so on (see Part 3). Netscape also has a strong e-commerce software suite called *CommerceXpert*. According to Dataquest, Netscape was the number-one vendor of Web server software in 1997; it has over 50% market share. So Netscape brings to the alliance the de facto NOS for the Internet. Note that Netscape only owns 6.8% of the HTTP server market; it holds third place after Apache (53.8%) and Microsoft IIS (23.7%).[9]

■ *A CORBA/Java Object Web.* As the owner of Java, Sun is in an excellent position to obtain a toe-hold on the client side with Java Internet appliances. Sun can also take advantage of Java on the server with CORBA/EJB. It now controls two Web application servers: NetDynamics and Netscape/Kiva's *Application Server*. By the time you read this, they should both be running EJBs.

As you can see, AOL/Netscape/Sun is a formidable combination. So what are the holes? First, it's unclear how Sun will differentiate its two application servers—Netscape/Kiva and NetDynamics. They, more or less, do the same thing. So one of them may have to go. Second, Sun is perceived to be a Solaris-first hardware vendor; it does not project the image of a cross-platform software solution provider. In Sun's hands, Netscape loses its status as a pure software company; it will be perceived to be a one-platform company, which is not a good thing. Server-side Java may help with the cross-platform story. However, there is more than just Java on the server. Finally, AOL/Netscape/Sun does not have an OTM for the mission-critical e-commerce transaction space. They will have a hard time competing with IBM and BEA for the high-end. They must fill this space to own the lucrative ISP and enterprise e-commerce business.

Microsoft

Microsoft has one thing nobody else has. They can give everything away free for the next 20 years.

> — *Eric Schmidt, CEO*
> *Novell*

Until December 1995, Microsoft appeared to be suffering from an uncharacteristic lack of clarity as it confronted the Internet. Perhaps it was hoping that MSN would replace the Internet in one fell swoop. Of course, this did not happen; MSN was a market failure. As a result, Microsoft decided that it could not continue to ignore the Internet. Its new Trojan Horse strategy seems to be to embrace the Internet and its standards and then morph them into COM+. As we explained in the last chapter, Microsoft has a very consistent Object Web story. So it can win big if its competitors deviate from a unified CORBA/EJB Object Web. Microsoft can afford to wait for the other side to make suicidal mistakes.

As Novell's Eric Schmidt points out, Microsoft has the deepest pockets in the computer industry. It can afford to bundle anything it wants with either Windows 98 on the client or Windows 2000 (née NT 5.0) on the server. The bundling of IIS and proxy server with NT made Microsoft an instant player in the Web server

---

[9] Source: Netcraft, *Web Server Survey* (December, 1998).

market. Microsoft's *Internet Explorer* is totally integrated within Windows 98. Windows 2000 is the mother of all bundles; it will add Active Directory, MTS and MSMQ to the NT bundle. Microsoft also supports the Internet via an impressive family of tools. It also has a suite of e-commerce server offerings—including *Commerce Server*, *Merchant Server*, and *Site Server*.

The bottom line is that Microsoft is a formidable player on the Internet, especially for low-end Windows-only shops. Microsoft brings to the equation a complete Object Web story. Microsoft's main weakness is that the story does not play well on non-Windows platforms. The Web is too diverse to become a Windows-only shop. So this is Microsoft's Achilles' heel. However, for the Microsoft "Windows everywhere" crowd, this may not be perceived to be a weakness. For them, the Internet simply becomes another Windows extension for which Microsoft sets the standards.

Bundling can be a two-edged sword. The other side is now countering the Microsoft bundle with Open Source. So Microsoft may have finally found its match. It's now competing against a very attractive (and free) Internet bundle that includes Linux, Apache, CORBA/IIOP, and Netscape/Mozilla.

IBM/Lotus

Like Microsoft, IBM is "very hard-core" about the Internet; it has become the center-piece of its client/server thrust. IBM is retooling its entire product line around what it calls *E-business*—a catch-all term for Internet, intranet, and E-commerce applications.

IBM's *Net Commerce Server* includes every conceivable Web service—including proxies and firewalls, electronic commerce services, security (SSL, S-HTTP, and SET), digital certificates, and system management. IBM's *WebSphere* provides an application server that supports CORBA and will soon support EJB. *Component Broker* will complement WebSphere by providing OTM-like services. *Project San Francisco* will provide EJBs for ERP that run on these platforms. And there is Domino 5.0—we explained what Notes/Domino 5.0 brings to the Internet in Part 6.

In addition, IBM has solid middleware products like MQSeries, TXSeries, and CICS. You can use IBM's *VisualAge* tool to visually assemble Web client and server applications that use all this middleware. Finally, IBM/Tivoli's *net.TME* provides object-based system management for these Internet applications.

IBM also has the system integration expertise, wide-area networking experience, and enterprise client/server know-how that makes it very credible with IS shops. This means that IBM is in an excellent position to become a "one-stop shop" for intranet client/server solutions. IBM is also in a good position to build and distribute

an Internet PC or Java machine; it has co-developed with Sun the *JavaOS* for these machines.

So, are there showstoppers? The main showstopper is that IBM still sells a bag of products instead of an integrated product line. IBM's solution to this problem is the Object Web. Eventually, CORBA/Java will integrate its entire product line. Every IBM product will become an EJB container; CORBA/IIOP will provide the common bus. So you will be able to run CORBA/EJBs on any of IBM's products. IBM's success as a Web software vendor will depend on how fast it can deliver this Object Web. Currently, you only have point products that provide different pieces of the solution.

Oracle

The Web server is just part of the database if you're Oracle, and just part of the operating system if you're Microsoft.

— **Brian O'Connell**

If the Internet turns out not to be the future of computing, we're toast.

— **Larry Ellison, CEO
Oracle
(October, 1998)**

Oracle is betting the company on the success of the CORBA/Java Object Web. The company is repackaging its entire ERP suite as Web-enabled CORBA/Java components. As we explained in Part 4, *Oracle8i* includes a built-in Java VM and supports CORBA/EJB. Oracle's *Application Server 4.0* provides a middle-tier platform that also supports CORBA/EJB. Oracle also has an e-commerce suite that includes a *Commerce Server* and a *Payment Server*. Oracle has a ton of consultants who understand the Object Web. And, as everyone knows, Oracle Chairman Larry Ellison is very excited about thin clients. So Oracle now lets you store any Windows file in its *Oracle8i* database with a simple drag-and-drop. Finally, Oracle provides visual Java tools—based on Inprise/Borland's *JBuilder*—to let you easily assemble pre-built components and create new ones. Your components can be tracked via the Oracle repository.

Oracle's approach to the Internet is very server-centric. However, it's a very interesting vision. Here's how the story goes: In the old days of 2-tier client/server, organizations had hundreds of servers deployed in every department. The clients were super-fat and hard to manage. The Internet introduced the 3-tier model, Java introduced mobile code, and CORBA provides the bus for components. So now you can make your clients thinner and also get rid of your departmental servers. Instead, you have a few superservers that are centrally managed, robust, and scalable. Users have easy-to-use Web browsers that invoke server-side applications written as CORAB/EJB components. Finally, you can run these components inside either *Oracle8i* or *Application Server 4.0*—they are both containers of beans.

At this point, you may be asking what about the millions of small businesses (and home businesses) that can't afford *Oracle8i* or superservers? Is Oracle giving up on these people? Absolutely not. Oracle offers very competitive Internet suites on NT, Linux, and NetWare. However, Oracle would prefer to see these small businesses outsource their Internet services to ISPs (or Oracle). This way they can get all the benefits of a professional IT-managed solution, but for much less money. The Internet—augmented with VPN technology (see Part 3)—makes these types of solutions highly feasible and very economical. By going the ISP route, small businesses can avoid major headaches. It's all very consistent.

With sales of $7.1 billion, Oracle is the world's second-largest software company. If the Object Web succeeds, Oracle could become the major supplier of intranet cross-platform server software—a game it plays well. So what is wrong with this picture? We obviously share Oracle's vision and we believe they will succeed. We also see two negatives. First, the company, early on, made a big deal about Network Computers. So their 3-tier Object Web became confused with NCs. Second, they still don't have a mission-critical solution for the middle tier. With all this concentration of server power, you need a mission-critical OTM that scales. Web *Application Server 4.0* is a great product, but it takes five years to create a seasoned OTM; like good wine, a good OTM must age.

BEA/WebLogic

We already covered BEA's *M3* OTM in Parts 5 and 7. So we won't repeat the story here. The question is: Why is BEA—a company that doesn't even sell a Commerce Server—included in this Web lineup? The answer is the Object Web. BEA has four great assets: 1) M3—a mission-critical CORBA OTM that scales, 2) WebLogic—the first EJB server on the market, 3) BEA is an OLTP company—it understands mission-critical software, and 4) BEA is a secular software company that specializes in multiplatform middleware.

So why is all this important? Today, there is typically a TP Monitor hiding in the back-end of almost every highly-scalable e-commerce application. For example both E*Trade and Federal Express use Tuxedo in the back-end. This TP Monitor is mostly invisible to Web users but it provides the scale and robustness that we described in Part 5. Of course, TP Monitors are being replaced with OTMs. An OTM

is a Web application server that scales. OTMs can directly run server-side components. Consequently, they are much more visible. They provide the heart of the Object Web. So BEA has two very hot properties: 1) a mature OTM, and 2) an avant-garde application server. It also has people who know how to support these mission-critical technologies around the clock. So where is BEA's e-commerce suite? It's the best-of-breed EJBs that third parties can provide on top of the OTM. They can develop their EJBs using WebLogic and deploy them on M3 when they need more power.

BEA is a relatively small fish, if you compare it with the size of its competitors. However, in the world of OLTP BEA is a giant; this is all the company does. In many ways, BEA fills some of the strategic holes that are in its competitor's products. So what are the negatives? First, BEA is a prime acquisition target; it has a set of CORBA/EJB products that many of the bigger fish may covet. Second, BEA needs to develop (or purchase) a suite of e-commerce EJBs that it can sell with its products. For example, it needs to provide suites of EJBs for consumer-to-business, business-to-business, and supply-chain transactions. Third, BEA must learn how to sell to ISPs—it mainly sells to IT and third-parties. Finally, BEA must create a low-entry package for the smaller ISPs—WebLogic may be the answer.[10]

CONCLUSION

There are more people on the Net every day than watch CNN. The number of households that can log on is about the same as the number of black-and-white televisions in 1950, and we expect the same explosion in growth.

— *Dennis Tsu, Director of Internet Sun*

To use Dennis Tsu's analogy, if today's HTTP Web is black-and-white TV, then the Object Web is color TV. We're starting to see some of that color with Java, but the best is yet to come. It will take the Object Web to create the kind of content that will bring the Internet to the masses; it will also do wonders for the intranet crowd. So does it ever stop? Not really. We did tell you that life on the Web is measured in dog years. Now you understand why.

---

[10] One of your authors is the VP of strategy at BEA. But don't worry—we made sure she did not write this section.

Part 9

Distributed System Management

An Introduction to Part 9

Managing the enterprise is an ugly, dirty, stinking problem.

— Ray Paquet, Analyst
GartnerGroup
(February, 1998)

You Martians have so far been getting the scenic tour of client/server computing. You've seen all the cool stuff—objects, groupware, database, and NOSs. But there's also a seamy side to client/server—the nasty little secrets that are normally kept out of the grand tour circuit. So what are these nasty little secrets? In a nutshell, the first generation client/server applications were "systems from Hell" when it came to keeping them up and running. These client/server projects were either single-vendor based or kept very small until we could figure out the kinks. Many of the early "Kamikazes" who attempted to build large scale open systems often fell prey to the technology; some never returned to talk about it. We call this nasty secret "client/server burnout."

So what is the cause of client/server burnout? The root cause is that we all got the scenic tour and fell in love with the promise of client/server. However, no one ever told us that we were *totally* on our own after we unwrapped the glossy packages from the different vendors. There was no single number to call when something went wrong. Yes, the different vendors gave us some rudimentary tools to manage their products, but these tools did nothing to help us manage the *sum of the products*. When something went wrong, it was always "the other vendor's fault."

We were left in the great "no-vendor's-land" of client/server, trying to make our systems work or face losing our jobs. Many of us burned the midnight oil trying to learn how to read the bits and bytes that flew over the network using Sniffers and other protocol analyzers. These early tools were real lifesavers—without them, we would have been totally blind. However, this is not the answer. We can't expect every client/server installation to have its resident TCP/IP, SQL, and object guru.

OK, you want us to get to the point—enough of this early "pioneer" talk. But we have news for you: We're *still* in the pioneer days of client/server. The *Distributed System Management (DSM)* technology—the topic of Part 9—*may* be the cure to client/server burnout. We say "may" because DSM products are just coming out of the labs; most are still untested in the battlefield. In addition, the success of a DSM platform depends on how easy it is for third-party tools to "snap into" it. And that won't happen overnight. So the good news is that there is a cure: DSM platforms. The bad news is that DSM platforms are in their infancy; you may have to pack a Sniffer back to Mars and be prepared to look at some bits and bytes.

Part 9 starts out by going over DSM platforms and what they can do for you today. Next, we spend time going over DSM standards and middleware. DSMs can only succeed by creating an open platform based on standards. Standards allow

management applications to "plug-and-play" into the DSM frameworks and access their agents anywhere in the intergalactic client/server universe. As usual, there are many standards from which you can choose. We will review the current standards for managing networks, desktops, systems, and applications—including SNMP, SNMPv3, MIB, CMIP, and DMI. We will also look at the Object Web standards for system management—including CORBA, CIM/XML, DEN, JMAPI 2.0, and WEBEM. So welcome to the seamy side of client/server. We hope that this won't be a Conrad-like journey into the "Heart of Darkness."

Chapter 30

Client/Server Distributed System Management

---

*N*ow that my applications have moved off the mainframe, how am I going to manage this mess?

— Anonymous MIS Manager

*T*he mere existence of a problem is no proof of the existence of a solution.

— Yiddish proverb

Client/Server has applied a giant chainsaw to centralized systems, slicing them into small pieces and scattering them all over the network. Then along came "open systems," which sliced up the software even further so that each piece comes from a different vendor. How do we manage the pieces? Management and support issues are the Achilles' heel of client/server computing. Even though the benefits of client/server systems are real—lower hardware and software costs, more flexible systems, easier to use front-ends—we're discovering that administration and support is far more costly than for centralized systems. Client/server computing disperses applications across multiple systems on a network and creates daunting

problems for all types of administrators concerned with keeping these systems running. The gap is widening between what users expect and what the support organization can deliver. It obviously doesn't make economic sense to ship a database and network administrator with every new client/server application that we deploy. So the rapidly escalating support burden of client/server systems must be brought under control, or the entire edifice may crumble.[1]

Are we in a no-win situation like the one described by the Yiddish proverb? Is there a solution to the problem of distributed system management in multivendor client/server environments? Until *very* recently, client/server management tools and products were totally inadequate for dealing with the complexities of distributed environments—they were always far less developed than their mainframe counterparts. You had to be a total masochist (or suicidal) to deploy a client/server solution in intergalactic environments. Departmental-sized solutions had slightly better success rates because somebody local was willing to put in the long hours of "volunteer" work. The first generation of client/server systems were mostly a "labor of love" by people who were willing to put in long hours to gain control over their local computing environment.

Fortunately, the situation may be turning around. Some very creative solutions to systems management are starting to come on the market. Most of them use client/server technology to help manage client/server systems. It's very recursive in that sense. Vendors of all sizes have finally come to the realization that no single system management product (or suite) can solve all the world's problems. The current trend is for vendors to create products that plug-and-play in one of the "open" distributed system management platforms—including HP's *OpenView*, Sun's *Solstice Enterprise Manager*, CA's *Unicenter/TNG*, Cabletron's *Spectrum*, Bull's *OpenMaster*, and Tivoli/IBM's *TME/NetView*.

These open management platforms can exchange management information with almost anything that lives on the network—including low-level devices, system software, and user applications—using standard protocols such as SNMP, CMIP, and DMI. The distinction between the network management and system management disciplines is quickly fading. Object-oriented user interfaces are providing Web-based single views of the managed environment. New Object Web management standards—such as CMI/XML—are providing common views of the managed data. Finally, management platforms can interoperate in all sorts of flexible arrangements, ranging from peer-to-peer to complex manager-of-manager relationships. This chapter answers some of the questions related to distributed management: Why the chaos? What needs to be managed? Next we explain the popular manager/agent paradigm for solving the world's problems. Then we look at the

---

[1] Tom Furey, the former General Manager of IBM's Client/Server efforts, estimates that "for every dollar you spend on client/server hardware and software, you'll spend five in maintenance, integration, and consulting."

management platforms that house these managers and the applications that launch their services. Finally, we take a quick look at the services that management platforms and applications must provide.

NEW WORLD DISORDER

In many large companies the network control center room seems as complex as the bridge deck of the starship Enterprise. Many systems are linked into the control center, but few are integrated...As a result, operations staff must be rocket scientists to integrate fault, performance, configuration, and other information gleaned from multiple management systems.

— GartnerGroup

System management is, of course, much more complex in distributed environments—especially heterogeneous ones. Unlike past generations of computers, client/server systems consist of three logically integrated but physically dispersed types of components: computer nodes, networks, and applications. The health of the system is dependent on the individual health of its component parts, as well as their interrelationships. All the problems associated with managing a typical computer system exist, and they are exacerbated by a substantial set of problems unique to the network itself.

Ironically, the multivendor diversity that's inherent in client/server solutions is also the primary obstacle to effective and affordable system management. You save money by buying components "a la carte," but you must turn around and spend what you just saved (and often more), making these components "whole" again. The great variety of vendors, networks, software packages, and system configurations make each client/server system different from the last one. And, until quite recently, vendors' management tools were customized for their own set of products and were generally targeted at the workgroup or departmental level.

As a result, client/server control centers in large organizations *do* look like the bridge deck of the starship *Enterprise*. So who takes care of the correlation between the different management platforms? The operators, of course. They must learn a different set of commands for each user interface and product. And they must continuously correlate information—such as fault, configuration, and performance—from the different management consoles. Because each system has its own separate management database, it's not unusual for the same information to be re-keyed multiple times. A single error may cause hundreds of different messages to flash on all the different consoles at the same time. In many cases, functions may overlap leading to more confusion. The first generation client/server systems were much too complex to manage—even in limited configurations with only a few vendors involved.

DEALING WITH CHAOS AND LEARNING TO LOVE IT

Sometimes the most vexing questions have simple answers: Distributed applications need distributed management.

> — **James Herman, VP**
> **Northeast Consulting Resources, Inc.**

In the early 90s, the industry began to realize that multiplying incomplete tools by multiple vendors created an unmanageable mess that threatened to derail the entire client/server movement. Something had to be done fast; the industry met that challenge and introduced many innovations very quickly. In the last few years, four generations of management architectures were introduced in rapid succession: *Manager of Managers, Distributed System Management (DSM), Open DSM,* and *Web-Based DSM* (see Figure 30-1). We cover these architectures in the rest of this section.

Manager of Managers

IBM's NetView was one of the first attempts to solve the problems of distributed system management at the enterprise level. NetView introduced the concept of

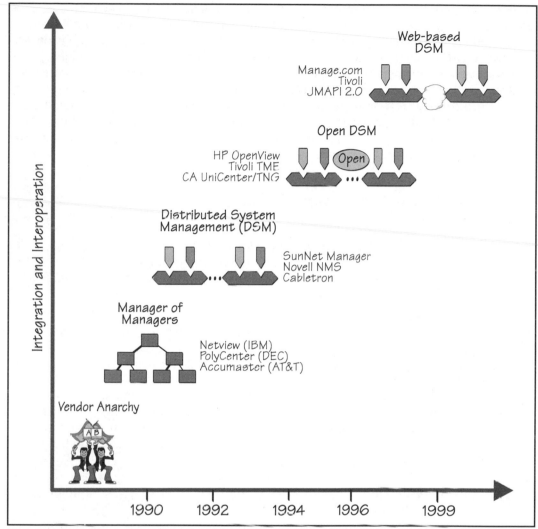

Figure 30-1. Four Generations of Distributed System Management Architectures.

Manager of Managers, which made it possible for a "mainframe in the sky" to oversee an entire enterprise. The idea was to create a single system image using a three-level hierarchy of management elements: low-level *entry points* that collect management information and send it upward; middle-manager *service points* that act on some of the information and send the rest upward; and *focal points* at the top that maintain a central database of management information and present a unified view of all the distributed resources. NetView/PC—the first *service point* product introduced by IBM—also served as a gateway that could convert management information from non-SNA devices into a format the mainframe focal points could understand using the SNA *Network Management Vector Transport (NMVT)*.

It didn't take long for Digital and AT&T to introduce their own Manager of Managers: *PolyCenter Framework* and *Accumaster Integrator*. Each product was based on a proprietary distributed management architecture. So the race was on between IBM, Digital, and AT&T to see who would be the first to manage the entire universe. It quickly became apparent that no one vendor—not even IBM, Digital, or AT&T—could possibly anticipate all the customer needs and requirements for a manager-of-managers product. There was just too much diversity for any one vendor to absorb—it was a huge and costly undertaking. IBM, Digital, and AT&T must have come to that same conclusion because they're now among the strongest proponents of open management platforms.

Distributed System Management Platforms

The next step in the evolution of management systems was the *Distributed System Management (DSM)* platform approach pioneered by Sun Microsystems' *SunNet Manager*, Cabletron's *Spectrum*, and Novell's *NetWare Manager System (NMS)*. These systems introduced two innovations:

1. ***The use of client/server technology in system management.*** Instead of a hierarchy of managers, these systems split up management applications along client/server lines. A GUI-based client workstation can work with any management server using RPCs to obtain management information. The servers collect their information from agents all over the network. The client workstation can provide a single view of the network by visually integrating management information that resides on multiple servers. Peer-to-peer or manager-of-managers arrangements among servers can manage the back-end data—the architecture is very flexible.

2. ***The use of "toaster" frameworks.*** The new DSM systems pioneered the concept of the "toaster" framework that allows management applications to plug into the platform and play. They accomplished that by creating a "barebones" management infrastructure consisting of published APIs, a starter kit of system management middleware, a system management workstation with integrated graphical utilities, and a management database on the server. The infrastructure was designed to entice third-party management application providers to write to the frameworks. The success of a framework is measured by the number of applications that it supports, the type of services these applications provide, and how well they integrate with other applications.

The combination of client/server and toaster frameworks caused a massive migration by third-party management application developers to the DSM platforms. The flexible client/server architecture provided scalability from entry level LANs to enterprise systems.

Open DSM Platforms

Control. It's what every IT manager wants—control over enterprise systems, user workstations, and critical applications—and control over access to all of them. Control is expensive—really expensive.

> — Sean Gallagher, Columnist
> InformationWeek
> (February, 1998)

The next step in the evolution of distributed management systems is *Open DSM*. Simply put, this is a DSM platform model that uses industry standards for its main interfaces. So where do these industry standards come from? The usual places, of course. Here's the list of standard bodies and consortia that *together* provide all the pieces needed to create a working distributed management platform: X/Open for management APIs and conceptual frameworks; OMG for ORBs and object services; OSI and the *Internet Engineering Task Force (IETF)* for network management; and the *Desktop Management Task Force (DMTF)* for managing the desktop and PC-attached devices.

In addition, most open DSM platforms use off-the-shelf RDBMSs (or ODBMSs) to store management data. This means that the database and the DSM server-side application code can run on different machines. Think of it as a 3-tier client/server architecture. Actually, DSM management is really a multi-tiered client/server architecture; it supports multiple layers of managers and agent/managers feeding each other. Examples of Open DSM platforms are HP's *OpenView*, Tivoli's *TME/NetView*, and CA's *Unicenter/TNG*.

Open DSM is not a panacea. It's certainly not the cure to all your system management woes. The current generation of Open DSM products is very powerful. However, these products are also very expensive and hard to deploy. For example, a DSM solution for managing 1,000 nodes starts at $500,000. Typically, it takes over a year to deploy such a solution—even with the help of system integrators. According to a 1997 GartnerGroup study, 70% of Open DSM projects never complete. In addition, the standards are not able to keep up with the rich set of features the DSM products provide. As a result, Open DSM is not really open.

Despite these problems, companies continue to spend billions of dollars on DSM software every year. Why? Because a successful DSM implementation can save you a bundle of money—about $5,000 per user over a five-year period. In addition, you need DSM to keep your systems running.

Web-Based DSM

The most recent step in the evolution of distributed system management is *Web-Based DSM*. The idea is to apply Object Web technologies to DSM systems. Figure 30-2 shows the five elements of a Web-based DSM solution:

1. ***Managed entities are represented using object classes.*** As part of its WEBEM initiative, DMTF has defined the *Common Information Model (CIM)* to represent managed objects over the Internet. This model defines core classes for representing common managed objects such as networks, routers, devices, desktops, operating systems, applications, and beans. You can also extend these classes to provide application-specific information.

2. ***CIM/XML is the universal interchange format for management data.*** DMTF defines XML tags—including their DTDs—for its CIM data objects. It is also defining XML tags for conveying management events, alerts, and reports. XML makes it possible—for the first time—to exchange management data

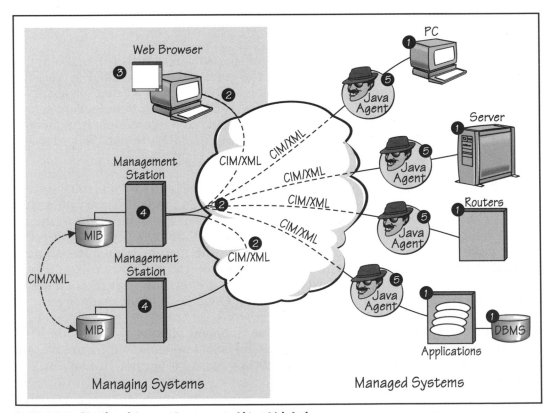

Figure 30-2. Distributed System Management, Object Web Style.

between: a) multivendor management platforms, b) agents and management platforms, c) Web browsers and management platforms, d) Web browsers and managed devices, and e) multi-vendor management databases. In addition, DOM lets you access this data from any language (see Part 8).

3. ***The management console is a browser.*** The Web browser becomes the universal visual interface for system management. We anticipate that DMTF will define XSL style sheets for displaying the XML-based management data. In addition, you will be able to use JavaBeans to process, correlate, and display management information inside a Web page (or shippable place).

4. ***Java-based management frameworks.*** The Java 2 enterprise framework is the ideal platform for Open DSM. Here's why: a) you can use Java's open APIs to store management information in any DBMS or ODBMS; b) Java's built-in CORBA and RMI ORBs can be used to collect management information from remote agents and also to invoke services on management platforms; c) Java provides a cross-platform rendering engine for displaying management data; d) Java provides a security system for mobile agents; and e) Java provides an open component model—Javabeans on the client and EJBs on the server—that lets third parties extend the management platform on both the client and the server. An example of a Java-based management platform is *Java's Dynamic Management Kit Version 4.0* from Sun; it is based on JavaSoft's *Java Management API 2.0 (JMAPI 2.0)*. Another vendor exploiting the power of CIM and Java technology is *Manage.com*. It provides a suite of management beans that includes configuration management, security scans, and inventory collection.

5. ***Mobile Java agents everywhere.*** Eventually, everything you deploy on the Web will be self-managing. Java's mobile code system makes it possible to deploy bean-sized agents on remote machines. These agents can use CORBA or RMI to communicate with their managing stations. JavaSoft's *JMAPI 2.0* defines an agent technology that integrates Web-based push/pull technologies as well as support for existing management protocols such as SNMP, and a range of communication protocols such as HTTP, RMI, IIOP, DMTF, WEBEM, and XML. In addition, Sun's *Jini* technology could be ideal for creating light-weight Java management agents.

In summary, Web-based distributed system management is where the action is. The idea is to use Object Web technology to create the next-generation Open DSM platforms. It lets system management take advantage of the ubiquity of the Web as well as its low-cost and easy-to-use technologies. The DMTF's CIM appears to be succeeding where DME (and others) failed—it provides a modern unified approach for the sharing of DSM data. Further on the horizon, DMTF will augment WEBEM with directory-based management. We will have more to say about DSM in the next chapter. We just wanted to let you know, early on, that the days of million-dollar DSM solutions may be numbered.

MANAGER TO AGENTS: WHAT'S GOING ON OUT THERE?

Mirror Worlds are software models of some chunk of reality, some piece of the real world going on outside your window. Oceans of information pour endlessly into the model (through a vast maze of software pipes and hoses): so much information that the model can mimic the reality's every move, moment-by-moment.

> — *David Gelernter, Author*
> *Mirror Worlds*
> *(Oxford, 1992)*

In his fascinating book, **Mirror Worlds**, David Gelernter defines five key ingredients that make up a mirror world: a deep picture that is also a live picture, agents, history, experience, and the basic idea that knits these all together. We found the "mirror world paradigm" to be very applicable to distributed system management. To make sense out of a chaotic distributed environment, we need to be able to grasp the whole and then move selectively into the parts. This is done by creating a mirror world of the client/server environment. Even though Gelernter does not mention it in his book, today's open management platforms provide the most advanced mirror world implementations.

So what does an open management platform do? It manages multivendor devices and applications on the network, runs management applications, interoperates with other managing stations, provides an integrated user interface of the managed components, and stores management data. How does it do it? By running an elaborate network of agents—it's like the CIA. The agents reside on the different managed entities on the network and report on their status. The management station can "parachute" its software agents anywhere on the network to look after its interests and gather the data it needs. The agents are also capable of executing commands on its behalf.

The agents help the manager create a "mirror world" of the client/server universe to be managed. Each agent monitors one piece of the universe. There could be thousands of agents parachuted throughout the network. They all run simultaneously, never stop to take a break, are always on the lookout for what may go wrong, and are always gathering data that may be of use to some manager. The manager software sifts through the massive amounts of real-time information it collects looking for the nuggets—the trends and patterns as they emerge. It must make sure the operator isn't overwhelmed with data. To do that, it must create a data model of the "chunk of reality" it manages. "Data refineries" must convert the data into useful information. A managing workstation should include either a relational or object database for managing and organizing the information that's collected and to remember past occurrences.

A mirror world isn't a mere information service—it's a *place*. You can stroll around inside the mirror world. To allow you to do that, the managing station uses iconic images to create visual computer representations of "what's going on out there." Multiple views allow you to zoom in, pan around, and roam through the network. You can read the screen like a dashboard when you need to see the status of a system at a glance, or you can wade through massive amounts of information organized in many views when you need to do some serious detective work. At every level, the display is live; it changes to reflect the changing conditions of the system as you watch. The way things are presented is a very important aspect of system management. Ideally, you should be able to see and control every aspect of a managed system from a single managing workstation. System management has the visual look and feel of an electronic arcade game, but in the background it deals with real agents that collectively control every aspect of a distributed system.

A management platform also provides the middleware needed for communicating with all types of agents. This ranges from simple agents that manage hardware devices (such as routers) to complex agents that chase after objects that roam on networks. The simple agents may be reached using a simple protocol like SNMP; the complex agents may be invoked via an ORB. In between, we have traditional agents for client/server applications that communicate using RPCs and MOM. In summary, distributed system management uses client/server technology to manage client/server systems. It's all very recursive. Mirror worlds are examples of how client/server technology will be used in the years to come. We can get a jump start by understanding the workings of the system management mirror world.

THE COMPONENTS OF AN OPEN DSM PLATFORM

Figure 30-3 shows the main components of an open management platform. It's a composite of the OSI, OSF-DME, WEBEM, JMAPI 2.0, and the UI-Atlas DM conceptual models of distributed management. More importantly, the figure is also a good composite model of commercial open management platforms such as HP's Open-View, IBM's Tivoli, and CA's Unicenter. Let's quickly introduce the management components of an open management platform before getting into the details. We start at the top of Figure 30-3 and work our way downward:

■ The *OOUI User Interface* provides visual representations of managed objects. The managing workstation should be able to automatically discover the topology of agents on a network, and then display them in a top view. You can use background maps to indicate the geographic locations of agents. Clicking on an icon representing a managed object displays a view of its current status and options for observing and controlling its state. You should be able to visually define event/action combinations—for example, an incoming event triggers some action on the management station. The managing workstation should provide an event browser with predefined event filters for traps, thresholds, status, configuration, and so on. Query dialogs should let you view information in the management database. You can use tree views to traverse information that's stored on any remote agent. A blinking element (or a color cue) indicates a trouble spot. You can click on that element to zoom-in on the trouble information.

■ The *Management Applications* are typically provided by third parties on top of the management platform's underlying facilities—including the user interface, the management database, the topology discovery services, and the facilities for communicating with remote agents and managed applications. The management applications fall into the following categories: problem management, change management, configuration management, performance management, operations management, and business management.

■ The *Management Information Database* is a database of information collected from the agents under the managing workstation's control. It can be implemented using an RDBMS or ODBMS. The database engine may provide active background daemons that monitor the historical data for trends and unusual developments. You can use triggers to proactively launch corrective actions. Note that a portion of the real-time management data is maintained by the agents themselves and stored in the local nodes they manage—the MIBs. So in a sense, we're dealing with a distributed database of hierarchical information. The data is spread on MIBs throughout the network. The managing workstation maintains aggregate snapshots of this distributed data. However, the data in the central database is not as up-to-date as the data kept in the remote MIBs (the point of capture).

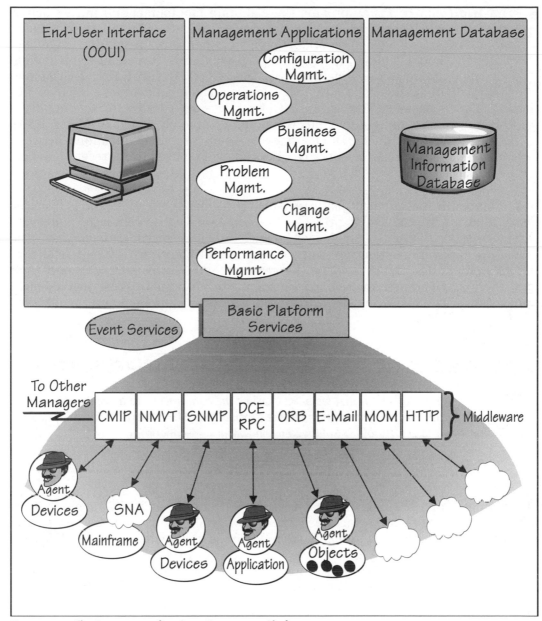

Figure 30-3. The Components of an Open Management Platform.

■ The **Basic Platform Services** provide high-level APIs that allow a managing application to communicate with agents, other managing applications, other managing platforms, and with the event management service. These APIs conform to open industry standards.

■ The ***Middleware Pipes*** provide the elaborate communication infrastructure needed by a management workstation and its applications to talk to distributed agents, other management workstations, and operators. A good management platform should support all the industry standards for agent-to-managing-station communications—including SNMP, CMIP, DCE, HTTP, RMI, DCOM, and CORBA/IIOP. It should also support legacy management protocols such as SNA NMVT alert packets. E-mail and MOM services are needed for sending asynchronous alerts and notifications to operators. Finally, either SNMPv3, CMIP, RPC, MOM, CORBA, or DCOM may be used for communications between management stations. Eventually, CIM/XML will be used to represent management data.

In summary, the management platform isolates the managing applications from the distributed environment and provides the common OOUI, database, and event services needed to create a single-system image of client/server management. The managing applications themselves are written by third parties. The more standard the APIs supported by a platform, the easier it is for third parties to port their applications. Of course, the real management work is done by these management applications—the platforms just provide the necessary plumbing and the installed base.

MANAGEMENT APPLICATIONS: COPING WITH DIVERSITY AND COMPLEXITY

With standardized APIs and what we believe will be the convergence to a small number of management platforms, an entirely new market is being created. A major opportunity now exists for the development of best-of-breed management applications.

— GartnerGroup

Management applications do the real work in distributed system management. They help us answer the following questions: How well is my client/server system performing? What is out there and where? Who is doing what to whom? How do I install new software? What went wrong? How do I fix it? Is everything being backed up? Can my system survive an 8.0 earthquake? In this section, we take a quick look at the categories of system management software that help us answer these questions.

How Well Is My Client/Server System Performing?

Collecting real-time information from various system components in a client/server environment and pinpointing the causes of performance problems can be a real headache for system and database administrators. The management software must

How Do I Install New Software?

The number of programs on each individual machine has risen dramatically over the last few years. Administrators have had a hard time managing this explosion; it's one of their top five headaches. *Software distribution and installation tools* let you download, update, track, and deinstall software packages on any networked machine. These packages can include anything from new operating system releases to end-user applications. Most of these tools can track the version number and status of the software. The better tools can perform unattended pushes from the code server to a particular client machine. *Software license management* tools can meter and enforce the use of licensed software. They typically support a wide range of licensing policies. This is an area where proper standards are important.

Users can subscribe to a particular software package and have it automatically delivered and installed on their machine. Of course, this delivery must be coordinated with the license metering application. A typical installation tool is divided into three components: clients or recipients of a delivery, the software package to be distributed, and the delivery schedule. You should be able to create distribution lists of recipients, making it easier to send software updates to a group of users. The delivery can be scheduled for a particular date and time. Clients can also perform installations on their own time—the *pull method*.

You should be able to define software distribution packages and subscription lists using a GUI (or preferably an OOUI). The "management by subscription" approach is used to automatically push the packages to all the subscribers. An OOUI allows you to create a subscription list by simply dragging and dropping individual host icons on a software package. The package typically consists of two component types: the files and directories that make up the software to be distributed, and the name of a program to be executed after the software is copied on each subscriber machine. Adding a new subscriber to a distribution list is just a matter of dragging a new icon and dropping it on the package.

Still missing is a "software vending machine" concept that lets clients browse from a wide selection of applications available on the server and try out an application before they buy. If they want to buy, the system should generate a purchase order, inform the licensing tool that it's OK to use this application, and update the inventory tool.

What Went Wrong? How Do I Fix It?

The number one headache of any administrator is, of course, how to deal wit'
The distributed nature of client/server systems—different transports.
databases—add several degrees of complexity. Failures can be caused !
component or from mysterious combinations of conditions. *Fault*

and help desk tools receive alarms, identify the failure, and launch corrective actions. The best tools can combine network, systems, and application-level management views. They help break down walls between database, network, and system management functions, making it easier to correlate failure symptoms. The tool should maintain error logs and issue *trouble tickets* to the people who need to know about the problem.

If an alarm occurs, a tool should be able to perform any combination of the following: send a notification, send an e-mail message, call a beeper, invoke a user-supplied program, update a log file, flash an icon, and pop up an alarm window. The better management systems provide scripting facilities that make it easy to automate the known corrective actions. Some tools provide mechanisms for associating events with actions (event handlers). It's a typical event-driven system—for each failure event, there is an event-handler action script. The event-handler script language should be able to call on other managing applications (for example, the configuration control tool) to perform some corrective action or to gather information on what went wrong. It's also important to provide sophisticated filters for events to narrow down the conditions that require intervention. Finally, the system must have enough smarts to recognize events caused by other events; it should then treat all these events as a single event.

Most tools do a good job of gathering real-time data on device and connection status, but then fall short on tasks like trend analysis, trouble ticketing, and reporting on network elements. The management software should continuously monitor the system for potential problems, and it must be able to automatically launch preventive or corrective actions to resolve problems before they occur. Instead of relying on problem *autopsy* and after-the-fact repair actions, potential problems should be avoided without requiring human interaction. This makes managing client/server systems less tedious and less susceptible to human error.

Can My System Survive an 8.0 Earthquake?

It's not just for disaster recovery anymore. Network backup is becoming part of a storage-management strategy that removes the weak link: you.

— *Michael Peterson, PC Magazine*

Data on the network is continually growing, leaving the administrator with another big headache: How can you manage this growth within the allocated budget, while keeping the data safe from disasters? Disaster recovery includes everything from scheduling daily backups to maintaining hot-standby sites. *Disaster backup, archive, and recovery tools* can initiate the backup or restore action where the source and destination of the operation can be located anywhere on the network.

These tools provide a user interface for scheduling the operations in unattended mode. The backup can be performed on any type of media. The better tools provide *hierarchical storage management* for multiple levels of storage—including memory caches, file servers, and an archive medium such as an optical juke box or tape drives. The tool should allow you to monitor where all the data resides and let you set policies like backup times. The best tools have the ability to learn from access patterns; they have some understanding of how information is related.

Chapter 31

Distributed System Management Standards

As we move to this new distributed client/server relationship, the question is: Are we going to have to put an administrator in each location? At $100,000 a year or so for each person, that gets expensive.

— *Gary Falksen*

This chapter introduces about a dozen distributed management standards and a gaggle of new acronyms. We first cover the traditional manager/agent standards—including SNMP, SNMPv2, SNMPv3, MIB, RMON, RMON-2, CMIP, XMP, and XOM. Next we cover standards for desktop management—the DMTF's DMI 2.0. Then we cover CORBA-based system management standards—including Tivoli and DME. We also cover JavaSoft's JMAPI 2.0. We conclude with the DMTF's WEBEM initiative and its new CMI/XML standard.

NETWORK MANAGEMENT

Two "standard" network management protocols have been defined: the Internet's SNMP and OSI's CMIP. Both are manager/agent protocols. Each of these protocols is capable of describing management information. The two protocols have much in

common (including a confusing similarity in terminology), but they differ in a number of important ways.

SNMP's approach is simple and straightforward, while CMIP's is both more powerful and more complex. The SNMPv2 protocol—first introduced in 1993—was never accepted by the market. SNMPv3—now a draft Internet standard—fixes many of the "simple" SNMP's shortcomings, but it cannot be called simple anymore. The new specification is huge. RMON-2—an extension of SNMP's MIB—is currently the market's darling; it has become an indispensable network management tool. To isolate developers from the underlying management protocols, X/Open defines the *X/Open Management Protocol (XMP)* API that works on top of either SNMP or CMIP.

The Internet Management Protocols

*T*he impact of adding network management to managed nodes must be minimal, reflecting a lowest common denominator.

— **Marshall T. Rose, Chairman**
SNMP Working Group

In 1988, the *Internet Engineering Task Force (IETF)* decided it needed an immediate stopgap solution to system management. The *Simple Network Management Protocol (SNMP)* was created to fill that need. IETF originally planned to pursue a two-track approach: SNMP in the short term, and the OSI *Common Management Information Protocol (CMIP)* in the long term. The OSI CMIP was far too complex for the needs of most devices; SNMP was simple and easy to implement.

To help the transition, it was originally intended that the SNMP *Management Information Base (MIB)* and *Structure of Managed Information (SMI)* be subsets of the OSI systems management. Eventually, that requirement was dropped, and each protocol went its own way; but they still retain a lot of common terminology. SNMP is the dominant network management protocol today. However, SNMP has a lot of deficiencies—it cannot meet modern system management needs. SNMPv3—introduced by the IETF as a draft standard in 1998—is intended to remove some of these deficiencies. In the meantime, many large corporations, telephone companies, and governments are committed to the OSI approach.

Defining Management Information: SMI and MIB-II

The Internet and OSI have introduced their own versions of a Data Definition Language for system management; in the process, they've also introduced a lot of strange and confusing terminology. To put it simply, the OSI and Internet people have created a language for defining the structure of the data that's kept on the managed devices. Their language defines a hierarchical (tree-based) database and names the components within the tree. The managing workstation uses this information to request data via a protocol such as SNMP or CMIP. The two protocols use the same type of architecture and terminology; however, CMIP is much richer and more complex than SNMP. CMIP uses richer data structures, more object-oriented data definition techniques, and a more sophisticated protocol for exchanging the data.

Both SNMP and CMIP use object-oriented techniques to describe the information to be managed; each resource to be managed is called a *managed object*. The managed objects can represent anything that needs to be managed—an entire host, a program, or just a variable maintaining a counter of received TCP packets. A *Management Information Base (MIB)* defines a structured collection of managed objects. The *Structure of Management Information (SMI)* defines the model, notations, and naming conventions used to specify managed objects within a particular protocol (such as CMIP or SNMP). If you view the MIB as a database, then the SMI provides the schema.

SMI identifies the data types and the representation of resources within a MIB, as well as the structure of a particular MIB. The ISO *Abstract Syntax Notation One (ASN.1)* is a formal language used to define MIBs for both SNMP and OSI management systems. ASN.1 describes the data independently of the SMI encoding technique used. The Internet's RFC 1155 defines a simple SMI to be used with SNMP MIBs; it only supports a subset of simple data types consisting of scalars and two-dimension arrays of scalars. (In contrast, OSI supports complex data structures and inheritance relationships for data.) An *object identifier* consists of a left-to-right sequence of integers known as subidentifiers. The sequence defines the location of the object within a MIB tree.

RFC 1123 defines *MIB-II*, which is a superset of MIB-I (RFC 1156). MIB-II adds additional groups of managed objects. Figure 31-1 shows the structure of managed objects that are defined in MIB-II. Objects are defined by their hierarchical location in the tree—for example, the IP object group is 1.3.6.1.2.1.4. New objects are always added "down and to the right." The ten object groups defined by the Internet are essential for either fault or configuration management. All devices that claim to be Internet managed nodes must implement the MIB; however, not all functions need to be present on all nodes. The *group* provides a convenient way to organize management objects according to the functions they provide. All objects within a group must be supported to be MIB-II compliant. For example, an implementation must include all objects within the IP group if it implements the IP protocol. The *experimental* node is used to introduce and debug new Internet-defined object categories before they become official MIB objects. The IETF believes that ideas must be proved in a working environment before they are considered for standardization.

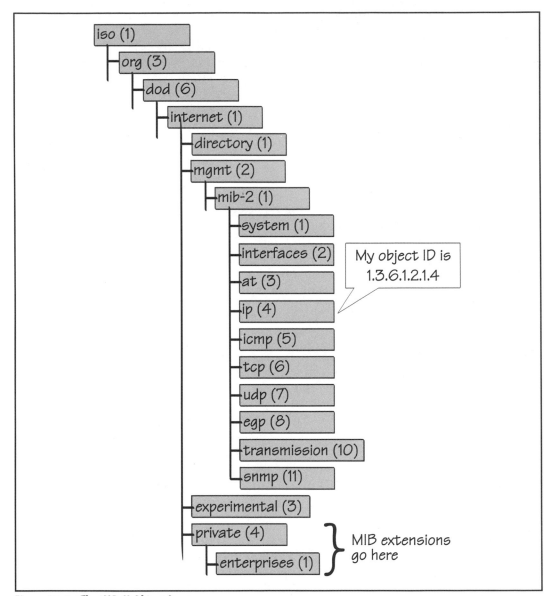

Figure 31-1. The MIB-II Object Groups.

The ten MIB-II object groups are not particularly thrilling. They contain several hundred low-level objects that perform TCP/IP network management functions from the transport layer down. The interesting system management stuff is left to the private MIB extensions.

New management objects are typically defined as MIB extensions in the *private* subtree; they allow vendors to create extensions that make their products visible to a managing station. The *enterprises* group is used to allocate *enterprise object IDs* to each vendor that registers for one. Vendors must describe their MIB extensions using formal descriptions—as defined in RFC 1155 or RFC 1212—inside a text file. Enough information must be provided to allow a managing station to load and compile the vendor-specific MIB definition and add it to the library of managed object descriptions. The managing station can only access information it knows how to ask for. The private MIB extensions are the heart of SNMP and OSI system management, but they're also the areas of greatest confusion. Users must make sure that the management platforms they select can handle the private MIB extensions for their systems. Different management systems are known to produce different results when managing the same MIB data; it's scary stuff.

Note that the MIB is one huge tree. The IETF has ongoing efforts to define mini-MIBs in different management areas—such as the application MIB, the printer MIB, the ADSL MIB, the entity MIB, and the MADMAN MIB (for mail and directory). These are all groups under MIB-II. By late 1998, there were nearly 100 standards-based MIB groups with over 10,000 defined objects. In addition, there is an even larger and growing number of vendor-specific MIB modules. MIB has become an industry treasure; SNMP is merely a protocol to access MIB data.

MIB Tools

The real value of SNMP comes from the MIB data it shuttles around. In practice, this means that you must be able to navigate the MIB trees—including the proprietary extensions—and understand their vocabularies. Unfortunately, there is nothing simple about MIBs or their arcane vocabularies. Consequently, most management platforms provide tools that make MIBs friendly. A MIB is, in essence, a form of hierarchical database that's distributed across managed stations. Like any database, it requires tools that make it accessible. Here are the typical tools that make it easier to work with MIBs:

■ A *MIB compiler* takes a file in RFC 1155 format and converts it to a format that can be used by the management station. The compiler is also used to update an existing MIB and add new vendor-specific definitions.

■ A *MIB browser* displays the MIB tree in a graphical manner; it allows you to search for objects by groups or attributes. You can refresh instance data from any managed node. The browser should allow you to create aliases for MIB objects (i.e., give them names that you find meaningful). The browser is really nothing but a specialized query tool for MIB databases. It lets you "walk the MIB." Some vendors allow you to overlay the MIB information on maps or on pictures of the objects you're interested in.

- A **MIB report writer** allows you to graphically create reports of the managed data. You can augment these reports with business graphs, maps, and other forms of visual presentation.

MIB tools are typically integrated with other visual management tools. For example, an agent discovery tool can display the location of the agents on the network, and you can use the MIB query tool to browse through the data they contain. You should note that MIBs are not very human-friendly. They were designed to be used by applications, not humans. So it's best to hide their details through graphic display tools.

The Internet's SNMP

The *Simple Network Management Protocol (SNMP)* is the most widely implemented protocol for network management today—it is supported by a constantly growing number of network devices. SNMPv1, as defined in RFC 1157, is designed to do exactly what its name suggests—it performs relatively simple management of the components in a network. It is used to alter and inspect MIB variables. SNMP is an asynchronous request/response protocol that supports four operations (see Figure 31-2):

- **GET** is a request issued by a managing station to read the value of a managed object. The get operation is atomic; either all the values are retrieved or none are. SNMP only supports the retrieval of leaf objects in the MIB.

- **GET-NEXT** is a request made by a managing station to traverse a MIB tree; it reads the value of the "next" managed object in the MIB.

- **SET** is a request issued by a managing station to modify the value of a managed object. This operation is often not supported because SNMP provides no effective security or ways to control who is allowed to perform SETs. The last thing you need are intruders causing havoc on the network using unprotected SNMP SETs.

- **TRAP** is a notification from a managed system to a managing station that some unusual event occurred. SNMP traps are very limited; they report one of seven events: cold start, warm start, link down, link up, authentication failure, external gateway neighbor loss, and enterprise specific trap. The traps use unacknowledged datagrams.

SNMP exchanges use TCP/IP's *User Datagram Protocol (UDP)*—this is a very simple, unacknowledged, connectionless protocol. It is also possible to support SNMP over the ISO stack using the connectionless transport system. Most SNMP agents are implemented as Daemon background tasks.

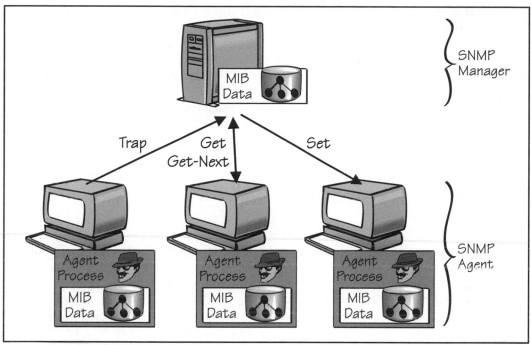

Figure 31-2. SNMP Manager/Agent Exchanges.

SNMPv1's Limitations

So what are the limitations of SNMPv1? The list is long; it's a classical tradeoff between simplicity and the complex requirements of modern management systems. Here's a quick summary of SNMP's more blatant shortcomings:

■ **SNMP is not secure.** The protocol provides a very trivial form of authentication; it is child's play for an intruder to break into the system. Most network managers do not allow the use of the SET command. This can be very limiting.

■ **SNMP is inefficient.** The protocol is not suited for retrieving bulk data; you must send one packet for each packet of information you want returned. SNMP relies on polling, which can swamp a network with traffic. Because the event traps cannot be extended, they cannot be used to create an event-driven environment. The server calls the agent and not the other way round. Polling limits the number of variables that can be monitored by a managing station, which translates into more cost.

■ **SNMP lacks important functions.** The protocol cannot be used to create new instances of MIB variables; it cannot execute management commands; and it does not support manager-to-manager communications.

■ *SNMP is unreliable.* The protocol builds on the UDP, which is an unacknowledged datagram mechanism. The traps are unacknowledged, and the agent cannot be sure they are received by the managing station. The SNMP designers believe that a datagram may have a better chance of reaching its destination under catastrophic conditions (that may be a bit far-fetched).

In summary, SNMP is excellent at its intended task—simple network management. However, it is too limited to handle the more complex functions of systems management.

Stretching SNMP's Limits: The RMON MIB-II Extensions

The *Remote Network-Monitoring (RMON)* standard defined in RFC 1757 is a very significant extension of MIB-II that stretches SNMP to its limits.[1] The moving forces behind RMON were the network monitor vendors; they needed extensions to SNMP that would allow their equipment to participate in the management of networks. A *network monitor*—for example, Network General's *Sniffer*—is a "promiscuous" device that sits on the network and can capture and view any packet, regardless of who sends it to whom. Clearly, these sniffer-like devices collect a tremendous amount of information that can be very useful to an SNMP managing station. Monitors are the ultimate "secret agent." They're tapped into the network and can see anything that moves on it. So the question is: How does a managing station obtain this massive information using SNMP? The answer is through the RMON MIB-II extensions.

What makes RMON so interesting is that it is the most intelligent entity ever defined by the Internet management protocols; it breaks the mold of the simple-minded and brain-dead managed device. A monitor must have enough intelligence to filter and act on the information it collects without directly involving the managing station for every action or swamping the network with massive amounts of bulk data transfers. Through *preemptive monitoring*, the sniffer (or *probe*) continuously runs diagnostics on the network traffic, notifies the managing station when a failure is detected, and provides useful information about the event. This activist style is a far cry from the typical SNMP philosophy that views each managed node as a set of remote MIB-defined variables.

RMON defines the conventions, using MIB-II extensions on standard SNMP, for telling a remote monitor what data to collect. Remember that SNMP does not support imperative commands, and it cannot create new instances of objects. So, RMON does it all via conventions that allow a MIB variable to represent a command

---

[1] RFC 1757—introduced in February 1995—supersedes RFC 1271; it extends the Ethernet-rooted objects in RFC 1271 to include Token Ring and FDDI.

and other variables to represent the parameters to the command; it's all very clumsy, but it shows what can be done in desperation. RMON defines a number of new MIB-II objects that represent commands. The monitor executes the command when the managing station writes to these objects using the SNMP SET command. The RMON specification defines how rows are to be added, deleted, or modified in a MIB setting. The bulk of RMON defines ten MIB-II object group extensions that are used to store data and statistics gathered by a monitor (see Figure 31-3).

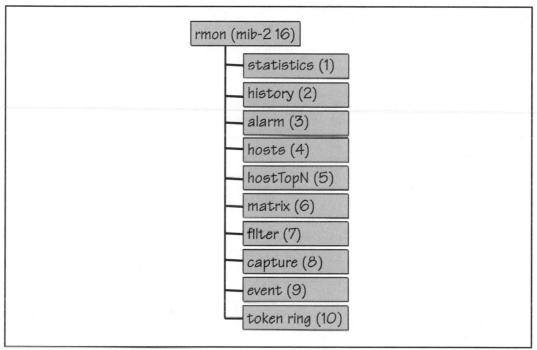

Figure 31-3. The RMON MIB-II Group Extensions.

Each of the ten RMON groups provide a set of control variables that allow a managing workstation to remotely control the operation of a monitor agent. These variables can be seen as state tables that tell the monitor what to collect and how to handle the events it generates. In a more modern setting, all of this could have been done using RPCs, MOM, or ORB invocations. RMON is a weird data-centric protocol that uses MIB variables to pass instructions, parameters, and control information between a managing station and an agent. It's a "kludge."

Here Comes RMON-2

In January 1997, the IETF introduced the RMON-2 standard defined in RFC 2021. The new standard adds ten new MIB groups on top of the ten already found in RMON

(see Figure 31-4). RMON-2 collects information on the workings of the all seven layers of the OSI model. For example, RMON-2 lets you track network traffic by application protocols. You can track the applications that generate the most traffic for each protocol—for example, RMON-2 can tell you which Website gets the most traffic. In contrast, the original RMON only deals with OSI layers one and two.

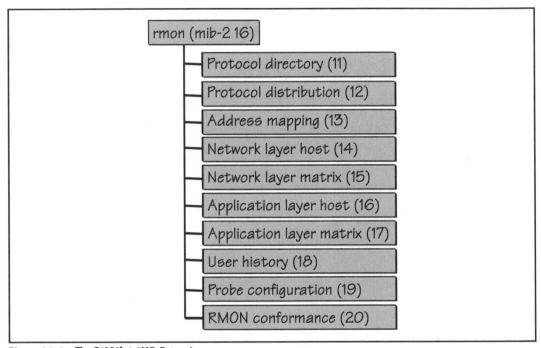

Figure 31-4. The RMON-2 MIB Extensions.

RMON-2 allows management tools to construct end-to-end views of the entire network. In contrast, RMON only deals with single network segments. With RMON-2, you can obtain a complete picture of how an entire network functions, not just the individual LAN segments. RMON-2 is more cost-effective than RMON. You don't have to place probes on each LAN segment to collect information. Instead, probes are embedded within routers and hubs, where they collect backbone traffic information.

As we go to press, all the major internetworking players—including Bay Networks, Cisco, 3Com, and Cabletron—have embedded partial RMON-2 probes into their routers and switches. So will this kill the standalone RMON probe industry? We do not think so. Standalone RMON-2 probes—from SolCom, Kaspia, HP, Bay, Frontier, Technically Elite, 3Com, and others—provide more complete RMON-2 implementations. They give you a much deeper view of the network than the built-in probes.

SNMPv2 and SNMPv3: What's New?

SNMP Version 2 (SNMPv2) became the Bosnia of standards. It was first introduced in March 1993 by Jeffrey Case, Keith McCloghrie, Marshall Rose, and Steven Waldbusser—the designers of the original SNMP and related Internet management standards. The proposed standard consisted of 12 RFC documents that totaled over 416 pages. SNMPv2 improvements over SNMP included a new security protocol, optional encryption, manager-to-manager communications, bulk data transfer, new SMI data types, new MIB objects, and the ability to add or delete table rows (a la RMON).

In March 1993, the SNMPv2 task force disbanded and vendors started to implement the protocol. Unfortunately, the vendors weren't too happy with some of what they found. They all seemed to agree with the majority of SNMPv2 features, but two areas proved to be overly complex—security and the administrative framework. The SNMPv2 working group was reconvened in December 1994 to fix these two problem areas. However, the group could not agree on a solution, so two competing security proposals emerged (see the next Soapbox). The IETF rejected both proposals and endorsed yet a third proposal, called *community-based SNMP* or *SNMPv2c* (see RFC 1901); it is SNMPv2 without a security framework. In contrast, the two other proposals—*SNMPv2u* and *SNMPv2**—had security, but not the endorsement of the IETF.

In 1997, the IETF convened an SNMPv3 working group to produce a *single* set of specifications for SNMP based on SNMPv2, SNMPv2c, SNMPv2u, and SNMPv2*. In early 1998, the new group published a draft standard for SNMPv3—see RFCs 2271 through 2275. Instead of reinventing the wheel, the SNMPv3 working group reused the SNMPv2 draft documents—RFCs 1902 through 1908. Then they added the missing link—security. As a result, SNPMv3 is really SNMPv2 with additional security and administration capabilities. Sanity prevailed at last.

The Great SNMP Wars

Soapbox

It's Bosnia. We've got Serbs and Croats.

— *Marshall Rose, SNMPv2 Co-author (March, 1996)*

When SNMPv2 access rights and security proved too difficult and cumbersome to implement, the original SNMPv2 working group went back to the mountain and returned with two competing security proposals:

- ***SNMPv2u—or User-based Security Model (USEC)***—is championed by Marhall Rose and Keith McCloghrie. USEC proposes a simple, minimalist security model (see RFCs 1909 and 1910). It's an agent-centric design that requires minimum involvement from the management station. Consequently, the security administration is also minimal.

- ***SNMPv2* (or "V2 star")*** is championed by Jeffrey Case and Steven Waldbusser (who is also the author of RMON-2). SNMPv2* introduces a security framework on top of USEC to make it "more complete." As Case puts it, "USEC has fewer features, but the question is, are there enough features in USEC?" Of course, Case must think the answer is no, which is why he came up with SNMPv2*; it offers multiple authentication and privacy services. In contrast, USEC's Rose thinks that SNMPv2* has the potential to become "the CMIP of the mid-90s—very capable, but extremely complex, large, costly, and ungainly."

In December 1995, the IETF disbanded the SNMPv2 working group to "let tempers cool down." So both sides went out to drum up support for their respective standards. But most vendors sat on the sidelines waiting for a winner to emerge before implementing products. In March 1997, the IETF convened an SNMPv3 working group to break the stalemate and come up with a unified SNMPv3 solution. In January 1998, the group published the first version of the "unified" SNMPv3 draft standard. Who said system management isn't exciting? ❑

SNMPv3 Operations

An SNMPv3 node can be both a managing and a managed object. This makes it possible to create manager-of-managers arrangements, and it allows SNMPv2 to share management information with its fellow managers. SNMPv3 is a "proper extension" of SNMPv2 and SNMPv1.

Here's the list of the old and new operations SNMPv3 proposes (see Figure 31-5):

- **GET** is identical to SNMP. The only difference is in the way responses are returned. SNMPv3 removes the atomic constraint, meaning that it will return whatever values can be returned—partial results are allowed. In contrast, SNMP either returns all the required variables or it posts an error.

- **GET-NEXT** is identical to SNMP, except that the atomic requirement is relaxed.

- **GET-BULK** is a new command issued by a managing station. It is similar to GET-NEXT. However, instead of just returning the next variable, the agent can return as many successor variables in the MIB tree as will fit in a message.

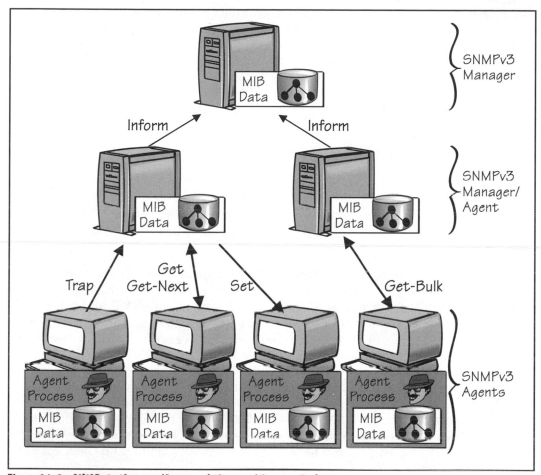

Figure 31-5. SNMPv3: Manager/Agent and Manager/Manager Exchanges.

■ **SET** is identical to SNMP. It is a two-phased operation. The first phase checks that all the variables in the list can be updated; the second phase performs the update. Like SNMP, it's an all-or-nothing proposition.

■ **TRAP** performs a role similar to SNMP, but it uses a different packet format (the SNMP trap header only recognizes a TCP/IP address type; SNMPv3 is more general). And, like SNMP, the trap is unacknowledged.

■ **INFORM** is a new command that's sent by an SNMPv3 manager to another manager. It is used to exchange management information. The messages can be sent to all the manager nodes specified in a MIB or to a particular manager. The management MIB allows a superior manager node to define the subordinate events it's interested in.

Like SNMP, SNMPv3 is connectionless; it uses a datagram service. The specification includes mappings to UDP. However, SNMPv3 can run on any protocol that supports datagrams, such as IPX, AppleTalk, and the OSI connectionless service. However, these protocols must provide a proxy gateway to UDP.

SNMPv3: Secure at Last

SNMP is the way we break into machines. Even if you don't have access to community strings, you can cause a lot of confusion.

— *Jeff Moss, Director*
Secure Computing Inc.
(November, 1998)

SNMPv1 and SNMPv2c provide security by sending passwords as clear text over the network—this approach is known as *community* passwords. These clear passwords allow any hacker with a sniffer to wreak havoc using SNMP as a back door. For example, a hacker can easily capture a community password and then use it to invoke SET operations on any networked device. According to Dan Backman, SNMP with community password strings stands for, "Security's Not My Problem."

SNMPv3 introduces a modular security architecture that can support multiple security models—ranging from the older community strings to a more modern distributed security model. SNMPv3 also introduces a security administration framework based on SNMP and MIBs. So you can use SNMP to manage SNMP. For example, a managing workstation uses its remote SNMP agents (and their MIBs) to enable access controls on networked devices.

SNMPv3 provides four mechanisms for dealing with security threats: 1) non-tampering, 2) confidentiality, 3) caller authentication, and 4) access controls. In practice, this means that SNMPv3 lets you encrypt all secured transmissions. In addition, the managing station that generates the request may be asked to authenticate itself to the target agent.[2] Finally, an agent can apply very granular access controls on all its operations and on its MIB variables.

An administrator can specify different levels of protection—including unsecured, authenticated, and authenticated with encryption. Unlike modern NOSs, the SNMPv3 security model does not support a security server, digital certificates, or directory-managed security. Instead, each agent and manager must maintain local copies of its access control lists within its MIB. A managing workstation uses SNMP to distribute the access control lists to all its managed devices. Without turning this

---

[2] In SNMPv3 every agent and manager has a unique *SNMP Engine ID*.

into a Soapbox, it seems that the management system is introducing yet another security model. And it doesn't look very simple.

THE OSI MANAGEMENT FRAMEWORK

Many of SNMP's deficiencies are addressed by OSI network management. Some, however, see this as a case of the cure being worse than the disease, given the complexity and the size of OSI network management.

— *William Stallings*

OSI distributed system management is defined by over 30 standards. Are you ready for a new dose of acronyms? In the OSI worldview, network management is divided into five application-level components called *System Management Functional Areas (SMFAs)*. These include fault management, accounting management, configuration management, performance management, and security management (see Figure 31-6). SMFAs rely on the services of 13 OSI-defined *System Management Functions (SMF's)*, which can be used by one or more SMFAs. The SMFs rely on the *Common Management Information Services Element (CMISE)*. CMISE is a combination of the protocols defined by the *Common Management Information Services (CMIS)* and the *Common Management Information Protocol (CMIP)*. CMIP, like SNMP, performs the actual exchanges between a managing station and an agent on the managed system. And like SNMP, it relies on a MIB to understand the capabilities of the managed agents and the data they store. OSI, of course, has its own CMI that defines information using ASN.1 notation; the basic unit of information is an object.

What's an OSI Object—and What Can It Do?

While SNMP was intended to be simple, immediately useful, and quickly deployed, the groups developing OSI management took a different approach. The goal of OSI management is to provide a comprehensive solution to the broad problems of network—and, to some extent, system—management. Because of its ambitious goals, OSI provides a comprehensive framework for defining *managed objects* borrowing heavily from object-oriented technology. The OSI notation used for describing managed objects is much richer than that used by SNMP. CMIP relies on a series of *templates* for defining managed objects and their attributes. You can specify the following characteristics for each managed object:

■ *Attributes* are variables that represent the data elements in a managed object. Each attribute represents a property of the resource the object represents.

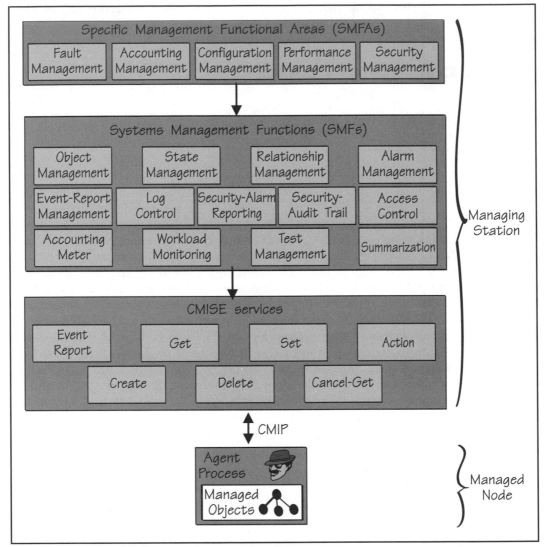

Figure 31-6. OSI Distributed System Management Overview.

- **Operations** are the actions that can be performed on the attributes of an object or on the object itself. The actions that can be performed on the object's attributes include *get, replace, set, add,* and *remove members.* The actions that can be performed on the object itself include *create, delete,* and *action.* OSI does not provide the semantics for defining the behavior of an object (i.e., method implementations or inheritance).

- **Notifications** are events that are emitted by a managed object—for example, when some internal occurrence that affects the state of the object is detected.

ISO defines a number of notification types, including the format of the data carried in a CMIP *event-report* and an object ID that uniquely identifies the source. Notification types include various alarms and violations, attribute value changes, object creation and deletion, and object state changes.

■ **Inheritance** is a managed object class that inherits all the characteristics of its parent class. ISO defines a number of object classes that can be used as parent classes for the purposes of inheritance, including an *alarm record*, *log*, *system*, *security alarm reports*, and an *event forwarding discriminator*.

The notation for defining objects is defined in *ISO 10165*; it is also know as **Guidelines for the Definition of Managed Objects (GDMO)**. The notation is commonly referred to as GDMO templates; it is substantially more powerful (and complex) than the simple language for defining SNMP objects. As we explained, ISO objects have a rudimentary level of object-oriented characteristics; in contrast, SNMP MIB objects are just glorified variables in a hierarchical tree. The GDMO is closer in intent to the CORBA IDL. However, CORBA provides much more advanced and comprehensive object semantics.

OSI Management Protocols: CMIP, CMOT, and CMOL

CMIP is really an abbreviation for the (overly) Complex Management Information Protocol.

> — *Marshall T. Rose, Author*
> *The Simple Book*
> *(Prentice Hall, 1991)*

CMIP is the OSI protocol for manager-to-agent and manager-to-manager communications. In sharp contrast to SNMP, *CMIP* is a connection-oriented protocol that runs on top of a complete seven-layer OSI stack. *CMIP over TCP/IP (or CMOT)* provides a skinnier version of CMIP for TCP/IP networks. *CMIP over LLC (or CMOL)* is the skinniest CMIP yet; it was designed by IBM and 3Com to run directly on top of the IEEE 802.2 logical link layer. CMIP is much richer in functionality than its SNMP counterpart. The CMIP protocol provides the following services:

■ **Get** requests data from the agent's management information base. The request may be for a single managed object or a set of managed objects. For each managed object value, one or more of its attributes can be requested.

■ **Event-Report** is a notification sent by an agent to a managing system indicating that some event has occurred. The service can optionally request a confirmation. Five parameters are passed with the notification event to specify the class of object and instance where the event originated, the type of event, the time it was generated, and any user information about the event.

■ **Action** is a request that directs a managed object to perform some particular action. The action is implemented by a procedure that's specified as part of the managed object. The *action-information* parameter, if present, can be used to pass input parameters and other information.

■ **Create** is a request made by a managing system to create a new instance of a managed object class.

■ **Delete** is a request made by a managing system to delete an instance of a managed object class.

All the CMIP services may be optionally performed with confirmation. To specify the context for the management objects of interest, CMIP employs two constructs: *scoping* and *filtering*. Scoping marks a node within the information tree where the search tree starts; filtering is a boolean search expression applied to the attributes of the scoped objects.

THE DESKTOP MANAGEMENT INTERFACE (DMI)

Not a single vendor adapter should be sold without a MIF...MIF everything in sight. MIFing now means users will be a lot less miffed later.

— *Jamie Lewis*
PC Week

At the other end of the spectrum, an industry consortium called the *Desktop Management Task Force (DMTF)* is defining standards to manage all components on a PC, Mac, or workstation—including hardware, OSs, applications, storage, and peripherals. The DMTF consortium consists of about 100 formal members; the leadership includes Compaq, Dell, HP, IBM/Tivoli, Intel, Microsoft, NEC, Novell, SCO, Symantec, and Sun. In October 1993, DMTF released the first version of its *Desktop Management Interface (DMI)*. The DMI is independent of protocol, platform, and operating system.

DMI solves a real problem: It makes it practical to manage the 10,000 or so PC components that are on the market. One of the reasons management hasn't proliferated down to PC components through SNMP is *cost*. To be SNMP-compliant, add-in vendors had to create a private MIB, work out the interfaces to SNMP agents, and negotiate with vendors of management platforms to have their MIBs interpreted. In addition, most PCs running DOS and Windows don't have enough RAM to support multiple SNMP agents or their protocol stacks. To compensate, proprietary agents were sometimes placed in adapter cards—for example, Ethernet cards from 3Com or Cabletron. With DMI, component vendors only have to "MIF" their device; DMI does the rest.

DMI support became widespread in 1996. It is incorporated into the wares of adapter vendors (Intel, Madge, and 3Com), PC manufacturers (AST, Dell, Compaq, IBM, and Apple), and system management vendors (Novell, IBM/Tivoli, Software AG, HP, and Sun). In addition, DMI is now supported by almost every LAN inventory program on the market. Finally, Apple, IBM, Sun, and Ki Networks have released a *common agent technology* that allows DMI-compliant components to be managed by existing SNMP-based management consoles. The common agents map between DMI MIFs and SNMP MIBs. IBM provides common agents for OS/2, Windows 95/98, and NT; Apple provides a common agent for the Mac; and Sun and Ki provide common agents for Solaris, HP-UX, and other Unixes. Note that Microsoft provides a partial implementation of the DMI standard in the Windows 95/98 plug-and-play feature.

The DMI Architecture

A DMI agent represents a PC and its managed resources to the rest of the world. The DMI interface allows these resources to be managed by SNMP, CMIP, or CORBA-based management applications. Using a concept called "slushware," the DMI agent can load and unload different pieces of code on demand, never taking up more than 6 KBytes. The agent is packaged as a terminate-stay-resident (TSR) program for DOS and as a DLL for Windows, NT, and OS/2; it only consumes RAM when activated. The agent loads on demand the code needed to manage a device. After it is loaded, the agent unobtrusively collects information while other applications are running.

The DMI architecture (see Figure 31-7) consists of four elements:

■ The **Component Interface** allows vendors of PC components such as memory boards, CD-ROMS, LAN adapters, and modems to register their devices and interfaces with DMI.

■ The **Service Layer** provides generic agent services. This device-independent layer interfaces to the local MIF database to deal with device-specific issues.

■ The **Management Interface File (MIF)** contains descriptions of the managed devices; it's similar in function to a MIB. The MIF is interpreted by the Service Layer, which uses the information to determine what actions to take on a managed device. The idea is that each of the 10,000 or so PC components will

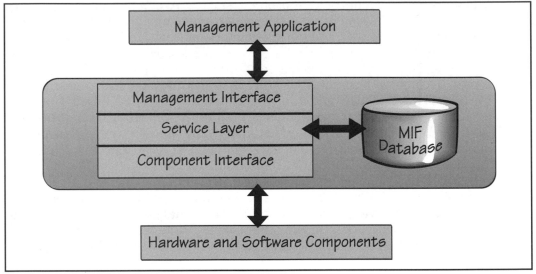

Figure 31-7. The DMTF Architecture.

have a MIF provided by the component vendor. The vendor supplies the MIF, and DMI handles the management.

■ The ***Management Interface*** provides a platform-independent API to the DMI services. The DMI agent can be externally accessed via SNMP, CMIP, or local applications; it provides the protocol to get to the MIFs.

DMI 2.0

Nearly 100% of enterprise requests for proposals list DMI 2.0 compliance as a requirement. So it is something we must have.

> — **Carol Rylander, Product Manager**
> **Dell Computers**
> **(February, 1998)**

In April 1996, DMTF published the *DMI 2.0* specification. In October 1997, it published a DMI 2.0 conformance specification standard. By late 1998, the DMTF gave its DMI 2.0 stamp-of-approval to over 200 shipping PCs and servers. DMI 2.0 defines a standard way for DMI agents to send management information across a network and ORBs. DMI 2.0 also defines IDL-specified APIs that can be invoked via the DCE RPC. The new DMI allows a component to define events within the MIF; it also defines an interface for setting event filters in the Service Layer. This means management stations are able to specify the types of events for which they want to receive notifications; they can also set severity thresholds.

One of the more exciting features in DMI 2.0 is its greatly expanded *Software MIF*. This new MIF makes it easier to manage, inventory, install, and uninstall software applications on your PCs, Macs, and workstations. The MIF specifies preinstallation file lists, software IDs and CRC signatures, version numbers, superseded products, installation dependencies, and support information. However, it neither collects real-time information nor maintains relationships between software components that run on both clients and servers. Instead, it focuses on an individual computer system.

Even with its shortcomings, the new MIF makes it possible for agents to check your hardware and software environment, install your applications, tell you where to get support, and finally uninstall the programs when you no longer need them. Generally, a software product will ship with one MIF file. The DMTF is also working on its XML-based CIM protocol to solve the application management problem (more on this later).[3]

X/OPEN MANAGEMENT STANDARDS

Wherever there are APIs, there's an X/Open standard lurking. So of course there are some X/Open standards for distributed system management calls. The idea is to provide a set of standard management APIs that isolate applications from the underlying management protocols (such as SNMP or CMIP). It's a very strange business we're in—we need standards to isolate us from other standards. X/Open defines two API sets: *XMP* and *XOM* (see Figure 31-8).

The X/Open XMP API

The *X/Open Management API (XMP)* is derived from an earlier interface called the *Consolidated Management API (CM-API)* from Bull and HP. The XMP API is used for standards-based, process-to-process communications between a managing system and a managed system. XMP defines a set of C API calls that allow access to both SNMP and CMIP. The interface semantics are more like CMIP than SNMP. Because of the differences in the representation of managed data, XMP does not make SNMP or CMIP totally transparent to the application. But as a compromise solution, XMP provides different XOM-based "packages" for use with the different

---

[3] The IETF is also working on an application MIB that provides more information about the state of a running application as well as describing associations between software modules.

Part 9. Client/Server Distributed System Management

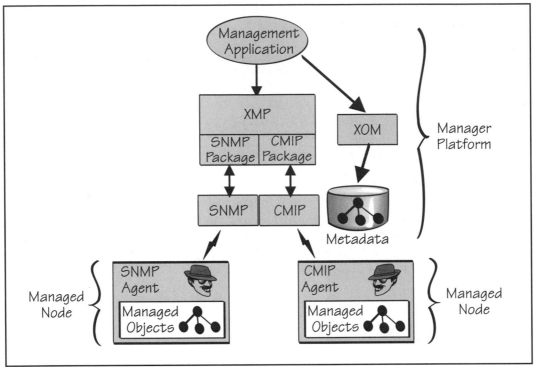

Figure 31-8. X/Open's XOM, XMP, and Metadata Database.

protocols (XOM is explained in the next section). One package is defined for standard SNMP operations, and one is defined for standard CMIP operations.

The X/Open XOM API

XMP relies on another X/Open-defined API called *X/Open Object Manager (XOM)*. The XOM API is used to manipulate the data structures associated with managed objects. The XMP data structures are prepared using XOM API calls. The current version of XOM provides a way to deal with complex ASN.1-defined types in C. Both SNMP and CMIP use ASN.1. XOM is general enough to be used by protocols that are not even related to system management. For example, DCE uses XOM in its Global Directory Services.

To support the more complex CMIP object hierarchies, X/Open includes a *Package Development Kit (PDK)*. The primary component of the PDK is a *metadata compiler*, capable of reading GDMO definitions and producing a package (which is actually a set of C data types). You can then use C structures with XMP and XOM. The metadata compiler populates a local database with information derived from GDMO definitions. The information about CMIP-managed object classes includes their superior and subordinate object classes, the attributes of the class, and whether a given object class supports create and delete requests. You can access the metadata database using normal XMP calls. This process is similar in nature to the CORBA IDL compiler and Interface Repository. But the CORBA architecture is generally much more consistent, and it provides more advanced functions.

THE OSF DME STANDARD

In July 1990, the OSF—now the Open Group—issued a Request for Technology (RFT) for a *Distributed Management Environment (DME)*, which was to provide a total solution for system and network management in heterogeneous multivendor environments. Anyone, OSF member or not, could respond. Twenty-five organizations submitted technologies. In September 1991, OSF announced the winners, which included HP's OpenView, Tivoli's WizDOM, IBM's Data Engine, and Groupe Bull's CMIP and SNMP drivers. In May 1992, OSF published a very comprehensive architecture that combined a traditional network management framework with a postmodern, CORBA-based object framework.

In late 1994, OSF "downsized" its DME effort. Instead of using the Tivoli ORB, OSF now specifies management interfaces to any CORBA-compliant ORB. It appears that OSF is putting most of its efforts in the management of DCE. As a result, open platform vendors are acquiring parts of the DME technology directly from its originators and incorporating them into their products. For example, IBM licensed parts of OpenView from HP, which got incorporated into NetView/6000 and LAN NetView. Digital then licensed NetView from IBM; it is the foundation for *Polycenter NetView*. Finally, IBM acquired Tivoli in early 1996. So Tivoli is now the foundation for IBM's CORBA-based system management platform called *TME 10*.

Despite its retrenchment, the DME system management architecture remains of great interest. DME provides a comprehensive framework for understanding distributed system management in its classical and postmodern approaches. The DME architecture uniquely reconciles these two approaches by using object wrappers and a CORBA-compliant IDL and ORB. This section provides a brief overview of DME's two design points:

- The **Network Management Option (NMO)** takes a classical manager/agent approach to system management.

- The **Object Management Framework (OMF)** provides a postmodern, object-oriented solution based on CORBA.

In addition, DME includes a *Distributed Services* component that provides an infrastructure for services in a distributed environment. It also includes a user interface component.

The DME Network Management Option (NMO)

DME's *Network Management Option (NMO)* provides a traditional management platform for applications that wish to access SNMP and/or CMIP. DME augments the traditional X/Open components with an *Instrumentation Request Broker (IRB);* see Figure 31-9. The IRB provides additional services on top of SNMP or CMIP. These services include the use of the DCE directory services to locate agents on the network, configurable retries, and a gateway service to the DME CORBA-based management environment. Via the IRB, objects will be able to access SNMP and CMIP managed resources.

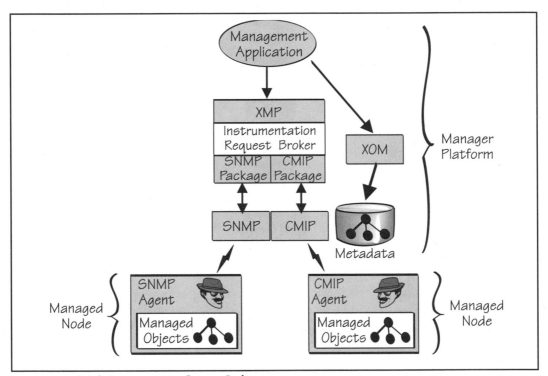

Figure 31-9. DME's Instrumentation Request Broker.

The DME Object Management Framework

Object orientation is particularly appropriate for creating network and system management software, where tasks are so varied and complex that no single vendor can hope to undertake more than a small subset.

— *Mike Hurwicz, Seybold Analyst*

DME's *Object Management Framework (OMF)* takes a radically new approach towards unifying network and system management; it builds on CORBA and the OMG services. The DME OMF is composed of multiple objects that cooperate and share information. The new framework goes beyond the traditional manager/object relationship. Instead, an object may at any time take either of two roles: a client requesting a service or a service provider. The DME *I4DL*—an upwardly compatible CORBA IDL with some extensions for event management and installation instructions—is used to describe the interfaces, attributes, and inheritance relationships of any management object. The communication between objects takes place over any standard CORBA ORB that uses DCE for its core communications (see Figure 31-10). DME calls this DCE-based ORB the *Management Request Broker (MRB)*.

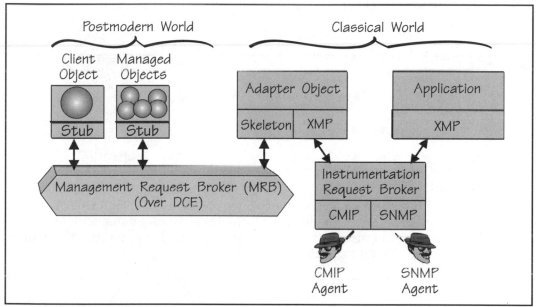

Figure 31-10. The DME Object Management Framework.

How does the postmodern, object-oriented DME incorporate devices that are managed using traditional protocols such as SNMP and CMIP? The answer is through special DME encapsulators called adapter objects (not to be confused with the CORBA object adapters used on servers). The I4DL is used to encapsulate legacy protocols and bring them to the object world. The adapter object looks like any other IDL-defined object. An application object can invoke operations on the adapter just like it does on any object using the typical remote invocations. Proxy methods invoked on the adapter call XMP to perform SNMP or CMIP functions. The adapter may define a set of operations that emulate the corresponding CMIP or SNMP calls, or it could augment them in some useful ways. For example, a CMIP adapter object might aggregate several CMIP operations on some managed object into one, providing a higher level of abstraction to the legacy object.

In summary, DME's OMF uses objects to encapsulate the implementation of any management resource. You can access a managed object only through an IDL-defined set of interfaces. The combined network and system management is modeled as the communication between objects that represent the resources of the system and objects that represent the user interface and managing applications. DME primarily deals with communication between management objects. Object adapters are used to encapsulate standard management protocols—such as SNMP, CMIP, and DCE. The DME Management Request Broker (with the help of the DCE directory services) provides a uniform naming space for all its objects (legacy or postmodern). It knows how to find them and invoke their services. So welcome to the postmodern world of system management with distributed objects. The commercial incarnation of this new architecture is the *Tivoli Management Environment (TME)*, which we cover later in this chapter. Of course, TME does not use DCE.

Open Group: The New OSF

Briefing

The OSF's new mission is to focus on architecture, subcontracting, and the distribution of standards-based infrastructure software. They no longer have a complete software development organization. The new OSF has adopted a secular approach to the management ORB—any CORBA-compliant ORB will do. When OSF members decided to move to a CORBA-compliant management ORB, they made the decision that OSF should leave the ORB business to OMG. Any CORBA-compliant ORB now qualifies as an MRB. ❏

UI-Atlas Distributed Management Framework

Unix International (UI) was the industry's other Unix consortium; its 270 members defined the requirements for the evolution of distributed software for Unix within an architecture framework called *Atlas*. In July 1991, UI published its *Atlas-Distributed Management (Atlas-DM)* requirements—distributed objects were the key unifying concept. USL elected to implement the first release of Atlas using existing Tivoli technology. The second release, which was due in 1994, was to be CORBA-based. The UI requirements, in the pre-Novell acquisition days, were implemented by USL (or whomever USL contracted out for the job). We're using the past tense because UI was dissolved on December 31, 1993. We still cover Atlas-DM in this section because it's an important architecture that helps us understand how distributed objects are used in systems management.

Architecturally, UI went even further than OSF's DME in its support of objects—the first release of Atlas didn't even bother with SNMP and CMIP. Atlas-DM, like the postmodern DME, defines management applications as collections of objects that interact with each other and with objects that represent the managed resources. The UI *Management ORB (MORB)* provides transparent access to managed objects across the network (see Figure 31-11). The objects represent generic resources in the distributed environment—including hosts, users, LANs, DBMSs, applications, disks, files, and OSs. A single dynamic API call—the Tivoli *objcall*—is used to invoke methods on objects (all parameters are passed as ASCII character strings). Object references can be passed at run time. In addition, Tivoli allows the dynamic discovery of objects and the operations they support. The second release of Atlas-DM would have used CORBA IDL stubs, dynamic method invocations, and a CORBA-compliant ORB. It was going to implement the X/Open XMP API for interfacing to SNMP and CMIP. Of course, Atlas-DM is now history.

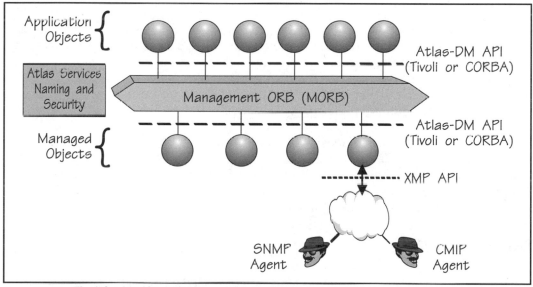

Figure 31-11. The Atlas-DM Object Management Framework.

So What Is CORBA's System Management Solution?

In 1995, the OMG started to define a CORBA *System Management Facility* that includes interfaces and services for managing, instrumenting, configuring, install-ing, operating, and repairing distributed object components. For a distributed component to be managed, it must implement IDL-defined management interfaces. The system management framework defines the following interfaces:

- **Instrumentation**—lets you collect information on a component's workload, responsiveness, throughput, consumption of resources, and so on.

- **Data collection**—lets you collect information on historical events related to a component. Any component may have a history—meaning a log of events. The data collection interface allows a managing workstation to query that log.

- **Quality of service**—lets you select the level of service a component provides in areas such as availability, performance, reliability, and recovery.

- **Security**—lets you manage the security system itself. It is distinct from the CORBA Security Service, which implements the security mechanisms.

- **Event management**—lets you generate, register, filter, and forward event notifications to management applications. It builds on the CORBA Event Service.

- **Scheduling**—lets you schedule repetitive tasks and associate event handlers with events. For example, you can schedule the execution of a task when an event fires or a timer pops.

- **Instance tracking**—lets you associate objects with other managed objects that are subject to common policies.

The technology for these services is X/Open's new *SysMan* standard. SysMan itself is based on the *Tivoli Management Environment (TME)*, which provides a CORBA-based distributed system management framework (see next section). TME 2.0 provides a set of CORBA-based technologies and services to create, maintain, and integrate distributed system management applications.

Tivoli and CORBA

Our idea was to build management applications around an ORB instead of network management protocols. So in 1989, we began working on a distributed object framework for managing applications.

— **Todd Smith, Chief Scientist**
Tivoli Systems

Tivoli is a tiny system management company that IBM acquired for a cool $743 million in January of 1996. Why did IBM pay this phenomenal sum to acquire a 300-person company with under $45 million in revenues? Because Tivoli is the best CORBA-based system management framework on the market. The Tivoli framework was exactly what IBM needed to complement its ORB-based suites for system management (also known as Karat and SystemView). The converged SystemView/ Tivoli management platform is called *TME 10*; it builds on TME. Tivoli has become the foundation platform for all the IBM system management products.

So what does TME look like? It consists of *Tivoli/Enterprise Console*, *Tivoli Management Framework (TMF)*, and a set of core management services (see Figure 31-12). Tivoli/Enterprise is a desktop management console that collects management events and provides a rules-based technology for automating management operations and event processing. TMF includes basic services for handling user-defined policies, scheduling tasks, instance tracking, instrumentation, and security. TMF also provides a set of system management classes (in the form of mixins) that managed and managing objects can multiple inherit from and customize. Tivoli has an active OEM program to license TME. Participants include Sybase, Informix, Sun, Unisys, and Siemens-Rolm. TME is the *de facto* and *de jure* (via X/Open) system management standard for CORBA ORBs. So, for all practical purposes, systems management for ORBs is mostly here today—it's called Tivoli (also see the next Soapbox).

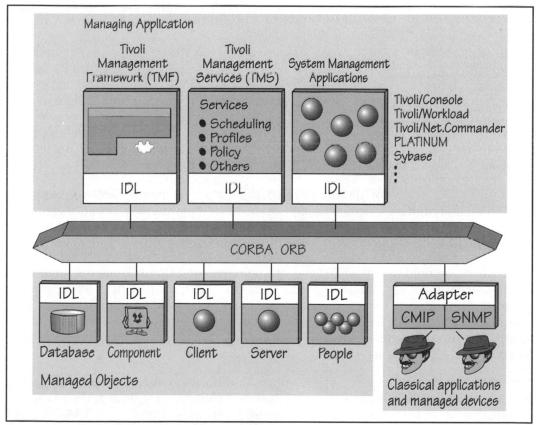

Figure 31-12. The Tivoli Management Environment (TME).

WEB MANAGEMENT: DMTF'S WEBEM AND CIM/XML

In June 1998—at the urging of Cisco, IBM/Tivoli, and Microsoft—the DMTF agreed to become the standards body for *Web-Based Enterprise Management (WEBEM)* and *Directory-Enabled Networking (DEN)*. WEBEM is an umbrella initiative to link intervendor management applications using Web technologies. A key component of WEBEM is the XML-based *Common Information Model (CIM)*; it describes a common way to represent management data—using object classes. DEN is an initiative to link network and systems directories. It was originated by Cisco and Microsoft.

The DMTF's WEBEM may become the mother of all system management standards. It will use a meta-layer of Object Web technology to integrate disparate standards developed by Microsoft, Cisco, IBM/Tivoli, JavaSoft, IETF, OMG, OSI, and Open Group (i.e., X/Open and OSF). It's a very timely initiative that solves a very big problem: How to manage the Web. If you think about it, the Web consists of multiple management domains that span networks and organizations. In this environment, a central point of control is no longer possible. So standards become the glue that holds everything together. The Object Web provides the unifying wrapper technology for managing the disparate pieces.

As we explained in the previous chapter, CIM uses XML to describe management information; it provides a common vocabulary for describing managed entities. CIM classes are defined using XML DTDs. CIM provides four immediate benefits: 1) a common data model and vocabulary for management information; 2) a common data interchange mechanism for multivendor management data; 3) an object model for describing relationships between the data elements—for example, a PC *contains* a power supply and a memory board; and 4) a way to subsume existing management information models such as SNMP MIBs, OSI's GDMO, and DMTF's DMI.

Note that CIM does not define APIs to the data. Typically, XML objects are manipulated using the language-independent DOM (see Part 8). In addition, CIM objects will require XSL support to be rendered. All this technology should be very familiar by now.

By the time you read this, the DMTF—with help from the Open Group—should have completed its CIM V2.1 and V2.2 specifications for managed devices, operating systems, desktops, networks, databases, LDAP directories, and applications. For example, CIM 2.2 will define application states, and support for the distribution, installation, updating, asset tracking, and configuration of distributed applications. As you can see, this effort is very ambitious.

Next the DMTF plans to work on defining CIM-based events and methods, as well as a CIM-based RPC and a Directory Access Protocol. Hopefully, they will not reinvent the wheel. This technology is currently available from the CORBA/Java and COM+ camps (see the next section).

JAVA MANAGEMENT API (JMAPI 2.0)

I never heard of that acronym—JMAPI. I guess you can take a J and put it in front of everything.

> — **Bill Gates, Chairman**
> **Microsoft**
> **(April, 1998)**

JMAPI 2.0—due in March, 1999—defines a component-based management platform based on ORB-based distributed objects, JavaBeans, EJBs, and Java 2. The previous version—*JMAPI 0.8*—was only a draft; it was never finalized. So why will this version do any better? The difference is that this time JavaSoft is not creating the standard in a vacuum. It is working with key system management vendors—including IBM/Tivoli, Computer Associates, SunSoft, and Tibco. It is also integrating the new standard with existing management standards.

JMAPI 2.0 is based on an open component model—JavaBeans on the client and EJB on the server (see Figure 31-13). Java 2 serves as the management framework; it

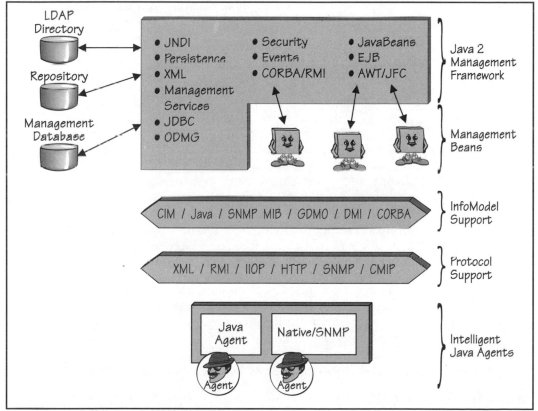

Figure 31-13. The JMAPI 2.0 Architecture (Source: Sun).

provides open APIs to DBMSs, ODBMSs, LDAP directories, and XML stores. JMAPI will augment Java 2 with a publish-and-subscribe event model, event filters, and a management repository. It will support multiple information models—including CORBA's IDL, DMTF's CIM/XML, SNMP's MIBs, CMIP's GDMO, and DMTF's DMI. It will also support multiple protocols—including XML, RMI, IIOP, HTTP, SNMP, and CMIP. Finally, it will support both Java agents and native SNMP agents. JavaSoft plans to provide test suites for JMAPI as well as a reference implementation based on Sun's *Java Dynamic Management Kit 4.0*. Sun will also ship a commercial version of the management kit.

What the Object Web Brings to System Management

Soapbox

A network management system is limited by the capabilities of the network management protocol and by the objects used to represent the environment to be managed.

> — **William Stallings, Author**
> **SNMP, SNMPv2, and CMIP**
> **(Addison-Wesley, 1993)**

JMAPI 2.0 brings together all the elements of Object Web management that we covered in this long chapter. JMAPI 2.0 includes both CORBA/Java and CIM/XML. It also encapsulates existing protocols like SNMP, CMIP, and MIB. Here's what the elements of the Object Web do for system management:

- **CORBA** provides a modern and natural protocol for representing managed entities, defining their services, and invoking their methods via an ORB. The CORBA Event and Notification Services bring object-based event services to system management. CORBA services—like transactions, security, the IIOP firewall proxy, collections, and relationships—are very useful in distributed management environments. These are all services that a system management platform would have to reinvent. Finally, CORBA provides the DOM for manipulating XML data structures.

- **Java** provides a component infrastructure—on both the client and server— for writing management applications. Java runs on almost every OS in existence, which is very important for ubiquitous systems management. Java is also ideal for managing embedded devices and Internet appliances— JavaOS, Java for PCs, and Jini were made for low-end devices. Finally, Java provides a mobile code system for distributing management agents.

- **CIM/XML** is the Object Web's answer to MIB. It is MIBs on steroids. You use CIM and XML to create modern renditions of MIB trees; DOM lets you navigate these trees. Finally, CIM/XML provides a universal mechanism for the exchange of management data between agents, managing platforms, Web browsers, and databases.

With the Object Web, managed objects can directly call the managing station when they have something significant to report (in contrast, SNMP relies mostly on polling). The Object Web can solve today's management problems. It is also the ideal platform for managing tomorrow's Web, which, hopefully, will consist of self-managing objects packaged as components.

Will Objects Replace SNMP?

SNMPv1—today's predominant management protocol—is too limited to address the requirements of total systems management. It needs to be replaced. This means that in the next few years, we'll be experiencing a large migration to more sophisticated management software. The three contenders for replacing SNMP are SNMPv3, OSI's CMIP, and the Object Web. All three require more memory and smarter processors than SNMP. So the question is: Which one do you choose?

What a surprise: We think it should be the Object Web. SNMPv3 and CMIP are both antiques and incredibly clumsy to program. MIBs are an anachronism in the age of IDL, CIM/XML, and object persistent stores. They require that management applications interact with a very large number of low-level attributes that they manipulate through *get* and *set*. SNMPv3 does not allow you to invoke methods on managed objects; CMIP does this very clumsily. We feel the "simple" SNMP was a wonderful, basic protocol that solved many real problems in the age of scarcity and simple network management. But now that we're moving to total systems management, the sooner the world moves away from SNMP, SNMPv3, and CMIP and replaces them with Object Web management, the better off system management will be.

Table 31-1 compares the features of SNMP, SNMPv3, CMIP, and Object Web management. SNMP and SNMPv3 place a minimum amount of event-emitting logic in the agents so that the managed nodes are simple. The smarts are in the managing station. As a result, traps (or events) are infrequently used, and the managing station must poll the agents to find out what's happening. In contrast, CMIP and CORBA are event driven, which means the agents are smarter; the managing station doesn't have to poll as much. As a result, a CORBA-based managing station can handle a much larger number of managed objects.

In general, CMIP or CORBA are better suited for the management of large, complex, multivendor networks than SNMP. Of course, SNMP's simplicity allows it to be deployed on more devices, which, in turn, makes it easier to manage large networks. The designers of SNMP understood these trade-offs very well. They opted for the least common denominator approach and were willing to live with the consequences. SNMPv3 makes the same architectural trade-offs as SNMP. Looking at the comparison table, we're not so sure SNMP is still the way to go. Systems management operational costs are just too high—the design point has shifted. We need smarter systems management software that knows how to deal with smarter objects anywhere on the intergalactic network. We believe the Object Web is the answer to the distributed systems management nightmare. ☐

Table 31-1. Comparing SNMP, SNMPv3, CMIP, and the Object Web.

Feature	SNMP	SNMPv3	CMIP	Object Web
Installed base	Huge	Very small	Small	Very small
Managed objects per managing station	Small	Small	Large	Very large
Management model	Manager and agents	Manager and agents	Manager and agents	Communicating objects
View of managed objects	Simple variables organized in MIB trees	Simple variables organized in MIB trees	Objects with inheritance defined in MIBs	Objects with IDL defined inter-faces; data is defined via CIM/XML
Manager/agent interactions	Polling. Infre-quent traps	Polling. Infre-quent traps	Event driven	Event driven
Explicit manager to agent command invocations	No	No	Yes	Yes
Security	No	Yes	Yes	Yes
Manager-to-manager exchanges	No	Yes	Yes	Yes
Bulk transfers	No	Yes	Yes	Yes
Create/delete managed objects	No	No (but can add table rows)	Yes	Yes
Communication model	Datagram	Datagram	Session-based	ORB
Application component model	No	No	No	Yes (JavaBeans, EJBs)
Management data in-terchange	No	No	No	Yes (via CIM/XML)

Table 31-1. Comparing SNMP, SNMPv3, CMIP, and the Object Web. (Continued)				
Feature	SNMP	SNMPv3	CMIP	Object Web
Mobile agent support	No	No	No	Yes (via Java)
Standards body	Internet	Internet	ISO	OMG, X/Open, DMTF, and Java-Soft
Approximate memory requirements (KBytes)	40-200	200-500	300-1000	64-2000

SYSTEM MANAGEMENT: MEET THE PLAYERS

According to Gartner/Dataquest, the total market for network and systems management will approach $10 billion by the year 2000—more than double 1997's $4.5 billion. Three groups of system management vendors are competing for this market:

■ *Mainframe system management vendors that are moving to Open DSM.* Heading this group is Computer Associates (CA) with *Unicenter/TNG*. In May 1995, CA acquired Legent for $1.78 billion. In May 1996, it acquired Digital's *PolyCenter.* In 1998, it acquired *Computer Sciences Corporation (CSC)*—a systems integrator—for $9 billion. CA must be on the right track. According to financial analysts, CA's TNG sales are expected to hit $1.6 billion in 1999, nearly triple 1997's $550 million. The mainframe vendors have a deep understanding of IS requirements for total systems management, especially at the application level. These systems typically provide accounting, security, storage, and workload management at the application level.

■ *Unix-based network management vendors.* This group includes SunSoft with *Solstice Enterprise Manager* and *SunNet Manager;* Cabletron with *Spectrum*, HP with *OpenView,* and IBM with *Tivoli/TME*. These are all system vendors with a long history in distributed system management and open frameworks. They all have large portfolios of third-party tools that run on their management platforms. In addition, these vendors are now extending their reach beyond network management; they now provide application and system management suites.

■ *LAN-based system management vendors.* This group includes Microsoft with *System Management Server (SMS)*, Intel with *LANDesk Management Suite*, Symantec with *Norton Administrator*, and Novell with *ManageWise*. These vendors have a long history in managing PCs, NOS servers, and depart-

mental LANs. The information they collect feeds the management food chain. Historically, these systems have not been able to provide enterprise-wide management solutions.

So who will win? It's too early to make this call. Look for acquisitions and mergers everywhere. Distributed systems management is far too complicated for a monolithic "one-size-fits-all" answer. Prebundled suites of monolithic products are not the answer either—they are too inflexible. The vendors that are best positioned provide open management frameworks based on Object Web technology.

Open frameworks can be complemented by hundreds of "plug-in" modules from third parties. Frameworks bring best-of-breed point management products together in an integrated customer solution. Together, these plug-ins (and their frameworks) should be able to manage PCs, LANs, WANs, applications, servers, and the Web. Future plug-ins will be built using Java component technology. *Manage.com*—a small start up—is a good example of system management, Object Web style.

CONCLUSION

Intergalactic client/server systems will fail if they cannot be managed. The spread of the Internet and intranets will further exacerbate the problem. Distributed management systems are still in their infancy. And their agents are from the Stone Age. For example, SNMP agents are totally passive—they speak only when spoken to. We need a new generation of smart agents that can act independently of the management systems. We need component-based management systems that are built on a distributed object and Web-based foundation. We need better object standards for managing applications. And we need it all now.

Unfortunately, the standards bodies are moving far too slowly. The IETF wasted five precious years on its SNMPv3 wars. The OSF's DME and UI's Atlas were aborted efforts. OSI's CMIP is a market failure. JavaSoft wasted two years on its aborted JMAPI 1.0 effort. The bright stars in this otherwise dismal picture are the Object Web management standards—DMTF's CIM/XML, Tivoli's *de facto* object standard for system management based on CORBA, and JavaSoft's JMAPI 2.0. So there is some hope. However, these efforts must learn how to move on Internet time. In the meantime, DSM is a system integrator's dream.

Part 10
Bringing It All Together

An Introduction to Part 10

The future is bright, fruitful, and positive.

— Bob Marley

Are you Martians still with us? All that talk of problem management and disaster recovery didn't faze you? We're reaching the end of our journey. We realize this tour was really long, but client/server is a broad topic. You probably want us to net it all out for you: Which technology do I pick? How do I get an application out in record time? What help can I expect? It turns out these are the million-dollar questions of client/server.

Which technology do I pick? This is like predicting the future. Anybody can predict it, but the trick is getting it right. We'll give you our two cents worth on where we think this technology is going. You Martians know how to surf now, so we'll throw in a wave theory of client/server. The idea is to look at technology cycles and figure out which wave to ride. If you read this book, you won't be too surprised by the answers.

How do I get an application out in record time? This takes us into the subject of tools. Here on Earth, we've had tools since the dawn of our civilization to help us with our work. The job of toolmakers is to look at all the raw technologies and create the tools that ordinary mortals can use to get a job done. With tools, we can develop client/server applications quickly. The better tools can even help us deploy and manage our client/server applications. Toolmakers are constantly trying to keep up with the technologies presented in this book, making them easier to use for the rest of us. Picking a tool is not easy. It locks you into a client/server paradigm. And we know that there's more than one way to do client/server; in fact, there are hundreds of ways to do it. So we'll answer the question by throwing a model at you on how to pick a tool. Then you'll have to decide which tool is best for your job.

What help can I expect? You'll need a good tool, a working methodology, and lots of good luck. You'll mostly be on your own—but that's when the real fun starts. This book provides a Survival Guide; it's just one more aid that will help you filter the signal from the noise in this overhyped field. Of course, you can always get the advice of consultants and attend seminars. But good advice doesn't come cheap. This final part gives you an overview of tools and methodologies. Are you Martians ready for your return trip home? Time does fly when you're having fun.

Chapter 32

Client/Server Tools and Application Development

---

*T*ool evaluation is fun. There are literally hundreds of products. How do you make a decision? One possibility is to stay in tool evaluation mode until you're told that the decision is due tomorrow. Then just pick one!

— **Anonymous MIS Developer**

The million-dollar question is: Which magical tool can take the pain out of client/server application development and deployment? And a related question is: Does client/server require a new approach to application development? All these questions are very dear to your authors' hearts. For many years, we were involved in building client/server application development tools. Our elusive goal was to create the perfect tool for developing, deploying, and maintaining client/server applications *quickly*. However, we learned the hard way that you have to make some serious compromises. There is no such thing as a "one size fits all" client/server tool. And there is no magical tool (including ours). So the next best thing we can do is leave you with a model for how to evaluate them. We'll even throw in our two cents on client/server development methodologies.

CLIENT/SERVER APPLICATION DEVELOPMENT TOOLS

Development tools are the linchpin in client/server. Tools encapsulate the client/server technology described in this book and make it easier for users to write applications. The best tools are highly visual. Most of today's client/server tools are used to create departmental decision-support systems. However, 3-tier Internet tools are just starting to take off. They may set the stage for blasting the tools market out of its departmental bunkers. So how do we classify those client/server tools? Which is the right tool for the right job? Like everything else in client/server, it seems everyone has an opinion on tools. So we present in this section a classification scheme that works for us.

The Latest and Greatest Model of Client/Server Tools

Yes, client/server tool evaluation can be a lot of fun. You're probably being bombarded with tons of glossy advertisements for tools that all promise to deliver instant and hassle free client/server solutions. At trade shows, you've probably watched those slick demonstrations that seem to create entire client/server applications with a few mouse clicks. But with over 200 tools on the market, which do you pick for evaluation? These days, we could probably safely assume that you don't have an infinite budget for tools or the time to evaluate all 200 of them. You could start pruning tools by platform, but most seem to run on all the popular platforms. Or you could prune them by price, but you could end up getting what you paid for. Or you could prune them by brand name and miss out on the most avant-garde tools with the latest and greatest features.

To help you with your evaluation, we propose a simple model that breaks the tool market around five axes (see Figure 32-1):

1. **Roots.** What's the tool's ancestry? At one end of the axis are tools that originated on mainframes; they tend to have a CASE-centric focus. At the other end of the axis are tools that originated on PC LANs; they tend to have a GUI-centric, event-driven focus. Somewhere in between are the supermini 4GL tools. The approach (or paradigm) a tool uses for application development is intimately tied to its roots.

2. **Distributed Technology.** What's the client/server technology? What applications does the tool create? The axis moves from fat clients with thin servers that specialize in decision support to thin clients with fat servers that do OLTP. In the middle are Groupware and Distributed Objects, which split the logic more evenly.

3. **Scope.** How much of the client/server function does the tool provide? The axis

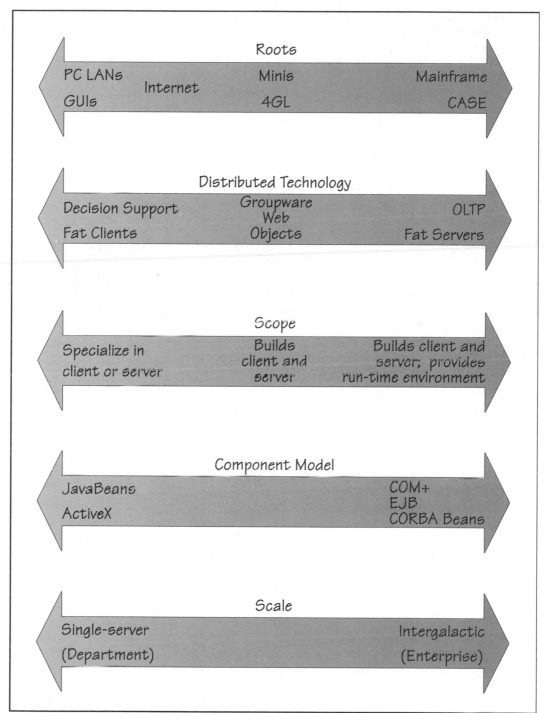

Figure 32-1. The Five Axes of Client/Server Tools.

ranges from tools that specialize in the client, the server, or the middleware to tools that provide all three (see Figure 32-2). Some tools may even go as far as bundling a run time that includes system management, an application server, a TP Monitor, resource managers, ORBs, and single point of installation. This may sound like heresy, but the more bundling the tool provides, the less integration you have to do. Integration is a major headache in client/server systems.

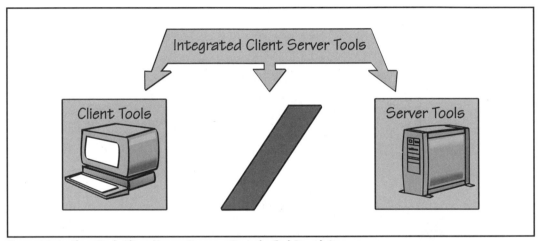

Figure 32-2. How Much Client/Server Coverage Does the Tool Provide?

4. *Component model.* What component model does the tool support? Which component types does it run in its palette? Which component foundation libraries does it provide? In the past many tools came with their proprietary component models. Today, for a tool to succeed it must support the de facto component standards we described in this book. Most fat-client tools support ActiveX in their palettes. Internet client tools support JavaBeans. On the server-side, most tools will eventually support Enterprise JavaBeans (EJBs) and CORBA Beans. Some will support COM+. Finally, some tools will even let you mix-and-match component models. For example, ActiveXs or JavaBeans on the client and EJBs on the server.

5. *Scalability.* How well does the tool scale for enterprise solutions? The axis moves from single-server tools to multiserver intergalactic tools. The middleware that the tool targets becomes an important factor in the more intergalactic tools.

You'll need all five axes to understand where a tool fits in the scheme of things and what it can do for you.

Will the Ideal Tool Please Stand Up?

The ideal tool is the one that does the job for you. For us, it's a tool that helps us create 3-tier client/server applications for the Object Web. No one is offering a complete tool, yet. However, many of the individual pieces are here today. Let's put together a set of requirements in the hope that someone builds the whole enchilada. So here's what we would like to see in an ideal tool:

- *A **visual place-builder for the first tier**.* The tool should let you build visual containers that you can then populate with components such as ActiveXs, JavaBeans, and Java applets. The container is either an XML compound document—with drag-and-drop support—or an ordinary Web page. The tool should provide prebuilt containers (or *places*) that we can then extend to meet our needs. Of course, these places must be portable across client platforms. They must also be *shippable*, which means the tool must provide hooks to associate security policies, itineraries, and rules with each place. Finally, the tool must package the places in certified JARs for distribution. Note that most Java tools come close to providing all of this today.

- *A **business-object builder for the second tier**.* The tool must provide server-side containers with object services such as persistence, security, transactions, locking, metering, and versioning (i.e., CORBA/EJB or COM+ services). You should be able to start with a raw business-object template and then extend it with the services you need via point-and-click. We also need a server-side programming environment to write business logic and associate it with the object. Finally, the tool should be able to create the server-side packages—EJB JARs, XML deployment descriptors, or COM+ packages—that contain the components and their support classes. The deployment descriptors specify the quality-of-service the components expect from an application server or OTM.

- ***Frameworks that encapsulate the third tier.*** The tool must provide frameworks that encapsulate existing server environments such as DBMSs, groupware, TP Monitors, MOM, ERP systems, e-mail, LDAP directories, and workflow. These back-end services are typically invoked by the middle-tier objects.

- *A **visual environment for assembling components**.* The tool must provide visual facilities for connecting (or assembling) objects across tiers and within tiers. For example, you should be able to associate a client event in the first tier with a CORBA or COM+ method invocation on a business object in the second tier. The CORBA IDL and Interface Repository can play a major role in tying together these components.

- *A **component repository**.* The tool must support teams of developers by providing a shared repository of reusable components, places, and server objects. The repository must, of course, provide check-in/check-out facilities and other such features.

We also expect the tool to provide run-time facilities that let you split the business objects at many different points—between the client, the server, and, more importantly, across servers.

We could keep this list going. But what are the odds of getting all these facilities in our current lifetimes? Actually, the odds are quite favorable. Most major tool vendors—including Inprise/Borland, Symantec, Microsoft, Oracle, Sybase, Dynasty, Forte, Penumbra, and IBM—are now adding support for both 3-tier client/server components and the Internet in their tools. So it's only a matter of time before their products provide all the features we've just described.

CLIENT/SERVER APPLICATION DESIGN

Mainframe application designers and programmers have had it easy. In the past, user interfaces were simple constructs driven by simple terminals. The primary focus was on the database and transaction code, leaving the human to simply respond, like an extension of the application. But with client/server applications, the tables have turned. The ultimate goal of client/server solutions is to provide mission-critical applications that have the ease-of-use and responsiveness of stand-alone PCs. In this section, we present a methodology for designing 3-tier client/server applications.

Client/server is primarily a relationship between programs running on separate machines. As such, it requires an infrastructure to do things standalone PCs never had to worry about. For example, robust interprocess communications over LANs or WANs must be included in the design. Graphical interfaces using GUIs and OOUIs must be exploited to make applications look and feel more like real-world objects instead of programming processes. User interfaces are becoming complex, responsive, ad hoc environments that put the emphasis on the human task. OOUI clients bring humans into the distributed loop, which inevitably adds a host of complications. Humans make lots of errors, do unexpected things, and typically require lots of information from diverse sources. The more advanced OOUIs—such as shippable places—turn the client workstation into virtual worlds where many parallel dialogs are conducted with a variety of servers.

OOUIs also give the user much more freedom than GUIs or terminal-based systems. Users are free to organize their visual objects (and desktop) in any way they please. They are not tied to the rigid logic of task-oriented applications. OOUIs have no main panels and navigation screens. They make it hard to tell where one application starts and another ends (or what an application object is versus a system object). There are just visual objects everywhere. This begs two important questions: Does client/server require a new approach to system development? Where design used to predominantly start at the database, which comes first now: the client or the server?

What Makes Client/Server Different?

Traditional (terminal-based) system design started with the data. The screens were developed primarily to drive the process of filling in the database, so they were designed after the transactions and tables were defined. Client/server applications, on the other hand, require a far more complex design approach:

■ The interface is more flexible than terminals, and the user is allowed more latitude.

■ The object-based, front-end designs place a lot more intelligence on the client-side of the application.

■ The messages between the client and the server are custom-built and application-specific.

■ The design must be optimized to take advantage of the parallelism inherent in the distributed application.

■ Reusable components can be used on both the client and the server.

This leads us to a design approach unique to client/server applications: You must start your design with both the client and the server. So, you have two starting points in a client/server application: the GUI/OOUI and the data (unless the data for a business process is already in place). The GUI/OOUI and data designs come together at the application objects in the middle tier. The application objects map the visual objects to the database, and vice versa. They encapsulate the shared data and the business rules. Does this seem complex? Don't worry: It's not nearly as ominous as it sounds.

Rapid Prototyping Is Essential

One way to avoid a "chicken and egg" situation from developing—like the one in Figure 32-3—is to use a rapid prototyping methodology. Rapid prototyping allows you to develop your system incrementally. You start with the client, and then work your way iteratively towards the server. You always move in small steps, constantly refining the design as you go along. Make sure to involve your end-user during all the stages of the interface design. In this form of delta development, the system is incrementally refined until you develop a working prototype that is mature enough

Figure 32-3. The Client/Server Chicken and Egg.

to be placed into production. This approach may place a larger burden on the programmer than the traditional approaches, which rely on up-front analysis and design. And, with rapid prototyping, you also run the risk that a cost-cutting management decision may place a non-optimized "working" prototype prematurely into production. At the other extreme, you may encounter another risk: the perpetual prototyping syndrome.

These risks are easily outweighed by the benefits that rapid prototyping provide in developing an OOUI client/server system. In client/server environments, it is difficult to determine beforehand how the system is supposed to work (the OOUI design, the network performance, and multiuser loading). It has been our experience that user specifications cannot anticipate all the needs of the users. They cannot adequately account for the potential OOUI technology offers. If you ask the users for guidance, the chances are that they'll give you the wrong answers based on existing solutions (GUI or terminal-based solutions). Instead, you should show them what the technology can do for them and what new visual dimensions OOUIs offer; then work with them on developing the application.

Invariably, OOUIs can capture more of the business process than either GUIs or terminal-based front-ends. A rapid prototype will help in the discovery of the application objects (or business objects). Users will find it easier to discuss visual business objects, and the visual prototype will help develop the design specifications.

So build a prototype and try it out. The trick is to be able to build the client application many times. It is easier to talk about something that can be demonstrated live and used. Moreover, it is important that the prototype be developed in an environment where the issues of client/server performance, network overheads, system management, and application server design can be tested live. Client/server systems require a lot of monitoring, fine-tuning, and administration. It is better for you to get acquainted with these issues early in the game.

From Prototype To Working System

The OOUI objects permeate the entire application and determine its shape. An application can be seen as a collection of visual business objects. The design of the application starts from the objects (and views) the user sees on the screen, and then works its way towards the server objects and the database structure. Prototypes are used to identify, with your customer's participation, the user model: What business objects are needed, and what do they do? Prototyping is an iterative activity with many false starts. Here is how the typical prototype evolves:

1. ***Understand the business process***. It is a prerequisite that you understand what the application is all about at the business level. So gather the requirements and study the tasks: What does the customer really want?

2. ***Design the visual places.*** Remember, a *place* provides the visual metaphor that ties together the components a user sees. It's the container that creates the virtual world. Or, if you prefer, it's the simulation of the real world. In a world of components, the place becomes your application. We recommend that you hire a visual artist to sketch out each place including its visual components.

3. ***Define the components or business objects***. What the user sees in a place are objects containing views that react to user input and actions. The objects are manipulated according to the requirements of the business process. You should create user objects that correspond to real-life entities; for example, a seat on an airplane. What are the main object types in the application? What other objects do they contain? What are the attributes of the objects? What functions do they have? How do they behave? What are the relationships between objects? What are the "composed of" relationships (is-part-of)? What are the dependency and collaboration relationships (is-analogous-to, is-kind-of, depends-upon)?

4. ***Work on the detailed object views***. What context menu actions apply to each object? What views are required? Are business form views required? Can the views be grouped in Notebook pages? What widgets controls—including input/output fields, list boxes, pushbuttons, menus, sliders, and value-sets—will appear in the views? What level of help is needed? What data validation at the field level is required? What level of triggers are required (on error, on message, and so on)? How are external procedures or methods invoked?

5.   ***Develop dry-run scenarios***. You can create your screen objects and animate the application (OOUI tools should provide this capability). Use the scenarios to validate the object model of the user interface. The scenarios should also help you identify the major event-driven interactions.

6.   ***Walk through a use-case system scenario***. Such a scenario should follow a transaction from its source through its execution. Identify the protocols that link the visual objects with the middle-tier server objects. Use Java introspection, CORBA IDL, or COM+ type libraries to define and document the object interfaces. Expand this scenario in areas that require more detail. Run an application scenario for each business object. Identify redundant behaviors. Which objects can be reused?

7.   ***Identify transaction sources***. A client/server system can be thought of as a client-driven event system. The server is, in a sense, passively waiting on requests from clients. The client, in turn, is driven by the user who is at the "controls" within the confines of the business process. The drag-and-drop of visual objects is typically the source of transactions. Information required upon opening a container or view may also be the source of a transaction. Object/action intersections almost always lead to the generation of a transaction. There is also a high probability that events such as data entry, menu selections, pushing a button, and action dialogs will generate transactions. The visual client interface will eventually be "brought to life" by writing the distributed object invocations that are triggered by the user interaction.

8.   ***Define your data (or entity) objects.*** You are now in a position to take a first stab at defining the database objects that correspond to the visual business objects you just created. Iterate on this step until you get it right. Many trade-offs are involved. The object/action orientation of the client design can help transform the visual objects into an entity-relationship model for database objects. The actions translate into method invocations on middle-tier server objects that encapsulate the persistent data. You can store the data in variety of datastores—including HTML files, DBMSs, ODBMSs, data warehouses, Lotus Notes, mainframes, and flat files. The middle-tier server object is the integration point for the data. Clients can only manipulate data by invoking these server objects. The server objects can choose to cache the extracted data in an ODBMS or keep it in memory. It's all transparent to the client.

9.   ***Publish the interfaces for the middle-tier server objects***. The publication of the server-side interfaces—including methods, properties, events, and expected quality-of-service—advertises to the world what a server object does. It's a binding contract between the server object and its clients. IDL defines the functions exported by the server object. It provides a higher level of abstraction than messages. Tools can use the CORBA interface repository, COM+ type libraries, and Java introspection APIs to discover on-the-fly server-side component interfaces. This lets you click on a server object within

a tool to visually inspect its interfaces, events, quality-of-service, and properties. Note that server-side components are highly-reusable IT assets. You should be able to reuse them from one project to the next.

10. ***Develop your code one business object at a time***. This means developing code on all three tiers for each object. Validate the user interface and the performance of the system with your customer.

11. ***Move from prototype to working system***. A working system is the sum of all the business objects it contains. It's the implementation of a place. You are developing your system incrementally, so you will have a full working system when you've coded your last business object.

We're not done yet. After you develop an acceptable prototype, you can then start experimenting with distribution issues. Where will the places be stored? How are they shipped from the server to the clients? How will you secure these places? These are the issues we covered in Part 8. So are we done? Not yet. You must also use the prototype to understand how to balance loads across servers. The beauty of 3-tier objects is that they scale both downward and upward. At one extreme, you run all your objects on a single machine. At the other extreme, you can give each object its own machine. So use your prototype to play with your loads. It's a dynamic load-balancing act between the clients and the server and between servers.

CONCLUSION

Client/server technology offers developers the potential to create revolutionary new visual applications. Creating these kind of applications requires the seamless integration of OOUI technology, operating systems, ORB technology, application servers, OTMs, TP Monitors, and DBMSs. To succeed, we will need new approaches to systems development that emphasize rapid prototyping, component reuse, and end-user involvement. Doing that will allow us to exploit the synergy between client and server objects. We will also be in a better position to understand, early in a project, the opportunities (for example, parallelism) and pitfalls (for example, performance and error recovery) introduced by splitting an application across a network.

The prototype-based approach to design eliminates the need for lengthy specifications. More importantly, this approach allows the customer to participate in the specification of the product and its stepwise refinement. The approach also lends itself well to the design of distributed applications because you can refine and fine-tune the distribution of function as you learn more about your system's real-life behavior.

So, the successful 3-tier client/server design starts in parallel with both the client and the server. The two starting points are the OOUI objects and the data objects. The "glue" that ties them together are the business objects in the middle. Remember, server-side business objects are highly reusable. So you should look at your existing inventory of business objects before creating new ones. The clients provide various views to these business objects. So start with the client and move towards the server, or vice versa. In either case, move in small steps and iterate. The visual prototype brings the design to life early. So, which comes first: the client or the server? They both come first!

Chapter 33

Which Way Client/Server?

This is the chapter that's going to bring it all together. We'll bring out our infamous crystal ball and speculate on where client/server technology is heading. We may even jump on a Soapbox and give you a fearless forecast of which technology wave looks most promising. Of course, there should be no surprises at this late stage of the book. You may have even guessed what we're going to see in this famous crystal ball. So what can we do to build the suspense? We'll tell you the following story.

Two of your authors teach a graduate-level course on client/server computing. In the course, we present all of the technologies that we cover in this book. Then we gave our students a choice of client/server projects. We tell them they can use any of the client/server technologies we cover for their projects—including file servers, DBMSs, TP Monitors, groupware, distributed objects, and Web application servers.

So which ones do they pick? Over 80% pick the Web for their client/server platform. In addition, the Web students spent an inordinate amount of time on their projects—they typically do a lot more work than we require. Some just camp out in our lab.

So what is the moral of this story? It says that client/server programming with the Web is very popular with our graduate students, many of whom are also professional programmers. In addition to being popular, programming for the Web can be addictive and fun. But as you know from this book, we need the Object Web to do real client/server work. Luckily, the Object Web is just as much fun to program, if not more. Most of our students stay with the program and learn how to program for the Object Web. So the Web is making client/server development fun. It is also bringing it to the masses in a big way.

WHICH WAY CLIENT/SERVER?

In Chapter 2, on page 30, we introduced the idea that client/server is transitioning from the *Ethernet era* to the *Intergalactic era*. We then spent most of this book going over the client/server technologies that can bring about this change. So what is the bottom line?

We offer Figure 33-1 as the answer to the question: Which way client/server? The Ethernet era of client/server saw a file-centric application wave (the NetWare wave) followed by a database-centric wave (the Oracle wave); TP Monitors and Groupware generated minor ripples. The Object Web is the next big wave. We believe that distributed objects combined with the Web technologies we described in this book

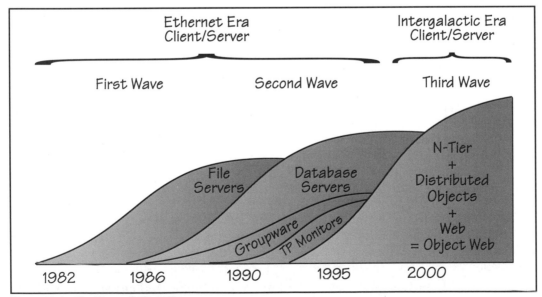

Figure 33-1. The Waves of Client/Server.

—including HTML, XML, DOM, HTTP, SSL, X.509, S-MIME, IMAP, firewalls, LDAP, and others—are essential for making the intergalactic client/server vision real.

Once the Object Web technology takes off, it will subsume all other forms of client/server computing—including TP Monitors, Database, and Groupware. Distributed objects can do it all, and better. Objects will help us break large monolithic applications into more manageable multivendor components that live and coexist on the intergalactic bus. They are also our only hope for managing and distributing the millions of software entities that will live on intergalactic networks. The Web is the killer application that will bring objects to the masses in a big way.

In this third edition, we showed many examples of the Object Web subsuming the more traditional client/server technologies. For example, TP Monitors have now morphed into OTMs and high-end Web application servers. DBMSs are becoming containers of Enterprise JavaBeans. Groupware is now based on Internet mail and distributed components. So the lines between these technologies are growing more fuzzy with each new edition of this book. Eventually, we will simply have the Object Web with specialized beans for groupware, system management, OLTP, e-commerce, ERP, data warehousing, OLAP, and a myriad of application-specific functions.

Which Wave Should I Ride?

We shouldn't have to get on a Soapbox to state the obvious: the Object Web is the future of client/server technology. Objects and the Web encompass all aspects of distributed computing—including OOUIs, compound documents, transactions, groupware, database, and system management. So the million dollar question is: Should you invest in interim technologies, or should you just catch the Object Web wave? It's a trade-off between using proven technologies and the ones that are at the "bleeding edge." We're really at a painful technological juncture. Mixing paradigms typically gives you the worst of both worlds. Like our students, we have the urge to immediately ride the Object Web wave and see where it will take us. However, we also hear a voice of caution that tells us the Object Web is still not ready for intergalactic prime time. The Web and objects will eventually morph, but do you want to be first to ride this wave? The good news is that you won't have to wait too long to safely ride this wave. All the pieces are coming together very nicely.

The Client/Server Scalability Issue

In addition to technology waves, we must factor the issue of scalability into the choice of a client/server platform. It is much easier to deploy client/server in small enterprises and departments. Over 60% of the existing client/server installations are single server and have less than 50 clients. The small installations are typically easier to deploy and manage. Almost all of the existing client/server tools address

that market. These tools can successfully be used to create client/server applications for decision support, e-mail, and groupware. They provide excellent facilities for building GUI front-ends and are adept at working with shrink-wrapped middleware and server packages (mostly SQL DBMSs and Lotus Notes). However, even at the low end, we don't have adequate tools for creating mission critical solutions. By this we mean applications you can depend on to run your everyday business operations. These types of applications, especially at the low end, must support transactions, built-in system management, and high-availability.

Intergalactic client/server is much more complex. It requires the sophisticated middleware described in this book—including MOMs, distributed transactions, ORBs, OTMs, and Web application servers. It requires proven tools that can take advantage of this middleware. Intergalactic client/server is by definition multiserver. So the tools should be able to deploy applications on multiple servers, manage transactions that are distributed across them, perform some form of load-balancing, deploy the software to the clients and servers, and manage the multiserver environment. To be open, these tools are expected to do all this on multivendor operating systems, multivendor resource managers, and multiple GUI front-ends. They must also use standard middleware and component models.

In short, IS people are demanding the level of cohesiveness and scalability they have grown accustomed to on single-vendor mainframe platforms, but now they want it for an open N-tier client/server world that runs on the Internet, intranets, and extranets. As we explained in this Survival Guide, much of the technology and standards that are needed to make this happen are finally coming together; it will be another year before the tools can catch up. Perhaps the Object Web is a bit premature. Yes, we can create client/server applications for it today using Java-Beans and visual tools that help build the front-end clients, but very few tools support EJBs on the server.[1] Within a year, we'll have the luxury of being able to create intergalactic client/server applications by pointing and clicking (or better yet, dragging and dropping).

IT'S TIME TO SAY GOOD-BYE

The only way to successfully predict the future is to invent it.

> — Alan Kay, PC Guru

Yes, the journey was a long, tumultuous one. We hope you enjoyed the guided tour as much as we enjoyed playing guides. To our friends from Mars, we hope you have a safe trip home—it was a pleasure having you here. We hope you'll find that

---

[1] To get a feeling for what you can do with this technology today see our book, **Client/Server Programming with Java and CORBA, Second Edition** (Wiley, 1998).

client/server gold somewhere. We're scratching our heads and trying to come up with some words of wisdom to leave you with at the end of this long tour. But we don't have much to add that wasn't already said. We just want to say that this was our attempt to make some sense out of this traumatic shift our industry is going through. It's a very painful shift for many of us; for others, it's the start of a new dawn in computing with the sky being the limit. OK, enough of that fluffy stuff. We'll say good-bye with a parting Soapbox on where things are going.

Soapbox

Can We Survive the Client/Server Revolution?

Yes, but to do that we need one million new beans. How did we come up with that number? Client/server technology makes it possible to redeploy most of our computer applications on commodity hardware, where the profit margins are razor thin. If we keep recomputerizing the same application base, using PC LANs, intranets, and extranets instead of mainframes, most of us will end up without jobs. This is because we're going after a downsized pie, where the profits are dramatically lower. If our profits are lower, we cut down on the research that helps us create these new technologies. And IT shops won't get new applications or technology. Everybody ends up losing. It's called the "cannibalizing effect."

Instead, we need to take advantage of client/server technology to extend the boundaries of computerization. In other words, we need to move on to new frontiers like the *Object Web*. But, can we create thousands of new client/server applications *quickly* to populate these new frontiers? To do that effectively, we need a technology base, standards, and tools. This Survival Guide makes the case that the technology base, standards, and some solid products are here today. We even have some embryonic tools that can help us create these applications more quickly. However, it's not enough to create the application; it must also be effectively packaged, deployed, and managed.

So who's going to package, deploy, and manage these applications? We can't expect everyone to read this entire book just to become client/server literate (don't get us wrong—we would love the sales). Instead, we need to simplify the packaging and distribution of our client/server products. Of all the technologies discussed in this book, the Object Web offers the best hope for creating—in record time—new client/server applications that can go where no other applications have gone before. So we're excited about the long-term prospects. However, in the short term, we must still write lots of code with little help from tools. And some of us are up to our eyebrows with Euro conversions and Y2K bug problems—we can't even begin to think about the Object Web. The good news is that after we get over this rough hump, we will be headed straight for a new gold rush. ❑

Where to Go for More Information

We compiled the following list of resources to help you find more information on some of the topics we covered in this book.

CORBA

The OMG meets every two months—usually in attractive locations—to continue its standards work. If you can't attend, the best way to find out what's happening is to visit the OMG Web site at *http://www.omg.org*. Here are some CORBA books you may find helpful.

■ Thomas Mowbray and Ron Zahavi, **The Essential CORBA: Systems Integration Using Distributed Objects** (Wiley, 1995). This book is on object methodology and design using CORBA. Tom Mowbray previously chaired the CORBA Common Facilities Task Force. So you will get a dose of valuable CORBA insights from reading this book.

■ Thomas Mowbray and Raphael Malveau, **CORBA Design Patterns** (Wiley, 1997). This useful book uses design patterns to explain CORBA programming techniques. It is the first design patterns book to cover distributed systems.

■ Roger Sessions, **Object Persistence** (Prentice Hall, 1996). This book contains everything you need to know about CORBA's *Persistent Object Service 1 (POS1)*. Roger Sessions was one of POS1's key architects. This standard is being replaced with POS2. However, this book still contains useful insights on object persistence.

■ Jon Siegel, et al., **CORBA Fundamentals and Programming** (Wiley, 1996). This book is a CORBA programmer's Bible; it covers multivendor C++ and Smalltalk CORBA ORBs.

■ Geoffrey Lewis, et al., **Programming with Java IDL** (Wiley, 1998). This book covers JavaSoft's *Java IDL*. Its authors are the Sun developers of the product.

■ Sean Baker, **CORBA Distributed Objects: Using Orbix** (Addison Wesley, 1998). This book covers advanced Orbix features such as filters and thread support. It briefly covers *OrbixWeb*.

■ Andreas Vogel and Keith Duddy, **Java Programming With CORBA** (Wiley, 1997). This is another CORBA/Java book.

■ Robert Orfali, et al., **Instant CORBA** (Wiley, 1997). This book by your authors is a gentle introduction to CORBA and its services for people who are in a hurry.

■ Robert Orfali and Dan Harkey, **Client/Server Programming with Java and CORBA, Second Edition** (Wiley, 1998). This 1000-page book, also by your authors, is an introduction to programming with Java and CORBA. It covers many of the Object Web technologies we described in this book.

■ David Curtis and Michael Rosen, **Integrating CORBA and COM Applications** (Wiley, 1999). This timely book demonstrates—through in-depth examples—that CORBA and COM can interoperate.

COM and DCOM

COM is covered indirectly in about a dozen Visual C++ and ActiveX books on the market. It's also covered in tons of online documentation from Microsoft—including the Win32 SDK. To get the latest on Java and DCOM, visit the following Microsoft Web Sites: *http://www.microsoft.com/visualj* and *http://www. microsoft.com/java/sdk*.

Here are some COM-specific books that you may find helpful:

■ Kraig Brockschmidt, **Inside OLE 2, Second Edition** (Microsoft Press, 1995). This second edition is still more complete in some places than the "official" Microsoft documentation on OLE.

■ David Chappell, **Understanding ActiveX and OLE** (Microsoft Press, 1996). This book is a very gentle guide to OLE and ActiveX. It's prerequisite reading for anyone interested in COM.

■ Dale Rogerson, **Inside COM** (Microsoft Press, 1997). This C++ programming book only covers COM.

■ Richard Grimes, **Professional DCOM Programming**, (Wrox Press, 1997). This very detailed C++ book covers both COM and DCOM.

■ Don Box, **Essential COM** (Addison Wesley, 1998). This is the latest and greatest COM programming book to hit the market. It covers C++ programming with COM in depth.

■ Roger Sessions, **COM and DCOM: Microsoft's Vision for Distributed Objects** (Wiley, 1998). Yes, this is the same Roger Sessions who wrote the CORBA Persistence book. This is the first Java/DCOM book on the market; it's also the first book that really covers MTS. As usual, Roger's style is wonderful. Of course, we strongly disagree with some of the positions Roger takes in his new book (but that's life).

Distributed Objects

There are tons of books on object-oriented methodologies and languages. However, very few of these books deal with distributed objects. Here are a few that you may find helpful:

- David Taylor, **Object-Oriented Information Systems** (Wiley, 1992). This book is a very approachable introduction to objects.

- Grady Booch, **Object-Oriented Analysis and Design, Second Edition,** (Benjamin-Cummings, 1994). This second edition of Booch's book is superb reading. It's also an introduction but with more emphasis on language constructs, methodology, and notation.

- Rick Cattell, **The Object Database Standard: ODMG 2.0** (Morgan Kaufmann). This is the published ODMG standard. To get more information on the Object Database Management Group (ODMG) contact *http://www.odmg.org*.

- Peter Eeles and Oliver Sims, **Building Business Objects** (Wiley, 1998). This book provides a general introduction to client/server business objects. Oliver Sims is the principal architect of Newi and an early pioneer of business objects. You should read this book, if you have an interest in distributed objects.

- Orfali et al., **The Essential Distributed Objects Survival Guide** (Wiley, 1996). This book is a gentle introduction to distributed objects and components.

Java

You should always start your Java quest with a visit to the JavaSoft Web Site— *http://www.javasoft.com*. In addition, there are now hundreds of books on Java. Here are the ones we found to be the most helpful:

- Cay Horstmann and Gary Cornell, **Core Java** (Prentice Hall, 1998). This is still our favorite introduction to programming in Java.

- David Flanagan, **Java in a Nutshell, Second Edition**, (O'Reilly, 1998). This is a must-have reference for Java programmers. It's a very handy guide to the Java classes and interfaces.

- James Gosling et al., **Java Programming Language, Second Edition** (Addison Wesley, 1998). After you read an introduction—for example, Horstmann—you may want to look at this insightful book by the creator of Java. It will help you consolidate your understanding of the Java language.

- Rick Cattell et al., **JDBC Database Access With Java** (Addison Wesley, 1997). This book is an introduction to JDBC by the JavaSoft team that developed JDBC.

Client/Server and Transaction Processing

This is a huge topic in its own right. Here are our all-time favorites:

- Jim Gray and Andreas Reuter, **Transaction Processing Concepts and Techniques** (Morgan Kaufmann, 1993). This book is the Bible of transaction processing.

- David Vaskevitch, **Client/Server Strategies, Second Edition** (IDG, 1995). Vaskevitch is Microsoft's VP of enterprise computing. This book provides an insider's view of Viper and Microsoft's client/server directions. Most of the meat is in the last part. The rest of the book is mostly about the business aspects of client/server technology. It's worth a read.

- David Linthicum, **Client/Server and Intranet Development** (Wiley, 1997). This book covers all aspects of client/server tools. It also has a good section on 3-tier and TP Monitors.

- Juan Andrade et al., **The Tuxedo System** (Addison Wesley, 1996). This well-written book is an introduction to the Tuxedo TP Monitor; its four authors are the key architects of the Tuxedo system.

- Philip Bernstein and Eric Newcomer, **The Principles of Transaction Processing** (Morgan Kaufmann, 1997). This book provides a good overview of TP Monitors and their underlying technology.

- Jeri Edwards, **3-Tier Client/Server At Work, Revised Edition** (Wiley, 1999). This fast-paced book by our coauthor presents nine case studies of some of the largest client/server systems in existence; it provides a ton of insight on how client/server technology is used in the real world.

- Dan Chang and Dan Harkey, **Client/Server Data Access with Java and XML** (Wiley, 1998). This book by our coauthor is the best introduction to XML and database architectures for the Web.

Index

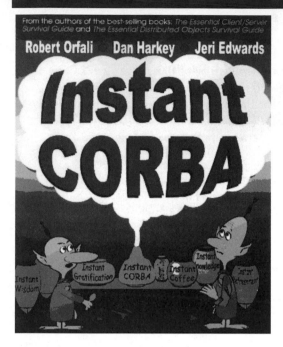

Client/Server Programming with Java and CORBA!

From the Authors of the best-selling books:
The Essential Client/Server Survival Guide and *Instant CORBA*

Robert Orfali ⚡ Dan Harkey

Client/Server Programming
with
JAVA™ and CORBA
Second Edition

Enterprise Beans · Server Beans · Client Beans · Mobile Beans · CORBA Beans · Intergalactic Beans

Contents at a Glance

I highly recommend it!

Whether you're a seasoned Java programmer, a distributed objects expert, or looking to be a little of both, this Second Edition of the enormously popular **Client/Server Programming with Java and CORBA** gives you the programming know-how you need to combine these two technologies into workable client/server solutions for the Object Web. Full of working code, tutorials, and design trade-offs, this one-of-a-kind book:

✔ Includes over 250 new pages on JavaBeans, CORBAbeans, and Enterprise JavaBeans. Shows you how to invoke CORBA objects from JavaBean tools such as Visual Cafe, JBuilder, and VisualAge for Java.

✔ Covers everything from simple ORB programming to exciting new areas such as CORBA's 3.0's POA, Object Pass-by-Value, IDL-to-Java, and RMI-to-IIOP.

✔ Uses tutorials and client/server benchmarks to compare CORBA and its competitors— including Java/RMI, Java/DCOM, Sockets, and HTTP/CGI, and Servlets.

✔ Covers in detail Netscape's ORB: VisiBroker for Java; it shows you how to use Caffeine to write CORBA/Java applications without IDL.

✔ Provides a Debit-Credit benchmark for JDBC databases to compare 2-tier vs. 3-tier client/server solutions.

✔ Provides a JavaBeans version of Club Med—a web-based, 3-tier client/server application that uses CORBA, Java, and JDBC.

✔ Shows how to use CORBA's dynamic facilities such as callbacks, dynamic invocations, object introspection, and the interface repository.

✔ Comes with a CD-ROM containing over 16 Java-based client/server applications (and other goodies).

Available at Bookstores Everywhere

For more information visit **http://www.wiley.com/compbooks**
ISBN: 0471-24578-X, 1020 pages, 1998, $49.99 US / $77.50 CAN

WILEY